THE ILLUSTRATED
HISTORY
OF MEDICINE

JEAN-CHARLES SOURNIA

THE ILLUSTRATED
HISTORY
OF MEDICINE

HAROLD
STARKE
— PUBLISHERS —

English language edition first published 1992
© Harold Starke Publishers Limited 1992
Translated from *Histoire de la médecine et des médecins*
© Larousse SA 1991 for this illustrated edition
© La Découverte 1991 for the text

Translation from the French by Louise Davies, Graham Cross and Lilian Hall
and typesetting by Andrew Wilson
in association with First Edition Translations Ltd, Cambridge, England

British Library Cataloguing-in-Publication Data.
Sournia, Jean-Charles
Illustrated History of Medicine
I. Title
610.9

ISBN 1–872457–05–3
Harold Starke Publishers Limited
203 Bunyan Court, Barbican, London EC2Y 8DH, England
and Pixey Green, Stradbroke, Eye, Suffolk IP21 5NG, England
Printed in Spain

The living are ruled by the dead.
Auguste Comte

History is a resurrection of life in its entirety, not superficially, but of its deep, inner structures.
Jules Michelet

One cannot practise a science well unless one knows its history. ·
Auguste Comte

There are two kinds of researchers: some who are just assistants, and others whose mission is to invent. Inventions should be made in all areas, even in the humblest search for facts or the simplest experiment. Science cannot begin to exist without personal and original effort.
Henri Bergson

CONTENTS

◆

CHAPTER I · *The diseases of Prehistory* 13

    I. From palaeontology to palaeopathology 15
    II. In search of palaeomedicine 18

CHAPTER II · *The continued existence of ethnomedicine* 21

    I. The modern Western world and ethnomedicine 23

CHAPTER III · *The archaeology of medicine* 31

    I. The medicine of the Fertile Crescent 33
    II. Egyptian medicine: early medicine 42

CHAPTER IV · *The Greeks establish our system of medicine* 59

    I. Medicine: between myth and philosophy 61
    II. Hippocratic medicine 70
    III. The doctrines of Alexandria 80
    IV. The Greeks in Rome 84

CHAPTER V · *The Middle Ages in Mediterranean countries* 95

    I. The Byzantines, heirs of Hippocrates 97
    II. The Jewish faith and prophylactic measures 110
    III. The Muslim digression 122
    IV. Universities and medicine in the West 138

CHAPTER VI · *Different types of medicine* 171

    I. The riches and contrasts of the Americas 173
    II. The traditions of India live on 189
    III. The magical powers of Imperial China 201

CHAPTER VII · *Anatomy in the Renaissance* 223

    I. The discovery of the human body 226
    II. A renaissance in all but medicine 244

CHAPTER VIII   *The seventeenth century and the Age of Reason* 261

     I. The fundamental principles of modern medicine 263
     II. A medicine still lacking in power 278

CHAPTER IX   *Medicine in the Age of the Enlightenment* 289

     I. The fashion for "systems" 291
     II. Erudite and fashionable experimentation 298

CHAPTER X   *Conversion to clinical medicine* 329

     I. The French Revolution and medicine in Europe 331
     II. The experimental revolution: from Magendie to Claude Bernard 348
     III. From prevention to public health 354

CHAPTER XI   *Laboratory medicine* 367

     I. Bacteriology: Pasteur extends our knowledge of "nature" 369
     II. Towards microscopic pathological anatomy 379
     III. New progress: from analytical chemistry to physics 386
     IV. Anaesthesia and asepsis lead to a revival of surgery 394
     V. The new specialists 400
     VI. Preventive medicine becomes well organized 412

CHAPTER XII   *From X–rays to penicillin* 419

     I. The radiology revolution 421
     II. Serums and vaccines after Pasteur and Koch 426
     III. Biochemistry transforms physiology 436
     IV. After enzymes: vitamins and hormones 442
     V. The fight against infections continues 447
     VI. Joint national and international responsibilities 452

CHAPTER XIII   *The explosion of knowledge and techniques* 459

     I. The triumph of biochemistry 463
     II. Medical physics 490
     III. Effective treatments at last 505
     IV. World health 537

Appendices 551

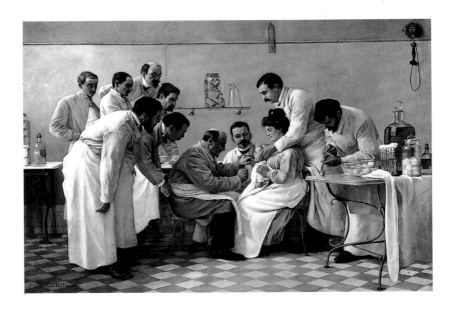

Georges Chicotot, Le tubage, *late
nineteenth century. Doctor Josias,
surrounded by his students, carries out an
intubation on a child with croup.
Public Works Museum, Paris, France.*

chapter I

The diseases of Prehistory

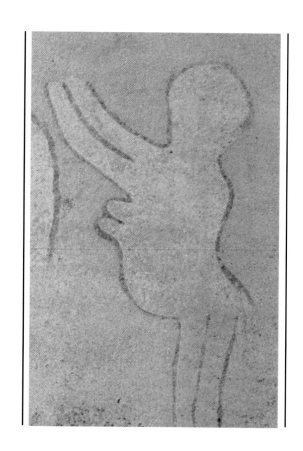

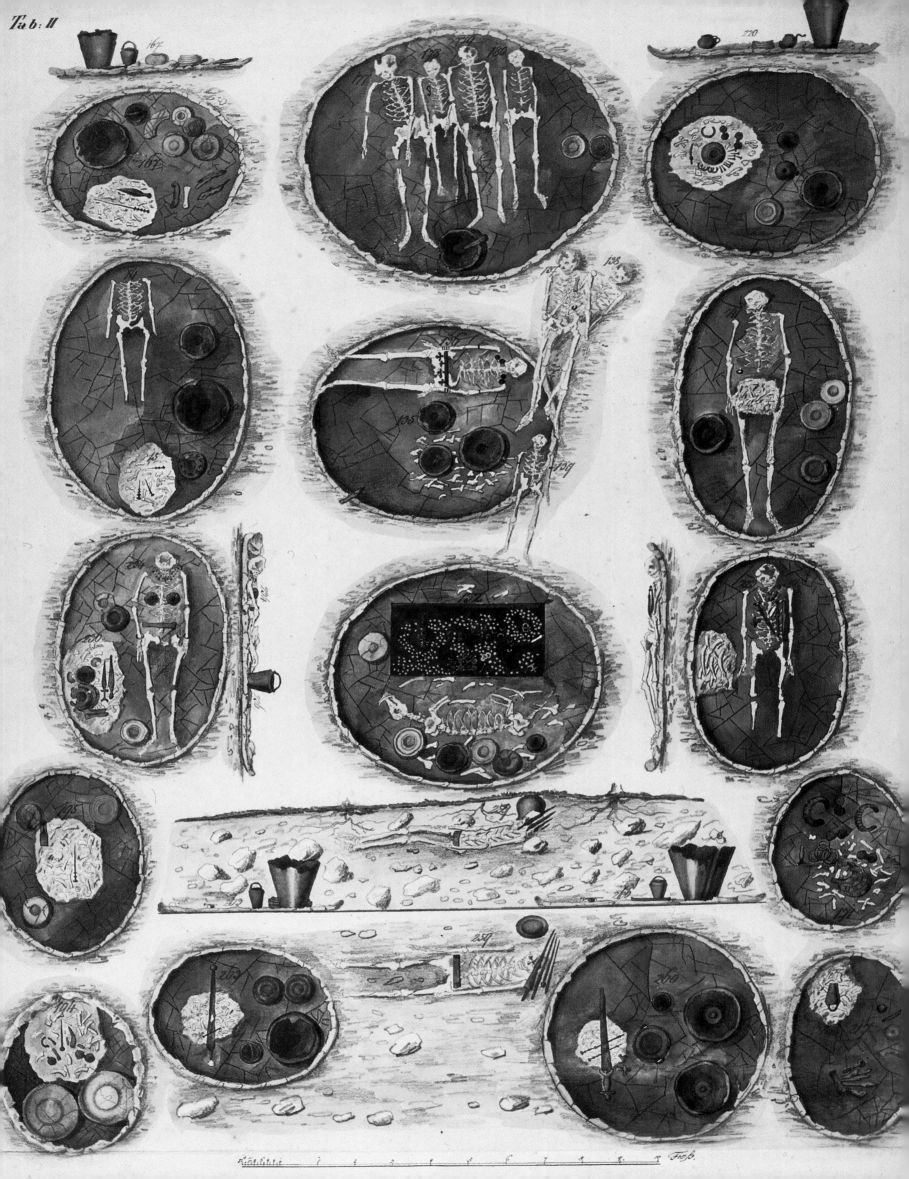

Tab: II

As we know him today, man (the member of the family of hominids whom we call *Homo sapiens sapiens*) is probably forty to fifty thousand years old, and it is likely that his overall physiology – that is to say, the working of his internal organs – has varied little during the course of the millennia. On the other hand, his morphology and perhaps the biochemical composition of his tissues have changed under the influence of his environment, his nutrition, his activities, his customs and his diseases.

We know almost nothing about prehistoric man since no written records exist, but it is reasonable to assume that the diseases from which he suffered were very similar to those of today. Everything we know about them we have learnt from fossils, bones and lower jaws discovered by palaeontologists during the course of excavations.

*P*alaeopathology, a science allied to palaeontology, is the study of the diseases of prehistoric man using bones preserved in different types of soils. By examining them, it is possible to identify some of the ailments which affected our ancestors. However, we have to be cautious when making assumptions about these *a posteriori* diagnoses because of the living conditions of those times which we can imagine were very harsh. The climate, the dense or parched vegetation, hunting for big game such as mammoths or rhinoceroses, the need for defence against predators that competed with man for the herbivores on which he relied for food, struggles between men for land which was hospitable and plentiful in game – all these are situations in which accidents could occur. Consequently, palaeopathologists find many signs of traumas, especially fractures of the

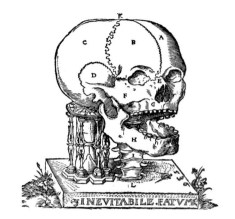

*F*rom palaeontology to palaeopathology

I.

long bones, of the spinal column or of the pelvis; arrow- or spear-heads lodged in bone, etc.

The bones also show the sequelae of rheumatic conditions which deform or fuse the joints. Other changes suggest tuberculosis of the bones and joints, but here too one has to be cautious; modern medicine teaches that bony tissue reacts in a similar way to different kinds of attack such as tuberculosis, certain conditions brought about by infestation with parasites, or attack by germs resembling the treponemas which cause syphilis. Some remains reveal bone cancer and others the skeletal changes associated with hereditary abnormalities of the haemoglobin. Some jawbone remains show poor sets of teeth: missing teeth and exposed roots are signs that serious gum infections were common.

Because of its resistance to decay, bony tissue represents the majority of the material available to palaeopathologists. Sometimes we chance upon soft tissue in varying states of mummification which we can rehydrate, X-ray, subject to radiocarbon dating or study under the electron microscope.

This panoply of modern methods also enables us to examine the viscera, and even sometimes the proteins of which they are composed. It is thus possible to determine the blood group or tissue type of individuals who have been dead for several thousands of years.

The burial site in ancient salt mines at Hallstatt (Austria), discovered in 1846 by Johann Georg Ramsauer, is one of the most important from the first Iron Age (about 1000 BC). 980 tombs and many objects were discovered, including pottery and remains of leather headgear. Watercolour by Isidor Engel, 1878.

15

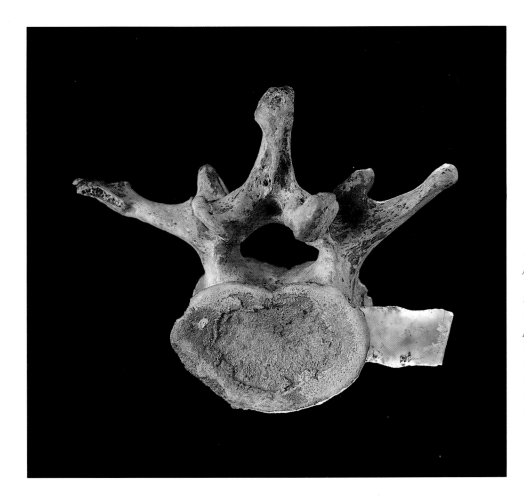

Human vertebra and flint arrowhead. These remains of a skeleton from the end of the Neolithic period reveal the significance of the traumas observed by palaeopathologists. Cave at Villenard, Somme, France.

"HOMO SAPIENS": A PORTRAIT

*T*wentieth-century palaeontology attempts to sketch a portrait of prehistoric man, assisted in particular by the discovery of some of his settlement sites. Prehistoric man lived in caves, sheltered from the rain and cold. He also lived in forests, on the savanna, or in huts of mud or foliage of which no trace remains. *Homo sapiens'* great advantage was his ability to adapt to his environment, all over the planet. As he adapted, *Homo sapiens* proliferated, migrating across all the continents, with the result that he still survives today.

Those remains that have come to light, mainly from communal burial places, show that *Homo sapiens sapiens* was small in stature. The human race has only recently grown in height, a development due to a more balanced diet rich in vitamins, improved standards of hygiene and better medical care. At birth, the same bony malformations existed in former times as do today: dislocations of the hip, dissymmetry in the development of certain bones, too many fingers or toes. Life was short, lasting on average only thirty years (skeletons of old people are rare). The

Pollen from a labiate, type of lavender. The microscope enables us to discover more about plants and people's diets in the Neolithic period.

family group therefore consisted of young individuals and, since girls reached puberty later than they do today, couples only had a relatively short time in which to reproduce.

The study of prehistoric settlements sheds some light on what people ate: food plants are revealed by palynology (the study of pollens), mineralized human faeces ("coproliths") are studied, as are animal bones scattered around the remains of fires. Our ancestors were hunters, fishermen and gatherers before they invented agriculture and reared livestock, and used metals to meet their needs. They had a poor diet that lacked some vitamins and afforded them an inadequate intake of calories. Harsh climatic conditions affected their physical constitution: in summer they suffered from dehydration, while winter brought great cold and heavy rain from which their rudimentary settlements provided no shelter. In addition, they shared their environment with bacteria and parasites, which inflicted upon them an enormous range of diseases that they did not know how to combat.

Progress and industrialization have enabled man to cope with inclement weather, and even with parasites and bacteria. Industrialized populations, and some peoples of the Amazon Basin and New Guinea, have learnt how to overcome such conditions over the centuries. They have adapted to the constraints imposed by the environment and have been able to modify it.

At least until the time of the French Revolution, writers continually evoked the myth, which still lives on today, of the Golden Age when man is said to have lived happily in the midst of a peaceful, serene nature. Animals and plants provided an easy source of food, and clear water was freely available from rivers and streams. Prehistory shows us that this reassuring Garden of Eden only ever existed in our imagination.

There are more than a hundred of these mutilated hand prints in the Gargas cave in the Hautes-Pyrénées: here the left little finger is missing. Is this simply a malformation or, as Leroi-Gourhan suggests, a Palaeolithic "hunter's code"?

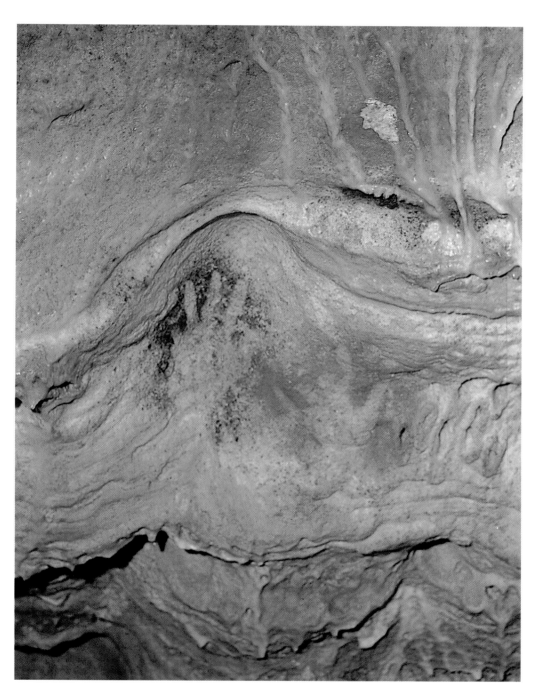

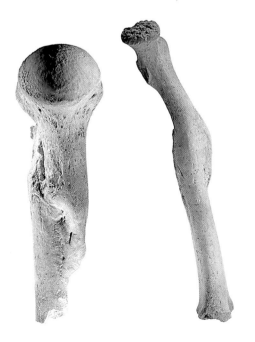

Child's femur (right) *and humerus* (left) *which have been fractured and have knitted well together through the formation of a callus, although shortening has resulted. Neolithic tomb, La Chaussée-Tirancourt, Somme, France.*

In search of palaeomedicine

II.

In the absence of written records, palaeopathologists have no documents from which to discover how man treated himself in the Neolithic period (10 000 to 4000 BC). Did Neolithic man use medicines? It is impossible to say. However, on the evidence of disinterred skeletons, we can state positively that he knew how to reduce fractures by immobilizing the broken bones and keeping them in line. But in the examples of healed bones, the fractured parts overlap, showing that he did not know how to apply traction to the broken extremities and so restore perfect alignment.

There is more doubt about lesions of the skull which have partly healed during the lifetime of the individual. Were they accidental traumas or deliberate wounds? We still do not know.

Did they have a religious significance, or were they aimed at mechanically treating a wound in which the skull had been depressed or a nervous disorder such as epilepsy or paralysis? In the latter case, we can assume that prehistoric man already attributed the origins of paralysis to the brain. Were they an attempt at alleviating mental disorders, which would enable us to deduce that prehistoric man thought that abnormal behaviour originated in the head?

These questions will probably remain unanswered, even though trepanned skulls are found throughout the world. Many museums around the world contain examples, and scientists have put forward a number of theories to explain these trepanations which are still practised by certain Black African ethnic groups.

Can we conclude that palaeomedicine existed? The word today is rich in meaning but, for all that, men with special knowledge did help other sick or wounded men and did practise precise procedures on their bodies to alleviate their suffering.

Trepanned Neolithic skull. Was this an accidental trauma or a deliberate operation with a religious significance, or did it simply have a mechanical therapeutic aim? Burial cave in the Petit-Morin valley, Seine et Marne, France.

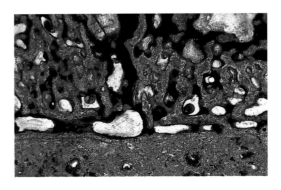

This macroscopic section shows the hypertrophying lesions of bone disease in the left humerus of an adult. La Chaussée-Tirancourt, Somme, France.

*Clearly, prehistoric man has only left us
"truncated messages", particularly as far as
his pathology is concerned.
This does not prevent painters from
using their imagination! This
panel is by Paul Jamin (1853–1903):
La fuite devant le mammouth!*

*This Neolithic statuette of a woman
symbolizes fertility. The theme is common
and goes back in its figurative form to the
Upper Palaeolithic period.*

chapter II

The continued existence of ethnomedicine

Where does one start a "history of medicine"? With the beginnings of rational medicine, founded on principles, methods and techniques which culminate in those of twentieth-century Western medicine? Or further back in history, with so-called traditional medicine? There is little information about the first "practitioners" who tried to bring medical relief to their companions who were suffering from pain, fever or wounds.

The early forms of medicine are thought to have borrowed greatly from magic before becoming sacerdotal and finally scientific. Each of these terms requires in-depth clarification since their pejorative or apologetic connotations probably do not tally with the fear of disease and suffering which mankind has felt for many thousands of years.

Thus the West, steeped in its superiority, considers the therapeutic principles still used today in the developing countries of Africa, Asia or the Amazon Basin to be "traditional".

In Western eyes, these forms of medicine are not based on experimental techniques which are comparable with those of modern medicine. However, all medical approaches, from whatever period or place, are inspired by traditions which have their source in the mists of time and are based on various methods developed over the centuries – methods that are often contradictory but may be used simultaneously.

As we move towards the twenty-first century, hospital and surgical medicine rub shoulders with country customs, bone-setters' techniques, herbalist practices, not to mention certain esoteric theories put forward by so-called "rational" doctors. All medicine, of whatever origin, is therefore

The modern Western world and ethnomedicine

I.

Statuette with magic uses from the Congo. On its front is a mirror of frosted glass. On its back, a small box contains a grigri. The object is designed as a reliquary. Private collection.

in keeping with tradition and is in this sense "traditional".

On the other hand, reservations may be made about the term "ethnomedicine", which is used to refer to medical techniques other than those that are practised in the West.

If one refers to any group of individuals who are bound by a culture, language and customs as an ethnic group, then all forms of medicine may be called ethnomedicine, including our own. It is generally acknowledged that medicine was first magical in nature, then religious, and gradually became scientific – that is to say, it resulted from precise and rational observation based on experimentation. Authors' opinions differ on exactly when this turning point occurred. Some date it back to the middle of the nineteenth century, with Claude Bernard, the French nineteenth-century physiologist, others place it to coincide with the discovery of bacteriology by Louis Pasteur, and still others as late as the 1950s.

Thus, Western medicine, which is today considered as the only universal medicine, was once an ethnomedicine similar to those forms practised in the developing countries, without observational procedures or experimental precision. From a state of ignorance, we have passed into a state of knowledge via successive flashes of inspiration. Even if the idea of this sudden progression remains respectable, we cannot deny the value of more primitive methods which have been abandoned because we consider them derisory, while other populations such as those of Africa or the Andes retain them. These primitive methods represent the first embryonic developments of a medicine which was to become exact, but they nevertheless respond to a permanency of the human spirit and to a constancy of human behaviour.

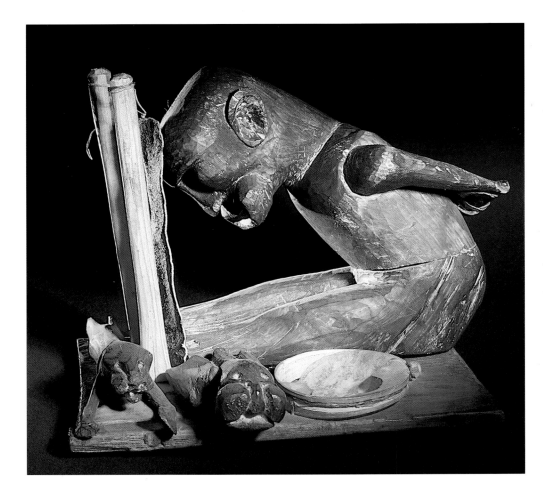

This little wooden figurine represents an Eskimo shaman. At its feet, two animal statuettes assist in the invocation of spirits. Danish National Museum.

A MEDICINE OF "INTERMEDIARIES"

Subjected as he was to daily necessities in order to survive in a world which he only partly understood, man felt the need for an intermediary between tangible, visible reality and the invisible which eluded him. Spirits or gods with a human face, whom he sought to placate so that they would be beneficent, fulfilled this role. "Religions", as we may call them despite the over-simplification, are therefore very varied and rely on human agents who serve as a link between ignorant men and sufferers, and the sovereign powers of heaven, who do as they please with the creatures of the earth. This "agent of communication" possesses knowledge or a talent. He exercises authority over the clan or the tribe by virtue of his wealth or inherit-ance. He becomes the appointed or elected spokesman and fulfils the role of priest or doctor, and sometimes both.

This kind of intercessor can still be found today among some African peoples. The Dogon, for example, have chosen the blacksmith as the village doctor. He is the master of form, since he straightens out bent and warped tools. He mends broken bones, removes tumours and makes the knife which incises a painful abscess or cuts maize to feed the family. The clan attributes magical powers to him since he forges knives from a raw, shapeless mineral, rather as the God of the Bible fashioned man from clay.

This is how the "witch doctors", the shamans of Asia, the juju men of Africa and the bone-setters of Europe came into being. All of them are distinguishable from the quacks, the sellers of medicines and illusory procedures who themselves know the inefficacy of their wares. Some years ago in France, Filipino healers who pretended to operate on an abdominal tumour or the chest without cutting the skin were praised to the skies. Their talents as magicians were only equalled by the gullibility of their patients.

The empirical experience of witch doctors and the knowledge accumulated by an ethnic group over several genera-tions can be considerable. These people, it is true, may not know the principles of Western experimental medicine as drawn up by the French physiologist, Claude Bernard, but they have observed over the

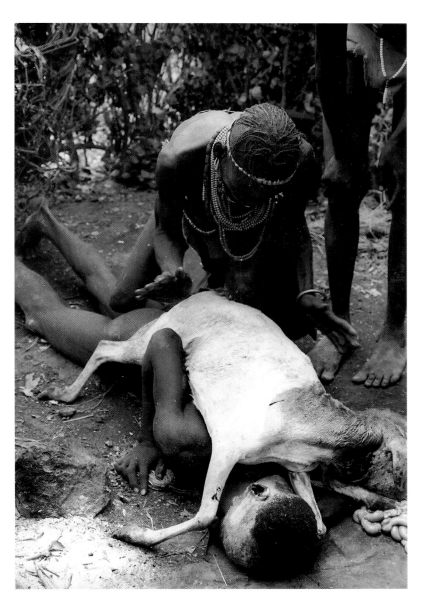

*Kamtchatkan shaman (Eastern Siberia).
Wearing ceremonial dress, he invokes
the forces of nature. Engraving with
watercolour, late eighteenth century.
Decorative Arts Library, Paris, France.*

*A "Nakaté" cure in Ethiopia.
The witch doctor touches the hide
of a sacrificed goat — whose viscera
can be seen bottom right — as it lies
spread out over the back of a sick man.
Museum of Mankind, Paris, France.*

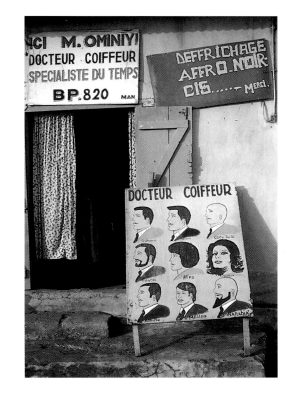

*Today, in the Ivory Coast, supernatural
and rational practices coexist.
Here, the shop of a "doctor-cum-
barber, weather specialist".*

centuries that the same causes often result in the same effects: a serious fracture may lead to gangrene and death; some well-studied and well-used plants relieve pain or induce sleep, while others poison or kill.

Witch doctors have also practised basic ethnosurgery for millennia, employing simple procedures that respond to obvious needs. They use branches to immobilize fractures, and mud to prevent pain and facilitate healing. They close wounds and stop haemorrhages with ashes, moss, cotton or latex. They suture with thread or thorns, and extract foreign bodies such

as arrow-heads with tweezers. Surgeons in the twentieth century employ the same procedures, using modern, improved materials.

In addition, the shaman is very familiar with the community he treats since he was brought up in it. He knows its organizations, its hierarchies, its methods and its collective behaviour, and he will not administer the same treatment to all members of the group. Moreover, the concept of illness varies from one people or generation to another. What may be normal to some will be pathological to others. Pain which is considered tolerable by one group will necessitate hospitalization in another. Sterility or infirmity may be accepted by some and rejected by others.

Thus, the shaman exercises a kind of archaic psychotherapy by matching the treatment to the patient, and by assessing the patient's social role, family ties, situation in the clan. He appreciates the true impact of physical or mental discomfort and makes a complete diagnosis of the condition of his patient, perhaps even more accurately than would a Western doctor who was too concerned with the disorders of one particular organ, or too preoccupied with an accurate biochemical analysis. For example, the griots (witch doctors) of Senegal practise a method similar to modern psychotherapy, employing suggestion and hypnotism.

Furthermore, this intermediary shares the beliefs of his group; he venerates the spirits of the spring or the baobab tree which make women fertile and crops grow well, or which spread diseases and plagues of locusts. Because of his knowledge, he alone is able to intercede with these gods, to make them look favourably upon men and to obtain their pardon if an offence has been committed.

Incantations, dances and offerings are addressed to the sovereign powers, while

Whatever his origins, man has always found reasons to believe in the elements, in the spirits which inhabit nature and in their intercessional powers.
Left: *in the Ivory Coast, trees shelter a fertility goddess.*
Below left: *somewhere in France, a spring with healing powers, from the* Journal des Voyages, *1901.*

medicines and amulets are given to the patients.

The barriers between the concrete world (pain, plant remedies, the sacrificial cock) and the supernatural world (the child who falls ill without good reason, the offended god, the food which has turned to poison) disappear, thanks to the "great witch doctor" who intercedes with the spirits. Even if we include all these methods in the term "fetishism" or "animism", they nevertheless have a curative power for millions of people with bodily afflictions and, as such, form part of medicine.

Underside of an African shaman's drum.
Museum of Mankind,
Paris, France.

*Medicinal plants (*above*)*
*and (*right*) fetishist grigris:*
heads of birds and antelopes' horns;
just some of the many so-called
"natural" forms of medicine used
throughout the world.

*M*odern man is suspicious of "natural" medicine, which was once termed "satanic" by both Christians and Muslims. However, even though he may be convinced of the superiority of modern medicine, he nonetheless adopts some unorthodox methods, especially when he is at a loss and all else fails. Proof of this can be found in the unchallenged success of the magi, sorcerers and other seers to whom we ascribe supernatural powers, which only goes to show that man attributes magical qualities to that which he fears or does not understand, or cannot apprehend in its totality.

So-called "natural" medicine thus retains a real prestige, as if the use of nature by man was not artificial. From this stems the fashion for natural "biological" foods, hot springs (already

David Ryckaert III (1612–1661):
The Witch Doctor, *1638.*
Fine Arts Museum, Valenciennes, France.

the subject of worship in the time of the Gauls) and herbal teas, all of which may be employed in preference to patent medicines.

From all this it can be concluded that Western man has difficulty in acknowledging the coexistence of different logical systems. Cartesian rationality is not necessarily universal, and each society creates its own system of medicine which suits its culture, beliefs, social structures and outlook, and which evolves over the course of time, linking magic to science. Some people choose to have themselves admitted to the most famous hospitals, but also go to Lourdes; others wear bracelets to ward off rheumatism, following the example of the bushman of the Kalahari desert and abandoning all rationality in the face of the unknown.

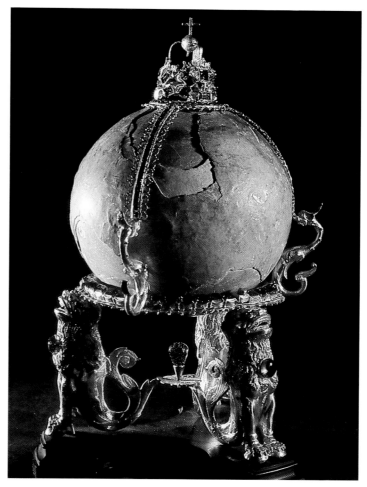

This stony concretion, or bezoar, which forms in the stomach of some animals, is richly mounted here in gold and emeralds, and was once used as an antidote. Spanish artefact of the sixteenth century. History of Art Museum, Vienna, Austria.

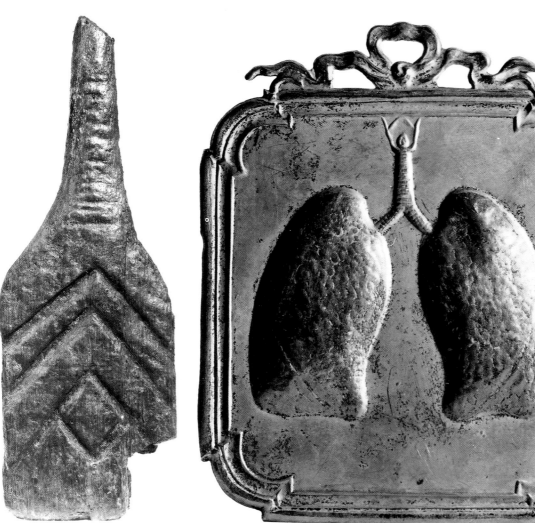

Two votive offerings of lungs, one Gallo-Roman from the source of the Seine, the other nineteenth century. Whether spirits or saints, the miracle-working powers of intercessors exert the same fascination upon men of all periods. Private collection and Archaeological Museum, Dijon, France.

chapter III

The archaeology of medicine

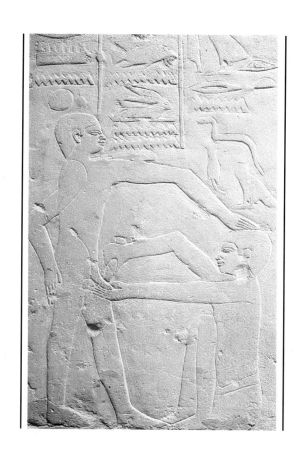

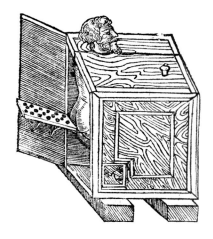

During the nineteenth century, archaeologists began to study the origins of Western civilizations in the Near and Middle East. In the sands of Egypt, Syria and Mesopotamia, they discovered the remains of ancient peoples who had developed the skills of agriculture and writing.

Among these remains were many texts on medical practices, but caution has to be exercised when interpreting tablets of baked clay bearing cuneiform characters, or hieroglyphic inscriptions, taken from the eight medical papyri known to date, and also the numerous funeral inscriptions found on stelae and on the walls of tombs.

Medicine in the Near and Middle East developed against a background of struggles between cities and empires. In the Fertile Crescent between the Zagros Mountains and the mountains of Armenia, the Mediterranean coast, the Sinai peninsula, the Arabian Desert and the Gulf, in the area centred on the valleys of the Tigris and the Euphrates that historians call, for want of a better name, Mesopotamia (literally, "between rivers"), there was a constant ebb and flow of people as dynasties rose and fell in dazzling succession.

The rivalries that developed between cities during the third millennium BC were succeeded by those between kingdoms and empires in which the Semites of central Mesopotamia were dominant and defeated by turns. Then, in 1100 BC, the city of Babylon, which rose to power under the great King Hammurabi, was breached by its formidable rival Assyria, the region in northern Mesopotamia comprising the cities of Ashur, Calah-Nimrud and Nineveh.

The medicine of the Fertile Crescent

I.

In Babylon, the gods were the guardians of the human body.
Opposite: *Malishipak II presents his daughter to Nana, goddess of health and medicine. Susa, 1200 BC.*
Right: *the grimacing demon Pazuzu, the evil spirit of the air, who was responsible for many illnesses such as pneumonia, pleurisy and fevers. About 1500 BC.*

First one and then the other of these two powers was predominant in Mesopotamia until Babylon finally conquered Assyria (in about 610 BC), before succumbing to the strength of King Cyrus and being annexed to the Persian Empire in 539 BC. There was a continuous coming and going of peoples and governments who, according to the texts, all showed uncommon cruelty towards the vanquished and were exceptionally relentless in their destruction. Nevertheless, all established themselves to varying degrees as builders and administrators.

A HIERARCHICAL SOCIETY

The texts, as well as evidence unearthed by archaeological excavations currently in progress, often provide information about the social structure of these kingdoms. At the top of the hierarchy was an overlord or king, who may have been deified, and who possessed varying degrees of power, being either the suzerain or vassal of neighbouring monarchs, depending on the vagaries of history. Beneath him were the influential castes of the priests, military chiefs and scribes; then came the merchants and landowners. The very lowest rung in the social hierarchy was occupied by farmers and manual workers. These were often slaves who, because of their humble origins, became the victims of wars and resulting deportations.

An examination of texts and tombs reveals that life expectancy was short. Those who survived the wars suffered continuously from attacks of malaria in marshy areas, from smallpox epidemics, diseases of the intestines and eyes, and from venereal diseases. And this is not to mention maternal and infant mortality. Famine does not seem to have been rife in Mesopotamia, since agriculture appears to have been secure due to the relative stability of the lowest water levels of the Tigris and Euphrates, whose spring and summer floods are less extensive than those of the Nile.

The texts that have survived date from about 3000 to 400 BC and take the form of collections of hundreds of tablets carefully numbered at the time they were written, or the form of stelae, statues or seals. These writings were not the last, nor the only ones; some of them were repeated century after century and bear witness not only to a perfect continuity of tradition but also to the fact that knowledge was transmitted from generation to generation by masters who taught in the most important cities.

BEHIND THE DISEASE: THE TRANSGRESSION

Have you sown discord between father and son,
between mother and daughter,
between brothers,
between friends,
Have you said "yes" instead of "no",
Have you used an inaccurate pair of scales,
Have you thrown out the legitimate son,
installing the illegitimate son in the home,
Have you moved a fence, boundary marker or
boundary,
Have you forced an entry into your neighbour's
dwelling,
Have you shared his wife's bed,
Have you expelled the virtuous man from his
family,
Have you stolen your neighbour's clothes,
Have you put honesty on your lips,
and treachery in your heart,
Have you committed crimes, stolen
or told someone else to steal,
Have you taken part in sorcery?

(*Quoted by* J.R. Zaragoza, Hist. de la Méd., Pharm., Art Dent. et Art Vét., SFEPMS, 1977, Vol. I, p. 94)

Seals with phallic symbols. Because of the magic power attributed to the sexual organs, these seals were thought to bring prosperity and ward off disease.

Tablet taken from an Assyrian medical "treatise". Examination of the skull and head. Each clinical form includes a favourable or fatal diagnosis. About 900 BC. Louvre Museum, Paris, France.

*Model of the liver
in clay, c. 1900 BC,
inscribed with magic
formulae. Hazor.
Idam Collections,
Jerusalem, Israel.*

DIAGNOSIS
AND RELIGION

*I*n ancient Mesopotamia, during the millennia that preceded the Christian era, man lived in an environment dominated by gods and religion. Marduk soon emerged as the chief god of Babylon, with his entourage of many spirits and demons who were responsible for the diseases suffered by man, and who had to be placated. Babylonian medicine was thus distinguished by the association of symptomatic treatments, which the Babylonians endeavoured to make effective, with incantatory practices that had more to do with magic and religious tradition than rational clinical principles.

The spirits were the companions of the gods and the guardians of both the home and the human body. All infringements of the rules that had been decreed provoked their anger. Disease was therefore endured as punishment for a sin: "Impurity has struck me. Judge my case, take a decision about me; eradicate the evil disease from my body, destroy all evil in my flesh and muscles. May the evil in my body, flesh and muscles leave today and may I see the light" (adapted from tablets of medical prognoses and diagnoses, about 2000 BC).

Thus, under certain circumstances, guardian spirits could do harm, and the Mesopotamians gave them specific names depending on the organ they attacked.

With this aetiology*, we understand that diagnosis and prognosis were on two levels: one hypothetical, the other truly medical. For example, clinical observation of the subject enabled the following diagnoses to be made: bouts of malaria, jaundice, intestinal occlusion, epileptic fits and strokes*. Clinical forms were specified for each of these diseases, including a favourable or fatal diagnosis. However, in parallel with this rigorous symptomatology*, a detailed inquiry was made into the previous history of the patient in order to discover the sin that had recently been committed, and to identify the spirit responsible for the disease.

To moral transgressions were added the causes of physical impurity: putting one's feet in dirty water, touching a man or woman who had unwashed hands, touching a dirty body, etc. Irrespective of whether a ritual value was accorded to this concept of "impurity", or whether cleanliness was considered to have a prophylactic effect against epidemics, the opportunities for becoming guilty were innumerable and – an example later followed by the psychoanalyst – the interrogation of the patient was carried out carefully since it was important to discover the root of the evil.

Several diagnostic methods of a divinatory nature were used: dreams, the flight of birds, the date of a flood, the colour and direction of smoke from a fire, the shape of a spot of oil, etc. The liver was considered to be the seat of thought and feeling. For this reason, hepatoscopy* became very popular, judging by the thousands of models in baked clay, wood or bronze which have been found during excavations. This practice of visceral divination was widespread and persisted for a long time, being still common among the Etruscans and Hittites. The depth of the liver's fissures and the shape of its lobes were studied to establish a prognosis for the disease under examination. Yet despite this impressive array of methods for identifying the trouble, the patient was often disappointed, as is demonstrated by this anonymous writer: "The diviner has not foretold the future by his divination; the consultant has not done me justice with his fumigation; I approached the necromancer but he did not reveal anything to me, and the magus did not deliver me from my anger with his ritual." Those seeking help were often swindled, and around 2800 BC, one of the kings of Lagash was known to have punished a number of diviners who were guilty of what today we would call "professional misconduct".

Hepatoscopy was one of the many divinatory procedures practised in Mesopotamia. These three models of animal livers are made of clay. Mari, about 1900 BC. Louvre Museum, Paris, France.

TREATING THE DISORDER AND PLACATING THE EVIL SPIRIT

Treatments based on such methods of diagnosis therefore proved to be of mixed value. The most significant form of medicine was surgery which reduced fractures, extracted foreign bodies, dressed wounds, amputated limbs, treated cataracts or sounded the urethra for a blennorrhagic stricture. Around 1700 BC the famous stela of Hammurabi, which can be seen in the Louvre Museum in Paris, fixed fees for various types of surgical intervention, providing they were successful, and penalties if the same treatments failed.

In parallel with surgical practice, medicines used in the treatment of disease were abundant and were based on plants, minerals, and decoctions of organs and animals of all kinds. Apart from oils and greases, there were potions, balms and ointments, covering all the requirements of medical, surgical and obstetric medicine.

The practices themselves were of course based on magic and religion. The first basic step consisted in naming the disorder, since identification of the disease both destroyed the mystery and indicated the god whom it would be advisable to invoke. The second step was propitiatory sacrifice, a substitution ritual which is found in many ancient and contemporary religions.

Some of the articles in the "Code of Hammurabi", king of Babylon, concern doctors and furnish proof of their eminent position in the social hierarchy. For example, shown here: "If a doctor has repaired the broken limb of a leading citizen... The patient will give the doctor the sum of five shekels (40 g of silver)." Susa, about 1750 BC. Louvre Museum, Paris, France.

WHO ARE THE "DOCTORS"?

In western Asia, it seems that the art of healing was never the province of a single profession that held the monopoly. Diviners, priests, sacrificers and doctors all treated the sick.

If the king's physicians were at the summit of the traditional hierarchy, the surgeons occupied an inferior position. There were also the midwives and wet-nurses in the service of the sacred prostitutes of the temples. Exorcists practised in the villages, while competent medical practitioners were held in high esteem, were well paid and were exchanged by kings as a token of courtesy.

Cylinder seal of the doctor Makkur-Marduk, named after the official god of Babylon, Marduk, who was the master of procedures capable of warding off the evils of life. Louvre Museum, Paris, France.

One point is worthy of particular note: an abundance of lists and nomenclatures has been discovered. It has therefore been possible to reconstruct from tablets a list of all the medicinal plants used by the Babylonians.

We know how they prepared syrups, pomades, ointments and infusions. We know that they were familiar with the properties of belladonna, and we possess a classified list of useful minerals. Nevertheless, indications for use are not given with every product, and we unfortunately do not have a treatise on Babylonian therapeutics as such.

THERE IS STILL MUCH THAT WE DO NOT KNOW

*W*hen reading the treatises and scholarly studies devoted to medicine, we cannot help but be amazed at the extraordinary continuity which emerges across centuries, languages and countries. Some documents date back to before the third millennium BC. Others, which are identical, to the fourth century BC. However, people's mentality and methods of artistic representation evolve over time. For example, take the attitude of society to the human body. In illustrations dating from the third millennium BC, the unclothed body was endowed with an honour which was reserved for the gods, while in centuries closer to our own, only slaves and the vanquished were shown in a state of undress. It would therefore be difficult to believe that medical customs did not change over the three millennia before Christ. We possess inscribed livers dating from both 2500 and 500 BC, the time of Xerxes, but does this mean that hepatic abnormalities were interpreted in the same way in both periods?

It would doubtless be better to admit our relative ignorance. The most well-informed Assyriologists cannot translate

One of the rare representations of the subject of mother and child. Nineveh, Palace of Sennacherib, Neo-Assyrian period. About 630–620 BC.

all the tablets at their disposal, and a bilingual anatomical dictionary does not exist. Some cities yielded hundreds of tablets from certain periods, among them the city of Mari, whose riches dating from 1800 BC have not yet been fully catalogued. Yet there are periods about which we know absolutely nothing concerning the same cities. It is therefore reasonable to assume that we will make generalizations as well as extrapolations. For example, some historians distinguish between two periods of Sumerian medicine: an upper period in the third millennium BC which was descriptive and empirical, and another, more recent period influenced by an obscurantist priesthood which favoured divination and astrology. This idea is no doubt rash and it is probable that the two modes of thought existed side by side during both periods.

To be sure, our knowledge is increased each year by archaeological excavations, but we have to be extremely guarded when analysing texts and finds: too many assertions sometimes encourage plausible interpretations, but these remain pure conjecture.

THE INFLUENCE OF MESOPOTAMIAN MEDICINE

Libation beaker belonging to Gudea, the patesi *of Lagash. The subject of the serpent entwined around a stick inspired our caduceus, which is today a symbol of beneficence. Tello, about 2120 BC. Louvre Museum, Paris, France.*

*W*ith its doctors, its treatises and its rituals, Assyrian medicine became widespread. Documents such as a work on diagnosis and prognosis, drawn up in the form of aphorisms during the reign of Ashurbanipal in the seventh century BC, exerted an influence on both Greek and Indian medicine. Moreover, relations with Egyptian physicians remained good, and it is right to emphasize the Mesopotamian origins of Hebrew medicine. Indeed, the closeness of the Semitic languages spoken in Palestine and Babylonia facilitated relations and exchanges between the two countries, whether diplomatic or warlike, commercial or cultural. Innumerable inclusions of Mesopotamian origin are to be found in the Talmud and the Bible, concerning secular and religious onomastics and prayers, as well as social, magic and medical rituals. They do not date from the short captivity of the Jews in Babylon (597 to 538 BC), but are the result of age-old contacts between the two peoples. Considering the influence that the Hebrew civilization still has on the Western world through Christianity, it could be argued that Sumerian medicine has a part to play even today.

Bronze exorcism plaque. At the top, the seven fearsome demons; below, the sick person is watched over by two "wise men" with fish tails. At the bottom, the wicked goddess Lamashtu, carried in a boat towards hell, torments the sick person. C. 750 BC. Louvre Museum, Paris, France.

Egyptian medicine: early medicine

II.

Egyptian medicine was practised for over three thousand years, and at first glance it is more accessible to the historian than the medicine of Mesopotamia. Unlike western Asia, with its unsettled history, Egypt – that is to say the valley of the Nile, its delta and the deserts which border it to the east and west – achieved a unity of population, language and, with the exception of a few periods of division between North and South, a political unity under the authority of an absolute sovereign. None of these features is found anywhere else in the Near or Middle East.

Hieroglyphics underwent continuous development, and historians are in possession of documents relating to each stage. Besides sculptures and seals – artefacts that are common to both Egypt and Sumer – Egypt has also bequeathed manuscripts on papyrus and leather as well as paintings on the walls of tombs and on artefacts.

These amount to a considerable body of writings of exceptional quality, while Sumer and Ashur principally left tablets of baked clay, which were small in format, and hence scribes had to use a concise style that is difficult to decipher.

Thus, despite inevitable gaps, we possess more information on the Nile than on the Euphrates, and Egyptologists are able to analyse the manuscripts of the third millennium BC as easily as contemporary historians are able to study the correspondence of Henry VIII.

About fifteen medical texts, drawn up at different dates, are available to us, the best known being the Ebers papyrus which is held in Leipzig. New York possesses the most interesting of them, the Edwin Smith papyrus, some fragments of which can also be seen in California, in the British Museum in London, in Copenhagen and in Berlin.

Apart from the Kahun papyrus, which dates from the twelfth dynasty (about 2000 BC), almost all the others belong to the eighteenth and nineteenth dynasties, or 1500 to 1200 BC. In actual fact, their origins are much more ancient.

Fragment of the Edwin Smith surgical papyrus. Injury to the nose and fracture of the jaw. 1500 BC. Eighteenth dynasty.

David Roberts (1796–1864), Main entrance of the temple at Luxor. *It was dedicated to Amun and, like many other temples, it accommodated the famous Egyptian "houses of life", which served both as the offices of scribes and as a place where medicine was practised. Attached to these houses of life were probably the "Sanatoria" where the god, assisted by doctor-priests, administered various treatments to pilgrims.*

The Ebers papyrus contains passages which most probably originated at the start of the third millennium BC, and which were then faithfully recopied. The papyri which we possess today therefore include elements which were taken up again with varying degrees of accuracy, and they occasionally include glaring errors.

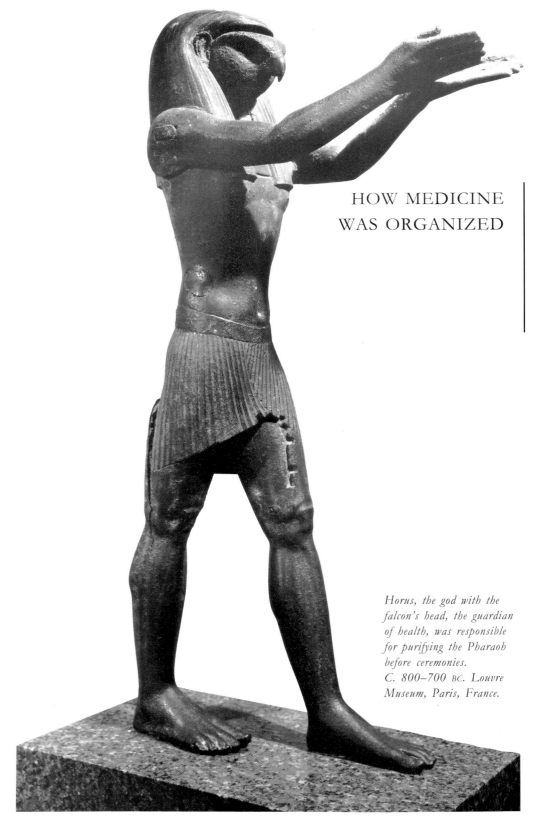

HOW MEDICINE WAS ORGANIZED

Horus, the god with the falcon's head, the guardian of health, was responsible for purifying the Pharaoh before ceremonies. C. 800–700 BC. Louvre Museum, Paris, France.

*T*his transmission of knowledge from generation to generation does not enable us to conclude that schools of medicine existed. Nevertheless, there were establishments known as "houses of life", where expert copyists deciphered ancient written forms, transcribing them into the writing of the period.

If comparisons can be made over the course of history, the activities of the Egyptian houses of life were closer to those of the monks of the Middle Ages than to those of the universities.

Medical practice does not seem to have been passed down from master to pupil, but from father to son, if not within the same family, then at least within the same caste.

Doctors formed part of an elite in a society whose various strata appeared to be strictly defined. They were on a level with the priests, the military commanders, and those responsible for the mines, agriculture and the public granaries. They also formed part of the hierarchy of the body of civil servants in the capital and the provinces, and bore titles such as "chief doctor", "head of the doctors", "medical inspector", "chief doctor of the South and North", "court doctor", "court medical inspector" and "chief physician to the king". Apparently they did not ask for fees, but were paid a fixed salary as civil servants, usually in the form of food and clothing.

Some practitioners called themselves doctor-magicians or doctor-priests. Many carried out official duties at court or in the temple, or devoted themselves to veterinary work, assessing the value of animals destined for sacrifice or human consumption. Others were attached to cemeteries, where they inspected embalmings and ensured that funeral rites were properly observed. Still others accompanied armies on campaigns, but we know of no ship's doctors.

Assistants of various grades helped these professionals. Thus, nurse-foremen cared for workers assigned to the mines and to the huge building sites created when temples and pyramids were being built or obelisks erected. It is easy to imagine how often accidents occurred among the thousands of men working under difficult and exhausting conditions.

Hesyre was a high-ranking civil servant of the third dynasty. Like many other practitioners of his time, he combined the medical responsibilities of "chief dentist" with those of "head of the king's scribes". Here he is represented holding the tools of a scribe in his left hand. Saqqarah, about 2700 BC. Cairo Museum, Egypt.

Canopic jars of Anpuhotep. These urns were placed under the protection of the four sons of Horus, who were patrons respectively of the liver, the lungs, the stomach and the intestines. They contained the viscera which were removed from the body as part of the embalming process. Saqqarah, about 1900 BC. Twelfth dynasty. Cairo Museum, Egypt.

This statue is probably of Imhotep, counsellor to Pharaoh Djoser (about 2800 BC), a scribe, architect, poet and doctor. The Egyptians venerated him for his healing powers and dedicated many shrines to him, in particular that of Memphis. 2600 BC. Louvre Museum, Paris, France.

Herodotus relates that the doctors were all specialists, some treating eyes, others the abdomen, and still others specializing in gynaecology. In fact we have to qualify this assertion, as we must the majority of contemporary accounts. In the fifth century BC, while the doctors of the capital were considered specialists, the same was not true of those in the provinces.

We know the names and biographies of several hundred doctors. However, none of them was as famous as Imhotep, who lived around 2800 BC. He was the prime minister of Pharaoh Djoser of the third Memphian dynasty (before the Old Kingdom), who built for his master the extraordinary mausoleum in the shape of a step pyramid which we can see at Saqqarah today. It is one of the earliest architectural stone monuments in the history of man. Imhotep was a high priest at Heliopolis and he bequeathed, by way of a will, moral instructions, and treatises on astronomy and medicine which had been added to over centuries. Later he was venerated as a healer, then deified and worshipped as a descendant of the god Ptah himself. Two thousand years later temples were built in his memory where the faithful sick used to practise nocturnal incubation*, hoping perhaps to be able to analyse dreams which were artificially induced, as was later also the practice in the *asclepion* of Athens and Epidaurus.

It is not so much the trading expedition to Punt (a country to the south-west of Egypt) led by Queen Hatshepsut which interests us here as the physical representation of Ati, the queen of Punt, who is suffering from a strange form of obesity with fatty hypertrophy of the buttocks and excessive incurvation of the spine. Deir el-Bahari, about 1490–1470 BC, eighteenth dynasty. Cairo Museum, Egypt.

PATHOLOGY
AND THERAPY

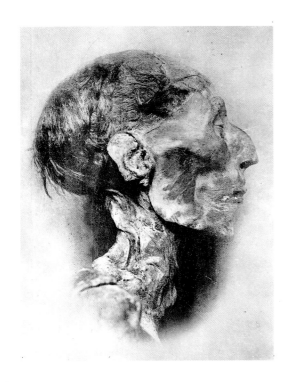

*Egyptian pathology is well known to us,
thanks to the embalming technique
described by Herodotus and the analysis of
mummies using modern techniques.
The mummy of Ramses II, nineteenth
dynasty, c. 1250 BC.*

*I*n all probability, Egyptian pathology
differed very little from that of Mesopotamia. However, we are able to learn
about it in more detail thanks to the
Egyptian mummies. These dried corpses
have been dissected, analysed and X-
rayed hundreds of times. We know about
the dental caries from which some pharaohs suffered. Doctors have diagnosed
rheumatism secondary to gum infections.
The imperfect calluses, osteomyelitis* and
Pott's curvatures* of the Egyptians of
three thousand years ago have no secrets
from us, any more than the bilharzia* or
ankylostomiasis* which were rife in a
country where water brought both life
and death. No other ancient civilization
offers such full information on human
pathology.

Gynaecology, and the didactic works
which doctors devoted to it, reveal to a
certain extent the sexual morality of the
period. Morals were fairly loose in Ancient Egypt, where women enjoyed considerable liberty and were important members of society. While marriage formed
the basis of the family, concubinage was
also virtually an institution, with adulter-
ous women encountering little suppression, and different forms of incest often
being tolerated, even glorified. It seems
that circumcision was practised during
various periods (the Hebrews doubtless
learnt the technique in Egypt), but it was
forgotten closer to our time. Some erotic
scenes such as dance scenes are also
worthy of mention. These decorated the
walls of tombs and accompanied the dead
into the next world.

*Anubis, patron of embalmers, "he who
wears the strip of cloth", prepares a corpse.
Deir el-Medina, tomb of Sennedjem,
nineteenth dynasty.*

Of course, this archaeological material, even though we can learn so much from it, only gives us an imperfect idea of the actual customs of the period. Nevertheless, we know that gynaecology was one of the main preoccupations of Egyptian doctors, with pregnancy often occurring early and being associated with numerous complications. It is possible to identify prolapse* of the uterus, for which pessaries* were prescribed; metritis*, vulvitis* and cancer of the womb, which were combatted with local injections, purgations and aromatic fumigations of which the precise composition is unknown.

The same uncertainty surrounds the vaginal contraceptive products which were recommended to Egyptian women. In the treatises, this subject occupies less space than the early diagnosis of pregnancy, which was made by observing the growth of two plants, one watered with water, the other with the urine of a woman who was thought to be pregnant. Today we marvel at the Egyptians' apparent prescience, because now we know that the hormones secreted by a pregnant woman can indeed stimulate plant growth. However, this rather hasty interpretation is in part erroneous. From the medical point of view, this test was only used to determine the sex of the foetus, and was an inexact analysis, since the effect on the plant proved to be the same, whatever the sex of the child. We cannot really call this prescience, but rather, postempirical magic. A plausible hypothesis would be the following: the Egyptians first discover that the urine of a pregnant woman stimulates plant growth. This experimentally established fact is then used not to confirm pregnancy – which is easy enough to do anyway if you wait a few weeks – but rather to make a magic prediction as to the sex of the child, this information being much more important from their society's viewpoint.

It is difficult to know whether circumcision (right) *was practised for reasons of hygiene or in observance of a purity ritual. Some rare texts describe the age "at which the sex has not yet been released", proving that this mutilation was carried out on young men at the approach of puberty. Saqqarah, mastaba of Ankhmahor, beginning of the sixth dynasty.* Above: *Thebes, tomb of Sennedjem.*

Thus, Egyptian medicine presents several examples of what today we would call "illogicalities". With the exception of aristocratic women, who used a special seat, Egyptian women gave birth in a crouching position, but the prescriptions recommended for a successful delivery consisted of prayers and incantations.

Ophthalmologists, some of whose names are known to us, were also held in high regard. There was Iri, the court oculist, for example, or indeed Kuy, the high priest at Heliopolis and inventor of an eye lotion whose composition has come down to us.

We know from a precise clinical analysis that a patient could have a squint following a fracture of the skull, and that blepharitis*, trichiasis and conjunctivitis were treated using eye lotions and various locally applied substances. Even if the Egyptians were familiar with cataracts, they do not seem to have practised surgery on the crystalline lens as envisaged by the Sumerians.

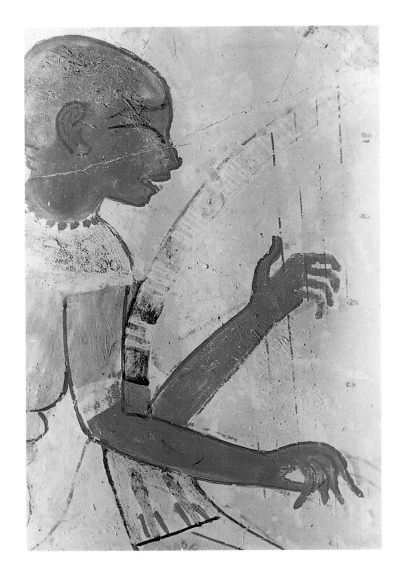

This blind harpist (right), and the treating the eye of a workman (below) show the attention paid by the Egyptians to ophthalmology. Gods were invoked in this connection: Thoth, as the doctor of the eye of Horus, and Amon. Thebes, tomb of Nakt, 1420 BC, eighteenth dynasty.

Sick man. Here the sufferer does not seem to be of a particular age or from a particular period. Bronze statue, New Kingdom. Vivenel Museum, Compiègne, France.

It is not possible to go into the details of the pathology and treatment of each organ here, but the manuscripts do reveal many interesting facts: older people were frequently affected by coughs, young children could suffer from asthma, no cure was known for putrid empyema. Various kinds of abdominal pain are also described, intestinal parasitoses (without the cause having been clearly identified), constipation, and so on. The Egyptians knew how to differentiate between disorders of the anus, a part of the body which is easy to observe. They diagnosed haemorrhoids and rectal prolapse and, in the team of court doctors, special mention is accorded to the "guardian of the king's anus". As for urology, the documents describe totally ineffective remedies for retention and incontinence, and for haematuria, a disorder which was often of parasitic origin and is still seen in Egypt today.

Two facets of Egyptian medicine – one religious,
the other scientific – expressed through
the subject of the child.
Above: *the goddess Isis, protectress of children,*
breast-feeding Horus.
Vivenel Museum, Compiègne, France.
Right: *amulet worn as protection against rickets*
in children, which is perfectly
represented elsewhere.

While the Ebers papyrus is the most famous, having been the first to be translated, it should be emphasized that the Edwin Smith papyrus is of great interest, since it gives an idea of Egyptian medical thinking. It is well preserved, dates from about 2000 BC, the beginning of the Middle Kingdom, and was perhaps inspired by Imhotep. It deals above all with external pathology*. The observations are listed in anatomical order, which always goes from top to toe. This type of presentation was also used later in the medical treatises of the early Middle Ages, and is still in use today in the lists of professional measures carried out by doctors. Each chapter describes a clinical case which is presented in a uniform manner: first, the surgeon carries out an examination which includes questioning the patient, exploring the lesion by simple methods such as palpation, probing the wound, mobilizing the segment of the limb and checking the arterial pulse. Then the surgeon tells the patient his diagnosis, comments on the prognosis – that is the chances of a cure – and finally there follows an account of the treatment, which usually consists of tricks that are as ingenious as they are effective, or of prayers and incantations in cases deemed to be incurable.

Without being anachronistic, we can qualify these descriptions of anatomical and clinical lesions: they were made on two levels, one simple, one complex. As an illustration of the complex level, where traumatic lesions of bone were concerned, a clear distinction was made between fissure fractures, incomplete fractures, green-stick fractures and comminuted fractures. Treatment consisted of a simple padded dressing, or a textile coated with adhesive which was used to draw together the lips of the wound. Wounds could be stitched and fractures immobilized by splints and a mixture of pitch and

LOGIC AND SURGERY

Metal pendant which was used to contain an oracular decree, namely a letter drawn up by a priest in accordance with the decision of a god on behalf of a human being. Here, protection is ensured by the magic of the writing. Tenth century BC. Louvre Museum, Paris, France.

TREATMENT OF ALOPECIA

combining exorcism with a pomade

"Remedy for warding off alopecia: 'Oh you the luminous one who does not stir from your course, you who fight against transgression, Aten, beware of him who has made himself master of the top of the head.' These words must be said over: yellow ochre, colocynth, alabaster, seeds known as 'eye of the sky' and honey. Reduce to a mass and apply to the head."

After G. Lefebvre, Ebers papyrus.

clay, a method recommended both for lesions of the long bones and for traumatisms of the cervical vertebrae in order to keep the head straight. Fractures of the bones of the nose were bonded by placing splints in each nostril in order to keep the fragments in a symmetrical position.

This brief presentation of the Edwin Smith manuscript leads us on to comments of a sociological, historical and scientific nature. First we should note the distance between medicine and surgery: external pathology lends itself to observation by eyesight, palpation or manipulation, while our senses do not perceive, or perceive inaccurately, internal pathology*. While the Egyptians knew the anatomy of animals in detail (three thousand years after the Smith papyrus, Galen was still only dissecting monkeys!), they knew nothing about man's anatomy, perhaps because of their respect for the human

This young man leaning on a stick is suffering from atrophy of the leg, which is typical of poliomyelitis. 1580–1330 BC, eighteenth dynasty. Carlsberg Collection, Museum of Sculpture, Copenhagen, Denmark.

appearance which they hoped to preserve for eternity by embalming the dead. For example, the skull of the deceased was emptied via the same nasal route which is used today to operate on the hypophysis, and the abdomen was eviscerated via a short, arch-shaped incision in the left iliac fossa. Such cramped routes do not provide scope for any observations relating to macroscopic pathological anatomy.

We could be tempted to contrast internal, hypothetical, magic or analogical medicine with surgery comprising effective observations and practices. In reality, the difference is not so great, and Egyptian medicine reveals a degree of acuity in examination, as well as empiricism, when it prescribes opium, henbane or belladonna for jactitation and painful conditions. At the same time, in certain surgical cases, it was recommended that traditional incantations be recited aloud to the god concerned: this could be Amon-Re, the supreme deity, or Isis, the mother goddess and protectress, or Tueris, the goddess with the head of a hippopotamus who presided over births. Following the example of Sumerian medicine, Egyptian medicine combined logic and magic. However, a distinction must be made between the two: currently, thanks to documents now available to us – and in spite of the caution which is necessary since a discovery which is imminent in Syria at Mari or Ras Shamra could overturn our opinions – we can assert that, in Egypt in 2600 BC, Imhotep was closer to ibn Nefis or the French fourteenth-century surgeon Guy de Chauliac than to the surgeons of Darius. However, the inhabitants of western Asia knew what they were about: despite the constant cultural and economic exchanges between the Nile valley and Mesopotamia, when a sovereign required the assistance of a doctor, it was the Assyrian who appealed to the Pharaoh, and never the other way round.

Lastly, let us beware of words which are used today in a sense that is in no way applicable to the people of 2000 BC. It is possible to comment at length on the association between "experimental materialism" and "magical and religious practices", but what would these terms have meant to a fellah or a court dignitary under Ramses or even under Nasser, when all matter was of divine origin and all phenomena obeyed laws which were laid down by the gods and to which the laws of men had to conform?

The distinction between magic and religion is derived from a system of references which is purely Western and moreover recent. In addition, three thousand years before Christ, the science of divination and oracles, was based on experience and on the repetition or conjunction of phenomena which were ascertained empirically.

Small stela of "Horus on the crocodiles". This was erected in a public place and was thought to provide protection against poisonous bites and dangerous animals. Sixth to fourth century BC. Louvre Museum, Paris, France.

WHAT HERITAGE?

We can never really get close to such an ancient form of medicine, about which history can teach us so little and yet so much. The pharmacopoeia alone would merit a more extensive exposition of its riches – similar substances were perhaps used by Western peoples in the Middle Ages, but they have been abandoned today – riches drawn from the study of viscera and animal excrement and plants from neighbouring and distant countries.

We should not smile at the mention of droppings, galls, amulets and exorcisms: this medicine decreed the precepts of hygiene and the therapeutic principles which still prevail.

The influence of ancient Egyptian medicine on other practices in other countries is obvious. In particular, the debt which the medicine of Hippocrates owes to Egypt has been understated.

However, one question remains: why, when in 3000 BC there were intellects capable of writing a treatise on minor surgery which was as intelligent as it was useful, were those who followed them so

The book of the dead of Userhetmos. Tueris, the goddess of fertility, appears here in the guise of a hippopotamus standing on its hind legs. 1320–1200 BC. Thirteenth dynasty. Cairo Museum, Egypt.

lacking in anything more than the ability to copy the manuscripts handed down by their predecessors?

Why did such precocity give rise to such stagnation? It is possible to establish this same phenomenon in other areas: for three thousand years, society retained the same castes, the same administrative structures, the same religion except for a few variants, the same funeral rites and the same tradition in which stories about magic and mythical voyages were repeated indefinitely from generation to generation.

Does intellectual opposition to change explain the fixedness of society, or is the reverse the case? Nobody can say. Nevertheless, we must not forget that our society and our Western science went through long periods of stagnation, with society and science by turns resisting that which today we call progress. The fact remains that, following on from the Edwin Smith papyrus, which is nearly four thousand years old, man and medicine have wasted time.

THE ARCHAEOLOGY OF MEDICINE
2600 – 323 BC

MESOPOTAMIA	DATE	DATE	EGYPT
		−2800	Old Kingdom
		−2700	First great pyramid Imhotep, architect and doctor
First Ur dynasty	−2600		
Sargon of Akkad Cuneiform tablets of remedies	−2300		
		−2100	Middle Kingdom Ptahhotep's prescription Edwin Smith papyrus
Hammurabi	−1730		
		−1580	New Kingdom
		−1375	Akhenaten
		−1354	Tutankhamun
The Hebrews in Palestine	−1300	−1300	Ramses II Ebers papyrus Chester-Beatty papyrus
Ashurbanipal The library of Nineveh	−670		
Jews are deported to Babylon	−597		
Great Persian Empire of Cyrus II	−550		
End of captivity in Babylon	−538		
		−525	Egypt under the Persian Empire
Alexander the Great takes possession of Persian Empire	−334		
		−332	Alexander takes possession of Egypt
		−323	Death of Alexander

chapter IV

The Greeks establish our system of medicine

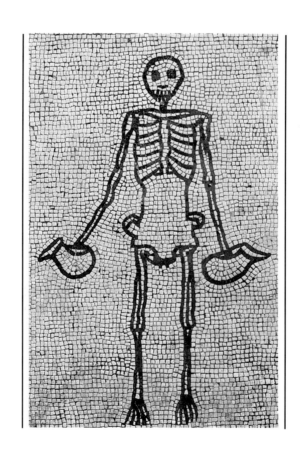

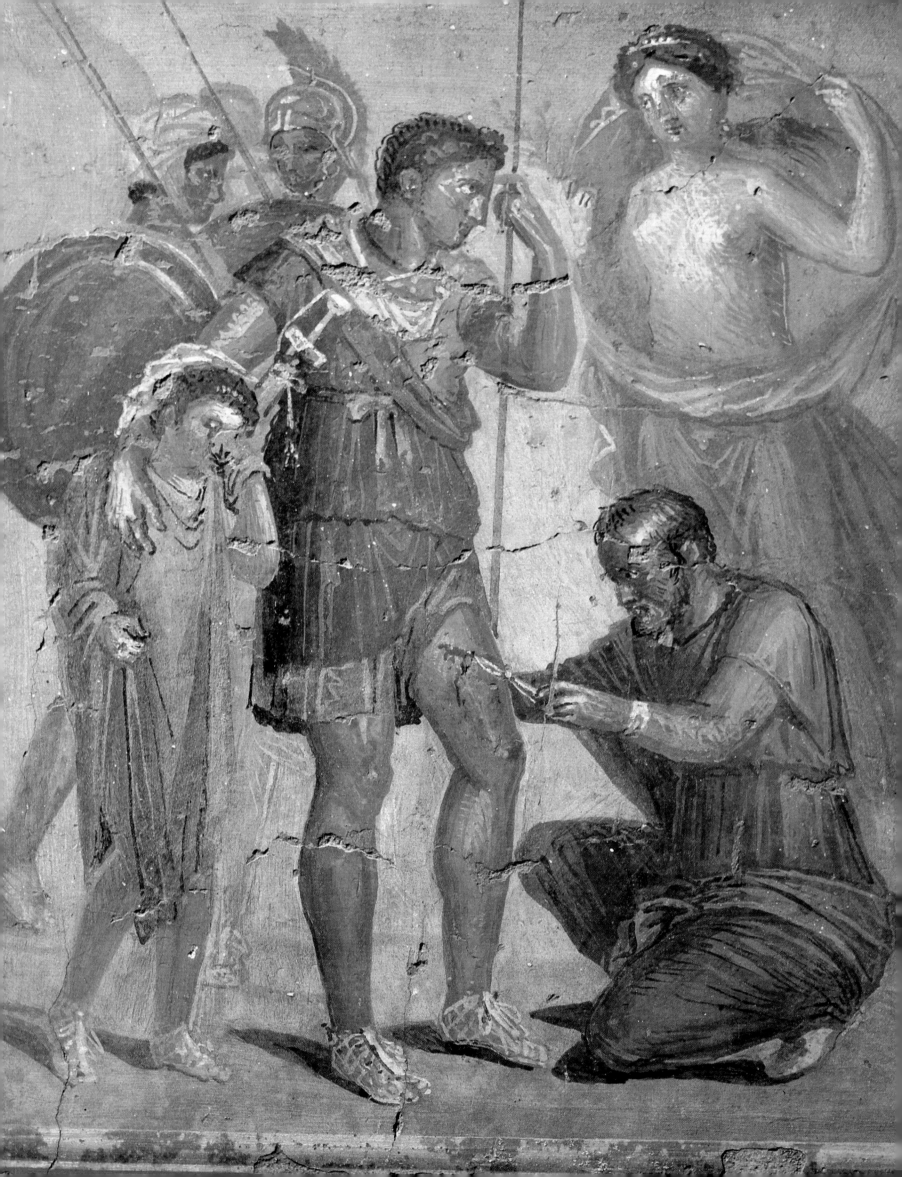

As we have seen, the beginnings of medicine were marked by uncertainties as the history of man passed through periods dominated by magic and religion, before arriving at a time when rational thinking prevailed. These uncertainties turn out to be even greater when we consider Ancient Greece, where there was no split between popular magic, practices of a religious nature and medical techniques, despite the influence of Hippocrates, who rid medicine in part of its philosophical and magic influences.

The pantheon of the Ancient Greeks included many gods and demigods who possessed powers of healing. While they could bring about disease when angered, seeking revenge or punishing a sacrilegious action, they could also cure illness. These gods almost always assumed human form, unlike the combinations of men and animals of whom the Sumerians and Egyptians thought so highly. They also behaved like men, whose passions they shared.

At their head was Zeus, the all-powerful. Apollo, master of the creative faculties and the arts, would heal if entreated to do so in the appropriate manner, but he could also decimate his enemies. His arrows spread the plague when the Greek

army was encamped before Troy. Similarly, the arrows given by Apollo to Heracles (whom the Romans called Hercules) were reputed to inflict incurable wounds.

Finally, the immortal Chiron, the most famous, wise and learned of the centaurs, taught medicine and himself practised surgery on Mount Pelion in Thessaly. He brought up Asclepius, and tended Achilles' ankle, which had been burnt as a result of his mother practising magic on him, by taking a bone from the skeleton of a giant.

Medicine: between myth and philosophy

I.

These two episodes in the Trojan war, as recounted in the Iliad *and the* Aeneid, *illustrate the stoicism and courage of Greek heroes.* Opposite: *the wounded Aeneas.* Right: *Achilles uses his javelin to close the purulent wound of Telephus. Fresco from Pompeii and bas-relief from Herculanum. National Museum of Archaeology, Naples, Italy.*

ESTAVRATION DV TEMENOS D'APOLLON

D'APRES
LES RVINES ACTVELLES ET LES TEX... ...IENS

Albert Tournaire (1862–1958),
Restoration in perspective of the
Temple of Apollo at Delphi, *1894.*
National College of Fine Arts, Paris, France.

ECHELLE

Apollo, who was worshipped at Delphi, was the mythical ancestor of Asclepius and Hippocrates. Here, as the "killer of a lizard", he symbolizes the end of disease and suffering.

ASCLEPIUS: A HEALING HERO

*A*mong the lower-ranking gods was Asclepius, also known in the West by the Latin name Aesculapius. According to legend, he was the son of Coronis and Apollo. Hermes is said to have taken him from his mother's womb when Coronis was already tied to the stake and succumbing to the vengeance of Artemis. The story goes that Asclepius went with Jason and the Argonauts to search for the Golden Fleece. As we have already

mentioned, the centaur Chiron is said to have taught him how to treat the sick using words, herbs and a knife. Thus, Asclepius, using therapeutic procedures still in use today, developed marvellous powers of healing.

According to tradition, he had many descendants. He had two daughters whose names still figure in our language today: Hygeia, who taught people how to lead their lives in a healthy way, and who gave us the word "hygiene", and Panacea,"she who heals all", the originator of medicines. Two of his sons are mentioned by Homer: Machaon, a gifted surgeon who treated the wounds of the warriors who laid siege to Troy, and Podalirius who devoted himself to medicine.

Asclepius remained vivid in the memory of the generations who followed his presumed existence, and his name gave rise to the word *asclepiad*, a term used by historians and a frequent source of misunderstandings. It can in fact be interpreted in different ways.

In its first etymological sense it means a descendant of Asclepius. As it is clearly all but impossible to verify the genealogies of the inhabitants of the eastern Mediterranean of three thousand years ago, we can hardly be surprised at the prolific numbers of descendants attributed to famous heroes by the story-tellers. Nor can we point a finger at practitioners of the healing arts who claimed to be descended from Asclepius in order to secure their reputation and their skills based on a heritage of magical talents.

Secondly, *asclepiads* were priests who were attached to the temples of Asclepius,

the *asclepions*, of which we will have more to say later. There they are said to have practised a "religious" medicine by invoking the benevolence of Asclepius. These priests are wrongly compared to the priests in charge of our Christian parishes, who devote themselves entirely to their ministry. By contrast, the job of an *asclepiad* was an honorary and costly post which was filled by laymen who were assigned to run the ceremonies of a place of worship for a limited period.

Finally, during the last two centuries before Christ and the first two centuries of the Christian era, it appears that *Asclepiades* became an appellation which was adopted by doctors or given to them by their patients, before becoming a name in its own right: thus, several men known as Asclepiades figured in Greek and Roman times, who were perhaps descended from each other and for whom it is difficult to establish a genealogical order.

Modern historians should therefore be cautious of over-using the epithet *asclepiad* and should not necessarily assume that it designates membership of a lineage, an organized clergy or a corporate body.

Opposite: Asclepius treats a young patient who has an injured shoulder. The subject is a classic one and is typical of numerous votive stelae from the Greek world. Museum of Piraeus, Athens, Greece.

With the stars keeping watch, Asclepius and Hygeia, his daughter, protect the owner of this intaglio amulet which was often worn in Athens. Medals Room, National Library, Paris, France.

NATURALIST PHILOSOPHERS

The West, which is keen on over-simplification, attributes the origins of philosophy to Socrates and the origins of medicine to Hippocrates. Yet the Greeks lived, fell ill and were treated long before the legendary Hippocrates. Unfortunately, however, his predecessors have left no traces.

Likewise, contemporary historians assign too important a role to the city of Athens whose predominance over the other Greek cities was brief. Before the sixth century, the philosophers, whose thoughts were to inspire the doctors of later centuries, expounded their ideas in Ionia (the western part of Asia Minor), in Sicily and in the south of Italy.

Without exhibiting bias, we should place Pythagoras at the head of these

Pythagoras, the first acoustician and music theorist, is also one of the "wise men" of antiquity who studied medicine. Theorica Musicae, 1480, Decorative Arts Library, Paris, France.

philosophers. Born in Samos, he lived for many years in Crotona. He was famous as a mathematician and throughout his life he pondered the existence of matter and the universe. With his disciples he established the universality of the four elements: earth, air, fire and water, which we also find in the human body.

His disciples prided themselves on belonging to a philosophical school, but Pythagoras distanced himself from them and contended with the mystery that surrounds learning: he held the teaching of knowledge to be the constant preoccupation of the scholar.

Pythagoras remained universally relevant, and had many followers. Thales of Miletus taught that a single method of analysis is suitable for all the activities of the mind; following the example of Anaximander of Miletus, he attempted to demonstrate that all life springs from water. Alcmaeon studied the origin of the human embryo and undertook to rule out cosmological and astrological considerations by founding good health on the balance of the four humours. We know that this theory of balance was to be successful for a long time to come, since it formed the foundation of psychological and biological sciences.

Heraclitus of Ephesus pondered the place of man in the cosmos and expressed the idea that all living phenomena are influenced by a form of "fire". He also attempted to split up substance into its component parts, and was alive when the doctrine known as atomism was propounded.

Zeno of Elea and his school developed the principle of the paradox in philosophical reasoning and its consequences on the study of nature: a thing may not exist at the same time as its opposite. While Empedocles of Agrigento wrote three treatises on *Nature* and a *Medical discourse*, Democritus, following on from Heraclitus, undertook to classify medicines.

*Are Asclepius and Hygeia feeding
their serpent mascot, the symbol of
prudence, or are they collecting
its poison to make a remedy?
Museum of Archaeology, Istanbul, Turkey.*

To Diogenes of Apollonia we owe a question which preoccupied scholars for years: is the vision of objects which the human eye affords a reality or a creation of that organ? How do our senses interpret nature and what confidence can we have in them?

All these men, who were curious about everything, formed schools which were sometimes rivals and sometimes allies. They established doctrines and constructed theories, among which were theories on the art of healing. Medicine did not represent an intellectually isolated discipline: it posed ordinary, everyday problems for these philosophers, who were curious about the composition of the universe, about the place that man could or should hold in it according to the wishes of a mysterious, unknown god, about the justification of life doomed inescapably to end in failure and death. All these were considerations which brought different interpretations to bear on human behaviour, and on the methods of reasoning which were accessible or useful to mankind. Naturally, doctors did not remain indifferent to them.

Apollo is also the god of terrifying punishments. By letting fly the arrows of plague, he condemns humanity to a slow death. Crater portraying the Niobids, Attic style, about 460 BC. Louvre Museum, Paris, France.

BEFORE HIPPOCRATES

Contemporary medicine probably assigns too important a place to Hippocrates and his work because of the absence of earlier documents. We have just mentioned a number of natural philosophers, and the books of Hippocrates reflect the theories they expounded. Moreover, it is probable that Hippocrates himself did not invent all the pharmaceutical formulae which he has bequeathed to us: older masters doubtless inspired the methodical precepts which he handed down to us, such as the fundamental principle of reasoned observation. Likewise, the Cretans possessed a specific art and culture several centuries before the Greeks did. In Homer's epic poem there are passages which are derived from legendary, sacred and prophetic narratives of Mesopotamia and the Nile valley. Hippocrates also drew inspiration from much older Egyptian papyri when he combined different plants or discovered medicines. The Greeks often had dealings with the Egyptians. They were fascinated by their political and administrative organization and the antiquity of their culture. Herodotus, in book II of his *History*, bears witness to this. It is therefore probable that, before Hippocrates,

Egyptian doctors, who were renowned for their observational talents and their *savoir-faire*, influenced the Greek practitioners who used their techniques.

Thus Plato attributes to Socrates some particularly eulogistic remarks on the competence of the doctors of King Zalmoxis. We do not know much about this king, but one question in particular comes to mind: did ties exist between the Greek practitioners and their colleagues in the East, in Europe and in Asia?

We do not possess any documents on the technical and intellectual roots of Hippocratic medicine. However, the interpretation of Homeric texts, from three or four centuries earlier than those attributed to Hippocrates, does provide answers to some of the questions posed at the start of this chapter. Homer certainly attributes a divine origin to the plague which attacked the Greek army, recounting that Apollo shot with his arrows the men who were guilty of sacrilege. Yet Machaon, Podalirius and other practitioners are described as tending wounds caused by sharp or blunt instruments. These were not magi, nor priests, but professional laymen, experts who carried out effective procedures learnt from former practitioners, without the aid of magic formulae or sacrifices to the gods.

Hippocrates (c. 460–377 BC), as depicted in a fourteenth-century miniature. He is shown inspecting urine, a procedure which epitomizes the doctor's examination of his patient at this period. National Library, Paris, France.

Paul of Aegina who, together with Hippocrates, was one of the "fathers" of medicine. From the frontispiece of a Galen manuscript, 1530. Library of the Old Faculty of Medicine, Paris, France.

Hippocratic medicine

II.

Tradition has it that Hippocrates was born in 460 BC on the small island of Cos, near the coast of Asia Minor. We can be sure of his historical existence from what Socrates has to say about his talents, but we know nothing about his life, despite legend attributing voyages and anecdotes to him. His name links him with the well-to-do class of the rural society of the time.

He is said to have stayed in Egypt and Scythia, and to have travelled through many Greek provinces. He refused to treat the Persian king despite a very attractive offer of "fees", and rehabilitated Democritus whom his compatriots considered to be mad. He is reported to have had many children, some of whom certainly became doctors, and to have educated many pupils who wrote about their former teacher and sang his praises throughout the Mediterranean.

We are not in a position to verify the authenticity of these events since, contrary to tradition, he was absent when the plague devastated Athens (in 430 BC). Thucydides would have written about him if he had played a part in it. Nor did he teach under the famous plane tree as legend relates, since the city of Cos did not exist in his day.

A LEGENDARY LIFE

*T*he fame with which his work was associated for many years after his death itself engendered new legends, in particular concerning his glorious medical genealogy. Hippocrates is said to have been the sixty-second descendant of Asclepius in a direct line, which would confer upon him a divine origin, since Apollo was the father of Asclepius. After him, his son-in-law, his sons and his grandsons allegedly treated all the princes of the ancient world, including Alexander the Great.

Hippocrates may well have belonged to a great family of doctors, especially since a "medical school" does seem to have existed on Cos. Its main concern was to theorize medical practice by laying down general rules based on observation, rendering it opposed to the school of Cnidus, which was more inclined to the study of individual cases without attempting to generalize.

According to tradition, Hippocrates died at the age of over one hundred.

The plane tree on Cos is legendary. Hippocrates is said to have held his consultations beneath it. Here, as pictured in a romantic engraving. Library of the Old Faculty of Medicine, Paris, France.

71

THE HIPPOCRATIC CORPUS

From the early Middle Ages onwards, doctors handed down a collection of texts which could be of considerable assistance in the practice of their profession. Numbering no more than sixty, these were grouped together under the title of *Corpus Hippocraticum*.

The form and content of these works vary. While some constitute actual documents treating a limited subject according to a logical plan – and we can indeed imagine that they were written by Hippocrates himself – others appear to be disordered clinical notes written in a succinct style such as a doctor might adopt today during his visits and consultations. The majority are written in the Ionian dialect of Cos.

Whatever the form of these "sixty" texts, all reveal a uniform didactic intention. They may not necessarily describe clinical cases complete with symptoms, data from the examination of the patient, even the patient's name and town, but they do lay down general principles.

The mode of expression is original: aphorisms summarize in a few words key ideas which apply to several pathological circumstances. They had to be learnt by heart and recited at a time when materials were limited to parchment for the instructors and wax for the pupils.

This type of teaching must have been genuinely successful, for not only were these aphorisms of Hippocrates taught up until the eighteenth century, but a large number of teachers wrote numerous treatises along similar lines to Hippocrates. Until the nineteenth century, teachers often drew up formulae which were easy to memorize, following the example of the Master of Cos.

The sixty Hippocratic books were therefore not written all one after the other, nor by the same man, and they certainly do not all date from the same period. In the nineteenth century Littré, the French lexicographer, organized various texts and fragments which were scattered throughout the libraries of the world and identified those which could have been linked with the school of Cnidus. It was also Littré who managed to date the various Hippocratic books with the greatest possible precision. Thus, some of the texts drawn up by the Alexandrian successors to Hippocrates are thought to date from several centuries later than the great doctor.

SOME HIPPOCRATIC APHORISMS

Many aphorisms written in Ancient Greek no longer make sense in the vocabulary of today. Others retain all their value and are evidence of good observation.
(Numbering by E. Littré.)

For the first time, Hippocrates frees medicine from philosophical ideas and above all from the magic with which it was encumbered. His teaching was to point the way for the entire history of medicine until the sixteenth century at least. Fifteenth-century manuscript. Library of the Old Faculty of Medicine, Paris, France.

A FAMOUS OATH

In the course of history, a famous passage has given rise to many exegeses, commentaries, adaptations and interpretations, be they true or false, namely, the oath which Hippocrates most probably did not draw up himself. Here is a translation:

"I swear by Apollo the physician, by Aesculapius, Hygeia and Panacea, and I take to witness all the gods, all the goddesses, to keep according to my ability and my judgement the following Oath:

To consider dear to me as my parents him who taught me this art; to live in common with him and if necessary to share my goods with him; to look upon his children as my own brothers, to teach them this art if they so desire without fee or written promise; to impart to my sons and the sons of the master who taught me and the disciples who have enrolled themselves and have agreed to the rules of the profession, but to these alone, the precepts and the instruction.

I will prescribe regimen for the good of my patients according to my ability and my judgement and never do harm to anyone.

I.1: Life is short, art is long, opportunity fleeting, experience deceptive, judgement difficult. One must not only do oneself that which is fitting, but also ensure that the patient, the assistants and external circumstances are willing to cooperate.

II.7: Restore slowly patients who have become thin slowly, and rapidly those who have become thin in a short time.

II.22: Diseases which are due to repletion are cured by evacuation, those which are due to emptiness by repletion, and in general the opposites by their opposites.

II.44: People who are naturally stout are much more at risk of sudden death than thin people.

V.6: Those who are afflicted with tetanus die within four days; if they live longer than this, they will be cured.

V.7: Epilepsy which occurs before puberty can be cured; but if it occurs at the age of 25 it will only cease on death.

VI.46: Those who become hunch-backed following asthma or coughing before puberty, will die (pulmonary and vertebral tuberculosis?).

The Hippocratic oath, taken from a fifteenth-century Greek manuscript. This famous text has been commented on repeatedly, and many versions have been made. Here, it has been annotated line by line in red ink. National Library, Paris, France.

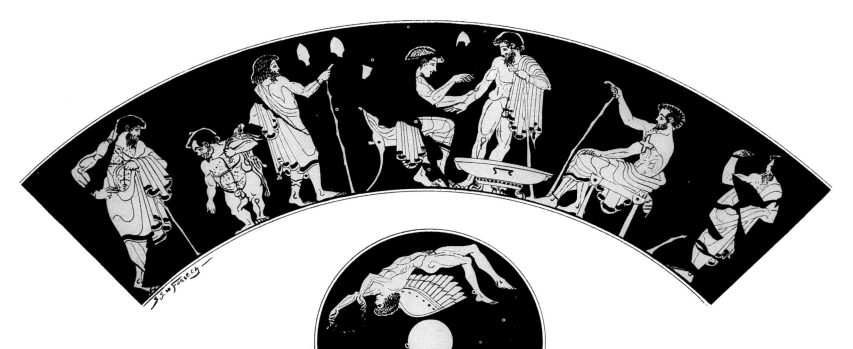

To please no one will I prescribe a deadly drug, nor give advice which may cause his death. Nor will I give a woman a pessary to procure abortion.

But I will preserve the purity of my life and my art. I will not cut for stone, even for patients in whom the disease is manifest; I will leave this operation to be performed by practitioners (specialists in this art). In every house where I come I will enter only for the good of my patients, keeping myself far from all intentional ill-doing and all seduction, and especially from the pleasures of love with women or with men, be they free or slaves. All that may come to my knowledge in the exercise of my profession or outside of my profession or in daily commerce with men, which ought not to be spread abroad, I will keep secret and will never reveal.

If I keep this oath faithfully, may I enjoy my life and practise my art, respected by all men and in all times; but if I swerve from it or violate it, may the reverse be my lot."

Some comments are necessary here. Let us forget the opening invocation and the final malediction. The first paragraph illustrates a desire for fellowship which is typical of the period, through the idea of mutual aid among the professional group of doctors and through the formation of

Hygeia tending cripples. On the left is a dwarf. We know of no women doctors of antiquity, with the exception of midwives, the mother of Socrates being one. Fifth century BC, from a nineteenth-century engraving.
Decorative Arts Library, Paris, France.

family-like relationships among its members. Some have seen in this the beginnings of a confraternity living in isolation, jealously guarding its privileges until it became, in the course of time, a narrow-minded, conservative corporate body. Many professions do indeed exist which practise the same customs and the same interdependences. When regulations or a revolution destroys them, they rebuild themselves immediately in another form.

If we place this passage in the context of the period, in which it obliged doctors to hand down their knowledge at a time when "technical schools" still did not exist, then doctors would have had to bring their profession out of the secrecy in which it had been clothed until then. The "Oath of Hippocrates" is a public text, accessible to all, that has nothing in common with the Eleusinian mysteries of which we are still completely ignorant. Not only did medicine not become a kind of freemasonry, but more generally, it obliged the holders of knowledge and techniques which were beneficial to man to impart them to following generations.

The second paragraph affirms the equality of men when faced with suffering and disease; it asserts that a doctor must above all protect life. Under no circumstances may he bring about death or provide poison for a suicide or murder. He will leave to others the responsibility for and the practice of abortion.

Finally, the third paragraph states for the first time the rule of medical secrecy, which does not constitute, as some would maintain, a professional privilege, but rather an elementary right of the patient and an obligation which the doctor must respect. This oath, drawn up some centuries before our time, reflects a number of moral rules which were in force in the Graeco-Roman society of the period. On the one hand, the doctor complies with a

Treating over-indulgence: an ephebe assists a drunken old man. Attic bowl, fifth century BC. National Museum, Copenhagen, Denmark.

number of constraints, and on the other, society demands from him a precise conduct: in this sense, the Oath of Hippocrates is a social contract. Doctors are still not allowed to be instrumental to murder or suicide, nor to provide access to toxic substances and, as in the past, medical secrecy is inviolable.

However, ways of thinking have evolved along with cultures and religions, and the precepts of Hippocrates which relate to abortion, for example, have undergone various modifications.

This oath, taken as guidance within the works of Hippocrates, is evidence of a definite continuity in the moral principles and ideals of our Western civilization.

A DIAGNOSIS OF LOVE

The young King Perdiccas of Macedonia was suffering from a malady with symptoms of languor which a doctor from Cnidus was unable to cure.
Fortunately, Hippocrates arrived from Cos, and his detailed interrogation enabled him to confirm that Perdiccas, without realizing it, was dying of love for a young concubine of his father's.
Once the cause of the disorder had been identified, the treatment was easy, and the king recovered. The same anecdote, but telling of other courts, was subsequently attributed to many doctors.

The medicine of Hippocrates seems obsolete today. The procedures with which he used to treat fractures and wounds remain valuable – so much so that he appears to us to be a better surgeon than doctor – but we cannot retain any of his prescriptions for medicines which were composed of substances from the animal, vegetable and mineral kingdoms. These medicines took the form of potions and ointments composed in the main of mixtures of simples. Doctors themselves prepared the decoctions, by pounding and grinding these substances, since pharmacists did not as yet exist. Hippocrates carried out cauteries and blood-letting, and administered purgatives and emetics. Such depurative procedures and substances remained in use until the end of the eighteenth century. In the same way, diet and lifestyle were carefully laid down.

THE HIPPOCRATIC METHOD

It is more rewarding to study the principles which were to guide the doctor's actions. In the first place, absolute priority was given to instruction. The doctor was expected to have read and to have learnt, and to have been educated by masters. He had to know the nature of the human body, its composition, anatomy and reactions to disease. On this account, Hippocrates condemns the ignorant, the charlatans, the magicians, the healers and the midwives who claim to treat the sick and who are more dangerous than effective.

In the second place, whatever the practitioner's theoretical knowledge, personal experience proves to be of prime importance. This advice, which is so obvious to us, was to fall into oblivion for centuries.

Lastly, nothing can replace questioning and examining the patient. The doctor must have a long discussion with the sufferer, looking at him, touching him, palpating his body. Only then can he form a diagnosis, consider the prognosis and suggest a treatment appropriate to the type of disease, to the age and disposition of the patient, the season of the year and to the climate of the country.

As we have seen, the Hippocratic method is based on pragmatism. Admittedly, in the *Corpus* we find ideas which are based on earlier philosophical doctrines. The composition of the universe, like that of the human body, is based on the four fundamental elements of the Pythagoreans: earth, air, fire and water. Four characteristics are associated with these four elements: dryness, humidity, heat and cold. Similarly, the human body also contains four humours: blood, phlegm, yellow bile and black bile. All these could be combined, although Hippocrates refused to become involved in this magic geometry. Indeed, this interpretation of nature was too theoretical for him, and he was of the opinion that only the examination which

A MUMPS EPIDEMIC ON THE ISLAND OF THASOS

"A swelling in front of the ears appeared on one side in some, but in the majority of cases on both sides, without fever. In all the patients, these swellings disappeared without incident... They were soft, large, diffuse, without inflammation or pain... They appeared in adolescents and in men in the prime of life; few women were affected... Some right at the start, and others later on, developed painful inflammation of the testicles, sometimes on one side, sometimes on both. The majority suffered greatly from this... The Thasians did not come to the doctor's surgery to seek help."

Above: *the king of Cyrene supervises the weighing of silphium, a plant with purgative properties which was grown in Cyrenaica and exported throughout the Mediterranean. Such was its importance that it was depicted on coins from the city of Cyrene (opposite). Cyrenian bowl, mid-fifth century BC. Medals room, National Library, Paris, France; tetradrachm, end of third century BC, Berlin.*

the doctor carried out, assisted by his knowledge and experience, could guide him in his decisions.

Hippocrates seemed apprehensive of doctrines which were adapted to disease, and thus was able to step back from a danger from which subsequent centuries did not escape.

Moreover, he chose, according to the pathological case, to employ two apparently contradictory procedures. Sometimes he thought that a disease had to be treated by its opposite; cold by heat, and vice versa, and at other times he acknowledged that disorders had to be treated by similar phenomena, such as serious diarrhoea by vomiting.

The constant improvement of knowledge, prudence in making decisions, the pursuit of balance in humours which have been disrupted by illness, the mistrust of abstract philosophies: these are the rules which are dictated by Hippocratic medicine.

MEDICAL CARE
IN GREECE

Despite the admiration which we feel for the seriousness, the methods and the thought which the *Corpus* conveys, we should not believe from reading it that all the people of Greece were treated in accordance with this moral code and these techniques. Alongside the doctors who claimed to be such, the rich and the aristocratic employed slaves or freed slaves with elementary experience of medicine. The common people who could not afford the doctors' fees resorted to mountebanks and village diviners and to barbers who sold charms, amulets and remedies of their own making. Plato's rationality did not win over Greece in its entirety and magic was still prevalent.

Neither did religion lose out. Everyone was able to invoke the god of their choice, but Asclepius became more prestigious as time went on. Already Homer had alluded to the temple consecrated to him at Trikka in Thessaly. After the crises of the fourth century BC, namely the Median wars and the Peloponnesian war – that is to say after Hippocrates, the *asclepions* became numerous in Greece. The most famous were at Epidaurus, Athens, Corinth, Cos, and later, Rome.

They were usually situated close to a spring and included baths, sometimes a theatre, an inn to accommodate pilgrims and their families, and houses for the priests. The sick left their offerings, spent

People came from all over Greece to the temple of Asclepius at Epidaurus to consult the oracles of the god. The many votive offerings which have been found illustrate the wide range of diseases for which they hoped to receive a cure. Alphonse Defrasse (1860–1939), General restoration, 1891–1893. National College of Fine Arts, Paris, France.

the night in the temple, and the following day the priests interpreted their dreams and prayed with the faithful. In this way, Asclepius, like Imhotep, was glorified until he too became a god.

At Epidaurus, inscriptions and votive offerings have been found which bear witness to the gratitude of the sick to Asclepius. They describe their suffering and their miraculous cures in simple terms: the blind who recovered their sight and the paralytics who recovered the use of their limbs. The *asclepions* reveal the psychosomatic and hysterical disorders of the people of Ancient Greece who were cured by suggestion or mental shock.

A clear distinction therefore emerges between "lay" medical practice and religious medical practice. Allusions to Asclepius are rare in the sixty books of the *Corpus*, which recommend a purely lay form of medicine that is inaccessible to both the ignorant and the charlatans. Besides, the priests did not teach. The *asclepions* had nothing in common with faculties of medicine and, contrary to a legend which dies hard, Hippocrates did not teach in the temple at Cos. A distinction must therefore be made between the care given by specially trained men who went in search of their patients, and that given by performers of religious practices.

At the time of Hippocrates, doctors were doubtless few in number. They

The asclepions were not only places of healing, they also served as places of entertainment. The theatre at Pergamum demonstrates this. Mid second century BC.

settled temporarily in a town where they entered into the service of a rich merchant or politician, before moving on to the next place. Hippocrates himself seems to have been familiar with this *periodeutic* way of life. Subsequently, some practitioners worked on behalf of a town council (*boule*), and it is usually known how much they earned. For most of the time, they cared for the slaves and the poor people of the town, assisted athletes of the palaestra and intervened when there was an epidemic, a war or an earthquake. They made their living by giving their services to groups or individuals according to a system which is still in use today.

The temples dedicated to Asclepius were generally built near a spring. The baths, which formed the basis of all the treatment, perpetuated an ancient ritual in which nature was worshipped. Here, the swimming-bath on Cos. Mid fourth century BC.

This statue of Victory on the asclepion at Pergamum bears witness to the care with which these establishments dedicated to Asclepius were generally decorated. Mid second century BC.

According to tradition, Hippocrates died in 377 BC. It is generally thought that his son-in-law and his two sons practised and taught medicine. However, none of their texts has survived.

Several authors whose work has come down to us are known as *dogmatists*. The highest ranking of these is Plato (428–348 BC). He was not a doctor, but he analysed all the known human sciences in his famous dialogues. He acknowledged the four elements which make up the universe and the human body, but attributed a major role in the functioning of the organism to the *pneuma*, a concept which was both energetic and immaterial, belonging to air and fire, which formed the

The doctrines of Alexandria

III.

breath of life. This breath of life gave movement to the organs and ensured their functioning. This Platonic idea was to enjoy a revival when it was taken up again in the seventeenth century by the *pneumatists*.

Diocles of Carystus, the author of the first herbalist manual, also had affinities with this dogmatist movement, as did Praxagoras of Cos, who studied the blood vessels. He was the first to distinguish between the arteries and veins and to study the variations of the pulse. However, his disciples did not adhere to the prudence of the former Master of Cos, and time and again they made rash deductions.

Conversation between a peasant and a philosopher by the side of a lustral bath, under the supervision of Asclepius, who is often portrayed as leaning on his traditional caduceus. Mosaic from the island of Cos, third century BC.

ΑΓΧΙΝΟΣ ΑΜΦΙΑΡΑΩΙ ΑΝΕΘΗΚΕΝ

ARISTOTLE: THE SUCCESSOR TO HIPPOCRATES?

A rebel of the school of the Athens Academy, Aristotle, who was born in Stagira, Macedonia, in 384 BC, was familiar with things medical as were many philosophers of his time. He surrounded himself with a group of *peripatetics*, and Alexander the Great was among his pupils. He first took an interest in zoology, then studied taxonomy, unfortunately applying to the anatomy of man information which he had acquired by dissecting animals. This method caused him to make numerous errors; for example,

Votive stela dedicated to Amphiaraus, fourth century BC. Museum of Archaeology, Athens, Greece.

he thought that the human heart had three chambers. He considered the heart to be the seat of the soul and the feelings, a doctrine which was perpetuated throughout the Middle Ages in the West. To him we owe such common expressions as "to have a heart" and "to wear one's heart on one's sleeve". He also thought that the body's warmth originated in the heart.

One of Aristotle's works deals with the origins of life and embryology, and the ideas put forward in it were also to be widely accepted for many years.

MEDICINE IN ALEXANDRIA

Alexander the Great's conquests brought about the decline of Athens and Ionia. The cultural policy under Ptolemy I and Ptolemy II then attracted the scholars of the Mediterranean to the new city of Alexandria. Two centuries of peace and good administration followed in the valley of the Nile. A new *mouseion* was built and dedicated to the nine Muses – namely to the arts and sciences – which perhaps resumed the ancient tradition of the "houses of life" of the time of the Pharaohs. The famous library of Alexandria grew until it contained more than seven hundred thousand manuscripts, so it is said. The religious eclecticism and tolerance of the Alexandrians opened the way for liberal policies which authorized, for example, dissection of the human body.

The library at Alexandria from a nineteenth-century reconstruction. A symbol of the accumulation of knowledge, it is said to have contained as many as seven hundred thousand volumes, with many works devoted to medicine among them.

This is why two anatomists were dominant during this period. Herophilus - born about 330 BC – is famous for his study of the nervous system and the meninges, and especially for his identification of the cerebral ventricles. One of the structures of the brain still bears his name. He established the seat of thought and feelings in the brain, leaving the heart to fulfil the simple function of maintaining body warmth. He practised both gynaecology and obstetrics, and described the internal genital organs of both man and woman.

Erasistratus, who was born in Chios in 320 BC, studied the vascular system. He asserted that the blood circulates from the arteries to the veins through invisible ducts and he corrected Aristotle's

SHEROPHIL9SERASIS'TRAT9

erroneous analysis of the heart. He was convinced that the role of the blood in the human body was of prime importance, and was opposed to blood-letting because of the resultant loss. Since he attributed most diseases to an excess of blood in the tissues, he is referred to as a *solidist*. He also examined the functioning of the peripheral nerves, and differentiated between the motor and sensory nerves.

His fame as a practitioner in the Hellenistic world was such that he was summoned to the court of Seleucus I, king of Persia, whose son Antiochus was wasting away. Erasistratus proved as perspicacious as Hippocrates, made the correct diagnosis and cured Antiochus. The progress made in human anatomy by Herophilus and Erasistratus was considerable, for the *Corpus Hippocraticum* contained only the rudiments of the subject. However, these two practitioners could not convince their colleagues. The *empirics* of Alexandria were not interested in anatomy. We know of some of them: Philinos of Cos, Serapion of Alexandria who tried to reconcile empiricism and dogmatism, and Heracleides of Tarentum who devoted himself to dietetics and techniques of preparing drugs.

The school of Alexandria began to decline in the first century BC. Even so, it included physicists, mathematicians, astronomers, pharmacologists and toxicologists. Among its doctors, disputes broke out between the different schools, and these were detrimental to the quality of their work. Pergamum, which boasted a botanic garden of poisonous plants, claimed to be the rival of Alexandria. In Alexandria itself, the conflicts between the disciples of Cos and those of Cnidus seemed to have been going on for centuries. Despite later interpretations, there is nothing which points to true collective teaching of medicine either in Athens, Pergamum or Alexandria.

Despite Hippocrates, magic and medicine were inextricably linked. On the right, a grimacing old woman foreshadows the witches of Macbeth. It is firmly rooted in tradition that sorcery must be carried out by ugly old women. Third century BC. National Museum, Naples, Italy.

In 47 BC, an initial fire, started during a riot, partially destroyed the library of Alexandria. Although its loss is often attributed to the Arab conquest, it vanished in the fifth century AD during bloody clashes between Monophysite and Orthodox Christians.

83

According to Ovid's Metamorphoses (Book XV), Asclepius took the form of a serpent when he came to rescue Rome from the plague. The metaphor is a beautiful one and illustrates the passage of medical knowledge from Greece to Rome. Eighteenth-century engraving. National Library, Paris, France.

The Greeks in Rome

IV.

The visit to the doctor. *Bas-relief from the first century* BC. *Museum of Roman Civilization, Rome, Italy.*

*W*hile the Greeks were evolving a complex form of medicine based on empiricism and intellectualism, the Italians were using prescriptions in which the traditions of folklore mingled with magic and religious sacrifice. Like many other peoples, they went in for ethnomedicine, the type of medicine which we call primitive or supernatural.

In Rome, little importance was attached to the profession of doctor or to the practice of medicine. Patricians entrusted such care to one of their slaves whom they regarded as competent, or sometimes to a barber. Thus, skilful and efficient slaves were able to get themselves freed and then open a shop. The Greeks, who were first slaves and then citizens, were soon to change this.

The first Greek doctor to come to Rome in about 219 BC, in order to practise, was Archagathus. However, it was Asclepiades, who arrived in 91 BC, who was the first to be hugely successful in attracting clients. He had been educated in Alexandria, and soon began to practise among high society. He became the friend of Mark Antony and Cicero, and taught Lucretius. His reputation grew still further when he interrupted a funeral procession and revived the "dead" man.

We can understand the fury of Cato the Elder at the favour won by this "charlatan", this seller of illusions, who belonged to a vanquished nation, was therefore unworthy of respect, and who claimed to treat the noble Roman citizens who certainly did not need his services.

Asclepiades, an epicurean, revived in Rome the *Methodist* School of Alexandria. As far as he was concerned, the body was only made up of matter, of small atoms circulating all around the body through invisible pores. Yet, materialist though he was, the *pneuma* appeared to him to be the source of all life.

We can understand that he won over his clientele by only prescribing the diets and medicines that pleased his patients. As for surgical treatments, he tried to carry them out "quickly, safely and agreeably": this Latin rule *cito, tuto et jucunde* was taught to students until the middle of the twentieth century, and still remains valid today.

Asclepiades probably adopted his name out of sheer boastfulness. On his death, an impressive influx of Greek doctors arrived in Rome. There were fourteen of the same name as he, either hoping to win the protection of the demigod Asclepius, or claiming to be the pupils of the fashionable Asclepiades.

Thessalus of Ephesus, who was a doctor at the time of Nero, did not enjoy the fame of Asclepiades. He was judged

ASCLEPIADES – A FASHIONABLE NAME

to be arrogant, scheming and a charlatan who advised his patients in accordance with their wishes so as not to make mistakes in his prescriptions.

Themison of Laodicea in Syria distinguished between three kinds of ailment: those which were caused by tension, those which were caused by relaxation, and those which did not fall into either category and were said to be mixed. He in turn took up the concept of the "crisis" which had been defined by Hippocrates, and so divided diseases into three phases: incubation, effect and abatement.

Soranus of Ephesus is still the most influential because of the impact of his teachings. After being educated in Alexandria, he came to Rome in about 100 AD. He was highly cultured, and he asserted his independence in a book against the medical sects, declaring himself to be connected with none of them. He also wrote a collection of biographies of doctors which we consider today as the first attempt at the historiography of the profession. Above all, Soranus of Ephesus is famous for his treatise on gynaecology and obstetrics in which he studies the different mechanisms of human generation, enumerates the causes of dystocia*, and recommends procedures for use in difficult labours, in particular when the umbilical cord appears before the foetus. He also gives advice relating to paediatrics and on how to feed and bring up small children.

Ivory box of Roman origin for containing medicinal powders. On the cover, Asclepius, Hygeia and the inevitable serpent. National Museum, Sion, Switzerland.

CELSUS' "DE ARTE MEDICA"

*M*ost of the doctors of this period wrote or dictated their works in Greek. Educated Romans knew Greek, as did the medical practitioners. Celsus broke free from this tradition by being one of the first to write in excellent Latin.

Following the example of Pliny the Elder, Celsus was a naturalist and encyclopaedist who practised medicine in first-century Rome. His treatise *De arte medica* is the first complete work on the medical profession. Like Soranus of Ephesus, he too claimed not to belong to any sect.

He listed all the illnesses, placing them in three categories according to whether they could be cured by diet alone, by medicines or by surgical intervention. At the same time as this study of therapeutics based on medical and surgical taxonomy, he established another anatomical and symptomatic form of therapeutics in which he differentiated between general and localized disorders. We can understand his interest in the treatment of patients, since, like Hippocrates, he neglected diagnosis in favour of prognosis. Celsus, "the Cicero of medicine", was the first to write an exhaustive treatise on human pathology. Unfortunately, he fell into unjustified oblivion, since the fame of Galen eclipsed his own.

A successful book – Natural History *by Pliny the Elder (23–79). Five books (out of thirty-seven) concern remedies made from plants, as demonstrated by these two illuminations dating from around 1500.*
Left: *the preparation of an ointment.*
Above: *its application to a wound. Marciana Library, Venice, Italy.*

THE PNEUMATISTS AND ECLECTICS

During the first century AD, several dozen Greek doctors made lasting names for themselves, either directly through their books or by being quoted by later authors. On the whole, all claimed to support the eclectic movement – that is, they did not belong to a sect or to a school – but, in following the Platonic idea of pneumatism, they moved away from the precepts of Hippocrates. At the same time, while displaying their freedom of spirit, they developed sympathies with the dogmatists of Alexandria, who held that all bodies, whether animate or not, possessed their own vital air which governed their destiny.

Archigenes of Apamea is famous for his surgical and gynaecological work. He seems to have been the first to use a vaginal speculum and, perhaps, to have applied ligatures to the arteries of a limb just before amputation. As for Rufus of Ephesus, he described with great precision bubonic plague and leprosy. His name remains linked with some original pharmaceutical prescriptions. We cannot say with certainty whether Aretaeus of Cappadocia, who was less well known, plagiarized or inspired Archigenes. A humoralist, who took his inspiration from Hippocrates, he studied the blood coughed up by phthisis sufferers, and commented that haemorrhages in one of the cerebral hemispheres are often accompanied by paralysis of the opposing side of the body.

An important contribution was also made at this time by Dioscorides. His main work, *De materia medica*, was written after he had travelled extensively, and describes mineral, vegetable and animal products with therapeutic uses, together with the methods of preparing and administering them. His prescriptions were to be followed to the letter, copied and adapted, from the time of Nero until the middle of the nineteenth century.

The seven wise men of antiquity: Plato, in the centre, Zeno, Aristotle, Pythagoras, Epicurus, Theophrastus and Socrates. In the Ancient World, medicine was not a separate discipline, but was closely linked with other forms of knowledge. Mosaic from Pompeii. National Museum of Archaeology, Naples, Italy.

Imaginary portrait of Galen, detail from the frontispiece of a fourteenth-century manuscript. National Library, Paris, France.

"GALEN WAS WRONG!"

*T*he strong personality of Galen dominated medicine in the second century AD. He was born at Pergamum in 131, where he commenced his education. He then travelled the Mediterranean region to complete it at Smyrna and Alexandria. In 163 he was living in Rome, but he left for political reasons. He came back two years later at the invitation of Marcus Aurelius, and died there in 201.

His contemporaries acknowledged his wealth of learning but did not like him, thinking him conceited, cruel and vindictive. As an eclectic, he ridiculed the medical sects, whether empirics or dogmatists, atomists or materialists. However, he could not help but be influenced by contemporary trends; he has been called a *naturalist* because, doubting the efficacy of his treatments, he expressed the idea of a benevolent nature, the mistress of healing, *natura medicatrix*. He thus inaugurated therapeutic scepticism, which is still alive today. We would call him an *organicist* – one who holds that all symptoms are due to organic disease.

Although he challenged Hippocrates and frequently held opposing ideas, he adopted his theory of the four humours: the blood, phlegm and yellow and black bile. A correct balance resulted in good health, so treatments aimed at restoring any imbalance.

The same applied to the system of temperaments, the number of which he fixed at four. The association of the four elements, four humours and four temperaments finally led to an absurd arithmetical form of medicine in the Middle Ages. If Galen borrowed these ideas from the Master of Cos, he distanced himself from him by believing reasoned diagnosis to be important, and associated himself instead with the pneumatists, particularly by insisting on the role of natural heat, which he believed was indicated by the pulse.

ypocras   manducare ut uuuá. Aly ítedút uuíc ut mádnicent   Jntéco eiz   Galien'

Or aícp uult q taruá cuftodire
clanitatez. cuftodiac fozu ncat
tibi necoffarui fte z hibcat abú

Hippocrates (on the left) and Galen in conversation. This miniature from the sixteenth century illustrates both the relationship between the medical knowledge of the two men, and the extraordinary durability of their teaching through the ages. National Library, Paris, France.

As well as being a theorist, Galen was also an experimenter, studying in the dog the effects of ligation of the ureters on the production of urine, and the functioning of the muscles after hemisection of the spinal cord at different levels. Unfortunately, he only dissected monkeys, and his examinations led to errors in his pronouncements on human anatomy.

He is responsible for the incorrect theory of the existence of direct communication between the two ventricles of the heart, a theory which was not questioned until the sixteenth century. William Harvey finally put an end to it one hundred years later.

The disdain with which Galen regarded surgery is due to the fact that he only came across it in the context of the care given to gladiators in the arenas of Pergamum and Rome, and to slaves who had been injured while at work. Such medical aid was also held in contempt by his contemporaries, and surgery did not recover from this prejudice until the late eighteenth century.

Finally, Galen did not escape the traditions of his time. He recommended the

interpretation of dreams by doctors and medical astrology. However, despite the errors committed by this encyclopaedic author, we must credit him with having made a remarkable synthesis of all the philosophical doctrines linked to medicine, while underlining the fundamental obligation of doctors to observe their patients well. He also initiated the idea of experimentation.

His influence was such that we still refer today to galenical medicines, and in any case he cannot be held reponsible for the rigid interpretations which were subsequently made on the basis of his teaching.

We can date the start of what today has become public health from Galen's time

Balneotherapy, like thalassotherapy, has always been popular. The Romans devoted monuments to their ablutions. Such buildings were sometimes lavish and were inspired by concern for the public good and by business sense. Above: painting found in the baths of Titus, Rome, Italy. Below: The thermae of Diocletian by G.P. Pannini (1691–1765). Corsini Palace, Rome, Italy.

in Rome. At that time, all the cities of the Empire had sewers, public latrines and fountains to provide clean water. Records from some of these towns mention payments to doctors known by the Greek name of *archiater*, who were employed to care for the poor and assist during epidemics. Doctors and surgeons accompanied armies on campaigns. *Valetudinaria*, or nursing establishments which accommodated veterans and the infirm, began to spring up, becoming the first hospitals. But these structures of health care and these buildings were only able to function under a well-managed administration which disappeared during the great barbarian invasions and the fall of the Empire.

THE GREEKS ESTABLISH OUR SYSTEM OF MEDICINE
776 BC – AD 476

POLITICAL SCENE	DATE	DATE	MEDICINE
Start of the Olympiads	−776		
Rome is founded	−753		
		−550	Cures at Epidaurus
Second Greek war against the Persians	−481		
		−430	Plague at Athens
		−460? to	Hippocrates' *Corpus Hippocraticum*
		−377?	Medical schools at Cos and Cnidus
Death of Socrates	−399		
		−390	Plato's *Timaeus* takes up Hippocratic subjects
Rome is taken by the Celts	−381		
Advent of Alexander the Great	−336		
		−330	Aristotle the naturalist
		−300 to −100	Heyday of the School of Alexandria
			Dogmatists and empirics at Alexandria
			An asclepion in Rome
		c. −219	First Greek doctors in Rome
Greece is annexed	−146		
Syria is annexed	−64		
		−60	Asclepiad and Methodist School in Rome
Gallic War	−58 to −51		
Death of Julius Caesar	−44		
		30	Celsus' *De arte medica*
Death of Christ	33		
		60	Dioscorides
		100	Aretaeus of Cappadocia
		131 to 201	Galen
Germanic invasions	260		
The Goths in Athens		287	Martyrdom in Syria of Cosmas and Damian, Christian doctors
Emperor Constantine I	306 to 337		
		325 to 403	Oribasius is doctor to Julian the Apostate
Christianity is the state religion	380		
			Hospitals in the Hellenistic world
Rome is taken by Alaric	410		
End of the Western Empire	476		

chapter V

The Middle Ages in Mediterranean countries

Many of our contemporaries regard the Middle Ages, from the end of the Western Roman Empire in 476 to the fall of Constantinople to the Turks in 1453, as a period of stagnation and obscurity, not to mention an era of obscurantism. They view it as an age in which man achieved nothing, discovered nothing and created nothing for one thousand years.

It is still difficult, even today, to appreciate the legacy of the Middle Ages. Many documents were lost and those which survived are difficult to interpret. Yet the medicine of 1453 in Europe was not that of imperial Rome; doctors did work, reflect, write and thus further their knowledge and perception of health and disease.

In 324, Constantine founded on the banks of the Bosphorus, a capital to which he gave his name.

The "New Rome", inaugurated on 11 May in the year 330 amid celebrations which lasted forty days, was soon to play a crucial role in the east of the empire: a political role, because of the constant presence of the emperor in the city; a religious role, as it became the seat of the patriarchy; an intellectual role thanks to the university founded in 330; and, last but not least, an economic role, for Constantine wanted to make Constantinople the great eastern metropolis of an empire which still remained centred on Rome.

He did not, however, foresee the imminent collapse of its eastern provinces when beset by successive invasions, from the sack of Rome by Alaric, in 410, to the reign of Theodoric one hundred years later. Thus, Constantinople became the true successor to Rome, and Greek gradually supplanted Latin.

The Byzantines, heirs of Hippocrates

I.

A sick person presents his bare arm. Illuminated initial letter from a Latin version of the Practicia *by Alexander of Tralles (525–605), one of the medical works of Byzantine origin most frequently translated in the West. Central Italy, mid twelfth century. National Library, Paris, France.*

The harvesting of medicinal herbs, from an Italian pharmacopoeia of the fifteenth century. Royal Library, Turin, Italy.

In the years following its foundation, Constantinople imposed itself as the capital of the Roman Empire, from the British Isles to the Crimea. But slowly its domain was reduced under the attacks of its neighbours.

The successors of Julian (331–363) lost in turn Gaul, Spain, Italy and part of the Balkans. Although Emperor Justinian (482–565) could boast of partial reconquests in the eastern Mediterranean, the imperial territory nonetheless shrank over time, despite individual successes since these were always countered.

In the eighth century, the Arabs, incited by the new religion of Islam, conquered Egypt, Africa and Syria. The Slavs and Bulgars occupied the Balkans and the Turks started to gnaw away at the banks of the Black Sea, Caucasia and ancient

THE RICHES AND WEAKNESSES OF THE EASTERN "ROMANS"

The Emperor Justinian I (482–565). Under his reign, some prestigious doctors lived in Byzantium: among them John the Psychrist and above all Alexander of Tralles, whose brother built the Church of Saint Sophia. C. 548, Church of San Vitale, Ravenna, Italy.

Persia. Gradually, the old empire was reduced to Greece and part of Asia Minor.

This Byzantine state bore little resemblance to our image of a modern nation. It had nothing to ensure its prosperity or survival and, with no system of succession, the emperors simply deposed each other.

It was a melting pot of races and languages and the foreigners on the throne were certainly not Greek. They were, furthermore, unable to impose any authority on the mercenary armies or the corrupt administration which grew rich at the expense of the State.

From early in the fifth century, Christianity was the sole religion in the Empire. This unifying factor could have helped create a certain cohesion, but instead major theological disagreements on the nature of Christ resulted in numerous schisms and heresies. Orthodox, monophysite, dyophysite and monotheistic clans wrangled over sees and patriarchates. Arians, Jacobites and Nestorians tore each other apart.

These "Byzantine" conflicts would not have had such serious consequences if politics had not been involved, for Greek orthodoxy and liturgy appeared to be intolerably authoritarian to the Egyptians, Levantines and Armenians, all of whom had their own languages and traditions and demanded their own bishops.

Thus, riots and civil wars ensued, due to different concepts of Christianity. In parallel to this, factors peculiar to the Empire conspired to weaken it and opened the way to foreign conquests.

Byzantium nonetheless produced a brilliant culture. Although it lost the two major cities of Antioch and Alexandria to the Arabs in the seventh century, it remained the centre of Mediterranean trade and the riches of Asia flowed to it: gold, gems, silk, carpets, spices, fruits and strange new animals.

From Byzantium, traders, artists and scholars travelled to the West. Architects designed Andalusian gardens and palaces as well as the castles of feudal lords; mosaics adorned Roman churches, and icon painters accompanied monks and bishops to Catalonia, Ireland and Moscow.

This capital was also a focal point for the cultural traditions of the Mediterranean basin: philosophy from Athens, law from Antioch and science and medicine from Alexandria. As the depositary of ancient knowledge, it was not only able to develop it – albeit modestly perhaps – but above all to transmit it to less privileged countries.

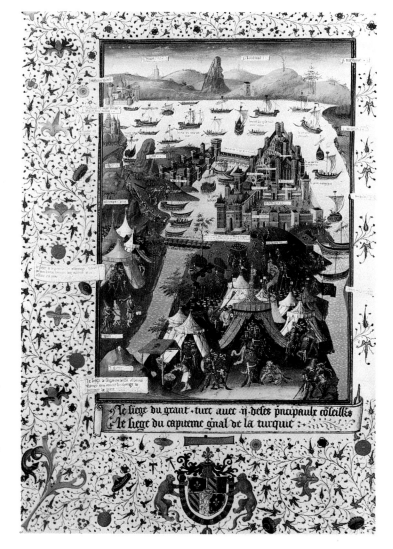

The conquest of Constantinople by the Turks, in 1453, marks the definitive collapse of the Byzantine Empire, mid fifteenth century. National Library, Paris, France.

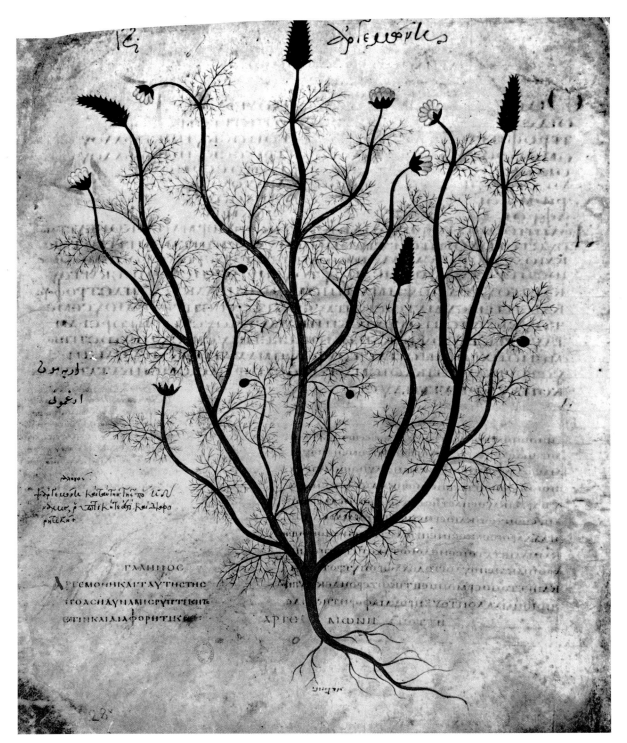

Pheasant's eye, usually used as a sedative, from a version of Dioscorides' De materia medica: *the* Codex Anicae Julianae, *one of the oldest illustrated botanical manuscripts of Byzantine origin still in existence today. Early sixth century. National Library, Paris, France.*

SOME BRILLIANT SUCCESSORS

*F*rom these early centuries, when the empire was no longer completely Roman but was not yet orientalized, dates the work of Oribasius (325–403) of Pergamum, the intellectual heart of the era. As master and companion of Emperor Julian, with whom he shared the return to paganism, he was to live in exile with the Goths for a number of years before joining the imperial court. It was there that he started work on a monumental medical encyclopaedia – only part of which has survived – and which is on a greater scale than the *Corpus Hippocratum* and Galen's treatises. Oribasius also included important texts written by several of his predecessors, such as Archimedes, Dioscorides and the surgeon Antyllus (who probably lived in the third century) and even perhaps Alexander of Aphrodisias. This erudite man, a commentator on Aristotle and as such considered a peripatetic, proved to be an excellent naturalist. He also asserted himself as an iatrosophist doctor (an

expert in remedies). Philosophers and doctors propounded abstract medical theories current in Alexandria during its decline: eclecticism, methodism, pneumatism, etc. Byzantine medicine was gradually to turn away from these scholarly disputes, intellectually stimulating no doubt but ineffective in the curing of disease. Oribasius, who was also interested in producing a pharmacopoeia, condensed his works into the form of a manual intended for the instruction of his son, a manual used for many years in the West.

Were it not for the compiler Aetius of Amida, a number of other doctors who were contemporaries of Oribasius would probably have been forgotten. Aetius of Amida had no hesitation in adding to a pharmacopoeia, which is now a classic work, magical formulae and invocations from the new Christian religion. He too concentrated on the essential accuracy of

Two plates from a Byzantine version of the Theriaca *by Nicander, a Greek writer of the second century* BC. *Treated as antique murals, they represent the parts of the plant to be picked and show their medical application.* Right: *the alkibios (*Echium rubrum*) used against snake bites. Eleventh century. National Library, Paris, France.*

diagnoses and developed uroscopy which was subsequently held in high esteem.

John the Psychrist (who died after 467) apparently inaugurated a function subsequently found in many courts: that of the emperor's physician. He won the admiration of his contemporaries and his successors with the efficacy of his therapeutics and the simple diets he prescribed for his patients, hence his merited appellation of "refreshing".

On a more serious note, Alexander of Tralles was a contemporary of Emperor Justinian (sixth century). Born at Ephesus, he travelled the empire from Armenia to Tangiers and Gaul, an empire which prospered once more for a short while, and settled in Constantinople where his brothers held high positions: one of them built the Church of St Sophia. In his *Twelve books of medicine*, he catalogues and methodically describes all known diseases and

Alexander of Tralles holding his "book of medical art", from one of the many Latin versions, from the Carolingian age, of his Practicia. *Early ninth century. National Library, Paris, France.*

then looks at traumatisms of the head and at fevers.

In contrast to his predecessors, he does not reproduce the work of ancient authors such as Hippocrates and Galen, despite his respect for them. He was one of the first to consider personal experience to be as useful and necessary as the knowledge of the Ancients. He thus produced an original work which merited greater attention from future generations.

In attaching such importance to diagnostics by questioning patients and examining symptoms, it was he who originated the precise description of a parasitic affliction of the liver: amoebiasis, causing the formation of abscesses. He also showed that extracts from poppy heads can relieve both coughing and chest pains, but that at too high a dose, they prevent coughing and expectoration* thus increasing blockages in the bronchi; and indeed today we now know that opiates* impair the respiratory function.

Paul of Aegina, who died around 690 at the time of the major Arab conquests and worked in the field of surgery, can be compared to Alexander of Tralles in the field of medicine. It was he who, in his *Summary of medicine* in seven volumes, divided the inventory of surgical diseases into two main sectors, as the surgeons of the twentieth century were to do later: afflictions of the soft tissue and those of the bones.

Paul of Aegina describes precise techniques: tracheotomy, ablation of the ganglions and superficial tumours, the treatment of traumatic aneurysms*, drainage of dropsy* of the stomach or hydrocele* in the *tunica vaginalis* of the testis.

Later, in the eleventh century, Michael Psellus, who owed his appellation to his speech defect, undertook a large-scale work on the subject of the natural sciences, which also covered versification techniques, the properties of stones, acoustics and the action of demons. He was in the imperial service and the scope and variety of his reflections, it is said, were equalled only by his vanity. His secretary Symeon Seth, a more modest man, studied the nutritive value of foods and judiciously commented on Galen's philosophy.

Following this rather summary list, it should be borne in mind that the authors did not rewrite their predecessors' texts but simply commented on them; in doing so, each one provided a new feature by describing a recent operating technique, adding an unknown plant to Pliny's herbal, supplementing Dioscorides' pharmacopoeia with a new composition learnt in Persia or India or revealing anatomical features not known to Galen, such as the salivary glands or the nerve of a small muscle in the hand.

In this way, they continue the classic Athenian tradition and each add their own stone to the monument of knowledge started by their ancestors.

FROM
VALETUDINARIA TO
HOSPITALS

However, Christian society, which took hold over the centuries, differed fundamentally from that of Socrates in the importance it afforded religion. Despite the presence of a patriarch, the emperor alone controlled the Church. Yet the clergy had considerable wealth and power, further enhanced by the development of monasticism which gave rise to monasteries and convents far and wide.

Although the Roman Empire did already have *valetudinaria*, establishments similar to hospices, later almost all the monasteries and convents in Constantinople, the major towns and the most remote country areas were to have their own inns for pilgrims, and hospitals. They appear to have been opened first at Edessa in Syria and Caesarea in Cappadocia

There are frequent healings in the Gospels. Byzantine medicine is a divine as well as a human task. First half of the fourteenth century, Monastery of Christ-in-Chora, Istanbul, Turkey.

in the fourth century, then in Constantinople and Jerusalem and soon more generally. Financed by donations and pious foundations, they welcomed the new-born and lepers alike, and illustrate the role of the Church in the medical life of the time, for until the nineteenth century, in Europe, the institution of the hospital was to remain in the hands of Christian charity.

Moreover, culture and instruction, not at all widespread at that time, already constituted a means of social advancement, and a large number of priests and bishops studied theology, philosophy, medicine and science. The number of medical clerics grew to such an extent that a patriarch in the twelfth century forbade his priests from practising medicine:

history does not tell us if he was obeyed.

However, the extent of the competition between men of the Church and court physicians and practitioners in the towns and armies who lived by their profession remains unclear. One thing is certain: the new religion left the former *asclepaeions* in ruin, and did not stop the sick from entering churches to ask God, Christ, the Virgin Mary or the thaumaturgic saints – all of whom have a specific power over certain diseases – to heal them.

While the Romans devoted a special cult to the twins Castor and Pollux, the Church in the East replaced them by Cosmas and Damian, two healers and brothers (martyred in Syria at the hands of Diocletian) who were to acquire a reputation as *anagyris*, i.e. providing treatment without receiving money. Western iconography was later to immortalize their most celebrated miracle: the replacement of the gangrenous leg of a father of a family by that of a man who had just died.

We must, however, tread warily for, during this long period in history, which we call Byzantine, surviving medical texts

The healing of the blind man (left) and the raising of Lazarus (right), two versions on the same theme of the miracle as therapy.
Byzantine manuscripts, twelfth century.
National Library, Athens, Greece and Earl of Leicester's collection, Holkham Hall, England.

do not combine medicine and religion. The study of nature and diseases was still a lay topic and we know of no doctor condemned by the Church for his theories. This was not so in later centuries when the clergy was, as is well known, to adopt a quite different position, for example, in the 1630s, when William Harvey's theory of the circulation of the blood was criticized and condemned.

The miracles of the thaumaturgical saints and healers accompanied those of Christ. Here, Saint Cosmas and Saint Damian, martyred under Diocletian and the patron saints of surgeons, replace a gangrenous leg by that from a black man. The change of colour helps the public perceive the miracle more clearly.
Fernando del Rincon (1455–1517).
Prado Museum, Madrid, Spain.

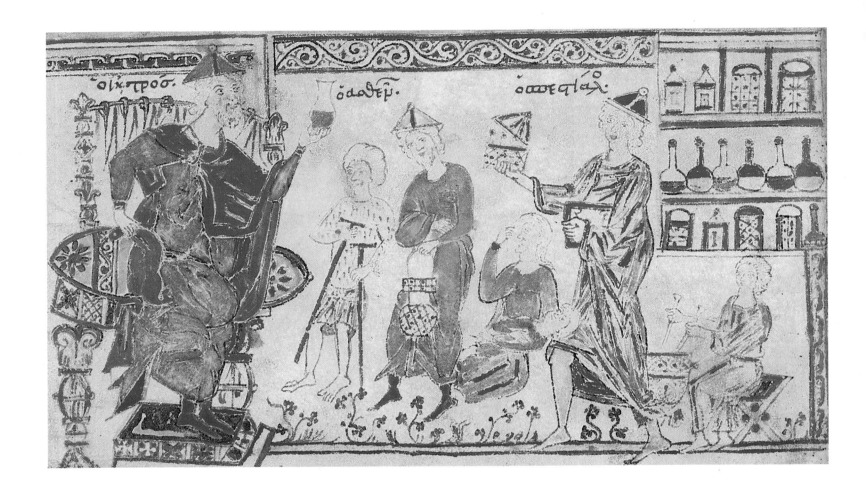

From the twelfth century, a number of phenomena conspired to accelerate the decline of the Eastern Roman Empire: in the east, the demographic growth of the Slavs, Bulgars and Hungarians, together with the military ardour of the Seljuk and then the Ottoman Turks; in the west, the religious fervour of the Christians, combined with the conquering spirit of the Frankish knights hungry for wealth, cleverly exploited by the trading republics of Italy who wanted to appropriate the warehouses of Syria and Constantinople and to divert trade from India and the Far East for their benefit.

THE LATIN RACES AND TURKS AGAINST THE BYZANTINE CULTURE

A doctor and a pharmacist in Athens in the fourteenth century, from a treatise on pharmaceutical preparations containing over 2600 formulae. Nicolas Myrepsus, De compositione medicamentorum, *1339. National Library, Paris, France.*

After the sack of Constantinople in 1204, a "Latin" emperor succeeded as *basileus*, but his domain was soon to be shattered into a mosaic of small states held by the Catalans, the Venetians, the Genoese and the Normans, expelled in turn when the throne was recaptured in 1268 by a Greek emperor, Michael Palaeologus.

These constant troubles prevailing in the eastern Mediterranean did not favour scientific progress or production. However, there were a few famous doctors, including Nicholas, from Alexandria, better known as "Myrepsus" (preparer of

ESCHVLAPIO · YPOCRATE · AVICENA · RASIS · ARISTOTILE

Serapione · Galieno · Diascoride · Alberto · m.

*The frontispiece of the book by
Giohanne Cademosto on the composition
of herbs: the eleven famous doctors of
Antiquity and of the Middle Ages, from
Asclepius to Albert the Great. Lodi,
first half of the fourteenth century.
National Library, Paris, France.*

107

drugs and perfumes). At the end of the thirteenth century, on his return to Constantinople with the Palaeologi, he published a major work on medicines, some simple, others complex, numbering two thousand six hundred, with formulations invented by him. Thanks to his erudition, Nicholas of Alexandria was able to add to the compilations already written by his predecessors and to use products from distant countries.

A century later, John Actuarius (the name is Latin for "accountant"), worked at the court of Andronicus III (1328–1341) and wrote one book on the examination of urine, another on the elements of diagnostics and, above all, a methodical treatise on therapy which contained all the medical data of his time.

However, the Turkish threat which hung over Constantinople prompted men of letters to emigrate. From the thirteenth to the fifteenth century, artists, jurists, mathematicians, physicists and doctors moved to the major cities in western Europe. Taking their books, their techniques and their learning, they taught their colleagues Justinian law and Euclidean mathematics. Of them, the following personalities stand out: Manuel Chrysoloras

On this ivory pyx lid, Christ and the paralysed man. These boxes usually contained plant-based prophylactic or curative powders. Byzantine art, seventh century. Cluny Museum, Paris, France.

(who died in 1415) in Rome, and in Venice Cardinal Bessarion (1392–1472) and Hermonynus of Sparta.

In 1453, the Turks captured Constantinople. Having taken their writing and religion from the Arabs, they now benefited from the general organization of the Byzantine Empire, its administration and its finances. But the new masters altogether neglected the many educational establishments and libraries and ignored the intellectuals who had stayed in the Empire.

This situation continued for some centuries and it was not until the nineteenth century that the first book on medicine was printed in Cairo. Thus the true heirs of Byzantium were in Christian western Europe. Arts, culture and science were to flourish in the western Mediterranean countries, the German Empire and later along the shores of the Atlantic.

One thousand years after the Arabs had taken Alexandria and four hundred years after Constantinople had been taken by Mahomet II, the didactic treatises of Hippocrates, Dioscorides, Oribasius and Paul of Aegina still formed the basis of education in the faculties of medicine throughout Europe.

Some plants from Asia Minor.
Their medical properties are given
in the text. Arabic version of
Dioscorides' treatise De materia
medica, 1228. Topkapi Library,
Istanbul, Turkey.

Basil and mediaeval belief. Top, *the
plant takes the form of serpents. Below,
it is used, after cooking, against spasms,
dizziness and migraines. Pseudo
Apuleius, Latin manuscript, thirteenth
century. National Library,
Vienna, Austria.*

The Mosaic tradition might have been nothing more than the religion of an unimportant people living in part of Palestine for several centuries, i.e. one of the peoples of the Near East who disappeared by merging into more powerful nations. But Jewish monotheism opened the way for the preachings of Jesus; Christianity spread the word of the Bible throughout the world, a Bible it called the Old Testament and which taught everyone about the history of the Hebrew people. When the Jews dispersed throughout the whole inhabited world, they took with them their unwavering loyalty to their faith which they spread wherever they went. Jewish doctors therefore also played a major role as propagators of their science, their customs and their religion.

In the early centuries of our era, two huge compilations brought together the documents of the Jewish tradition: the Talmud of Jerusalem and in particular that of Babylon (fifth century), the richest and most complete in all fields. Indeed, the Talmud represents the whole of the Bible — where the law of Moses is expressed principally in the Pentateuch — and all the commentary and teachings given by the rabbis over the centuries. The Talmud reflects the Jewish people's vision of the world, expressed via a religion, a philosophy, a history, an ethic, an astronomy and a way of life.

This view of the world is based on belief in a single, omnipotent and omnipresent God, master of life on earth, with laws to be obeyed by man. Man, furthermore, does not exist as an individual, firstly because he is simply one of God's creatures and God disposes over him, and also because he is but one part of God's people. Numerous consequences regard-

The Jewish faith and prophylactic measures

II.

HYGIENE IN THE TALMUD

ing the physical sufferings to which the human body is subject result from this concept of human life within a community living only by God and for God.

The Bible teaches that all human suffering comes from heaven. Thus, every individual illness or collective epidemic is the result of divine will, either to test man — as was the case for Job, shown seated on a heap of manure, whom the Lord beset with ills although he was just and respected His law — or to punish him because he had sinned and transgressed His law. Miriam, Moses' sister, was smitten with leprosy because she plotted against her brother; David's wife became sterile for deriding her husband's fervour; the idolatrous Philistines were decimated by the plague while the Hebrews were spared.

Tintoretto (1518–1594), Susannah bathing. *Scenes of ablution appear in the Apocrypha. Up to the sixteenth century, as portrayed in this illustration, hygiene was synonymous with luxury and wealth. Art History Museum, Vienna, Austria.*

Other examples, of which there are many in the Bible, could be cited. It is true that the Talmud sometimes mentions natural origins of diseases but they are related to divine judgements or moral causes.

The concept of disease as punishment was, of course, particularly anchored in Assyro-Babylonian medicine. Nor must one forget the captivity of the Jewish people in Mesopotamia. The cultural and linguistic affinity between the Semitic peoples, the war and trade links around the shores of the Mediterranean and those of the Arabian Gulf, the intellectual activity of the Jewish communities which was to continue until the early Middle Ages – all this explains the perpetuation of the concept of sanction. As God is just, He acts in wisdom and if man is unhappy, it is because he deserves to be.

This idea is found, of course, among all religious peoples. Conversely, it means that man can beseech the divinity to show clemency and put an end to his misfortunes. Judaism, however, passes it on in its entirety to Christianity – the Golden Legend contains just as many chastisements as the Old Testament – and today too, many of the faithful and many priests regard disease as legitimate punishment for faults committed against God or Christian ethics.

Moreover, God decides on the start of a disease, and so on its end too. Thus, is not any attempt to alter its course a sacrilege? Does man think he is powerful enough to thwart the divine will, as if he were equal to the Lord? The believers of the three monotheistic religions expressed indignation at human intervention in the course of disease. In the Islamic countries, highly competent doctors were even condemned for witchcraft.

The Bible's teaching that we are all in the hands of the Divine Providence leads

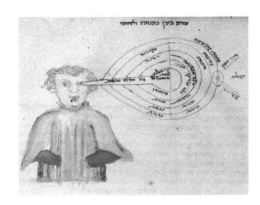

Treatise on optics and ophthalmology.
Hebrew manuscript, 1181.
National Library, Paris, France.

inevitably to fatalism, though not without a certain wisdom. But the will to live, generally so widespread and enduring, thwarts it to the extent that no society has deliberately denied itself doctors; even the Talmud accepts them.

This attitude to suffering is in radical contrast to Hippocratic medicine which attributes great importance to prognosis. Basically, why would a doctor concern himself with prognosis if the patient's fate – recovery or death – is preordained?

As the individual exists only as part of the group, it is understandable that the rules of collective hygiene should occupy such an important place in the Talmud, rules upheld for ethical reasons and inspired by Mosaic Law, where any breach of them constitutes an offence to God. One of these obligations regarding hygiene is circumcision, which seals the covenant of the people with the Lord. Some people today attempt to regard this as a means of protecting against sexually transmitted diseases, such as cancer of the penis, or cancer of the cervix for the female partners of circumcised men. These hypotheses, however, have never been confirmed statistically. It appears that circumcision perpetuates a tribal rite, of prehistoric origin, common to a number of peoples in Africa and western Asia.

Additionally, the fundamental distinction between the pure and the impure governs all acts in life – human activities and man's relations with nature, plants and animals.

Any human excretion, even resulting from a physiological process and thus intended by the Creator, such as tears, urine or menstrual blood, is impure.

This concept of impurity was to govern Western medicine for centuries and was to lead to the proliferation of evacuation treatments, enemas, purges and bloodletting.

Collective rules of hygiene feature largely in the Talmud. Every act of everyday life is covered: from feeding to excretion (the latter considered unclean). Here, a chapter heading for a reasoned analysis of the Talmud, by Asher ben Yehiel. Hebrew manuscript, fifteenth century. National Library, Paris, France.

Thus, certain animals were deemed impure, such as shellfish, and others pure, such as cloven-hoofed ruminants: the pig, which is cloven-hoofed but not a ruminant, is thus considered impure.

Such taboos undoubtedly constitute totemic memories particular to the Semites, with most of the world's peoples having their own. Likewise, the flesh of licit animals can only be consumed if certain rites are observed at their slaughter, rites which dictate not only the method of killing but also which knife should be used. Faecal matter must be carefully buried and the carriers of certain diseases isolated from the group to prevent the transmission of their impurities. Thorough purification follows any contact with a corpse. Thus every act of life is codified and categorized: food, sexual life and the cultivation of the fields.

These rules have been interpreted by some as expressing a clear understanding of the natural origin of disease, an early form of prevention and collective hygiene even before this concept had been invented. The isolation of the sick reflects, according to these rules, an understanding of contagion, while the taboo on pork eliminated from the diet a meat which carried parasites – as if all animals did not contain them – and the proliferation of micro-organisms and putrefaction which occurred immediately after death would explain the impurity of corpses. In other words, Moses anticipated Pasteur!

אֱלוֹלֶר אֶלְדִי יִזְדָאד לֵלוֹאַר תַּרְמָיִיהוּ וּגְטִיע אֶלְבֶנָת תַּעְאִישׁוּ :

וָאת

הַארוּ בִּרָא וְרָאֶל מָא חֲכוּשׁי יְתַּוֵּיוּ גְטִיע עֶלָא כָּאטָר כָּיף יוֹלְדוּ זָדְטִיהֹם פֶּל וָאד

There are many sexual taboos in the Talmud, even between spouses. Engraving from 1864, taken from a Venetian liturgical book of 1609. Alliance Israelite Universelle, Paris, France. Right: a Jewish doctor, from a drawing of 1568.

Similarly, the taboo on sexual relations with a woman for two weeks during and following her menstrual period, thus restricting relations to two weeks a month, leads modern medicine to conclude not only that this was a form of contraception as it reduced sexual relations, but also that it encouraged procreation by increasing sexual relations in the fertile period.

All these interpretations highlight a medical anachronism witnessed all too often throughout history. While the Bible contains some brilliant clinical descriptions of epilepsy, myocardial infarction or hemiplegia, the Talmud is not a medical treatise. Furthermore, the vocabulary used is that of two thousand years ago. How can we be sure that the Hebrew or Aramaic terms, translated by the words "leprosy" or "plague" correspond to today's diseases? There are no indications that the Jews before our era explained the method of transmission of certain contagious diseases, not knowing that they were due to parasites and germs.

It is reasonable to assume that the distinction between the pure and the impure rests, not on a wondrous prescience of what would one day be the septic and aseptic, but rather on the perpetuation of tribal customs based on magic and witchcraft, which date from an age when the Jewish people were desert nomads.

Factors to be borne in mind concerning hygiene as preached by the Talmud, however, are the isolation of the sick, the cleanliness of their camps and villages achieved by the burying of bodily waste, and certain other measures of this kind. Another noteworthy factor is that learned men examined a body in cases where death gave rise to legal action, described the wounds and distinguished between blood and a coloured substance, in other words a form of "expert witness", the beginnings of forensic medicine.

However, although, according to the law, man and nature can only be studied through God, not all Jews view the

114

Medecin Juif

Talmud as the summary of all knowledge.

Even before the birth of Christianity, Jews emigrated to all known parts of the world, in particular to Morocco, the Yemen and India. They were to embrace other schools of thought; the Jews in Palestine became Hellenized while others studied and taught in the intellectual world of Alexandria. While remaining true to their faith, following the destruction of the Jewish kingdom of Palestine in the first century and the scattering of the persecuted people throughout the world, these cultured Jews were to create a long tradition of brilliant doctors, which exists to this day.

DEONTOLOGICAL COUNSEL OF JEWISH DOCTORS

Assaph of Tiberias (sixth century, Syria) repeats the words of Hippocrates:
"You shall not prepare poison for a man or woman who wishes to kill their neighbour. You shall not give the composition thereof nor pass it on to anyone. You shall say nothing."
Ishaq ibn Sulaiman (tenth century, Tunisia) wrote a "Doctor's Guide" where we read:
"Do not forget to visit and care for the poor, nothing is more noble... Comfort the patient by the promise of healing, even if you do not believe this: coming from you, this affirmation can help nature... Demand your fees when the disease is at its peak, as once cured the patient will forget what you have done for him."

The name of the doctor Assaph of Tiberias seems to us to be the most characteristic of this period of philosophical turmoil. His writings constitute a testimony to the various rival systems in Alexandria: gnosis from Neoplatonism, Aristotelism and even the sequels of occultism and mysticism which sometimes co-exist. The Judaism of the period could not escape, either, from the effects of Zoroastrianism in Persia and Babylon.

In the sixth century, Assaph, in his treatises, attempted to avoid these abstract concerns. Although he contradicts it from time to time, he was imbued with Galenism, affirmed that the blood circulates, differentiated the arteries which have a pulse and the veins which are immobile and, contrary to the Talmud, identified the central point for the blood

JEWISH DOCTORS IN ISLAMIC COUNTRIES

Two Jewish doctors from Constantinople examine urine. Water-colour, late sixteenth century. Private collection.

as the heart and not the liver. The variety of his interests led Assaph to write a treatise on the pulse and on urine, a therapeutic work intended for the poor, and another describing digestive diseases, but he cannot be considered as the person who discovered the circulation of the blood.

In addition, Assaph has the merit of being the first person to address the problem of medical translation in a language with a small vocabulary — a difficulty which was to be encountered on numerous other occasions in the future. Ancient Hebrew did not have the academic, anatomical or physiological terms created by the Greeks. He, however, invented them, forged new words and described the medical science of his time in elegant Hebrew.

Although he did not risk expressing his ideas openly, for fear of offending those of his faith, he highlighted a fundamental dilemma in the history of human thinking: can the teachings of the sacred texts be considered as the absolute truth if at the same time the manifestations of nature and the functions of the human body are examined rationally? Since Assaph, religious minds have still not resolved the dilemma between faith and reason.

In the seventh century, the Arab invasion spread Islam to the southern shore of the Mediterranean and almost the whole of the Iberian peninsula. This was to give rise to a society in which the Jews, in a minority, were to be forced to live as second-class citizens, surrounded by Muslims who held power and also practised a monotheistic religion in a fairly similar language. This is why, until the end of the Middle Ages, a number of Jewish doctors were to write in Arabic as well as Hebrew, or even in Latin so as to be understood by Christian scholars.

In the East, the Omayyad and Abbasid caliphs encouraged the development and

Maimonides (1135–1204), "the eagle of the synagogue", the most famous Jewish doctor, born in Cordova, author of numerous medical treatises. Eighteenth-century print. National Library, Paris, France.

the teaching of the sciences – as we shall see later – but it was particularly in the Maghreb and in Spain that medical traditions became embedded in Jewish communities.

Ishaq ibn Sulaiman al-Israeli went from Alexandria to Kairouan in the early tenth century. He wrote his books *The Mind and the soul*, *Urine*, *Food* etc. in Arabic or in Hebrew. Soon translated into Latin, his work was taught in Europe until the sixteenth century.

Hasdaï ibn Shaprut (915–970) was minister to the then Caliph of Cordova, Abdel-Rahman III. The emperor of Byzantium had sent the caliph a Greek manuscript of Dioscorides' treatise on medicinal plants; Hasdaï translated it into Arabic with the help of a monk, which proves that at that time harmony reigned between Judaism, Christianity and Islam. Hasdaï also used his ministerial authority to create an academy of sciences at Cordova.

Benjamin of Tudela (in Navarre) was known less for his medical work than for the account of his journey to Italy and his description of the Jewish colonies and doctors he encountered.

THE GOOD DOCTOR AS SEEN BY ALI IBN RABBAN AT-TABARI (ninth century)

"In all things, he will choose the best and the fairest. He will not be brazen, verbose, flippant, proud or disparaging. His body will not smell unpleasant, nor will he be perfumed, nor vulgar, nor affected in his dress. He will not be infatuated with himself, placing himself above others, he will not wish to dwell on the faults of those who exercise his art, but will instead conceal their errors..."

The common presence of three masters of medicine, Jewish, Arab and Christian, illustrates the multiplicity of influences on medical knowledge by the various religions, in particular as a result of the work of translators, Lyons, 1515. Library of the Old Faculty of Medicine, Paris, France.

We know the names of other Jewish doctors who wrote and taught in the Muslim world in the Middle Ages, in both the East and West. Their work, frequently inspired by Greek authors, is somewhat lacking in originality, with the exception of that of Moses ben Maimon, known as Maimonides. He was born in Cordova in 1135, fled the town for Fez because of the intolerance of the new princes, moved to Cairo with the Sultan Saladin, died there in 1204 and was buried in the Holy Land. With his wide cultural knowledge – theological, philosophical and medical – he left behind a considerable quantity of works covering aphorisms, books on dietetics, poisons, coition and commentaries on Hippocrates and Galen.

In contrast to his Jewish colleagues, he produced an original work, recommending moderation in his prescriptions, and emphasizing the healing effects of a combination of medicine and psychology. His *Guide for the perplexed* can be regarded as a religious compendium as well as a treatise on good health.

His reputation as a rabbi and doctor was to assume such vast proportions in the two communities – Jewish and Christian – that he was called "the eagle of the synagogue".

But soon the dwindling Arab territory in Spain and the formation of a mosaic of small rival states in the Maghreb and in the East resulted in the loss of the intellectual, religious and medical climate which, in conjunction with the metaphysical zeal, had stimulated Jewish doctors challenged by their Muslim colleagues, for several centuries. The Sephardic Jews then halted their scientific output for some considerable time. This was regrettable as, under the sometimes tolerant and sometimes oppressive Muslim authority, they had formed a solid community, characterized by a very particular ritual and liturgy, which was expressed through a poetic language often stamped with the mark of hedonism.

With their emigration, due to the changing policies in the states, and their subsequent expulsion from the Iberian peninsula at the end of the fifteenth century, Arabist Jewish doctors moved to Constantinople, Prague and Amsterdam. They were nonetheless able to keep their individuality in the face of Ashkenazi Judaism.

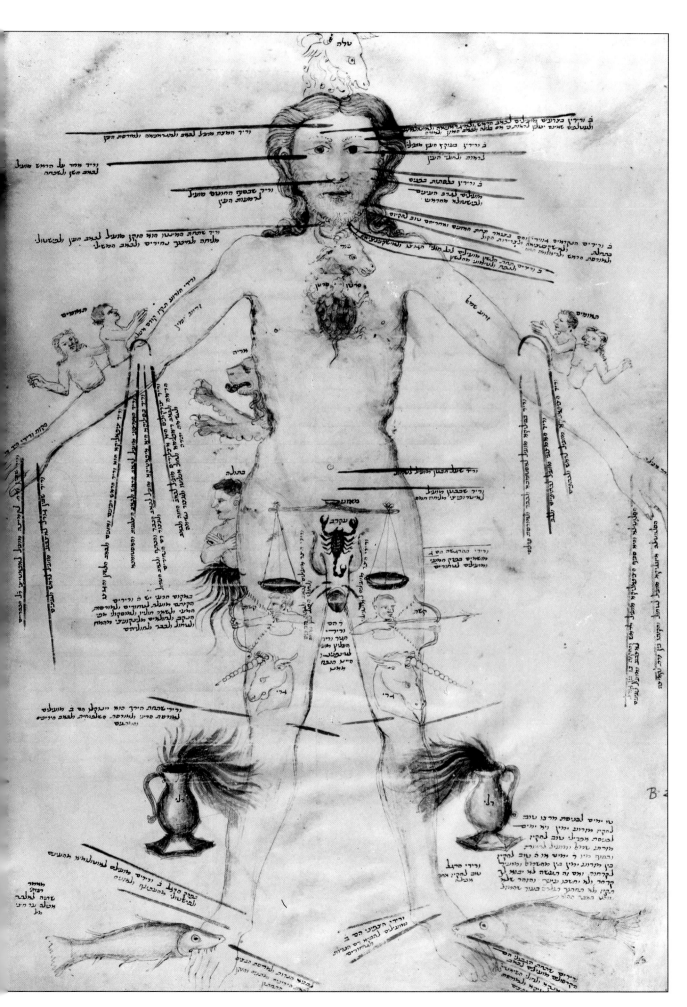

Zodiac man. Every part of the body is placed under the influence of a sign of the zodiac. Muslims, Jews and Christians recognized, in the Middle Ages, the existence of cosmic influences on health. Hebrew manuscript, fourteenth century, southern France.

Gold Jewish amulet. Italian workmanship, seventeenth century. Max Berger Judaïca Collection, Vienna, Austria.

JEWISH DOCTORS IN CHRISTIAN COUNTRIES

*I*n the early centuries of our era, Christianity became quite distinct from its Judaic origin. From the tenth century, when sovereigns established Christianity in both the East and the West as the only religion allowed by society, the Jews' lives became more fraught with difficulties than in Islamic countries.

Standing between the Muslim and Christian worlds, they were the topic of conversation throughout southern Europe and beyond. The earliest Jewish doctor whose writings we know was called Shabataï Donnolo; he was born in Otranto and lived in the tenth century. His book on medicinal plants owes much to the works of Dioscorides and Assaph of Tiberias. Jews were later involved in the foundation of the School of Salerno in the eleventh century.

From this point onwards, Christian Europe had hundreds of Jewish doctors; we cite a few below by way of example: Gershon ben Judah at Metz in the tenth century, Sephradi at the court of the king of Castile in the eleventh century, Jacob Benacosa in Padua in the thirteenth century, Gershon ben Shlomo in Arles, also in the thirteenth century, and many more.

At Toledo and elsewhere in Spain as it was gradually reconquered, Jewish doctors passed on to the Christians the Greek medicine which their Arab colleagues had taught them. They were the first teachers in the universities of Montpellier and Bologna, and went on to Regensburg, Frankfurt, Augsburg, Flanders, Cracow and Moscow.

The Jews were persecuted from the Middle Ages onwards. Expelled from Spain in 613 and Merovingian Gaul in 629, they returned because they were needed, only to be banished once again, from England in 1290, from France in

1394, Spain in 1492 and Portugal shortly afterwards. Italy and the papal domains around Avignon showed more tolerance: the synagogues in Cavaillon, Carpentras and Bologna remained active for centuries. The faithful trod the paths of Europe and, even after the Middle Ages, many European courts sheltered Jewish doctors, prudent and polyglot, adapted to the cultures of the countries in which they lived, learned in medicine and philosophy. The descendants of Jewish doctors, long since converted, were to teach

MEDICAL AXIOMS OF
JEAN MÉSUÉ (ninth century)

1. In medicine, the truth is a goal which can never be attained; and treatment based on what books prescribe, without the advice of a skilled doctor, is dangerous.

...

7. Suspect anyone who is not interested in the foundations of medicine, in the sciences of philosophy, the laws of logic, the bases of mathematics, and who gives himself to worldly pleasures, especially in the art of medicine.

...

42. It is important that the doctor does not forget to ask the patient about anything, internal or external, which could have given rise to the disease; then he judges which is the strongest influence.

...

81. If someone consults a large number of doctors about his disease, he can easily fall into the error of each of them.

...

98. It is important that the doctor's state be balanced: neither turned totally to our lowly world, nor totally rejecting the world beyond, so that he stands between the desire for one and the fear of the other.

From the French translation.

Page from a Hebrew manuscript translated from the Arabic original after 1300. It reproduces some of Maimonides' medical aphorisms, in semi-cursive Hebrew script in the Spanish style, adorned with floral motifs and grotesques. National Library, Paris, France.

at the faculty of Montpellier until the nineteenth century.

Without demonstrating any great originality – certainly less than their Muslim counterparts – they nonetheless played a considerable role as intermediaries in the transfer of knowledge from the ancient and Greek East to the less-developed Latin West. Although no more intelligent than the hosts who sheltered them with varying degrees of willingness, they displayed unequalled energy in their desire to see their community survive. And as sovereigns forbade them ownership of land and membership of trade guilds, they exploited their ingenuity in banking, commerce and medicine – the areas left open to them.

The Muslim digression

III.

Tradition would have us call the huge production of written texts in Arabic left by doctors since the great conquests of the seventh to the fourteenth century "Arab medicine". In fact, many of these doctors did not come from the Arabian peninsula, since the majority of them were natives of various provinces in the Greek and Persian Empires. In the West, Berber, Iberian or Visigoth blood flowed in their veins; in other words, their mother tongue was not Arabic. Moreover, some of them were Christians, of Zoroastrian or Jewish tradition, and not Muslim.

But they belonged to a vast territory in which the Arabic language, which reached its most accomplished form in the Quran (612–632), formed the basis for a single cultural world. The Arab-Islamic Empire, from the Indus to the Atlantic and the Pyrenees, was not unified for long, as ethnic and dynastic disputes, resistance by indigenous peoples and foreign invasions rapidly decimated it. However, the Arabic language and likewise Islam, the religion of princes, helped to unify this vast scientific world and served as a link for medicine and doctors within this universe.

The Arabs, thanks to their numerous translations, played an essential role in the passing on of manuscripts in Greek to the Christian West. Dioscorides' De materia medica *is doubtless the best example of this. It is shown here in a contemporary copy of a miniature representing a pharmacy. Topkapi Museum, Istanbul, Turkey.*

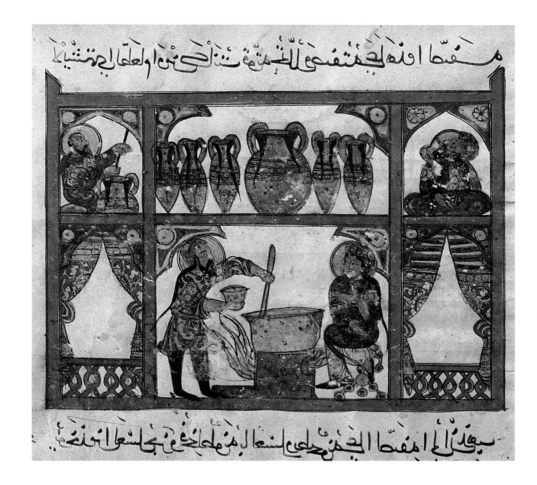

The same pharmacist's dispensary, from another Arabic version of Dioscorides' De materia medica. *As in the previous copy, the pharmacist himself is under the patronage of two haloed masters. Baghdad, thirteenth century. Metropolitan Museum, New York, USA.*

HYGIENE IN THE QURAN

*S*ome written documents have survived dating from the Bedouin civilization before Muhammad's preaching in the seventh century, and parts of them can be found in the Quran. The Arabs thus used the same therapies as those of all the nomadic peoples of the Near and Middle East.

Natural divinities were beseeched to heal the sick, magic formulae recited and pilgrimages made to Mecca. Learned men set fractures and made potions with herbs from the desert, while midwives helped at childbirth.

In view of the fact that the inhabitants of the town of Medina practised Judaism when Muhammad was young, it can be assumed that certain principles of hygiene found in the Talmud survived in other towns, in the oases and even perhaps in the tents of Arabia. In any case, some practices are common to the Semitic peoples from the Mediterranean to the Indian Ocean.

Thus, the Quran orders circumcision, like the Bible, and forbids the consumption of pork for the same reason, doubtless of prehistoric totemic origin. Rightly, it recommends moderation in the diet and in the consumption of intoxicants such as wine, cannabis and hashish. The Quran also contains rudimentary principles of dietary and bodily hygiene.

Today, in Islamic countries, the faithful base their medical education on a "medicine of the Prophet". Although some manuals written at a much later date, probably in the thirteenth century, claimed to be by the Prophet, they certainly cannot pretend to be of a sacred origin and are even less help in relieving the sick of the twentieth century.

123

RESPECT FOR GREEK BOOKS

The conquering Arab tribes, strong from their recent union and their new faith, invaded, without too much difficulty, the Sassanid Persian and Greek Empires, disorganized by religious, linguistic and dynastic disputes. In Syria, Palestine and Mesopotamia, they met related peoples speaking similar languages because the migratory movement from South Yemen to the "Fertile Crescent" dated back several centuries. And above all, from the Nile to the Iranian plateau, they experimented with administrative, fiscal and military structures, of no use in the context of earlier Bedouin anarchic society. Thus, the first four caliphs to succeed Muhammad, who died in 632 – Abu Bakr, Omar, Osman and Ali – followed by the Omayyad caliphs, built on these founda-

A master explains to his pupil the properties of plants according to the secular precepts of Dioscorides. Arabic version of Dioscorides' De materia medica. *Topkapi Museum, Istanbul, Turkey.*

tions organizations which enabled them to extend the domain of believers even further.

In 762, the dynasty of the Abbasids, in establishing its capital at Baghdad, marked its originality by three centuries of relative peace in regions previously often in turmoil. This was achieved by rigorous centralization, enforced islamization and an arabization frequently accepted without demur.

These Abbasid caliphs were all enamoured of culture. In the early ninth century, Al-Mamun had a House of Science built in Baghdad where all the manuscripts they had bought throughout the Empire and in Constantinople were to be collected; he sought out doctors and scholars, took them into his court and paid them well, whatever their religion. And he had no difficulty in finding them. Likewise in the old Persian provinces, the caliphs discovered at Gundi-Shapur a school of medicine founded by Nestorian Christian doctors expelled by the Orthodox emperor of Byzantium and welcomed by the Zoroastrian Persian sovereign. The majority of these doctors, like their colleagues from the old Byzantine provinces, attempted for three hundred years to translate the old Greek books into their own language, Syriac, so that their pupils would be able to understand Hippocrates, Dioscorides and Galen without difficulty. We therefore know, over a number of generations, certain families of these doctors who remained true to their faith, their profession and above all to the teaching of ancient Greek medicine which had been passed on from Byzantium to Islam.

These Nestorians in the Persian Empire displayed an adventurous and proselytic spirit and their monks spread throughout Central Asia, gave the Mongols an alphabetic script and brought about lasting conversions with the result that Genghis Khan's mother joined this Christian rite in the twelfth century.

The caliphs' benevolence with regard to the doctors of the old Byzantine and Persian Empires is associated with two major factors. On the one hand, the Arabs taught the Chinese how to make paper from vegetable fibre which was stronger and easier to work on than papyrus and less costly than parchment. On the other, they borrowed from India the transcription of numbers, adding the wonderful invention of the zero. These two factors were to revolutionize the transmission of knowledge.

The caliphs brought together in Baghdad scholars hitherto scattered throughout their empires and encouraged them to continue their work on all the scientific disciplines of the Graeco-Roman world. Coming from the Greek via Syriac, or translated directly from Greek into Arabic, these texts required the formation of new terms in the fields of physics, mathematics, medicine and astronomy, unknown in the original Bedouin language. Where the translators did not have an Arabic root from which to derive a term, or where they did not understand the Greek word, they transported it as it stood into Arabic. Thus, the Arab world was also to know Aristotle, Archimedes and Pythagoras, songs with actions celebrating the Greek hero Alexander and the Persian Rustum, and the Indian medical treatises of Susruta.

Stages in the development of the foetus according to a Latin translation of Rhazes' Tractabus de medica (c. 860–923), fourteenth century. Marciana Library, Venice, Italy.

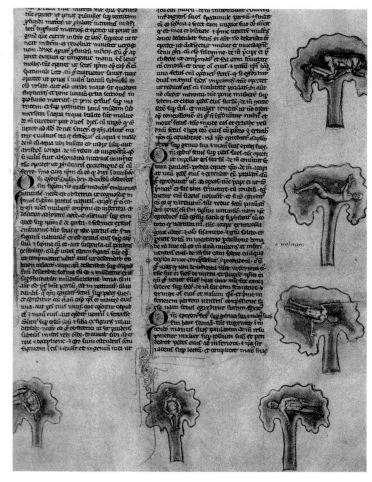

CLINICAL PRACTICE AND PHILOSOPHY

Few Greek medical books escaped the translators' zeal: Hippocrates, Galen, Rufus of Ephesus, Paul of Aegina, Oribasius, Alexander of Tralles and others. The most prolific of them was, without doubt, Hunaïn ibn Ishaq (Johannitius). Others also taught and created works of their own, for example the Nestorian Yuhanna ibn Masawayhi (known as Mésué), who came from a Gundi-Shapur family, a doctor to six caliphs, who left us aphorisms in the style of Hippocrates, a major pharmacopoeia, notes on gynaecology and obstetrics, a description of the anatomy of the monkey, etc.

After him, Ali ibn Rabban at-Tabari (800–870) wrote a major book, *The paradise of wisdom*, which covered the fields of medicine and sociology, embryology and

Arab doctors in their studies read or talk with their disciples. Arabic version of Nicander's Theriaca, *thirteenth century. National Library, Paris, France.*

astronomy. It testifies to a sound know-ledge of Indian medicine and the four basic elements of Empedocles are found combined with the four humours of Hippocrates.

From the end of the ninth century, all doctors of renown practised the Muslim religion, even though they were not of Arab blood; for example Abu Bakr Muhammad ibn Zakarya al-Razi, known as Rhazes. From Ray, near Teheran, he studied medicine late in life from Ali ibn Rabban at-Tabari, was called to Baghdad to build a hospital there and died in 920. He wrote a number of works on gout and kidney and bladder stones. Not afraid of contradicting Galen, he differentiated be-tween a number of eruptive diseases and wrote a treatise on smallpox and measles.

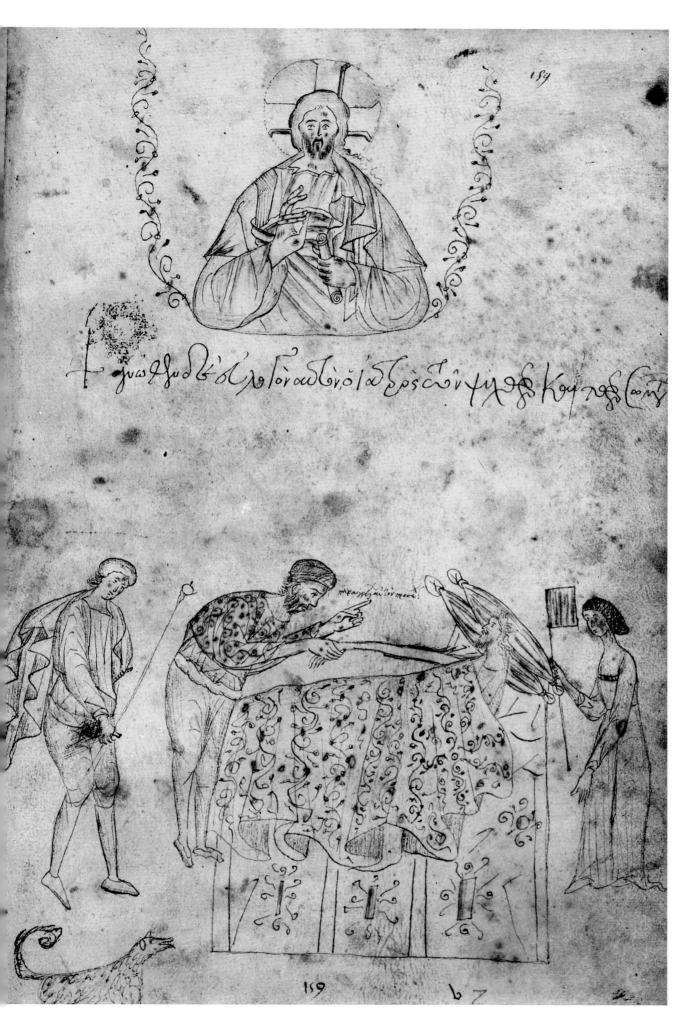

The De peste *can be considered the most innovative work by Rhazes. It contains the best clinical observations of eruptive infectious diseases, from which the patient shown opposite is probably suffering. Greek version fifteenth century. National Library, Paris, France.*

DIAGRAM TAKEN FROM AVICENNA'S CANON

It establishes the correspondences between the basic qualities of the body, the seasons, the humours, ages, movements of the soul, etc.

To satisfy Avicenna, the following should be added: the temperaments, main medicines, planets, etc.

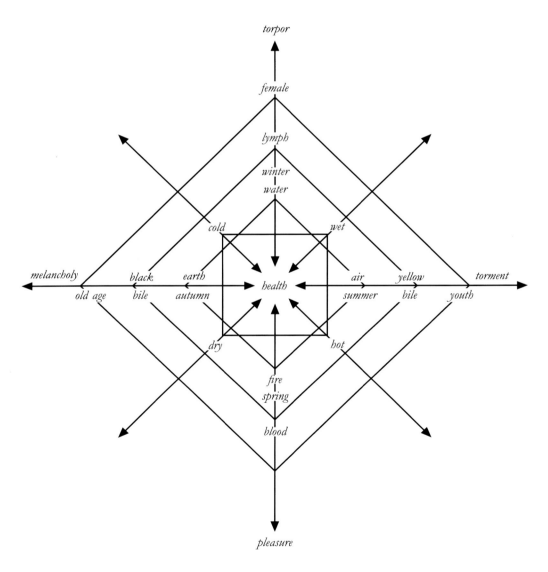

After his death, his pupils extracted from his teachings clinical lessons collected in a book entitled, in Latin, the *Continens*, i.e. a sort of medical encyclopaedia, in which Rhazes showed himself to be a most shrewd and scrupulous clinician who recommended examining the patient thoroughly before prescribing a prudent treatment.

Affirming the need for a sound medical culture and the priority to be given to experience, his pharmaceutical prescriptions are not encumbered with philosophical or astrological considerations, but simply recommend drugs which he has shown to be effective. Moreover, he displays good sense in what he says, such as "medicine is only easy for imbeciles; serious doctors always discover difficulties", and his clinical descriptions reveal a certain talent for observation, whether for hay fever or vesicular lithiasis.

Although the Abbasid regime flourished until the middle of the eleventh century and many doctors' names passed into posterity, none acquired prestige comparable to that of Abu Ali ibn Adillah ibn Sina, known as Avicenna. Born in 980 at the extreme east of the Empire, at Bukhara, to a high-ranking civil servant and a Tadzhik mother, he learnt the natural sciences from a Christian teacher and then studied medicine, entered into the service of a number of local lords under whom he suffered alternately fortune and disgrace, became passionately interested in all known sciences and lived his final days in Isfahan in 1037, exhausted by "his works and the joys of the flesh".

Throughout almost two hundred works, he developed his knowledge in such varied fields as astronomy, mechanics, acoustics, music and optics. He produced a summary of philosophical theories current at the time, assimilating the nuances of Aristotelian and Neoplatonic

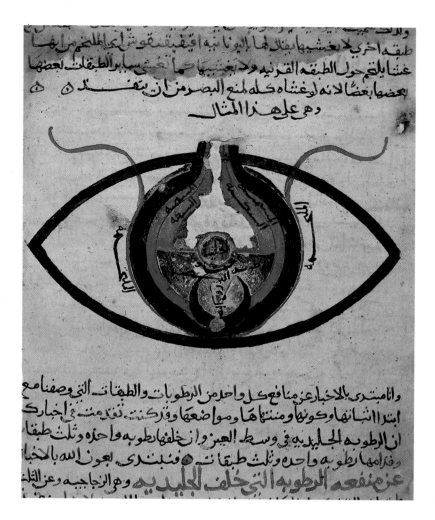

Various Arab representations of eye diseases (above), and the lungs (right), from the Anatomy of the eye *by Al-Mutadibih (thirteenth century) and Avicenna's* Canon *(fourteenth-century version). National Library, Cairo, Egypt and National Museum, Damascus, Syria.*

Left: *a teacher and his pupils (Persian manuscript, seventeenth century).*
Above: *symbolic representation of man in the cosmos (Turkish manuscript, sixteenth century). Museum of Islam, Cairo, Egypt and Museum of Turkish and Islamic Arts, Istanbul, Turkey.*

to foot. Nothing is forgotten, love is classed as a cerebral disease like amnesia or melancholy, though easier to cure.

Regarded for eight centuries of Western medicine as one of the foundations of truth, the *Canon* was part of the required teaching in universities. Yet, to our eyes, it seems an obscure hotchpotch from which no useful deduction can be made for the sick. Let us then hold Avicenna in high esteem as a philosopher but reserve our admiration for Rhazes as a clinician.

Nonetheless, Avicenna is the most legendary doctor in the Middle Ages: in 1980, almost twenty countries joined with Unesco in celebrating the thousandth anniversary of his birth with great fervour.

After the eleventh century, renowned Arabic-speaking doctors became a rarity in the East. We have their names, even though they contributed little to medicine. Ibn al-Baïtar (1197–1248) wrote a treatise on medicinal substances in which he mentions plants from India and the Far East. Ibn Butlan, a Christian from Antioch, wrote the *Tables of health*, the pattern of which was to be imitated for the next eight centuries. Ibn Nafiz of Damascus (1210–1296?), chief doctor in the city's hospital, is the author of an encyclopaedia on medicine, to which he adds law and philosophy and he describes the minor pulmonary circulation fairly clearly in his comments on Avicenna's *Canon*. He can be regarded as the predecessor of Servetus and of Harvey.

When Baghdad was captured by the Mongols in 1258, and then under the rule of the Ottoman Turks, doctors, although they continued to write, no longer displayed their skill or their capacity for attention and reflection. Administrative authority and religious conformism extended over the Empire and stifled the talent of doctors in the East.

ideas; this summary helped to make his life's work one of the world's monuments to philosophy: no philosopher or metaphysicist in Europe in the Middle Ages could ignore his arguments, and all either adopted or refuted them.

Unfortunately, in the field of medicine, Avicenna seems to fall prey to the intoxication of a total monism: according to which the movement of the heavenly bodies governs the dates for bleeding and the prognosis of the sick, the geometry of polygons determines the healing of wounds and the pulse counted with a water clepsydra is a guide for diagnosis.

One of his works is the *Qanun fit' tibb'*, known in the West as the *Canon* of medicine, which is a comprehensive review of all the diseases of man from head

Animal sacrifices and techniques of healing merge. A hen is used by an Arab doctor to heal a snake bite. Fifteenth-century Persian miniature. Topkapi Library, Istanbul, Turkey.

TEACHING HOSPITALS

*T*he silence which fell over the Arabic East, after the splendour of such excellent practitioners, can be regretted all the more since at that time medicine rested on fertile foundations in terms of both skill and education.

In 932, the Caliph al-Muqtadir made a preliminary examination compulsory before practising medicine and he gave one of his doctors the task of organizing the tests. Pupils could be trained either by an apprenticeship with a master, whom they

Pages from an Arabic pharmacopoeia and from the Book of Calila el Dimna, *both fourteenth century. Malek Library, Teheran, Iran and National Library, Cairo, Egypt.*

paid, or by attendance at a hospital school.

Indeed, following the example of Greek hospitals, or at the suggestion of the old doctors of Gundi-Shapur, from the eighth century, the caliphs and then the emirs and sultans gave their towns hospitals. According to Ibn Batuta, who in the fourteenth century travelled the world from Tangiers to China, there were thirty-four hospitals in the East; some of them can, incidentally, still be visited in

بزان واتی تواند شد و انرا سبب شفا شمرد وباز اعمال خیر و سخن توبه آخرت ازعلت کنه ازار
گونه شفای دهذ که معاودت صورت نبندد ومن یحکم این مقدمات ازعلم طب نبرآ نمعلوم ق

نهمن برطلب دین صرف کرده ایم والحق راه آزادان وبی بایان یافتیم سرآ سرخنا ومضایوق دکاه سه

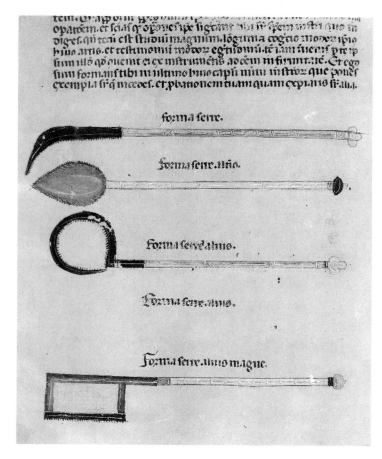

Baghdad, Aleppo and Cairo. The caliphate of Cordova, alone, possessed forty, of which little survives today.

These spacious establishments were divided into four, one quarter being for the insane, and included a pharmacy and a library, a small mosque and a Quranic school. Their construction can be regarded as a holy work deriving from the alms collected from the true believers. They were run on the basis of endowments giving the caliphs income from fixed assets such as fields, mills or shops.

Qualified doctors cared for the sick. Furthermore, these establishments had a social role too, as the poor and pilgrims were sheltered there; they also supplied teaching facilities. The pupils, after selection, had to examine the sick and then entrust them to more experienced assistants before the master confirmed the diagnosis and prescribed the treatment.

In the tenth century, there was, in Cairo, a famous dispute between two professors, one extolling the superiority of theoretical education and the other, examination at the sick-bed. The discussion ended in a compromise, but for four centuries at least the Muslim world had enjoyed teaching hospitals for which the Christian West had to wait until the eighteenth century.

These doctors and teachers were involved in the life of their institutions of which they became the historians; thanks to them, we have today a series of medical biographies, from the ninth to the thirteenth century: four hundred years of the history, if not of medicine, then at least of doctors.

This hospital medicine from the height of the Arab Middle Ages was practised in the context of an extraordinary blossoming of science. In the space of a few generations, Al-Khwarizmi gave his name to logarithms and developed algebra and trigonometry, Al-Farghani expanded on

the Indian concept of sine and invented the tangent, and a successor calculated cosine and tangents. Astronomy broke away from astrology, geography flourished thanks to navigators, Al-Idrisi produced maps with longitudes and latitudes and Arab sailors used the Chinese compass.

The optician Alhazen established that angles of incidence and reflection were equal. He studied the sky and came to the conclusion that space was organized in nine concentric circles, an idea borrowed by the West and used by Dante in his *Divine comedy.*

The Afghan Al-Biruni, for his part, travelled across Asia and described its flora, fauna, minerals, customs, religions and heavenly bodies, but this did not prevent him from becoming passionately interested in physics and calculating the weight of hot and cold water.

Arab medicine thus experienced several centuries of peace in which an intense intellectual ferment was matched by great religious tolerance (Al-Biruni's agnosticism, for example, was given free rein).

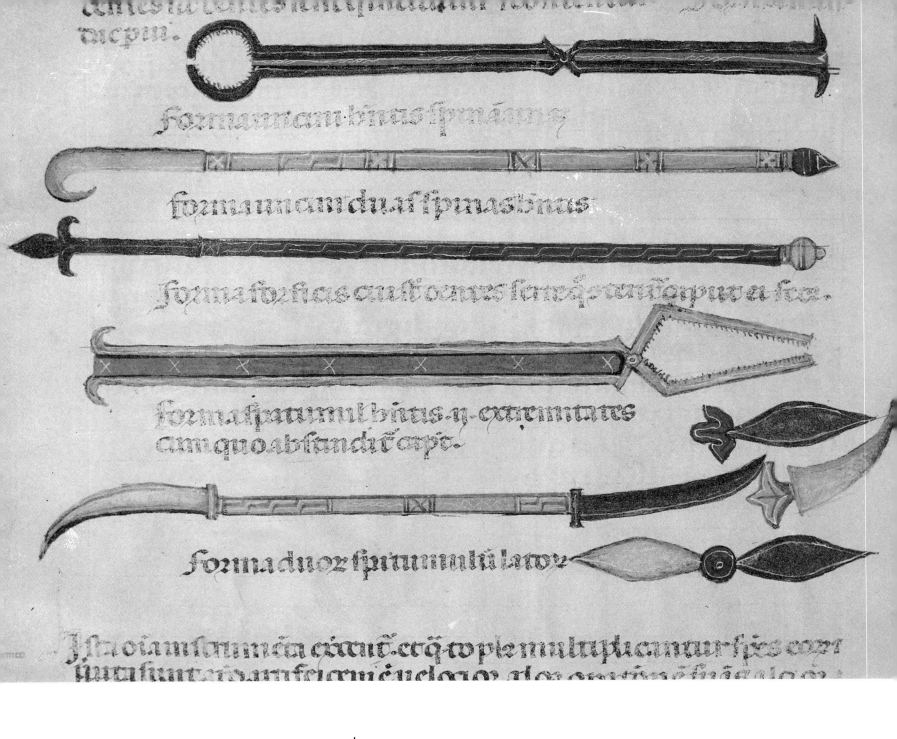

ARAB DOCTORS
IN SPAIN

At the other end of the Mediterranean, the Maghreb and Spain, where Muslims and Arab-Berbers mixed, experienced the same prosperity followed by the same troubles. Glorious descendants of an Omayyad refugee in Cordova cultivated the arts and sciences in a climate of brilliant military successes, and then left the power in the hands of their mercenaries who incited revolts, secessions and wars of succession, and left the way open to invasions from the Sahara. Finally, the battle of Las Navas of Tolosa in 1212 marked the beginning of the end of Christian rule; the prosperous caliphate of Cordova became the minute realm of Granada, which, in turn, disappeared in 1492.

The originality of Abulcasis' plates was such that they were reproduced – and transformed – constantly up to the sixteenth century. They served generally as models for printers. Atger Museum, Montpellier, France.

Nonetheless, Cordova did shine like few other Christian seigneuries for a few centuries. Scholars, poets and doctors frequented a library as rich as that of Alexandria had once been.

In the mid tenth century, Ibn Juljul wrote a *Life of doctors and philosophers* and improved the Arabic translation of Dioscorides' treatises, while Al-Wateb el Kurtubi (which means "the Cordovan") wrote a remarkable treatise on obstetrics and paediatrics.

Shortly afterwards, Abul Kassim al-Zahrawi, known as Abulcasis (936–1013), made his name as a brilliant surgeon in that era. Although his work in thirty volumes, *At-Tarsif*, is inspired by Paul of Aegina, it is innovative in many respects.

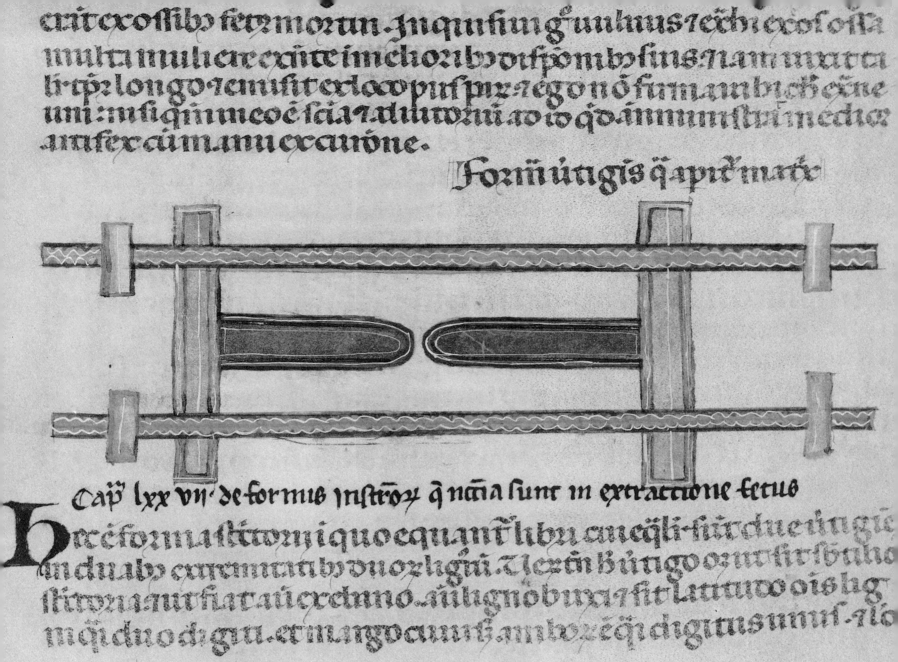

Forma ûtriglis q̃ apꝛ mãtie̅

Cap̃ lxx vn̅ de forme͂ı instꝛoꝝ q̃ n̅cia sunt in extractione fetus

This instrument of traction and counter-extension, invented by Abulcasis, was used in the treatment of dislocations and fractures. Atger Museum, Montpellier, France.

He affirmed first of all that there is no barrier between medicine and surgery, as the good surgeon needs to know both. This principle was to be forgotten in the West, as was the need for a good knowledge of anatomy. He recommended certainty of diagnosis before any intervention, developed instrumentation, clinically analysed various types of fracture, listed the different methods of extraction of arrow tips, etc.

He can therefore be considered one of the true creators of surgery, by his prudence and by his powers of observation. Future surgeons, such as Guy de Chauliac or Ambroise Paré, were to copy him without any hesitation, yet they only rarely acknowledged all that they owed to him.

Abu Marwan ibn Zuhr, known as Avenzoar (1073–1162), distinguished himself principally by his critical nature and by the disdain in which he held Galen and Avicenna's ramblings.

On a totally different level, Averroes (Abu Walid ibn Rushd, 1126–1198) divided his time between Cordova and Marrakesh. As a jurist, physician, theologian and doctor, he distinguished himself by the discovery of the role of the retina in sight and by the observation that smallpox never attacks the same person twice. His main work was to cause a major upheaval in the philosophical thinking of his time, as it concerned the difficulties of reconciling reflection and faith. Thus, the Muslims rejected him on grounds of

135

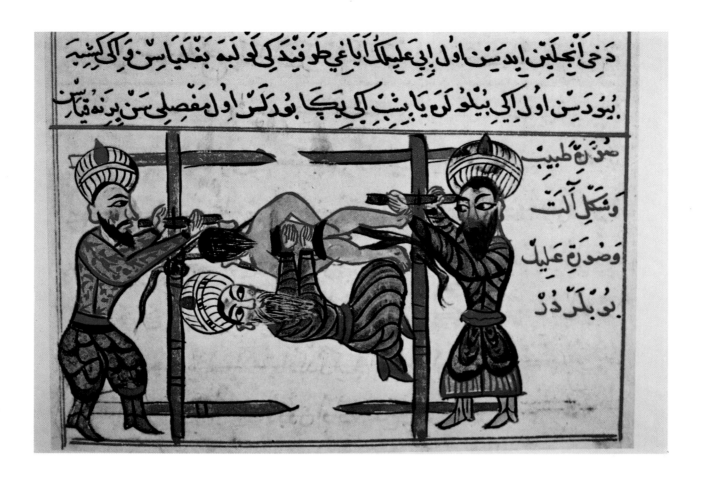

اَکشن آلَت

وَ نُظَرِ عَلِيلٌ

بُو بَکَرُ دْرَ

atheism and Saint Thomas Aquinas was to refute his works in detail (he was studied in Paris and Padua); Rome condemned him in 1240 and 1513.

We should also mention Ibn al-Khatib and Ibn Khaldun. The former, who was born in Granada in 1313 and died by strangulation at Fez in 1374, left us an excellent account of the great plague of 1348. The latter, a great Tunisian explorer, worked in an area we would today call medical geography.

The role of Jewish doctors in the development of medicine and the eminent place held by Maimonides have already been mentioned. When Granada was captured in 1492 by the Catholic kings, the Arab and Jewish medical tradition continued in other centres of culture which already existed, such as Fez, Marrakesh, Tunis and Kairouan.

Andalusian doctors isolated and identified numerous diseases and developed methods for their diagnosis, invented unprecedented surgical operations and, by means of a manual dating from the ninth century, established professional ethics which were independent of

Plate from the earliest Turkish surgical manuscript, 1465. A surgeon and his two assistants manipulate the spinal column of a patient. Fatih Museum, Istanbul, Turkey.

religion. It must be stressed that Muslim doctors and surgeons had no special liking for compilations, summaries or encyclopaedias. They did not produce any themselves, but commented freely on the work of their predecessors, correcting, contradicting and thereby adding the fruit of their own practical experience in the art of healing.

The Arabs also raised the fundamental question which still preoccupies believers in this century: how can a truth revealed, be it Christian or Muslim, be reconciled with the real and the rational, how can dogma accord with science? Does the doctor have the right to interfere in phenomena about whose development God decides?

Christian scholasticism was to use Avicenna's and Averroes' arguments and, at the end of the twentieth century, doctors and some religious people still do not agree on the ways of helping one's neighbours.

Finally, it would be incorrect to think that Arab doctors, isolated by their language and their writing, lived apart. In contrast to a generally propagated idea,

the major cultural exchanges did not take place during the crusades, from 1099 to the fall of Saint Joan of Arc two centuries later, but in Spain during the five centuries of the *Reconquista*.

Indeed, prosperous Andalusia attracted traders, visitors, Christian monks and clerics, all of whom had something to learn from the Muslims, while the Muslims had no reason to travel northwards. The countless travellers from the north to the south of Spain crossed frontiers which were only occasionally battlegrounds, and quickly learnt Arabic and Hebrew. To have their successors benefit from their knowledge and their travels, they translated into Latin the old Greek books, from texts which they obtained in Arabic.

It is easy to imagine that the passing on in this way of ancient knowledge via several languages (from Greek to Syriac, then Arabic or Hebrew, to end in Latin) gave rise to errors, contradictions and inconsistencies.

It is, however, of little import that monks from Scotland or Dalmatia, Germany or France were sometimes mistaken.

From the same manuscript by Sharaf ed-Din. Surgical treatment of female genital problems. National Library, Paris, France.

Gerard of Cremona (1114–1187) spent most of his life in Toledo and not in Italy; Constantine, called the African because he was a Muslim from Tunisia, travelled the world before dying as a monk at Monte Cassino.

The Normans and Emperor Frederick II of Hohenstaufen, after conquering Sicily and Naples, surrounded themselves with Muslim scholars and doctors. The first medical schools were established on the shores of the Mediterranean in Montpellier and Salerno.

These exchanges multiplied over a period of some four hundred years. The outcome was that, thanks to the Arabs, the Christian West was to know the ancient Greek authors, Plato and Aristotle, as well as Hippocrates and Galen.

Arab-Latin relations lost their intensity from the fourteenth century, when Greeks immigrated increasingly from Constantinople to the Christian countries, bringing with them ancient, scientific and philosophical literature in its original form. In the meantime, the Arabs had enriched this ancient culture and had allowed the West to profit from it.

From the fifth century, from Germania to Sicily and Spain, princes assumed powers and territories without, however, creating states. With the end of the Western Roman Empire (476), the phenomenon of the great invasions grew: the Burgundians, the Huns and the Alamans, then the Franks, the Avars and the Lombards, not to mention the Normans and Hungarians, in turn swarmed across Europe. Dialects were established everywhere from a mixture of low Latin and the local Scandinavian or Germanic language. The general ignorance of Latin, the only basis for scientific knowledge, combined with the difficulty in communication. Nevertheless this scientific knowledge survived and circulated.

In these countries in total political chaos, Christianity spread in its Latin form and only the educated propagators of the religion were able to read the ancient authors who looked at diseases and how to cure them. This area of reading left to the monks is all the more noteworthy in the medical field as medicine did not constitute a particular intellectual discipline, for it was part of an authentic general culture and belonged to a global vision of the universe, a vast reality in which man has his place, whether he is well or ill.

The development of monachism following the proselytizing of Saint Benedict of Nursia in the sixth century further emphasized this isolation of knowledge in clerical society; while the secular clergy and even the bishops remained poorly educated, in the monasteries there were men able to read, write, speak and interpret scholarly texts, some of which were on the subject of medicine. However, this monastic medicine was to re

Universities and medicine in the West

IV.

THE RELIGIOUS AS GUARDIANS OF KNOWLEDGE

main, for almost another three centuries, a medicine passed on without any creative capacity.

The names of some clerics have thus survived thanks to their medical works among other more philosophical treatises: Boece (480–524), Cassiodore (468–523), Isidore of Seville (c. 570–636), the Venerable Bede (674–735). It was perfectly normal for these erudite men from various countries in Europe not to consider the art of healing as a human activity different from any other, for it was based on pragmatism and reflection, the concrete and the abstract. Today, too, medicine cannot dissociate itself entirely from physics, chemistry, fluid mechanics, sociology, psychology and ethics, and it was not until the early nineteenth century that some governments reserved its practice to certain people recognized as competent. But the fact that the Church became, willingly or otherwise, the repository of the medical knowledge of the time, was to link faith to medicine for many centuries to come; the Vatican has still not renounced its right to intervene in this area.

In the ninth and tenth centuries, the spread of education among ordinary people marked the Carolingian renaissance. The fact that the emperor himself was only semi-educated was irrelevant: by his symbolic wish to recreate the old Roman Empire, he also sought to re-establish a vast political community, using Latin as the unified language and vehicle of the transmission of knowledge. During the alternating periods of stagnation and creation which humanity experiences throughout its history, this revival of education at periods which are contemporary to within a few decades can be observed in the Carolingian West, in the Abbasids empire of Baghdad, in the caliphate of Cordova and in Byzantium under the authority of the Macedonian dynasty.

APOLLO   MEDICVS

The monks in their monasteries or sometimes at the courts of princes were knowledgeable about medicine as well as theology, mathematics, botany and architecture, where they did not busy themselves with alchemy. And, because of this knowledge, they involved themselves as much in politics or administration as in the catechism. The Englishman, Alcuin, was to become the extremely active counsellor of Charlemagne; and, throughout

Isidore of Seville (c. 560–637) was without doubt one of the last fathers of the Western Church. His twenty books on etymology, as seen here, under the patronage of Apollo, constituted the most comprehensive encyclopaedia of profane and religious knowledge of his time. Ninth-century manuscript. Chapter Library, Vercelli, Italy.

Western Europe, Benedictine monasteries would shelter eminent intellectuals. In Wearmouth in England, the Venerable Bede attempted to codify blood-letting; in Mainz, Raban Maur, the abbot of Fulda, recorded medicinal plants, as did Odon de Meung at Saint Martin's abbey of Tours. The names of other monks could also be cited, at Saint Gall, at Einsiedeln, Canterbury and Marmoutier, and even the name of Bishop Fulbert of Chartres.

The School of Salerno, at the crossroads of
Arab and Latin culture, the only school in the
eleventh century to teach exclusively medicine,
from an imaginary representation taken from
Avicenna's Canon. Fourteenth- or fifteenth-
century engraving. Municipal Library, Bologna,
Italy.

THE CROSSROADS OF SALERNO

While the educated monasteries corresponded with each other, exchanged monks and manuscripts, but confined their activities to a closed circle reserved for clerics, the School of Salerno clearly had other ambitions.

The historian still suffers from a lack of information about its origins, buried in the mists of time; legends about it reflect the prestige ascribed to it in centuries to come. For example, the links which are supposed to have associated Salerno with Monte Cassino, an abbey founded by Saint Benedict in 529, seem to have more to do with a wish for annexation of the School by the Church than with historic fact. Likewise, the account of the foundation of the Salernian group by an Italian, a Greek, a Jew and a Saracen reflects the desire for a flattering universalism proper to later centuries and has no documentary foundation.

In any case, from the early eleventh century, rumours abounded in Europe about this little port of Salerno, in southern Italy, where doctors taught their

One of the most celebrated works of the School of Salerno: the Regimen sanitatis, *a sort of code of health and hygiene, written in Neapolitan dialect.*
Right: the doctor knows he must choose the best astral configuration to collect plants. Second half of the fourteenth century. National Library, Naples, Italy.

discipline in Italian, Greek, Latin and Arabic, accepted passing students, whatever their religion, discussed ancient texts and expressed their curiosity about any new medical concept. Two facts, which were not to be repeated for many years, characterize this seat of culture. On the one hand, only medicine and a certain amount of law were taught. No other discipline was tackled and the School of Salerno was not to produce any philosophical work during this period. On the other hand, the teachers were not clerics but lay people who practised medicine.

Scholars from the whole of Christian Europe and Jewish and Muslim Spain went to be educated at Salerno, including Constantine the African, whom we have already mentioned, considered to be the most celebrated translator of Arabic into Latin. For several centuries, under the Lombard, Norman and Swabian regimes, southern Italy and Sicily were to become fevered areas of transition from Greek to Latin culture, via Arabic, as were Cordova, Seville and Toledo.

History gives us names such as those of Warbod Gariopontus, who wrote a vast medical encyclopaedia, Jean Platearius, the author of a book on "the passions of women before, during and after childbirth", and Roger of Parma, famous for his treatise on surgery. Some people think that until the eleventh century, the School adopted methodism, then developed towards humourism, but the description of this change seems artificial as throughout the whole Middle Ages doctors adhered to Hippocrates' principle of the four humours.

The place held by women in the teaching corpus also comes within the field of legendary controversy. Apart from a certain Trotula or Trota, the author of a treatise on gynaecology and obstetrics, there were supposedly other women whose names are passed down by tradition. Whatever the truth of the matter, ten centuries were to preserve the memory of Trotula in parallel with this derisory polemic: "Was she really a doctor or simply a self-educated midwife?" The prestige of the School of Salerno was to continue for a few centuries before it faded. Although Frederick II, in the thirteenth century, granted it the exclusive right to award diplomas to doctors and, later, it was authorized to perform the dissection of the human body, the golden age of Salerno was coming to an end; there were fewer pupils in the School and fewer ships in port. The commercial

Regimen sanitatis. Left: *a copier works on a manuscript.*
Right: *a scene depicting culinary art. Second half of the fourteenth century. National Library, Naples, Italy.*

and the intellectual circuits had shifted elsewhere.

Nevertheless, one work from this School, which we would describe as a treatise on hygiene, was to survive until the present day: the *Regime for health*. This compilation of rules for good health dealt with diet, lifestyle, sexual activity and moderation in all things and inspired hundreds of popularized works adapted for all languages, all climates and all levels of culture. This formula of popularization of a *Regimen sanitatis* is still just as successful today.

Despite the School of Salerno, in the twelfth century the Church had a monopoly in knowledge. The rich regular clergy kept in its monasteries clerics who copied texts (and sometimes illuminated them), thus reducing the price to the pupils. Bishops were encouraged to develop their "cathedral schools", open to children from various social classes.

The clerics then became so enthusiastic about medicine that they became its practitioners, placing their Hippocratic erudition at the service of the sick. This phenomenon took on such massive

In this French version of a Salernian surgical treatise, the doctor, on the left, also dispenses medicinal herbs and remedies. On the wall, a receptacle used to collect the blood from blood-letting. Thirteenth-century manuscript. British Museum, London, England.

proportions that some acquired prestige, authority and wealth at the expense of their religious functions. The Church of Rome objected to this and, in 1130, the synod of Clermont forbade members of the clergy and communities from practising medicine (as did the Church in the East). Clearly, the monks did not obey immediately, as this decision had to be frequently repeated. However, these measures did not result in the secularization of medicine as such. Firstly, medicine was only one branch of science, which could not escape religion, and secondly, educated people were subject, by their training, to certain rules proper to the ecclesiastical discipline: for example, in Paris, it was not until 1452 that doctors were no longer obliged to be celibate.

The centre of political and commercial activity shifted in the course of these decades. The crusades, the first of which was crowned by the capture of Jerusalem in 1099, continued in the Mediterranean, but their main thrust came from Northern Europe: capital and ships were provided by Augsburg or Venice and no longer by Salerno, Amalfi or Bari. The "Franks", the Western Europeans, discovered the Byzantine civilization and became aware of their intellectual limitations. Monachism then became aggressive, the templars fought even more against the infidel by word than by the sword, while the Hospitallers of Jerusalem praised in Palestine the concept of an establishment which cares for the wounded, but they did not develop this new form of medical aid.

At the same time, the character of philosophical preoccupations changed, moving beyond the limits of the faith but not divorcing itself from it. Intellectuals grappled with a question which appears to us futile or artificial because it is badly stated: do races and species exist *per se*, is their existence anterior to that of the

Blood-letting, as practised in the fifteenth century to prevent the plague. Tractarus de pestilentia, *fifteenth century. University Library, Prague, Czech Republic.*

individual, are they superior to the individual? This "quarrel of the universals" expresses in abstract terms other philosophical difficulties already raised by Plato and Aristotle. It concerns the links between reality and thought and in the final analysis between the body and the mind. Neither religion nor medicine could remain totally divorced from this debate.

Abelard (1071–1142) attempted to resolve the dilemma. Neither he nor any of his successors was able to settle the matter and the theological and philosophical jousting soon gave rise to separate paths of reasoning which were to isolate the individual disciplines from each other.

SALERNIAN HEALTH REGIME

Extracts translated from an eighteenth-century versified version in French:

Breathe a serene air, with purity bright,
With no exhalation to dim its light;
Flee odours and vapours which can infect
                                        or impair,
And rising from the gutters, corrupt the
                                        air...
If you wish to prolong your pleasurable
                                        successes,
Then of vice and at table, avoid all
                                        excesses...
The greater the ill, the harder art's chore:
Easier to prevent than a patient restore.
Air, rest, sleep, food and pleasure
Keep man healthy, taken in due measure:
These innocent joys, abuse turns to ill
Which ravages the body and troubles the
                                        will...

THE BIRTH OF
THE THIRTEENTH
CENTURY

The science of medicinal herbs, from the translation by Gerard of Cremona of a treatise by Galen. Italy, late thirteenth century. Municipal Library, Laon, France.

The concerns which were evident at the end of the twelfth century appear to have provoked the explosions which rocked Europe in the early decades of the thirteenth century. Catholic armies took Constantinople from the Orthodox Byzantines in 1204, confirming definitively the ruin of the East to the profit of the West. In 1212, the Christian North of Spain crushed the Muslim South at Las Navas de Tolosa, thus sealing the end of a hitherto dazzling culture. In 1214, France triumphed over the Germanic Roman Empire, thus forcing it to renounce for ever its European supremacy. In 1215, the English imposed on their king the *Magna Carta*, which was a precedent for a new distribution of power between a sovereign and his subjects.

These events transformed the relationships between cultures, religions and states. The Mongols laid siege to Baghdad in 1258, helped Turkish power to gain a stranglehold over the old Arab world and shattered the fertile links which had until then united Christianity and Islam.

Following these geopolitical upheavals in the Levant, Greek intellectuals departed for Europe, which could now assimilate ancient philosophy without any intermediary.

Like Bologna, which had created a "university" with its masters and pupils — a simple intellectual community — other towns endowed themselves with institutions to teach the "universality" of knowledge in all areas of philosophical reflection, covering the study of thought and nature, or in other words "physics". We do not have any conclusive documents establishing whether the University of Bologna or Montpellier is the older, but this question is largely irrelevant: they were both immediately and equally successful. In just a few decades, the major towns of Italy, and then France, Spain and England all had their own universities.

From the time of their foundation, their development and the exchanges which they fostered created intellectual Europe: initially confined to imperial Roman Europe bounded to the East by the Elbe and Danube, it spread rapidly to Hungary and the Slav and Scandinavian countries.

While Catholic Europe was born as a result of the movement of clergy from the north to the south, to Andalusia and to the Byzantine East, as a result of the crusades, from the thirteenth century, cultural Europe was inspired by lay people, although it could not entirely escape the Church. Although the universities were founded and financed by towns or administrative districts which were making their presence felt, or by the local lord or the bishop, the Church closely monitored the teachers and the educational system which they dispensed. However, the method of recruitment of teachers, based on their skill and no longer centred on the orthodoxy of their beliefs, soon gave rise to problems in the ecclesiastical hierarchy.

FOUNDATION OF UNIVERSITIES

(Some of these dates are uncertain)

1188(?)	**Bologna**
1209	**Valencia**
1214	**Oxford**
1215(?)	**Paris**
1220	**Montpellier (confirmation of a previous foundation)**
1224	**Naples**
1228	**Padua**
1229	**Cambridge and Toulouse**
1230	**Salamanca**
1245	**Rome**
1261	**Pavia**
1279	**Coimbra**
1290	**Lisbon**
1300	**Lerida**

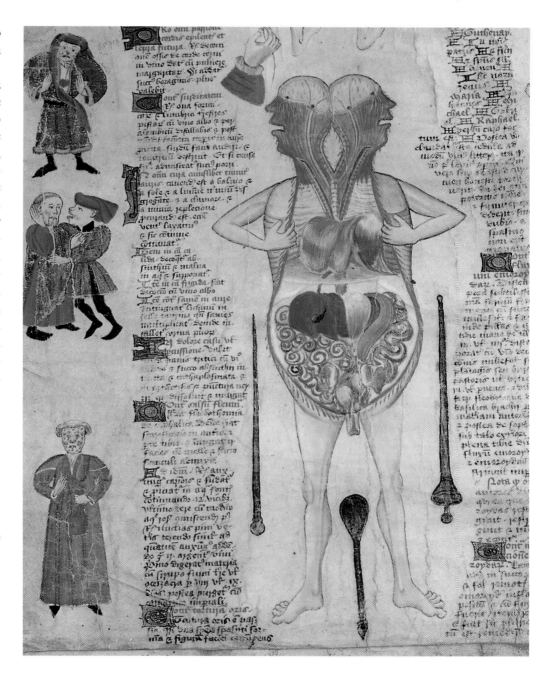

In the Middle Ages, anatomical plates were still rare and still fanciful. Here, a corpse, sawn along its length, reveals its internal organs. In the margin, on the left, a few humorous scenes concerning skin disease. From John Ardane of Newark, De arte phisicali et de chirurgia, *1412. Royal Library, Stockholm, Sweden.*

147

A fourteenth-century university. The fact that the majority of students were clergy testifies to the pressure the Church exerted on education at that time. Fourteenth century, Italy. Municipal Library, Cambrai, France.

BETWEEN FAITH AND REASON

The problem was still that of reconciling the findings obtained by the study of nature and the truth as revealed by the Church's teachings. The Muslim ulemas had already regarded Averroes with suspicion when he expressed his doctrine of the two truths inspired by Aristotle; Averroism thus based on a rationalist ambiguity was soon in favour in Pavia and Paris and the Church was forced to condemn it on a number of occasions.

However, it was through Avicenna and Averroes that Aristotle penetrated the Latin world. Thus, Albert von Bollstaedt of Cologne (1200–1280), to whom posterity was later to give the name Albert the Great, established a convincing interpretation of the whole analysis of Aristotle's ideas, an interpretation soon taken up once more by Thomas Aquinas (1227–1274).

In 1222, the bishop, William of Auxerre, also gave a most satisfactory reading of Aristotle and (as the Church had already accepted these, in some cases ancient, works) authors such as Hippocrates,

Visit by a doctor to the hospital Santa Maria della Scala in Siena. Founded c. 1090, it was considered in the fifteenth century to be one of the first to develop a real health policy. For example, every patient was to have his own bed. Pinacoteca, Siena, Italy.

Aristotle and Galen became the favourite reading of students. The ecclesiastical authorization did not mean that these teachings were always faithfully followed. In Paris, Roger Bacon (1214–1294) doubted the infallibility of the Aristotelian doctrine. However, the hierarchy was so distrustful of any theological and philosophical deviations that the strict adherence to the ancient authors, copied many times over, was to become one of the causes of a centuries-long medical stagnation. Neither Hippocrates, Rhazes nor Avicenna had sought such an intellectual inactivity.

The vainly sought unity between metaphysics and the sciences of observation was also reflected in the single method of discussion and education: scholasticism. With the help of a syllogism, or based on two different propositions, a dialogue is commenced in which the arguments of the two theses are set against each other with victory going to the most generally held opinion or that accepted by the dogma.

Albert the Great (c. 1193–1280). His teaching, which aided the rehabilitation of Aristotle, was to have a strong influence on Saint Thomas Aquinas. Like the majority of philosophers at that time, he was also interested in the properties of plants and metals. National Library, Paris, France.

The result of such jousting was that the better orator was not the one who based his arguments on data from observation derived from method or reasoning, but the one who was able to show the consequence of adverse theses with the greatest skill, however artificially.

It can be said that this didactic method encouraged intellectual agility and abstract eloquence but did not contribute to the development of knowledge of the reality of the universe.

However, the number of universities increased because towns regarded them as a mark of prestige and an attraction to students who went there to spend their allowances. The Church preferred to create and control them rather than to tolerate them and, in particular in the fourteenth century, their numbers multiplied under the Maecenas princes who used them for their propaganda purposes. Thus, in addition to prestigious universities such as those in Bologna and Padua, Montpellier and Paris, small towns in France were endowed with universities where an inadequate number of professors dispensed a mediocre education and awarded diplomas of little worth.

The better schools, for their part, had medical students take regular tests over five or six years of studies, and awarded them in turn the rank of bachelor, graduate and master or doctor. Each test obliged the candidates to give gifts to the school's personnel, vergers, professors — gifts in cash or in kind, such as hats, gloves or banquets. The conferring of these ranks was marked by a religious ceremony which testifies to the pressure exerted by the Church on science as well as on society, and once again the graduate offered candles, a panel or furniture to the town's medical "college" chapel, not forgetting a substantial offering to the "poor in the parish".

Medical studies were therefore long and expensive, but the "doctor" could be proud of his title and demand high fees. If he came from a reputable university, he was welcomed in other schools and colleges to practise there, but if his title was more modest, he had difficulty leaving his own province.

In Europe, this university system and these official and customary hierarchies were to continue and become even more complicated until the early nineteenth century: the rigidity of institutions exacerbated the effects of routine on education and thinking.

A cripple who has had his right hand and leg amputated seeks asylum. It was for him and those like him, and by charity, that the hospitals of the time were intended. Relief from a pew in the church of Saint Lucien in Beauvais, 1490. Cluny Museum, Paris, France.

THE CHURCH AND
THE HOSPITAL

From the start of Christian monachism, in the sixth century, monasteries devoted themselves to learning, prayer, manual work and also to helping the poor and deprived as taught by Christ. This is why so many monasteries used one of their buildings as a hospital.

In fact, it is difficult to distinguish the hospital from what, in our eyes, seems to resemble a hostelry. It was not so much the sick in the locality who went there, but travellers and above all pilgrims who found a safer refuge in the monasteries than in the inns on the main highways. The rich, who were accompanied by their servants and escorts, would stay there for a few days and pay for this facility.

*The hospital and the church.
Franciscan monks care for lepers in a
hospital, probably in Italy. From the*
Franceschina, *sixteenth-century
illuminated manuscript. Augustea
Library, Perugia, Italy.*

Accounts are known of pilgrims who set out from Gaul to make their devotions and seek healing either in Rome at Saint Peter's tomb or in Jerusalem at the Holy Sepulchre, even before Palestine fell at the hands of the infidel in 638. The commercial relations between the two extremities of the Mediterranean, and then the crusades swelled the tide of these journeys, both pious and therapeutic, thanks to well organized "tourist agencies".

Then, at the culmination of the Middle Ages, the cult of miraculous relics became a current Catholic practice. Monasteries, convents and churches boasted of the remains of a local saint which attracted

On the road to Santiago de Compostela, the monastery and the hospital receive pilgrims. Left: *the capital of a column in the cloisters of Tudela, Spain.* Below: *pilgrims praying. Master of Saint Sebastian, late fifteenth century. Barberini Palace, Rome, Italy.*

the sick and infirm, and pregnant and sterile women alike.

Religious communities obtained considerable resources in this way, as the income from the accommodation added to the holy offerings. From the late tenth century, the most famous pilgrimage, together with that of Rome, was that of Santiago de Compostela in Galicia where, it was said, the clothes of the apostle James had been found when the Saracens left the region.

Throughout Europe, even from distant Friesland and England, pilgrims lined the roads to Galicia, following well-worn routes, marked by other shrines of prayer and monastic inns, of which a few hundred

are known. By the time of the Renaissance, these hospitals scattered along the
roadsides, where so little care was provided, were no longer frequented. The
monks, however, added to their excellent
hospitality more therapeutic activities:
many of them grew rare plants with
curative properties in the enclosure around
the cloisters. These constituted the first
botanical and pharmaceutical gardens,
guided by manuals from Ancient Greece
and Arabia.

Religious communities also founded
urban hospitals. Etymologically speaking,
they received "guests" rather than patients and also took in the homeless poor,
the infirm and the insane. If someone fell
ill, the doctor or surgeon was called. This

A Paris hospital in the fifteenth century.
As in Siena, the dietary regime constitutes
the basis of therapy. Every patient has a
jug and a plate (in the background).
Ordonnance des chrétiens, *printed by*
Antoine Vérard, 1490. National
Library, Paris, France.

institution had no therapeutic objective
nor any didactic purpose, as links with the
local university, in the large towns, were
very rare.

It should be noted that the cult of relics
and the reputation acquired by certain
shrines preserved, in the Christian rite,
the old pagan devotions to healing heroes.
We saw earlier how Saint Cosmas and
Saint Damian succeeded Castor and Pollux.
Likewise, at the site of springs once
worshipped by the Gauls, churches were
erected where the faithful brought votive
offerings to pray for miracles or to give
thanks for a recovery. Magic and religion
coexisted at all levels of society, together
with medical practices which were still
not clearly distinct from them.

THE MISFORTUNE
OF THE TIMES

*T*he doctors of the time can hardly be reproached for not knowing how to deal with diseases which we are still not able to control today, one thousand years on.

Leprosy was widespread throughout Eurasia at the culmination of the Middle Ages, perhaps even before the Christian era if our interpretation of the Old Testament is correct. The healthy held it in such terror that very early on efforts were made, by governmental decisions, to isolate lepers in leprosaria or leper houses. They numbered, apparently, over one thousand in the kingdom of France in the twelfth century.

A jury composed of representatives of civil and religious authorities and a doctor or surgeon would examine the sick person suspected of having leprosy. There were doubtless many incorrect diagnoses resulting in people with harmless skin

The "plagues", sent from heaven in the form of fantastic animals, swoop on the town. Vincent de Beauvais, Le Miroir historial. *Condé Museum, Chantilly, France.*

diseases being wrongly imprisoned. This internment often led to exclusion from civilian society and the religious community, as well as loss of income.

We now know that the ways in which this disease is transmitted do not warrant such a rigorous segregation. Fortunately, the Christian world did not always implement these measures. It is said that cases of leprosy increased enormously at the time of the crusades; in any case, from the fifteenth century, its frequency gradually declined, with leprosaria admitting very few patients. In the sixteenth century, almost all of them closed and their assets were dispersed or put to other uses.

Smallpox too is a very old disease. Until vaccination, in the early nineteenth century and its disappearance in 1977, it was one of the most deadly diseases of the human race. In the Middle Ages, it raged

The Middle Ages made scapegoats of lepers,
although they were only mildly contagious. A
sort of living dead, this leper announces his
passage by waving a rattle. The city gates are
closed to him. Barthelemy the Englishman,
Des propriétés des choses, *late sixteenth
century. National Library, Paris, France.*

in short periods of virulence, killing principally the very young and the old. It became, in time, a common endemic affliction, an inevitable scourge to which one becomes accustomed.

The plague, however, proceeded by spectacular upsurges and left even more dramatic memories in the minds of the people than smallpox. The "black death", which we now know is usually transmitted by fleas on rats, appeared in the form of small black marks around each bite and ganglions swelling in the neck, groin and armpits, and the patient would be dead within a few days. In other cases, where a healthy person was infected by the spittle of someone suffering the plague, death came even sooner, within the day.

"Saint Anthony's fire", here in the form of death riding on horseback, from a fifteenth-century woodcutting.

It had already struck in the sixth century under Justinian and then been forgotten when, coming from Central Asia, it struck the Black Sea ports, followed by Constantinople and Syria, before arriving in Messina and Marseilles in 1348. Travelling along the main channels of communication, it reached the whole of Europe including Scandinavia and Moscow. It is estimated to have killed between one third and one quarter of the European population in just a few years, sowing terror everywhere, wiping out communities and whole villages. Mortality on such a grand scale necessarily disturbed the equilibrium between towns and states, transformed social contacts by decimating families and creating new

Page of a herbal from an abridged adaptation of Plaetarius' Circa instans. Northern Italy, fifteenth century. National Library, Paris, France.

A patient, doubtless from a noble family, afflicted by boils prepares to experience the benefits of a medicinal bath. Large illumination by Evrard d'Espinques. Barthelemy the Englishman, Des propriétés des choses, late sixteenth century. National Library, Paris, France.

rich people, prompted the transfer of populations between towns, rural areas and regions spared or only slightly afflicted and also affected trading circuits.

The plague struck at the imagination of the people of that era by the number of lives it claimed and by the random way in which it attacked both young and old, the powerful and the poor. Thus, if on the one hand there was no shortage of "scapegoats" in the form of the new arrivals like the Jews or the lepers who were massacred in many provinces, on the other, the manifestations of atonement constantly multiplied, from the resurgence of pilgrimages, to pious endowments, donations to the Church and ceremonies with processions and collective flagellations.

Baths, as well as diet, formed the basis of mediaeval therapy. Here, a bath-house attendant removes cupping glasses from the backs of his patients. In the background, a bather rests. Abenzohar, Tractatus de pestilentia, *fifteenth century. University Library, Prague, Czech Republic.*

The plague, however, would continue to rage until the end of the eighteenth century in certain European countries, in the form of short epidemics, despite the isolation of those afflicted and the administrative procedures such as the incineration of their goods, the fires of aromatic plants lit at the crossroads in towns, the quarantines imposed in the ports and frontier posts to prevent access to healthy areas by those suspected of having the disease.

It is easy to understand why the plague, which is still endemic in certain parts of the globe, left the regions no longer affected by the illness so profoundly marked.

In addition to the other infectious diseases – such as measles and mumps – from which we still suffer and which can sometimes prove fatal, the population of that period suffered the consequences of a poor diet.

The paucity of means of transport and storage meant that major production fluctuations in different regions due to weather conditions could not be counteracted, so that fatal famines were a regular occurrence. The diet did not contain all the substances required by the body and deficiencies in certain vitamins resulted in diseases such as scurvy or rickets, and lowered resistance to infection.

Due to the archaic nature of agricultural techniques or the poor preservation of foodstuffs, there were frequent cases of poisoning. The most formidable was ergotism, caused by a poison found in the "ergot", a parasitic fungus on rye. This disease attacks the small arteries in the limbs and causes pains and intolerable burns, followed by spontaneous amputations. It was hoped that this "Saint Anthony's fire" could be cured by devotions and pilgrimages to the saint – which ensured the prosperity of communities of Antonian monks.

A patient and his doctor, from the illuminated Latin version of a book by Galen. France, fourteenth century. National Library, Paris, France.

INEFFECTUAL MEDICINES

*I*n the face of these misfortunes – and many more could be cited – doctors "shone" by their powerlessness, despite the wealth of universities and the intensity of the purely theoretical education they dispensed, for the respect shown to the texts of Hippocrates, Galen or Avicenna did not allow anyone to stray from the concept of the four basic humours of the human body, with disease caused by their imbalance which needed to be redressed.

Furthermore, there were insufficient diagnostic processes: visual inspection of the patient, his general demeanour, skin, face, the feeling of the pulse, the characteristics of which were recognized although its regularity was not measured, and examination of the urine using a specially shaped receptacle. This point of the medical consultation proved to be essential. It was how doctors could establish remote diagnoses, based on large numbers of widely available and discussed treatises on "uroscopy". The iconography of the Middle Ages, as it has reached us, has no shortage of scenes of

The reputation of the hot baths of Pozzuoli, near Naples, was such that Peter of Eboli celebrated them (c. 1212–1221) in a poem dedicated to the Emperor, Frederick II. A significant detail: men and women bathed there together, which was not the case later, at the Church's request. Peter of Eboli, De balneis duteolaneis, fourteenth century. Municipal Library, Rheims, France.

doctors with their urine receptacle, a symbol of their profession.

While diagnostic aids may have been limited, therapeutic aids were, in contrast, as numerous as they were ineffectual. The basis for any prescription rested on the regime of the patient's life, in accordance with the Salernian tradition: the doctor advised a certain type of physical activity, a certain range of food called a "diet", involving a selection of dishes depending on whether they were lean or fat, purgative or stringent, and prescribed wines on the basis of their colour or the ground from which they came. From the thirteenth century, at the instigation of Raymond Lull and Arnold of Villanueva, alcohol made from wine, held to have invigorating properties, was even used as "*eau-de-vie*".

Doctors also included bathing in their regimes. There was no shortage of water in the towns at that time; some springs, known in Roman times, were reactivated. The "bath-houses" thus received large numbers of customers, accepting women and men together.

The virtues of plants, from phantasmagoria to practice! Left: *wild lettuce used against eye complaints.* Right: *the strange mandrake with its anthropomorphous roots was commonly regarded as an aphrodisiac.* Pseudo Apuleius, De medicaminibus herbarum liber. *National Library, Vienna, Austria. Herbal, from Plaetarius,*

Once his regime was decided, the doctor advised on medicines, of which he had a large range, in the three kingdoms of nature.

In the tenth and eleventh centuries, the encyclopaedic works listing and describing minerals and animals increased in number: herbals, "bestiaries" and lapidaries, the most famous of which is that of Bishop Marbod of Rennes (1035–1123). Initially written as simple inventories, they nonetheless constituted an attempt at systemization which, while supplementing Pliny's work, was the precursor of what was later to become botany, zoology and mineralogy. They supplemented the work of the Ancients by adding large quantities of information. Substances in powder form were catalogued, sometimes precious stones and even gold and mercury, depending on the magic virtues attributed to them, or depending on their colour: red stones were said to counteract the loss of blood and correct pallor.

In addition to the hundreds of plants appearing in Dioscorides' pharmacopoeia are those proposed by the Salernian Platearius and those which the Arabs had learnt about from India and China. Here too, similarities imposed their logic: the sap of yellow flowers was a remedy for jaundice, the bulbs of certain plants corrected flagging virility and guaranteed procreation.

Doctors were also interested in the animal kingdom; mammalian testicles, scorpions' pincers, offal, bile, furs were all indicated. Even human ear wax and nail clippings were collected. The digestive tract of certain animals sometimes contain chalk stones or bezoars to which were attributed virtues against "poisons", i.e. perfectly normal indigestion.

Apothecaries also used the excreta of certain animals, faecal matter or urine: this copro-pharmacy was to remain in vogue until the end of the eighteenth century. All the products taken from the animal kingdom were combined in innumerable ways, each apothecary having his "theriacal*" recipe, which he kept secret and which he guaranteed as a panacea.

It would not be accurate to regard these medical prescriptions as the result of gratuitous, irrational or arbitrary fantasies or phantasmagoria. They have to be seen as part of a general view of the universe

The twelve signs of the zodiac, from Aries to Pisces, surround the sun. Cornelius Celsus, Zodiacs. *Central Italy, eleventh century. National Library, Paris, France.*

in which all the components were thought to be interdependent and linked by affinities governed by the Creator; where man is only a microcosm in the cosmos, all the parts of which correspond to each other: every plant, every organ of an individual, every star is part of an immense system of coherences which the doctor had to know how to use in his treatments; for example, the correct function of the liver depended on Saturn, like the flowering of vegetable plants. It was not important that these "signatures" could not be supported by proofs for they reflected the divine will.

Books of the time certainly reflected this global view of creation. In the portrait of "zodiac man", for example, each human limb and organ corresponds to the image of a planet. And since the effect of any particular constellation changes with each individual's date of birth, what we now call astrology governed therapy. It is therefore not surprising that doctors were knowledgeable about astronomy. The universality of education in the universities constituted all the knowledge which the doctor had to acquire. He could not be ignorant of any of the branches of natural science, or in other words "physics": it is for this reason that in England a doctor was called a physician.

Today, the frontiers of this complex knowledge seem somewhat vague, from esotericism to astrology, magic and even the witchcraft observed and condemned by the Inquisition. The stake was never far away. At the slightest suspicion of non-conformity with the dogma, practitioners soon took on the air of suspects.

The life of Arnold of Villanueva (1235?–1315?) illustrates these uncertainties. A Catalan, educated at Salerno, he attended, as was normal at the time, the majority of the most important European universities, absorbed all the sciences and performed various political and diplomatic tasks at the service of different sovereigns

Vision of Saint Hildegard. Man, subject to the mysterious forces of the universe, remains in God's protection. State Library, Lucca, Italy.

before being accused of witchcraft by the Dominicans. Rescued by a pope whose suffering from urinary lithiasis he had relieved, he settled in the most cosmopolitan town at that time: Montpellier. There, he wrote a *Breviary* and a *Regime of health* in which he attempted to bring together current medical doctrines and all known medical flora.

SKILFUL SURGEONS

Doctors acquired their knowledge thanks to the scientific disciplines of the time. Because their studies were long and costly, medical practitioners were few in number and worked only in the major towns for high fees. Inclined principally to theoretical debates, they scorned manual practice, leaving to others afflictions requiring action with a more immediate effect than prescriptions and advice. Thus, doctors and surgeons – the latter, in etymological terms being those who "acted by the hand" – constituted two distinct groups, in contrast to Arab doctors for whom medicine and surgery formed the two inseparable parts of a single art. It was not until the French Revolution that surgeons and doctors were to be reunited.

The barbers who shaved and practised blood-letting did not shrink from lancing

A public dissection at the Faculty of Montpellier. In the fourteenth century, this was still simply a spectacle without any didactic purpose. Guy de Chauliac, Chirurgia, 1363. Atger Museum, Montpellier, France.

abscesses and setting fractures. Some specialized in more precise areas and gradually, in the course of the twelfth century, new professional groups, quite distinct from each other, emerged and developed: barbers, bone-setters, with no instruction other than their practical experience; barber-surgeons, with short gowns, who had undergone a form of apprenticeship; and surgeons with long gowns, dressed similarly to doctors, who had undergone training with an experienced surgeon and had been admitted to their professional "college" following certification by their master and a practical test. For example Guido Lanfranchi (Lefranc), who originally came from Bologna (?–1315), and was forced to flee Italy because of bloody internecine fights between towns, took refuge in Paris, and,

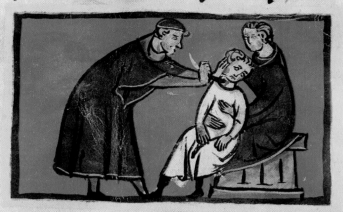

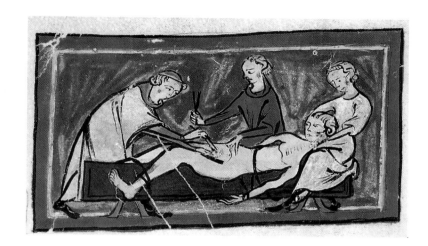

Some surgical operations in the Middle Ages:
1 — *incision of an abscess on the neck*
2 — *operation on a scrotal hernia*
3 — *extraction of a javelin*
4 — *application of points of fire on the forearms*
5 — *intervention in the abdomen*
6 — *dental care*
Thiringia magistri rogerii, *fourteenth century. Atger Museum, Montpellier, France.*

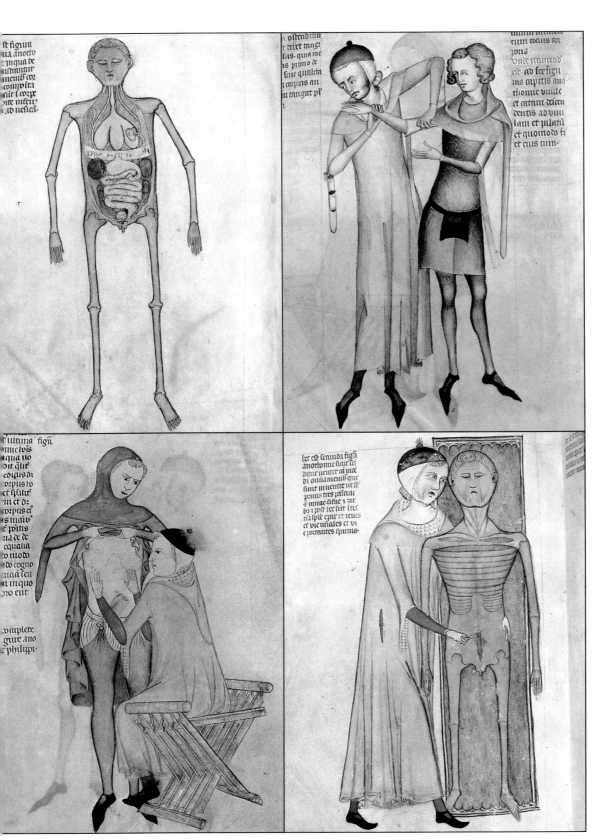

Clockwise from top left: *rough anatomy of the organs in the trunk; treatment of a luxation of the neck; palpation of the abdomen; start of an autopsy. Guy de Pavie, 1345. Condé Museum, Chantilly, France.*

although considered a reputable surgeon throughout Europe, joined the Saint Cosmas and Saint Damian College as he had not been admitted to university.

It will be noted that while the treatment of internal diseases stagnated, during the millennium, that of external diseases improved constantly. Developing the teaching of Paul of Aegina, enriched by Abulcasis, surgeons drained running sores, removed superficial tumours, treated hernias and some malformations, sutured wounds, curetted fistulas, removed foreign bodies and projectiles such as arrow tips, or stones from the bladder, stopped haemorrhaging sometimes by binding the bleeding vessels, reduced dislocations and displacements of the ends of the bones in the case of fractures, which they immobilized in their correct position, carried out the amputation of gangrenous limbs and operated on cataracts. They had no hesitation in trepanning in the case of cranial traumatisms and they developed surgical and dental instrumentation, often poorly suited, so that they could carry out the necessary work. They even knew how to relieve the sufferings of patients undergoing operations by having them breathe in the fumes from sponges saturated in the sap of poppies and hashish, or in other words containing opium: an inadequate empirical procedure.

One area however remained outside the field of activity of doctors and surgeons, that of obstetrics which remained solely in the hands of midwives, trained to a greater or lesser degree by older women.

It is also surprising that a field of investigation as wide and necessary as anatomy did not interest surgeons, although Abulcasis had written that good surgery is impossible without a perfect

knowledge of the human body. Neither the Church nor Islam had, in fact, formally forbidden the dissection of corpses. Yet, although human bodies were dissected – usually the bodies of those sentenced to death – in the presence of members of the public and of students, no one in the Middle Ages thought to benefit from these operations by writing accurate anatomical works, carefully studying the functioning of the organs, or simply improving surgical practice.

Certain modern historians have endeavoured to find different and even contrary conduct by the surgeons of the time. Henri de Mondeville (1260?–1320?) studied at Bologna and Paris before teaching at Montpellier and following Kings Phillip IV and Louis X at the Court of France. He wrote a work entitled *Surgery* which became famous among practitioners and apprentices. By recommending the immediate suturing of wounds, he displayed his superiority over one of his successors, Guy de Chauliac, according to whom wounds produced firstly a "beneficial and pure" pus before they healed.

Guy de Chauliac (1300?–1368) also studied at Paris and Bologna, and stayed for a time in Paris, Toulouse and Lyons before settling in Montpellier. With a lesser knowledge than that of Henri de Mondeville, he practised in Avignon in the employ of the pope, where he was able to describe the ravages of the plague of 1348, although his failure in the face of the epidemic incurred the wrath of Petrarch. However, he owes his great celebrity to his treatise entitled *Chirurgia magna*, directly inspired by Abulcasis, which was to serve rightly as a guide to generations of surgeons over the next four centuries.

167

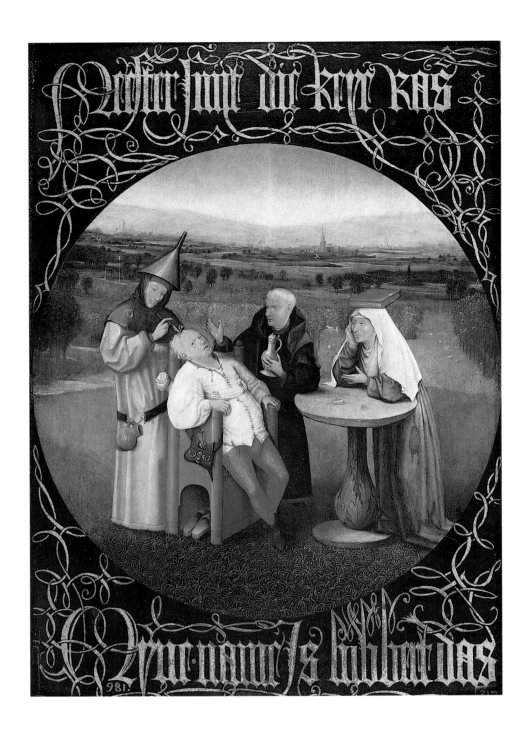

Madness emerged in the late Middle Ages as the epitome of all fears. Here, the Excision of the "stone of madness", *by Hieronymus Bosch (1450–1516). Prado Museum, Madrid, Spain.*

Be that as it may, there was no basis for the dispute between Mondeville who sutured immediately and Chauliac who left an infected wound to weep initially. Yet it was to crop up again six hundred years later, during the 1914–1918 war. In fact, it all depends on the form and the origin of the wound, the extent of the lesions, whether any foreign bodies are present, etc.

The most striking feature during this millennium which constitutes the Middle Ages is the relative conservatism of medical practice in Europe, while surgical techniques, for their part, slowly improved.

The professions concerned with the healing arts gradually organized them-selves, with the better educated and more active doctors establishing their social superiority over the rougher, poorer yet more effective surgeons. The Church, for its part, seemed to have settled the various contradictions inherent in the field, between science and metaphysics, faith and reason, by imposing on medicine its traditional concepts and its rigorous and frequently capricious discipline.

However, in the mid fifteenth century, new ideas emerged which were to overturn the moral and intellectual order previously thought to be permanently established. As at the start of the Christian era, Italy triggered the change, but many other sciences were to benefit from it before medicine would.

THE MIDDLE AGES IN MEDITERRANEAN COUNTRIES
476 – 1453

POLITICS AND CULTURE	DATE	DATE	MEDICINE
End of the Western Roman Empire	476		Nestorian doctors in Persia
			Plague epidemic in the Mediterranean
		525–605	Alexander of Tralles, doctor to Justinian
Reign of Justinian	527–565		Smallpox epidemic in France
			First hospitals in Lyons and Paris
		c. 600	Paul of Aegina
			Leper houses in Europe
The Hegira: Muhammad leaves Mecca for Medina	622		
The Omayyad Empire from Persia to Tunisia	630–670		
The advent of the Carolingians	751		
Independent emirate of Cordova	756		
Charlemagne Emperor	768–814		
		777–859	Jean Mésué
		860–923	Rhazes
Foundation of Cluny	910		
		936–1012	Abulcasis in Cordova
Foundation of the Germanic Holy Roman Empire	962		
		–597	Avicenna at Isfahan *Canon of medicine*
Hugues Capet King of France	987		School of Salerno
		1015–1087	Constantine the African in Salerno
		1073–1162	Avenzoar
Foundation of the University of Bologna	c. 1088		
Jerusalem taken by the Crusaders	1099		
Foundation of Clairvaux	1120		
		1126–1198	Averroes at Seville and Cordova
		1135–1204	Maimonides
Constantinople taken by the Crusaders	1204		
		1210–1288	Ibn Nafiz
Las Navas de Tolosa	1212		
Catholics reconquer Muslim Spain		1240–1313	Arnold of Villanueva at Montpellier
The Turks take Baghdad	1258		
End of the Latin States of Syria	1291		
Start of the Hundred Years' War	1339		
		1346	Start of the Plague in Europe
		1360	Guy de Chauliac, doctor to the popes of Avignon *Grande chirurgie*
		1377	First plague regulations in Ragusa
The Turks take Constantinople	1453		
End of the Hundred Years' War	1454		

chapter VI

Different types of medicine

In the West, we tend all too often to regard ourselves as the sole originators of the medicine which today is accepted worldwide. Yet in reality, the whole of humanity has contributed to it, each community adding the fruits of its ingenuity and its natural environment.

Three of those peoples who, in the course of history, have fashioned their own healing arts merit particular attention: the inhabitants of the Indian sub-continent, those of the great plains of China in the immense continent of Asia, and the Amerindians of the New World.

*I*t is generally accepted that around 30000 to 40000 BC, migrants from eastern Asia settled in Alaska, which they reached via what is now known as the Bering Strait. They gradually occupied the whole continent of America as they moved southwards in successive waves. According to another hypothesis, intrepid sailors from Melanesia and Polynesia colonized parts of Central and South America.

Whatever actually happened, these migrations probably continued for several thousand years. Colonies of the new arrivals, doubtless small in number and scattered over vast territories, each formed their own individual cultures which differed greatly from one another. When we speak collectively of the "Amerindians", therefore, we must never forget their diversity. In Central America, in the late fifteenth century, the Arawaks and Caribs were still in the Stone Age, yet they were close, in geographical terms, to the Aztecs who had a highly organized empire, with beautiful cities. Likewise, in South America, the naked cannibals of Brazil differed in every respect from the richly clad Inca princes.

Until 1492, humanity evolved in two groups on the two continental shelves of

Eurasia and America, each entirely ignorant of the other and each weaving its own cultural fabric. Although both were of the species *Homo sapiens*, and therefore had the same mental and intellectual blueprint, they developed into widely divergent types of people.

*T*he riches and contrasts of the Americas

I.

Left: *the various sakras of the human body are centres of energy through which the body communicates with the gods and the universe. India, Rajasthan, nineteenth century. Private collection, Paris, France.*
Right: *this Mexican statue made of volcanic rock represents a priest (?), his hair cut to resemble a sacred hallucinogenic mushroom. Civilization of the Pacific coast. Photographic library of the Museum of Mankind, Paris, France.*

DISCOVERY AND DESTRUCTION

The sixteenth-century invaders of the so-called New World found populations who knew neither iron nor the wheel, who carried goods over vast distances without any beast of burden other than the delicate llama, and who traded without the use of money. But they did have gold and silver, which Spain and Portugal were to seize, helped by their horses and their arms, when they reduced millions of people to slavery.

Only a few remains of the Maya, Aztec and Inca civilizations survived in the wake of the conquistadors: majestic temples buried in the virgin forest, the city of Machu Picchu and the walls of Cuzco at a tremendously high altitude. Most significantly, these conquerors carried away to Europe all that they could, and partly destroyed what they did not understand, in particular the books written on sisal-grass paper in a script which today is still not fully understood; in this way many treatises about local sciences disappeared, sciences which in Europe were called astronomy, physics, agriculture – and also medicine.

All that remains therefore are a few documents written in Quechua (from Peru) or Maya (from Mexico and Guatemala). Amended over the years, these texts, some of which are illuminated, are scattered throughout the libraries of the world. However, they do not include treatises on pure medicine, for this discipline was inseparable, in the minds of the Amerindians, from other realms of knowledge. In the same way, medicine was taught together with other subjects in the early European universities.

In parallel with these few texts, manuals were written by the conquistadors themselves – some of them being mestizos, the products of the first marriages between the indigenous peoples and the Europeans – as they understood the local languages and collected the tales of the literate indigenous population. Two men of the Church made their names in this field: Sahagún and Bartolomé de Las Casas. From the early sixteenth century, they established themselves as protectors of the Indians and their cultures. They were followed by representatives of sovereigns, military men, members of religious orders, explorers and doctors, who passed on to the West their discoveries and the fruits of their curiosity in books written in Latin or their own mother tongues.

Incidentally, researchers are still learning about the life of the peoples of the American continent before the conquest as they make new archaeological discoveries: since the nineteenth century in particular, they have been interpreting the remains of sculptures, temples, inscriptions, domestic items, pottery, ceramics and jewellery discovered in the forests.

Opposite: *a sumptuously clad person perforates his tongue with a stick. This is doubtless a ritual scene of self-sacrifice. Huilocintlia (Veracruz), Huastec art, National Anthropological Museum, Mexico.*
Right: *plate from a Peruvian manuscript, late sixteenth century. Private collection, Paris, France*

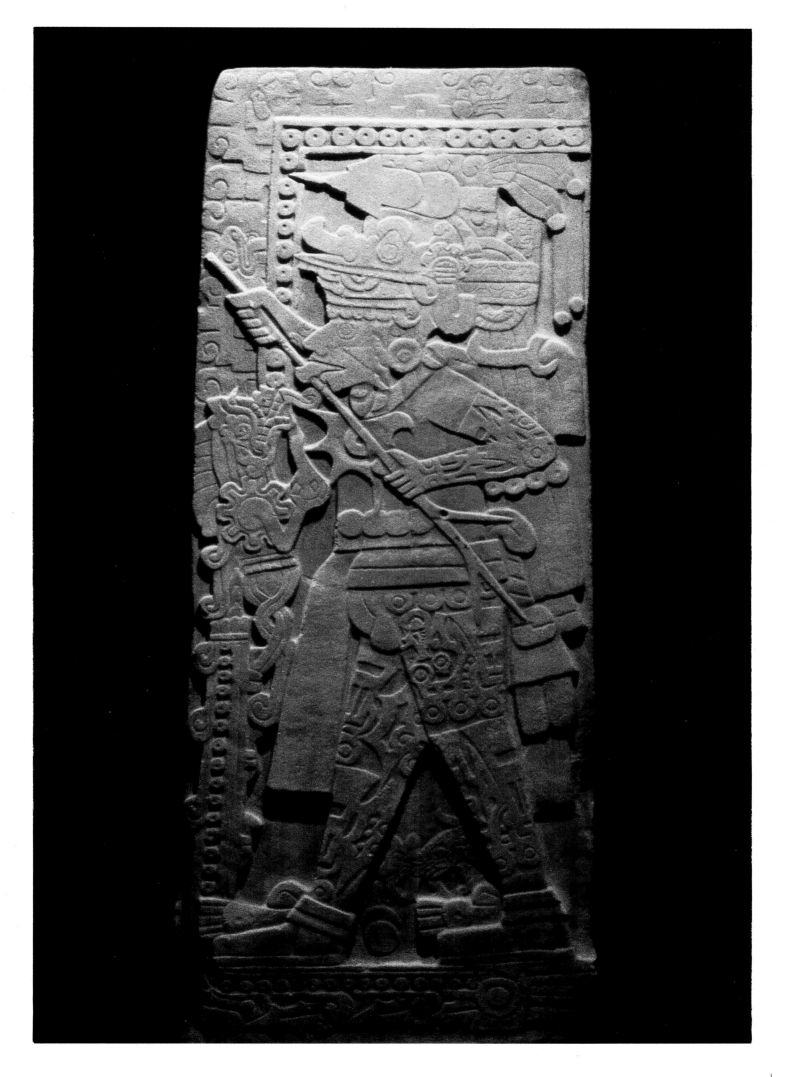

CUSTOMS AND HEALTH

*I*t is as difficult to ascertain the diseases of the pre-Columbian population – just five centuries ago – as it is those of the Egyptians of the Ancient Empire six thousand years ago. Although the inhabitants of Peru mummified their dead in funeral urns, curled up, adorned in their ceremonial clothing and jewellery and accompanied by the plates and dishes they used every day, the Mayas and the Aztecs, on the other hand, burnt their dead with the result that only a few corpses remain for examination.

We can, however, deduce that the men of the New World had no easier a life than the peoples of the European continent. They died young, having worked a barren, tropical or marshy land in the plains, or an arid one on the terraces at a high altitude. They frequently fought each other and in their society legal sanctions took the form of mutilations. Likewise, harsh religious practices imposed "voluntary" amputations: a finger, a limb, an ear, the nose.

They sometimes demanded death. Thus, in Mexico, human sacrifices – in the form of the surgical removal of the heart – were carried out to honour the victors in the game of pelota. War was sometimes waged for the sole purpose of acquiring prisoners who could be sacrificed to appease the gods.

These peoples suffered from numerous tropical diseases, parasitic infestations, tuberculosis and disfiguring rheumatisms. Many women died in childbirth; they were honoured in the same way as the gods.

Inadequate communications meant that the effects of bad weather and regional differences in harvests could not be mitigated against. We do not know whether, before the conquest, there was any contact at all between the Aztec emperors of Mexico and the Incas of Peru. But we do know that famines took their toll. However, in the south and north, the populations lacked neither vegetables nor carbohydrates, some having certain varieties of beans, others potatoes, and all growing maize. As they did not keep sheep, goats, cows or horses, they doubtless ate little meat although they did have hens, turkeys, aquatic birds and dogs. Peru alone had a few *Camelidae* – the llama, for example. Nor did they have fats, such as oil.

These pre-Columbian peoples seemed to have a greater predilection than those in the Old World for fermented drinks, hence the frequent incidence of drunkenness. Like the inhabitants of Mesopotamia and Burgundy, they had a taste for beverages made from plants. They made a kind of beer called *chicha* from maize, and they also used agave juice for this purpose.

It is difficult to say what effects these alcoholic drinks had on the population's general state of health. The Aztecs severely reprimanded drunkenness in the young but old people could drink at their own discretion. Maté drunk as an infusion and chewed leaves of the coca plant grown on the high plateaux, both contain cardiac stimulants which help people to live at a high altitude. Tobacco, which was smoked from the Mississippi to Brazil, having come via the Caribbean, gave a sensation of euphoria valuable in cult ceremonies.

The great variety of plant life resulted in another form of intoxication, using hallucinogenic substances: mescaline produced by a cactus, and peyote or psilocybin from a mushroom. The use of these substances, varying according to the people and their age, was either widespread or kept secret – reserved for diviners and priests for their oracles, or consumed in a group at ceremonies where there were collective trances.

Even today, these poisons are widely used in North America as well as in South America, which soon lost its monopoly.

The practice of human sacrifice was to persist among the Aztecs until the end of the fifteenth century. It was halted by the conquistadors as it was contrary to the Christian religion.
Above: Tudela codex, 1553. Museum of America, Madrid, Spain. Left: Nutall codex, National Library, Paris, France.

Although the Amerindians did not pass on any written theology, we know that they wondered about the universe, the mechanisms driving it and the relationship between the visible and the invisible. Thus, they developed a pantheon of gods and spirits, each of which presided over certain natural phenomena or human activities. By observation of the stars, they established a calendar which governed both ritual ceremonies and seasonal occupations. Man represented but an infinitesimal part of the infinite cosmos, each of his organs living under the influence of a planet, and each of his actions being interpreted by a naturalistic polytheism in which the deity concerned had to be honoured and respected. Thus, in Mexico, Tlaloc, the god of rain and water, also controlled the urine and caused or healed dropsy. The goddess of fertility governed the abundance of maize harvests, and also births. Ancient manuscripts generally represent her crouched in childbirth with the baby's head emerging from her vulva.

We can see, therefore, that on the two sides of the Atlantic man had a different concept of himself and his place in the universe. In antiquity, as for the monotheists of the Middle Ages, he was God's most perfect creation, the microcosm representing and justifying the macrocosm: he was both the centre and the purpose of the world. For the Amerindians, on the other hand, he constituted but one element among many in the universe, of the same substance and subject to the same laws (this is doubtless still the case today for the descendants of these peoples); Tlaloc controlled rainfall

SUCKING OF WOUNDS, INFUSIONS AND STEAM BATHS

Originally, this "sun stone" in the image of the god Tonatiuh, was placed in the holy chamber of a temple and reminded every citizen of the need for blood sacrifice, which alone could give the gods the strength to ensure the movement of the sun. End of the Aztec empire. National Anthropological Museum, Mexico.

in the same way as he controlled water in the abdomen of the sick person. But although cosmogonic views differed on the opposite shores of the ocean, medical practices were very similar.

In the New World foreign bodies were extracted with instruments made of wood, as these people had no hard metal. Trepanning with stone tools was practised, for the same obscure reasons as in the Old World. Abscesses were lanced with hard stones, but this operation was followed by sucking – which was also the treatment for wounds and animal bites – being almost routine practice, whatever the nature of the blood, venom or pus to be sucked. Wounds were sutured with human hair threaded in bone needles, or by using the jaws of giant ants, which were decapitated once attached.

If the wound did not heal, it was irrigated with *chicha* blown from the full mouth of the doctor and dressed with honey or latex sap, unknown in Europe. Fractures were splinted with wood.

Apart from these surgical procedures, the human body remained a mystery. No religious practice – neither the human sacrifices of the Aztec priests who, to remove the heart which was offered to the gods, cut open the abdomen or the thorax; nor the eviscerations of the Peruvians, who removed the entrails of the dead and fumigated them (as we today smoke hams) before burying them; nor even the shrinking of heads practised by the Amazonian tribes who removed the bone of the skull while keeping some of those of the face – formed a basis for learning.

178

Handle of sacrificial
knife made of hard stone
(Tumi). Inca origin.
Private collection.

The goddess of maize in childbirth (above)
and Tlaloc, the god of rain (below) dressed
in their ceremonial costumes: like the gods of
nature and fertility in other civilizations, they
were the most important to the Aztecs.
Codex Borbonicus, early sixteenth century.
Bourbon Palace Library, Paris, France.

.20.

A common health measure among the North American Indians in the sixteenth century (above) and in the nineteenth century (opposite): fumigation combines the benefits of sweating with those of the medicinal plants which are burned. Théodore de Bry, Indorum Floridam. Frankfurt, 1591, and print by Catlin. Private collection.

*Two examples of ritual deformations, of the skull (*left*) and the teeth and ears (*right*). The reasons for such practices are still not fully explained: are they for aesthetic reasons, or do they relate to consecration to a chosen divinity or to rites of passage? Diego Rivera collection, Mexico.*

Doctors diagnosed internal diseases by examining the skin, the eyes, the complexion, the teeth and the pulse. Urine and faecal matter do not appear to have been used in this way. Therapy was based principally on the use of plants from which medicines were extracted. They were dried, boiled or fermented, and isolated or combined to make thick syrups or infusions; the patient drank them or the doctor sprayed them directly into the mouth or even the anus; some used a cannula or an animal's bladder.

Magical value was attributed to annointing the body and the rubbing of painful areas with human blood. In the world of the Amerindians, prisoners supplied what was in effect material that was easily obtainable and that pleased the gods.

As in Western Europe, baths and evacuations of the body in the form of vomiting, purging, bloodletting and sweating – practised in various ways – were

An Aztec human sacrifice according to a Spanish chronicler. Diego Duran, Historia de las Indias, *1579. National Library, Madrid, Spain.*

Imaginary portrait of a native doctor priest of California. Print by Labrousse, from Jacques Grasset de Saint-Sauveur. L'encyclopédie des voyages, *eighteenth century.*

recommended. An earth hut or a tent, similar to those of the Turkish baths in the East or of the sweating-rooms of Europe was used for steam baths; fumigation involved placing the patient on a grid over glowing embers, as was also done for dead bodies.

It is clear that these practices were the result of religious and magical preoccupations rather than of any empirical verification of their efficacy: the patient was subjected to incisions, scarifications or mutilations of the limbs or the extremities. The significance of the dental practices so highly esteemed in Mexico is still unclear: the teeth were filed, the incisors were sharpened, they were encrusted with gems and precious metals and sometimes were removed. Was this a form of therapy against caries and mouth infections? Or a beauty treatment reserved for the rich and for dignitaries? Or even a magical practice? We can ask the same questions about the deformations carried out on the skulls of some newborn babies, the perforations of the nose or lips and so on.

Of course, these rites were accompanied by incantations, prayers to the deities concerned and animal sacrifices. We suppose, therefore, that the people responsible for treating the sick were skilled in medicine, religion and witchcraft. They did, though, have varying status among these American peoples of the pre-Columbian age. In some societies, healers were considered to be sorcerers in close contact with the world of spirits – like the griots in black Africa today – while among others, such as the Aztecs, no particular status seems to have been attached to doctors, apothecaries and herbalists. In South America doctors were also priests. The rank of the healing profession clearly varied from one region to the next, depending on the prevailing attitude.

EXCHANGES OF DISEASES AND REMEDIES

When the European conquistadors invaded this unknown world, seeking easy wealth, they encountered peoples with cultures and intellectual capacities which they did not understand, and thought they could take all and give nothing in return. But in fact, unforeseen exchanges did take place.

Unwittingly, the Europeans passed on to the Amerindians the germs they carried and to which they had been accustomed for centuries: the colds of the former became the influenzas or fatal pneumonias of the latter. In a few decades, measles, German measles, smallpox and influenza caused epidemics which devastated the populations to whom these fevers were hitherto unknown. This catastrophic decimation by disease was compounded by the bad treatment meted out to the

One of the medicinal plants brought from the New World, gayac wood, was used against syphilis. Print from Jean Stradanus (1523–1605). National Order of Pharmacists, Paris, France.

indigenous populations by the new arrivals: there had been motiveless massacres, deportations and forced labour in the fields and mines. The millions of inhabitants of the South American continent before the conquest were reduced to but a few hundred thousand one hundred years later.

In exchange (although some would disagree) everything seems to suggest that syphilis came from the New World. From the time of Christopher Columbus' first visit, there were relations between the sailors and the indigenous women, and the latter seem to have transmitted venereal diseases to the former. It is possible that the Amerindians had long become immune to syphilis and were little affected by it. However, once it was imported into Europe, the disease became

Aztec dental treatment, as visualized by the Mexican artist, Diego Rivera (1886–1957). Decoration in the Document Room of the National Agricultural School of Chapingo (1926–1927), Mexico.

an epidemic. Today, some people doubt that the disease originated in America although numerous historical arguments support this view. In fact, a number of non-venereal afflictions, caused by a protozoic germ similar to that which causes syphilis, were already rife on both continents; hence the difficulty in being more definite about the origin of the disease.

The same uncertainties as to the direction of transmission are true of other diseases: from Europe and Africa to America, or the other way round. Thus, the mosquitoes which carry malaria exist on both sides of the Atlantic and the origin of the transmission of yellow fever is also unclear. As the facts seem to support both hypotheses, we will doubtless never be sure of the exact truth. The same question arises in relation to other parasitic infections such as certain leishmaniases, and to rickets and even amoebiasis*. It does, however, appear certain, that the discovery of America constituted an essential stage in the process of worldwide pathological uniformity.

The conquerors attempted to recreate their normal diet in New Spain and in New Castile, and later in New England and then in New France, by importing domestic animals.

In reverse, they brought to Europe not only food plants, fruits and vegetables, but also plants for medicinal use: ipecac against diarrhoea, guaiacum against syphilis, cinchona against fevers, tobacco and cacao as stimulants, sarsaparilla as a diuretic, datura as a sedative, and so on.

This transfer of medical plants to the Old World grew to such an extent that by the late eighteenth century, on the eve of the birth of extractive chemistry, one third of the whole European pharmacopoeia proved to be of American origin. The pharmacopoeia therefore was enhanced more in the space of three hundred years, thanks to Christopher Columbus, than

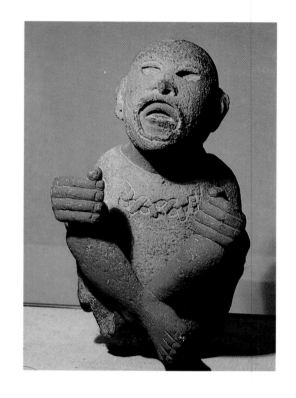

*Two examples of
sacrifices.
Left: a mummified
Inca child sacrificed at the
age of ten.
Right: statuette of an
Aztec high priest wearing
the skin of a prisoner.
Santiago Museum, Chile,
and Basle Museum,
Switzerland.*

over the previous four millennia since
Imhotep, and over the seventeen centuries since Dioscorides. Doctors in Europe, when using these plants, did not
innovate in any way, but followed the
recommendations and the traditions of
the native South Americans.

Surprisingly, the various species of
plants and animals became familiar in
Europe over widely differing timescales.
Turkeys were bred in France from 1560;
Bossuet praised tobacco in his teachings;
and the Court in England, before that of
Louis XIV of France, recommended the
use of cinchona. Yet it was not until the
end of the eighteenth century and the
beginning of the nineteenth that maize –
after arriving in Cyprus – and the potato
– after a halt in Germany – spread
throughout the European continent, where
they were to revolutionize the diet of man
and of domestic animals.

It was not until the early twentieth
century that Hevea, which provides a
substance just as useful as rubber, was
introduced into South-East Asia – and
then almost illicitly.

*Gayac, from the
Blackwell Herbarium,
Nuremberg, 1757.
Library of Decorative
Arts, Paris, France.*

It is inevitable that historians and archaeologists tend to study civilizations which have left evidence in the form of majestic architecture or sumptuous objects, rather than other, more "modest" peoples. However, in addition to the illustrious civilizations, like those of Mexico and Peru, we should not forget the millions of other people who populated the American hemisphere, although they did not construct solid buildings, did not have any writing, and were in many cases nomadic or lived in small tribal communities grouped into federations which were in a constant state of flux.

The Europeans discovered them over the centuries: first came the Spanish, then the Portuguese; and then the French followed in Carolina, Brazil and Canada, and finally the Dutch and the English, the last to explore this immense world. All these adventurers, with various interests, obtained from their travels, trials, captivities, evangelistic missions or administrative experience – information

An Inca priest and healer, beside a patient. State Museum, Berlin-Dahlem, Germany.

about the customs and the medicine of the indigenous peoples. In fact, we are still in the process of learning as there are large gaps in our knowledge of the Amazonian Indians, the Inuits of Hudson Bay and even the "Indians" of the High Plateaux, although they are now integrated into the populations of modern states with Hispanic and Christian traditions.

Their way of life may have been different and their miserable populations may have been on the bottom rung of the ladder in the eyes of the Europeans, but their medical practices were similar: the naturist cults were the same, with people plunging into steam baths in the tents of the north and in the mud huts of Yucatan; human sacrifices differed only in their form; healers made use of local plants; and witch-doctors offered incantations in the languages of their communities, which addressed the same prayers for healing to Great Manitu and to Tlaloc.

What is the situation today? In North America, the Inuits (Eskimos), the

Cheyennes and the Apaches have settled, whether in the Great North, the Rockies, the shores of the Pacific Ocean, the Great Plains or the swamps of Louisiana and Florida. The populations are growing slowly in their reservations or territories; tuberculosis, imported by the Europeans, has more or less stabilized while alcoholism is still on the increase. When ill, they accept modern medical treatment which they supplement with their ancestral customs.

However, in South America, the decimation of the populations continues. The Amazonian Indians are plundered and massacred while their natural environment is transformed. In the southernmost tip of the continent, the numbers of Araucanians, the Patagonians and the Fuegians from the Tierra del Fuego are in rapid decline. Although the European peoples have instituted an effective medical system, they show no mercy to those who do not rapidly become integrated in their religious, political and economic institutions.

Right: *an Aztec goddess of fertility generally associated with Tlaloc, the god of rain and water. British Museum, London, England.*
Top: *gold funeral mask of Inca origin. Museum of Fine Art, Dallas, USA.*

The traditions of India live on

II.

We can measure the isolation of ancient America and our ignorance of its past by looking at Indian medicine, the development of which we can follow from before 2000 BC. Surviving texts are written in Sanskrit, a script discovered by European philologists in the late eighteenth century which is the original source of Indo-European languages.

Moreover, since ancient times, men and ideas have constantly been on the move throughout the vast continents of Asia and Africa. If Hippocrates was not directly inspired by Indian medicine, his ideas were nonetheless imbued with its concepts; it left its mark on the Arab authors of the Middle Ages and there was a constant and fertile interchange between Chinese and Western medicines.

Thus, although we know little about Aztec medicine other than the pharmacopoeia from the environment which Europeans have so abused, by contrast, the medicine of the Indian subcontinent is one of the cornerstones of modern medicine.

VEDA AND AYURVEDA

The Vedas are compilations of old texts dating from before 1500 BC; they are philosophical and religious poems rather than medical instructions, nonetheless they incorporate one of the bases of later Indian medicine, that is, the impossibility of distinguishing between the soul and the body, of dissociating the visible from the invisible, as both are energized by the same life force.

These Vedic hymns seem to have been imported into the old Dravidian India at the time of the immigration of the Indian population and are therefore older than Greek medicine. They reflect the influence of the Iranian Avesta and perhaps of Mesopotamia. Disease is regarded as being the result of a transgression of the rules

Right: *the preparation of drugs following the precepts of Ayurvedic medicine, at Udaipur in the eighteenth century (*top*), and today in Rajasthan. Udaipur Museum, India. Left: the god Hanuman, symbol of devotion, eighteenth century. Slim Gallery collection, Nepal.*

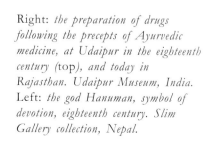

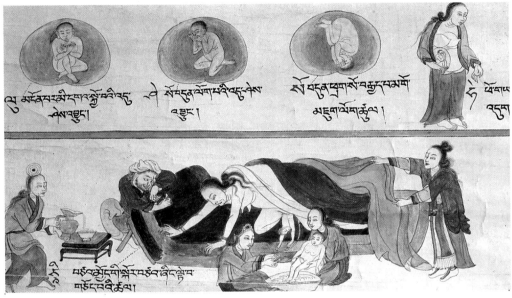

governing the world, and the deity offended by this sin is seen as causing the ill but also able to heal it.

Little information can be gleaned from these extremely vague texts concerning the therapies used and it is even difficult to distinguish, from the pathological conditions described, between what is probably malaria and other cachectic conditions.

From the sixth century BC changes in the manner in which such cures were documented became evident. This period also, incidentally, marked a major philosophical and religious development in the Old World, with a number of remarkable figures appearing within the space of a few decades: examples are Confucius, Buddha, Zarathustra, Socrates and

Hippocrates, each of whom was to spread his teachings throughout the whole world.

The medical system, which went under the name of Ayurveda, spread alongside Buddhism and reached all the countries of South-East Asia. Ayurvedism was similar to Buddhism insofar as moral rigour and bodily health were connected: correct behaviour, goodness, respect for others and modesty involved strict bodily cleanliness and moderation in the pleasures of the flesh.

Bodily hygiene therefore required frequent bathing, regular washing of clothing, the cleaning of the teeth and the rinsing of the nasal cavities. Likewise, the diet was to be adequate and varied, with the healthiest drink being water – a fifth century treatise tells us that alcoholic

Feminine hygiene in
India during the
Mogul period.
Left: *a woman at her
toilet, early nineteenth
century, private
collection.*
Below: *the gopies
bathe in the Yamuna,
eighteenth century,
School of Kangra.
National Museum,
New Delhi, India.*

The priest and the devotee: a Brahman, also a doctor, places the mark of Tilak on the brow of his patient as a sign of benediction. In India medicine and religion were intertwined. Pahari School, late eighteenth century. Shandrigarh Museum, India.

drinks (fifty-four varieties of which are described) can inspire joy and increase energy. Man was exhorted not to abuse sexual activity, which combines the benefits of procreation with the mutual satisfaction of the partners. We can see how the development of certain aspects of the Ayurveda later resulted in Tantric and Zen Buddhism.

It would, however, be wrong to regard these recommendations as a system of preventive medicine before such a thing existed – an all-too-widespread anachronistic interpretation. They suggest, rather, a philosophy of life, an individual and collective morality, Ayurveda being quite different from the health regimes recommended by the School of Salerno.

The religious dogmas of Buddha never-

theless did not eradicate the complexities of Hinduism, which adapted to the Ayurveda following the eclipse of Indian Buddhism: Hinduism was then regarded as the result of the wishes of the god Siva, passed on to men by his wife Parvati. It also introduced certain dietary taboos such as that on the eating of beef.

Over the centuries, the Ayurvedic compilations, which were passed down through the generations, were copied, and information from neighbours in the west and north was added. Conversely, they were translated into Pahlavi in Sassanid Persia, into Arabic (Rhazes was clearly inspired by it), and into Chinese; the evidence for this is that Indian drugs, some of which came from the Arabs, are mentioned in contemporary treatises.

Left: *an avatar of the god Vishnu,
often invoked for healing purposes. Eighteenth
century illuminated text. National Library,
Paris, France.*
Above: *diagram of a man, from the manuscript
of Hatha-Yoga, eighteenth century. Each
part of the body is adorned with a magic sign.
British Library, London, England.*

CHARAKA AND SUSRUTA

*T*wo physicians who lived in the last years of the first century BC, Charaka and Susruta, who have since become legendary figures, explained the Ayurvedic doctrine in two collections of Sanskrit texts. They were based on previous works and numerous additions were made subsequently. The texts are not methodical but are the culmination of an oral teaching tradition; they nonetheless constitute a coherent whole, reflecting the physiological and therapeutic concepts of the time, which are based on medical knowledge and observation: gods, spirits and demons have a lesser role in the occurrence of disease than in the ancient Vedas and there is an underlying desire for rationality in the Susruta collection. These writings still incorporate the four basic elements of the universe: air, earth, fire and water, to which a fifth – space – is sometimes added. Life was thought to be generated by the simultaneous action of wind, fire and water, the movement of which was triggered by a "breath", similar to the Greek *pneuma*. In addition, the human body was composed of seven living substances: the blood, the chyle, the flesh, fat, bone, marrow and sperm. Good health depended on their equilibrium; any surfeit or deficiency would cause ill health. The art of the doctor, then, consisted solely of re-establishing the harmony which reigned prior to the illness.

At certain times, the dissection of corpses was permitted in India: this was carried out after soaking the body in water for five days. The practice did not bring

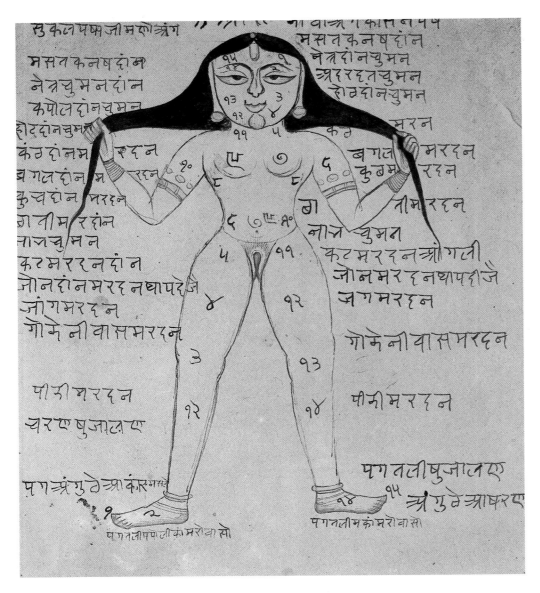

Medicine and the heavenly bodies according to the Kama Sutra. *The sensitive points of the female body vary depending on the lunar calendar. Kumar Sangram Singh collection, Jaipur, India.*

about any improvement in anatomical knowledge. There was confusion between the blood vessels and the nerves, and the function of the organs was explained on the basis of theory rather than by consideration of what they actually did. The heart was regarded as the seat of the conscience; it was animated by the same "breath" that made blood circulate and produced the pulse. Associated with fire, this "breath" cooked the food in the stomach and governed all the body's activities. This vital energy was regarded as fragile, for there were thought to be one hundred and seven points on the body where it was in jeopardy.

Before reaching a diagnosis, the doctor would question the patient, paying attention to his voice and any anomalies in his movements; he would also listen to his breathing and examine his general appearance, his skin and his tongue; he would study the smell of his sweat and his urine, which he would even sometimes taste in order to detect any sweet flavour. The study of the characteristics of the pulse, on the other hand, was only recommended in texts after the eighth century, doubtless influenced by Chinese techniques.

As in all protomedical systems, animals, plants and minerals were used to make drugs: the most comprehensive treatise includes sixty-four products made from minerals and fifty-seven made from animals, while over four hundred plants were used on the basis of six fundamental flavours which were to be extracted: sweet, sour, salty, pungent, bitter and astringent. They were chosen according to which vital elements were thought to be disrupted by the disease, using a classification with a therapeutic, rather than a descriptive or botanical, purpose. The coherence between the visible and the invisible created a system of correspondences which the skilled doctor had to take into account, reflecting man's

The goddess Mariadale, invoked against smallpox. Eighteenth-century miniature. Private collection, Paris, France.

desire to establish a cohesion between the world around him and the cosmos. The Ayurvedic pharmacopoeia was evidently regularly revised over a period of fifteen centuries, during which time new plant species were being discovered. Today too, it continues to be taught and treatises are still written, with many vendors of medicinal herbs singing its praises on the market stalls throughout the Indian subcontinent, particularly in the south.

It is thought that, in the fourth century BC a surgeon with the name of Divaka was in Buddha's entourage; his supposed work has been augmented and, indeed, is still being updated today: the treatment of sores, superficial tumours, urine retention and malformations was clearly more developed than treatment of those conditions in Europe at the same time. A surviving mediaeval catalogue derived from his work describes and lists one hundred and twenty-one instruments required by the good practitioner.

Mutilations of the nose appear to have been frequent in the Middle Ages in India, as they were also elsewhere, due to the

Left: *opium smokers. Eighteenth-century miniature. Udaipur Museum, India.*
Right: *preparation of medicines, perhaps opium too, according to the Indian pharmacopoeia.*

torturing of delinquents or prisoners of war, or following leprosy or lupus. Some surgeons repaired such disfigurements by transposing pieces of skin from the forehead. This "Indian plastic surgery" – long scorned in the West – has now been returned to favour and, of course, is enormously successful.

For almost one thousand years, Indian doctors formed a profession which, if not organized, was at least hierarchized. Educated doctors worked at the courts of rulers and local princes, others were employees at care centres financed by the nobility, and healers with varying degrees of skill practised everywhere. Doctors learnt their profession from gurus who dispensed a practical and theoretical education and perpetuated a very rigid code of professional ethics. Within this fixed system of castes and classes, which still characterizes Indian society, pupils came from the upper social strata and were able to read and write old Sanskrit and the local languages, or alternatively they came from families with a tradition of entering this profession.

ANCIENT FORMS OF MEDICINE IN MODERN INDIA

The Muslim invasion from the north-west in the twelfth century halted the continuous progress of Ayurvedic medicine, just as the Mongols had halted the spread of Arab medicine after the capture of Baghdad in 1258.

Nonetheless, the new Arab-Persian rulers were proud to have physicians with the prestigious title of wise men (*hakim*) in their ranks. They also took up the heritage of ancient Greek science, perpetuating the principles adopted by Hippocrates. They practised a medicine called *yunani*, which is the Arabic word for "Greek".

In the Tamil region in the south-east of India where the Hindi language and Islamic religion have not gained much of a foothold, a form of "Siddhar" medicine which is thought to date from the pre-Aryan Dravidian culture, is still practised today; its particular features are the greater significance given to the characteristics of the pulse, and its distinctive pharmaco-poeia in which mineral substances, classed as male and female, hold an important position.

Yoga developed alongside the Ayurveda and it was highly acclaimed by Europeans of the period who saw it, wrongly, as a therapeutic technique. Governed since

Yoga is a method of both meditation and relaxation, useful for the "diseases" of the soul and the body.
Left: *from an eighteenth-century miniature, School of Mewar. Private collection, Udaipur, India.*
Above: *today.*

the first century by precise (frequently revised) texts, yoga constitutes a discipline of the body and the mind. It presupposes a healthy body and maximizes the effects of controlled breathing, energies and vital fluids. A yogi acquires perfect control over his respiration by means of clearly defined postures learnt through apprenticeship; he can even control his heart rate, thus slowing his circulation to the point of unconsciousness.

In the same way a yogi can even achieve power over certain muscles which are normally beyond human control, for example over the functioning of organs

A scene from the life of Vikramaditya. On the right, a goddess prepares ambrosia, an elixir of life similar to a medicine. Pahari School, early nineteenth century. Museum of Bharat Kala Bhavan, Benares, India.

constituting part of the vegetative, and therefore unconscious, life: a yogi can take liquids into the bladder via the urethra and into the rectum via the anus (in which situations these organs are functioning in the opposite direction to the physiological norm). Today, such possibilities are merely described without any real explanation being given. Yoga can be useful in treating illnesses defined as psychosomatic, but its medical use can scarcely be extended beyond that area.

The physical control which the wise man had to acquire included control of the sexual act, which Tantric Buddhism

raised to the level of a hymn to nature. The *Kama Sutra* is not a medical book any more than it is a collection of erotic writings; it is in fact a guide to the perfect discipline of the body and the mind. Anyone following its principles achieves total equilibrium and thus good health.

Modern India is a vast melting-pot for its huge population of disparate origins and languages, cultures, religions and resources. Any practices are worthwhile if they help relieve the immense misery and the diseases which are all too prevalent. Although India aims to educate the majority of its doctors in faculties where

At Benares, a healing divinity receives offerings from a noble couple, eighteenth-century illuminated text.
National Library, Paris, France.

Western science is taught – this being the most appropriate means of fighting endemic diseases, epidemics, parasitoses and the deficiencies suffered by the population – it nonetheless supports schools for yunani medicine and schools which bring the Ayurvedic tradition up to date. Furthermore, in rural areas the population still turns to healers who practise archaic customs. We can see from this that India is definitely the one country in the world which really perpetuates the principles and techniques which the healing art has employed ever since certain men decided to treat one another.

名醫華佗

壽亭侯關羽

一勇齋
國芳画

彫庄

*T*he wonders of Imperial China

III.

*O*f all the medical traditions which developed in the Middle Ages beyond the Middle East and Europe, none has had an impact on such a large proportion of humanity and over such vast territories as has Chinese medicine. It is far removed from Irano-Greek concepts as it reflects a different vision of the world from that of Indo-European peoples.

It is difficult for the modern historian to describe Chinese medicine because of the structure of the Chinese language and its development over two thousand years. Translations produced by erudite Europeans three centuries ago in some cases contain incorrect interpretations. And because of its own development – having undergone many changes, both political and religious, and having absorbed doctrines from India and from Europe – Chinese medicine inspired such a wealth of literature.

THE UNIVERSE OF NUMBERS

*C*hina practised the same rudiments of medicine as other peoples in prehistoric times. Thirty thousand years ago, a few thousand inhabitants of north-east Asia crossed the continent to settle in Alaska – taking with them the witch-doctors who were later to be called the medicine men of the North American Indians. The populations left behind in this part of Asia were treated by "shamans". This term, of Mongol origin, has over time gained universal meaning and it can rightly be said that all population groups had their shamans – the term could, in fact, also be applied to village sorcerers in Europe. Still very much in favour today in Tibet, Shamanism is practised by people with mysterious powers, who use incantations, herbs, ritual ceremonies and certain body treatments.

We know of Chinese texts about medicine dating from the first millennium BC.

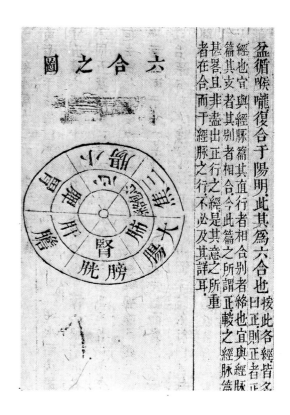

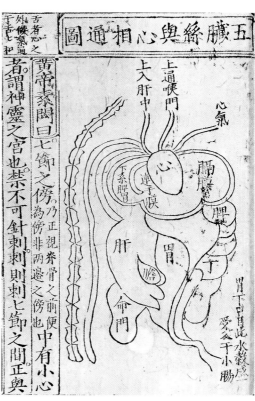

The Orient and medicine. Left: *the famous surgeon Hua T'o treats the wound of the hero Kuan Kung. Japanese print.* Above: *pages from an eighteenth-century Chinese medical manuscript. Wellcome Institute, London, England, and National Library, Paris, France.*

Subsequently, they have been constantly revised and supplemented – probably the most detailed from that era is the *Yi-king* treatise from the fourth century BC.

The main characteristic of Chinese medicine is its fascination with numbers. It delights in the indexing, classification and numbering of every element in the universe in order to fit it into definitive and permanent categories. No analogy, however, can be drawn with the theory that was subsequently much vaunted in the West, that only the measurable is scientific: the Chinese method of allocating numbers is not based on any scientific doctrine and does not constitute any wondrous prescience. We will be looking at a few examples where an apparent resemblance conceals the absence of any fundamental similarity.

Consulting a mandarin doctor in the last century. The young woman's wrist rests on a small cushion. For reasons of etiquette and modesty, the doctor feels his patient's pulse with the tips of his fingers, and above all avoids looking at her. Water-colour on rice paper, nineteenth century. Wellcome Institute, London, England.

In the Chinese system nothing escapes enumeration – the fateful element – it determines the life of the cosmos until the end of time, for man and for matter. Numeromancy or divining by numbers was a crucial guiding force in everyday life in China. Man, on the other hand, was regarded as no more than one element in a world governed by two universal principles: Yin and Yang. The former is positive, male, dark and evolutionary, and the latter negative, bright and female. While they are opposites they are not in conflict. They are complementary and are therefore considered essential for the movement of the stars, the climate, the rhythm of the seasons and life itself.

The world is made up of five elements: earth, water, iron, wood and metal. It thus conforms to different combinations of

Yin and Yang with the five elements, man being but an infinitesimal particle within the infinite cosmos.

One illustration of this system dates from a bygone age, and shows trigrams, joined together in pairs, forming sixty-four hexagrams. This pattern was not simply decorative and may have played a part in the development of Chinese writing; later, it in time acquired a symbolic value, illustrating universal life.

The movement of the most remote heavenly bodies was thought to govern every moment, every action and every organ of man. An excellent knowledge of astrology had to be acquired since in China as in the rest of the Asiatic continent, astrology was thought to control human life. The study of nature therefore forged close links between a plant, a stone, an animal and a man in a precise situation in life, for example, when suffering a disease, since the principles of Yin and Yang were apparent in any of them. In fact, the use of the symbolism of correspondences for practical purposes is a feature which can be observed in all protomedicines.

The Chinese concept of the origin of the world differed from that of other peoples: they did not invent one or more gods who regulated the universe and men, the latter being merely at the mercy of their whims. Buddhism was a code of behaviour and not a theurgy based on an inspired text. Similarly, the doctrine of Confucius can be regarded as a guide to social, family and political ethics. Although the Chinese did not altogether avoid personifying invisible powers in the form of spirits or demons incarnating rain or drought, typhoon or earthquake – following a tendency common to the whole of humanity – these divinities nonetheless obeyed a universal order which was superior to them (even where an individual or part of his body was "possessed").

Cosmological representation of the material and moral world with the trigrams and Yin and Yang.
Wellcome Institute, London, England.

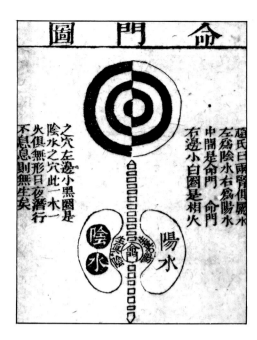

Medical diagram showing the kidneys, on either side of the spine, eighteenth-century Chinese medical manuscript. National Library, Paris, France.

A PHYSIOLOGY WITHOUT ANATOMY

Since everything was regarded from the perspective of the Yin-Yang pair, the dichotomy of concrete and abstract was not an issue and man was not thought to have a body and a soul, as was visualized in the West; these distinctions or opposites were meaningless to the Chinese. The crux of the matter was not to know the composition of the human body, nor where its organs were located, but to observe how man functioned in the universal scheme. Thus, Chinese medicine, until the end of the nineteenth century, was not interested in anatomy; dissection would have revealed only a form that was of no value for a true understanding of disease.

The perception of the human body which developed was therefore based on an imaginary physiology. It identified three regions, five organs, six receptacles and three cauldrons. Three hundred and sixty bones, equal in number to the days of the year, constituted the skeleton. These organs made up systems, the composition of which is sometimes surprising: while it seems logical that the liver and the gall bladder should belong to the same system, the association of the colon with the lungs is more difficult to understand.

All these components intercommunicate, not via the arteries, veins, nerves, lymphatic vessels or tendons (none of which was identified by the Chinese), but along invisible channels. Likewise, each organ has, in addition to its Yin and Yang, both its own *k'i*, similar doubtless to the Greek *pneuma* and the Indian *prâna*, and a system of channels which connects it to its counterparts. Symmetrical organs such as the kidneys are in contrast, one being Yin and the other Yang.

As everything in the universe is connected, every component – organ, bone or joint – is associated with a clearly defined area of the skin, which is but a reflection of the life going on beneath it. Action can be taken therefore on very precise points on the skin in order to produce an effect on the organ concerned.

YIN AND YANG
OPPOSITE – COMPLEMENTARY

	YIN	YANG	
	earth	sky	
	moon	sun	
	north and west	east and south	
	water	fire	
	cold	hot	
	rain	wind	
	blood	life force	
	bestiality	intelligence	
	woman	man	
	stomach	back	
	right side	left side	
	chronic	acute	
	diseases	diseases	

From Huard et al., Le Seuil, 1977.

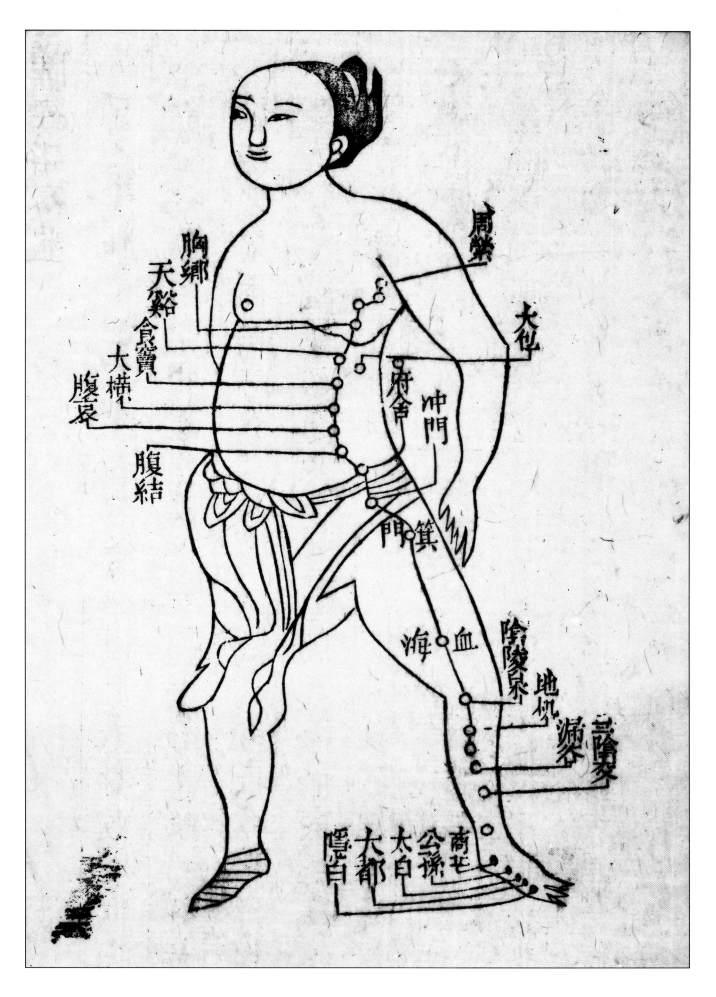

An acupuncture meridian, from the left armpit to the big toe. Chinese medical manuscript, eighteenth century. National Library, Paris, France.

Acupuncture, with its professed anatomical basis, is the product of this concept.

The openings in the cutaneous envelope were thought to be the routes via which the organs communicated with the outside world and therefore received influences from the world and the heavenly bodies. The Yin of the solid organs such as the liver and the spleen escaped via the anus and the urethra; the Yang of the hollow viscera via the sensory organs.

The body's whole system was regarded as operating under the effect of the circulation, not of the blood, but of the energy driven by the vital breath, and it only reached its maximum strength if all the forces present were in total equilibrium. This notion of equilibrium, although common to Graeco-Latin culture and Chinese medicine, was not the result of either influencing the other.

Any element affecting the equilibrium of the Yin-Yang duo was thought to result in disease, just as anything impeding the circulation of the vital breath caused plethora or slowed the correct functioning of the organs, or even emptied the "transportation vessels". Men and women could master the correct circulation of the breath by observing certain rules in their physical and moral life. As in Indian medicine, perfect health was associated with hygiene in the individual's social and private life, for not only could winds and their poisons, and likewise the cold, disrupt harmony, but so too could the seven emotions, from which the wise man needed to know how to protect himself if he wanted a long life.

The pulse was studied, as this proved that breathing kept a certain rhythm, for the alternation of wakefulness and sleep is essential to humans just as they depend on the seasonal harvest of plants to provide them with their nourishment. All these factors were considered proof that the whole universe obeyed cosmic rules. Chinese sages thus combined various rhythms of observation, which were easily established thanks to their passion for numbers. They wrote numerous treatises on rhythmology and numeromancy, of no value today in the study of chronobiology – a topic still to some extent shrouded in mystery.

OBSERVATION OF THE PATIENT

When examining the patient to whom he was called, the Chinese doctor first had to make the best possible use of his theoretical knowledge about the functioning of the human body as his scope for examination was severely restricted. Propriety prevented him from asking members of the nobility to undress, and these formed the greater part of his clientele, for poor people generally consulted the village witch-doctor.

The doctor studied the patient's complexion, assessed his breathing, and appraised his vigour; he asked to be shown nasal secretions, saliva and possibly tears; he looked at the face as a whole, the hands and the nails, and all the external organs which were thought to reveal the state of the internal organs. If the complexion was bluish or flushed, or white or black, he deduced that the liver, heart, lungs or bladder were affected.

The orifices via which Yang escaped were of particular importance: the mouth, tongue and nostrils. In addition, the pupils reflected the state of the kidneys, the whites of the eyes, the lungs, the eyelids were associated with the spleen and the pancreas. Similarly, the earlobe revealed the condition of the kidneys and the heart, the extreme edge of the external ear – poetically called "the jade balcony" – showed the state of the liver. It should be stressed, however, that these correspondences date only from the eighteenth

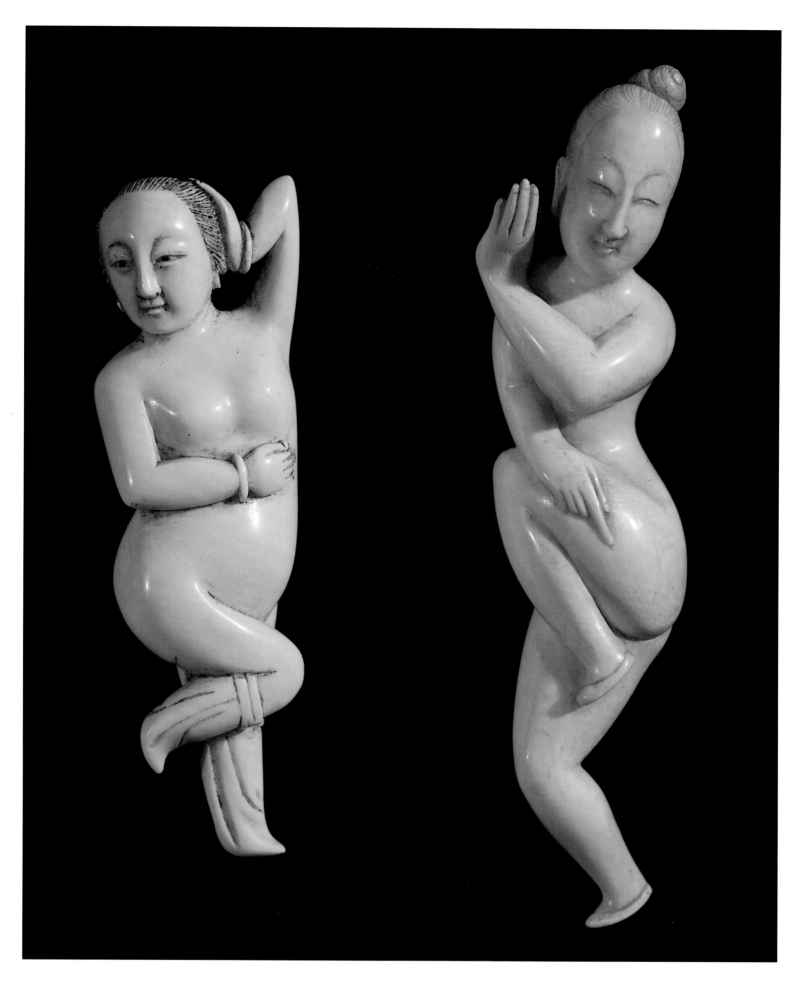

Two ivory medical statuettes. They were used by women to show the place which caused them pain. Private collection, Paris, France.

century, for they reflect a grasp of the anatomy of the abdomen obtained from the teachings (or interpretation) of visitors from the European continent.

Nor did the doctor neglect the orifices via which Yin escaped. He therefore inquired about the urine and faecal matter, and the state of the anus and the genital organs. He attached great significance to the sperm in particular, which was the best possible reflection of vital energy.

Emphasis on the external examination of the human body and its secretions is far more marked in Chinese medicine than in Western medicine. It is a pity that Chinese doctors were not able to correlate the data from their examinations with lesions appearing on internal organs; if they had they could have developed, via the careful examination they undertook, an anatomical and clinical semeiology which would have been beneficial and advantageous to future generations.

The doctor's examination was accompanied by questioning. He would obtain information about the patient's recent physical history – pains suffered, the quality of sleep, appetite, digestion, menstruation, urination and defecation. During this dialogue, he would listen attentively to the tone of the voice, the respiration, coughing and expectoration, laughter, singing, sobbing or crying, and even vomiting, as all these sounds provided him with valuable information. However, the doctor's listening activity did not include applying the ear to the patient's chest or any form of auscultation.

It is clear that, although meticulous, the physical exploration of the patient's body was restricted and confined to a rudimentary feeling of the abdomen through the clothing. The Chinese doctor did not investigate the volume of the liver or the spleen or even any abnormal tumefaction. Instead, he assessed the quality of hypothetical channels between the various

A mandarin doctor writes a death certificate. Water-colour on rice paper, nineteenth century. Wellcome Institute, London, England.

parts of the body. In terms of medicine today, the only technical procedure was the taking of the pulse on the wrist. What we call the "other arteries" remained unexplored, but observation of the radial pulse alone did provide a great deal of information: its rhythm was analysed as was its regularity, and its strength, at three different points along the artery, by compressing it to a certain level which enabled a distinction to be made between the underlying pulse and the superficial pulse. By exploring the left and right wrists in this way the doctor recorded twelve different pulses, the characteristics of which indicated the organs affected; he then had to determine their colour, their flavour and their sound, but we do not know how this sensory assessment contributed to the study of the internal organs.

THE RANK AND FUNCTIONS OF THE ORGANS

(The body is structured like society and like the world)

ORGAN	RANK	FUNCTION
heart	*emperor*	*discernment*
lungs	*minister of state*	*administration*
liver	*general*	*reflection*
spleen pancreas abdomen	*officer of the public granaries*	*digestion*
large intestine	*super-intendent*	*transformation of products*
kidneys	*officers of work*	*erection creation*

From Huard et al., Le Seuil, 1977.

208

CODE OF GOOD
HEALTH

Having learnt anatomy from a book, the Emperor Taitsong tells the torturer how to spare certain organs. Water-colour, from the Book of emperors, *eighteenth century. National Library, Paris, France.*

Before reaching the stage of prescribing treatment for a disease, the doctor would endeavour to keep the patient in good health by following precepts of hygiene basically concerning the diet, which was to be as varied as possible with no excess of meat or alcoholic drinks. Moderate physical exercise undertaken on a regular basis was to keep the body in a satisfactory condition. Perhaps through influence from India, the control of respiration was to be learnt, including its amplitude and its rhythm, by using certain postures aimed at relaxation. Baths and massage were also recommended.

The individual's harmony was not maintained solely by his physical health but also by the role he played in society, through ensuring a balance between his civic and military virtues. He therefore practised martial arts which, although defensive, obeyed a moral code of discipline and respect for others. This controlled violence led, over the centuries, to the identification of particularly vulnerable points on the body where impact could result in unconsciousness or death; at the same time, rigid rules of etiquette between opponents allowed for the development of effective resuscitation techniques.

The control of the vital energy also extended into the area of sexual activity. Although customs allowed a prosperous family to have a number of concubines – albeit hierarchized – and although homosexuality was tolerated, the Chinese were recommended not to abuse sensual pleasures, which were sources of enjoyment

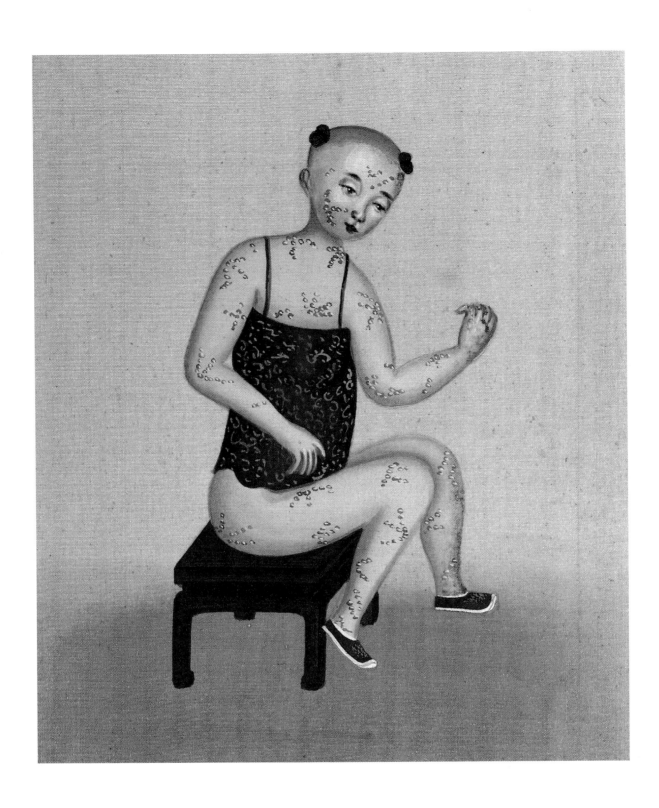

for partners. Thus, numerous "treatises on the bedroom" were written. These very popular works were supplemented over the centuries and incorporated some of the erotic practices of the Indian *Kama Sutra*.

In these manuals, men were encouraged not to surrender their seed to their partner, as the sperm represented vital energy which should not be squandered: *coitus interruptus* did not, it was taught, prevent shared pleasure, and the man thereby kept his strength and controlled his senses. These precepts of a moral and

A smallpox rash, from a nineteenth-century Chinese water-colour. National Library, Paris, France.

physical nature should not, however, be interpreted as a form of preventive medicine, except in the case of variolization. This technique, which consisted of introducing pus from smallpox victims into a small scarification of the skin to trigger a more benign smallpox than if it had been contracted by contagion (in which case it could be fatal), seems to have been used in China by the upper classes from the eleventh century onwards. It later became more widespread in the rest of Asia and was introduced in Europe in the eighteenth century, thanks to the Turks.

*F*ollowing the example of other doctors in antiquity, the model for whom was still Hippocrates, the Chinese reached prognostic rather than diagnostic conclusions. Their deterministic view of the world, in which the fate of the individual is preordained, did not however prevent them from attempting to intervene and change it by recourse to therapeutic measures.

As stated earlier in this chapter, a healthy dietary regime was recommended in order to maintain balance between the essential influences. In addition, they had a rich pharmacopoeia, administered in forms common to all races: plasters for blistering purposes, unctions, pills, syrups, powders, granules and solutions in the form of drinks or enemas.

Use was made of the animal, vegetable and mineral kingdoms for making drugs. Soils, minerals, salts and mixtures of powders were particularly valued by the Chinese; as were metals such as gold, iron and mercury. Similarly, animal organs were prescribed for specific cases: shark fins or stag antlers as analogues to human parts; the genitals which revived masculine ardours; and animal excreta from which subtle preparations were made.

Human waste also figured in apothecaries' dispensaries: over thirty-five human products with curative properties have been counted, examples including body hair and nails.

It goes without saying that plants constituted the main resource. The extreme diversity of climate in this vast subcontin-

ent gave rise to an extraordinarily varied flora which doctors exploited to the full for therapeutic purposes. They used even the most insignificant bud offered in profusion by nature, ground roots, chopped stalks, dried leaves, and sometimes macerated or fermented leaves, bark, seeds and luscious fruits from which an alcoholic elixir was extracted.

After examining the face and pulse, and the nature of the imbalance, the doctor chose medicine not for its efficacy but on the basis of a code adopted in accordance with universal harmonies drawn from the senses. Every substance was included in a classification based on the five senses,

Some items from the traditional Chinese pharmacopoeia, in the eighteenth century and today: ginseng, buffalo horns, etc. National Library, Paris, France.

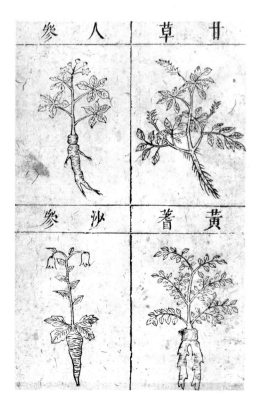

the five colours and the five smells and each one had three "qualities" which made it appropriate to remedy the discords between Yin and Yang, the five elements, and so on.

Depending on the gravity of the individual case, a special receptacle for potions was used: a goblet made of copper or amber, or even a carefully selected type of wood.

The vast pharmacopoeia naturally formed the subject of treatises, which were called *pen tsao*. They were first written before the Christian era and were supplemented over the centuries. The most complete one specific to Chinese medicine, prior to any additions from Asia, is the *pen tsao kang mou* dating from 1590.

When the Europeans, in the seventeenth century and in particular in the eighteenth century, discovered the wealth of the Middle Empire, they could not but admire the scale of this pharmacopoeia, the ingenuity of its preparations and in some cases its poetry. This explains why the *pen tsao* were translated into numerous languages, first those of Asia and then those of Europe.

In view of the profusion of medical prescriptions, the surgical techniques of the Chinese appear particularly poor for such an industrious people. They could have learnt much from their Indian neighbours.

Moxibustion, an unknown technique in the West, is more original. A moxa is a small cone of dried mugwort which was applied to the patient's skin and ignited. These fragments burnt without a flame, like tobacco in a cigarette. The burning produced a sore which acted as an exutory to the ill. The sore was then dressed until it healed. Alternatively, in order to avoid the burning, an onion ring or a few pieces of paper were placed between the skin and the moxa.

FROM ACUPUNCTURE TO MESOTHERAPY

*A*cupuncture, which already has been mentioned earlier in this chapter, is peculiar to China. Acupuncture and moxibustion stem from the same idea: each organ, receptacle or cauldron contained under the skin is linked to an area of the skin by an invisible communication which translators have called, as an approximation, the *meridian*.

Chinese doctors inserted very fine steel needles into the skin, to a depth of several centimetres, at the points at which the meridians for the particular organs concerned ended.

This process was to be used for two thousand years, to treat conditions whose location was difficult to pinpoint within, the thorax, the abdomen or the head, and for more specific osteo-articular pains or even fractures.

Generations of mandarins, convinced and convincing, attributed enormous curative power to acupuncture and they consiered that the theory of links between the inside and the outside of the human body was corroborated: the human mind is easily swayed to judge by appearances.

Acupuncture therefore played a fundamental role in the development of an understanding of human anatomy which is peculiar to Chinese culture.

Medical works appeared from the early centuries AD, illustrated both by meridians and drawings of the body, some of them accurate and others showing fantastically shaped organs which were the reflection of pure conjecture.

European visitors to China were interested in this supposedly medical system. In the seventeenth century, they started to export the idea and later a competent and sincere popularizer, Soulié de Morant (1878–1955), shared it with the general public. Today, acupuncture has become the focus of renewed attention and approval in the West.

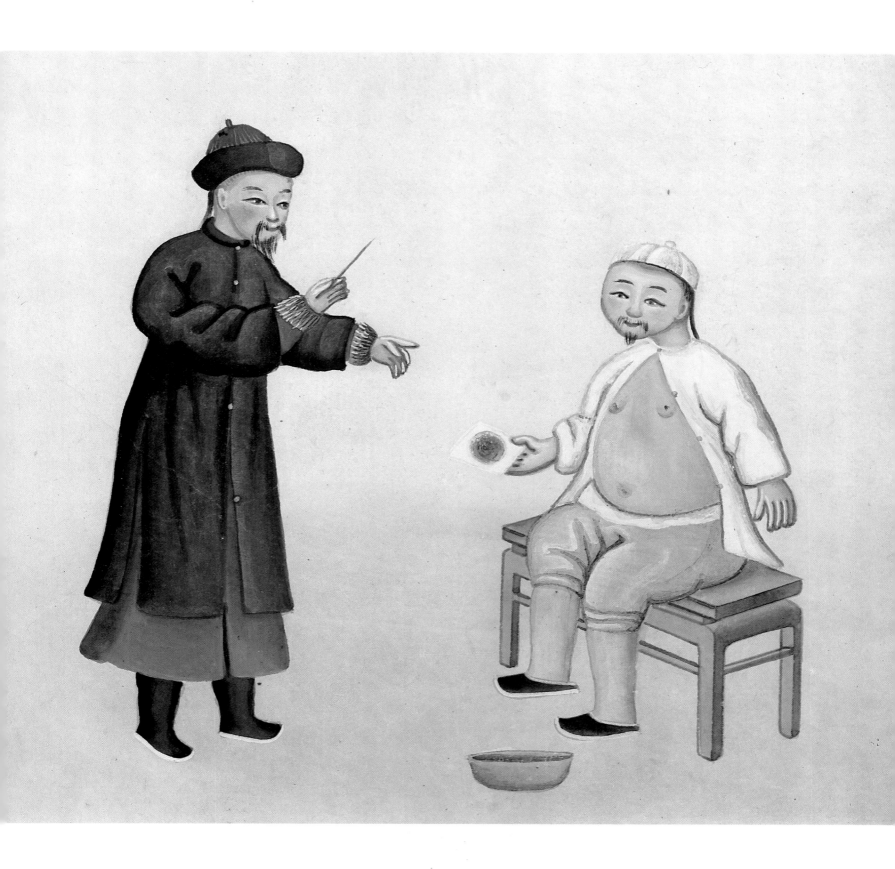

*A scene of acupuncture against dropsy,
from a Chinese water-colour,
late eighteenth century. National
Library, Paris, France.*

It also gave rise to neurophysiological studies; it would appear that the puncturing of particular areas of the skin triggers motory phenomena which form the basis of reflexotherapy. It may also produce, in the internal organs, reactions which are difficult to define, due to synaptic (interneuronal) links which are, however, still hypothetical.

The recent identification of endorphins* produced by the organs following certain stimuli proves that the various areas of the skin do indeed differ and can transmit messages of a neurological type.

Finally, it is true that Chinese acupuncture applied at the specified points produces an analgesia (not an anaesthesia) such that surgery, on the abdominal organs for example, can be carried out.

This discipline, born in China centuries ago, produces individual phenomena which

Western medicine is as yet unable to explain. Acupuncture is used today to treat certain psychosomatic illnesses and this clearly raises the question as to whether the Chinese were not in fact correct in refusing to dissociate the soul from the body. What about the technique of mesotherapy* currently in vogue in the West, based on the same procedure of numerous small needles that was used by Chinese doctors?

By using the same theory of a mysterious system of communication between the internal organs and a particular area of the skin, this technique introduces a product in a specified section of the dermis. However, the efficacy of mesotherapy or acupuncture cannot be demonstrated by modern statistical principles. Nor can their action be explained by anatomy and physiology.

Acupuncture in China and Korea: on the left on a model, on the right on an anatomical plate. Each organ corresponds to a precise point on the skin. Korean manual, nineteenth century. British Library, London, England.

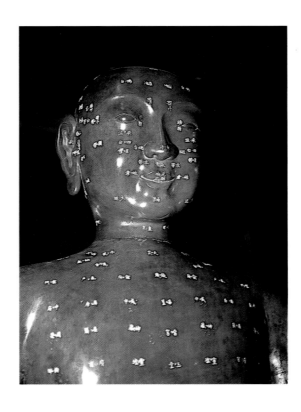

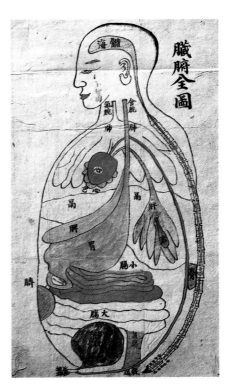

"STANDING ON ITS OWN TWO FEET"

Although the practices of Chinese medicine developed over the centuries, the fundamental principles remained unchanged for almost two thousand years.

Indeed, although Pien Ts'io (a semi-mythical Chinese doctor, ?400–200 BC) was famous among his peers in the fourth century BC, it was not until the glorious Han dynasty (206 BC to AD 220) that the doctrine acquired its definitive form; Tchang Tchong King (142–220) was deservedly called the Chinese Hippocrates. Shortly afterwards, Huang Fu Mi (215–282) codified acupuncture in a treatise which set the standard for all subsequent manuals.

In the early centuries AD, the professional doctors gradually distanced themselves from the world of witch-doctors, herbalists, magicians and also Buddhist and Taoist priests and monks. In the

This child's hat, bearing the face of a good genie, protects against "evil spirits". China. Museum of Mankind, Paris, France.

twelfth century, one of the emperors created a special class for doctors in Chinese society with its strict hierarchy; he granted them a special school, bringing their practice under state control. An imperial office of medicine was even created in the Sung dynasty (960–1280). China then experienced a Golden Age as printing, the compass and the use of gunpowder were developed. In the same period, the first herbal was published, adorned with colour illustrations of the most commonly used plants; this work was widely distributed.

The long reign of the Mongol Yüan dynasty (1276–1368) enveloped China in an immense unified empire extending from the China Sea to Russia. Curiosity prompted some doctors to explore hitherto unknown lands, and Chinese, Indian, Persian and Arab scholars met at Tabriz, the western tip of Asian culture.

A Chinese woman carries her harvest of medicinal plants to market. Right: a doctor treats a sore on the arm caused by an arrow wound. National Library, Paris, France, and University of California, Los Angeles, USA.

This century was to witness the first contacts between doctors of the Middle Empire and those of Europe, without, however, producing any notable results.

Two centuries later, during the Ming dynasty (1368–1644), relations between these two worlds were to intensify; they continued to develop under the Manchu Ch'ing dynasty (1644–1912), right through to modern times. As exchanges flourished, visits from travellers, traders and evangelists led the doctors of the Celestial Empire towards a new understanding of disease and of the functioning of the human body.

On the other side of the world, a veritable Sinomania took hold during the eighteenth century. Stories and documents written by missionaries were eagerly read and Europe learned that this civilized, organized and powerful country was capable of developing coherent scientific doctrines quite foreign to the Western, monarchic system based on Aristotelian logic and Christianity.

While the West marvelled at China's culture, Chinese medicine, for its part, staunchly resisted foreign influences. The Chinese elite's conviction of its intellectual superiority did not waver. Moreover, the coherence between its vision of the world, of the country's social organization and of human physiology was so great that the acceptance of any European idea would have completely upset the Empire's equilibrium.

Chinese doctors remained incredulous and resolute, despite the fact that Wang Ts'ing Sen dissected the corpses of cholera victims in 1798 and found that the human anatomy closely resembled that described in Western treatises, and despite his efforts to propagate the idea of the circulation of the blood and knowledge that the brain controls the functions of the heart.

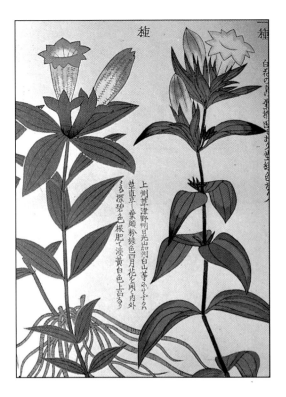
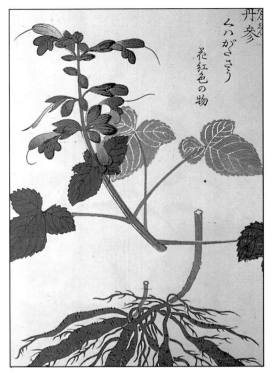

Nonetheless, due to the decline in imperial power under the assaults of Western forces, and later to the Second World War – factors which resulted in the disintegration of the old social structures – schools of Western medicine gradually appeared along the east coast, then further inland.

By the mid-twentieth century, the French, Americans, Germans and English were teaching the basic rules of medicine and prevention of disease in faculties and missions.

While the People's Republic of China threw off the "yoke of foreigners", it did not completely renounce all Western influences, neither did it abandon its traditional medicine. According to one of Mao Tse-tung's sayings, China was "standing on its own two feet".

The rather unfairly dubbed "barefoot doctors" treat the majority of the population – a billion citizens; they are paramedics concerned with hygiene and prevention of disease rather than with treatment and prescriptions. Their job is to check on the cleanliness of workshops, farms and villages, the removal of rubbish and the installation of latrines.

They are also involved in the control of insects and birds which pillage crops, and of vermin, and they teach others how

Plants from a treatise on the Japanese pharmacopoeia. Left: Gentiana algida; Right: Salvia nipponica. *Water-colours, 1830. Private collection, Seoul, Korea.*

to filter water and give small children a healthy diet. They are drawn from the community and carry out their functions alongside their normal jobs in agriculture and industry.

Herbalists, bonesetters and sorcerers still treat the population with their herb teas, acupuncture, charms, horoscopes and magic ceremonies – but these practices have not prevented the Republic of China from establishing hospitals and faculties of traditional medicine while at the same time developing Western medical institutions run by professionals with many years' training in China or abroad. The latter practise sophisticated techniques with costly medicines and instruments, inaccessible to the general population.

Clearly, the Chinese spirit of pragmatism, used to the inevitable compromise between Yin and Yang, sees no contradiction between the two types of medicine. A Chinese person may benefit from the skill of doctors in the treatment of first-degree burns, the reattachment of limbs amputated in accidents or the treatment of cancer of the oesophagus, while at the same time asking his family to offer sacrifices at the nearby temple to appease evil spirits. Europe, too, witnesses similar types of contradictory behaviour.

CHINA IN THE FAR EAST

China's traditional conservatism within its frontiers did not prevent it from exercising a strong influence to the west among the people of Asia, to the east across the China Sea and to the south-east in the Indo-Chinese peninsula, thanks to emigrants, imperial diplomats, traders, Buddhist missionaries and conquering armies.

Thus, Japanese medicine was so imbued with Chinese medicine that it adapted itself to the language, script and customs of the latter. But when Portuguese navigators introduced different books and methods in the sixteenth century, the Japanese accepted them with their characteristic avidity. A few Japanese doctors started to translate medical treatises, but the expulsion of the Portuguese in 1638 temporarily closed the door on any European influence, at least until the early eighteenth century. Then the Dutch arrived, replaced Catholicism with Calvinism and a Latin language with their Germanic one, and also brought in their luggage a medicine – the tradition of Western medicine.

The Chinese ban on dissection and the repulsion felt in connection with it were not shared in Japan. Japanese doctors practised dissection on the corpses of those sentenced to death and thus recognized that the anatomical plates in European books illustrated the human body better than Chinese books did. Although they initially concluded from this that Japanese people were made differently from Chinese, experience soon revealed the inaccuracy of the Chinese books.

Following this revelation, Japanese medicine constantly sought to adapt to Western medicine, with all the obvious translation difficulties, and with hesitation and progress alternating, depending on the political relationship between the Japanese government and the European powers or the United States throughout the nineteenth and twentieth centuries.

Today, we can say that modern Japan has totally assimilated Western medicine; it uses its vocabulary and its most complex and costly techniques. However, the majority of the population has not renounced the Sino-Japanese medical traditions, nor the religious customs based on magic and on acupuncture. The latter differs in practice from Chinese acupuncture: the Japanese acupuncturist uses very fine needles which penetrate the body. It is not clear what this procedure owes to Chinese acupuncture.

Thailand, on the other hand, adopted Chinese medicine in its totality, although acupuncture did not enjoy the same privileged position there. As in China, it

The "great cooking-pot" personifies the functions of digestion, from a Japanese etching by Utagawa Kunisada (1786–1866). University of California, Los Angeles, USA.

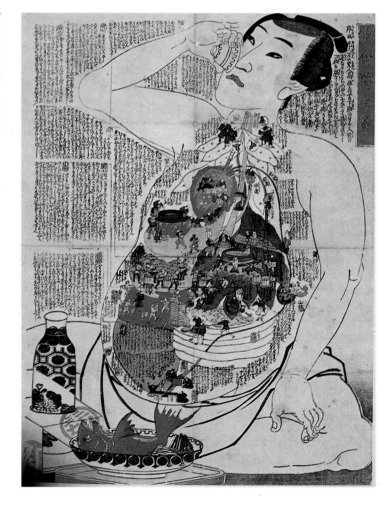

Huang Tui, thought to be the author of the oldest treatise on Chinese medicine, in conversation with Shen Nung, one of his disciples. Ivory figurine. Wellcome Institute, London, England.

was thought that every joint or internal organ communicated with a particular area of skin which could easily be treated. But from this shared background different procedures emerged: instead of inserting needles at particular points, the Thais massaged the area concerned. This led them to develop a range of manipulative techniques, from simple contact through to *tapotement* and *petrissage*. Thai doctors also preached advice on everyday hygiene; this involved sexual conduct which Europeans were soon to call "Thai massage" and which acquired enormous notoriety.

The Indo-Chinese peninsula was subject to many foreign invasions and colonizations, by peoples with different languages, customs and cultures. Its history is therefore extremely complex. Nonetheless, from the fifteenth century, with the end of the Chinese and Khmer Empires, we can talk of a Sino-Vietnamese medical tradition, thanks to the reputation of Tue-Trinh, who brought back, from a long stay in China, some *pen-tsao*, the pharmacopoeia of which he adapted to the flora of his country, which is far more tropical than that of China.

Another major figure was Hai-Thung Lan-Ong (1720–*c.*1785). European visitors admired his therapeutic skill and several generations revered him as a master. From the nineteenth century, Indo-China came under the influence of foreign doctors who accompanied the occupying forces of various nationalities. French doctors vaccinated even the remotest populations and trained indigenous doctors. A Pasteur institute which specialized in the study of local diseases was created.

Modern Vietnam, like other Asian countries, has kept its medical heritage based on ancient traditions – because the people set great store by it – while at the same time developing modern institutions along European and notably French lines.

SYSTEMS OF MEDICINE
1400 BC – AD 1912

FAR EAST	DATE	DATE	INDIA	DATE	PRE-COLOMBIAN AMERICA
		−1600	The Aryans in India		
Writing	−1400		The first Vedas		
Confucius	−555, c.−479				
First medical texts		−536, c.−486	Buddha		
The warring states	−480				
Taoism					
Treatise on the pulse					
The Ch'in kingdom	−230	−230	The Asoka empire		
The Han dynasty	−206–209	−200	Development of Hinduism		
The Chinese in Korea and Tonkin	−100	−100	Treatise on yoga		
Pharmacology books					
		100	Buddhism in central Asia		
The Three kingdoms	220		Charaka		
China reunified under the Chin	222				
Treatise on medicine by Ko Hung					
		320–480	The Gupta dynasty		
Buddhism spreads	350				
		400	Susruta		
Buddhism in Japan	550				
Addition to the *pen-tsao*				630	The first Maya empire
T'ang dynasty	618	647	India divided up		
Barabudur	750				
				830	The Mixtecs
Angkor, Khmer capital	900				
End of the T'ang dynasty	908				
The Sungs reunify China	960			987	New Maya empire
Imperial medical encyclopaedia		1150	Decline of Buddhism		
		1200	Islam and the Ganges	1200	The Incas in the Cuzco valley
Genghis Khan in Peking	1215				
Marco Polo in China	1275			1325	The Aztecs in Mexico
Start of the Ming dynasty	1368				
		1398	Tamerlane in Delhi		
				1440	New Maya empire
The Portuguese in Japan	1542			1492	Christopher Columbus in Haiti
				1520	Hernan Cortes against the Aztecs
Expulsion of foreigners from Japan	1630			1524	Francisco Pizzaro against the Incas
The Dutch in Japan	1641				
Manchu dynasty of the Ch'ing	1644				
		1658	Aurangzeb, the Great Moghul		
The Meiji era in Japan	1867				
		1876	Victoria, Empress of India		
End of the Empire in China	1912				

chapter VII

Anatomy
in the
Renaissance

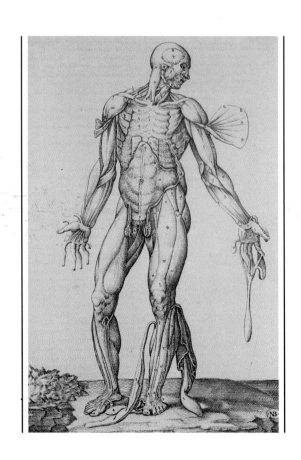

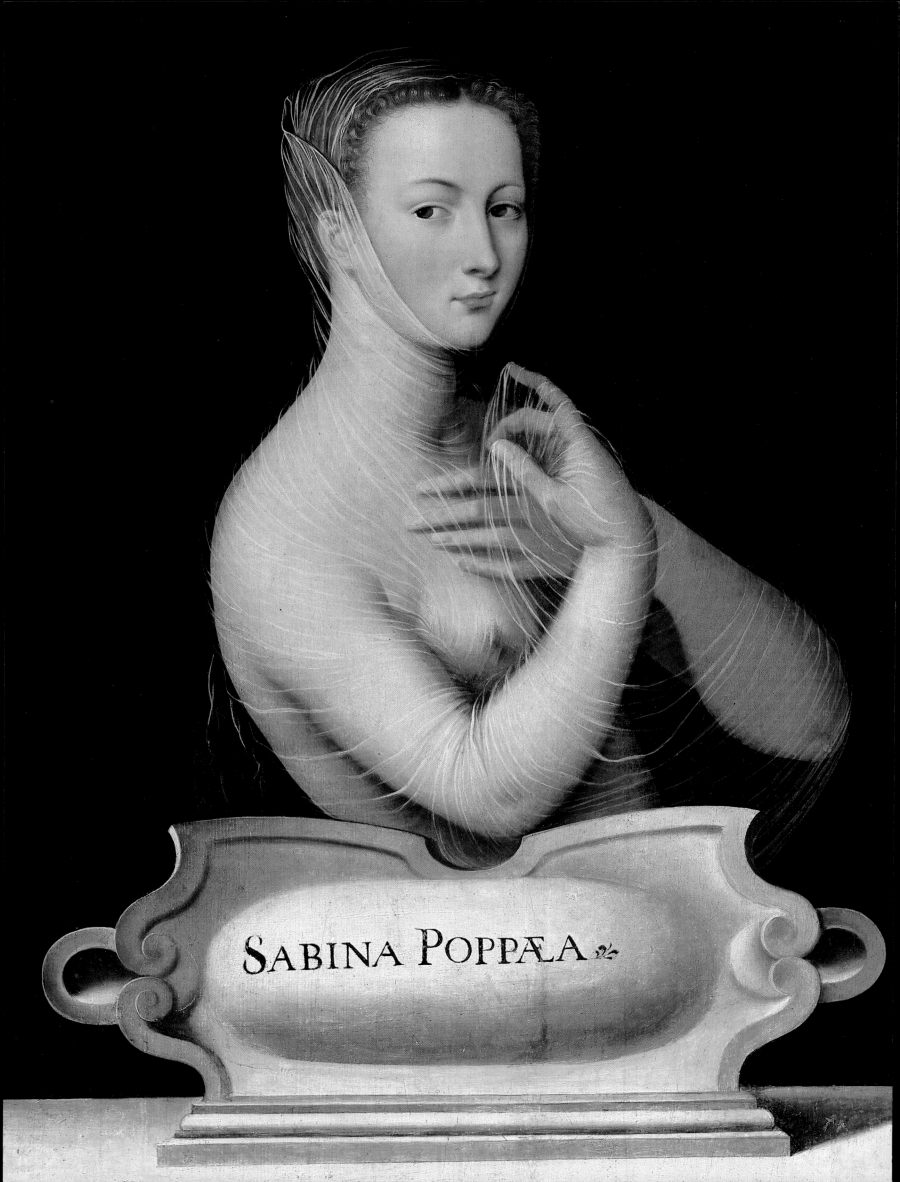

SABINA POPPÆA

At the end of the fifteenth century, and throughout the sixteenth, Western thinking underwent a considerable change. This was due to a number of discoveries which called into question the ideas that underpinned philosophical and intellectual thought in the Middle Ages.

Henceforth, mankind was to view the universe differently. The finite world of Aristotle or Plato and its "sphere of fixed stars" expanded with the discoveries of the Danish astronomer Tycho Brahe and his Polish counterpart Nicolaus Copernicus. The immutable cosmos was growing larger, as was the planet Earth — with the invention of the compass and the advances in shipbuilding, men were now able to sail around it. New routes opened up, and Columbus tried to reach the "Indies", discovering new lands as he sailed.

The conquest of these new worlds, with their variously attired peoples and their different religions, shook Western belief in the infallibility of the Old and New Testaments. Western man was no longer the unique creature described in Genesis. Doubt arose, and along with doubt came criticism. The Reformation weakened the once unshakeable authority of the Roman Catholic Church. Religious wars, which raged on and off throughout the sixteenth century, redrew the map of Europe. States regrouped as traditional alliances were forged and broken. At the same time, the religious unrest and feeling that had been stirred up by the Reformation and Counter-Reformation, the Huguenots and Papists, revived the atmosphere of intolerance. Witchcraft trials were numerous, for the Devil was everywhere: in the villages, where his presence was sometimes manifested by hysteria or by people being "possessed by the Devil", and in the cities, where scholars sometimes opposed the conformism of religious thinking.

From painting the human body to anatomy. During the Renaissance, the body, especially the female body, which until then had remained hidden or had been treated in a purely religious manner, became the subject of both literature and painting. Here, the artist pays special attention to the hands and the breast of his model. Sabina Poppaea, *Fontainebleau School, sixteenth century. Museum of Art and History, Geneva, Switzerland.*

To the conquests of new lands were added commercial and economic conquests. The world became a huge territory which the countries of Europe divided between them. The seas were constantly crossed and recrossed by Portuguese, Spanish and Dutch ships. Gold and silver, the standards of state power, gave rise to merchant banks. Merchants settled in the cities and influenced government policy.

This tremendous expansion, to which can be added the invention of printing in fifteenth-century Germany, intensified communication. Techniques for printing texts were simplified, and the characters used by the printing works of Europe became standardized. Latin ceased to be the only officially recognized language of scholarship, and authors began to write in the language of their country. The Ancients were rediscovered with the arrival in the West of Greek refugees, who brought with them texts written in their original language — texts which had not been corrupted by successive translations into Latin and Arabic. Greek, which had long been poorly understood and badly translated, came back into favour. Marsilio Ficino founded an "academy" in Florence which was inspired by Platonic ideas. Italy abandoned scholasticism which, by its rigidity, was hampering the intellectual life of the universities and the colleges.

The Renaissance, that great sixteenth-century outpouring of thought, had its source in Italy. A few decades later, it reached France and northern Europe. The image of the scholar was changing. The "humanist" of the sixteenth century had a new view of the world: he questioned the great dogmas and, while respecting the Ancients, whose writings remained sacrosanct, he judged them, criticizing and reconsidering their ideas.

Humanism permeated all branches of knowledge in sixteenth-century Europe, including medicine.

225

The changes in morals that followed these new developments in thinking began in the Italian principalities, and were inspired by Baldassare Castiglione's book *Il cortegiano*. Fashions changed. There was less austerity. Poetry began to exhibit a more subtle eroticism than that of the fairly *risqué* stories and *fabliaux* which had been popular in the Middle Ages. A literary genre known as *le Blason des corps* or blazonry idealized the body of the beloved and celebrated each part. Gradually, relationships between men and women evolved.

The idea of the nude in painting and sculpture was also changing. Fifteenth-century representation of the human body had been diffident, but was now becoming bolder. The subjects were at first religious – the martyrdom of the saints or Adam and Eve – yet they enabled both men and women to be painted. Adam and Eve, in the painting by Lucas Cranach, wander about the terrestrial paradise almost naked. Michelangelo, who was more daring, painted and sculpted Christ, the man and son of God, completely naked (the Counter-Reformation modestly veiled his masculinity).

The representation of the human body was to intensify and change in its conception as the taste for antiquity and mythology spread: Hercules, Apollo, nymphs and sylphs were the subjects of stories whose moral or symbolic significance sometimes eludes us today. Artists also drew their inspiration from Ovid's *Metamorphoses* and from Old Testament stories. The choice of heroes of antiquity allowed them to paint the human body: the fashion for depicting nudes spread among the studios and gave rise to new aesthetic criteria. Proportions were fixed according to precise canons that were not to be contravened in the search for perfection. The head had to be a precise fraction of the total length of the body, and likewise

The discovery of the human body

I.

Two didactic diagrams by Albrecht Dürer. The human body is converted into numbers and letters and ideal measurements. School of Fine Arts, Paris, France.

the size of the limbs and the width of the shoulders. The idea of the "golden section", which is applicable both to the body and to architecture, is nowhere better illustrated than in the drawing by Leonardo da Vinci which shows a well-proportioned man in a circle, the symbol of ideal beauty.

Thus the Renaissance readopted the universal order of the Greeks: everything corresponded to the grand numeric and geometric order of the universe.

These new preoccupations gave rise to works of art that were destined for a limited public, yet they bear witness to a new view of the human body. If the Reformation and Catholicism tried to answer the questions that concerned man's place in the divine creation and his duties towards God, the men of science and in particular the doctors wanted to know what this body, which people were now prepared to represent, was made of.

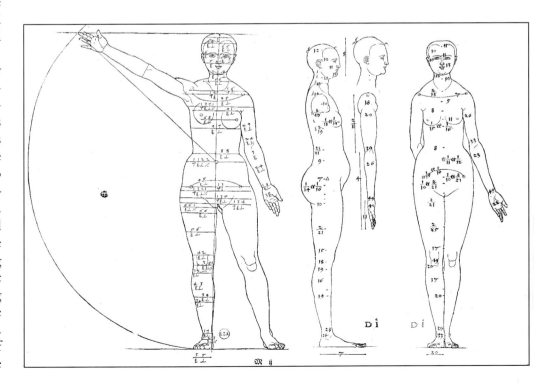

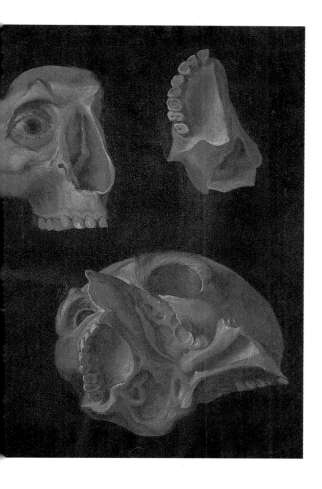

Horror and ideal beauty. Different ways of treating anatomy are found in the Renaissance. Above: the desire to be scientific, as shown by the different views of the bony masses of the face and the base of the skull, by Fabricius ab Aquapendente (1533– 1619), professor at Padua University. Right: art through mythological subjects provides a pretext for nudity, like this Venus by Cranach the Elder, along aesthetic lines which are very different from those of Dürer. Private collection, Marciana Library, Venice, Italy.

Maistre Arnoult de ville noue.

DISSECTION IS REGULARIZED

Two opposing principles dominated the entire period. The first held that the mortal remains of God's creature, man, merited religious respect and any interference with it was sacrilegious. The second, man's insatiable curiosity and the progress he was making in caring for patients, pushed him to dissect corpses. Islam still today has not decided what its policy should be on this subject.

In Christian countries during the Middle Ages, the desecration of graves was a serious crime. However, the guardians of public order knew of dissections being practised under the authority of doctors in the Italian universities and in the French cities of Paris and Montpellier. Well-known medical figures were present at such dissections without being pursued for colluding in the offence. The corpses being studied were not merely those of executed criminals whose bodies had not been claimed by next of kin. There were also corpses which were taken from

Humanism, the Renaissance and the printed book. Here, the frontispiece from the Trésor des pauvres *by Arnaud de Villanueva (1235–1313), translated into French and printed in Lyons in 1527. Library of Decorative Arts, Paris, France.*

cemeteries in varying stages of decomposition. The Church and the Inquisition turned a blind eye to the large numbers of corpses, far in excess of those authorized by law, which were being dissected. This tolerance, which may appear to some as a form of social hypocrisy, was to continue to be shown for many years.

A tutor who had a corpse at his disposal immediately made this known to his students. The news spread, and dissection was quickly commenced before putrefaction set in. Only in the nineteenth century was the technique introduced of injecting the corpse in order to prevent both microbial proliferation and the death of the investigator from infection via small wounds received during dissection. The sixteenth century saw the introduction of the term "anatomy" to designate the static disposition of the organs in the human body, the study of them, and the dissection which enabled such a study to be made. Expressions evolved such as "to perform an anatomy", or "anatomize", and victims of infection died of an "anatomical puncture".

Because of the smell, dissections were conducted in the open air, weather permitting. In winter they were carried out where there was plenty of space, for example in a church, where temporary tiers of seats would be arranged. The tutors very often did not wish to touch the putrefying viscera and preferred to sit high up on a rostrum, from where they talked about Galen while a demonstrator pointed out the parts revealed by an assistant. There was thus a strict hierarchy, with each of the three individuals

Two portrayals of doctors at the beginning of the Renaissance. One shows a doctor in his study, surrounded by books which mostly date from the Graeco-Roman period, the other a doctor on his rostrum during a dissection. A subordinate demonstrator is entrusted with describing the parts as they are revealed. Learning is still rated more highly than practical skills. Fasciculo di medicina, *Verona, 1494. Library of the Faculty of Medicine, Padua, Italy.*

playing a well-defined part. Other tutors preferred a more direct method, believing that one can only explain that which one observes oneself. Mondino di Luzzi (1275–1326) was already using this approach in the fourteenth century. These two methods of teaching coexisted for many years, and it was up to the tutor which one he chose. Once the method had been decided upon, the dissection was carried out in a sequence determined by the speed of decomposition of the organs. After the abdomen and the digestive tract came the thorax with the heart and lungs. The skull was then opened, and finally the limbs were dissected. This procedure took several days.

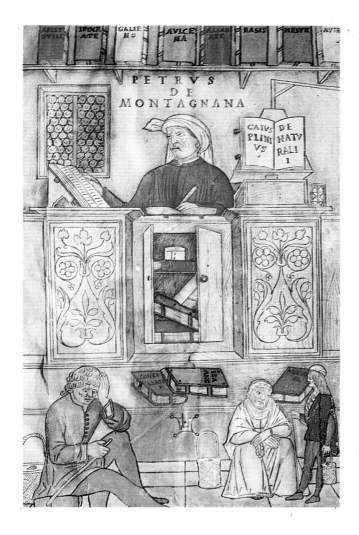

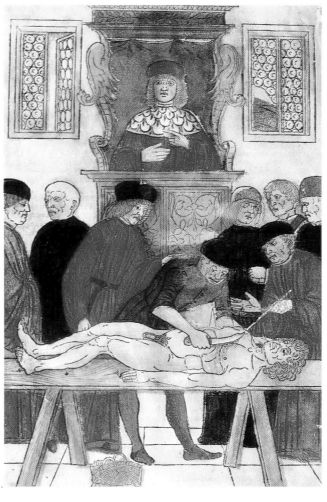

ILLUSTRATED BOOKS

Illustration showing the main muscles used in mastication after Fabricius ab Aquapendente (1533–1619). Marciana Library, Venice, Italy.

Since dissections were rare and their audiences limited, documents were needed for the education of future doctors. Until then, the only drawings at their disposal were inspired by Galen and had been recopied time and again by students, becoming distorted in the process. The invention of printing enabled commentaries to be added to the woodcuts that had already been used and reproduced in an imprecise manner in the fifteenth century. In Italy, Berengario da Carpi (1470–1530), a professor at Bologna, set an example by having printed loose sheets which illustrated and explained anatomy.

The use of perspective in the representations of the human body soon caused problems. Painters knew and used the rules of perspective, but the first anatom-ical engravings, published in 1491, ig-nored them. The drawings were flat and the absence of relief did not correspond to reality. From 1517, the creators of anatomical drawings started to use per-spective, but this only became widespread after 1529.

Some tutors were opposed to such a technique of graphic representation, claim-ing it was inexact. Their spokesman, Jacques Dubois (known as Sylvius), de-nied the value of such illustrations by arguing that the image was not a substi-tute for the object. It seemed that the artist did not regard the human body in the same way as the scientist. One strove after aesthetics, the other after precision and strictness. Titian painted, Vesalius observed. No anatomy book of the six-teenth century was to belie this argument.

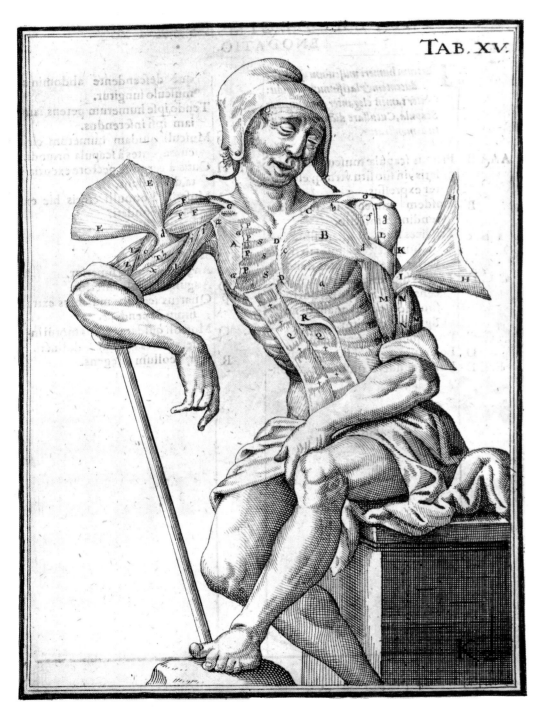

TAB. XV.

The écorché, *or anatomical figure without skin, is designed to teach "surface anatomy".* Tabulae anatomicae, *Frankfurt, 1632.* Right: *study of nudes by Michelangelo (1475–1564). Louvre Museum, Paris, France.*

RENAISSANCE ANATOMISTS

Jacopo Berengario da Carpi c. 1470–1530	Realdo Colombo 1516–1559
Jacques Dubois (Sylvius) 1478–1555	Cesare Aranzio 1530–1589
Charles Estienne 1504–1564	Gabriello Fallopio 1523–1562
Bartolommeo Eustachio c. 1510–1574	Constanzo Varolio 1543–1575
Giovanni F. Ingrassia c. 1510–1580	Fabricius ab Aquapendente 1533–1619
Leonardo Botallo 1530–1571	Adriaan van den Spieghel 1578–1625
Andreas Vesalius 1514–1564	Johannes Bauhin 1541–1613
	Giulio Casserio 1552–1616

All these doctors added to the works of their predecessors, educated students and almost all identified anatomical structures which still bear their name today. They all lived in Padua at some time as students or professors.

231

The first "illustrated books" to be printed can be placed in the category of "surface anatomy". Michelangelo (1475–1564) and Dürer (1471–1528) portrayed the human body (the first anatomy book, based on Dürer's forms, was published in 1534), but they drew and sculpted according to aesthetic criteria. Their lines do not always follow the exact form of the muscles which can be guessed at beneath the skin. As for Leonardo da Vinci (1452–1519), even though the structure of the muscles is exact, he was more interested in how the organs functioned, and drew as an engineer would. Also, these reproductions only reached a limited audience, despite being distributed widely from the 1570s onwards. An account of such works would not be complete without mentioning the drawings of Charles Estienne (1504–1564) – a French doctor who came from a family of scholars and printers – which appeared in 1546, after those of Vesalius.

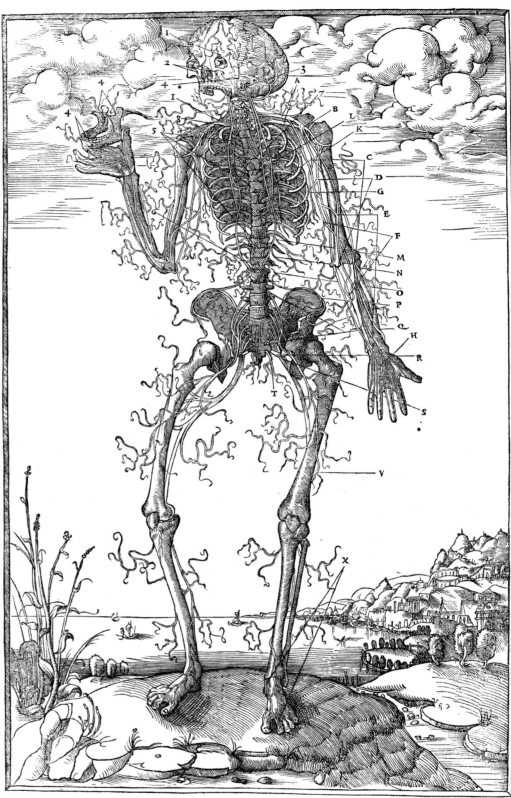

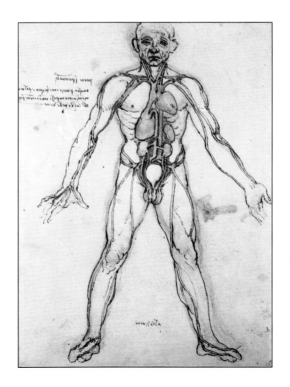

Charles Estienne (1504–1564), like Vesalius, questioned Galen's ideas on anatomy. On the basis of this plate from De dissectione partium corporis humani, *published in 1545, he gives a good description of the phrenic nerve and the sympathetic chain. Library of the Faculty of Medicine, Paris, France. Left: anatomical figure by Leonardo da Vinci, British Royal Collection.*

VESALIUS
(1514–1564)

Vesalius, who became a famous anatomist, was born in 1514 in a small town in the north of the Netherlands, where he adopted his Latinized name. He left an extensive collection of original works in which the precision of line and the attention paid to observation bring his anatomical drawings to life. His adventurous life took him as far as the Holy Land; he died in 1564.

He came from a family of doctors and apothecaries and studied medicine in Paris under Gontier d'Andernach, who was famous for his adaptations of ancient authors, and then under Jacques Dubois, commonly known as Sylvius. Among his fellow disciples were Michael Servetus, Charles Estienne, Laurent Joubert and Fernel. Before taking his doctorate in Padua in 1537, Vesalius chose Galenic

Andreas Vesalius (1514–1564), the author of De humani corporis fabrica *and greatest anatomist of his generation. Here he is shown surrounded by his pupils in Padua, in a somewhat fanciful painting by Édouard Hamman (1819–1888). Fine Arts Museum, Marseilles, France.*

therapy as the thesis for his first examination. Later he succeeded P. Colombo as professor of anatomy in Padua, teaching for a few years before leaving the post to Realdo Colombo. His famous work *De humani corporis fabrica* was published in Basle in 1543 under the direction of his friend Oporinus.

At the request of Cosimo de Medici the Elder, he took the chair of anatomy in Pisa, then decided to lead a roving life travelling through Europe. He left Italy, married in 1544 in the Netherlands, followed Emperor Charles V and the great men of the court of Augsburg to Brussels, then Madrid, where he became Philip II's physician. As well as being an academic, he also cared for patients, dissected corpses and animals, published the second edition of his *Fabrica* (1553–

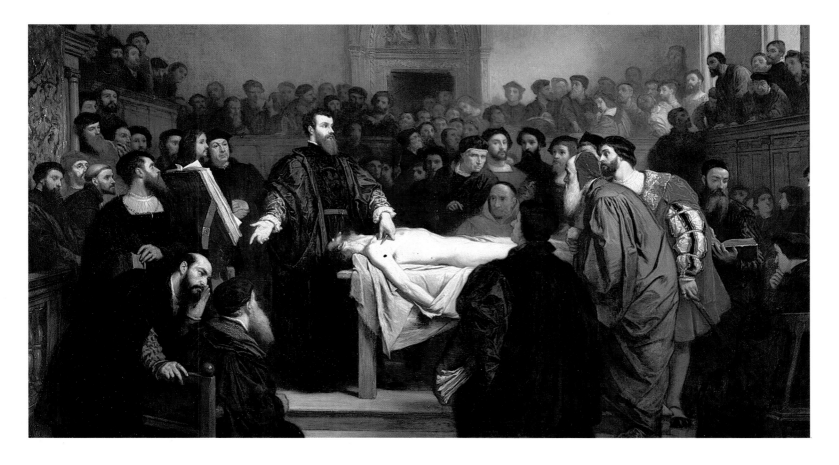

Without doubt the most authentic portrait of Andreas Vesalius, by Pierre Pons (1574–1640), which formerly hung in the old hospital of Orleans. Fine Arts Museum, Orleans, France.

1555), wrote but then destroyed commentaries on a book by Rhazes, and replied to critiques by his master Sylvius and his pupil Fallopio. He died on the small Ionian island of Zante on his return from a pilgrimage to the Holy Land that he undertook for reasons which we do not know.

The anatomical works of Vesalius, which are famous primarily for being anti-Galen, surpass those of his predecessors in their concern for rationality and verisimilitude. While his drawing and commentaries conflict with the tradition of Galen, he nonetheless retains a certain degree of hesitancy and there are some discrepancies between the text and the engravings. In particular, he adopts Galen's idea about the communication between the ventricles of the heart, but does not reproduce it in his diagrams.

His originality also lies in his constant preoccupation with establishing an anatomical nomenclature. Because he observed and detailed the structures of the human body, he realized that some organs had several names while others had none.

Consequently he made choices and took decisions which are often judged to be arbitrary or inopportune. He drew on ancient Arabic, Greek and especially Latin authors when inventing his new names. Moreover, Latin is the main language of his *Fabrica*. His choices resulted in some inconsistencies of terminology, and his successors and imitators did not necessarily follow him in everything.

However, Vesalius did not ever completely break free from the teaching of the great Galen, which is unfortunate because he possessed far greater practical experience of the human body and of dissection than Galen and his predecessors. A millennium of scientific conformism and veneration of Galen still weighed too heavily on him.

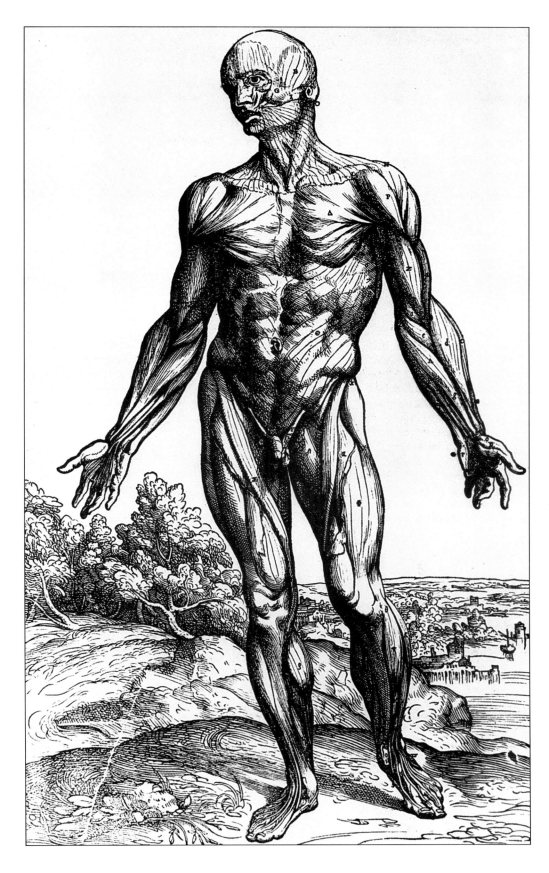

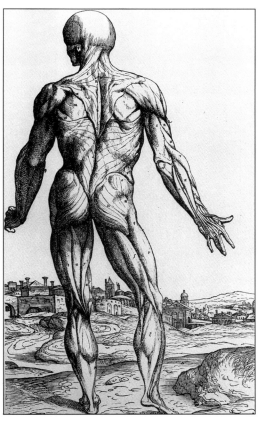

ANATOMY AFTER VESALIUS

Vesalius' work spread rapidly and his *Fabrica* was imitated throughout Europe. Since copyright did not yet exist, plates and drawings were copied in France, Germany, Spain and Britain, in the printing works which Aldus Manutius had founded in Venice and in those of Plantin at Antwerp. His nomenclature, which was thought to be too heterogeneous, was also simplified.

However, care should be taken not to commit an anachronism by looking at Vesalius' illustrations with an expert eye too concerned about anatomical accuracy. He was consistent in striving after an aesthetic effect in his technique and, over the centuries that followed, his engravings were admired more than his texts were read. The paradox remains in the fact that Vesalius set more store by the written description than by the engraving, and did not give his engravers much information.

The blocks were cut in pear wood using a special method. The engravings bear different signatures: Calcar, Campagnola and even Titian. Charles Estienne certainly displayed his collaboration with La Rivière, Rosso and the Fontainebleau School in this connection.

Anatomical painting in the Renaissance did not escape from the debate which had already been alluded to by Sylvius concerning the difficulty in reconciling rigor-

Frontispiece from the same edition of De humani corporis fabrica. *A dissection under the authority of Vesalius. Library of the Faculty of Medicine, Paris, France.*

ous scientific observation with the sensibility to which the artist is committed. Mannerism, too, left its mark on anatomical iconography in the sixteenth century: long, almost stretched bodies, heads which were often too small, undulating silhouettes which did not justify the pose or the gesture which the artist wanted to represent. The baroque style was also to influence anatomical representation in the same way during the century which followed.

The technique could not free itself from aesthetic preoccupations, nor could it remain indifferent to religious and philosophical concerns. Vesalius and his successors worked for the glory of God and to the glory of His most perfect creation, as represented in the *Fabrica*. All life implies imminent death and man cannot escape from his condition. This was all the more so for people in the Renaissance, who had not forgotten the horror of the great plagues of the fourteenth century. *Écorchés*, mutilated figures with lacerated flesh and skeletons in despairing poses all testify to this.

The only ray of light in this universe of death was the art of illumination as practised in the tradition of ancient manuscripts. Calcar left his mark on all the illuminations of the second editions of the *Fabrica* by including *putti* in them. These merry cherubs carry out dissections, clean bones, remove corpses from graves, practise vivisection, cauterize wounds and trepan skulls. Colombo's

One of the seven works of mercy: the giving of aid to the poor. A painting by the Master of the Prodigal Son. Flemish school, sixteenth century. Museum of Valenciennes, France.

illustrator chose mythological subjects to decorate the start of each chapter: Apollo rubs shoulders with Isis, the nymph Io, Orpheus and Leda. These subjects reflect the taste of the period, but they probably also hold symbolic meanings.

This illustration of the body filled the public with enthusiasm. Thus, little by little, dissection lost its air of secrecy. Many medical faculties kept records of the numbers of dissections conducted. Authorized dissections increased during the winter months, when the corpses would be better preserved. Civil and religious authorities authorized the construction of buildings reserved for the purpose. The provisional amphitheatre of anatomy at Padua, which was built in 1490, was replaced by a permanent building, with tiered rows of seats and a barrier separating the central table from the press of spectators. All Europe soon followed Padua's example, although Paris still had to make do with temporary premises until 1617.

THE SURGEON
AMBROISE PARÉ

*T*oday, surgeons have to be thoroughly familiar with anatomy. Albucasis and others had stated this principle in the Middle Ages, but in the sixteenth century this fact was forgotten. Doctors had exclusive access to new knowledge, and surgeons only practised dissections in secret.

However, they were confronted by hitherto unknown wounds caused by the new firearms. The huge bombards of the Hundred Years' War started to be replaced at the end of the fifteenth century by the wheel-lock arquebus, followed in the sixteenth century by the musket and light arms. These arms, which were initially called "hand cannon", emitted small, low-velocity projectiles. They nonetheless produced jagged wounds which presented surgeons with new problems.

Various prostheses made or designed in the sixteenth century by Ambroise Paré (c. 1509–1590). Two great military leaders of the period had iron hands: in France, the Huguenot La Noue, and in Germany, Götz von Berlichingen, who was called "the Iron Hand" (1480–1562), and who was immortalized by Goethe and also figured in Jean-Paul Sartre's Le diable et le bon dieu. *Wellcome Institute, London, England.*

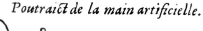

Poutraict de la main artificielle.

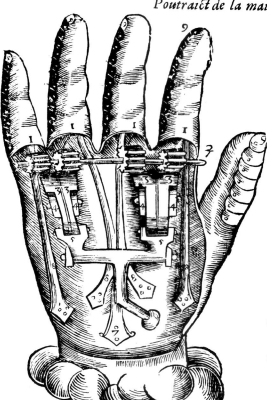

Description de la main de fer.

1   Pignons feruans à vn chacun doigt, qui font de la piece mefne des doigts : adiouftez & affemblez dedans le dos de la main.

2   Broche de fer qui paffe par le milieu defdits pignons, en laquelle ils tournent.

3   Gafchettes pour tenir ferme vn chacun doigt.

4   Eftoqueaux, ou arrefts defdites gafchettes,, au milieu defquelles font cheuilles pour arrefter lefdites gafchettes.

5   La grande gafchette pour ouurir les quatre petites gafchettes qui tiennent les doigts fermez.

6   Le bouton de la queüe de la grande gafchette, lequel fi on pouffe, la main s'ouurira.

7   Le reffort qui eft deffous la grande gâchette feruant à la faire retourner en fon lieu, & tenant la main fermée.

8   Les refforts de chacun doit, qui ramenent & font ouurir les doigts d'eux-mefmes, quand ils font fermez.

9   Les lames des doigts.

La figure fuiuante te montre le dehors de la main, & le moyen de l'attacher au bras & à la manche du pourpoint.

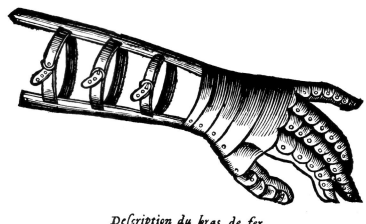

Description du bras de fer.

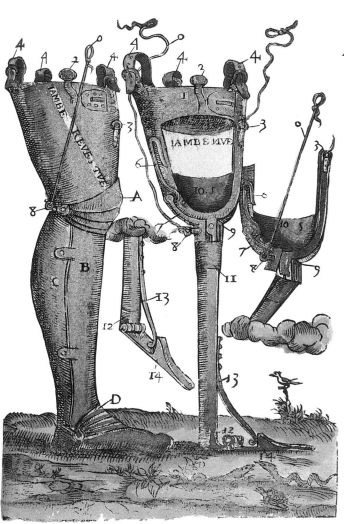

239

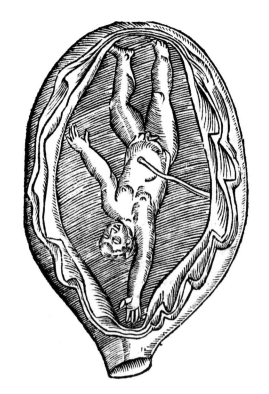

The Germans were the first to attract the attention of their colleagues to this development, and they took advantage of the spread of knowledge brought about by the invention of printing. Brunschwig published an important book in 1497, followed by H. von Gersdorff in 1517. For the first time, books were being published not in Latin but in the vernacular.

Ambroise Paré, who was very well known in France, devoted his first book to this subject. The son of a country box maker, he was born in 1509 (?) near Laval, and served his surgeon's apprenticeship with a Paris practitioner. After entering the service of the French king, Henry II, he followed him as a military surgeon to all the battlefields in the north and east of France, from Metz to Hesdin. He profited from considerable support, thanks to his shrewd judgement allied to a circumspect attitude to treatment. Late in life he was admitted to the powerful College of Surgeons of Paris. He died rich and respected in 1590 in Paris, after writing many works, in particular his *Cinq livres de chirurgie* of 1571. Anecdotes concerning his life abound. King Charles IX is said to

Some of Ambroise Paré's "imaginings".
Right: *two foetuses in an inverse position* in utero.
Left: *a hermaphrodite foetus with breasts already well developed. Library of the Faculty of Medicine, Paris, France.*

have hidden him under his bed on the night of the Saint Bartholomew's Day Massacre, since his sympathies were with the Huguenots, but there are no documents to confirm this.

In actual fact, Ambroise Paré owes his fame to his human qualities and to his encyclopaedic work. Although he did not quote his predecessors, he nonetheless borrowed much from Guy de Chauliac, Mondeville and Albucasis, some of whose

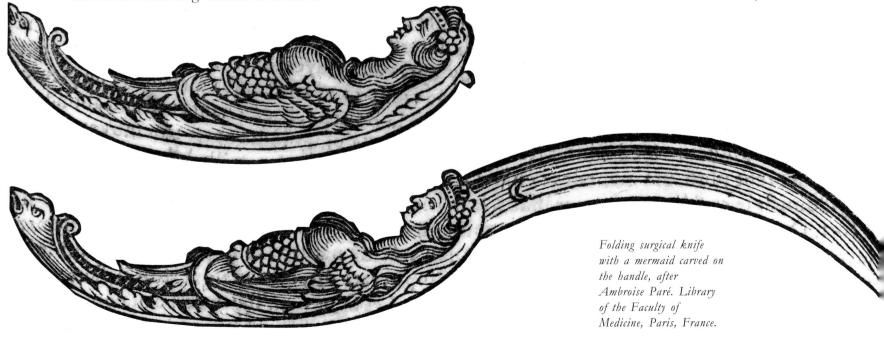

Folding surgical knife with a mermaid carved on the handle, after Ambroise Paré. Library of the Faculty of Medicine, Paris, France.

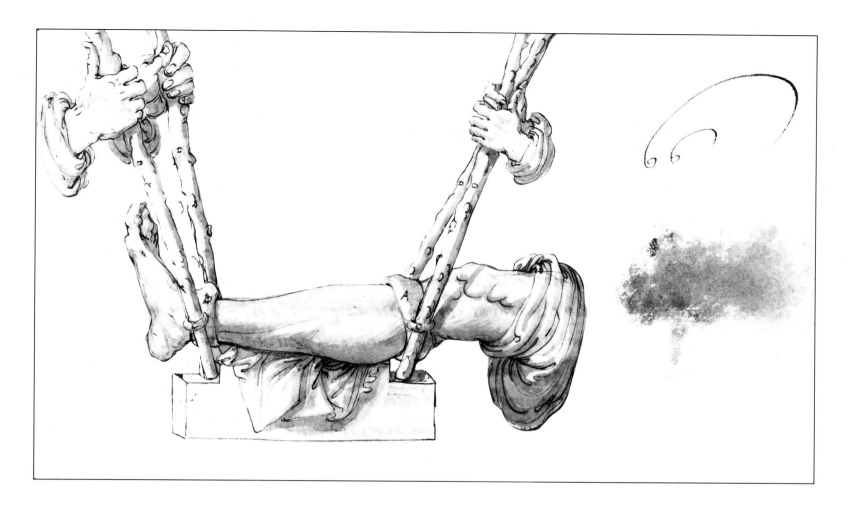

techniques he used. Likewise, it is difficult to attribute to him the procedure for ligation of the blood vessels which bleed during an amputation. However, it is thanks to him that the old method of cauterizing wounds using boiling oil or a red-hot iron was abandoned in favour of a dressing he invented. By contrast, one of his Italian contemporaries, Jean de Vigo (1460–1519) believed that wounds caused by gunpowder had to be treated by fire, which was the only way, in his opinion, of avoiding the hypothetical risk of poisoning, a hypothesis totally lacking in foundation. Also, cauterization by fire is very painful, and the type of bandage used did not do anything to prevent ultimate suppuration of the wounds.

In his books, Ambroise Paré deals with questions that are relevant to surgery, such as childbirth, abnormalities and congenital malformations. In one of his works, *Les monstres*, he describes the most bizarre cases, often exaggerated by popular rumour, which resulted from the coupling of two men, of animals and of diabolical creatures of the collective imagination. However, although he continually affirmed that experimentation and observation were of prime importance, he

This drawing, attributed to Francesco Rossi, is an illustration from the translation by the Italian surgeon Guido Guidi of the works of Hippocrates which was given to François I in about 1540. It shows the reduction of a fracture along its length in order to correct the overlap of the pieces of bone. National Library, Paris.

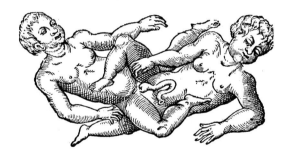

A FAMOUS APHORISM

In relation to one of his noble clients, Ambroise Paré wrote:

"I dressed him and God healed him."

The modesty and originality of this statement have been much admired. In reality, from the time of the first Capetian kings, the sovereign, who had just been consecrated at Rheims, touched the abscesses of patients with scrofula, saying to each:

"I touch you, God heals you."

All the books on Arabic medicine from the Middle Ages bore the formula: "After this treatment the patient will be cured, God willing."

241

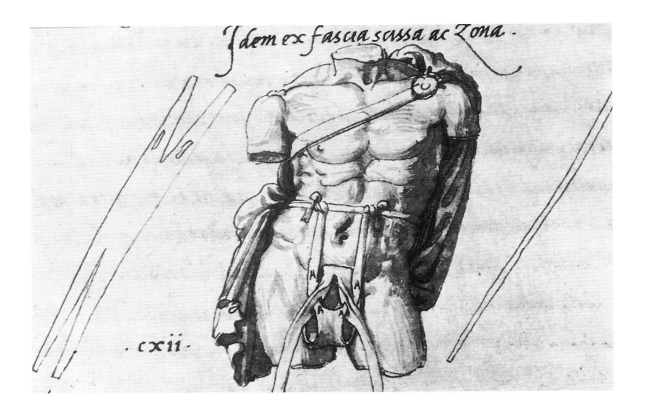

Above: *Guido Guidi, Latin translation of Hippocrates. Various types of truss are illustrated in a drawing attributed to Primaticcio.* Right: *from the same work, a dramatized drawing attributed to Francesco Rossi showing the treatment of a shoulder lesion. National Library, Paris, France.*

succumbed like so many others before him to the influence of the Church and the ideas of his time. In particular, he had a high regard for relics; yet, on the other hand, in some of his books he did not hesitate to denounce the use of sham invalids and other deceits in demonstrations of healing powers.

Ambroise Paré gave little recognition to the ancient masters, and was equally neglectful of his contemporaries, but this did not prevent him from borrowing some techniques, such as the treatment of hernias without castration, which he owed to Pierre Franco (1506–1579?). Franco, a Huguenot from Provence who spent much of his life in Switzerland because of his religious views, left behind a number of original works. While the name of Ambroise Paré is associated with the establishment of surgery in France, his colleagues from previous centuries should not be forgotten. In actual fact, Paré owed his fame to the moral principles which guided his long career and to his prolific writings which encompass the extent of surgical knowledge in his century. He wrote in French, and his books were widely read. Despite being famous in France, his reputation did not spread abroad. In Italy there were practitioners of equal worth, such as Guido Guidi (1509–1569). Germany boasted Fabricius Hildanus (Wilhelm Fabry of Hilden) (1560–1634), Switzerland Felix Würtz (1518–1574) and Conrad Gessner (1516–1565), Britain William Clowes (1544–1604) and Peter Lowe (1550–1610), to name but a few.

Another Italian, Gaspare Tagliacozzi (1545–1599), made himself famous by introducing a new procedure for surgically repairing amputated noses which involved taking a pediculate piece of skin from the arm, a technique already being used in India. In Italy, such mutilations were due to war wounds, duels, and perhaps also to syphilis and tuberculosis luposa.

However, neither the doctors nor the surgeons were able to use their knowledge of anatomy. Intervention was impossible in the case of the deep viscera because of the risk of infection, and the doctors remained ignorant of the funtioning of the organs they had discovered. Some of them did not understand the interest being shown in the dissection of human corpses.

Despite everything, the discovery of descriptive anatomy marked an indispensable and irreversible stage in the evolution of medical science. From this point on, the study of the human body would never cease. More knowledge was gained by each successive generation, not only by scholars but also by the many artists who were involved in studying man and his physical representation, and of whom the sixteenth century could be justly proud.

At the end of the fifteenth century, medicine was still associated with the branch of knowledge which today we call philosophy. It had not yet asserted its individuality: doctors owed their degrees more to philosophy, theology, mathematics, astronomy and optics than to medicine itself.

Some authors have escaped oblivion: Thomas Linacre (1460–1524) in England, Brissot in France, the renowned Pico della Mirandola in Italy, who never practised medicine, and his compatriot Nicolo Leoniceno (1428–1524), who openly condemned the favour which Arabic authors were enjoying and who gave the first clinical description of syphilis.

The generation that followed was dominated by three personalities, one French, one Italian and one German, who each left their mark on the century for different reasons.

*F*ernel was the son of an innkeeper in the north of France, and for a long time taught mathematics before becoming passionately interested in astronomy and geodesy. He constructed his own astrolabe, and then invented a way of measuring the terrestrial meridian. As far as he was concerned, all these disciplines came under the heading of philosophy. His father-in-law later made him study medicine so that he could earn enough to support his family. He subsequently published *Universa medicina*, which ran to many editions.

Very early on, Fernel was aware of the sterility of a scholasticism which produced excellent dialecticians but did not contribute to the development of knowledge. From the start, he gave priority to the observation of phenomena, followed by deduction. Like Aristotle, he considered the senses to be of great impor-

A renaissance in all but medicine

II.

JEAN FERNEL (1497–1558)

tance, and he borrowed from him the term "physiology" to designate the larger part of his *Medicina*. He proceeded by stages, starting with physiology and progressing to therapeutics. He expanded Hippocrates' medical teachings and, in attempting to classify diseases, made progress in nosology.

This work might have led to revolutionary progress in medicine, but for the fact that Fernel was unable for intellectual, and probably political, reasons to free himself from tradition. He stood by the sometimes confused theories of Galen, and considered indisputable the idea of the four humours of the body and the four elements with their characteristics. His forebears of the School of Alexandria would have called him a "humourist" or "pneumatist", because he believed in vital spirits that enabled the organs to function. In addition, Fernel did not manage to discern the specific nature of medicine, which for him was always a subsidiary branch of philosophy. The mediaeval primacy of discourse over fact continued.

A hospital scene from a bas-relief in enamelled terracotta. First half of the sixteenth century. Uffizi Gallery, Florence, Italy.

Allegory with pilgrims on the way to Santiago de Compostella. Saint John the Baptist and Saint Rock are here seen as anonymous pilgrims asking for help from the Church. Giovanni della Robbia, enamelled terracotta, first half of the sixteenth century. Ceppo Hospital, Pistoia, Italy.

THE DOCTOR IS EXPECTED TO KNOW EVERYTHING

"As medicine discusses and explains the admirable structure or the fabric and nature of man, in the same way it inquires into and recognizes the birth and failure of all things, the properties and the virtues of animals and plants;... it considers all things that emerge from the open entrails of the earth, from the rotation of the skies and the stars, and the influences which arise from them and govern the world below."

"No beginner should try his hand at medicine who has not already been well versed in these disciplines and who has not been completely steeped in them (mathematics, dialectics and grammar)..."

"It is appropriate to call it the universal art."

Fernel, "Physiologia"

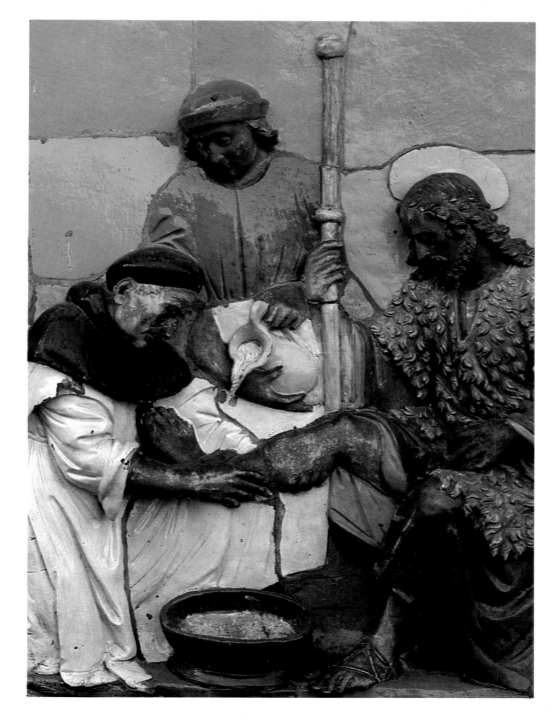

FRACASTORIUS
(1483–1553)

*L*ike Fernel, the Verona professor Girolamo Fracastoro, known as Fracastorius, had more than one string to his bow. He was an astronomer, and a mathematician, and was interested equally in geography, music, poetry and etymology, as well as in clinical practice.

A poem which he published in 1530, *Syphilis, sive de morbo gallico*, was a great success. This long mythological narrative, written in Latin verse in the manner of Ovid, describes a shepherd, Syphilis, who was punished by Apollo. The god inflicted on him the suffering and hideous wounds of this "French disease" which was then raging throughout Europe, and which we still call "syphilis" more than four and a half centuries later, a term which soon replaced the scholarly name proposed by Leoniceno, "*lues gallica*". The clinical description which Fracastorius gave proves that the disease was much more serious and had a much more rapid course than is the case in Europe today.

Fracastorius' other work, *De contagione et contagionis morbis*, went almost unnoticed at the time of its publication in 1546. In the sixteenth century, doctors thought that epidemics were the result of unwholesome air exerting an influence upon the organism, this being the origin of the Italian term *influenza* which is still used

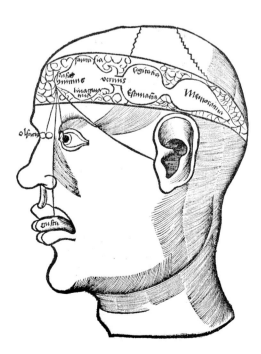

today to designate acute viral infections of the respiratory tract. Hippocrates' ideas concerning air therefore still persisted. Basing his analysis on several diseases, Fracastorius distinguished between two modes of transmission of the infection: direct contagion by which one individual catches phthisis (consumption) or leprosy from another, and indirect contagion due to germs, "seminaria", which are transported through the air, on clothes, everyday objects, etc. This was the case with the plague which repeatedly manifested itself in Europe, and with typhus, which was carried by the French armies to Italy. He therefore dissociates two different types of contagion relating to epidemic diseases, a distinction which is still made today. However, he was still unable to provide experimental proof, and thus it is difficult to think of him as the founder of modern bacteriology. Nor was he able to draw any conclusions from this with regard to prophylaxis or therapy. He nevertheless contributed to spreading doubt among scholars, and prompted the administrative authorities to establish systems of quarantine. The debate between contagionists and anti-contagionists was to last until the end of the nineteenth century and, on this account alone, Fracastorius certainly left his mark.

A village surgeon operates on an abscess behind the ear. He keeps his surgical instruments in a sack hanging from his belt. This is a far cry from the beautiful anatomical models of Vesalius or Estienne. Lucas of Leyden (1489–1533). Petit Palais Museum, Paris, France.

FAMOSO·DOCTOR PARESELSVS

PARACELSUS
(1493–1541)

A contemporary of Fernel and Fracastorius, Paracelsus, whose real name was Theophrastus Bombastus von Hohenheim, was a restless character who led a picaresque life. He was born in Switzerland and studied for a time at Ferrara under Leoniceno, who warned him against the teaching of the Ancients, and in particular that of Pliny. Paracelsus demonstrated that he had not forgotten this lesson when he burnt the works of Galen in public. He became a professor at Basle, a doctor to Tyrolean miners and a military surgeon, travelling throughout Europe. He wrote medical treatises in German which were full of aggressive attacks on his opponents. He drank, fought duels, and was probably assassinated in Austria. This colourful character took the name of Paracelsus, and as such we know him today.

His anti-conformist views won him the sympathies of some and the animosity of others, but he was never treated with indifference. Many studies have since been made of him. His work is both significant and varied, and sometimes contradictory. Generally speaking, he rejected Aristotle and Galen and even made this the principal theme of his teaching.

An apothecary's shop in the sixteenth century. The jars of medicines are labelled with symbols rather than with names spelt out in full, so that illiterate assistants could find the right one. Woodcut. Library of the Faculty of Medicine, Paris, France.

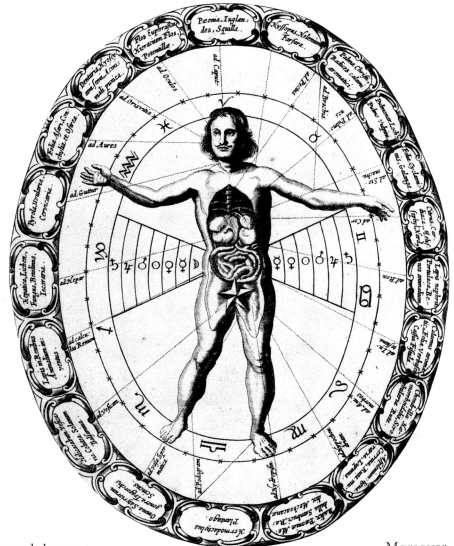

Medicine in the Renaissance continued and complemented that of the Middle Ages. On this man-zodiac by Athanasi Kizcheri, engraved about 1600, each internal organ corresponds to an astrological sign, a symbol or a medicinal substance. National Library, Paris, France.

More precisely, he improved the treatment of gunshot wounds, developing emollient dressings which were not painful. He used the experience he gained in the mines to introduce minerals into the pharmacopoeia, and he recommended the use of metals and metalloids for treating many clinical conditions. In particular, he strongly recommended the use of salts of antimony, and this started a debate which lasted for a century at the Paris Faculty between the "spagyrics" or "iatrochemists" and the conservatives. He also encouraged the study of anatomy by carrying out experiments on animals.

His name would have had a place in history equal to that of the father of pharmaceutical chemistry had he not mingled mediaeval ideas with his own original and innovative views. Paracelsus held that the human organism represented an inferior reflection of the macrocosm, with each internal organ being reciprocally associated with a star or planet: the heart with the sun, the liver with Jupiter, and so on. Metals were a reflection of the planets, and so his chemistry did nothing more than perpetuate mediaeval alchemy and astrology.

Some medicines in tablet form from a water-colour plate in a sixteenth-century medical treatise. Marciana Library, Venice, Italy.

Moreover, Paracelsus was convinced of the coherence of the universe and saw its "signatures" in everything about him, imagining that yellow flowers were suitable for treating jaundice, red earth for treating haemorrhage, and so on. While he did not believe in the *pneuma* of the Ancients, he nevertheless explained the activity of the organs as being due to a mysterious vital principle. He was a rationalist, but also an occultist, a member of the Rosicrucians, and the author of a treatise on nymphs and sylphs. He was a mystic and a poet, and sang the praises of nature, of which man is both master and slave, the riches of the earth and the harvests, the enigmas of the sky and the flight of birds.

He also left behind a strange collection of stimulating works which provoked numerous controversies. German-speaking countries acclaimed him, Italy ignored him, his books were not translated into French until the end of the sixteenth century and even then the French did not think much of him. As for the English, they coined the adjective *bombastic* to refer to a grandiloquent and vacuous personality such as that of Paracelsus.

THE "BREATH OF LIFE" THEORY IS CHALLENGED

As the sixteenth century progressed, doctors acquired a better knowledge of visceral anatomy. The exact role of the "breath of life", about which the Ancients had written and which nobody had ever seen, therefore became an increasingly important issue. What was the energy that controlled the regular beating of the heart and the pulse? Many Renaissance doctors were able to supply parts of the answer well in advance of Harvey and his discoveries.

Michael Servetus (1509–1553) was born in Aragon and studied and practised medicine in various French towns, hence he is also known by the Gallicized name Michel Servet. He was a competent doctor, and he affirmed that venous blood arrives in the lungs where it is purified before returning to the heart by ways which he did not dare to specify, doubtless for fear of contradicting Galen's theories. Already, in thirteenth-century Damascus, Ibn Nafiz had put forward this idea, which had since been forgotten. Unfortunately, Servetus also studied theology and questioned Catholic dogmas. As a result, he was forced to take refuge in Geneva, where he was finally burnt at the stake together with his books on medicine.

A pupil of and then successor to Vesalius, Realdo Colombo added to Servetus' theory by describing the route of venous blood towards the right ventricle of the heart, its passage to the lung via the pulmonary artery, and its return to the left ventricle via the pulmonary veins. He thus analysed the circulation of the blood in a precise manner. Galen still held sway, however, and this idea, despite its success in the scientific world, did not lead to unanimity when confronted with Galen's concept of small pores connecting the two ventricles.

Andrea Cesalpino (1519–1603), a pupil of Colombo, continued his master's work and coined the term "circulation". He thought that this perpetual motion was accomplished during sleep, but he did not establish the connection between the perception of the pulse and the flow of blood through the lungs.

At the turn of the sixteenth century, another Italian, Santorio Santorio (1561–1636), a pupil and friend of Galileo, invented a machine for taking the pulse and assessing the variations in it with "mathematical certainty". Santorio also contemplated measuring the temperature of the body, and he made a balance with which to weigh a person over several consecutive days, enabling food consumption to be measured, and also weight losses as a result of sweating and excretion.

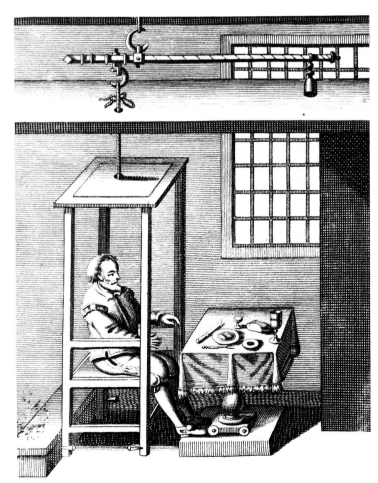

Santorio (1561–1636), a Venetian doctor, one of the founders of experimental physiology, on a balance he invented, sitting in front of his food for the day. De statica medicina, 1612. The engraving is taken from an English edition by John Quincy, 1722. Library of the National Natural History Museum, Paris, France.

THOSE WHO ADMINISTERED TO THE SICK

*W*hile medicine was making progress, therapeutics was hardly evolving at all, although plants brought back from the New World had enriched the botanic gardens of the medical faculties. Tincture of guaiacum was used to treat syphilis, as were mercury salts, whose deleterious effects on the buccal mucosa were soon noticed. Doubtless under the influence of the School of Padua, near to which were the thermal springs of Abano, balneotherapy became very fashionable. Montaigne, for example, frequently stayed at Bagno di Lucca in Italy, hoping thereby to cure his kidney stones. The usual diseases were rife, with epidemics break-

ing out from time to time. In towns, temporary establishments were gradually being equipped to provide accommodation during periods of contagion. Over time, urban communities took the place of the Church in administering the hospitals because of the financial difficulties encountered by the latter. The progressive secularization of such institutions, at least from the point of view of administration, took place in both Catholic and Protestant countries.

Leprosy had already begun to decline during the previous century, and now its disappearance was confirmed. The leper houses no longer had a purpose and so

Lucas von Valckenborch (1535–1597),
Emperor Rudolf II taking the waters.
*Under the influence of the School of Padua,
balneotherapy, already an ancient practice,
developed apace throughout sixteenth-
century Europe. Art History Museum,
Bern, Switzerland.*

his magnificent engraving of 1514,
Melancolia I.

Even if they did not belong to the
nobility and were not men of power,
doctors earned a good living and belonged to the well-to-do middle classes.
Rembrandt, in his two *Anatomy lessons,*
painted doctors in rich clothing. They
received money from their well-off patients, but cared for the poor without any
payment. Some, like Rabelais, belonged
to the retinue of important personages.
Others were paid in kind by village
communities for the care they gave to the
plague-stricken, or which they gave in
hospitals and prisons, or for the control
they exercised over the pharmacies. Doctors also enjoyed tax benefits in most of
the countries of Europe.

Naturally, levels of education and wealth
varied depending on their qualifications
and also on the areas where they practised, from capital cities to the countryside. The head of a faculty, who was held
in high regard by his pupils, earned
considerably more than a doctor – even

Pontormo (1494–1556), Scene
from hospital life, *1514.*
Academy Museum, Florence, Italy.

their buildings were turned over to hospital use. As before, the hospitals or
hospices were used more commonly to
house the poor and infirm than as places
for the care of the sick. Saint Bartholomew's
Hospital was established in London in
1123, but it was not until the Reformation
that it was endowed by Henry VIII and
assumed the role of healing the sick.
Special rooms were soon set aside for the
insane – the Swiss doctor Felix Platter
(1536–1614) reserved a special section for
disorders of the mind in his classification
of diseases. Historians referred to the
sixteenth century as the "century of melancholy", a theme adopted by Dürer in

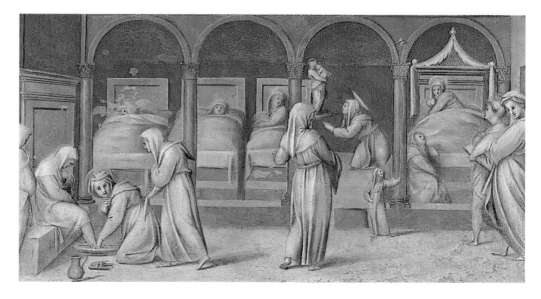

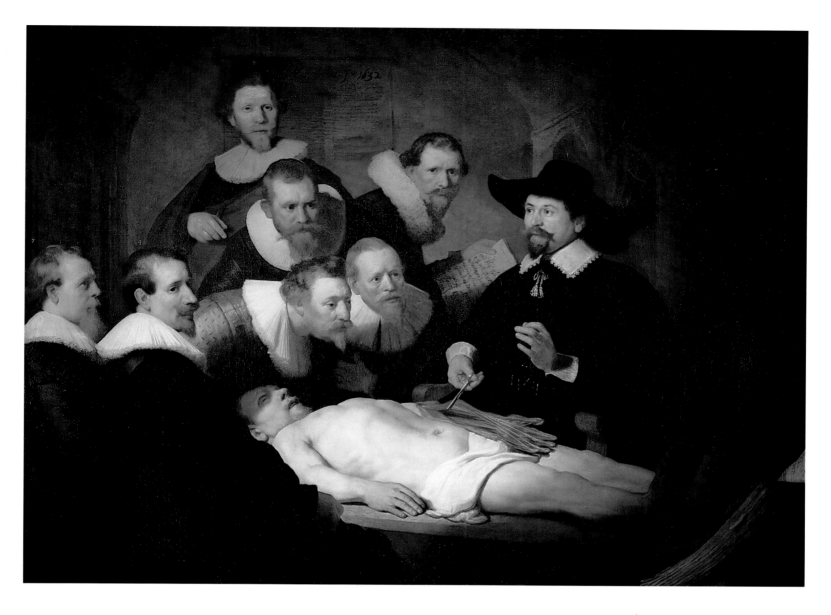

The sixteenth and the seventeenth centuries were both very important in the history of anatomy. Rembrandt van Rijn is the only one to paint the subject several times. Here, his Dr Nicolaes Tulp's anatomy lesson, *1632. Mauritshuis, The Hague, the Netherlands.*

a fully qualified one – practising in a small town. Doctors therefore felt the need to band together in "colleges" to guarantee the stability of their profession. These brotherhoods flourished everywhere, in the city states of Italy, in the principalities of Germany, in the French or Spanish provinces, and in London where the *Royal College of Physicians* was founded. Each community jealously guarded its own specific character. Intellectual conservatism became allied to social conservatism, while the distance separating doctors from surgeons grew. Even as members of the medical profession, the latter earned little, did not speak Latin and carried out manual work in contrast to the doctors, who were highly educated, fairly rich and had smooth tongues. This distinction between the two types of practice was to persist for two centuries. But whether

This famous engraving by Albrecht Dürer, Melancolia I, *1514, portrays madness born of an excess of reason and of the anxiety engendered by the progress in anatomy and surgery, among other fields, during a sixteenth-century split between the risks of discovery and the temptation of reassuring conservatism. Petit Palais Museum, Paris, France.*

they were titled practitioners or simple craftsmen, members of both these branches of the medical profession were still few and far between, and the wounded and sick were often cared for by others. Monks and nuns distributed remedies to the faithful, lords of the manor and their wives cared for the people of their estates, and their memorials bear witness to their charity, which was often tinged with paternalism. In the villages, bone-setters, truss-makers and quacks practised alongside women illegally established as midwives. The term "charlatan" was coined: it is derived from the Italian verb *ciarlare*, which means to "cry" and refers to those who sold remedies called *Orvietans* (quack medicines) or *Venice treacle* – also of Italian origin – from platforms set up at fairs or in marketplaces, attracting their clients by loud cries.

Treatment for an eye disease: strands of wool soaked in healing water are passed using a seton through the eyelids.
Engraving from Augendienst *by Georg Bartisch von Königsbrück, Dresden, 1568. Library of the Faculty of Medicine, Paris, France.*

VERNACULAR LANGUAGES AND ERUDITE MEDICINE

*R*enaissance society is striking because of the contrast between its thirst for knowledge, which was experienced by all classes, and the narrow-mindedness shown by the academies, colleges, universities and faculties, which clung to an identity that was based on hierarchy, degrees and the Latin language.

In France, the politicians soon took up a stance against the isolationism of the scientific world by creating a Royal College and naming the professors who were in charge of teaching, to the great displeasure of the Sorbonne. It recommended and sometimes enforced the use of the French language, which could be understood by all.

In Italy, doctors set the example by publishing books in the Tuscan dialect which prevailed over the Venetian spoken in Padua. Fabricius Hildanus and Paracelsus in Germany used High German, while in England John Caius (physician and second founder of Gonville and Caius College, Cambridge, 1510–1573) used English rather than French, which had been fashionable a century earlier, or Latin, the language spoken at university. Another Frenchman, Laurent Joubert (1529–1583), the Chancellor of Montpellier, specialized in the study of folklore and denounced "common fallacies". The phenomenon appears to be connected to the development of printing and to the efforts of the promoters of this new industry to enlarge their clientele.

While this popularization was beneficial to the people, it provoked the acrimony of the universities which opposed the diffusion of knowledge in the vernacular languages. Their anger showed itself especially towards the surgeons who

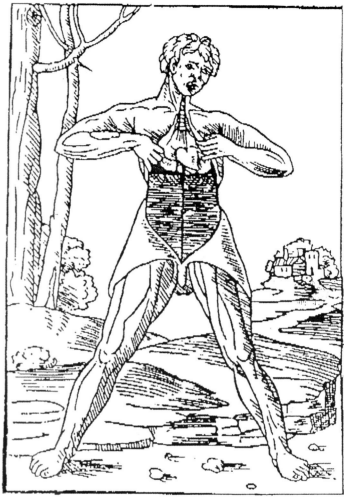

did not know Latin and claimed to be useful to the wounded and to soldiers on campaigns by speaking the language of their patients.

The clergy were not long in joining in this linguistic dispute. The Protestants preached and wrote in the local language, following Luther's example. The Catholics clung to Latin, fearing bad translations of their texts which could give rise to heresies.

At the end of the sixteenth century, the situation regarding medical books varied from country to country. Treatises on food hygiene and healthy living were common in all languages. By contrast, English and German doctors remained faithful to Latin (the latter until the twentieth century), while in France, French was the main language of medical treatises.

Left: an arrowhead is extracted on the field of battle, from one of many engravings illustrating scenes of military surgery. Hans von Gersdorff, *Der Wundartzney, Strasbourg, 1540. Library of the Old Faculty of Medicine, Paris, France.*
Right: an anatomical plate by Mondino de Luzzi, Paris, 1532, Estienne and Vesalius were to do better! Library of the Old Faculty of Medicine, Paris, France.

SOME "COMMON FALLACIES" ACCORDING TO JOUBERT

Port-wine stains:

"Sometimes babies, boys as well as girls, are born with red marks on their faces, necks, shoulders or other parts of the body. It is said that this is because they were conceived while their mother had her period... But I believe that it is impossible that a woman should conceive during her menstrual flow."

Conception − contraception:

"Against those who are always making love in order to have children, and those who do so less often in order to have fewer: the vulgar ignoramus deludes himself in both cases, acting totally contrary to his intentions."

THE DECLINE OF
ITALIAN AUTHORITY

In France, at the start of the sixteenth century, books, which were mainly printed in Lyons, thrived, thanks to the Italian wars and the fashion for all things Italian which spread throughout Europe, from Poland to Flanders. However, the Lyonese influence was not to last. In the seventeenth century, the main printing works specializing in medicine were located in Paris.

The development of trade links with America promoted the growth of ports and money markets on the Atlantic coast to the detriment of northern Italy. Padua and Bologna took a back seat while Paris, Nuremberg, Cambridge, Salamanca and Coimbra flourished. Medicine, after being centred for so long around the Mediterranean, moved north. European medicine was becoming standardized, as witnessed by Felix Platter, a German-speaking Swiss

who left accounts of his visits to many of Europe's medical faculties.

Like other disciplines, medicine benefited in part from the complete revision of traditional ideas and from the revival which resulted. It gradually freed itself from the yoke of philosophy, whose artificial means of expression had held it back for many years. It resorted increasingly to the factual with its emphasis on anatomy and observation. However, the impression left by the past lived on: if the former idols had been shaken, they had not been toppled. Vesalius did not contradict Galen. Paracelsus, who was opposed to him, fell into esotericism. The Renaissance continued to bear witness to the profound duality of reformism and traditionalism. It was not until the following century that rationality based on observation and verification finally saw the light.

These two plates by Antononio Salamanca, taken from Anatomia del corpo humano, *are écorchés, a common form of illustration in anatomical treatises of the sixteenth century. Library of the Faculty of Medicine, Paris, France.*

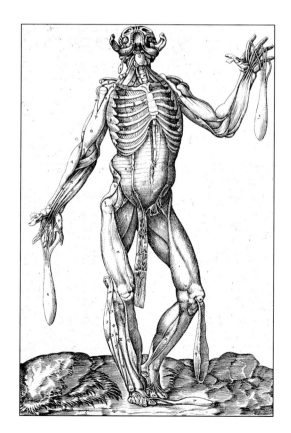 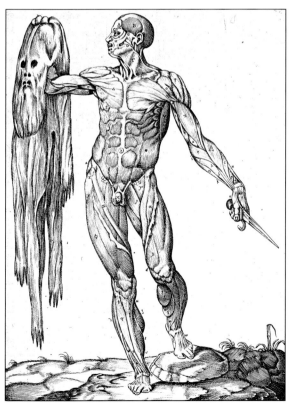

ANATOMY IN THE RENAISSANCE
1450 – 1590

POLITICS AND CULTURE	DATE	DATE	MEDICINE
First printed book attributed to Gutenberg, using lead characters	*1450–1455*		
		1477	First medical books printed in German
Marsilio Ficino founds an academy in Florence	*1480*		
		1490	Theatre of anatomy at Padua Epidemic of sweating sickness in northern Europe Syphilis in Europe
Christopher Columbus in Haiti Granada is taken by the Catholic kings and end of the *Reconquista*	*1492*		
Savonarola burnt in Florence	*1498*		
Michelangelo paints Sistine Chapel	*1508–1512*		
Luther publishes his 95 theses	*1517*		
		1518	College of Physicians founded in London Van Hutten treats the pox with guaiacum
Charles V, Emperor and King of Spain	*1519*		
		1526	Paracelsus at Basle
		1530	Fracastorius names syphilis
Machiavelli's *The Prince*	*1532*		
		1536	Cardano describes typhus
		1537	Rabelais becomes a doctor in Lyons
Foundation of the Society of Jesus	*1539*		
		1543	Vesalius, *Anatomy*
Council of Trent	*1545–1563*	*1545*	First book by Ambroise Paré Charles Estienne, *L'anatomie*
Death of François I and Henry VIII	*1547*		
		1497–1558	Jean Fernel
Abdication of Emperor Charles V	*1556*	*1556*	Franco, *Surgery*
		1558	Colombo, *Anatomy*
		1561	Fallopio, *Anatomical observations*
First of the wars of religion in France	*1562*		
		1568	Ambroise Paré, *Traité de la peste*
Battle of Lepanto	*1571*		
St Bartholomew's Day Massacre	*1572*		
		1573	Book by Varolio on the nerves
Montaigne, *Essais*	*1580*		
		1583	Cesalpino, *Medicinal plants*
		1590	Death of Ambroise Paré
Death of Philip II of Spain Edict of Nantes	*1598*		

chapter VIII

The seventeenth century and the Age of Reason

If, in the eyes of the modern observer, the sixteenth century was a time of religious unrest, the seventeenth century was by contrast relatively stable. Various forms of Protestantism were becoming established in a number of European states, while the Catholicism of the Counter-Reformation spread widely throughout Poland and the New World. Absolute monarchies were flourishing alongside the semi-democracies of the Swiss cantons, the United Provinces of the Netherlands, and some republics of the Italian peninsula.

Disputes of a metaphysical nature were yielding to reasoned argument and to a view of the world that was increasingly based on materialism. Even if the universe was still being regarded as the result of divine creation, it now appeared to be a coherent whole which lent itself to methodical study using the new instruments of observation. From now on, people would believe in "reason", and only that which could be verified, analysed or felt was held to be rational. Thus the intellectuals of the seventeenth century rapidly succumbed to an obsession for "reasoning", which was certainly fascinating, but often abstract and artificial, after the manner of mediaeval scholasticism.

Some brilliant men who participated in both these trends left their mark on the century. Francis Bacon (1561–1626) can rightly be considered the father of experimentation and observation. Isaac Newton (1642–1727) built on the discoveries of Galileo, deduced from Kepler's heliocentrism the laws of universal gravitation and perfected the mathematics associated with it. However, he venerated the alchemy of the past and doubted the

The fundamental principles of modern medicine

I.

The contradictions of a hesitant seventeenth century in which ancient practices coexisted with the modern.
Left: *a doctor inspects a patient's urine, a practice that was centuries old, from a painting by Gérard Dou (1613–1675).*
Right: *a transfusion from arm to arm such as would have been carried out three centuries later, engraving by G.A. Mercklin, Nuremberg, 1679. Louvre Museum and Library of the Old Faculty of Medicine, Paris, France.*

doctrine of reliance on the senses expounded by his friend Locke (1632–1704). Leibnitz (1646–1716), who also developed infinitesimal and differential calculus quite independently of Newton, nonetheless adopted an optimistic finalism in which the human being is made up of minute active and thinking "monads". Descartes (1596–1650) thought of the human organism as a perfect machine, but he imagined that its functioning was due to mysterious animal spirits. One cannot help but observe that this work, which bears witness to bright, well-organized and incisive intellects, reflected a new embodiment of the ancient doctrines of the *pneuma* and of vital air.

Although the thinkers of this brilliant century were still feeling their way and sometimes displayed inconsistencies, they did establish the fundamental principles of future science and medicine.

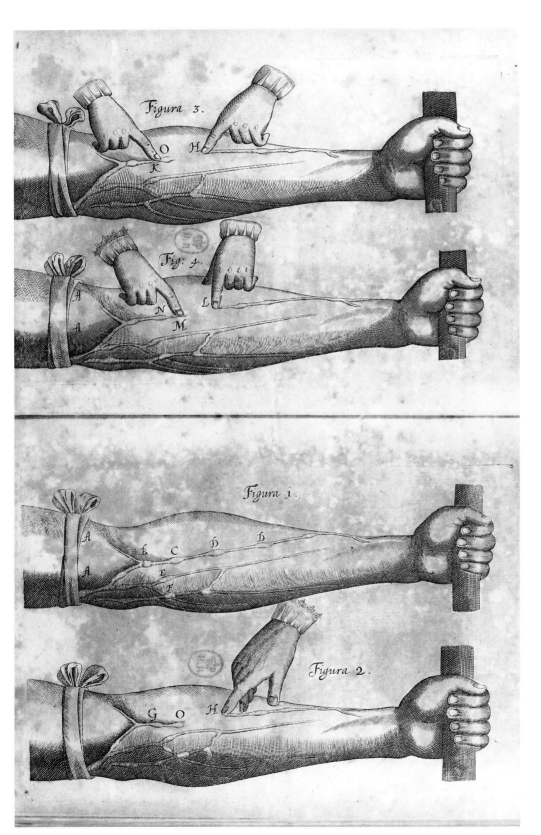

The Englishman William Harvey (1578– 1657), above, *from the portrait by Rolls Park (1627), based his theory of the circulation of the blood on a series of simple and irrefutable experiments in which he studied venous blood flow using a tourniquet and digital compression, as shown,* left, *in the plates from his most famous book,* Exercitatio anatomica de motu cordis, *which was published in 1648. National Portrait Gallery, London, England and National Library, Paris, France.*

ARISTOTLE'S PRINCIPLES AS REFORMULATED BY HARVEY:

"One should believe in reason as far as one's proofs agree with the facts perceived by the senses; but when the facts appear to be satisfactorily proven by them, one should accord more credence to them than to reason."

HARVEY AND THE DISPUTE ON THE CIRCULATION

William Harvey (1578–1657) published his *Exercitatio anatomica de motu cordis et sanguinis in animalibus* in 1628 and thus made known the greatest discovery of the century – a discovery which was to upset traditional ideas about the body, namely the circulation of the blood. Harvey was born in Kent, studied at Canterbury and Cambridge, spent some time in Padua with Fabricius ab Aquapendente, was a professor in London, and ceased teaching when Cromwell seized power.

His work is a model of deductive reasoning carried out on the basis of personal observation. He probably ignored the works of his predecessors such as Ibn Nafiz or Michael Servetus, but was familiar with those of the Italian masters. He dissected corpses, experimented with bandaging limbs, and took cross-sections

William Harvey explains his theory of the circulation of the blood to King Charles I of England. *Robert Hannah (1812–1909), Royal College of Physicians, London, England.*

of blood vessels in live and dead animals, such as the snakes and fallow deer of the royal parks. In doing so he demonstrated that the "circulation", a term he borrowed from Realdo Colombo, could not be other than as he described it. Coming from the veins which criss-cross the organism, the blood accumulates in the right auricle, then in the right ventricle of the heart. From there it passes into the lungs via a large artery, and returns to the heart through the left auricle and left ventricle; from there it is propelled via the aorta throughout the body.

He thus contradicted many widely accepted ideas using arguments based on practical study. For example, he observed that the motor reservoir of the blood is not situated in the liver, but in the heart; that the arteries contain blood and not air;

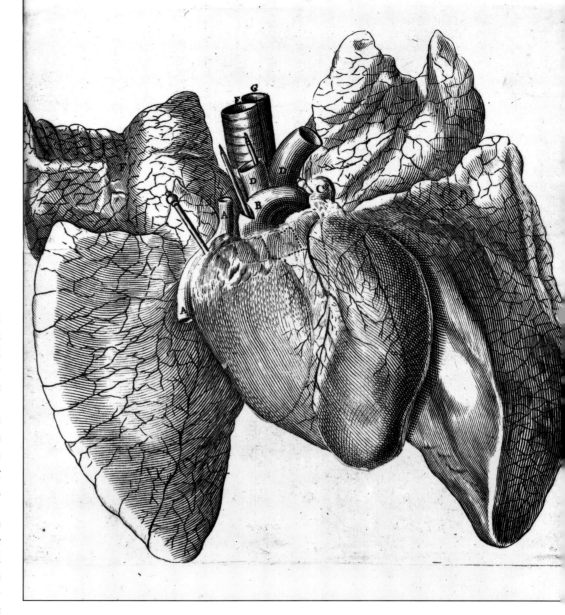

that the blood does not flow back and forth along the veins, but circulates through the arteries and veins in one direction; and that blood does not continuously replenish itself but represents a constant volume which is always on the move.

The coherence of his description is such that to deny a single part of it is to reject the whole. Thus, while Descartes remained faithful to the idea of vital air to explain the movement of the blood, Harvey rejected it totally.

He did not lack opponents amongst the traditionalists: Jean Riolan the Younger (1577–1657), who taught at the Royal College of Paris, rejected all Harvey's theories outright in a courteous correspondence with him which was soon made public. Also in Paris, Guy Patin (1601–1672) contradicted Harvey strongly, calling his supporters "*circulateurs*" and likening them to itinerant doctors who travelled from town to town selling dubious potions.

Throughout the whole of Europe, those for and against the circulation theory published lampoons and scurrilous pamphlets in which the unyielding traditionalists and those convinced of the value of experimentation and logic confronted one another. In England, James Primerose, an Irishman born in France who had studied under Riolan and was now teaching in Hull, refuted Harvey's theories, as did Hofmann in Germany. Others who defended him included Paul Schlegel and Conring, both Germans, Steensen the Dane, the Englishman Lower, the French-

The glaring errors in these sections of the heart (above, from Descartes' De homine figuris, Leyden, 1662) and the viscera (opposite, from the book by Aselli, the discoverer of chyliferous vessels, De lactibus sive lacteis venis, Milan 1627), do not detract from the quality of the drawings and the engraver's skill. Library of the Old Faculty of Medicine, Paris, France and University Library, Padua, Italy.

man Vieussens, and the Dutchmen Jan de Wale and De la Boë. The king of France was eventually to put an end to these arguments: in 1672, forty-four years after the publication of *De motu cordis*, Louis XIV ordered Dionis to teach the circulation of the blood at the Jardin du Roi (the forerunner of France's Museum of Natural History) to the great displeasure of the Faculty of Medicine. The opponents of the circulation theory had to concede defeat, and the king's decision represented the first intervention of political power in the life sciences.

Despite having done the groundwork, Harvey did not have at his disposal all the means of observation necessary for the description of the different stages of the

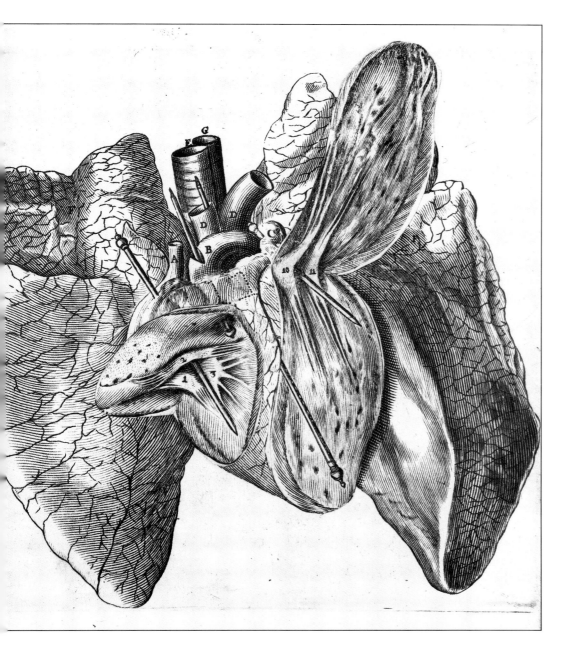

CIRCULATION, THE STEPS TO ITS DISCOVERY

13th *Ibn Nafiz – Damascus*
16th *Michael Servetus – Lyons*
      Realdo Colombo – Padua
      Cesalpino – Pisa
      The term "circulation".
1628 *William Harvey – London*
      The greater and the lesser
      circulation.
1649 *Henry Power – Cambridge*
      The capillaries between the
      arteries and the veins.
1651 *Jean Pecquet – Paris*
      The lymphatic circulation.
1661 *Marcello Malpighi – Bologna*
      The pulmonary capillaries.

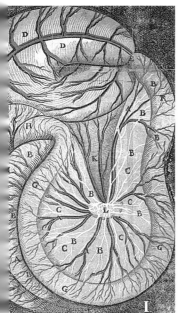

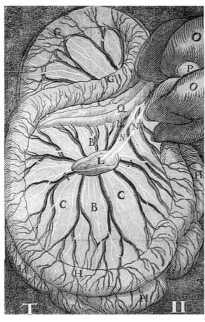

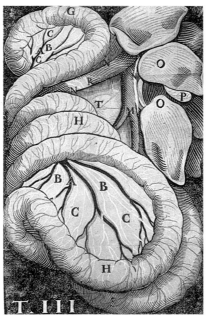

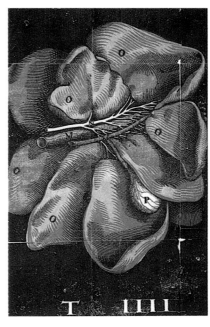

Different theoretical examples of blood transfusions. Above: using a dead dog, Amsterdam, 1672. *Opposite:* using a lamb, Leipzig, 1692. *Library of the Old Faculty of Medicine, Paris, France.*

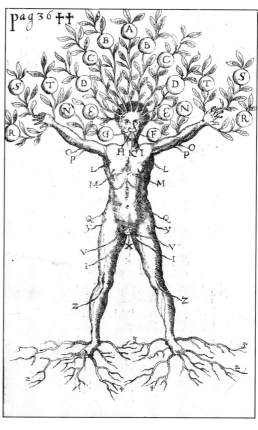

pag 36 ††

circulation of the blood, and these gaps were to be filled a few decades later. He also concerned himself with another of the body fluids, the lymph, without being able to discover its circulatory system.

In Pavia in 1622, Gasparo Aselli had already identified the lymphatic vessels of the mesentery during digestion, while a century earlier another Italian, Bartolomeo Eustachio, had described the thoracic duct. However, it was to be the Parisian Jean Pecquet (1622–1674) who discovered the lymphatic circulation by studying the role of the lymph glands, the termination of the "lacteal vessels" in the abdominal cistern which still bears his name, and finally, the discharge of this lymph into the subclavian venous circulation. This second circulatory system was to arouse as much controversy as the first before

Above right: this representation of the points where veins could be cut for blood-letting (which remained a basic form of treatment, unlike transfusion which was still at the experimental stage) was inspired by the traditional diagram based on plant life, the Tree of veins, which had been passed down from the Middle Ages. Odios, De arte medica. Ulm, 1642. Library of the Old Faculty of Medicine, Paris, France.

finally being accepted by European scholars.

Hippocrates' theory, which was based on the four humours, was thus being brought into question. The discovery of separate blood and lymph systems led to their dissociation: the white and black bile which emerged from the liver flowed into the intestine without exiting again, while the blood circulated in the arteries and veins, with which the lymph was connected. One could therefore no longer conceive of a "balance" between these four substances which had now been shown to exist, had been precisely identified, and yet were shown to be anatomically independent of one another. The very foundations of treatment, foundations that had inspired medical practice for centuries were now in doubt.

Antonie van Leeuwenhoek (1632–1723), the inventor of the microscope and father of modern microscopy. Frontispiece to Arcana naturae, *Leyden, 1722. Library of the National Veterinary School of Maisons-Alfort, France.*

FROM THE MICROSCOPE TO THE MYSTERIES OF GENERATION

*D*uring the sixteenth century, anatomists had made their observations with the naked eye, and their analyses had been limited accordingly. However, the seventeenth century brought the development of a new instrument: the microscope. Galileo had already been able to make a close examination of parts of insects using the lenses of his astronomical telescope. In Holland, opticians had made increasingly successful attempts at creating a microscope, but it was Antonie van Leeuwenhoek (1623–1723) who finally succeeded in building the instrument that revolutionized scientific observation as a whole, and medicine in particular. It was to undergo continuous refinement over the years, resulting in the tremendously powerful microscopes we know today. Scholars seized the opportunity it offered to launch themselves into the study of ever smaller living creatures, and of increasingly minute structures of the human organism.

Leeuwenhoek studied all the fluids that nature had to offer, and discovered in his own blood the tiny corpuscles we call red blood cells. The microscope revealed hair-thin anastomoses between the blood vessels, which he named "capillaries", whose existence Harvey had already surmised between the veins and the arteries

in the peripheral tissues, the mesentery, and the lungs in humans and other animals. With this discovery, all the elements of the circulation of the blood which Harvey had propounded were now in place. The microscope also enabled Marcello Malpighi (1628–1694) to make further progress in the study not of minute elements, but of the structure of living material. He confirmed Robert Hooke's observations on the composition of plants, and identified in the human viscera the juxtaposition of cells (a term he invented) which he compared to a honeycomb. Malpighi thereby inaugurated the histology of the kidneys, the skin, the liver and other organs.

The doctrines of Aristotle, which had been altered only slightly by Soranus of Ephesus in the second century, had settled the question of human procreation: that man's semen consists of tiny, already formed human beings, and that woman's uterus serves only as a nourishing environment in which they grow. Harvey examined embryos of different animal species at various stages of development and concluded that living beings are born from an egg, and that this principle applies equally to viviparous and oviparous creatures. However, his observations were inevitably limited, and at the

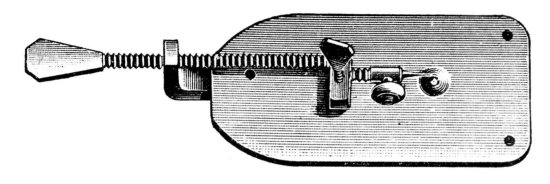

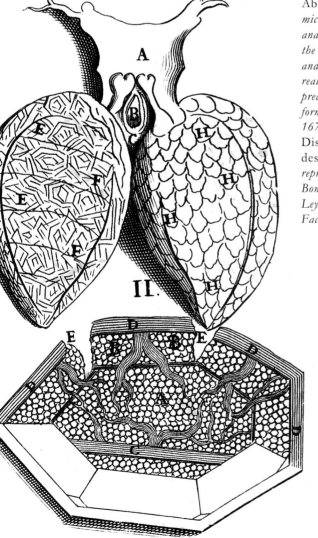

Above: *a model of a seventeenth-century microscope.* Left and below: *various anatomical representations bring together the improbable (the shape of the lungs and the crude view of the placenta), the realism of the pulmonary alveoli and the precise representation of the different forms of sperm drawn by Leeuwenhoek in 1678. The lungs are from Malpighi,* Discours anatomique de la structure des viscères, *Paris, 1683. The representation of the foetus is from Bonaciolus,* De conformatione foetus, *Leyden, 1641. Library of the Old Faculty of Medicine, Paris, France.*

end of his life he expressed regret that he had not been able to penetrate the mystery of reproduction.

With the aid of a microscope, Leeuwenhoek was able to confirm the analysis made by one of his Dutch predecessors when he observed the presence of animalcules in human semen. The Dane Niels Steensen (1638–1686) or the Dutchman Reijnier de Graaf (1641–1673) – it is not known who was the first – identified a kind of vesicle on the "female testicle" or ovary. Their contemporaries considered this follicle, the Graafian follicle to be like a tiny egg. If so, surely the complete miniature being which would grow into a baby was located in the follicle, but, if this was so, was the sperm's only function to give it the "breath of life"?

Steensen played an active part in the controversy. He was both a first-rate anatomist who had contradicted Descartes' ideas on the structure of the brain, and a great theologian who had been converted from Lutherism to Catholicism. One of his areas of specialization was the study of secretory glands. However, the debate on the functioning of the ovary was to continue for almost another two centuries.

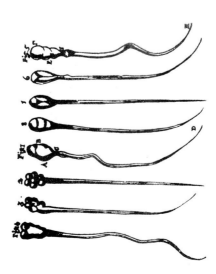

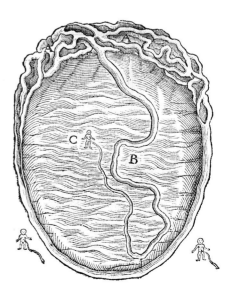

The patient, *Wolfgang Heimbach (seventeenth century), Gallery of Fine Art, Hamburg, Germany.*

TOWARDS THE STUDY OF LESIONS

Giovanni Borelli (1608–1679) continued the studies made by Santorio who, at the end of the preceding century, observed the functioning of the human machine by measuring a person's weight at different times of the day. He represented the muscles as levers, as Leonardo da Vinci had done, and looked for other numerical data by introducing a thermometer into the visceral cavity of animals.

Harvey's successors experimented by using various techniques on the blood vessels. They carried out therapeutic intravenous injections, and blood transfusions from animal to animal (research by Richard Lower in England), and from animal to man (research by J.B. Denis in France). These attempts resulted in setbacks because of inadequately developed instruments.

In the fields of physiology and pathological anatomy one great name came to the fore, that of Richard Lower (1631–1691). He continued Harvey's work, showing that venous blood becomes red when it mixes with the air drawn into the lungs. He also demonstrated the existence of anastomoses between the two arterial systems of the heart, and furnished proof of the justification for and efficacy of blood-letting in cases of severe failure of the left ventricle. He observed the connection between pulmonary and cardiac disorders, as well as the possibility of restoring the vitality of the tissues by means of new vicarious arteries in cases where the main artery of a limb had been obstructed.

The name of Lower remains indisputably linked with the history of cardiovascular disease. Cardiology today is not only a major medical specialty, but is also the oldest, since it has its roots in the seventeenth century.

However, Lower was not alone. In a few decades, men such as Albertini followed by Lancisi, Malpighi and Baglivi in Italy, Vieussens in France (1641–1715), and Wepfer in Switzerland were to make considerable advances in medicine. They established correspondences between certain clinical manifestations and observations made during autopsies. They studied the repercussions between pulmonary and cardiac insufficiency; lesions of the heart valves; disorders of cardiac rhythm which may accelerate or slow down; the difference between aneurysms and cardiac dilatation; and cerebral haemorrhages which cause paralysis or sudden death.

Obstetrics, which had long been neglected, gradually began to develop, and surgeons and doctors were called to attend serious cases or to be present when distinguished ladies were giving birth. Louise Bourgeois (1564–1644) opened the first systematic training establishment for midwives in France. Following her example, François Mauriceau (1637–1704) instituted training for several students, and in England the Chamberlen family developed forceps which were placed around the head of the foetus to extract it if the delivery was proving diffult. This instrument, which was soon in common use, was to be improved by subsequent obstetricians and it led to a definite advance in obstetric techniques.

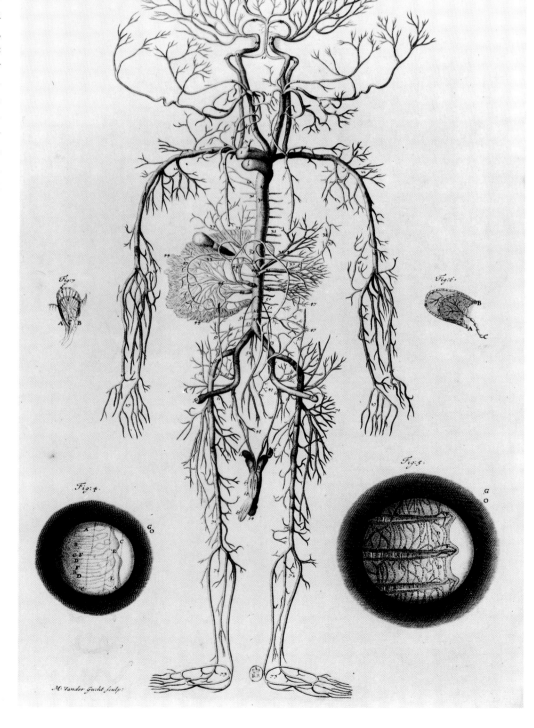

Diagram of the main arteries in man, after William Cowper, the English anatomist (1666–1709). Only one cartouche in four is clear. National Library, Paris, France.

New horizons were being opened up by the microscope and the autopsy, but this did not distract doctors from caring for the sick and from relieving suffering and disease. Like their illustrious predecessors, they remembered the necessity for observing their patients and the value of experience gained at the bedside. The origins of clinical practice as we know it today can be traced back to the seventeenth century, the term "clinical" being derived from the Greek word for the bed upon which the patient reclined.

Thomas Sydenham (1624–1689), who was educated at Oxford, Cambridge and Montpellier, and then taught in London, left behind a considerable body of medical writings. He wrote in Latin, and after his death his son translated his work into English, publishing it as *Doctor Sydenham's Practice of Physick* in 1695. It was to be used as teaching material for many years, and

A delivery in a rich Parisian family. The role of the midwife in the foreground is clearly shown. From an engraving by Abraham Bosse (1602–1676). National Library, Paris, France.

includes a precise and still relevant description not only of the symptoms of gout and kidney stones from which he suffered, but also of a large number of metabolic, infectious and nervous diseases. While his contemporaries and his students valued the accuracy of his analyses, his patients were grateful to him for being moderate in his prescriptions, since he preferred purgation and dietary measures to blood-letting.

Doctors from various different countries emulated him: especially Hermann Boerhaave (1668–1738), a Leyden doctor who treated many of the crowned heads of Europe and whose reputation extended as far as China. While keeping abreast of the innovations that arose from the development of techniques, he was guided by the ancient principles expounded by Hippocrates. He believed in the beneficial role of fever, and adopted the idea

Gabriel Metsu (1629–1667), Doctor
visiting a patient; *as was usual, the
doctor decides on his diagnosis by inspecting
the patient's urine. The Hermitage,
St Petersburg, Russia.*

that disorders in the functioning of organs,
whether qualitative or quantitative, were
characterized by a lack or an excess which
he termed "plethora". Also following the
example of Hippocrates, he cultivated the
literary form of the aphorism.

Sydenham and Boerhaave continued to
be influenced by the teaching of the
illustrious Greek master. They did not
renounce the notions of the temperaments, the changes in the humours, and
the influence of the air and climate on the
course of disease.

Finally, we should emphasize the influence of the Leyden school of medicine,
where Boerhaave succeeded Franciscus
de la Boë (1588–1672), whose teaching
spread throughout Europe, building the
foundations of modern medical practice.

WHAT DID THE PARIS DOCTORS READ?

*The inventories made of their libraries
after their deaths tell us much about
their medical knowledge.*
*Galen is quoted forty-five times in the
notarial archives which we studied,
Hippocrates one hundred and twenty-one
times, Dioscorides thirty times, Paul of
Aegina twenty-three times.*
*Works by Aëtius, Alexander of Tralles,
Oribasius, Pliny the Elder and Celsus are
also mentioned.*
*Arabic authors are represented: twenty-
seven doctors possessed a work by Ibn
Masawaih, and thirty-nine one by
Avicenna. Some authors from the
preceding century were familiar: Girolamo
Cardano is recorded fifty times, Fernel
forty, Vesalius fifteen. Contemporary
authors were much less frequently
consulted.*

*(From F. Lehous, Le cadre de vie des médecins
parisiens aux XVIᵉ et XVIIᵉ siècles.
Ed. Picard, Paris, 1976)*

CINCHONA IN THE TREATMENT OF FEVER

*I*f the circulation of the blood was the major discovery in the field of physiology, the use of cinchona bark was to be the principal innovation in therapeutics. This product, called cinchona by the Peruvian Indians who used it to treat fever, was brought to Europe by the Jesuits, who theoretically retained the monopoly of its supply. A far-sighted Englishman, Robert Talbor, was soon to use it to treat the King of France and members of the French court. In buying the remedy from him they immediately conferred respectability on the consumption of cinchona. Despite the opposition from the Paris Faculty, which persisted in denying its benefits, all of Europe was soon to be consuming it in increasing quantities.

Apothecaries prepared a solution using unspecified quantities of the raw material which was imported from America. For almost two centuries, until the extraction of quinine, apothecaries' shops sold potions in which the concentration of active substance was very variable. The result was malpractice, even fraud, and it was the patients who suffered. Cinchona was reputed to be excellent against "fevers". We use this term today to mean raised body temperature, but in the seventeenth century doctors still had no way of measuring this and the word was used to mean any general malaise accompanied by a feeling of excessive internal heat. The list of "fevers" was therefore large.

Since the time of Hippocrates, practitioners had described fevers in which paroxysmal attacks occurred at regular intervals. Depending on the number of days that separated these crises, they referred to fevers as double, tertian, quartan, mixed, and so on. It is almost certain now that some of these fevers were due to malaria, which is transmitted to man via certain kinds of mosquito. Of course, it is impossible to furnish parasitological or statistical proof of this, but it seems that malaria was widespread in seventeenth-century Europe, reaching as far as northern Scandinavia. The excellent anatomist Thomas Willis (1621–1675) describes the ravages it caused in England.

Many Italian doctors specialized in the study of this disease, the most famous being Giovanni Lancisi (1654–1720). He seems to have glimpsed the role that the mosquitoes played in spreading it, and adopted Hippocrates' argument that there was a connection between the development of fevers and the "bad air" emanating from marshy areas (hence the name, derived from the Italian *mala aria*). He also recommended that the marshes in the countryside around Rome should be drained.

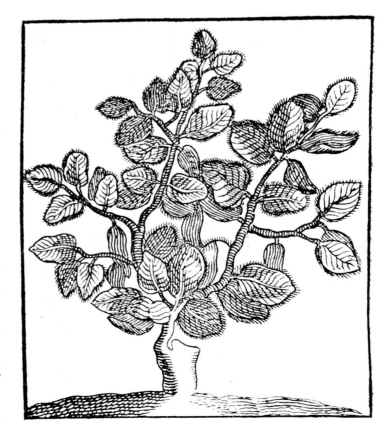

Cinchona became accepted as the universal remedy for fevers throughout the seventeenth century. Engraving by Lemery, seventeenth century. Library of Decorative Arts, Paris, France.

Franckfurter
Apotecker-Tap

A well-stocked pharmacy in Frankfurt-am-Main at the end of the seventeenth century. German engraving, Museum of Munich, Germany.

A *medicine still lacking in power*

II.

Despite its virtues, cinchona was ineffective against numerous fevers which were rife, often as epidemics or endemics. One such was smallpox, whose frequent and deadly outbreaks were almost a normal part of daily life.

In the first half of the seventeenth century, food shortages were common because of poor harvests and difficulties in transporting grain. Falls in production, high prices and famine caused malnutrition, dietary deficiencies and increases in infant mortality. To these trials were added the ordeals of war, immortalized by the French artist and engraver Jacques Callot. The Thirty Years' War caused suffering throughout Europe. Food shortages and the ravages of war combined to create conditions in which epidemics thrived. The risks of infection were increased still further by the growing numbers of vagrants and beggars on the roads, and by constant troop movements.

THE CONTINUANCE OF PLAGUES

The plague was rife throughout the century in all of Europe, bringing in its wake misery and terrifying mortality. The epidemics of 1660 in Milan and 1665 in London in particular left a lasting impression on people, whose accounts are scattered among the literature of the time. In order to combat the scourge, governments reinforced their border controls and quarantine regulations in ports.

In England, which was particularly badly affected by the great plagues of the seventeenth century, the parishes kept records of deaths, and these mortality lists were the first steps in demography and medical statistics, from which grew the modern science of epidemiology.

Large cities built institutions to provide temporary accommodation in which to isolate the sick during epidemics. The

David Ryckaert III (1612–1661), The alchemist (1634), or rather a doctor passionately interested in anatomy, in his study. The detail of the composition (hourglass and skulls) is reminiscent of the "vanitas" which were in vogue in the seventeenth century. History of Art Museum, Vienna, Austria.

Saint-Louis Hospital in Paris, built by Henry IV, is one example. In addition to the epidemics and civil wars in England and France, the Thirty Years' War, which bathed in blood the whole of Europe from Livonia to Catalonia, led to large numbers of hospitals being built in the first half of the century. The decades of conflict brought about so much misery that people's generosity was aroused. In France, Saint Vincent de Paul, a chaplain to galley slaves, set the example by founding the Sisters of Charity. Everywhere, secular authorities and religious congregations began to found institutions to provide charity and care for the sick.

Leprosy had disappeared, and with it the leper-houses that would have added to the hospital provision. Unfortunately, most of these establishments had been converted to other uses – in France, Louis XIV's minister Louvois handed a number of them over to the army.

It is interesting to note that the role of the hospital institution was becoming increasingly ambiguous. It was commonly held that only unfortunate people who could not be cared for at home resorted to hospitals. At this time, many suffered from the combined plight of destitution and disease. To such people were added beggars, cripples, the senile, the insane, the maimed, prostitutes and even delinquents. In France, Louis XIV therefore decided to establish a "general hospital" in all the large cities for the confinement of such unfortunates and other individuals who were unable to fend for themselves. The sick and the social outcasts were therefore gathered together in hospitals, and this gave rise to the misconception, which is still sometimes encountered today, that hospitals exist to serve a dual social and medical purpose.

Since they did not have to resolve this problem of public order, the French army and navy established the first permanent

The Jardin du Roi in Paris in 1623 (above). Many medicinal plants were grown there and were used to treat patients in the Hôtel-Dieu (right). Library of the Arsenal and Carnavalet Museum, Paris, France.

hospitals for their wounded and "fever" patients, an administrative nicety which was to last for three centuries.

Other infectious diseases such as typhus spread throughout the world, and in Europe the troop movements of the Thirty Years' War exacerbated the problem. Laryngeal and anginal forms of diphtheria were recorded for the first time (a Neapolitan doctor suggested tracheotomy to treat croup in the laryngeal form). A disease called *vomito negro* or yellow fever appeared in the West Indies and soon spread to Europe.

Baglivi established the efficacy of another plant from America, the root of the ipecacuanha shrub known as ipecac, in the treatment of diarrhoeal fevers. As with other roots, ipecac only had a symptomatic effect by decreasing the frequency of evacuations and did not act on the germs which were responsible for the disease.

Top left: *In his* Recueil des plus illustres proverbes *(1657), Jacques Lagniet (1620–1672) gives a blunt account of the foundation of the general hospital in Paris in 1656, and of the confining of the poor. National Library, Paris, France.* Bottom left: *the nuns of Port-Royal-des-Champs have no scruples about blood-letting. Attributed to Madeleine de Boulogne (1648–1710), Château de Versailles, France.*

La belle saignée, *water-colour engraving by Arnoult, about 1700. Decorative Arts Library, Paris, France.*

RUDIMENTARY
THERAPEUTICS

*U*nfortunately, in the seventeenth century, cinchona and ipecac were the only innovations in treatment. As for antimony, which was recommended by Paracelsus, the Paris Parliament passed a decree putting an end to its prohibition by the Faculty. The French displayed great wisdom in authorizing its use in certain doses for treating specific diseases. Medical practitioners also prescribed various other metals: mercury, which had already been used to treat syphilis; iron in cases of anaemia (from the Greek, meaning "lack of blood"); copper sulphate or zinc for skin disorders, and so on. In the use of iron we find again the ancient idea of similitudes: since rusty iron is red like blood, it should palliate anaemia.

Generally, there were no codes of practice governing the preparation of medicines, and no controls or regulations issued by any authority or royal power. Each apothecary made up his own mixtures according to the criteria he thought fit, or according to local tradition.

Doctors and herbalists alike sold "miraculous" potions at fairs. These methods brought medicinal treatment into disrepute and aroused both sarcasm and scepticism.

Patients therefore remained loyal to purgations, cupping, blood-letting, and dietary measures which could be as fanciful as they were contradictory. As for the rich, they went to take the waters in the spas of Europe.

THE ILLUSIONS OF IATROPHYSICS AND IATROCHEMISTRY

Materialist thinking, which was prevalent in the seventeenth century, brought back into favour the terms which had been borrowed from the ancient Schools of Alexandria. The iatrophysicists explained the functioning of the human body in terms of the laws of physics, and Descartes, despite the distinction he made between the mind and the soul, went along with such ideas, whose most ardent supporters were the Italians. They concerned themselves with making measurements of weight, temperature, muscular exertion and other phenomena.

Iatrochemistry was more popular in northern Europe, thanks to Jean Baptiste

Along with blood-letting, the enema was one of the most common treatments of the seventeenth century, and was often more dangerous than effective. Le clystère, engraving by Abraham Bosse (1602–1676), National Library, Paris, France.

van Helmont of Louvain (1577–1644). This extraordinary chemist discovered a number of elements, coined the term "gas", was opposed to the theory of the circulation of the blood despite believing in scientific observation, and likened the transformations that take place in an organism to chemical processes which were already known at the time such as calcining and boiling. For example, he asserted that digestion takes place with the help of six types of fermentation. If it is improper to consider him as the originator of medical chemistry, he nonetheless introduced into physiology terms which we still use today.

Nevertheless, van Helmont did not escape the influence of Paracelsus and followed him in believing that small living entities were in charge of all the bodily functions according to a precise hierarchy. This concept of the "archeus" (a term derived from an old mediaeval word) was to be moderately successful in learned circles for almost two centuries.

Some scholars such as Boerhaave tried to establish syntheses from these sometimes justified, sometimes artificial ideas. They tried to reconcile the chemists, who proposed alkaline and acid diseases, with the natural philosophers who opposed solid bodies and humours. Even Sydenham, despite his attachment to clinical practice, made concessions to imaginary theories.

This ferment of ideas increased the divergence of opinion. Traditionalists were unable over the space of a few decades to free themselves from the theories of Hippocrates, Galen and Avicenna on which medicine had been based since ancient times, and they endured with difficulty the agitation stirred up by innovators. The Paris Faculty of Medicine in particular displayed a very narrow form of conservatism and was opposed to such novelties as the idea of the circulation of the blood, and treatment with antimony and cinchona. It was supervised closely by the Church of the Counter-Reformation,

and was subject to the rituals of examinations and ceremonies which had remained unchanged for centuries. It hindered all forms of progress in technique and in the organization of medical discipline. Molière and Boileau found the Faculty a source of choice subjects when writing their satires.

Théophraste Renaudot (1585–1653) by contrast represented the opposition to the traditionalists. He was a great innovator who developed free consultations for

The medical professions in the seventeenth century were strictly hierarchical and organized into corporations. The engraver Larmessin chose to poke fun at them after the manner of Arcimboldo. The two surgeons (far left) carry the badges of their profession, top left: *the pharmacist carries jars and ointments; the doctor,* bottom left, *the highest in the hierarchy, has nothing to offer other than his bookish learning. Seventeenth-century engravings. National Library, Paris.*

BOSSUET THE IATROMECHANIC

In his encyclopaedic work for the education of the Grand Dauphin, son of Louis XIV, the bishop of Meaux wrote: "There is no type of machine that is not present in the human body. In order to suck a liquid, the lips serve as a pipe and the tongue as a piston. The trachea is attached to the lungs like a kind of smooth, specially shaped flute which, as it is opened by varying amounts, modifies the air and changes the sounds... The vessels have their valves or valvules which point in all directions; the bones and the muscles have their pulleys and their levers...
All these machines are simple; they are easy to operate and the structure is so delicate that all other machines are crude by comparison."

the poor, started a pawnshop modelled on Italian lines, an advertising service and a daily news sheet covering court and world events. By not behaving like a traditional doctor, he threatened to undermine society and as a result he died in poverty; his works did not survive him.

Surgeons, who exercised a manual and therefore less scholarly profession, were also subject to the pettinesses of the Faculty. Doctors in positions of power wasted no time in proclaiming them to be little more than barbers. The Paris Faculty was the victim of derisory conflicts and gradually brought discredit upon itself, while that of Montpellier at the very same time was looking favourably upon the new ideas which found a large audience among its members. However, medicine was changing in spite of conservative faculties. Since these possessed neither laboratories nor hospitals, the researchers, chemists, clinicians and natural philosophers communicated their scientific discoveries in the newly founded Academies, even though these were mainly

Théophraste Renaudot (1586–1653), a doctor, journalist, historiographer to the king and founder of a pawnbroker's shop, from an engraving by Michel Lasne, 1644. National Library, Paris, France.

literary establishments. The *Journal des savants* founded in 1665, published medical articles. The *Journal des nouvelles découvertes sur toutes les parties de la médecine* was started in 1679 by a surgeon, and therefore had no connection with the Paris Faculty of Medicine.

Medicine in Europe was evolving. Though medical practitioners continued to travel between European cities according to the ancient tradition, teachers now resided permanently in the main cities and remained attached to the schools in which they had been students. Steenson the Dane taught in Italy for a time and was thus an exception. National characteristics became more pronounced in the medical field at the expense of the Europeanization which had been prevalent in the Middle Ages.

At the same time, Italian and French medical sciences were spreading through northern Europe to England, Flanders and Germany. From this time on, discoveries were no longer the exclusive domain of the old Catholic world. It may be imagined that the ignominy suffered by Galileo and the supercilious mistrust shown by the Church towards the universities curbed initiative, and slowed the impetus of scientific discovery in Mediterranean Europe, even though Protestantism in the North was not always tolerant and open.

The doctors of the seventeenth century, though steeped in logic, materialism and reason, saw their analyses limited by the absence of adequate and sufficiently advanced instrumentation. They often resorted to intellectual suppositions which falsified the interpretation of properly observed facts. Thus we can explain the paradox presented by seventeenth-century medicine which, though founded on precision, research and realism, at the same time included theories that were purely speculative and arbitrary.

THE SEVENTEENTH CENTURY AND THE AGE OF REASON
1603 – 1699

POLITICS AND CULTURE	DATE	DATE	MEDICINE
Shakespeare, *Hamlet*	1600		
Death of Elizabeth I, Queen of England		1603	
Cervantes: *Don Quixote*	1605		
		1607	Jean Riolan, first physician to Maria of Medici: *L'anatomie*
		1609	Louise Boursier: *Observations sur la stérilité, accouchements et maladies des femmes*
Death of Henry IV, King of France	1610		
Galileo invents the telescope			
Dynasty of the Romanovs	1613		
The Thirty Years' War	1618–1648		
The *Mayflower* in Boston	1628	1628	Harvey: *Description of blood*
Death of Gustavus Adolphus of Sweden	1632		
Rembrandt: *Dr Tulp's anatomy lesson*			
Descartes: *Discours de la méthode*	1637		
The *Jardin du Roi* established in Paris	1640	1640	Cinchona is introduced into Europe
Execution of Charles I, King of England	1649		
		1651	Jean Pecquet: *Dissertation anatomique sur la circulation du sang*
		1655	Richard Lower: *Treatise on the heart*
		1662	General hospitals founded in France
		1665	Malpighi discovers red blood cells The Great Plague of London
		1666	Foundation of the Academy of Sciences, Paris
		1668	François Mauriceau: *Traité des maladies des femmes grosses...*
		1673	De Graaf discovers the ovarian follicle
Peter I, Tsar of Russia	1682		
Newton's Law of Gravitation		1683	Leeuwenhoek discovers bacteria
Revocation of the Edict of Nantes Emigration of French Protestants	1685	1685	Complete works of Thomas Sydenham
Locke: *Essay concerning human understanding*	1690		
Charles XII, King of Sweden	1697		
Treaty of Ryswick between France and European coalition		1699	Lémery: *Pharmacopée universelle*

chapter IX

Medicine in the Age of Enlightenment

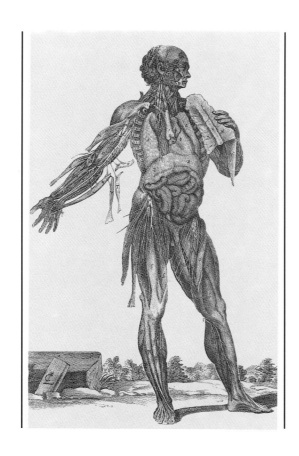

In many respects, the medicine of the eighteenth century was an extension of that of the previous century. There were the contradictions between competing theories, and the study of such sciences as physics and chemistry continued. The taste for experimentation grew and scholars, entranced by novelty, took their place alongside traditional practitioners. These conflicts were to continue until the early nineteenth century.

Medicine, however, became increasingly secular. The Europe of the seventeenth century was built on religion: thus the frontiers of the Westphalian peace bore the mark of religious antagonisms, and likewise cultural life as a whole was subject in varying degrees to the influence of the Churches.

In the eighteenth century, the sciences gradually emerged from the shadow of metaphysics; although it was said that "philosophy is the queen of sciences", the meaning of the word had changed. The philosopher of the eighteenth century studied both concrete and abstract disciplines; he became sceptical but did not yet dare to be an unbeliever. Philosophers' doubts went hand in hand with the relaxation of morals.

The new Masonic lodges, originating in Protestant countries, then diffused an intentionally anticlerical deism, while the Society of Jesus, adjudged too influential, was expelled from Catholic countries. In France, Gallican Jansenism was in favour once again.

This new attitude, which would not have been tolerated by the civil or the religious powers in the previous century, found its expression in the Encyclopaedist movement. Many doctors joined it, and philosophers, led by Diderot, turned

The fashion for "systems"

I.

A fashionable experiment in the eighteenth century: the air pump, designed by the English physicist Robert Boyle in 1658– 1659. Wright of Derby, 1768. National Gallery, London, England.

eagerly to the study of medicine. Intellectual expansion continued in the second half of the eighteenth century, with the birth of enlightened despotism. The new type of sovereign widened his power at the expense of the Church and the aristocracy and thus encouraged science, manufacturing, trade and agriculture to contribute to the prosperity of the people. Princes, philosophers and doctors each, therefore, in their own way furthered progress and universal happiness.

The intellectuals of the time were greatly influenced by the principle of universal gravitation developed by Newton, in the wake of Kepler and Galileo. It was cited by them as an explanation for all manner of hitherto incomprehensible phenomena.

The French mathematician Maupertuis (1698–1759) placed man at the centre of a vast cosmogony, thereby providing a rational basis for the mediaeval theory which saw in the human microcosm a reflection of the universal macrocosm. The philosopher La Mettrie (1709–1751), in his work entitled *L'Homme machine*, reduced man to an object, which won him the condemnation of the Catholic and Protestant Churches.

Then Hermann Boerhaave (1668–1738) demonstrated, thanks to his friend Fahrenheit, that any chemical reaction is accompanied by thermal phenomena, and that the functioning of the human body is therefore totally dependent on the laws of physics, thus rendering the conflict between iatrophysics* and iatrochemistry* invalid.

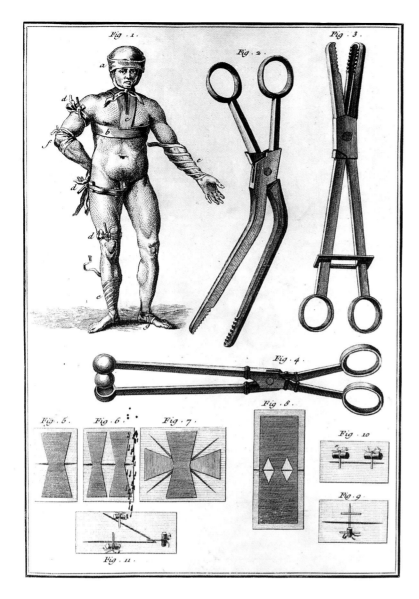

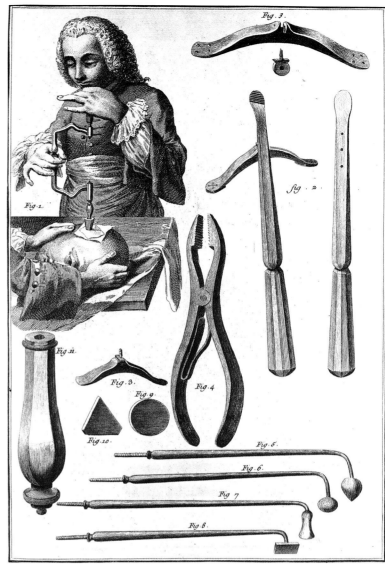

MECHANISTS AND VITALISTS

*T*he great minds of the time, having operated for so long in a world dominated by religion, had difficulty in accepting these mechanistic theories. Even Voltaire, the French eighteenth-century apostle of free thinking, could not imagine that "the clock that is the world" did not have a clockmaker – hence, in the eighteenth century, the number of schools tending more or less towards metaphysics.

The chemist Georg Stahl (1660–1734), from the Pietist University of Halle, for example, affirmed that mechanistic theories did not explain life. According to him, life is dependent on a "sensitive soul" (*anima*) which governs all changes in the body and prevents death.

This animism in fact was simply a revival of the ancient idea of benevolent nature which must be allowed by the doctor to take its course until recovery. Of course, this view did not conceal his

Among the one hundred and fifty contributors to Diderot's Encyclopédie, *published in thirty-five volumes from 1751 to 1772, there were many doctors. These two plates from the article entitled "Surgery" illustrate various instruments and,* right, *a trepanning operation. National Library, Paris, France.*

metaphysical ambition, which prompted the positivist Littré to say, a century later: "nature, another name for God". Stahlism spread throughout the northern European countries; in the south, it took another form.

For his part, John Brown (1735–1788) distinguished himself as one of the many figures from the prolific Edinburgh Medical School. As he conceived life to be the result of nervous forces responding to a greater or lesser degree to excitations – and that the disruption of these forces was due to various diseases, some sthenic and others asthenic – Brown recommended the sedative opium for sthenic complaints and the stimulant alcohol for asthenic complaints. The Brunonian system, which had an air of wisdom about it and accurately simplified therapeutics, won many followers in Britain, Germany and Italy.

The statue of Asclepius, in a rural landscape, appropriately appears as the frontispiece of the series of surgical plates in the Encyclopédie. *Library of Decorative Arts, Paris, France.*

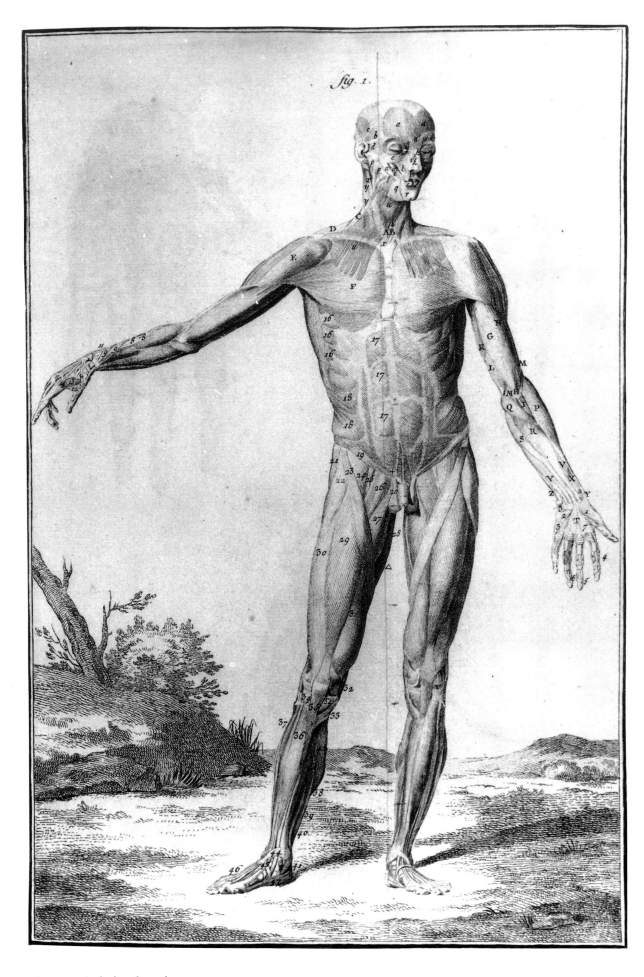

*An anatomical plate from the
Encyclopédie. Since Vesalius,
illustration of the human body had become
more serious and accurate. Library of
Decorative Arts, Paris, France.*

France, however, was divided between the mechanists and the new "vitalists". It was in Montpellier – not Paris, which displayed less curiosity for novelty – that this school of thought developed. According to Théophile de Bordeu (1722–1776) and Paul-Joseph Barthez (1734–1806), life responds to specific phenomena, which may be indefinable; they cannot be explained by animism, which does not take account of the physical and chemical exchanges which are, after all, easily observable, nor by pure mechanism which is too simplistic.

Vitalism, by recognizing that life is of an irreducible nature, is in a midway position between the two systems. One cannot help but feel that Bordeu's "vital impulse", which cannot be isolated and, by definition, materialized, closely resembles the *pneuma* of the Ancients. The vitalists did not, in fact, make any further progress in the explanation of vital phenomena than did the Ancients. After eighteen centuries of Christian theology, the scholars of the Enlightenment simply dressed the preoccupations of pagan antiquity in a new vocabulary.

These modes of thinking filled scholars with enthusiasm at the time and inspired many dissertations. They still astonish us today by their artificiality – they have no effect on the treatment of the sick – yet they cannot be dismissed simply as a philosophical pastime since they formed a framework for experimentation. Furthermore, they had a far-reaching effect on medical thinking, and a hidden vitalism still permeates the so-called "biological" sciences.

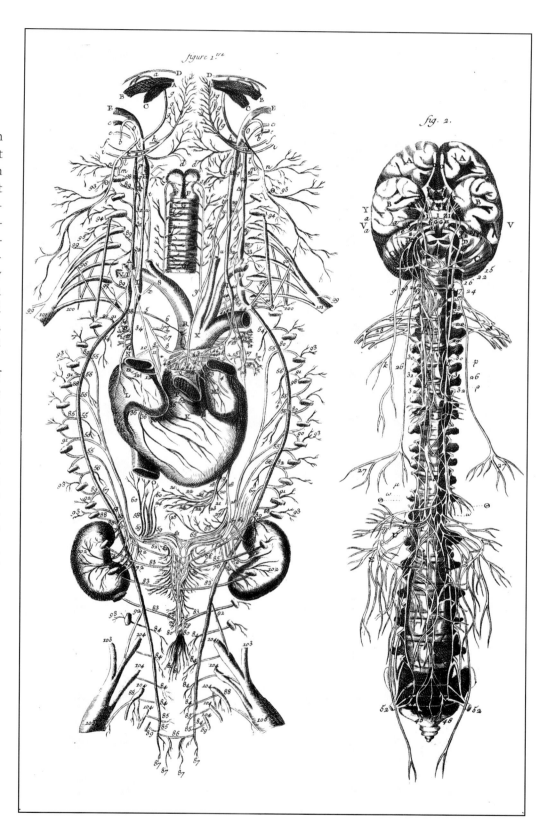

The "Neurology" plates from the Encyclopédie, *from Vieussens,* Neurographia universalis, *1684. The description, general and not very instructive, is somewhat dated. Library of Decorative Arts, Paris, France.*

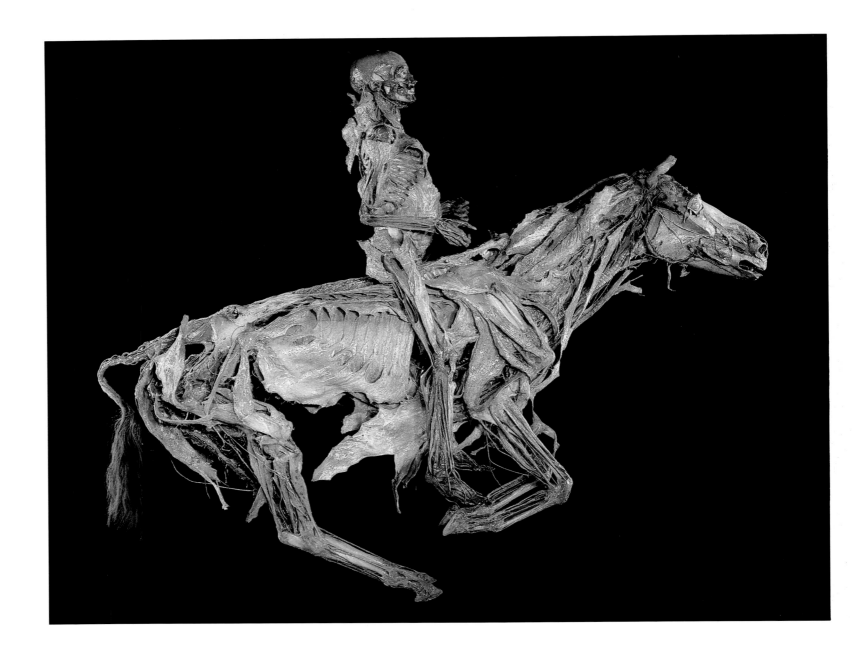

CLASSIFICATION AND WORLD ORDER

Anatomical wax models were in vogue in the eighteenth century. This anatomical work by Fragonard takes the form of a horseman of the apocalypse. Veterinary School of Maisons-Alfort, France.

Even at the height of the Middle Ages, efforts were made to classify human diseases by characterizing them according to one of the four humours which might be impaired, the patient's temperament, the season of the year, the climate, and so on. In the eighteenth century, new concepts of the human body and how it functions and the new view of man's place in the universe gave rise to new classifications in which the living world of plants and animals was presented as an ordered universe, organized in the same way as human societies were, with nature (or the Creator) leaving nothing to chance. Work of this kind, undertaken by Linnaeus for plants and Buffon and then Jussieu for animals, had a profound effect on the scholars of the eighteenth century. Medicine itself could not escape this concern

for classification; a number of people are worthy of mention in this connection.

William Cullen of Edinburgh (1712–1790) divided diseases into classes and orders, depending on the way in which the solids and fluids of the body were affected, whether there was a deficiency or plethora, and so on. However, today it is very difficult to identify the afflictions in question as they were not precisely defined. What are spasms and why do they come next to madness? What do intumescences* and impetigo* have in common? These are unresolved questions.

This type of classification was to be repeated a number of times subsequently; this was not unjustified as the choice of medicines depended on it. The variety of adjectives used to describe medicines, linked to the action attributed to them, is

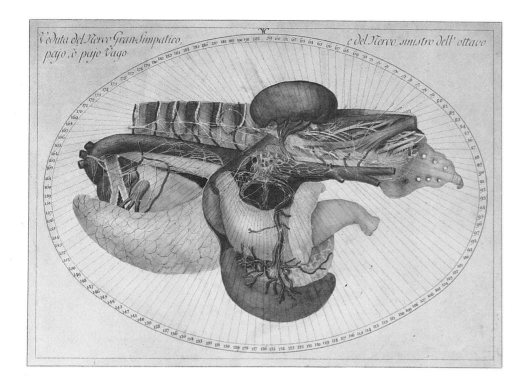

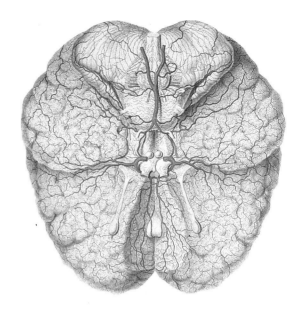

Arteries of the lower surface of the brain. Drawing, late eighteenth century. Library of the Old Faculty of Medicine, Paris, France.

surprising: examples are emollient, discursive, carminative and sarcotic.

These are terms which we no longer understand and which describe supposed properties not proven by experiments. This lexical abundance faded over the centuries as medicines became more efficacious.

In France, it was in Montpellier again that Boissier de Sauvages established his authoritative classification which he presented in his Latin *Pathologia methodica* (1759), soon translated into French. This naturalist doctor grouped diseases into ten main categories, drawing from the works of Carl Linnaeus (1707–1778), with whom he corresponded. In turn, the latter published his *Genera morborum* in 1763. Published towards the end of the century, Philippe Pinel's *Nosographie philosophique* was based on different principles.

Today, we have great difficulty in finding any justification for the types, classes and species of diseases imagined by the "nosographists" (who described diseases) and the "nosologists" (who classified them) two centuries ago.

What was the reality behind the various "putrid fevers" catalogued by Boissier de Sauvages, in view of the fact that the meaning of the word "fever" has changed

The desire to go into too much detail despite the level of technical progress resulted in somewhat confused illustrations of the nervous system. Here, the sympathetic nerves. Water-coloured print. Medical Surgical Academy, Austria.

and the adjective "putrid" is now scarcely ever used in medicine?

The very concept of disease has changed. Doctors in the Age of Enlightenment applied this term to conditions which had in common a few easily recognizable symptoms and sometimes a similar prognosis; but they made no reference to the causes of morbid phenomena nor to their humoral manifestations, nor to the internal lesions associated with them. The criteria for the identification of diseases have since changed and indeed are still evolving.

DISEASES ARE OF THE SAME ORDER AS NATURE

"He who conscientiously observes the season, the time and the hour at which the onset of quartan ague commences, as well as such phenomena as shivers, extreme sensations of heat and cold, perspiration and all the symptoms which accompany such a fever, will have as many reasons to think that this disease is a species as he has to believe that a plant is a species because it always grows, flowers and perishes in the same way."

Adapted from Thomas Sydenham (1624–1689)

These attempts to classify diseases, however, marked an important stage in the history of medicine for they testify to a change in the attitude of doctors with regard to the problems facing them. Breaking with the theoretical nonsense of past decades, renouncing the Hippocratic systemization of the temperaments which regarded every patient as a special case, practitioners categorized their patients, so that they could then be studied collectively.

Nosology* thus responds to an organized concept of the universe as well as to a desire to organize knowledge.

The ingenuity of some seventeenth-century researchers was to inspire many followers during the Age of Enlightenment, and one can consider the century as the founding age of modern physiology. Two concepts are relevant here. First, experimentation, that is, all the methods and techniques governing the implementation of laboratory experiments; in this regard, Lazzaro Spallanzani (1729–1799) can legitimately claim a certain glory. Second, the term a "man of experience" meant then, as now, a man who had acquired wisdom, prudence and knowledge thanks to his worthwhile activity; Giovanni Battista Morgagni (1682–1771) fits this description.

The cleric Lazzaro Spallanzani taught in a number of Italian towns, spent some time in Paris, travelled throughout the Mediterranean and found the time to explore numerous areas of physiology. He had a passionate enthusiasm for the natural sciences, and he corresponded with a number of friends in Germany and Switzerland, who shared much of his curiosity for a great many topics, but who frequently held different opinions from

*E*rudite and fashionable experimentation

II.

PHYSIOLOGY, THE FRUIT OF EXPERIMENTATION

From natural sciences to chemistry: two celebrated eighteenth-century researchers: the Italian Lazzaro Spallanzani (above); and the Frenchman Antoine-Laurent de Lavoisier with his scientific instruments, painted by Jacques Louis David, 1788 (right). Medicine was to benefit enormously from their work. Library of Decorative Arts, Paris, France and Metropolitan Museum, New York, USA.

his own. Spallanzani is often cited for the diversity of his knowledge and the ingenuity of his experiments, but he has greater significance than that. By detailing the hypotheses which he wished to counter or confirm, listing first the possible causes of error and the means of avoiding them, requiring the repetition of experiments under the same conditions or changing certain of the conditions, and by his awareness of the caution required when interpreting results, he holds a place in the theory of experimentation in the life sciences which is seldom recognized. The nineteenth century was to be indebted to this Italian, a man of genius, although it rarely paid him any tribute. This was particularly true with respect to his work on the circulation of the blood.

THE MAN MACHINE
OF LA METTRIE

Man is a Machine so complex that it is impossible, firstly, to have any clear idea of it and consequently to define it. This is why all research by the greatest Philosophers has been in vain a priori, that is to say in that they have tried to use the wings of the Mind so to speak. Thus it is only a posteriori, or by seeking to extract the Soul, through the Organs of the body for example, that one can, I do not say, discover with evidence the very nature of Man, but achieve the greatest possible degree of probability on this subject.

Let us then take the stick of experience and leave History there, with all its vain Philosophers' opinions. To be Blind, and to believe we can do without this stick is the pinnacle of blindness. A Modernist may well say that vanity alone does not draw from secondary causes, the same advantage as from the first! One can and one must even admire all these wonderful Geniuses in their most futile studies; the Descartes, the Mallebranches, the Leibnitzs, the Wolfs, etc. but what fruit, I ask you, has been harvested from their profound Meditations and all their Works? Let us start then, and see, not what they have thought, but what needs to be thought for peace of mind in life. So many different temperaments, minds, characters and customs. Even Galen was aware of this truth, which Descartes took further, stating that Medicine alone could change Minds and customs with the Body. It is true that Melancholy, Bile, Phlegm and Blood, etc. according to their nature, abundance and the various combinations of these humours, make of each Man a different Man.

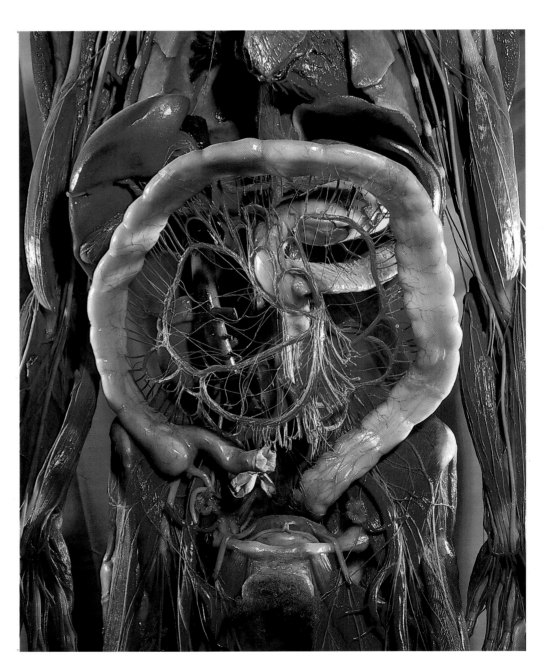

Detail from an anatomical wax model by the Italians Paolo Mascagni and Felice Fontana, Florence, 1785. Wax models, generally very expensive, usually adorned the studies used by amateurs rather than the anatomy lecture theatre, used by students. Medical Surgical Academy, Vienna, Austria.

Although in 1707 the Englishman Sir John Floyer (1649–1734) demonstrated the purpose of counting the pulse against time, and although in 1733 blood pressure was measured in the dog by using a water-pressure gauge, Spallanzani was the first to affirm the importance of the cardiac systole which causes the pulse in the arteries, the first to attempt to measure the speed at which the blood circulates, and, using the microscope, the first to detect the passage of red globules from the arteries to the veins via the capillaries.

It was a Frenchman who explained the detailed mechanisms of respiration. Richard Lower already suspected that the red colour of arterial blood came from the fact that it mixed with air from the lungs; Stephen Hales in his turn thought that air combined with the blood by a sort of "combustion".

Lavoisier was to advance research even further. Antoine-Laurent de Lavoisier (1743–1794) was one of the numerous polymaths of the eighteenth century: chemist, naturalist, economist, member of the Constituent Assembly, he was also a farmer general (a profiteer from tax gathering), for which he was guillotined in 1794.

It was Lavoisier who gave oxygen – discovered by Pierre Bayen and Joseph Priestley – its definitive name; he was the founder of a coherent and rational chemical nomenclature, abandoning the picturesque names in favour of compounds inherited from mediaeval alchemy. He also demonstrated that air is composed of nitrogen and oxygen, and that only oxygen combines with the constituents of the blood.

He found that during respiration the body absorbs oxygen and gives out carbon dioxide: enclosed under a bell-jar, a sparrow dies when it has consumed all the oxygen.

Julien Offray de La Mettrie (1709–1751), one of the leaders of the French materialist movement, compares man to a machine. Eighteenth-century print. Carnavalet Museum, Paris, France.

Spallanzani discovered the intricate mechanism of asphyxia which is due not to circulation problems but to a lack of oxygen in the nervous system. He also revealed the existence of cutaneous respiration.

The knowledge of digestive phenomena, however, progressed more slowly, because of ignorance about organic chemistry. Therefore the mechanical transformation undergone by food had to be explored instead. According to Philippe Hecquet (1661–1737), the stomach's sole function is that of trituration, but the Parisian Jean Astruc (1684–1766), although very traditionalist in other respects, adds that juices such as saliva and bile and the secretion from the pancreas also play a role in the denaturation of food.

René de Réaumur (1683–1757), by making buzzards swallow perforated tubes, was able to show that digestion is based on chemical processes and not only on mechanical mixing. Spallanzani, on the other hand, preferred to use domestic fowl, which he induced to swallow a sponge attached to a thread. He then removed the sponge to study the fluids collected.

It was perhaps in what we call the physiology of reproduction, and particularly in fertilization, that the progress of the century is most marked. What are the roles of the male and female? Where does the embryo come from? These are two of the major questions asked at the time.

In this field too, Spallanzani displayed his ingenuity by studying the reproduction of frogs and toads, in which males and females expel their sperm and eggs into water, where fertilization takes place. By fitting the males with waterproof "pants", he observed the circumstances in which tadpoles were produced. He also observed that the spermatic fluid kept its reproductive properties if kept cool, but that heat destroyed those properties. He

In parallel with anatomical wax models, a fashion for cheaper, terracotta figurines developed. This is a somewhat acrobatic foetus. G. A. Galli, 1776. University of Bologna, Italy.

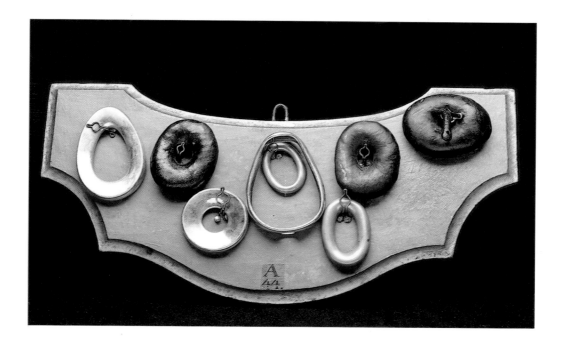

Various intravaginal instruments used to treat certain complaints and malformations of the uterus. University of Bologna, Italy.

was the first to carry out artificial fertilization with sperm, by introducing them into the vagina of a dog.

This shrewd researcher showed that contact between the eggs and sperm was necessary for reproduction, but he attributed the fertilizing property to the spermatic fluid and not to the spermatozoa. Many scholars in fact only touched on the truth although they actually had available to them all the means necessary to discover it fully.

Spallanzani left the question of ontogenesis* unresolved; he thought, no doubt – like others of his time – that the embryo is already formed in the ovum and that the male fluid triggers its growth.

It was Caspar Frederich Wolff (1733–1794) who, while defending epigenesis*, was to demonstrate that no tissue or organ could be detected in the egg, and that structures gradually develop in it after fertilization.

Little by little, the mechanism of movement was discovered; muscles and joints of course function like levers, but how does the muscle work? A sudden movement can result in its contraction; this is a reflex, a word created by the French doctor, Jean Astruc. Albrecht von Haller (1708–1777) established that the muscle is irritable, while sensitivity is the property of the nerves.

Electricity had been known for almost a century when, in Italy, Luigi Galvani (1737–1798) and later Alessandro Volta (1745–1827) developed electrophysiology, resulting in the birth of neurophysiology. Their experiments on the central and peripheral nervous system of frogs contain much of value for neuromuscular physiology and remain an example to modern students.

EXPERIMENTATION IN THE EIGHTEENTH CENTURY – DIFFICULTIES AND CONTROVERSIES

Albrecht von Haller states some principles:

"No experiment, no procedure shall be carried out just once; and the truth can only be revealed by a constant result from repeated experiments. There are numerous external factors which affect experiments; these factors are eliminated by repetition because they are foreign, and the phenomena in the pure state remain, which occur perpetually in the same way because they derive from nature itself."
Yet Haller was perhaps himself not rigorous enough, for at the same time another naturalist wrote to Spallanzani: "If Haller had consulted authors less, he would have consulted his head more; he would have reflected more and discovered more still."

M. D. Grmek, Florence, Italy, 1982.

Between medicine and charlatanism: a scene of magnetism c. *1785, using Mesmer's method. English water-coloured print. National Library, Paris, France.*

Jacques Bénigne Winslow (1669–1750), Danish anatomist, the first to describe certain parts of the portal vein, which still bears his name. National Order of Pharmacists, Bouvet collection, Paris, France.

In the eighteenth century, magnetism had many therapeutic applications. Patients were "electrified" to cure all manner of problems, while magnetism sessions had soldiers or society people forming chains.

The Austrian Franz Anton Mesmer (1734–1815) started a considerable craze in Vienna and, even more so, in Paris. Although he did, in fact, achieve a certain success with diseases which we call psychosomatic, his failures were far more frequent.

Magnetization gave Jean-Paul Marat (1743–1793), a graduate of Edinburgh, a reputation in society. The subject was fashionable and inspired a wealth of medical literature in the decades preceding the French Revolution.

However, studies by the Faculty of Paris and the Royal Medical Society were soon to denounce this practice as being one of charlatanism and suggestion. The method retained its disciples for a time before being generally discredited.

In the field of general physiology, the eighteenth century proved to be a positive period in the main. Many scholars were equally interested in anatomy, clinical practice, chemistry and the functioning of the organs, their weight and their temperature (an area in which Fahrenheit and Celsius won many disciples). Many works entitled *Physiologia* appeared, demonstrating the areas that interested researchers and their progressive abandonment of purely theoretical medical concepts.

The term "pathological anatomy" was coined by one of the polymaths, a certain Friedrich Hoffmann (1660–1742) from the productive University of Halle. Normal anatomy had attracted enormous interest in the sixteenth century, in the seventeenth and eighteenth centuries there were outstanding scientists working in this area, such as the Dane, Jacques Bénigne Winslow (1669–1750), who was based in Paris and converted to Catholicism. However, all these dissectors noted lesions in corpses they examined.

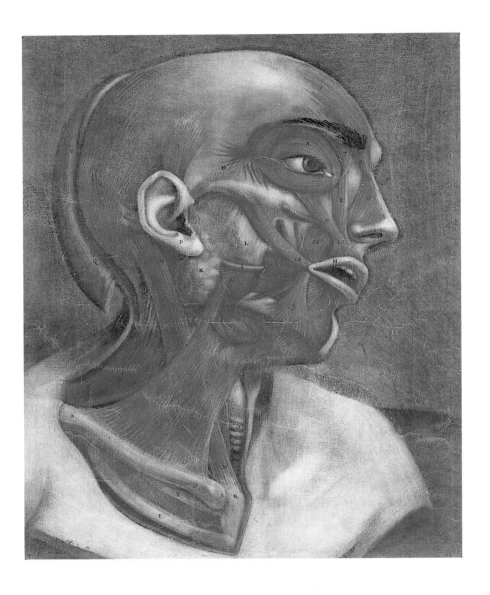

Therefore, alongside normal anatomy, pathological anatomy merits more than a passing mention; Giovanni Battista Morgagni (1682–1771) advanced it into a discipline which is an essential part of medicine. Having studied at Bologna under Valsalva and then taught at Padua, he published in 1761 a voluminous work entitled *De sedibus et causis morborum per anatomen indagatis*, in which he gave accounts of over six hundred autopsies undertaken by him or his superior. Many of the corpses were those of patients under his care; one of the autopsies was to become famous: that of a Venetian nobleman who died from alcoholism.

As good an observer of the dead as of the living, Morgagni was the first to establish a retrospective link between lesions found in the body and clinical symptoms.

Two anatomical plates by Jacques Gautier d'Agoty (c. 1745): the muscles of the face (above) and the rib cage (far right). The other inclined muscles on each side form wings, hence the name of this famous plate: "The anatomical angel". Library of the Old Faculty of Medicine, Paris, France.

Without elevating it to a general dogma, he helped to spread the idea that any "disease", characterized at that time only by the signs obtained from observation of the living, had corresponding characteristic anatomical lesions, and that the signs and lesions related to each other. His work, which was published in Latin and several other languages, presented his observations in descending order from head to foot, according to a tradition dating from ancient times.

Reading his list, it appears that no organ of the body has escaped his notice; he also identified normal organs or varieties of normal anatomy of which his predecessors were ignorant. For instance, he established that apoplectic attacks were the result of a deterioration in the cerebral blood vessels, and that some cases of pulmonary breathlessness and

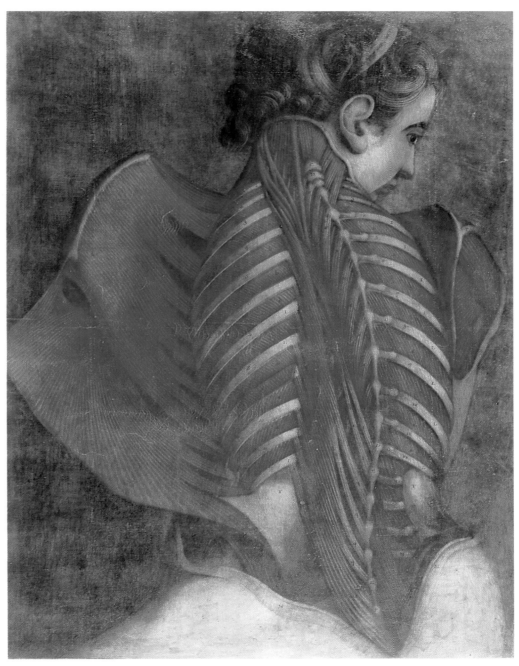

dropsy were secondary to indurations* of the valves of the heart; he described the damage caused by venereal diseases, and so on. A number of his findings were to help in the creation of the new science of forensic medicine.

Morgagni also developed autopsy techniques, and he taught how to estimate the weight, volume and colour of a solid organ and the diameter and length of a hollow organ; how to differentiate between factors occurring prior to and subsequent to death and how to link these findings to the pain experienced by the patient and the observations made by the doctor in attendance.

All his successors, up to the present, were to respect him as the father of anatomical pathology; today, in France, the expression "*chez Morgagni*" is a euphemism for the autopsy room.

Above left: *Giovanni Battista Morgagni (1682–1771), the first to relate a patient's symptoms to the pathological anatomical lesions particular to a disease.*
Palazzo del Bo, Padua, Italy.

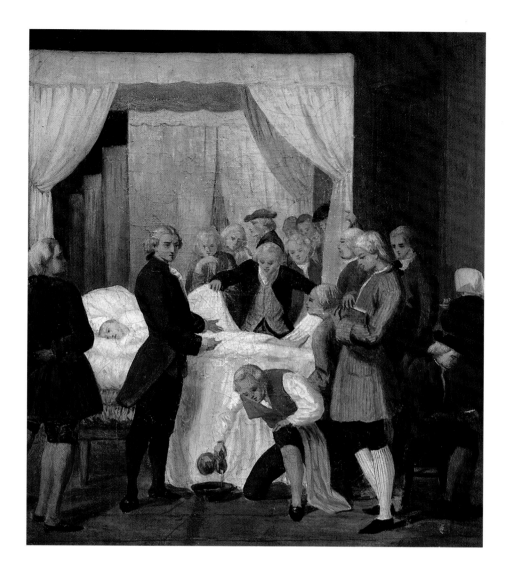

CLINICAL PRACTICE AND FAME

One thing is certain: the identification of diseases, in the modern sense of the term, owed more to pathological anatomy than to simple clinical practice because doctors' means of observation at the bedside were so limited. The questioning of the patient about the nature, the symptoms and the duration of his problems was however as precise as Hippocrates had recommended. Doctors studied the pulse and began noting the pulse rate.

The complexion, eyes, mouth and teeth were examined. The appearance of urine continued to be taken into account, though the quantity produced in a given period was no longer measured; in contrast to the Middle Ages, urine was no longer the central factor in diagnosis.

The examination was normally confined to seeking the information mentioned above. There was no auscultation. Some reckless characters dared to palpate their patient's abdomen, but the assessment of the volume of the liver and the

The changes in eras, countries and customs did not bring about any changes in traditional medical practices, be they the examination of urine or that of the pulse. Opposite: the German doctor Sansanietto examines a patient's urine; eighteenth-century print by Springer. *Above:* the doctor's visit, eighteenth-century painting. Museum of Medical Art, Rome, Italy.

search for the spleen hidden beneath the ribs remained exceptional practices. The doctor did not in general place his hands on the patient; any act of this kind, considered to be vulgar, was solely in the field of competence of the surgeon who, by definition, worked with his hands.

Over the centuries, surgeons produced their own symptomatology* and vocabulary. They knew how to feel a tumour, how to estimate its superficial and underlying connections, its consistency, mobility and volume; since the eighteenth century, they have continued to assess it by comparison with a vegetable or fruit rather than to measure it!

In searching for a fracture in a limb, they attempted to detect an abnormal movement, a creaking or friction; in joints, they identified the stiffness of ankylosis, and, finally, they practised buccal, vaginal and rectal examination. They effectively invented a symptomalogical system of which doctors, who declared

THE HYGIENE OF CLOTHING

Doctors in the eighteenth century concerned themselves with all the behaviour and conditions of everyday life: the habitat, cleanliness of the body and house, the diet and so on.
Winslow, a Dane who lived in Paris, denounced the corset:
"Winslow had carried out anatomical studies on the functions of the ribs and diaphragm in normal respiration (1738). This led him to protest violently against the whims of eighteenth-century fashion which, by imposing ever tighter whalebone corsets, was the cause of harmful postures and functional impairment. Although they were no longer the iron corsets of the Renaissance, but simply very tight silk tubes, the psychological reason for wearing them was the same: to have a wasp waist and the bosom uplifted, creating between the breasts what the gallant Teutons of the rococo period called 'the blessed well'. All believers were offended, especially where this heaving cleavage harboured jewellery and especially precious crosses decorated with diamonds or golden crucifixes."
Winslow however stated that these wasp-waisted corsets were worn by those suffering from jaundice, gastralgia, digestive obstruction and even chlorosis. Not only did these corsets compress the abdominal organs but they even flattened the curve of the chest and the rib cage, constricting and reducing the function of the lower ribs, while the excessively tight shoulder straps impaired the mobility of the shoulders and arms. As all these drawbacks can be found to occur in two to four months, is it not disastrous to observe such abuse in healthy young

women! He felt that compression was the principal cause of chlorosis and the pale complexions were due to the compression of the lymphatic glands. He was particularly concerned about the poor functioning of the ribs and diaphragm, as the constriction of the

rib cage created a very poor point of support for the elevation of the diaphragm.

From E. Snorrason: The Anatomist J. B. Winslow, *Copenhagen, Denmark, 1969.*

310

A busy pharmacy. In the foreground, a number of assistants are at work. In the background can be seen the traditional garden of medicinal plants. Painted panel, mid eighteenth century. Beaune Hospice, France.

themselves more scholarly, were ignorant.

However, even with their restricted means of observation, doctors managed to describe sets of symptoms which always had a logical connection, for instance, attacks of angina pectoris, with the distressing prognosis that often accompanies them, and "plethora", wherein we find the polymorphic manifestations of arterial hypertension. They identified a number of types of renal affliction, categorized skin complaints, and so on.

But doctors were not all equally talented. As is the case today, the wisest were not those who published the most books, nor those with the greatest number of patients. It was at this time that the myth of the celebrated doctor emerged: the doctor who, in his lifetime, treated the greatest number of patients or trained the greatest number of students, who was known by his works, and whose name passed into posterity thanks to much repeated biographies. His fame, most easily acquired in a court or reputable university, his renown, justified to a greater or lesser degree, lived on for centuries, whatever the actual value of his teaching to future generations. The sociological category of "great doctors", which can still be observed in the West, dates from this period; it is not appropriate to discuss its origin here, and it is the task of the historian to sift through the names of those whose memory is venerated in the different countries of Europe.

Albrecht von Haller (1708–1777), a memorable personality in eighteenth-century Europe, came from Switzerland. After studying under Boerhaave in Leyden, Winslow in Paris and Bernoulli in Basle, he finally settled in Berne and revealed himself to be a physiologist, poet, anatomist, chemist and researcher; he put his prodigious erudition to good use by writing a major work and keeping up a regular correspondence with a large number of scholars. In the study of muscular contraction, he developed, *inter alia*, the concept of irritability, which he distinguished from that of sensitivity.

311

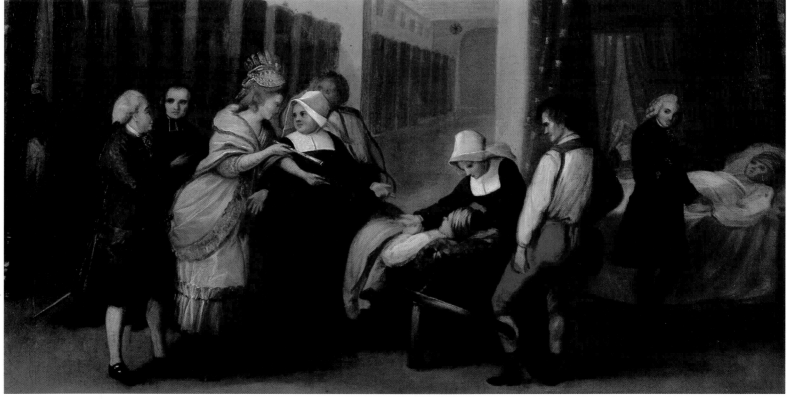

Théodore Tronchin (1709–1781), from Geneva, was enormously successful, with a clientele in a number of courts in Europe, especially in Paris. Voltaire respected him greatly for having cured him of imaginary diseases. Tronchin distinguished himself particularly through his indefatigable propaganda for variolization.

From the Netherlands came Hermann Boerhaave (1668–1738). Although he was a good chemist and excellent botanist who corresponded with Linnaeus, he owed his prestige to the clinical education which he dispensed over several decades in the hospital of Leyden.

Despite the fact that he was not the author of any major discovery in symptomatology or in therapeutics, Boerhaave exercised a profound influence on his students – who were to spread to the far corners of Europe – through his method of patient examination. The Edinburgh School in Scotland, cultivating the tradition of Sydenham, owes much to Boerhaave, as well as to Cullen, Monro and others. We can pick up his trail in Göttingen and especially, in Vienna, where his compatriot Gerhardt van Swieten (1700–1772) settled.

England reveres the memory of John Fothergill (1712–1780), an austere practitioner with a vast clientele, enriched by court officials, who rubbed shoulders with the poor, whom he treated as an act of charity. He made no real contribution to the development of medicine, in contrast to William Withering (1741–1799), who was an altogether more modest yet more productive doctor; it was he who was to learn from a peasant woman that an infusion of leaves of the common foxglove is effective against dropsy and in certain heart conditions. Digitalin, which was initially extracted from the plant and then made synthetically, still features in the arsenal of cardiopathic remedies. Withering's discovery is, in fact, one of

The foxglove was so named because of the shape of its flowers, closely resembling the fingers of a glove. For over two centuries, it has helped relieve the sufferings of cardiac patients. From Jean Robin, Le Jardin du Roi, *1608. National Library, Paris, France.*

In France, the number of private initiatives in the field of public health increased. Top left: *a vaccination session in the château of Liancourt, in the Oise,* c. 1820. *Painting by C. J. Desbordes (1761–1827).* Bottom left: *the wife of the Director General of Finances, Necker, visits the hospice of La charité in Paris,* c. 1780. Public Works Museum, Paris, France.

the main therapeutic achievements of the eighteenth century, achievements which were somewhat thin on the ground. Georg Stahl did call for the simplification of the pharmacopoeia and the suppression of innumerable remedies with an exaggerated reputation, but this fell on deaf ears.

John Hunter (1728–1793) was a person of an altogether different ability. A Scot living in London, he distinguished himself in the fields of human anatomy and comparative anatomy and proved to be a brilliant surgeon; indeed, some of his techniques for the treatment of aneurysms are still valid today. A surgeon colleague of his, Percivall Pott (1713–1788), was to give his name to tubercular osteo-arthritis of the spinal column.

In Austria, Leopold Auenbrügger (1722–1809), a pupil in the school of van Swieten, made his mark by publishing, in 1761, a small treatise in Latin on the percussion of the thorax. In this he demonstrated that he could infer a pulmonary, pleural or cardiac lesion from the sounds he heard, supported by knowledge gained from autopsies. Thanks to him, doctors who had previously used only sight, smell, sometimes taste and hardly ever touch, could then make use of hearing. Unfortunately, his work remained unnoticed in other countries until it was translated into French by Corvisart in 1808.

Italy has already given us a number of celebrated names; that of Bernardino Ramazzini (1633–1714) must be added to the list. By his original observations on the muscles, he made a contribution to what we now call ergonomics. Above all, as a clinician, he established the link between certain diseases and the occupation of patients: specifically lead colic in painters using white lead, the problems of enamellers using antimony, and even damage to the skin and teeth of doctors

The surgeon Desault (1738–1795). Print after Kimly, early nineteenth century. Library of the Old Faculty of Medicine, Paris, France.

who frequently treated their syphilitic patients with mercury!

Furthermore, he was one of the first since Paracelsus to make an inventory of occupational diseases. He was not, however, prompted by any legal or social concern and it would therefore be an exaggeration of his role to present him as the prophet of industrial medicine.

In France, few doctors merited reknown, but one who did was Jean-Baptiste Sénac (1693–1770), Louis XV's doctor, who produced a remarkable summary of current knowledge about the diseases of the heart, and its rhythm and operation. At the end of the century, on the other hand, Paul-Joseph Barthez (1734–1806) enjoyed fame, income and favours from those in political power which seem out of all proportion to the contribution which he made to medicine.

Specialists in surgery were more innovative. Some discovered new instruments and unprecedented channels for the extraction of bladder stones – which were frequent, due to the rich diet of the time.

Others were among the pioneers of operative ophthalmology practising, like Jacques Daviel (1693–1762) – who treated over two hundred patients – the extraction from the eye of the damaged crystalline lens responsible for cataracts; until then, it had simply been pushed back into the aqueous chamber of the eye.

A doctor's bag: forceps for childbirth, miscellaneous clamps, enema canula, eighteenth century. Museum of Medical Art, Rome, Italy.

It was Pierre Fauchard (1678–1761) who introduced odontostomatology into the field of medicine. The extraction of teeth had, for thousands of years, been the monopoly of charlatans wandering from fair to fair, who had no knowledge of general pathology nor anatomy; Fauchard was the first to introduce methodical observation, rationality and caution into the art of dentistry.

This brief list would be incomplete without Pierre-Joseph Desault (1738–1795). In his career as a surgeon, he was not, admittedly, a great innovator; his experience was in operating quickly and advising against trepanning which was carried out all too often at that time to treat cranial traumas. On the other hand, when teaching surgery at the bedside of patients in the Parisian hospitals, he proved to have the stature that Boerhaave had in the field of medicine. Desault disappeared in the midst of the Revolution. However, through the precision of his examination techniques, his care in prescribing surgery and the skill of his operations, he was to exercise considerable influence on the development of medicine in the decades to come.

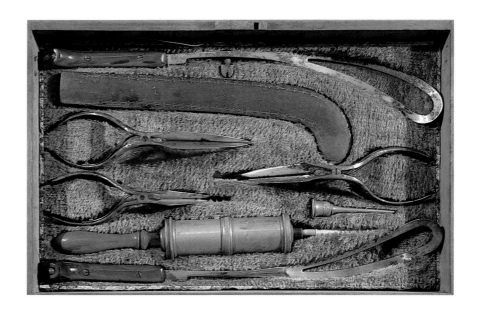

MEDICINE, NUMBERS AND HYGIENE

While doctors theorized or experimented, the population of Europe grew throughout the eighteenth century, despite the diseases for which medicine had no cure.

For some decades, the plague seemed to have abandoned Europe, but it suddenly struck Marseilles, Provence and the upper Languedoc in 1720. The considerable mortality and panic which it engendered in the country prompted most European governments to make more stringent quarantine regulations, frontier checks and penalties for breaching the plague barriers more stringent.

At the same time, other epidemics continued their ravages: diphtheria, skin diseases, whooping cough and mumps for instance. Boissier de Sauvages catalogued the symptoms characterizing typhus, and all the ports of the Americas were hit by yellow fever which later reached Europe. Malaria also continued to advance.

La peste de Marseille en 1721, Michel Serre (1658–1733). The history of "plagues" extended well into the Enlightenment. In Marseilles, of a population of seventy-five thousand, forty thousand died in the period 1720–1722, despite the quarantine measures imposed by the authorities. Atger Museum, Montpellier, France.

Likewise, during the eighteenth century, fatal outbreaks of smallpox occurred, decimating the Court of France, and on one occasion claiming the life of Louis XV. But Lady Montague was to import from Constantinople the process of variolization: by inoculating a healthy subject with pus from someone recovering from smallpox, the healthy person was given a benign form of smallpox, which was much safer than the spontaneously contracted disease.

The method was not without its risks as it could cause virulent smallpox; however, despite fierce opposition, inoculation spread rapidly throughout northern Europe. Hesitant for a considerable time, France was converted late in the day, thanks to the celebrated Swiss doctor Tronchin, who managed to inoculate the members of the court of Versailles. Variolization was therefore on its way to

L'ORIGINE de la VACCINE

becoming the first mass medical treatment, its effect being not to eliminate a disease or to prevent it being caught, but to make it less serious. The discovery by Edward Jenner (1749–1823) was to supplant it.

A country doctor in England, he observed that farmers' wives and farm labourers whose hands bore the scars of an infection caused by a disease of cows' udders – cowpox – did not contract smallpox during epidemics. To test his hypothesis, he decided to conduct meticulous experiments including tests and checks before presenting his idea to his peers: he found that the introduction into the human body of pus from cowpox protected that person against contracting smallpox. Although many scholars were highly sceptical, vaccination spread in all social environments in England, and, at

Vaccine and humour, or how to popularize a practice which, around 1800, still aroused the mistrust of the people. Ceramic plate. Institute of Vaccine, Paris, France.

the end of the century, French inoculators became vaccinators.

In addition to infections, many fell victim to deficiencies, notably scurvy. This was found in particular in the crews of both the merchant navy and the marine forces, who were often at sea for several months and frequently had a diet based on food preserved in salt. The lack of fresh fruit and vegetables was first suspected as a cause of scurvy when James Lind (1716–1794) found that lemon juice, which provided the essential vitamin C, was a remedy. At the same time, another vitamin deficiency in the diet which led to pellagra was also identified.

In England, there was a move toward denouncing and combating excessive alcohol consumption. In Savoy, François-Emmanuel Fodéré (1764–1835) described

Demi-crétine du valais.

Tresca sculp.

Goitrous cretinism in the Valais, from a rather unpleasant print by Tresca. J.-L. Alibert, Physiologie des passions, early nineteenth century. Museum of the History of Medicine, Paris, France.

POOR HEALTH IN THE COUNTRYSIDE

The population of France increased overall in the eighteenth century; however, some provinces were hard hit by poverty, famine and epidemics. This is illustrated by figures for the two Breton districts of Paimpol and Saint-Brieuc.

Dates	Births	Marriages	Deaths	Surplus Births	Surplus Deaths
1776	247	50	260		13
1777	235	56	222	13	
1778	280	53	207	73	
1779	272	46	498		226
1780	227	49	372		145
1781	294	67	251	43	
1782	237	49	376		139
1783	256	62	351		95
1784	239	60	246		7
1785	268	54	205	63	
1786	268	56	303		35
1787	253	72	286		33
1788	314	44	212	102	
Total	3 390	718	3 789		
Annual average	260	55	291		

From Meyer: **Le personnel médical en Bretagne à la fin du XVIIIᵉ siècle,** *p. 200, 1972, Mouton ed., Paris, France.*

Doctors had their detractors in the eighteenth, as in the seventeenth, century. In this satirical procession, the doctor and the apothecary ride alongside the priest, the patient and death! Private collection, Paris, France.

goitrous cretinism, which he observed in certain regions.

These findings led doctors to ponder on the pathology of certain communities. At their instigation and sometimes at the request of the authorities, studies were conducted and published about living conditions on board ship, in hospitals and prisons, or wherever a large number of individuals lived together in a confined space.

Data and figures abounded. The German economist Gottfried Achenwall (1719–1772) managed to show that a good government required the use of records: details of births and deaths, diseases, epidemics and epizootics; as well as those of agricultural and mining resources, manufacturing and shipping, and so on. This was how health statistics, which were to serve as an aid to the health of nations, were born.

Doctors were all the more incapable of controlling diseases because their treatments were ineffectual and because there were so few of them. Most, coming from the upper middle classes who could afford to pay for the long years of study, settled in the major cities. Peasants and the poor remained in the hands of bonesetters and diviners, not to mention witches and village gossips who subjected them to ignorant traditional practices.

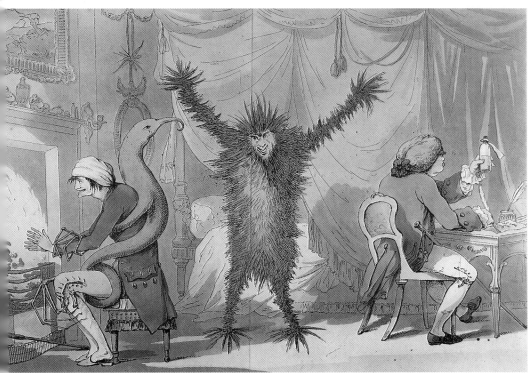

Some caricatures of medical scenes. From left to right and top to bottom: *Goya,* The doctor as an ass*; Rowlandson,* The hallucinations of the hypochondriac *and* Suffering and fever, c. *1792; Woodward,* The funeral mute and death, c. *1798. National Library, Paris, France and Museum of Arts, Philadelphia, USA.*

The doctors knew classical literature, both Greek and Latin; they were interested in the new sciences, and they often proved to be better read than the notable religious and lay people with whom they rubbed shoulders in the academies recently founded in the provincial capitals. They met erudite men of all disciplines within the scholarly societies which were then springing up throughout Europe. This period also witnessed the birth of scientific reviews in which researchers reported their work in Latin or their own language.

Doctors were not alone in practising the healing art with varying degrees of success. They still needed the collaboration of surgeons for a whole range of interventions, for in the eighteenth century medical practioners still did not know how to bandage, reduce a dislocation, lance an abscess, set a fracture or remove a tumour.

In comparison with doctors, surgeons appeared to be more numerous, less well-read, less affluent and less respected in society. After an age-old battle against doctors and a number of derisory disputes, some of which even went to court, they were rehabilitated in France in the eighteenth century. They dissociated themselves definitively from any professional relations with barbers, succeeded in

The foundation by Louis XV in 1731 of the Royal Academy, intended for surgeons, established the social advancement of this profession in France in the eighteenth century. Pierre-Antoine Demachy (1732–1807), La construction de l'Académie Royale de Chirurgie *(today the Faculty of Medicine), water-colour,* c. *1780–1789. Private collection, Paris, France.*

creating the Royal Academy of Surgery – despite the fury of the Faculty of Paris – and thus, like doctors, could then endorse theses and in fact become doctors. Finally, in Paris, doctors and surgeons found themselves side by side in the Royal Society of Medicine, which the Faculty soon accepted.

Although in France apothecaries constituted a well organized profession, distinct from herbalists, the line of demarcation from doctors was less clear in England, due to old traditions. A compromise was finally reached which still survives today, whereby apothecaries have certain rights regarding prescriptions and treatment. Eventually, in a desire for modernization, the title "apothecary" was replaced by the more scholarly "pharmacist".

Quarrels between professionals were compounded by complaints from doctors about the inequality of their education. Some ten faculties issued controlled diplomas following serious studies: Paris attracted students from bordering countries, likewise Göttingen and Halle; Padua, Bologna and Montpellier drew students from the Mediterranean countries; northern Europeans went to Leyden and Americans to Edinburgh. But, in addition to these reputable universities, many others, with inadequate teachers, provided only a rudimentary education.

Large theriaca jar for the poor (contained an antidote for venomous bites). This model, dating from 1751, comes from the Hôtel-Dieu. Collection of the Faculty of Pharmacy, Paris, France.

Over the centuries, pharmacy gained large numbers of new, equally ineffective, products: compilations of recipes became ever more voluminous, the shelves of dispensaries ever more replete. Saint-Roch Museum, Issoudun, France and Museum of Medical Art, Rome, Italy.

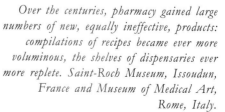

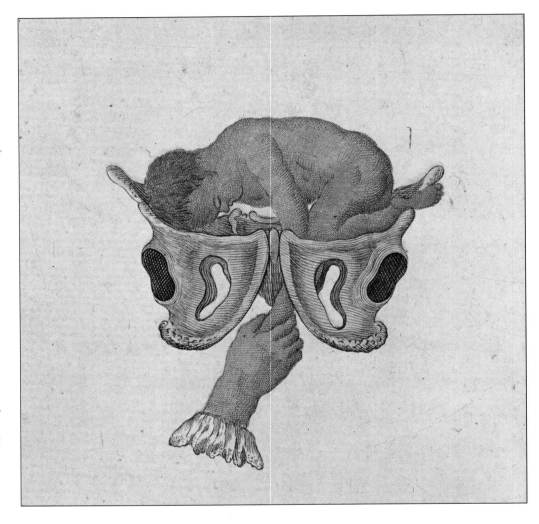

Two plates showing how to extract an incorrectly presented foetus. Angélique-Marie Le Boursier du Coudray, Traité des accouchements, 1759. Library of the Old Faculty of Medicine, Paris, France.

THE AUTHORITIES, EPIDEMICS AND EPIZOOTICS

" – *Granaries need to be built where grain can be stored in years of plenty and which can be opened in years of famine. Another real resource against many epidemic diseases would be to provide the poor with rice and to increase cultivation of the right type of potato from which bread could be made when wheat stocks are inadequate or when wheat is too dear.*

– It must be ensured that excreta is taken at least one league from the large towns, and likewise any things which could taint the air with harmful and alkaline fumes, such as those associated with butchers' shops, and cemeteries, must be removed.

– The government cannot pay too much attention to epizootic diseases; individuals owning infected animals must be forced to kill them when they first become ill."

From Le Brun, *op. cit.,* Theoretical treatise on epidemic diseases...., *1776.*

Even in hospitals, the respective positions of doctors and surgeons remained uncertain. In these institutions, which owed their existence to the benevolence of municipal authorities or individuals and were usually subject to some religious authority, practitioners were not regarded as indispensable. A study conducted in France by Tenon (1724–1816) revealed the extraordinary dilapidation of these dirty and overcrowded institutions where the sick, invalids, young delinquents, prostitutes and undesirable beggars mixed with those suffering from major diseases or cancer and also with the insane. The

hospital at this time still served as a refuge, prison and asylum as well as a place of care.

True hospitals, in today's meaning of the word, owe their existence in England and France to the initiative of armies and navies: they arranged for treatment as well as providing a sound practical education, thanks to experience gained on the battlefield and in distant countries. The Royal Hospital at Greenwich was opened as a hospital for seamen in 1705. Guy's Hospital in London was built in the 1720s.

The malaise in medical institutions, with structures dating back to the Middle Ages, explains their difficulty in adapting to scientific progress, despite the fact that many doctors did address this issue.

Among the "philosophers" and "physiocrats" who, inspired by progress, developed innumerable projects for the advancement of manufacturing, agriculture and commerce to improve the prosperity of the people, were a number of doctors: François Quesnay (1694–1774) is the best example.

In France, the monarchy felt the same concern. Administrators were obliged to inform the minister about epidemics and epizootics occurring in their provinces; they made doctors responsible for finding out about any disturbing situation and notifying the authorities accordingly. Food and medicines were distributed in the most severely affected regions.

Upon its foundation, the French Royal Society of Medicine was expressly obliged to keep the government informed about the health of the country: thus, its permanent secretary, Félix Vicq d'Azyr (1748–1794), decided to form a national network of correspondents responsible for notifying him of any untoward events or epidemics – even local ones – relating to bad weather, the population's general state of nutrition, habitat, everyday hygiene, and so on.

Moreover, the details in parish registers show that mortality at birth and during infancy was still quite considerable in the eighteenth century. In order to train midwives destined to replace the untrained village midwives, the local officials encouraged the instructional activities of Angélique Le Boursier du Coudray (1712–1789), who illustrated her courses using a model she had made. At the same time, the colleges of surgeons in many towns were developing obstetrics education.

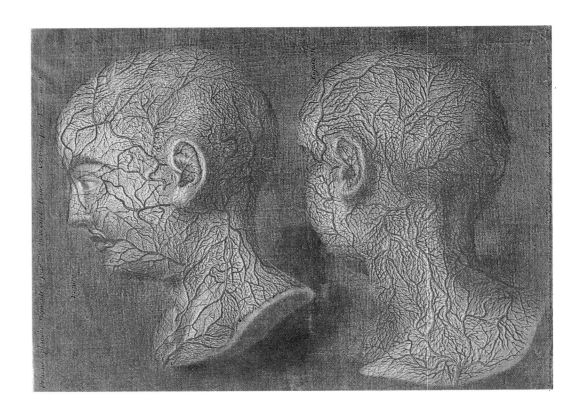

THE AUTHORITIES AND FOOD HYGIENE

"–Workers must be prevented from drinking the water with which the mines are cleaned, and these water courses must be diverted so that they do not mix with those normally used for drinking water by the inhabitants.

– Mines shall only be opened at a fairly considerable distance from highly populated areas.

– The Public Ministry shall ensure that frequent visits are made to wine merchants to check that their wines are not kept in lead or tin vessels.

– It would be easy to forbid the sale of any type of fruit before it was fully grown.

– Magistrates shall devote attention to the preservation and the quality of grain, and reject that which is mouldy, infected with worms, etc."

From Le Brun, op. cit., 1776.

Jacques Gautier d'Agoty (c. 1745), illustration of the superficial arterial vascularization of the head of a child. Museum of the History of Medicine, Lyons, France.

Under the influence of *Émile* by Jean-Jacques Rousseau (1712 – 1778), theories about the upbringing and education of children became fashionable; doctors gave advice about the way to wrap them in swaddling clothes and feed them, and the first books on children's diseases appeared.

The increasing preoccupation with public health was reflected, towards the end of the century, in the publication of numerous works: André Tissot (1728–1797), from Lausanne, wrote *Avis au peuple sur la santé*; Fodéré, in 1798, *Traité de médicine légale et d'hygiène publique*. There were calls for regulations governing potentially dangerous establishments such as chemical factories and slaughterhouses; some, like Sébastien Mercier in his *Tableau de Paris* published in 1781, proposed moving cemeteries to the periphery of conurbations; while others called for the provision of sewers in urban areas. At the turn of the century, the Austrian Johann Peter Franck (1745–1821) published a major treatise proposing a comprehensive

The four stages of cruelty, *by the celebrated English caricaturist William Hogarth (1694–1764). Water-coloured print,* c. *1750–1751. Museum of the History of Medicine, Paris, France.*

health policy. He attributed to the political powers responsibility for the health of their people and many duties of intervention. Medicine had already started to find its way into all areas in the name of hygiene: an unimaginable concept one hundred years earlier!

Thus, despite a muddled development, contradictory tendencies and artificial controversies, medicine underwent considerable changes at the dawn of the French Revolution. Society witnessed the birth of reliable medical systems, although these were often received with some scepticism because of their lack of clear organization. The knowledge

The morbid interest in monstrous malformations did not abate in the eighteenth century. From a work by Geneviève Regnault, Les écarts de la nature, *1775. National Library, Paris, France.*

acquired about the functioning of the human body, thanks to the sciences used in experimentation, and to the study of lesions, cast light on physiology, a subject which had remained something of a mystery until then. Many existing theories were shown to be illusory, opening the way to a new concept of disease.

The instruments invented (by physics) (for the measurement of temperature, weight, rhythm and flow) as well as those developed by mathematics (for the study of demography, epidemics and their frequency), combined with other discoveries in the service of medicine and introduced numbers and quantification into the life sciences.

MEDICINE IN THE AGE OF ENLIGHTENMENT
1700 – 1799

POLITICS AND CULTURE	DATE	DATE	MEDICINE
		1696	Giovanni Battista Morgagni, *Anatomical notebooks*
Philippe V of Anjou, King of Spain	1700	1700	Bernardino Ramazzini writes a treatise on the diseases of artisans
Foundation of St Petersburg	1703		
Newton, *Opticks*			
		1707	Georg Ernst Stahl publishes his *Theoria medica vera*
		1708	Hermann Boerhaave and iatromechanics
Frederick William, King of Prussia	1713		
George I of Hanover, King of England	1714		
Louis XV, King of France	1715	1715	Raymond Vieussens, *Livre sur le coeur*
		1717	The medical work of Tournefort
		1718	Pierre Dionis, *Traité des accouchements*
		1720	Lady Montague brings variolization to London
			The plague in Provence
		1728	Pierre Fauchard, *Traité des dents*
		1736	Jean Astruc and venereal diseases
Frederick II, King of Prussia	1740		
Maria-Theresa, Empress of Austria			
		1743	Astruc and the reflexes
			Foundation of the French Academy of Surgery
			James Lind describes and treats scurvy
First volume of the *Encylopédie*	1751		
Condillac, *Traité des sensations*	1755		
Seven Years' War	1756–1763	1756	First suburban hospital in Plymouth
		1757	Albrecht von Haller, *Elements of physiology*
		1759	Classification of Boissier de Sauvages
		1761	Leopold Auenbrügger is the first to have the idea of using percussion
Catherine II, Empress of Russia	1762		
Rousseau, *Émile ou de l'éducation*			
		1763	Carolus Linnaeus and the classification of diseases
Start of Scheele's chemistry	1770		
		1777	Antoine-Laurent de Lavoisier: experiments on respiration
			Anne Charles Lorry, *Treatise on diseases of the skin*
		1779	Johann Peter Frank writes, in German, the first book on public health *System of medical policing*
Kant, *Critique of pure reason*	1781	1781	Jean-Louis Baudelocque, *Traité d'accouchements*
Start of the French Revolution	1789		
George Washington, first president of the United States			
Execution of Louis XVI	1793		
Third partition of Poland	1795		
		1796	Jenner carries out the first vaccination against smallpox
Bonaparte in Egypt	1798	1798	Philippe Pinel, *Nosographie philosophique*
Bonaparte's *coup d'état*	1799	1799	François-Xavier Bichat, *Traité des membranes*

chapter X

◆

Conversion to clinical medicine

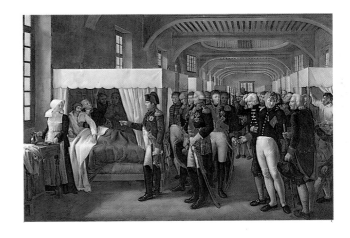

Building on the efforts of previous centuries, medicine became truly scientific in the nineteenth century. The publication of a number of books with titles containing the word "rational" is characteristic of the spirit of the age; it was not that previous periods did not use "reason", but there are subtle differences in the meanings of the words "rational" and "reasonable", and the different interpretations of the word "reason" in various countries and cultures are a veritable quagmire for the unwary.

As became apparent when looking at the eighteenth century, Western medicine cannot be regarded as an isolated entity. Its development in the nineteenth century was also dependent on the economic, social and political development of the era. World-wide economic organization favoured the emergence of vast industrial and commercial enterprises, along lines which would later be described as either "capitalism" or "liberalism". Wealth was invested in the development of mining (coal and iron ore) and manufacturing (spinning, weaving and metalwork) and, in conjunction with the shipping companies, colonialism extended its powers beyond Europe.

Labour concentrated around towns: the working-class suburbs, in which employers provided cheap housing, schools and churches to keep the "moral order", created a new social order. Poverty became visible; the structured eighteenth-century society, in which there were nobles and commoners, gave way to the nineteenth-century society of social classes, which was just as discriminatory in terms of income. However, in the latter half of the nineteenth century, medicine was to reach everyone, the fortunate and the destitute, the colonizers and the native people of the colonies.

The French Revolution and medicine in Europe

I.

Power and medicine. The Empire was concerned with the quality of the surroundings and the care given to the wounded, as this visit by Napoleon I to the Invalides hospital in February 1808 testifies. Painting by Véron-Bellecourt (1773?–1838?), Museum of the Palace of Versailles, France.

Although it was not their intention to abolish medical institutions, the French revolutionary assemblies nonetheless made a *tabula rasa* of the past under the banner of liberty and equality. The government abolished the faculties of medicine, their titles, and their degrees, as well as academic societies and the journals responsible for publishing an account of their activities, and the academies, colleges of doctors and surgeons. The art of healing became open and accessible to all.

In 1789, French hospitals were in a sorry state, a state incidentally denounced in a report by Jacques Tenon in 1788. Reforms were clearly needed. The Constituent Assembly discussed the matter in two committees but, lacking awareness of the dual social and medical role of the hospital, failed to come to a decision. Various measures – such as the secularization of the clergy's assets, then those of hospitals, and the abolition of the small amount of funding provided by local governments – further exacerbated the misfortunes of these establishments.

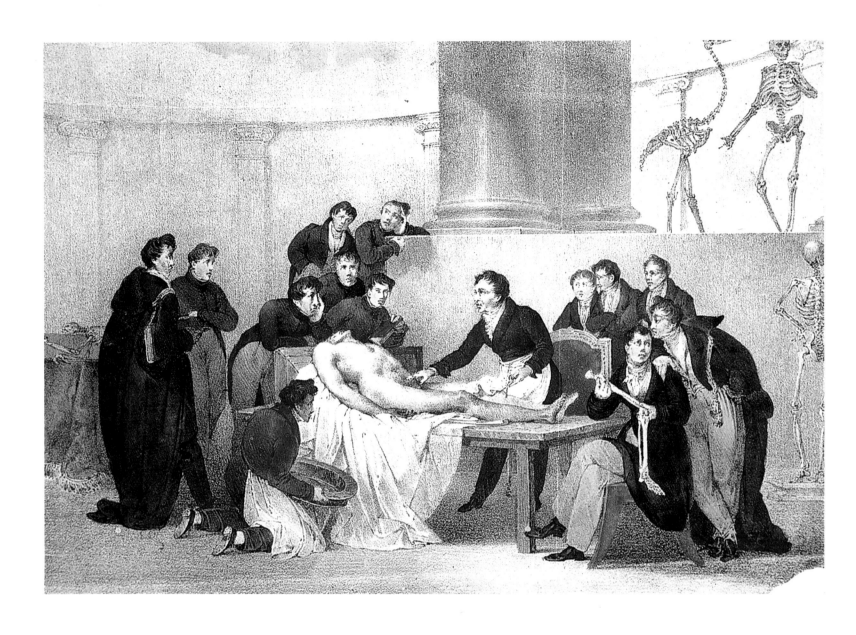

ESSENTIAL REFORMS

A lesson in anatomy in 1826. The Revolution undoubtedly valued practical teaching in medical faculties. Carnavalet Museum, Paris, France.

The whole system therefore had to be rebuilt. The chemist and doctor Antoine de Fourcroy (1755–1809) reorganized the educational structure and, a few months after the fall of Robespierre, persuaded the Convention (or national assembly) to allow the re-establishment of three schools of health – in Paris, Montpellier and Strasburg; these schools had professors appointed and paid by the state, chairs for the individual disciplines and set numbers of students.

After Antoine de Fourcroy, the reorganization of medical education continued under the Consulate (government by consuls), thanks in particular to the influence exercised on the government by ideologists such as the doctor Pierre-Jean

Georges Cabanis (1757–1808) and the chemist Jean Chaptal (1756–1832).

The effect on French medicine of these major reforms can still be felt today. Once the quarrels between physicians and surgeons were settled, the art of healing proceeded with one and the same aim. Similarly, students followed the same type of education, whatever their subsequent speciality.

Moreover, the theoretical education dispensed by the old Faculty was now accompanied by practical training in the form of dissections and regular and compulsory visits to hospitals. "Medicine of observation", as it was called at that time, became the general rule. This compulsory association between school and hospital

Two famous doctors from the Revolutionary age. Left: Georges Cabanis (1757–1808), also an ideologist philosopher.
Right: Jean-Louis Baudelocque (1746–1810), who made a scientific discipline of obstetrics. Library of the National Academy of Medicine, Paris, France.

henceforth became an established method of teaching. The twelve teaching beds which Herman Boerhaave had in the hospital of Leyden and likewise the educational visits and the examinations which the surgeon Desault required of his students were no longer the exception. The rare excursion into the realms of practical experience of pre-Revolution times became the standard procedure in France.

Professors of clinical medicine were then appointed by the state in hospitals which had become municipal establishments and whose financial stability was slowly improving. Furthermore, students were only awarded diplomas if they actually attended classes in dissection halls and hospital wards. The hospital was no longer the refuge of misery; it became a place of learning: it was there above all that medicine progressed and widened its field of knowledge.

The clinical departments thus created included one for obstetrics; this specialism, neglected by the old faculties and practised mainly by surgeons, became, after the Revolution, a fully medical discipline.

The chair at Paris was entrusted to Jean-Louis Baudelocque (1746–1810), author of *L'art des accouchements* (1782). The reputation of the maternity ward which he created at Port-Royal, like that of his school of midwives, is unrivalled even today, after more than two hundred years in existence.

With education thus unified throughout the country, the state issued a diploma ratifying a single type of education and only those with this qualification were allowed to practise medicine. At the same time, Latin was finally and definitively abandoned in favour of French and became the symbol of an obsolete style of education. In making these changes, France spearheaded an innovation. The rest of Europe proved to be somewhat more reluctant to change from Latin to their own national languages.

Finally, the Church ceded control of the running of faculties and hospitals. Doctors could henceforth express

Philippe Pinel (1745–1826) embarked on the path of "moral treatment" of madness and is regarded as the founder of modern psychiatry. He is shown here releasing the inmates of Bicêtre from their chains. Painting by Charles Müller (c. 1840–1850). National Academy of Medicine, Paris, France.

hypotheses and theories without regard to dogmas and ecclesiastical suspicions. Although secularization was attacked in France under the Restoration and the Second Empire, as in various other European countries and in the United States, it nonetheless became the *sine qua non* of scientific independence.

In reality, most of these ideas already existed under the *Ancien Régime*. The Revolution, simply imposed them definitively in France, and eventually throughout Europe. This was largely because, having stood the test of time, of events and of medical experiments, they proved to be logical, coherent and effective.

HOMOEOPATHY

Christian Samuel Hahnemann (1755–1843) observed that when he took tincture of quinine he experienced feverish symptoms in himself which were similar to those which the drug cured. He concluded that diseases should be treated with drugs which give rise to the same symptoms as the disease itself. This was the basis of his "law of similars", which Hippocrates had already formulated in another way without extending it to all diseases in general.

Hahnemann also believed that it was the nature of a drug and not the quantity which was responsible for its effect (which means that very small concentrations can be used).

The homoeopathic doctrine, which is similar to some of the fanciful systems of the eighteenth century, quickly found great favour among the non-medical public. A hundred and fifty years after the death of its originator there is still no scientific proof of either its principles or its effectiveness.

Honoré Daumier (1808–1879),
Les médecins homéopathes,
1837. This caricature sums up the
new therapy of homoeopathy,
created by the German doctor
Hahnemann. National Order of
Pharmacists, Paris, France.

A NEW
VISION
OF DISEASE

*M*en born in the eighteenth century could not suddenly abandon the systems and theories on which they had been brought up in favour of a teaching based solely on the clinical study of patients and the dissection of corpses. In the early nineteenth century, the medical profession was still unable to accept this sudden change of emphasis from theory to practice.

Philippe Pinel (1745–1826) epitomizes this intermediate generation, which is a phenomenon that recurs throughout history. Although he was a clinician as much as an ideologist, Pinel is today famous as a mental specialist, for it was he who is generally thought to have freed the mentally disturbed inmates of the hospices of Bicêtre and la Salpêtrière from their chains. But this measure was actually taken before his time by an official, not a doctor, at the General Hospital. During the course of his career, Pinel managed the first French psychiatric school. He was, furthermore, one of the main propagandists for vaccination against smallpox.

He was also the author in 1798 of *Nosographie philosophique,* which revived the draft classification developed in previous years. In it he catalogued a considerable number of "fevers" which were characterized by their visible symptoms and classified according to theoretical criteria. This system was totally artificial and took account of neither new methods of patient examination nor discoveries resulting from autopsies. It is therefore hardly surprising that it was very quickly abandoned.

La salle des folles à la Salpêtrière.
Gouache by Daniel Vierge (1851–1905).
Public Works Museum, Paris, France.

The title of the work is particularly significant. By using the adjective "philosophical", Pinel revived the old notion that philosophy covers all the sciences, including medicine. However, during the nineteenth century, medicine definitively renounced its connection with philosophy; it moved away from abstraction in favour of observation, facts and the so-called "exact" sciences.

In this generation of French doctors, from the *Ancien Régime* to the First Empire, there were many remarkable intellectuals; they showed how correct observation of patients and the study of organs after death could contribute to medicine. Many of them died young, paradoxically the victims of tuberculosis.

François-Xavier Bichat (1771–1802) was one of these luminaries. Although he died

Two of the leading lights of French surgery during the Revolution.
Left: *Pierre Desault (1738–1795), whose career was devoted solely to practice and teaching, and* (right) *his pupil and friend, the anatomist François-Xavier Bichat (1771–1802). Library of the National Academy of Medicine, Paris, France.*

at the early age of thirty-one, he still found time to win over many of his contemporaries by the breadth of his intelligence and his insight, and by his abundant medical output. Among his most famous works are the *Traité des membranes* (1801) and *Recherches physiologiques sur la vie et la mort* (1802).

Without even the use of a microscope, Bichat identified in the human body classes of membranes (we would call them tissues), each with its own structure and above all a particular role in the working of the body: he attributed to them an anatomical and functional significance and was the first to expound on the need for physiological studies. Like Pinel, Bichat also remained attached to the abstract theories of the Age of Enlightenment. To him, organs were ma-

chines which obeyed precise mechanical principles and which caused disease if not correctly tuned.

At the same time, Jean Nicolas Corvisart (1755–1821) emerged as a remarkable teacher when surrounded by his students at the sickbed. This shrewd, eloquent and indolent man is famous as the doctor chosen by Napoleon on account of his vast clientele. He is also remembered because he was a good cardiologist and, above all, because he had translated into French a book published by Auenbrügger in 1761 and since forgotten: this Austrian doctor recommended percussion and used it to diagnose thoracic complaints. Thanks to Corvisart and the authority he enjoyed, a new sensory domain was opened to medical observation. Two of Corvisart's pupils merit particular mention: Gaspard

René Laennec (1781–1826) was the popularizer of the method of auscultation, practised (above) *on a child. Painting by Robert Thom, 1954.*

Bayle (1774–1816) and especially Théophile-René Laennec (1781–1826), both of whom died of consumption after studying this disease.

It is of no particular relevance that, in perfecting the procedure of *mediate auscultation*, in 1819, Laennec was influenced by Auenbrügger's percussion, or that, for reasons of modesty, he would not place his ear on a young woman's chest, or that the inspiration for his invention came from children who, in the gardens of the Tuileries, amused themselves by whispering to each other along some pipes on a building site. It was nonetheless Laennec who, by introducing the stethoscope, provided doctors with an instrument which was to enhance their diagnostic capabilities more than he could have imagined.

By his observations at the Hôtel-Dieu hospital and his necroscopic findings, he established the identity of various manifestations of tuberculosis, regardless of the organ affected, and described a number of diseases of the abdomen including a type of cirrhosis of the liver which, curiously, is not the one which now bears his name.

Laennec, a monarchist, extremely religious, sickly and reserved, had no more vigorous an opponent than François Broussais (1772–1838), who was a professor at the military hospital of Val-de-Grâce, a republican and atheist with an aggressive edge to his language and writings. His verve, authority and prolific written output won him, in his own lifetime, a reputation which astonishes us today as none of his works has survived.

Although Broussais was quite right to denounce those whom he called "ontologists", those who, like Pinel, created fictional entities or diseases, he went too far in tarring some of his colleagues with the same brush – colleagues like Corvisart, Bayle and Laennec who identified organic diseases on the basis of objective reasoning. Although he rightly developed the concept of inflammation, he was wrong in supporting the distinction between sthenic and asthenic diseases, based on the contractability of certain tissues.

Finally, he was wrong in attributing most physical complaints to "gastroenteritis"

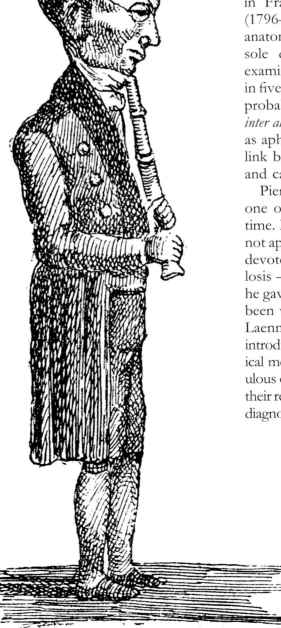

– in doing so becoming himself something of an "ontologist" – and then treating them simply by diet, leeches and profuse bloodletting. As a result, despite the fact that Broussais spent his life replying in an often virulent way to his opponents, even his own pupils soon forgot him when he died.

Another great name among the doctors in the first half of the nineteenth century in France was Jean-Baptiste Bouillaud (1796–1881), an ardent protagonist of anatomical and clinical medicine, and the sole doctor able to boast of having examined twenty-five thousand patients in five years – a record, incidentally, which probably still stands. Bouillaud studied, *inter alia*, certain nervous conditions such as aphasia* and above all established the link between inflammatory rheumatisms and cardiac conditions.

Pierre-Charles Louis (1787–1872) was one of the most original doctors of his time. Misunderstood in his day, he is still not appreciated today. Because he initially devoted himself to the study of tuberculosis – as well as typhoid fever, to which he gave its definitive name – his work has been viewed in conjunction with that of Laennec. His main achievement was the introduction of what he called the "numerical method", which was based on a scrupulous observation of symptoms in a patient, their repetition and their frequency. He drew diagnostic and prognostic conclusions from

Left: *Laennec and his trusty stethoscope, as portrayed by himself in 1824.* Right: *a plate from the* Traité complet de l'anatomie de l'homme *(1831–1854) by Jean Bourgery: bleeding of the jugular and cephalic veins. Library of the National Academy of Medicine, Paris, France.*

340

Pl.5

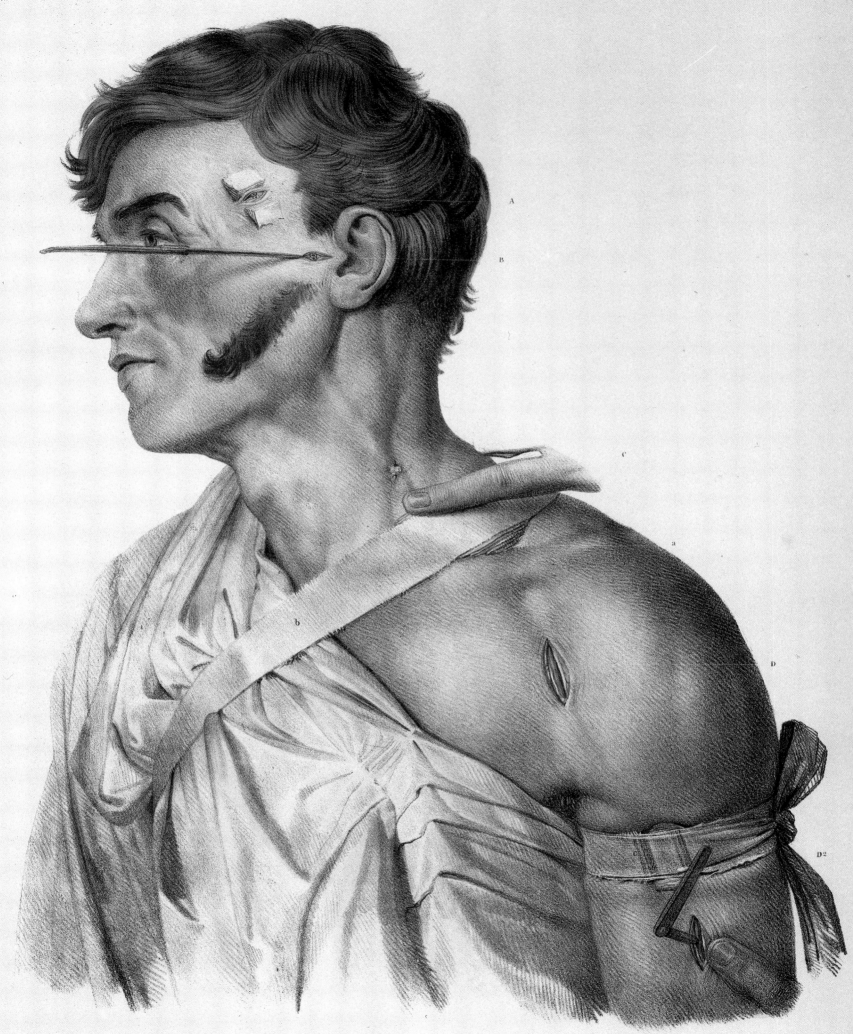

Dessiné d'après nature par N.H. Jacob

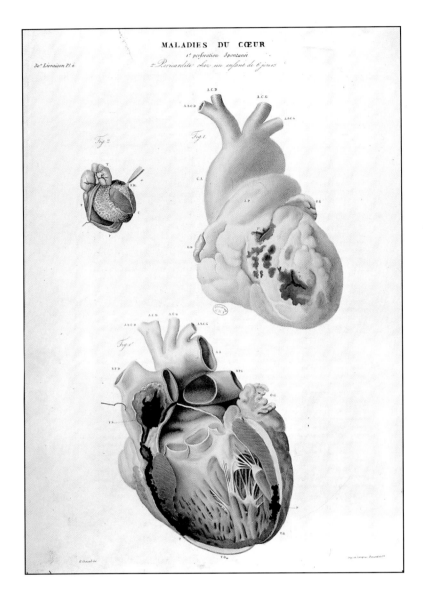

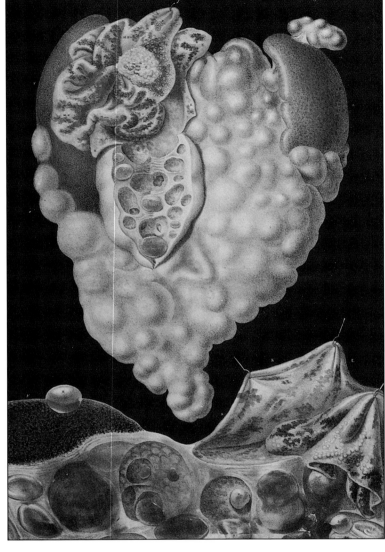

the resultant calculations. In the same way, he ensured that results obtained by therapy were carefully quantified, using the figures alone to testify to the efficacy of the various treatments applied. However, one hundred and fifty years later, this method is still not generally used.

Louis in effect had the audacity to introduce the calculation of probabilities into medicine, thus mixing mathematical rigour with human suffering. Although he was criticized by his contemporaries – in particular by Claude Bernard – he was nonetheless a precursor of medical statistics.

By the continuous comparison of clin-

Jean Cruveilhier (1791–1875),
Anatomie pathologique du corps humain *(1828–1842).*
Left: *diseases of the heart.* Right: *diseases of the liver and spleen. Library of the Old Faculty of Medicine, Paris, France.*

ical symptoms and organic lesions, doctors were able to associate a particular disorder of the tissue with a particular sign and a particular symptom. Each disease could therefore be identified by a set of specific data which was not common to any other disease. This concept of "specificity *" was subsequently to be developed quite brilliantly in other scientific disciplines.

This long list of French doctors from the first half of the nineteenth century cannot be exhaustive, such was the blossoming of inventive and observant minds, passionately involved in their profession and

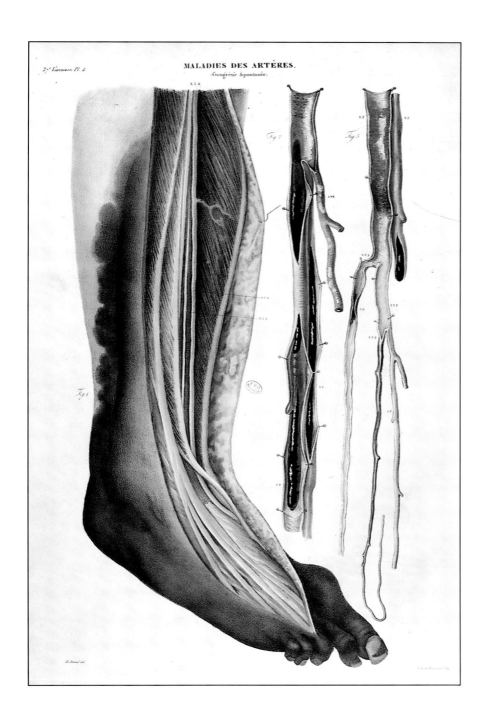

inspired by this new form of medicine. Most of them not only attracted large numbers of students from the Old and the New World, but also enjoyed immense prestige, and soon had imitators, rivals and pupils, some of the most notable of whom were English and Austrian.

In Vienna, the successors of Van Swieten and Stoll naturally could not remain indifferent to innovations: Karl Rokitansky (1804–1878) and his pupil Josef Skoda (1805–1881) emerged as active heads of medical schools and were quick to start teaching percussion and auscultation. Moreover, Skoda distinguished himself

Jean Cruveilhier: description of a case of spontaneous gangrene. Library of the Old Faculty of Medicine, Paris, France.

by a sceptical attitude to healing which was to set the tone in medicine over the next one hundred and fifty years: in the past, doctors had been confident of their drugs, although these were usually ineffective, but nineteenth-century doctors concentrated on diagnosis and prevention, at the expense of therapy.

In Germany, with the exception of Lucas Schoenlein (1793–1864), practitioners professed a medicine known as "romantic", inspired by the Brunonian system (see p. 292) and the mediaeval respect for an essentially benevolent nature. However, this view was abandoned in favour of observation and direct experimentation. Clinical schools sprang up throughout Germany.

In history, actual events and events which did not occur can be equally interesting: why, for example, did Italy not figure in the development of anatomical and clinical medicine at that time, although it had long been prominent on the European medical scene? This can perhaps be partially explained by the stagnation into which it was plunged by the Treaty of Vienna in 1815. The Holy Alliance re-established the authority of the Church and of the monarchies everywhere, while the old and enormously innovative faculties of Pavia, Padua and Bologna came under the strict control of Austria and the pope.

Economic development, forging ahead in Great Britain, northern France and the west of Germany, did not reach the Italian towns, which had earlier had the stimulation of a dynamic bourgeoisie.

The intellectual climate in Italy was certainly not conducive to medical imagination, and anatomical and clinical medicine appeared perhaps, in the eyes of the authorities, too revolutionary to be tolerated. In any case, physicists such as Volta and Galvani had no equivalent in the field of medicine.

343

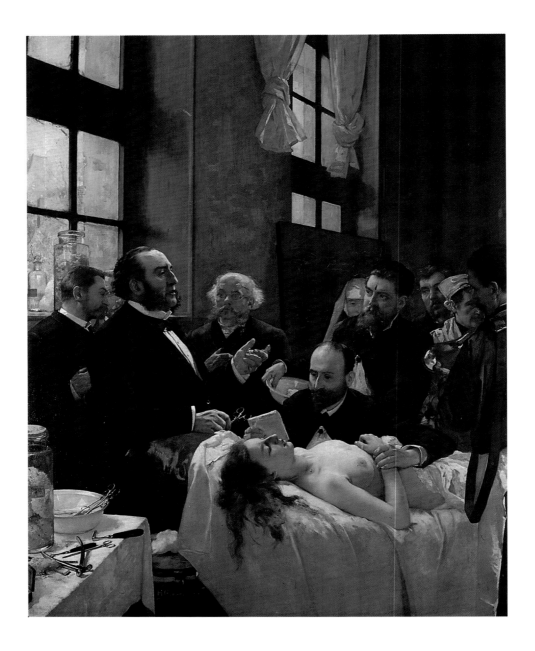

SURGERY– STILL A HASTY AFFAIR

When the Convention decided to merge medicine and surgery into a single discipline, it favoured surgeons at the expense of physicians. As age-old adversaries, the former had the sense not to try to take advantage of the situation. The hidebound attitudes of the faculties were thus finally condemned and surgical dynamism was rewarded.

Surgery gave medicine a new sphere of action: the manual exploration of the body, hitherto forbidden to doctors. All students henceforth learnt to explore a tumour, assess its size, its connections, its links with neighbouring tissue, its mobility, the appearance of the skin covering it, its temperature, and so on. Surgical terminology, rich and precise, infiltrated the field of medicine.

This situation was due to the fact that, for decades, surgeons had endeavoured

Henri Gervex (1852–1929), Avant l'opération, *or surgery as seen by an academic painter. The operating theatre is a sort of fashionable meeting place and, as we might have guessed, the patient is young... and beautiful. Public Works Museum, Paris, France.*

to develop "observation" and had taught this to their apprentices and pupils. They even introduced it in hospitals, thanks to the powerful personality of Pierre Joseph Desault (1738–1795), a surgeon at La charité and then the Hôtel-Dieu hospitals in Paris. An indefatigable and impartial worker, devoting his entire life to the poor rather than to his more affluent patients, he led his students at break-neck pace from the bedside of a patient through to the anatomy theatre, requiring them to keep daily records of their patients' progress. His clinical lectures were published posthumously by Bichat, and his teaching methods were imitated by every professor of clinical medicine and of surgery, each of whom occupied a post created by Fourcroy in the new medical schools.

Desault's pupils were young surgeons sent, immediately upon graduating, to the armies of the Republic and the Empire; one of their number, Dominique Larrey (1766–1842), was soon honoured by Bonaparte. Larrey, who was involved in the Egyptian campaign, faced one of the major difficulties of wartime surgery in the desert climate early on in his career: the transportation of the wounded from the battlefield to the place where they could be treated. By using camels in Egypt, mules in the Alps and sledges in Russia, he became the first surgeon to advocate the use of ambulances in wartime.

Another – perennial – problem of wartime surgery was one which Larrey was unable to resolve: whether to amputate or attempt to save a damaged limb. Amputa-

Left: Jean-Nicolas Corvisart (1755–1821), Napoleon's chief doctor, shown (right) in conversation with wounded soldiers. "Honour to unfortunate courage". The political message of this print by Épinal is quite evident here. INRP, historical collection.

tion resulted in many sudden deaths due to haemorrhaging and infection, while conservation caused many lingering deaths from tetanus, gangrene or generalized infection.

It is said that, by amputating too readily, Larrey created too many invalids who could have recovered without this cruel sacrifice, but we will never know the number of wounded who would have recovered without amputation, nor the number of those saved from death because of amputation.

Of Desault's contemporaries and pupils in Paris, Joseph Récamier (1774–1852) and Jacques Lisfranc (1790–1847), Joseph Malgaigne (1806–1865) and Auguste Nélaton (1807–1873) all enjoyed a certain renown, but none achieved the glory of Guillaume Dupuytren (1777–1835).

La chirurgie au secours de la Grande Armée. *Dominique Larrey (1766–1842), the Great Army's chief surgeon, working during the battle of Hanau in 1813. He was above all the creator, in 1799 in Egypt, of the first system of military ambulances, using camels. Museum of Val-de-Grâce and Library of the Old Faculty of Medicine, Paris, France.*

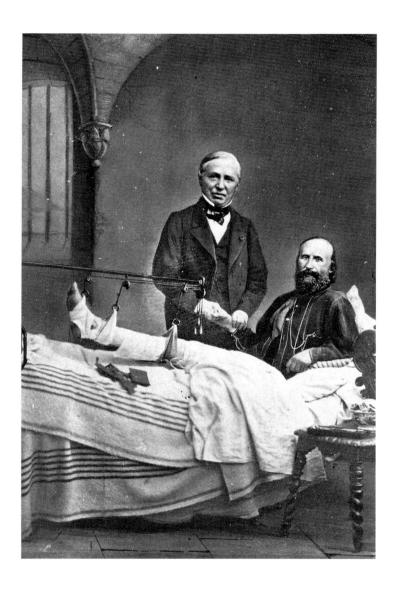

any illusions about surgery at that time. These surgeons did, admittedly, become more adventurous; they invented new amputation and disarticulation techniques better suited to lesions and better able to save limbs; they dared to remove organs such as the rectum and the uterus, they knew when and when not to trepan when faced with cranial traumas, and also how to correct the unfortunate consequences of difficult labours, such as painful fistulae between the bladder and the vagina. But, whatever their dexterity and their speed, their patients continued to suffer horribly in their hands despite laudanum – a barely effective potion containing opium. Also, for the first days following the operation the patient usually had to suffer a suppurating wound which was slow to heal, at the cost of further suffering – if it was not fatal – when the infection spread throughout the body. Pain and infection were still the two major obstacles against which surgery constantly fought, without any apparent remedy.

Hard-working, jealous of his colleagues, ambitious, despotic, hungry for honour and wealth, Dupuytren was an admirable surgeon, restrained yet efficient. Although he wrote little, he trained numerous pupils who all aspired to emulate him.

The brilliant French school of surgery had its following in England in the person of Astley Cooper (1768–1841), in Scotland in the person of James Syme (1799–1870), in Germany in the person of Bernhard von Langenbeck (1810–1887) and in the United States in the person of Jack Marion Sims (1813–1883).

This catalogue of prestigious surgeons must not, however, be allowed to create

Dr Nélaton at the bedside of Garibaldi in 1870. Surgeon to Napoleon III, Nélaton was also the inventor of probes used in urology.

THE CONCERN FOR PROGRESS DOES NOT PREVENT SCEPTICISM

In medicine: Magendie ridiculing his pupils' prolific prescriptions for drugs:

"It is clear that you have never tried to do nothing."

Skoda greeted every new product with the words:

"Ah, it's all the same thing."

In surgery, Jean Marjolin (1770–1849). A surgeon in Paris, brilliant, titled and rich and proud of himself:

"Surgery has reached a point where there is little more to be learnt."

Although the theories and systems so prized by doctors in the eighteenth century had been discredited, they did not simply vanish from the minds of the time. Stahlism, rejecting the Cartesian view of man as a machine – like the Brunonian system, classifying diseases as "sthenic" or "asthenic" – still had its disciples in Europe. In France, vitalism inspired many works – not solely of a scientific nature. For instance, in his meditations on life and death, Bichat clearly showed that he was a vitalist.

The first works of the young François Magendie (1783–1855), in contrast to those of Bichat, appeared to be a materialist bomb. He quickly became a doctor at the Hôtel-Dieu hospital in Paris, alongside Dupuytren, but his fixed ideas and his rebarbative character – on a par with that of Dupuytren – prevented him from entering the academy, though not from being elected professor of the College of France. Magendie had the merit of being able, throughout his entire career, to reconcile his role of hospital doctor with that of laboratory director and teacher.

He felt that progress in medicine could only follow advances in physiology, and that these could only be achieved by experiment. "I cannot conceive," he said, "of any line of demarcation between the laws which govern living bodies and those which govern inert bodies." Magendie thus decried both animism and vitalism. Furthermore, what some observed on the autopsy table, Magendie sought by experimentation. In denigrating purely anatomical and clinical medicine, he swelled the ranks of his enemies, and by calling for experiments on animals as an indispensable research procedure, he outraged the protectors of animals as well as those

The experimental revolution: from Magendie to Claude Bernard

II.

MAGENDIE AND HIS PATHOLOGICAL PHILOSOPHY

François Magendie (1783–1855), the French physiologist, is one of the founding fathers of modern medicine. College of France, Paris, France.

who declared animal physiology inapplicable to man. Despite his many detractors and despite obvious errors – for example, when he denounced the utility of the microscope and the existence of red blood corpuscles – his work was nevertheless important.

His first discoveries were concerned with the action of strychnine, extracted from an exotic plant by Pelletier and Caventou in 1818, and then emetine extracted from ipepacuanha: his technique was the genesis of experimental pharmacology. He then turned to the formation of the image on the retina, the peristalsis of the oesophagus and the consequence of the absence of certain substances in the diet (touching on the notion of deficiency). He worked for some considerable time on the nervous system, described the circulation of the cephalo-rachidian fluid and confirmed the sensory role of the posterior nerve roots of the spinal cord just as, before him, the Englishman Charles Bell (1774–1842) had established the motor role of the anterior roots; he also studied the quadrigemina tubercles of the base of the brain.

Following in the footsteps of Haller and Spallanzani, Magendie then took a further step forwards in experimental procedures to advance human physiology, by denying empiricism and its "fantasies" and by making physics and chemistry the basis of physiology.

Lithograph by H. N. Jacob of a nasal operation, showing sections of the face, taken from the voluminous work by Jean Bourgery (1797-1878) entitled Traité complet de l'anatomie de l'homme.

Next to him, his contemporary Pierre Flourens (1794–1867) appears a rather colourless figure. An average but over-rated researcher, he particularly made his name in the field of exploration of the nervous system, thanks to his description of the "vital centre" of the *medulla oblongata*, injury to which causes death because of the suppression of certain vital functions. Similarly, Flourens studied many specific areas of the brain, the role of the semi-circular canals in maintaining equilibrium and the anaesthetic effect of chloroform. He was, finally, the author of worthy popularizations to which he owed his reputation among the general public.

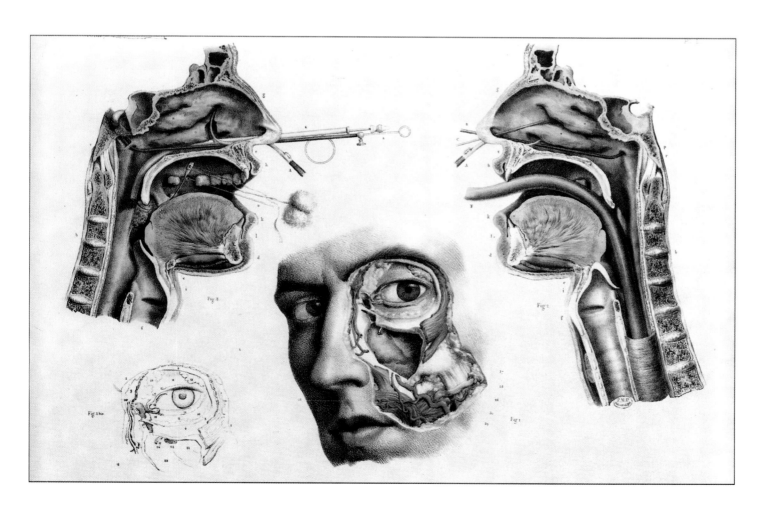

The physiologist Claude Bernard. His Introduction à l'étude de la médecine expérimentale, *1865, sets out the basic principles of modern scientific research. Portrait by Auguste Mengin. College of France, Paris, France.*

CLAUDE BERNARD
(1813–1878)

*T*hanks to his powers of judgement and despite his faults, Magendie had the enormous merit of laying the foundations for the career of his successor in the College of France, Claude Bernard (1813–1878), who had, in fact, at one time considered a career in the theatre. A researcher with an insatiable curiosity – as his logs of experiments prove – a great worker despite periodic health problems, dogged by domestic problems (for his wife, religious and jealous, could not accept the honours heaped upon her husband for his "cruelty" to laboratory animals), Claude Bernard rose above this difficult personal situation, carried out an enormous amount of research and wrote a great deal, often retiring for this purpose to the house in Beaujolais where he was born.

Although, in the Second Empire, he no longer had to fight against vitalism, which had become rather outmoded, he nonetheless had to contend with spirituality. In society at that time, frivolous and avid for material gain as it was, there was still a general belief in God. As in previous centuries, scholars had to temper their views. The sceptic Jules Renan and the positivist Auguste Comte and his disciples, such as Émile Littré, were also subject to much criticism.

Through prudence or because of a lack of personal religious conviction, Claude Bernard also established a clear distinction between the field of science and what lay outside it: "It is not the task of science to prove or disprove God; it is not concerned with this question. Materialism which states that there is nothing beyond matter is not within the bounds of science." He could not, however, escape the eternal question which men of science ask themselves: is life something special which

material laws cannot explain? "There is, in all the functions of the living body without exception, a conceptual aspect and a material aspect. The conceptual aspect of the function is associated by its form with the unity of the plan of creation or construction of the organism, while its material aspect responds, by its mechanism, to the properties of the living matter." The statement is not clear; vitalists would not have denounced "this plan of creation", but Claude Bernard distanced himself from vitalists as well as from the devout or excessive materialists.

In any case, within the field of science with which he was concerned, he believed in the unity of science and the union of all its disciplines: "The *sole* truth, the search for which is the aim of science, will only be attained by the interaction of all the sciences. Physiology is an intermediary science, lying between the sciences of

Sketch with water-colour by Claude Bernard showing a sub-maxillary ganglion in the calf. College of France, Paris, France.

THE GERMAN SCHOOL OF PHYSIOLOGY

Johannes Müller (1801–1858)
The specificity of the sensory nerves: the optical nerve and the acoustic nerve can only transmit sensations of one kind.
Work in the field of embryology.
Eduard-Friedrich Weber (1806–1871)
The speed of the pulse.
The concept of inhibition in neurophysiology.
Emil Du-Bois-Reymond (1818–1896)
Founder of electrophysiology.
Hermann Helmholtz (1821–1894)
Law of the conservation of energy.
Geometrical optics.
Carl Ludwig (1816–1895)
Physiology of cardiac mechanics and circulation.

the mind and those of nature; it is intended to bring them together, especially today now that it has made such enormous progress."

It is not possible to list here all the areas of human physiology addressed by Claude Bernard. His work on the secretions of the pancreas is the most well known, but other studies should be mentioned, such as those on the antagonist roles of the sympathetic nervous system and the pneumogastric nerve, on vasomotricity, on the transformation by the liver of sugar into glycogen, and on the glands which secrete directly into the bloodstream (endocrine glands), such as the thyroid, and those which secrete on to external or internal body surfaces, such as the sweat and intestinal glands.

He established the concept of "function", that is, the role fulfilled by each

One of the volumes of the Traité complet de l'anatomie de l'homme, *by Jean Bourgery, was jointly signed by Claude Bernard. This illustration of the nerves of the pyloric end of the stomach is taken from it. Library of the Old Faculty of Medicine, Paris, France.*

tissue or organ in the human physiology to maintain life, a role which the body accelerates or checks as necessary: Bichat only glimpsed this concept, Claude Bernard explained it; he may well have denounced the usefulness of the history of medicine, but he could not help but be influenced by the works of his predecessors, consciously or otherwise.

He also described the "internal medium", that is, the physico-chemical substance which bathes the tissues of the body, inside the blood vessels and outside them, in such a way that a change in the medium at a given point can have repercussions on a remote organ. On the one hand, life depends on the equilibrium of this internal medium, and on the other, is characterized by the various mechanisms which sustain it. It was at this time that Littré translated Hippocrates: the old

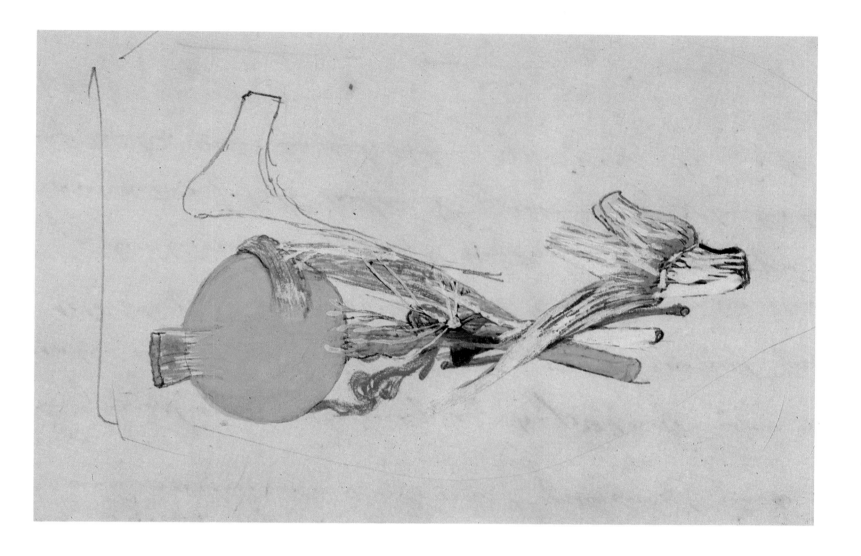

Greek master would have been happy to see Claude Bernard's physiology confirm his doctrine of the balance of the humours.

It was only after years of work and after discovering a number of functions that he decided to commit his principles to writing: his *Introduction à la médecine expérimentale* appeared in 1865.

This book soon became the bible of physiology: this was because Claude Bernard was not content simply to catalogue the rules to be followed in experiments to restrict the numbers of errors as far as possible; he also set out the criteria for a teaching based on sound physiological facts, as well as philosophical reflections on the healing art.

For decades, the *Introduction* served as a guide to physiologists world-wide. Today, Claude Bernard appears somewhat outmoded. Like anyone setting out definite

Drawing by Claude Bernard, taken from one of his experiment logs (May 1842), showing the nerves of a cat's head. Archives of the College of France, Paris, France.

principles, he could not resist making what he considered reasonable exceptions to them: for example, why did he not believe in Pasteur's methods? Subsequent generations are unwilling to pardon the errors of their ancestors although they continue to repeat them.

Claude Bernard wrote: "In physiology, any researcher can make unexpected findings provided that he is fully aware that theories are so incomplete in this science that in the current state of affairs there is as much chance of discovering facts which overturn them as there is of finding facts which support them."

If, like all scholars, Claude Bernard was at times mistaken, his work nonetheless established the fundamental rules for biological research, incontrovertible rules which his successors were to supplement and apply in other areas.

In the course of the nineteenth century, doctors gained insights from the interpretation of diseases by means of clinical and anatomical medicine and, in laboratories, physiologists gained a better understanding of the human body. Yet the sick continued to endure their ills despite the increasing number of doctors who, with conviction, lavished on their patients medicines which often had no effect on the course of their sufferings.

Of all the diseases prevalent at that time, the epidemic ones are those which we can most easily identify today and those which affected the largest number of people.

Thanks to Jenner having proved his theory of vaccination in England in 1796, a decisive step was made in the fight against smallpox in the final decade of the eighteenth century. In France the first vaccination using his method took place in 1799; Pinel, Guillotin, the new School of Health in Paris and General Bonaparte were its main advocates and consequently schools and whole regiments were vaccinated. The clergy co-operated and devoted their Sunday sermons to the subject of vaccination. The practice soon spread throughout Europe.

The method, consisting of introducing into the human body pus from cowpox, which is harmless to man, to give protection against the serious disease of smallpox, certainly raised a few eyebrows: it was regarded with suspicion and legitimate scepticism. However, the public authorities – and this was not the least of their merits – did their utmost to convert the opposition.

In France, successive Ministers of the Interior and *Préfets* acted: doctors were

From prevention to public health

III.

THE CRUSADE AGAINST SMALLPOX

One of the first vaccinations by Edward Jenner (1749–1823), against smallpox, c. 1796. In France, the number of vaccination campaigns increased during the nineteenth century, with Napoleon's blessing. Painting by Gaston Melingue. Library of the National Academy of Medicine, Paris, France.

persuaded to conduct vaccination campaigns in the countryside. They obtained the vaccine from the purulent vesicles of children in orphanages. Doctors, paid by district councils and sometimes even awarded public honours, were involved at every stage.

But the fees they were paid did not cover the costs they incurred. The product used was not always of good quality and the doctors' enthusiasm gradually waned. Vaccination, which was definitely in vogue, nevertheless spread through the various social strata and, in the second half of the nineteenth century, there was a slight abatement in smallpox epidemics generally.

We have already mentioned tuberculosis. It started to be a real problem in the late eighteenth century in England, before reaching France. Among the many historical figures afflicted by this disease were the Dauphin (the eldest son of Louis XVI), Gaspard Bayle, François-Xavier Bichat, Théophile-René Laennec, the son of Napoleon I, and many others besides.

But above all, tuberculosis eventually became an integral part of the French romantic tradition, for the young man in the literature of the time – portrayed as evanescent, prematurely melancholic, already mourning his life which has barely commenced – was in fact suffering from tuberculosis.

This statement may seem rather dry and strictly medical, but the hero – or the romantic heroine as epitomized in Dumas' *La dame aux camélias* (later appearing in the Verdi opera *La traviata* based on the same story) – was often more severely afflicted by tuberculosis than by some existential "world weariness".

In France, the endemic disease abated only in the late nineteenth century, before spreading to Germany.

Alongside tuberculosis, eruptive diseases – known as "exanthematous" because of

Ernest Hébert (1817–1908), La malaria. *Parasitical diseases were one of the major scourges of the nineteenth century. Drainage programmes (as in the Landes and the Poitevin marsh), carried out in the second half of the nineteenth century, gradually got the better of the disease although it was not possible to eradicate it entirely. Musée d'Orsay, Paris, France.*

the red rashes they produced on the skin – continued their ravages: scarlet fever, measles and rubella were all described too vaguely for us to be able to establish today the part that was played by each of them.

Malaria also persisted more or less everywhere, despite the efforts made and the proliferation of public drainage works throughout Europe which punctuated nineteenth-century history. These were carried out particularly in Holland and the papal states, with the reorganization of the Roman countryside, and in south-west France with the drainage and afforestation of the Landes region. So rife was the disease that the painter Ernest Hébert achieved a notable success in the salon of 1850 with his Romantic painting entitled *La malaria.*

We do not know much about the numerous diarrhoeic diseases, prevalent at the time yet little analysed diseases that are today identified by the germ causing them. A little more is known, on the other hand, about typhoid fever, thanks to the talent for observation of Pierre Bretonneau (1778–1862).

This unassuming doctor from the Touraine region is credited with attributing to a single disease a whole range of pathological symptoms found throughout the body: a sore throat, a rash of a

SPECIFICITY ACCORDING TO BRETONNEAU *(well before Pasteur):*

"A special germ peculiar to each contagion gives rise to every contagious disease. Epidemic scourges are only caused and disseminated by their reproductive germ..."
"Specific diseases develop under the influence of a contagious principle, a reproductive agent..."

particular pink colour, haemorrhaging, pains in the joints, peritonitis due to perforation of the small intestine, hepatic and renal problems and sometimes even cardiac problems.

Bretonneau showed that this generalized infection had its origin in abnormal patches on the mucous membrane of the intestine, and gave this disease the name "dothienenteritis", which was soon replaced by that of "typhoid", invented by Louis.

Bretonneau was able to discover a single cause for these disparate problems, thus helping to develop the concept of *specificity*: a disease is specific in that it has a cause and apparently unconnected symptoms which have a single prognosis; thus diagnosis is simple and treatment must be tailored to the disease.

In a few decades, Pinel's abstract nosology was brushed aside by anatomical and clinical findings – findings which enabled Bretonneau to attribute to diphtheria alone a certain type of tonsilitis, the appearance of grey membranes and a suffocating laryngitis – life-threatening in the young – followed by paralysis of the eyes and the soft palate.

Bretonneau was therefore the archetypal non-university doctor who helped to identify diseases on the basis of anatomical and clinical thinking.

Finally, he was distinguished by the quality of his pupils, in particular Armand Trousseau (1807–1867), also from Touraine, one of the most brilliant professors of clinical medicine of his age, who received patients from all parts of the globe and was personally able to influence his numerous pupils in the Hôtel-Dieu hospital in Paris with his exceptional teaching ability.

Europe which, in contrast to earlier centuries, no longer suffered from the plague – it was by then confined to the Far East – was suddenly hit by two hitherto

Despite the fear of cholera, the disease was still ridiculed. The epidemic which broke in Europe from 1830 prompted many caricatures. Art Library of the Prussian Cultural Heritage, Berlin, Germany and National Library, Paris, France.

Venereal diseases spread in the wake of armies. Following the allied occupation of Paris, in 1815, the frequent "visits" by soldiers to the Palais Royal had to be followed by medical advice! Museum of the History of Medicine, Paris, France.

unknown epidemics. The most deadly was cholera, which came from Afghanistan, via Russia and Scandinavia, to England and reached Paris in 1832, from where it invaded the rest of Europe. This severe diarrhoea caused by contaminated water aroused fear because of its epidemic nature and yet its contagious aspect was not generally accepted. It was to ravage intermittently and briefly in various countries until the end of the century.

The other new disease was yellow fever. Seamen knew it well in Central America, where it raged in the form of violent epidemics, yet remained in endemic form between each attack. It was to spread by sea to the ports of the Iberian

peninsula, to Cadiz where it decimated Napoleon's troops, and to Barcelona in 1821 where a number of French doctors devoted themselves to treating its victims, and in turn died of it.

This list of scourges should not cloud our view of world-wide population growth: numbers grew steadily, even in the countries of Africa and Asia, where nutrition was poor and epidemics were more common than in America or Europe.

In the latter continent, life expectancy at birth gradually increased. However, the particularly strong demographic growth in France and Germany at this time cannot be attributed solely to medical progress.

THE EMERGENCE OF PUBLIC HEALTH

The main cause of the improvement in health undoubtedly lay in a better diet. In France, and indeed in Europe as a whole, cereals and agricultural produce were now being transported more rapidly and more easily and the consequences of poor harvests could be prevented. From the eighteenth century onwards, maize from America, easier to grow and with a high yield, gradually spread throughout Europe from Italy. The potato, initially adopted by the Prussians, likewise gained ground.

Thus, the nineteenth century in Europe was not, like the eighteenth, a century of famine. Only Eastern Europe, Scandinavia, and above all Ireland – where an epiphytic disease of the potato caused famine and consequently a large-scale emigration of the population to the United States – were still severely affected.

Concerns about public health were reflected after the Revolution by a co-ordinated project, on a national scale in France, instituted by Dr Joseph-Ignace Guillotin (1738–1814), the president of the Health Committee to the Constituent Assembly, and ratified under the Consulate by the laws of 1802 and 1803.

In this regard too, France led the way. The *communes* (the smallest administrative areas) were given responsibilities in the field of health: they had to ensure that citizens were supplied with drinking water and keep a list of insanitary accommodation and "insalubrious and dangerous" establishments: newly created chemical factories, butchers', slaughterhouses, knacker's yards, mines, tanneries and dye works, and so on. The principle of these "classified establishments" still applies, but the list is much longer today.

The *communes* also had to help the poor, have their hospitals managed by an administrative committee, and provide assistance and drugs for inhabitants who were sick. They were obliged to have doctors at their service. At district level doctors were responsible for advising the *Préfets* of the state of health of the population, and of epidemics and epizootics.

Thus, the government acknowledged its responsibilities in maintaining the nation's health, and doctors, in turn, developed an interest in community hygiene. Chairs of hygiene were created in universities, where men such as François-Emmanuel Fodéré (1764–1835) shone. Another illustrious figure, Louis-René Villermé (1782–1863), undertook a vast survey throughout France of the health of silk- and cotton-mill workers. Armand Parent-Duchatelet (1790–1836) concentrated on the working-class areas of Paris and the problems caused by prostitution, while Adolphe Quételet (1796–1874) was involved in the industrial development of the Liège basin.

The *Revue de médecine légale et d'hygiène*, which dealt with matters involving medicine and various public regulations and the law, enjoyed a large audience from the

Florence Nightingale (1820–1910), the famous British nurse, became involved in the running of hospitals during the Crimean war (left) and helped to improve the army's health services. She then concentrated on the training of female medical personnel in hospitals (right).

outset and was influential throughout Europe, and in 1851, a doctor created the concept of "social medicine".

The Consulate also organized medical practise in France. Only graduates from medical schools were allowed to practise medicine. Unfortunately, under the influence of Cabanis and in order to provide the army with a sufficient number of doctors – albeit poorly trained – to deal with the volatile situations arising in France's troubled years, and to ensure that care could be provided in rural areas, a "provisional" category of health officers was created. With but a few years of study behind them, they were only semi-qualified. The incompetent Charles Bovary (the husband of Gustave Flaubert's heroine) was the most famous literary figure among their ranks.

Eduard Ritter (1808–1853), Le musicien malade, *1847. The family doctor, as he was until just a few years ago, first appeared in 1830–1850. From that point onwards, the respected doctor had friendly relations with his patients and their families. Austrian Gallery, Vienna, Austria.*

This unsatisfactory situation was nothing new; the old adage "a little learning is a dangerous thing" is clearly applicable to these inadequately trained health officers, yet the system lasted for one hundred years – long enough to be revived and copied by tsarist Russia.

This was the era in which medicine became hierarchized: in hospitals with competition for studentships, in the faculties by means of rigorous examinations creating associate professors and full professors. This organization, and likewise the thirst for knowledge stimulated by anatomical and clinical medicine, lent the French medical profession a certain dynamism which was reflected in the creation of a large number of academic societies as well as in the publication of a number of medical journals.

The doctor's social prestige, which became established in the nineteenth century, did not extend to the official but inferior rank of health orderlies, and even less to the shady world of bonesetters and charlatans. Top: *J. Léonard*, Le médecin des pauvres. Below: *Albert Anker (1831–1910)*, Le charlatan. *Fine Arts Museum, Valenciennes, France and the Public Art Collection, Basle, Switzerland.*

Voùlez-vous déjeuner avec nous, la mère Pilon?

Gérard Grandville (1803–1847), Une dissection, *taken from the series entitled* Métamorphoses du jour, *1829. This caricature is aimed at doctors, metamorphosed into crows or griffon vultures.*

Membership of the French Academy of Medicine, established in 1820 by Louis XVIII at the instigation of Antoine Portal (1742–1832), was also much coveted. It brought together representatives from all the disciplines involved in people's health: doctors, surgeons, physicists, chemists and other appropriately qualified people.

In its long history, medicine had never experienced a breakthrough as brutal as that of the nineteenth century. In the space of a few decades, disease changed – it was no longer a subject for discussion, but a subject for practical observation. Man was no longer an exceptional being; his life force was no different from that of any other living creature and, from the study of animals, deductions could be made about the functioning of the human machine.

A breakthrough of such proportions was not to be witnessed again until the mid twentieth century, when the pharmacopoeia was suddenly to benefit from the addition of a large number of effective substances.

France was fortunate in having had, for half a century, remarkable clinicians, excellent observers of the living and the dead, and ingenious researchers who developed theories about their methods. This explains the superiority of French medicine in Europe, a superiority which slipped from its grasp in the second half of the nineteenth century.

CLINICAL MEDICINE
1801 – 1865

POLITICS AND CULTURE	DATE	DATE	MEDICINE
		1801	Bichat: *Traité d'anatomie générale*
Napoleon I, Emperor of France	1804	1802	Cabanis: *Rapports du physique et du moral*
Lamarck: zoological philosophy	1809	1808	Broussais: *Traité des phlegmasies chroniques*
Zenith of Napoleon's Europe	1811	1810	Gaspard-Laurent Bayle: *Recherches sur la phtisie pulmonaire* François Gall: *Anatomie et physiologie du système nerveux*
Fall of Napoleon I First then second restoration of the Bourbons The Holy Alliance	1814–1815	1815	Joseph Hodgson describes aortic insufficiency
		1816	François Magendie: *Précis de physiologie élémentaire*
		1819	Laennec invents the stethoscope *Traité de l'auscultation médiate*
Brazil gains independence, casting off Portuguese dominance	1823	1820	Foundation of the Academy of Medicine in Paris
		1824	Antoine-Laurent Bayle founds the *Revue médicale*
		1825	Pierre Louis develops the numerical method Matteo Orfila applies toxicology to forensic medicine
		1826	Pierre Bretonneau: *De la diphtérie* Foundation of the British Medical Association in London
The "Three Glorious Days" Start of the July monarchy	1830	1830	Cholera reaches Russia
		1832	Corrigan and Hope work on diseases of the heart
Victoria, Queen of England	1837–1901	1838	French law on the mentally ill
		1840	Heine and infant paralysis
		1843	Robert Graves describes exophthalmic goitre Ferdinand Hebra develops a new system for the treatment of skin diseases in Vienna
		1846	William Morton pioneers the use of ether in anaesthesia
Karl Marx and Friedrich Engels write the *Communist Party Manifesto*	1847	1847	Article by Semmelweis on infection
"Liberal" and national demonstrations in Europe. The Second Republic in France	1848	1849	Huss invents the word "alcoholism" Claude Bernard publishes his first studies on the glycogenic function of the liver
Louis-Napoleon Bonaparte is declared Emperor of France	1852	1852	First international congress on hygiene
		1860	Charles Pravaz develops the syringe for injections
War of Independence in the United States	1861–1865	1861	Paul Broca locates aphasia in the brain Florence Nightingale trains the first nurses

chapter XI

Laboratory medicine

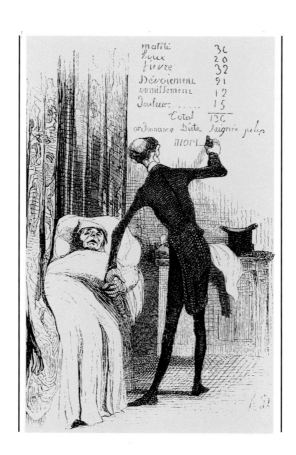

Clinical anatomy conquered the world in the space of twenty years, and it took no more than twenty years to depose it, for in that time the other sciences had developed powerful tools for revealing the structure of living tissue. Chemistry described the changes of the "humours" which were so dear to Hippocrates, physics analysed the movements involved in certain basic functions, and Pasteur discovered a world which until then had been completely unknown.

In the medical world, the last few decades of the nineteenth century saw the start of a still unresolved debate. Which is the more important: the doctor who questions and examines his patient, and conducts a person-to-person relationship which is in itself therapeutic; or the anonymous laboratory, with its equipment for measuring and quantifying physico-chemical processes?

The microscope had been greatly improved since its invention by Leeuwenhoek in the seventeenth century; but strangely, naturalists were making much more use of it than doctors, and pathological anatomy still remained macroscopic. Pasteur was one of those who forced medicine to adopt the microscope. Medicine after Pasteur was to be very different from medicine before Pasteur. He discovered an invisible world – invisible to the naked eye at least – about which only very few people had had a vague intuition. This was the world of micro-organisms: germs of life and germs of death.

The son of a tanner in the Jura Mountains, Louis Pasteur (1822–1895) trained as a chemist under Jean-Baptiste Dumas (1800–1884), and worked in this capacity for much of his life. He first discovered the asymmetry of crystals which can bend

*B*acteriology: *Pasteur extends our knowledge of "nature"*

I.

rays of light to varying degrees. Then the wine manufacturers and brewers of northern France, where he was living in the 1850s as Dean of the Faculty of Lille, asked him to investigate ways to make their products last longer. Thus he was to penetrate the chemical mechanisms of fermentation in a factory which made sugar from sugar beet, and to identify microscopic yeasts without which such fermentation cannot take place.

Silkworm breeders in the Languedoc then asked for his advice when an epidemic devastated their silkworm rearing-houses, and he was able to identify the tiny micro-organism responsible.

Pasteur and the legend. Opposite: *his laboratory in the rue du docteur Roux, Paris.* Above: *a card designed both to advertise and to educate, which was probably given away free with a bar of chocolate. It illustrates an episode in Pasteur's career: his discovery of the law of fermentation.*

Louis Pasteur in his laboratory, *Albert Edelfelt (1854–1895). Pasteur Institute, Paris, France.*

CHOLERA AND RABIES

*F*or several years, the scientific world was fascinated by the debate that centred around Louis Pasteur and Félix-Archimède Pouchet (1800–1872). The latter believed in "spontaneous generation", namely the potential that certain germs have of appearing by themselves in inert surroundings. Pasteur, unlike Pouchet, knew that germs had to be present for life to exist: "gas, fluid, electricity, magnetism, ozone, things that are known and things that are hidden; there is nothing whatever in the air but the germs it carries along, which are a requirement for life..."

By varying the circumstances and conditions in a number of experiments, Pasteur showed that moulds do not grow inside flasks which are kept in a vacuum, and that fermentation does not take place in them, and that conversely all these phenomena occur as soon as contact is re-established with the surrounding atmosphere. He declared that "spontaneous generation is a figment of the imagination". Just as Harvey had demonstrated that "all eggs are born from an egg", after

Pasteur it was possible to assert that life can only be born of life. However, the problem of the definition and origin of life still remained unresolved. Pasteur's demonstration reinforced its mysterious nature, and gave further justification to the special character of "biology" (a term invented by the German Treviranus and applied to the new science by Lamarck in 1802).

Pasteur went on to identify the micro-organism responsible for fowl cholera, and stock breeders then drew his attention to anthrax in sheep. He confirmed the pathogenic role of *Bacillus anthracis*, which Davaine and Rouyer had discovered in 1850 in the blood of ewes that had died from anthrax, and demonstrated that the disease is transmitted from one animal to another. Pasteur was certainly not the first to identify micro-organisms; Leeuwenhoek had seen them, and others who followed him had also demonstrated the contagious nature of glanders which is transmitted from one horse to its stable companions and to stable boys. However,

Pasteur was to be given the credit for showing the universality of microbial life, for advising surgeons to operate only with sterile instruments, and to use only dressings that had previously been sterilized.

In May 1881, Pasteur and his assistants succeeded in preventing anthrax from developing in sheep by inoculating healthy ewes with an attenuated bacterial culture. He called this technique "vaccination", a word which he borrowed from Jenner, thus paying tribute to the Englishman, even though Pasteur's method had nothing to do with smallpox or with disease in cows. Jenner's vaccination consisted of injecting people with a virus which produced a disease largely resembling smallpox, and which unfortunately could lead to its own complications (such as fatal encephalitis), whereas Pasteur's vaccination used the actual pathogen of the disease which was to be prevented, once its virulence had been attenuated by various processes.

Pasteur's most impressive success, and the best known, is undoubtedly his vaccination in 1885 of a young shepherd who had been bitten by a rabid dog. When he injected the boy with extracts from the spinal cord of a dog with rabies, Pasteur did not know whether he would actually give him the disease. However, the procedure succeeded, and the method is still used today to vaccinate livestock and foxes.

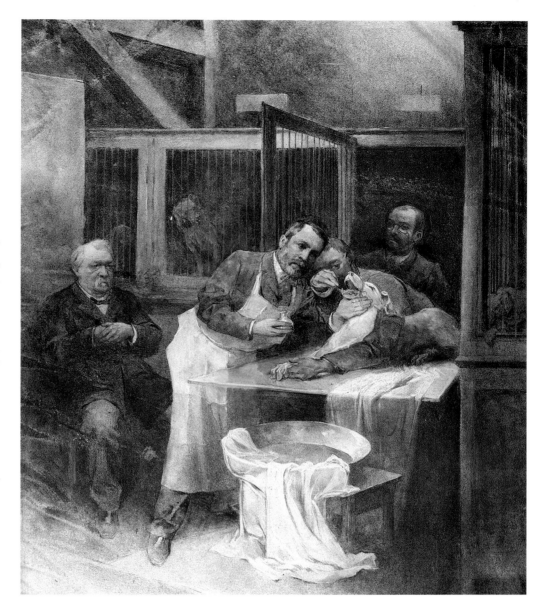

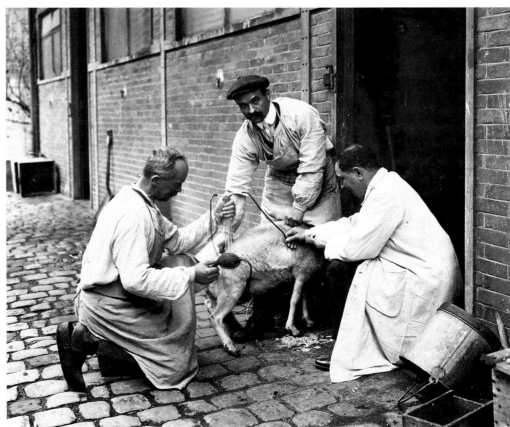

Two of Pasteur's experiments. Top right: *taking a sample of saliva from a dog (charcoal drawing by Alphonse Mucha).* Bottom right: *vaccinating a sheep against anthrax. Pasteur Institute, Paris, France.*

The greatest honours were heaped upon Pasteur during his lifetime. He was and still is celebrated throughout the world, and rightly so, as one of the great benefactors of humanity. Through the acuteness of his observations and the rigour of his experiments, he opened up to man an immense area of nature which until then had been unimaginable – the realm of the very small. In the seventeenth century, Pascal rested a metaphysical argument on the mite, a tiny arthropod which he held to be the smallest living creature that could be observed. Pasteur made it possible to study the parasites which live off the mite.

Naturalists who were working at the start of the century – such as Lamarck, Cuvier and Geoffroy Saint-Hilaire, who did so much work on palaeontology, reconstructed the history of living animals, classified them, and ordered them

KNOWING HOW TO INTERPRET CHANCE

One day, one of Pasteur's colleagues, Émile Roux (1853–1933), happened upon a culture of the bacteria that cause fowl cholera, which had been kept in a cupboard for several weeks under poor conditions of preservation, with no oxygen and no light.

To check on the quality of this "aged" culture, Roux injected it into some hens: they did not die.

In order to make a comparison, Roux injected the products from a fresh culture into these same surviving hens: once more, they did not die.

With Pasteur, he concluded that the aged bacteria had an attenuated virulence and protected the animals against the normal virulence of the microbe.

This was how Pasteur's "vaccination" came about.

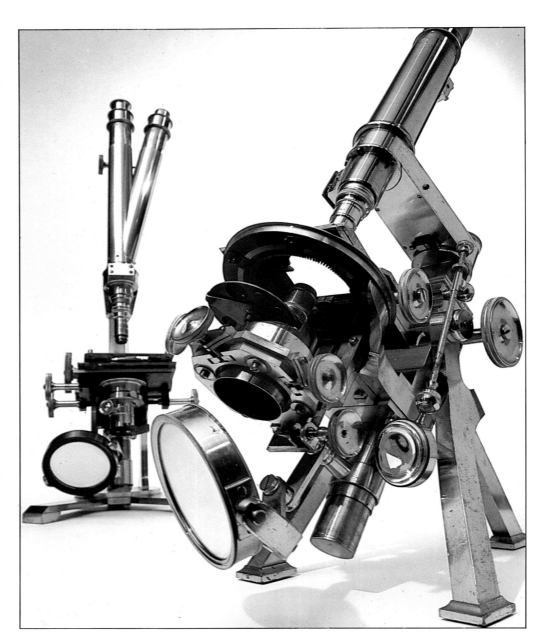

Two types of microscope made in England (left, Abraham, 1865; right, Powell and Lealand, 1899). The microscope on the left was one of the first to enable binocular viewing. Arthur Frank Collection.

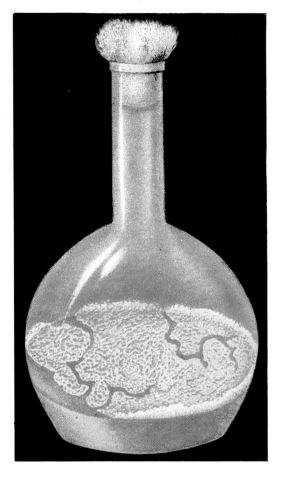

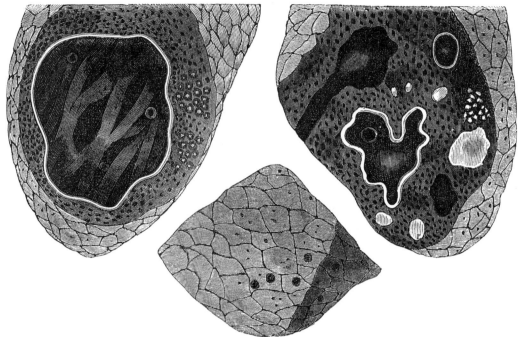

in a hierarchy – never imagined that such a wealth of microscopic life was possible.

The time was not far off when it would be necessary to study fossil bacteria several million years old in order to seek out the origins of life itself.

Pasteur's colleagues perfected special filters to collect the bacteria that they wanted to study, but they also noticed that the filters invented by Chamberland (1853–1908) allowed "filterable viruses" to pass through, which themselves often caused disease.

At the Pasteur Institute, founded in 1888 with the help of generous public donations, Pasteur's successors lacked the means of observing these viruses. They nevertheless surmised that viruses were alive and were most probably susceptible to sudden morphological change. There then arose, in relation to the infinitely small, the issue of mutation which Charles Darwin had raised in 1859 in his famous book, *Origin of species*.

Pasteurian bacteriology also troubled

Above left: *a tubercle bacillus culture on the surface of glycerinated culture medium, from I. Strauss,* Tuberculosis and its bacillus, *1895. Above right: one of the first academic representations of tuberculosis lesions, taken from* La médecine illustrée, *1888. Library of the Old Faculty of Medicine, Paris, France.*

minds for another reason: microbes could cause disease, but they did not explain everything – other species were necessary for certain vital chemical reactions to take place. Not only did microbes represent another form of life, they were sometimes essential to the life of higher species. The many aspects of Pasteur's work were not without their surprises, and his ideas met with a certain amount of resistance. As is always the case with scientific innovations, there were plenty of sceptics, and debates could be stormy.

However, Pasteur soon mastered the art of polemics, and was able to promote his ideas in such a way as to convince the hesitant, with the result that bacteriology soon became an indispensable branch of medicine. The most impoverished hospitals opened laboratories and bought microscopes. The success which Pasteur had had in preventing some diseases would doubtless be possible with others: the observation of bacteria therefore led to a new form of medicine.

Chez Bauger R. du Croissant, 16

Imp. d'Aubert & Cⁱᵉ

L'EAU DU PUITS DE GRENELLE.

– Décidément cette eau chaude est très mauvaise à boire.
– Oui, mais il y a beaucoup de petits insectes dedans !

ALL THE MICROBES IN THE WORLD

*P*asteur was responsible for establishing another fact that is central to the history of medicine: the proof of contagion in the case of some diseases. Since the time of Hippocrates, man had been aware of epidemics; that is, diseases which suddenly affect a large number of individuals within a limited area. However, for centuries doctors had been wondering whether disease was in fact transmitted from person to person. Some claimed to be contagionists (such as Fracastorius in the Renaissance) and had excellent arguments for their time; and there was no shortage of others who proclaimed themselves to be anti-contagionists. Whatever the scholars may have thought, general opinion and public authorities had acknowledged the existence of contagion for almost a thousand years. All this was to change in the second half of the nineteenth century.

In 1837, Pierre Rayer confirmed the contagious nature of glanders with the aid of many epidemiological observations. Jean Antoine Villemin went further by transmitting tuberculosis to animals using purulent flesh from patients who had died from the disease. Nonetheless, some were to reject this evidence when it was published in 1865.

By proving the existence of pathogenic micro-organisms which lived in the air or

The French artist Daumier is acting here as spokesman for the mixed reactions which the theory of germs provoked, from disbelief to passionate interest. National Library, Paris, France.

in water and could therefore attack all the people in the area, Pasteur and his followers put an end to the controversy: contagious diseases were finally acknowledged to exist.

Scientific curiosity and the widespread use of the microscope led to the discovery of micro-organisms all over the world. People started to see microbes everywhere, and all human illnesses, from rheumatism to cancer, were attributed to as yet undiscovered bacteria. Even madness was attributed to the spirochaete of hereditary syphilis.

THE SUFFERING OF OTHERS

"One does not ask a poor wretch, 'What country do you come from, or what region are you from?' One says. 'You are suffering, that is all that matters; you belong to me, I will make you feel better.'"

Louis Pasteur.

This attitude towards another's suffering was not invented by Pasteur, but he had to remind his contemporaries of it. Slavery had only just been abolished, theories about the "inequality of the human races" were widespread, and there were signs of the first excesses of colonialism.

It is hard to assess whether or not the misconception that there was a germ for every disease gave research a fresh impetus. In any event, it was only a few decades before scientists identified the germs which were responsible for many of the epidemic, endemic and contagious diseases that had been taking their toll of humanity for centuries. By using the same conditions of observation and identification they had employed for microbes, doctors discovered a number of parasites, even multicellular ones that had until then escaped the microscope. Expeditions to distant lands and the colonizing activities of Western powers also enabled doctors to describe the microscopic flora and fauna of the tropics.

All this curiosity and rivalry led to extraordinary developments in bacteriology, from the pathology associated with fungi, to the pathology of the mites that cause scabies and of intestinal worms such as the various tapeworms and filariae.

The most inventive mind of this period, and one comparable to Pasteur, was

Robert Koch (1843–1910) in his laboratory. His remarkable work on tuberculosis in the 1880s, and his discovery of the bacillus which bears his name, laid the foundations for the research work carried out by Calmette and Guérin that resulted in their famous BCG vaccine.

the German Robert Koch (1843–1910). Contrary to the supporters of bacterial polymorphism, he asserted the existence of species among these unicellular creatures, with each species having its own characteristics, producing its own toxins, and triggering its own specific pathological phenomena. The concept of specificity that had been so dear to some authors at the beginning of the century was reaffirmed in Koch's work. He maintained that each disease was due to a given micro-organism which could not cause any other disease.

Koch identified the tubercle bacillus, enumerated its modes of transmission, and produced a brilliant confirmation of the work that Villemin had done thirty years earlier. During his travels in India and Egypt, he isolated the cholera vibrio, and in Africa he studied sleeping-sickness and the plague.

In the space of forty years, from 1870 to 1910, progress in bacteriology made a spectacular leap. Löffler described the causative agent of diphtheria, Eberth that of typhoid fever, and Laveran that of malaria, the disease responsible for those famous tertian or quartan fevers of the past.

However, one difficulty still remained. It was not yet known how the pathogen of some diseases penetrated the human organism. Sometimes it was inhaled and there was direct contagion from human to human, as in pulmonary plague or influenza; it could also be ingested when drinking or eating food; in other cases, it penetrated via a wound. Nevertheless, these explanations remained inadequate.

The ingenuity and observational skills of a number of doctors were still needed before the role of "insect vectors", as we call them, could be discovered. The mosquitoes were the first to be blamed when Ross demonstrated their role in the transmission of malaria, Manson their role in the transmission of filariae, and Beauperthuy and Finlay their role in the transmission of yellow fever. Then the tsetse fly was identified in Africa, and shown by Bruce to spread sleeping-sickness.

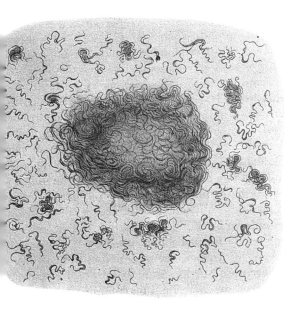

Robert Koch in 1906 during one of his trips to East Africa. Left: *one of the first representations of Koch's bacillus, from I. Strauss,* Tuberculosis and its bacillus, *1895. Library of the Old Faculty of Medicine, Paris, France.*

Émile Roux (right), *one of Pasteur's faithful colleagues who continued his work, could have posed for the photograph* (below) *with these Russians from Smolensk, who were treated against rabies in 1886 in the laboratory of the rue d'Ulm in Paris.*

AU PAYS DU SOLEIL
Le moustique. — Sors donc de ton garde-manger, eh! feignant!   Dessin de Doës

Bacteriology and parasitology thus revealed some complex mechanisms of communal life, with man living in the midst of a mysterious microscopic world of which he was sometimes the victim, and against which he had to defend himself. Once again he felt hunted and surrounded by elusive enemies; but now, in the enthusiasm of triumphant science, he glimpsed the means of overcoming these new dangers.

Once Louis Pasteur and Émile Roux had discovered how to give protection against diseases caused by microbes, by decreasing their virulence and vaccinating healthy people, many vaccines soon started to be manufactured. Another procedure was then devised. Since the higher mammals are able, like man, to generate substances to protect themselves against

Above right: *the mosquito, which was blamed for all kinds of illnesses following the work of Ross, Manson and Beauperthuy on parasites, as seen by the magazine* Le rire, *31 August 1901. Decorative Arts Library, Paris, France.*

germs, it was decided to transmit an attenuated disease to animals and to inject people with elements from the blood of the animal which had been thus vaccinated. These serums, as they were called, were soon perfected and their use became widespread, sometimes with a prophylactic and sometimes with a curative aim.

This fight against infection is certainly one of the great innovations of the second half of the nineteenth century, and it took place in an atmosphere of euphoria. The general public persuaded themselves that every germ would soon be defeated in the fight against insect vectors, in the suppression of microbes, and in the prevention or destruction of their harmful action. The number of successes continued to increase in the early years of the following century.

Among the medical triumphs of the nineteenth century, we frequently forget to mention Rudolf Virchow (1821–1902), a doctor who was little known outside Germany. However, he exhibited a rare perspicacity while pursuing many activities in addition to practising as a doctor.

Virchow was born in Prussian Pomerania and studied medicine, history and Arabic poetry. He was soon obliged to leave Berlin because of his political opinions. He taught for a while at Würzburg before being summoned back to Berlin. He took part in Prussian political life, in which his secularism and nationalism caused him to oppose the actions of Bismarck. He was passionately interested in archaeology, and helped

Towards microscopic pathological anatomy

II.

Schliemann carry out the famous excavations at Troy. He was attracted by anthropology, denied the existence of clearly defined human races, and therefore refused to acknowledge that anti-semitism had any racial basis.

While doctors, and the French in particular, were content to record lesions which they observed with the naked eye on the autopsy slab, Virchow studied microscopic lesions. He paid tribute to his predecessors, Lazzaro Spallanzani and Giovanni Battista Morgagni, by borrowing from the seventeenth century the word "cell", which had formerly been applied to plants. He was also the grateful pupil of Johannes Müller and colleague of Rudolf von Kölliker (1817–1905).

Rudolf Virchow (1821–1902), from the portrait by the German painter Hugo Vogel. Rudolf Virchow Hospital, Berlin, Germany.

VIRCHOW AND CELLULAR THEORY

Virchow owes his reputation to the book he published in 1858, *Die Cellularpathologie*. He attributed disease to a disorder which could be located in an organ, and demonstrated that each form of tissue has its own particular type of cell: the cells belonging to each of the organs are alive in their own right, are nourished by the blood and discharge waste. Most importantly, each cell is born from a similar cell, whether during the growth of an individual or during the continuous renewal which the human body undergoes.

Returning to Harvey's maxim *omne ovum ab ovo*, he declared *omnis cellula a cellula*. One of his predecessors invented the term "histology" to designate the study of the tissues. Now Virchow was to devote himself to the study of pathological histology. Virchow directly continued Bichat's work by concluding that it is the cell which gives the tissue its specificity.

Throughout his long life he identified many diseases which produce typical microscopic anomalies, such as some kinds of leukaemia and tumours. However, he did not use the term cancer, even though he explained the development of metastases by the transfer of tumour cells via the blood or the lymph.

He revealed himself to be deeply materialist. Just like the Paris "positivists" such as Émile Littré (1801–1881), the author of a medical dictionary, or Charles Robin (1821–1885), a professor of histology, Virchow was opposed to all systems, and was careful never to construct an artificial theory. He thus had the opportunity of disproving the ideas of Jean Cruveilhier (1791–1874) who, doubtless due to the particular condition of the corpses on which he carried out autopsies,

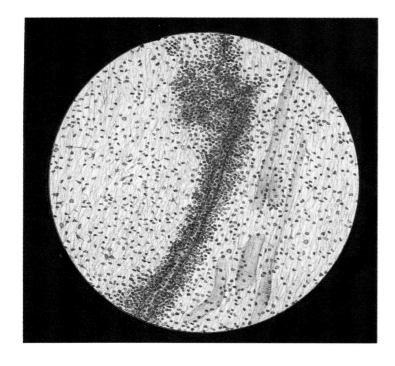

A tissue section carried out by Theodor Schwann (1810–1882), the famous German naturalist who founded the cell theory. Berlin, Germany.

SOME OF THE PATHOGENS IDENTIFIED OVER THIRTY YEARS

1875	Leprosy	Hansen	Norway
1875	Amoebiasis	Loesch	Germany
1878	Boils	Pasteur	France
1879	Puerperal fever	Roux	France
1879	Gonorrhoea	Neisser	Germany
1880	Malaria	Laveran	France
1880	Typhoid	Eberth	Germany
1882	Tuberculosis	Koch	Germany
1883	Cholera	Koch	Germany
1884	Tetanus	Nicolaier	Germany
1887	Brucellosis	Bruce	Britain
1889	Chancroid	Ducrey	Italy
1894	Plague	Yersin	France
1901	Sleeping-sickness	Dutton	Britain
1905	Syphilis	Schaudinn	Germany
1906	Whooping Cough	Bordet	France
1909	Typhus	Nicolle	France

attributed all illnesses to "phlebitis", that is to say to inflammation and obstruction of the veins. Virchow did not deny the existence of phlebitis, but he showed that it was only one lesion among many, and therefore not responsible for illnesses in general.

Claude Bernard was sceptical about Virchow's "pathophysiology", just as he was about Louis' "numerical medicine" or Pasteur's microbes. In fact, Bernard considered the physiology of the body to be so important that he did not see the relevance of the microscopic study of cells. Virchow's great merit and work consisted in assimilating all the discoveries of his contemporaries: for example,

Une leçon de Claude Bernard, 1889. Among those present we can make out, from left to right, Dumontpallier with the white beard, Paul Bert, turning towards the former, and Dastre, seated on the right. All these men left work of value to posterity. Léon Lhermitte (1844–1925), National Academy of Medicine, Paris, France.

the glycogenic function of the liver described by Claude Bernard can only take place within the confines of the hepatic cell. Did a contradiction really exist between the many unicellular organisms discovered by bacteriologists and the life of the cell as identified by Virchow?

This does not mean that Virchow was never wrong. The distinction he made between two major kinds of epidemic appears to us to be based on the very theories he abhorred. According to him, "natural" epidemics such as dysentery or malaria were linked to a change in the climate or in living conditions, while "artificial" epidemics such as typhus, cholera, scurvy and tuberculosis had physical or

SCIENTIFIC MEDICINE ACCORDING TO VIRCHOW

"The position which we propose to adopt ... is simply that of the exact sciences ... the precise and lucid development of anatomical and clinical experiments will be our first and essential duty. These experiments will gradually lead to the true theory of medicine, pathophysiology."

"The scientific researcher only knows bodies and the properties of bodies; he calls transcendental all that which lies beyond, and considers transcendentalism to be an aberration of the human mind."

"The human mind is only too inclined to abandon the tedious path of scientific reasoning and lose itself in reverie."

Rudolf Virchow in good company in his institute of pathology at the Charité Hospital, Berlin, Germany, in 1900...

even mental side-effects and could be blamed on society. This vision of the epidemic demonstrates that at this period, despite Virchow's far-sightedness, the causal link between germs and contagion was not an easy one to accept.

Virchow did not only work with the microscope. From 1848 onwards he took an active part in the struggle against the traditionalism of the Holy Alliance in Prussia, and later against the moral order of Bismarck. He observed at first-hand an epidemic of typhus in Upper Silesia, was interested in cholera and trichinosis, and fought for the education of women. He was interested in anthropology, and studied the anatomy of six thousand school-children. He also contributed to the cleaning up of Berlin by participating in the improvements which were made to its network of sewers.

*...and receiving Lewis Wilkens,
a giant-sized anthropological
wonder from America.*

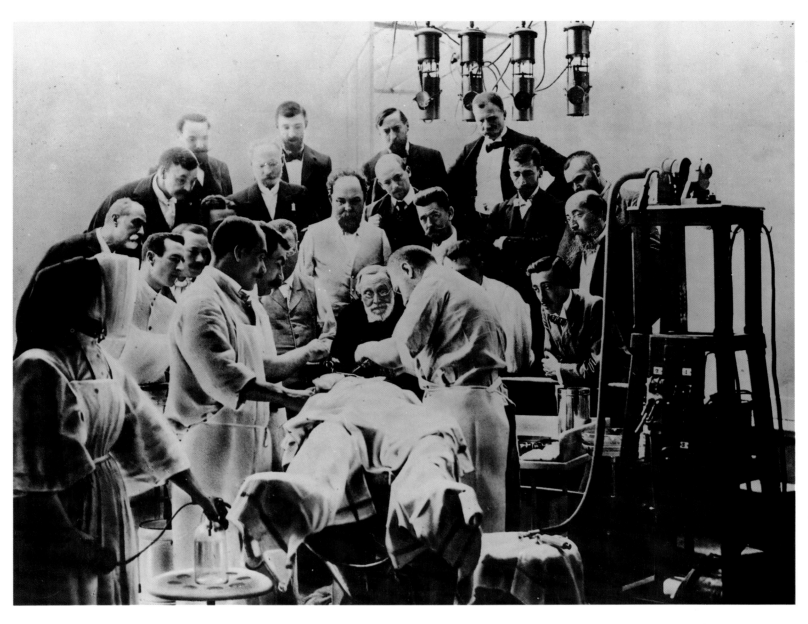

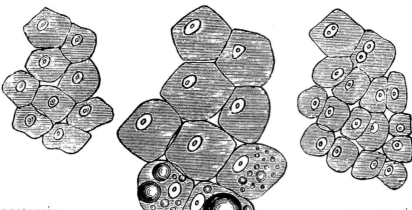

The early days of cellular pathology. A diagrammatic representation of liver cells from a lecture given by Virchow on the foundations of pathology in 1858.

By founding a journal of anatomico-pathological anatomy which was published for more than a century, and above all by refusing to appear as a systematist, Virchow disseminated without too much resistance his theory which became known as the "cellular theory". He considered the cell to be "the basic form of life, the organic unit". Each cell has its own function, which it carries out through its structure: structure and function are closely linked and constitute the specificity of each cell. A change in one or the other engenders "cellular pathology" and eventually disease in the organism.

Subsequent discoveries which challenge Virchow's work are rare. His clarity of exposition, the precise terminology which he invented, and his public work enabled him to convince many of his contemporaries and to educate brilliant students. For more than half a century he ensured the success of the German school of anatomy, which included such figures as Friedrich von Recklinghausen (1833–1910), Julius Cohnheim (1839–1884) and Paul Ehrlich (1854–1915).

In the second half of the nineteenth century, microscopic pathological anatomy developed all the more rapidly in Europe, due to the fashion for carrying out post-mortems which had become widespread since the beginning of the century. In a short space of time, an immense amount of data was accumulated on the structure of organs. Clinical anatomy in the 1820s therefore found a new justification. New instruments were invented, such as the microtome, which enabled increasingly thin sections of tissue to be cut for microscopic study. The microscope was improved, and methods of fixing and colouring tissues were perfected. All this allowed for the identification of cellular structures whose existence had hitherto not even been suspected. This microscopic morphology naturally necessitated

Top left: in Paris, on 2 August 1900, Virchow was present at an operation on the skull. Bottom left: Paul Ehrlich, a microbiologist and one of Virchow's students, winner of the Nobel prize in 1908, in his study in 1910.

new terminology: almost all the nomenclature covering the features of blood dates from this period.

Even clinical practice was to be influenced by anatomico-pathological anatomy, which lost its status of theoretical activity. From now on a diagnosis could no longer be made solely on the basis of observation of the lesions on the autopsy slab; confirmation had to come from the microscope. The same instrument also enabled diagnoses and therefore prognoses to be made more precisely in the case of lesions in a living person. Cells taken from a skin abnormality enabled the disease responsible to be precisely identified, and it was with this aim in mind that the French dermatologist Ernest Besnier (1831–1909) invented the practice of removing cells for study, giving it the name of "biopsy" – a sample of cells taken from a living patient – as opposed to "necropsy" or "autopsy", the dissection and examination of a dead body.

Virchow probably never suspected that, because of him, microscopic pathology would become one of the foundations of medicine a century later; it will undoubtedly remain so for a long time to come.

MEDICINE AND POLITICS ACCORDING TO VIRCHOW

"The doctor is the natural advocate of the poor man."

"If medicine really wants to fulfil its great task, it will be forced to intervene in political and social life, and it will have to denounce the obstacles which prevent the normal blossoming of vital processes."

385

The work of Priestley and Lavoisier in the Age of Enlightenment stimulated scientific research. Scientists were encouraged during the time of the French Revolution and subsequently by profound changes in the teaching of medicine, changes which were being introduced for strategic as much as for scientific reasons. The work of chemists was becoming clearly differentiated from that of physicists, as they tried to extract from plants the active substances which doctors had been using as medicines for centuries. Consequently, analytical chemistry made rapid progress.

In 1806, morphine was isolated from opium. This was followed by codeine and heroin. Pierre Joseph Pelletier and Joseph Caventou identified emetine, strychnine, quinine and caffeine. A large number of products were extracted from plants at this time, including theobromine, theophylline and ergotamine, which was extracted from rye plants infected with the fungal disease known as ergot and responsible for gangrene of limb extremities.

The valuable lesson which Withering received in 1785 from a farmer's wife, who suggested that he use the leaves of the foxglove to treat dropsy, was furthered by Homolle in 1864 and Claude Nativelle in 1869, who demonstrated the effect of digitalin. The discovery of this first cardiotonic product was followed by those of sparteine and strophanthin. In about 1830, salicylic acid was extracted from willow bark, which was already known to be a febrifuge. Today it has the highest consumption of any drug in the world, and is known by the name of aspirin.

Until the end of the nineteenth century, the search for active substances was continued among the plants of the medi-

*N*ew progress: from analytical chemistry to physics

III.

ANALYTICAL AND SYNTHETIC CHEMISTRY

aeval pharmacopoeia, and some brilliant discoveries were made. This progress slowed in the middle of the twentieth century, when the industrial manufacture of synthetic products took over, but natural remedies are now beginning to regain favour.

Doctors stimulated the curiosity of researchers by now having at their disposal a new method of introducing a product into a patient's body, for the syringe had been invented. Hitherto, potions had been taken by mouth, enemas administered via the rectum, and inhalants via the respiratory tract. With the syringe, injections were now possible.

More and more pharmacists possessed their own laboratory. Here, Christian Rosenberg in Copenhagen, 1863. Museum of Historical Medicine, Copenhagen, Denmark.

It was Charles Pravaz (1791–1853) who perfected the smallest and most practical syringe – initially made of metal, and later of glass. From then on, the new liquid drugs could be injected subcutaneously or intramuscularly.

For administering solid drugs, *cachets* and compressed tablets were invented, along with pessaries to treat gynaecological disorders, and suppositories which could be absorbed by the rectal mucosa.

There was frequent rivalry between France and Germany in the field which was then coming to be known as pharmacology. The most famous name in this field was Justus von Liebig (1803–1873) who, in addition to his work on drugs, studied many metabolic phenomena. We

The great German chemist, Justus von Liebig (1803–1873), in his laboratory at the Institute at Giessen in Hesse. Research in Germany went hand in hand with the development of the chemical industry at the end of the nineteenth century. After Wilhelm Trautschold, c.1840.

have him to thank for identifying the three classes of food required by man: fats, proteins and carbohydrates, a classification still fundamental to dietetics today.

Another German, Friedrich Wöhler (1800–1882), synthesized urea in 1828. This chemical, which is extracted from urine, is nothing more than a waste product excreted by the kidneys. However, Wöhler succeeded in making urea, the product of one of the vital activities of the human body, from its constituent parts. At the time, this achievement seemed revolutionary, for it showed that organic chemistry was but one branch of chemistry, and the new romantic vision of the meaning of life disappeared overnight. The laws of inorganic chemistry could now be applied to all chemistry; life had become nothing more than a chemical activity. However, even if only because of its implications for the patient, biochemistry retained its interest: Liebig was to be its principal pioneer.

From now on, synthetic chemistry gradually replaced analytical chemistry. For example, we owe to synthetic chemistry the extensive range of barbiturates which includes barbitone and phenobarbital.

Henceforth, the fate of pharmaceutical research was to be closely linked with industrial chemistry. The intensive exploitation of coalmines in England, France and Germany provided chemists with an unlimited supply of a carbon-based raw material which opened up possibilities for investigation in all areas. It was in Germany in the 1880s that the pharmaceutical industry was born and began to develop.

Portrait of Justus von Liebig, *one of the founders of the chemistry of human nutrition, Wilhelm Trautschold (1815–1877). E. Merck AG Collection, Darmstadt, Germany.*

$\mathcal{A}$ll the innovations in the physical and chemical sciences during the course of the century were to be employed by scientists in their efforts to learn more about the precise functioning of the organs in humans and animals.

In the field of chemistry, mention should be made of the exploration of the functions of the liver – work which continued that of Claude Bernard. As regards renal activity, the conjunction between chemistry and clinical practice proved to be particularly marked. Richard Bright (1789–1858) in Great Britain, Fernand Widal (1862–1929) in France, and Franz Volhard (1872–1950) in Germany studied the composition of urine and the damaging effects of excess urea in the blood. They established a connection between the disordered excretion of urea and certain cardiac symptoms.

MEDICAL PHYSICS AND PHYSIOLOGY

Chemistry also enabled researchers to penetrate the detailed mechanism of the breaking down of food substances and their assimilation into the organism which is continually creating new cells. The metabolism of these products, with a catabolic phase followed by an anabolic phase, shed new light on nutritional phenomena.

It was perceived that certain substances are necessary for chemical reactions to take place: they may be used in small quantities, but they are found again almost intact at the end of the reaction. These "ferments" – an ancient term borrowed from traditional methods of wine and beer manufacture – were dubbed "enzymes" in Germany and "diastases" in France. It is now known that the great majority of biochemical changes are connected with enzymatic activity.

At the end of the nineteenth century, making a diagnosis was still a summary affair. Laennec's stethoscope was still not being used on a regular basis.

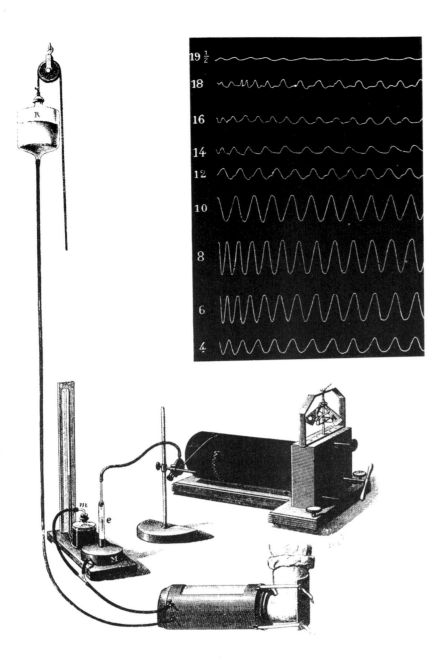

In thermodynamics, scientists began to use smaller and more accurate thermometers, and the relative constancy of the temperature in the large mammals forced a review of Lavoisier's concept of the body as a heat machine. Physiologists studied the variations in temperature of the human body which result from its activities and may be brought about by disease. In the middle of the nineteenth century it gradually became customary to take the temperature of a patient at least twice a day.

From then on, the term "fever" was no longer used to refer to diseases. Instead, fever – or high temperature – became a simple sign whose presence and course were characteristic of certain disorders. Since the beginning of the century, doctors had been in the habit of taking the pulse with the aid of a pocket watch. They now noticed that an acceleration in the

The ancestor of the sphygmomanometer. Using this apparatus, which was assembled in 1858 by a genius of a handyman, Étienne-Jules Marey (1830–1904), "one can, with an adequate degree of accuracy, assess the absolute pressure of the blood in the human arteries". Museum of the History of Medicine, Paris, France.

pulse occurred in parallel with an increase in temperature. However, some diseases manifested themselves by the lack of concordance between these two signs.

The dazzling technical progress which marked the nineteenth century therefore did not exclude medicine. Advances in optics led in 1851 to the invention of the ophthalmoscope and in 1854 to the development of the laryngeal mirror, which was used to examine the vocal cords.

The ingenuity of Thomas Edison (1847–1931) prompted researchers to use electricity to explore the dark cavities of the body, since the manufacture of small light bulbs had now been perfected. Endoscopy developed rapidly over a few years, with the invention of a laryngoscope, a cystoscope which could be introduced into the urethra to examine the bladder, and a rectoscope for studying the lower section of the large intestine. At the end of the nineteenth century it was even possible to carry out bronchoscopy and oesophagoscopy.

After teaching physiology in New York and London, Charles Brown-Séquard (1817–1894), Claude Bernard's successor to the chair of the College of France, used electricity in his neurophysiological experiments. It enabled him to excite the nerves or sectioned fascicles of the spinal cord and to determine their functions. Brown-Séquard also applied himself to describing the activity of the endocrine glands, the sexual organs and the adrenal glands; he thus became the father of modern endocrinology. He also invented "opotherapy", the use of extracts from glands to treat cases of disordered glandular function or insufficiency. The idea proved to be a good one; today, for example, we treat diabetes with insulin extracted from the pancreas. He even injected himself with extracts from the testicles of animals in order to alleviate

the effects of ageing. He was naïve enough not to be able to resist the old myth of eternal youth. Others after him were to be beguiled by the same illusion.

Along with electricity, other techniques were being used in the advancement of physiology. Jules Marey (1830–1904), who used photography to study man's movements in detail, was the pioneer of medical cinematography. The development of chart recorders meant that it was now possible to record several sets of data simultaneously, such as movement, changes in pressure in a cavity, the flow of a liquid, and so on. This information could also be combined with successive chemical analyses. The veterinary surgeon Auguste Chauveau (1827–1917) introduced probes into the hearts of animals and made some valuable discoveries concerning haemodynamics and the physiology of cardiac contraction.

Hermann Helmholtz (1821–1894), German physicist, acoustics expert and physiologist, with his optical instruments. After Ludwig Knaus, 1881. National Gallery, Berlin, Germany.

The work of doctor and physicist Jean-Louis Poiseuille (1799–1869) contributed to advances in fluid mechanics, and enabled Pierre Potain (1825–1901) to perfect an instrument for measuring arterial pressure on the forearm. Another form of numerical data was thus added to the list of those which doctors could already obtain from their patients. Potain's sphygmomanometer is still in use today.

Electricity was to be the inspiration for another technique, namely that of electrocardiography. As soon as it was possible to record the electric currents produced by the contraction of muscular tissue, those of the heart muscle were studied. The Dutchman Willem Einthoven (1860–1927) constructed the first instrument capable of recording the electrical activity of the heart. Today, the electrocardiogram is the principal means of diagnosing most forms of heart disease.

During the nineteenth century, experimentation in physiology became increasingly complex, but almost all the methodical rules laid down by Spallanzani and Claude Bernard remained valid. At this time of intense scientific development, the German school was particularly active – notably with Emil Dubois-Reymond (1818–1896), Carl Ludwig (1816–1895) and Hermann Helmholtz (1821–1894), but we cannot leave this topic without mentioning the Russian, Pavlov.

Ivan Pavlov, (1849–1936), became famous for his physiological and psychological studies of the digestion. His experiments led him, for example, to make a little pocket from part of a dog's stomach so that it opened out onto the skin. Using this technique of the "little stomach", he was able to measure the qualitative and quantitative variations in the secretion of gastric juices as a function of time and of certain stimuli. Once the dog became accustomed to the administration of food being accompanied by the sound of a

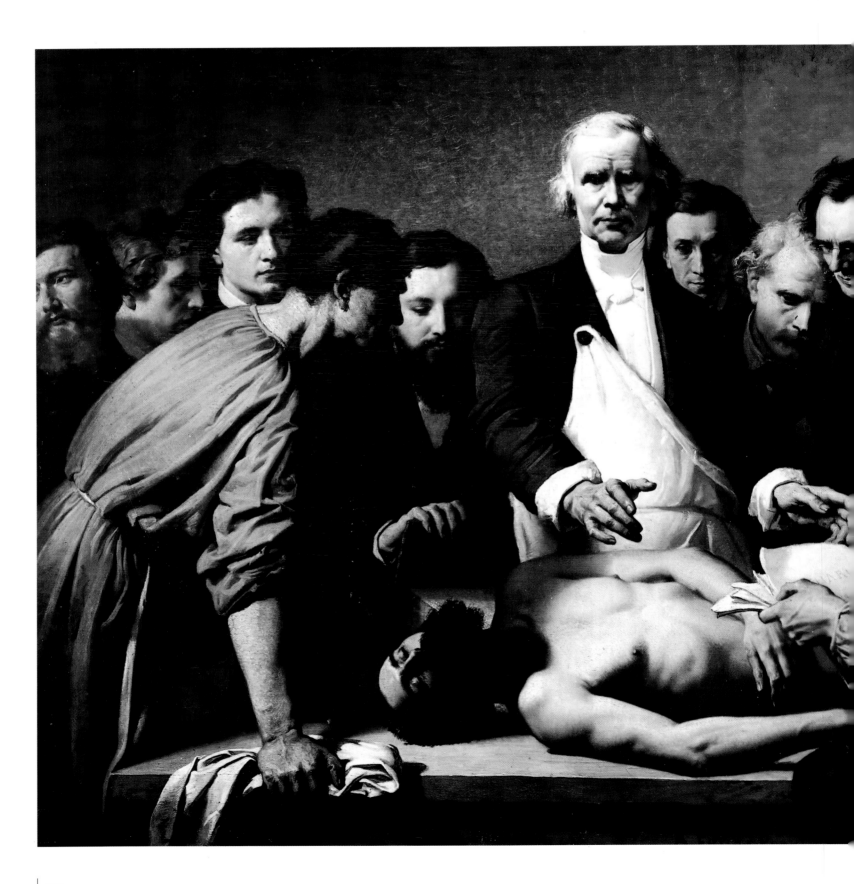

tinkling bell, its stomach secreted juices as soon as its ears heard the sound.

Pavlov used the term "conditioned" to describe these reflexes of the autonomic nervous system when they are subjected to external conditioning. He deduced from them a neurophysiological theory which was able to account for certain types of behaviour in animals and man. In time, Pavlovian theory was to give rise to many exaggerated interpretations, and it led to confused political and ideological interpretation of physiology. However, Pavlov's theory influenced Soviet biology and medicine, as well as psychology and psychiatry, for almost a century.

La leçon du professeur Alfred Velpeau. *The artist had no qualms about imitating Rembrandt in the great tradition of anatomy lessons of the Dutch school of the seventeenth century. François Feden-Perrin (1826–1888), Fine Arts Museum, Tours, France.*

THE ETERNAL SCEPTICS

In opposition to his colleagues who were enthusiastic about the new anaesthesia, Alfred Velpeau (1795–1867), a distinguished master of surgery in Paris, declared with all his authority:
"Avoiding pain is a will-o'-the-wisp that is no longer pursued. We must accept that sharp instruments and pain during surgery are two things which will always be linked." A colleague said gloomily: "Anaesthesia has put an end to the surgical temperament".
A century later, René Leriche (1899–1955) was to remark: "The pain of others is generally easy to bear."

393

For thousands of years, doctors had been trying to relieve pain. When they had to carry out a painful procedure on a patient, they first administered wine, brandy or opium depending on the period and the country, but without much success. In any event, these products were only available in limited quantities and could not be used on a large scale, particularly on the battlefield. The nineteenth century introduced mass production of more effective drugs which were to revolutionize medical practice.

Since the time of Priestley and Lavoisier it had been known that the lung was able to absorb gases which then penetrated the whole body. In the United States in 1842, a doctor in Georgia carried out his operations after making his patients inhale ether. He showed this technique to one of his friends, the dentist Horace Wells (1815–1848), who adopted it, but replaced the ether by nitrous oxide. Wells had noted that pleasure-seekers at fair grounds who inhaled this mirth-provoking gas did not suffer pain if they were injured while under its effect. He gave a public demonstration of the technique in a hospital, but failed to anaesthetize his patient.

Anaesthesia and asepsis lead to a revival of surgery

IV.

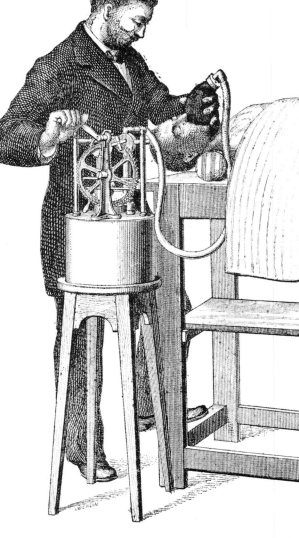

1846: the birth of anaesthesia. Methods are still antiquated.
Above: a pump with complicated cog-wheels.
Left: a small, portable apparatus.

An operating theatre in a German hospital in 1890. Anaesthesia and gas lighting ushered in the modern age of surgery.

WILLIAM MORTON
AND THE BIRTH
OF ANAESTHESIA

*W*ells' colleague William Morton was luckier. On 16 October 1846, in a large hospital in Boston, he anaesthetized with ether a young man who had to undergo surgery to the neck. This time the attempt was entirely successful. But Charles Jackson, who claimed to be the inventor of this method, took Wells to court. The outcome of this story was sad. Wells, Morton and Jackson, the protagonists in the case which was to revolutionize surgery, were all to die in pitiful or tragic circumstances.

The news of the discovery spread throughout the medical world. From 1846 onwards, anaesthesia was successfully used in England. French and German surgeons adopted it a few months later. They either used ether or chloroform, depending on their preference, and not without unfortunate consequences for them. Chloroform could have adverse effects on the liver, and ether could lead to fainting fits. After half a century of experimentation with different mixtures, the medical profession finally reverted to the original choice of nitrous oxide, since it was easier to manage.

Apart from nitrous oxide, other substances were used to combat pain. The effects of the leaves of the coca plant had been known for many years. The alkaloid extracted from it – cocaine – was subsequently used in injections as a painkiller.

ANAESTHESIA "FIT FOR A QUEEN"

In 1853, Queen Victoria was anaesthetized with chloroform by James Simpson (1811–1870), who was an Edinburgh gynaecologist, for the delivery of her son Leopold. Once it had been demonstrated in this way that the product was effective and harmless, anaesthesia using chloroform became fashionable.

This volatile liquid was administered using a sponge which was continually moistened by a drip: this technique, which had been used for the queen, was long preferred over various forms of apparatus that enabled the dose to be measured more accurately. In France, the use of the mask, perfected by the surgeon Louis Ombredanne (1871– 1956), survived longer than other methods.

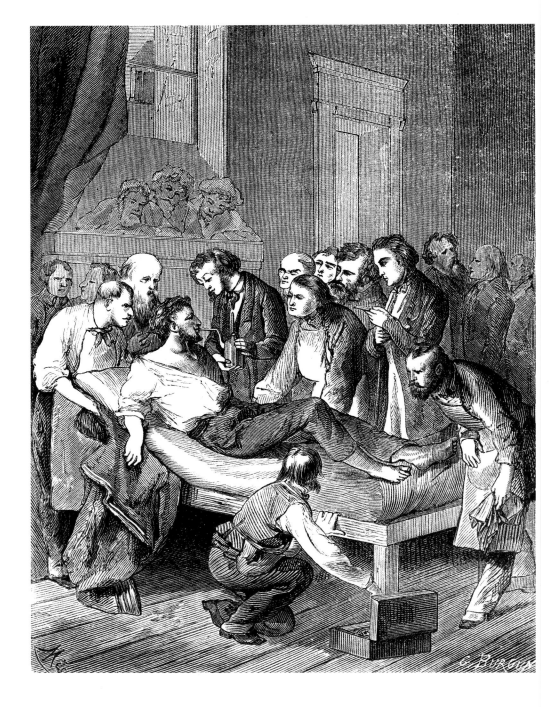

There was a forty-year gap between the invention of general anaesthesia and that of local anaesthesia, which came about by two very different processes of discovery. General anaesthesia was more complex and more dangerous, while local anaesthesia was much more simple.

While the surgical act had thus been facilitated by the suppression of pain, there were still serious risks associated with the period following an operation because of the threat of infection. The idea gradually gained acceptance that germs were responsible for the suppuration of wounds and for contagion amongst surgical patients. In the first few decades of the nineteenth century, "gangrene"

The dentist T. G. Morton carries out the first public demonstration of surgery without pain using ether at the Massachusetts General Hospital on 16 October 1846.

and "hospital gangrene" were talked about without their cause being fully understood. However, certain products were used for impregnating dressings in an attempt to diminish the terrible mortality rate which, in some institutions, meant that two-thirds of those who underwent surgery died.

Thus in France, in about 1862, Jules Lemaire emphasized in a number of his communications the good results he had obtained with dressings containing different derivatives of tar such as phenol, which had been discovered in coal tar by Runge in 1834. However, he did not have the means to continue his research and nobody else repeated his results.

At the same time, Joseph Lister (1827–1912) was working on the subject in ignorance of Lemaire's contribution. While practising as a surgeon in Edinburgh, Glasgow and finally London, Lister began using the microscope to follow the development of inflammation in tissues. It was exceptional at the time for surgery and microscopy to be practised in parallel. He too discovered the disinfectant properties of carbolic acid (phenol), made great use of it, and began to urge his colleagues and students to be meticulously clean. Until then, surgical gowns usually bore traces of pus, blood and sanies from previous operations.

Lister only used instruments which had previously been soaked in carbolic acid and he dressed wounds with compresses moistened with the same product. With the aid of the microscope, he discovered that the silk and cotton used for sutures and ligatures were no longer resistant to blood or lymph after a few days, and he therefore decided to replace them with an organic material. He started using gut violin strings, then catgut, a resorbable thread which he soaked in carbolic acid.

LISTER AND SOMMELWEIS: ANTISEPSIS AND ASEPSIS

Doctor Dupuytren's surgical instrument case. Ivory instrument handles were to be replaced by steel with the advent of sterilization. Public Works Museum, Paris, France.

When Lister heard in 1865 of Pasteur's work on the role of micro-organisms, he realized that he was on the right path and laid down his principles in the form of an antiseptic method which he expounded in public in 1867 before the British Medical Association. The mortality rate among his surgical patients decreased spectacularly. The Frenchman Just Lucas-Championnière (1843–1913) was very impressed, and France and Germany soon adopted the same technique.

The obstetrician Ignaz Sommelweis (1818–1865), who made the same observations as Lister in Vienna and Budapest, decided to declare war on puerperal fever, which caused so many deaths in maternity wards. He demanded meticulous cleanliness of his assistants and thereby reduced the mortality rate of his patients. However, he was not as highly qualified as Lister and he was less persuasive. He was unable to endure the incredulity of his colleagues and superiors, and was not taken seriously. Despite his disinterested zeal and the success of his methods, he succumbed to insanity and died a lonely man.

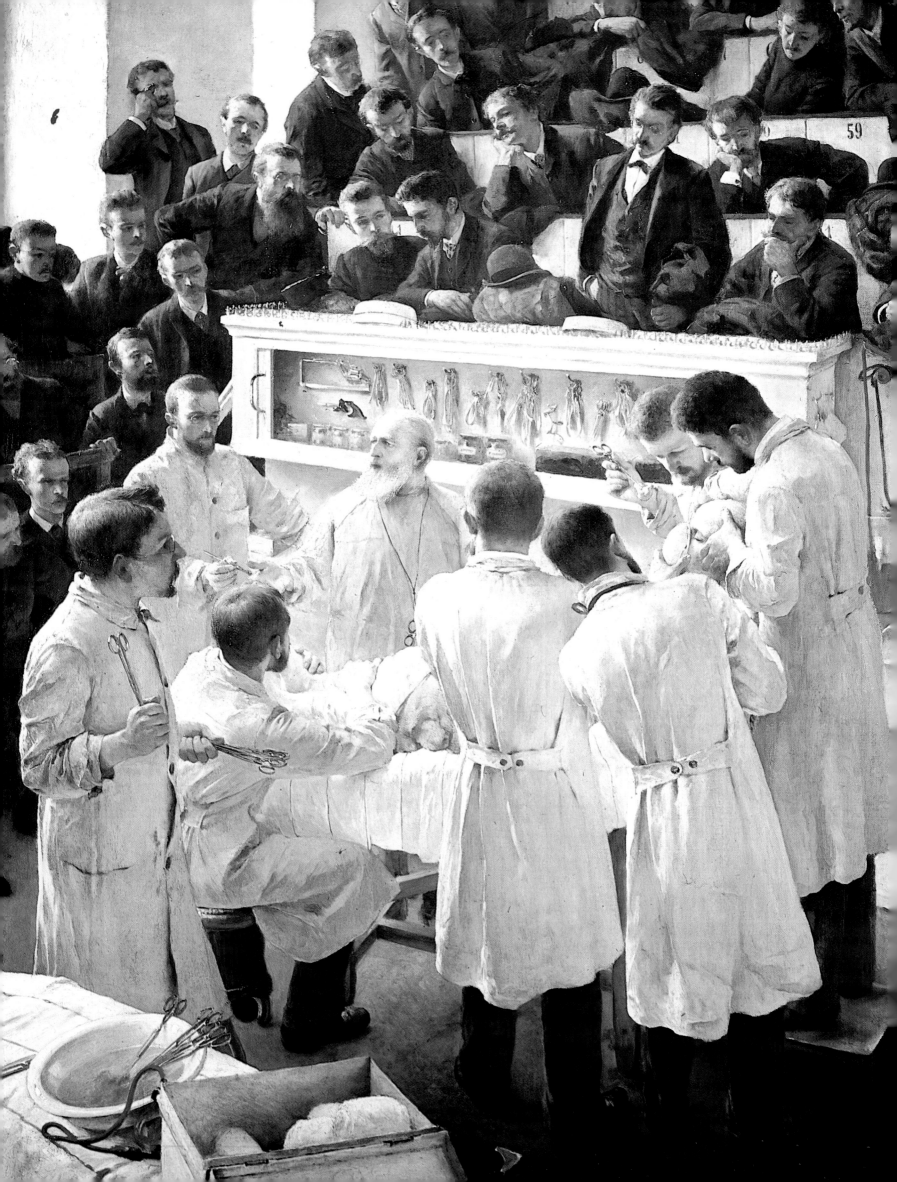

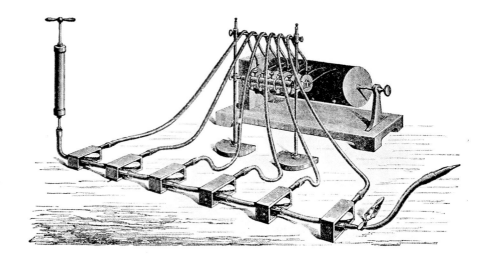

As we have seen, by this time antisepsis* had not made a great deal of progress, and so it was the new science of bacteriology which came to the aid of the surgeon. On the advice of Pasteur, measures were gradually adopted that enabled surgery to be carried out in the total absence of pathogenic organisms. The germs which caused suppuration were identified, and the healing of wounds was observed with the aid of the microscope. While surgeons still used antiseptic in the traditional way to dress wounds resulting from trauma, they gradually changed their practices when it came to operations.

The surgeon's hands and the patient's skin were carefully cleaned using disinfectants. The ligature material, instruments and compresses were sterilized according to Pasteur's procedures, which involved boiling them or placing them in a vessel in which the temperature exceeded 100°C. Surgical gowns underwent the same treatment.

Thus aseptic surgery came into being, and the rules which governed it became increasingly strict. Felix Terrier (1837–1908) contributed to securing the respectability of sterilization, as Lister had done for antisepsis.

Pain and infection were now under control, and hitherto unforeseeable advances were made in surgery. Surgeons perfected their instruments. Eugène Koeberlé (1828–1919) in Strasburg, Jules Péan (1830–1898) in Paris, and Theodor Kocher (1841–1917) in Bern developed artery clips which were easy to handle and had safety catches. Tubes made of rubber or glass allowed secretions to be drained away.

Electricity enabled surgeons to illuminate the operative field using a shadowless lamp. In Baltimore, William Halsted (1852–1922) made the wearing of sterilizable rubber gloves compulsory, thus guaranteeing asepsis* of the hands. A large number

Apparatus for recording the pressure of a liquid propelled along a tube. It can also be used to study the pressure in human blood vessels.

A stomach operation in Vienna in 1881. Theodor Billroth and his assistants wear immaculate white coats, but they are still not wearing gloves, and the sterilization of their instruments leaves much to be desired. Painting by Adalbert Seligmann, Vienna, Austria.

of surgeons were now able to operate on the least accessible organs.

J. M. Sims in the United States (1813–1883), Theodor Billroth in Austria (1829–1894), Jacques Reverdin in Switzerland (1848–1908), Victor Horsley in Great Britain (1857–1916), Nicolai Pirogoff in Russia (1810–1881), Octave Terrillon (1844–1895) and Jules Péan (1830–1898) in Paris were just a few of those who became pioneers of visceral surgery, which had been out of the question before the advent of asepsis. Tumours were removed and abcesses drained in all parts of the abdomen (stomach, liver, large intestine). Calculi and cancers of the kidney were treated, as were abnormalities of the uterus. The pleura was drained, appendectomy became a routine operation, and surgeons were even able to suture wounds to the heart.

The skull was opened to reach the brain, and it became possible to correct disorders of the endocrine glands by operating on the thyroid.

At the end of the nineteenth century, while doctors were still lamenting the lack of convincing results from drug therapy, surgeons could be proud of their operations. But although there seemed to be no limit to their skills, in reality there were still many problems.

Their radical approach and their extirpations sometimes led to new difficulties. Infection had not totally disappeared, anaesthesia presented risks, and indications for surgery had yet to be rigorously formulated. Most significantly, post-operative morbidity and mortality remained considerable; surgery was still not over its teething troubles.

The new specialists

V.

Discoveries made in the laboratory did not detract from clinical medicine. Teaching at the patient's bedside, the giving of lectures, the complexities of diagnosis, studying the history of diseases, and the acquisition of rich and titled clients – all these still retained their prestige.

In English-speaking countries, this period was dominated by the personality of William Osler (1849–1919). He first practised in Canada, then taught in the United States where he contributed to the launching of the medical school at the Johns Hopkins University in Baltimore.

With his colleague, the surgeon Halsted, he trained many students who were to be the medical elite of the United States for several decades.

Then, doubtless tempted by the universal authority which Victorian Britain enjoyed, Osler completed his career in London. Through his talents as a writer and teacher, his humane qualities and his gift for clinical observation, he left a deep impression on three great countries with similar cultures. He is still venerated by Canadian, American and British doctors today.

In France, Georges Dieulafoy (1840–1911) had a profound influence on the Paris School. He was convinced of the importance of medical laboratories and set up a laboratory in his clinic at the Hôtel-Dieu in Paris. He understood the usefulness of surgery in particular cases, and supported intervention in the case of acute appendicitis.

If the doctors treating the French prime minister Léon Gambetta had followed his advice, the politician would not have died when he did, since the autopsy confirmed Dieulafoy's diagnosis.

Dieulafoy was a brilliant symptomatologist and the author of a large treatise on pathology. Despite his authoritarianism, he was not without charm. His imposing appearance and his wealth contributed to his powerful influence. His arrival by carriage at the Hôtel-Dieu was marked by a great deal of clatter and bustle, and his visits to patients were accompanied by much ceremony. People came from all over Europe to consult him and hear his lectures, and his brilliant teaching inspired several generations of doctors.

The many scientific disciplines employed by medicine contributed to its blossoming. Practitioners gradually became used to specializing in certain parts or functions of the body. Previous medical tradition had only recognized two kinds of specialist: lithotomists who removed bladder stones, and oculists who corrected disorders of vision and operated on cataracts, but now other specialized disciplines were coming into being.

Left: *Professor Delorme (1847–1929) and his students at the Val-de-Grâce Hospital in Paris in 1894. The painting shows the progress made in military surgery during the second half of the nineteenth century. Val-de-Grâce Museum, Paris, France.*
Right: *the stages of a cataract operation.*

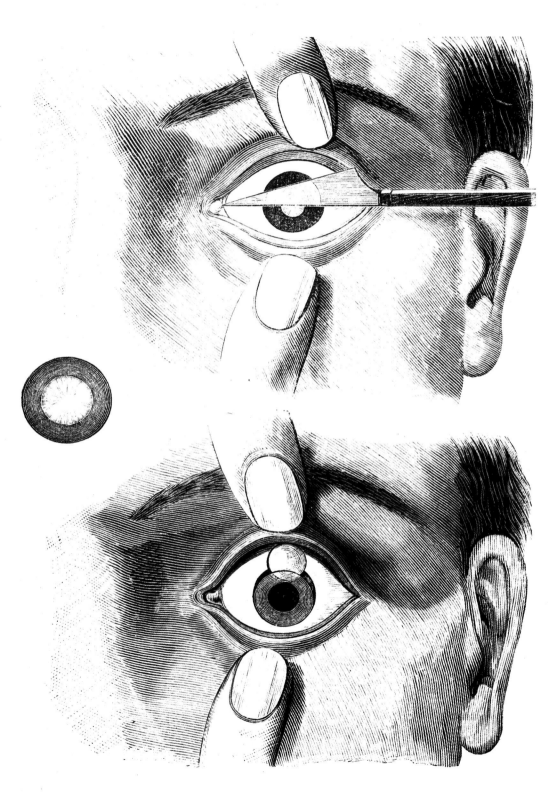

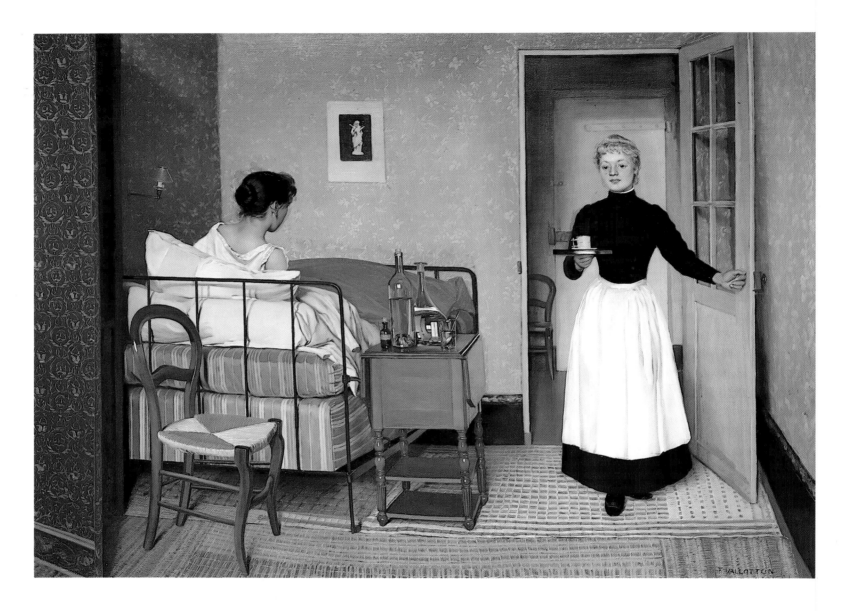

Félix Vallotton (1865–1925), La malade, *1892.*
Private collection.

PRECISE INSTRUCTIONS ARE GIVEN CONCERNING DIET

A strict diet was often prescribed during serious illnesses at the end of the nineteenth century. Dieulafoy, on a visit to a young girl who was recovering from typhoid fever, gave permission for a gradual reintroduction of food to be made and authorized an apple. The mother replied, "Doctor, my daughter prefers pears, does it matter?" Dieulafoy responded indignantly, "Madam, do you want to kill her?"
We do not know whether the doctor said this out of naïvety, or was merely being ironic.

However, dental care paradoxically retained a lower status and a pejorative image in most European countries. This would explain the delay in odontology and stomatology becoming established as medical specialities, despite being concerned with a part of the human anatomy which is no less worthy of interest than any other.

Physiologists were already fairly familiar with the phenomenon of the conduction of nervous impulses when a modest French practitioner, Guillaume Duchenne of Boulogne (1806–1875) began to take an interest in patients presenting with symptoms of paralysis in the clinic at the Hôtel-Dieu run by Armand Trousseau (1801–1862). Duchenne undertook to describe the tiniest signs which resulted from impairments of the smallest bundles of nerve and muscle fibres. He drew up a symptomatology which is still valuable today, both for the peripheral nervous system and for lesions of the spinal cord.

Jean-Marin Charcot (1825–1893) came within the same neurological tradition, but the scope of his work was different. At the Salpêtrière Hospital in Paris he founded a school which was to be famous world-wide. He was a precise clinician, and described several diseases that still bear his name. He, too, enjoyed great fame. He had a number of rivals, those in France being Jules Déjerine (1849–1917) and his wife, who was one of the first women doctors, Pierre Marie (1853–1940) and Joseph Babinski (1857–1932), and in England John Jackson (1834–1911).

Almost at the same time, the study of cerebral lesions underwent rapid development. At the start of the century, the German Franz Josef Gall (1758–1828) became famous in Paris by inventing phrenology which, by about 1810, had become very fashionable. He tried to establish a parallel between the shape of

The name of Jean-Martin Charcot (1825–1891) is especially connected with the study of hysteria, which at the time was considered to be a suggestive disorder. Caricature by Luque in Les hommes d'aujourd'hui, *late nineteenth century.*

Above: *Charcot presents a hysterical patient to his colleagues at the Salpêtrière Hospital in Paris, by André Broussais (1857–1920).* Right: *a collective hypnosis session, Saint-Louis Hall, in 1891, by the specialist in mental illness, Jacques Moreau of Tours. In Charcot's opinion, hysteria, unlike other mental disorders, was not of nervous origin but rather the most psychological of the effects of neuroses. Neurological Hospital, Lyons and Carnavalet Museum, Paris, France.*

a person's skull and his or her intellectual ability, a technique which became the subject of jokes. However, Gall also put forward a more plausible theory when he attributed particular functions to certain areas of the brain.

Jean-Baptiste Bouillaud (1796–1881), and most importantly the surgeon and anthropologist Paul Broca (1824–1880), adopted his ideas. By studying language disorders (aphasia) which were of vascular or tumoral origin, the latter succeeded in attributing specific functions such as speech, thought and memory to precise areas of the brain and cerebellum.

Until then, no distinction had been made between nervous and mental disorders. In the latter field, the start of the century was marked by the work of Pinel in France, Benjamin Rush (1745–1813) in the United States, and Thomas Trotter (1760–1832) in England. They can be considered to be the first specialists in mental illness.

The Frenchman Jean Esquirol (1772–1840) showed himself to be a worthy pupil of Pinel by founding schools at the Salpêtrière Hospital and Charenton Asylum which subsequently thrived. In 1838 he was the instigator of a law passed under the July Monarchy which proved to be exemplary in Europe. It instituted legal protection for the mentally ill who previously had too often been subjected to excessive confinement and inhumane treatment. The same law, some aspects of which are still in force in France, required each administrative district to provide an asylum for the insane.

Augustin Morel (1809–1873) also joined this movement for the protection of the mentally ill. This unfortunate man put forward the theory that those with a hereditary or congenital, physical, mental or even moral defect were suffering from "degeneration". He even considered abnormal social behaviour to be proof of

A maniac during an attack. Esquirol, Des maladies mentales considérées sous les rapports médical, hygiénique et médico-légal, *1838. Library of the Faculty of Medicine, Paris, France.*

Telemaco Signorini (1835–1901), the San Bonifacio Asylum in Florence, Italy, 1865.

such degeneration, which could show itself to be hereditary. He therefore drew up a long list of diseases for which he could envisage no treatment whatsoever.

Some specialists in mental illness such as the Frenchmen Valentin Magnan (1835–1916) and Jacques Moreau of Tours (1804–1884), the German Emil Kraepelin (1856–1926) and the Russian Sergei Korsakov (1854–1900), who were otherwise sensible clinicians, believed in this myth, which they also extended to sufferers from venereal diseases and their children.

According to this thesis, alcoholism was evidently due to degeneration. Once the term "alcoholism" had been coined in 1849 by the Swede Magnus Huss (1807–

Madness was a main preoccupation of doctors and psychiatrists in the nineteenth century, from Pinel to Charcot. The photographs of patients with mental or nervous illnesses – here a hemiplegic taken in 1878 – are some of the first instances of the use of photography for teaching purposes. Photographic collection at the Salpêtrière Hospital, Paris, France.

1890), doctors from all over Europe soon assembled under this heading numerous digestive, mental and nervous disorders which had been caused by the excessive consumption of alcohol. At their instigation, many temperance societies were set up in Europe and the United States. In France, Magnan and Marcel Legrain became the principal organizers of this "crusade" against alcohol, which was also inspired by religious conviction.

Degeneration, with the social consequences it entailed, naturally led on to a new branch of study, namely criminology. The Italian Cesare Lombroso (1836–1900) founded this new discipline on the basis of the theory of degeneration. By spreading the idea that the criminal often

While Freud's supporters recommended psychoanalytical cures for the treatment of the mentally ill, others resorted to electric shock therapy or to the injection of chemical substances. Above: *the shock treatment room at the Salpêtrière Hospital, Paris, France.*

exhibits physical signs of his or her criminal character and possesses criminal tendencies that are hereditary and incorrigible, he also contributed to the success of a form of determinist justice which supported the moral and social order prevalent in Europe at the time.

Also during this period, neuropsychiatry came into being under Charcot at the Salpêtrière Hospital in Paris. On the basis of a number of spectacular manifestations which he observed in women presenting with neurological and psychological symptoms, Charcot isolated hysteria. Not only did he describe the signs of hysteria during his lectures, but he also induced convulsions and fainting fits in a woman before a large audience of European

doctors who were won over and dumbfounded by the demonstration. Hysteria thus became one of the great neuroses of the feminine sex. After a few decades, this syndrome also began to be applied to men, before it was dropped entirely from nosology. It is interesting to note that Sigmund Freud (1856–1939) was present at Charcot's lectures and also attended the school of psychiatry at Nancy which was led by Hippolyte Bernheim (1840–1919).

Chemistry made a spectacular entry into medicine when the Minorcan Matteo Orfila (1787–1853) became the head of the Paris Faculty of Medicine. Orfila carried out his duties in a climate of political agitation. He was appointed as an expert witness in several notorious criminal

SOME FAMOUS FRENCH DOCTORS: 1840–1900

Joachim Albarran 1860–1912
Urologist
Gabriel Andral 1797–1870
Clinician
Jules Baillarger 1809–90
Psychiatrist
Michel Billard 1800–32
Paediatrician
Alfred Binet 1857–1911
Paediatrician and physiologist
Anatole Chauffard 1855–1932
Clinician
Jean Darier 1856–1938
Dermatologist
Eugène Doyen 1859–1916
Surgeon
Hubert Farabeuf 1841–1910
Surgeon and anatomist
Joseph Grancher 1843–1907
Paediatrician and hygienist
Félix Guyon 1831–1920
Urologist
Victor Hanot 1844–1896
Clinician
Étienne Lancereaux 1829–1910
Clinician
Charles Lasègue 1816–1883
Neurologist
Auguste Nélaton 1807–1873
Urologist
Jules Parrot 1809–1883
Paediatrician
Paul Poirier 1853–1907
Surgeon
Stéphane Tarnier 1828–1897
Obstetrician
Charles Troisier 1844–1919
Clinician
Théodore Tuffier 1857–1929
Surgeon

Sigmund Freud, who found Charcot "literally fascinating" when he attended his lectures as a young student.

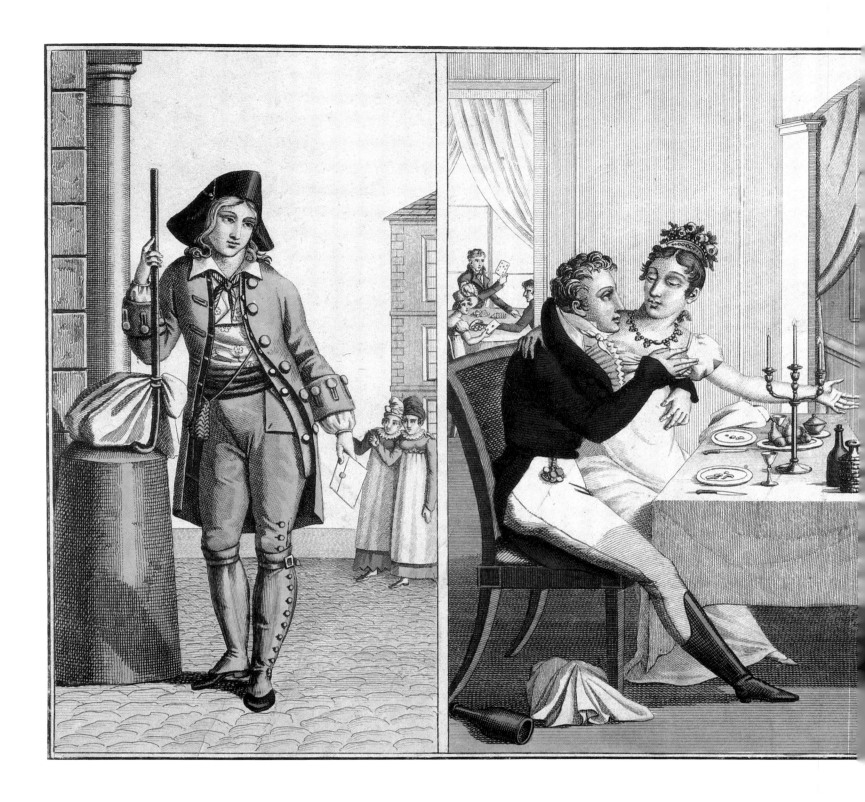

trials, and contributed to the establishment of two medical specialities – pharmacology and forensic medicine.

Today we may regret that, due to the inadequacy of scientific knowledge at the time, Orfila may have brought about the conviction of innocent people. However, he should be credited with having convinced the courts that medicine, which had been brought in to assist the course of justice for thousands of years, was now based on reliable scientific data. Orfila founded a reputable school of forensic medicine together with Ambroise Tardieu (1818–1879) and Paul Brouardel (1837–1906). After that, Great Britain and Germany had to take notice of this legal innovation.

Another medical discipline emerged as a result of the invention of the microscope, namely dermatology. Jean-Louis Alibert (1766–1837) was its pioneer. Paul

The dangers of syphilis. These three episodes from The life of a handsome young man in Paris *have captions that are short and to the point – "arrival", "escapades", "hospital". Carnavalet Museum, Paris, France.*

Unna (1850–1929) in Hamburg and Raymond Sabouraud (1864–1938) in Paris followed in his wake, but it was in venereology rather than dermatology that the medical school of the Saint-Louis Hospital in Paris was to make its name.

The microscope gave fresh impetus to this discipline. On the basis of microbiological discoveries, Philippe Ricord (1799–1889) and Jean-Alfred Fournier (1832–1914) made the distinction between the different venereal diseases of the period. Their views were soon confirmed when, in Rome, Augosto Ducrey (1860–1940) identified the micro-organism responsible for chancroid, and in Breslau, Albert Neisser (1855–1916) discovered the gonococcus responsible for gonorrhoea. Finally, in Hamburg, Fritz Schaudinn (1871–1946) discovered the spirochaete which causes syphilis. Those who, like Fournier, established the syphilitic origin of tabes, or, like the German Erb and the Englishman Hutchinson, demonstrated that syphilis can be hereditary, were not only men skilled in laboratory techniques, they were also experienced clinicians.

It would take too long to enumerate all the various medical specialities which acquired separate identities during this period. Their development, with a timelag of a few years, was to be the same in the various European countries and in North America. "Specialists", as they came to be known, soon founded their own groups and started societies which published journals. Among these specialities, whose names had not all yet been firmly fixed, were infantile medicine (later to become paediatrics), ophthalmology, urology, gymnastics or physical medicine or physiotherapy, gynaecology which joined forces with obstetrics, then separated from it again, and orthopaedics which did not, as its etymology suggested, only apply to children. Infections which were common to the ear, nose and throat in themselves justified the creation of otorhinolaryngology.

Practitioners were not as closely connected with their discipline as the specialists of today. All worked in the laboratory as well as at the bedside, and all of them, whether doctors or surgeons, were interested in fields that were related to their own. This open-mindedness explains the keenness of their clinical perspective and the success of their teaching.

By necessity, such technical and intellectual ferment led to certain changes in the exercise of the health professions. Gradually, most European countries came to admit to the medical profession only those who were officially qualified. They also regulated the profession of pharmacist, since medicines prepared according to doctors' prescriptions henceforth contained dangerous substances.

Midwifery training became progressively widespread and was available from medical faculties and private institutions. The education of the kindly staff of hospitals, who were frequently monks and nuns, often left much to be desired. To remedy this, a nursing school was opened in the Rhineland in 1836, which became the model when Florence Nightingale (1823–1910) started a campaign to

P*reventive medicine becomes well organized*

VI.

train nursing staff throughout Europe, after she experienced the suffering endured by soldiers in the Crimean War. In the space of a decade, the nursing profession developed, took into account the new techniques of antisepsis and asepsis, and enjoyed a certain amount of respect. Henceforth, skilled nurses became indispensable in all aspects of caring for the sick.

Apart from the national learned societies which doctors had created for their various specialities, the profession as a whole gradually adopted the habit of meeting at scientific congresses or gatherings of international societies. One of the first of these international societies transformed itself into a vast league against tuberculosis. In parallel with these groups, whose preoccupations were essentially of

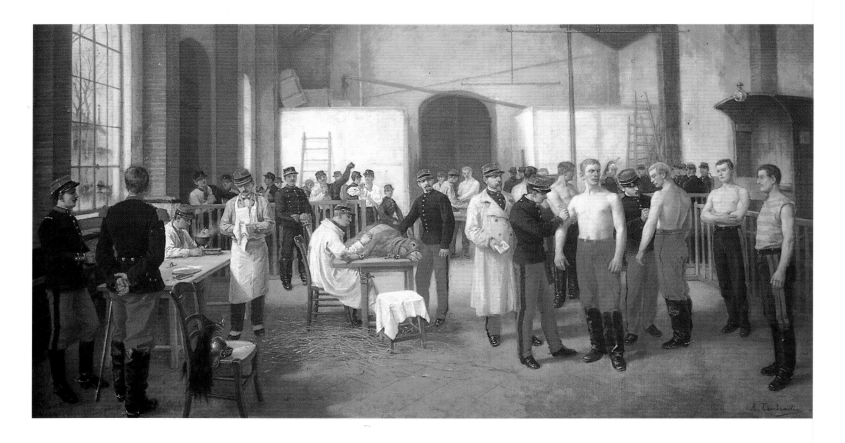

a technical nature, doctors also founded associations which were intended to maintain order within the profession and defend its material interests.

This appeared to be a necessary step since public authorities were increasingly calling upon doctors to care for the poor, to go about the country vaccinating people, and to carry out technical tasks in matters of hygiene that were entrusted to local communities. Practitioners were often paid too little and too infrequently for their trouble.

The associations of doctors which sprang up almost everywhere in Great Britain, France, Germany and the United States aimed to institute a moral discipline within the profession, to help families in difficulty, and to defend common interests in the face of government. However, in France, medical trades unionism was prohibited until 1892 by the law of Le Chapelier (1791).

Since the nineteenth century was the century of industrialization and urbanization, a public health policy proved to be essential. Even before Pasteur's bacteriology had proved the existence of microorganisms, a large public health movement was developing during the thirty years from 1820 to 1850. When it tailed off rapidly elsewhere, Great Britain took up the cause under the energetic influence of Edwin Chadwick (1800–1890).

The need was enormous. The large conglomerations of poorly paid workers around the new mills led to a proliferation of hovels where the working classes lived without sanitation. Poverty, contagious disease and delinquency were rife and threatened public order. England saw the start of a European campaign to provide better distribution of drinking water, to clean up working-class districts, build sewers, provide health education in primary schools and implement new vaccination programmes.

The battle against contagious disease and industrial accidents intensified in the 1890s. The French Republic looked after its soldiers (opposite), *but not so its workers, who resorted to founding mutual benefit societies. Generally speaking, until 1898, workers bore their own medical expenses unless they were able to prove that their employer was at fault.* Séance de vaccination au Val-de-Grâce en 1900, *A. Plonchon. Val-de-Grâce Museum, Paris, France.*
Above: La forge, *Maximilien Luce. Petit Palais, Geneva, Switzerland.*

Factories at Creusot, France, in 1866. It was here that the first workers' funds to provide aid for the victims of illness or accident were set up in the 1830s. Water-colour by Bonhomme, private collection.

Town planning, public health, moral order and bodily hygiene were the motives given for the refurbishing of Paris under the authority of the *Préfet* Georges Haussmann (1809–1891), and for that of Munich under the technical direction of Max von Pettenkofer (1818–1901).

Once again, it was industrial development which encouraged the founding of mutual aid societies in the case of illness or industrial accident. In the iron-ore and coal mines, and the steel works and cloth mills, protection funds were set up, sometimes on the owner's initiative, sometimes in the form of workers' mutual benefit societies. These private associations gradually amalgamated and in the Germany of the 1890s urged Chancellor Bismarck to start the first nationwide system of social security in the whole of Europe. Industrial medicine was organized, free care was guaranteed to workers in case of illness or accident, and pensions were assured. This vast government enterprise was aimed at pacifying a working popula-

tion which was becoming progressively more aware of its political power in the newly formed trades unions, but it also responded to a number of worthy humanitarian concerns. In any event, this Prussian form of social security set a fashion.

However, government initiatives were not enough to banish the poverty which was prevalent in industrialized countries. Many private charitable movements thus came into being, as they had done over the course of the previous centuries. People's dispensaries (a term which had been coined in England at the end of the eighteenth century) were opened in every large city. They addressed themselves to the population of a district or a parish and combated specific illnesses such as tuberculosis or venereal disease. They were often concerned with child welfare: in France, milk dispensaries and Grancher's system of removing children from families infected with tuberculosis dated from the end of the nineteenth century.

The Red Cross was also founded by private initiative. Henri Dunant (1828–1870) had been appalled by the sight of the wounded and dying after the battle of Solferino (1859), just as Florence Nightingale had been by the typhus patients in the Crimea. He aroused public opinion sufficiently to bring together several governments for the purpose of signing the Geneva Convention in 1864. This convention guaranteed protection for prisoners of war, the wounded and the sick and for medical personnel. From this initiative the International Red Cross was born, and also the League of National Red Cross and Red Crescent Societies.

But there were earlier signs of international co-operation. The cholera epidemic, which decimated Europe from 1830 onwards, brought back the nightmares which had been associated with the plague in previous centuries. As it had done in the past, cholera came from the East, and the idea spread throughout France that international co-operation would be useful in avoiding the repetition of such a scourge. The political situation also lent itself to such an enterprise, since the Ottoman Empire was starting to crumble and was losing its power.

The first international conference on health met in Paris in 1851 and brought together doctors and diplomats. It sought to decree and impose strict quarantine regulations to combat the spread of plague, cholera and typhus. These quarantine regulations, which imposed isolation for a fixed period upon travellers, ships, crews and merchandise coming from a contaminated region, are no longer in use today.

Although it can be said that miasmas are no respecters of frontiers, these frontiers do have their uses. At the time of the cholera epidemic in 1854, the doctors of Nice who believed in contagion had the region guarded by the Piedmont army,

Allegory of the plague, *1898. Old fears were revived by the cholera epidemics of 1832, 1849 and 1892 – Chateaubriand wrote of "that great black death armed with its scythe". Arnold Böcklin, Museum of Art, Basle, Switzerland.*

From 1830 to 1900, medicine was to prove increasingly effective in the fight against cholera. In Hamburg in 1892, boiled, and hence sterile, water was distributed to the population.

and not without success, while Marseilles, which had not taken the same measures, was extremely badly affected.

From about 1850, international health conferences met periodically in the various capitals of Europe. The discovery of the micro-organisms responsible for the dreaded epidemics and the proof that contagion occurred added justification to their existence. Government agreements were reached on the duration of quarantine and on health and customs checks, and leper houses were established on the Red Sea and at each end of the Suez Canal, which had recently been opened to shipping.

Health offices under the control of the great powers were opened in Alexandria, Tangiers and Constantinople, and also in Bucharest to cover shipping on the river Danube.

At the end of the century, the fruits of this co-operation could be clearly seen: cholera had disappeared from Europe. Muslim pilgrims from the Far East, the Indies and Morocco who gathered in the holy city of Mecca no longer returned home with the plague. Finally, an end had been put to the ravages of yellow fever in the Americas. A new order of international health was coming into being.

At the dawn of the twentieth century, medicine had thus been revolutionized by the invention of the laboratory, the microscope, chemistry and electricity. Doctors worked in a completely different way, and no longer based their diagnoses purely on clinical observation. As for therapeutics, other than the spectacular successes achieved by surgeons with the aid of anaesthesia and asepsis, only a few active substances were as yet being used, and medicines were generally ineffective, although vaccines and public health measures gave rise to hope based on the generalized prevention of infectious disease.

Despite the considerable advances made in laboratory medicine, fame resided with the great clinicians. They were experienced academics from England, France and Germany who inspired the popular press and travelled the world at the request of the maharajahs of India, the pashas of Egypt and the *nouveaux riches* of the United States.

In Europe, the authority which France had won in the first half of the nineteenth century began to decline, since the French remained too attached to clinical medicine. In the faculties, the professors who taught the so-called fundamental sciences occupied an inferior position in the university hierarchy, which was headed by the professors of clinical medicine. The examinations set by hospitals, especially the provincial ones, were more sought after and more difficult than the competitive examinations which those aspiring to teach at *lycées* and French universities had to pass.

This mentality and these practices continued until the middle of the twentieth century. France gradually faded from the scene as Germany came to the fore. There, the exact sciences were taking precedence over clinical practice. Great Britain, and then the United States, were soon to follow suit.

LABORATORY MEDICINE
1859 – 1909

POLITICS AND CULTURE	DATE	DATE	MEDICINE
Battle of Solferino	1859		
Bismarck, Chancellor	1862		
		1864	The Geneva convention recognizes the role of the Red Cross
		1865	Villemin demonstrates that tuberculosis is contagious Mendel's laws
Marx, *Das Kapital*	1867	1867	First international medical congress
Opening of the Suez Canal	1869	1869	Lister sets forth his antiseptic theory Classification of the elements by Mendeleev
Fall of the French Empire Creation of the German Empire	1871		
Alexander Graham Bell invents the telephone	1876	1876	Alfred Fournier, tabes due to syphilis
		1878	Pasteur and the first microbes
		1879	Pavlov and the reflexes
		1880	Laveran and the haematozoon
		1881	Lewis and the electrocardiograph
Nietsche, *Thus spake Zarathustra* First petrol-driven motor car First system of social security in Germany	1883		
		1887	Falot, cardiac malformation of "blue babies"
Kaiser Wilhelm, Emperor of Germany	1888	1888	Foundation of the Pasteur Institute
The fall of Bismarck Clément Ader, first flight in an aeroplane	1890		
		1893	French law concerning free medical assistance
		1897	Ross demonstrates the role of the female anopheles in the transmission of malaria
Spain at war against the United States	1898		
		1900	Role of the mosquito in yellow fever
Death of Queen Victoria	1901		

chapter XII

F*rom* X–*rays*
to
penicillin

In the course of its history, every scientific discipline passes through stages of rapid development and other, slower, stages of relative stagnation. But more often than not, the stillness is only on the surface. This was one of those periods during the course of which previous innovations were improved, while the ground was prepared for future discoveries. The first decades of the twentieth century provided a contrast to the fertile inventiveness of the previous half-century, and of the one to come. This less spectacular episode nevertheless produced much of value.

One evening in the autumn of 1895, Wilhelm Röntgen (1845–1923) found that a barium platinocyanide screen, which had been left by accident in his small laboratory at Elberfeld, became fluorescent whenever he passed a high voltage electrical current through an almost empty tube enclosed in an opaque envelope. In this way mysterious rays, soon to be called X-rays, showed that they could pass through metal walls. Röntgen took a photograph of the image obtained. The image of his wife's hand, with a wedding ring virtuously proclaiming her allegiance, was soon to be seen all over Europe. At the same time, and this is not a mere coincidence, in Paris the Lumière brothers were demonstrating their cinematograph for the first time!

The history of medicine knows of no other discovery which has been adopted as quickly as X-rays, without any controversy, scientific rivalries, or quarrels between schools. Within a few months the entire medical profession in Europe was aware of it. In 1896 Armand Imbert (1851–1922), in Montpellier, published a book on the technique of radiography,

*T*he radiology revolution

I.

Édouard Vuillard (1868–1940), Le cardiologue H. Vaquez et son assistant, *1917. Public Works Museum, Paris, France.*

and in 1897 Antoine Béclère (1856–1939) began a course of röntgenology[*] (as radiology was then called) in Paris. The world took to röntgenology with much greater readiness than to bacteriology. Hospitals, for example, were much quicker to equip themselves with X-ray equipment than with laboratories provided with microscopes and chemical reagents. It was only later that the first users discovered the hazards to which they were exposing themselves, their patients and their assistants. There were many victims in the first decades of the twentieth century, particularly among doctors. Thus Charcot's colleague, who became an assistant in the radiology department at the Salpêtrière Hospital, died within a few years, riddled with cancer.

With the discovery of X-rays by Röntgen, the human body was never to be seen in the same way again. Until then only its outer appearance had been known. Its interior had only been explored on the operating table by surgeons – who were necessarily hurried and only had access, for prudence's sake, to a small area – or on the autopsy table by pathological anatomists. With these new rays the body became transparent, in both sickness and health, and life and disease were displayed to the physician without him in any way affecting the body under examination.

X-rays make a different impression on a fluorescent screen or a photographic plate depending on the density of the bodies through which they pass. Thus they first found application above all in the diagnosis of lesions of the skeleton, where the bones are impregnated with opaque calcium, and in monitoring changes in lesions such as fractures and tumours. Then interest turned to foreign bodies made of metal which were lodged in the body. Those wounded in the First World War derived the benefit as bullets and shrapnel were located and removed.

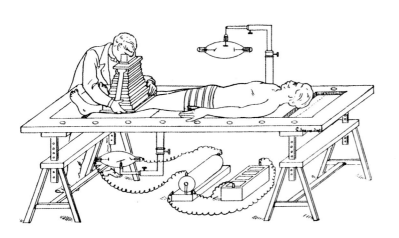

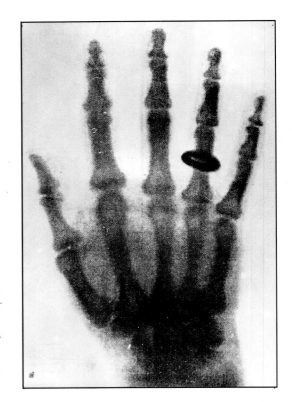

From Ruhmkorff's coil (1851) to Séguy's operating table (1897), the first tentative steps in radiography are epitomized in a single image — that of the hand of Röntgen's wife, photographed by her husband in 1895, using X-rays for the first time.

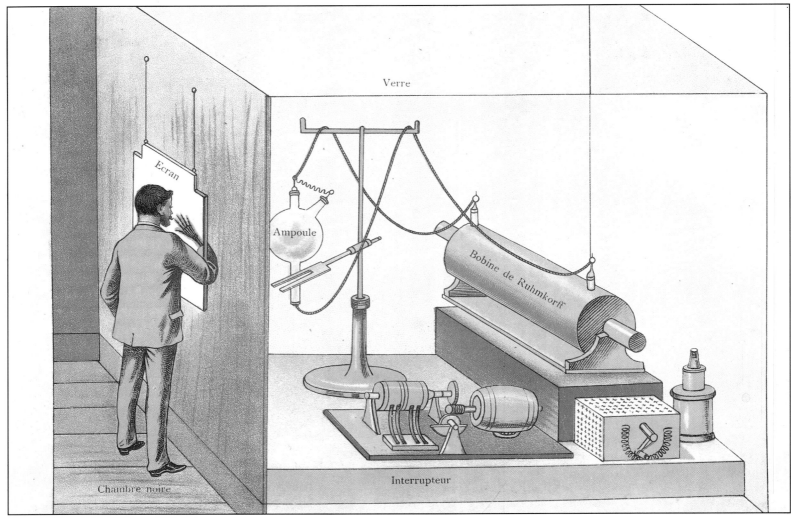

Verre

Ecran

Ampoule

Bobine de Ruhmkorff

Chambre noire

Interrupteur

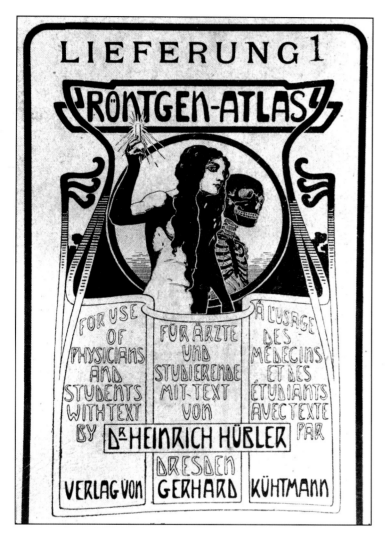

However, the soft parts of the human body have their own different densities. For example, lungs which contain air do not produce a uniform image if they harbour lesions, and the pleural cavity can be seen when it contains fluid. Thus, the voids due to tuberculosis could be seen in living patients. Up to then they had been suspected by auscultation, and confirmed on autopsy.

It now became possible to diagnose tuberculosis of the lungs both by the presence of the Koch bacillus in sputum, and by radiological signs. Thanks to

Radiography and its increasing use. Left: the cover of a radiological atlas published in Dresden around 1900 by Dr Hübler. Right: radiology at the Val-de-Grâce Hospital, as seen by Fargeot, published in an illustrated magazine at the time of the Great War.

X-rays, Karl Ranke (1870–1926) was able to describe the three stages of the natural history of this disease. By obtaining screen images or radiographic plates from a large number of people, both those who were thought to be healthy and those who presented worrying symptoms, doctors were able to establish the causes of the disease and the ways in which it spread. They also found that this "consumption" affected all classes of society, all countries and all ages. These new discoveries gave birth to major efforts to control the disease in the early years of the century.

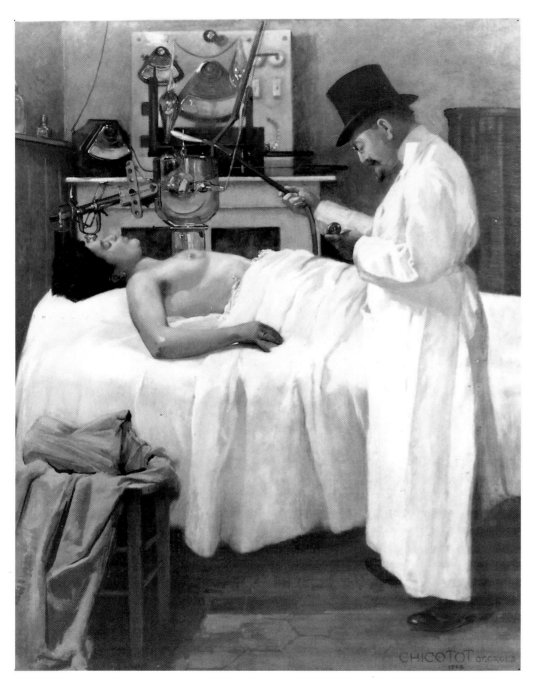

One of the first attempts at treating cancer with X-rays, in 1908. Dr Georges Chicotot, an amateur artist and the painter of the illustration on the cover, here provides his self-portrait.
Right: *equipment for treatment with X-rays, in 1897.*

In Europe these continued until the 1950s.

The effects of the revolution brought about by radiography continued to be felt for more than half a century. New equipment provided better protection for patients and the teams looking after them. Different ways of examining the body, the appropriate voltages and currents, the wavelength of the radiation used, the exposure time – all these were gradually refined.

With each improvement doctors had to learn the new anatomy of a black and white image on a flat plane. Soon air was injected into fluid-producing cavities: first the pleura, then the abdomen, then the ventricles in the brain. A liquid containing barium, which is opaque to X-rays, was administered by mouth or via the rectum to explore the patient's alimentary canal. Iodine-containing substances were introduced into the vascular system, and the circulation of the blood and the lymphatic system was revealed. Through the new techniques of cinematography doctors could then follow the varying progress of the substances they used as they were passed along by peristalsis in the oesophagus and the intestines.

Tomography then provided images of the internal organs centimetre by centimetre, detecting smaller and smaller lesions. The same procedure of injecting an iodine-containing material into a vein made it possible to follow the rate at which this was eliminated by the kidneys or the liver, minute by minute.

Thus, little by little doctors developed a new symptomatology for deformations in both solid and hollow internal organs. At the same time these images provided them with physiological information about the functioning of the organs. X-rays provided a new link between the shape of organs and their action. For example, it was found that some kidneys which

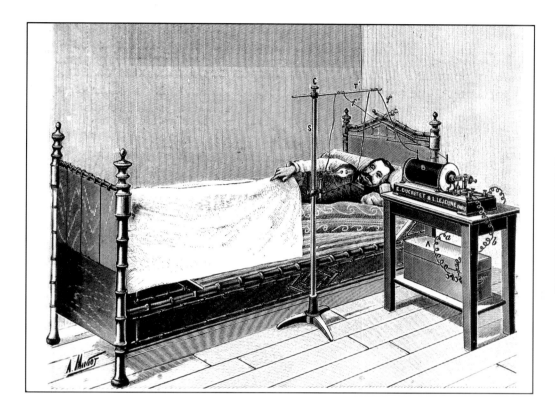

*Marie Curie,
who discovered a new
radiation from radium in
1898, followed in the steps of
Röntgen and Becquerel.*

appeared anatomically normal were not performing their excretory function because this could not be seen to be happening on radiographic plates. This visual medicine brought an image-based language of symptomatology into being.

In addition to this, it was found that these rays can destroy tumours almost as soon as they appear. The rays became a "magic power" essential to all medical work because they contributed both to diagnosis and to different forms of treatment.

Hardly had Röntgen identified his radiation when yet other forms were discovered. Henri Becquerel (1852–1908) proved that uranium emits ionizing radiation, and then Pierre Curie (1859–1906) and Marie Curie (1867–1934) discovered radium. Many other radioactive minerals were discovered in the wake of these. Radium in turn can be used to destroy cancers, so radiotherapy and radium therapy both came into use.

By the middle of the twentieth century research workers had made progress in understanding the structure of the atom. The particles with their different energies which go to make up the atom had been isolated, and the potential and some of the hazards of the radiation which they produced were known.

Doctors set great store by these discoveries, and in many cases their hopes were fulfilled during the second half of the twentieth century. But at that time they still did not know that these same forms of radiation could become agents of death, or could cause terrible bodily damage.

425

Serums and vaccines after Pasteur and Koch

II.

For a century the recently founded Pasteur Institute became one of the major centres of biological research, particularly in the fight against infectious diseases. It trained generations of French and foreign scientists, and many institutes with the same aims were set up in imitation of it, or under its guidance, throughout the world.

Koch too had many pupils, and it can be said that up to the mid-twentieth century bacteriology and serology were primarily French and German sciences.

As is well known, Pasteur produced the first vaccine, against anthrax, by using a spent culture of the bacterium. Subsequently other vaccines were manufactured using different physical and chemical procedures to reduce the virulence of the micro-organism concerned. In this way vaccines were obtained against typhoid and paratyphoid fevers, cholera, typhus, bubonic plague, whooping cough, yellow fever, and so on.

But the effectiveness of these vaccines varied. Gradually people learned how to purify them, store them, and remove inactive substances from them. In 1921 great hopes were raised with the development of a vaccine against tuberculosis from a bovine bacillus by Albert Calmette (1863–1933) and Camille Guérin (1872–1961). The BCG (Calmette and Guérin bacillus), which does not provide complete protection against attack by Koch's bacillus, nevertheless remains one of the

The traditional image: a sanatorium in the first decade of the century, or fresh air for sufferers from tuberculosis.

main instruments for the prevention of tuberculosis, particularly in underdeveloped countries, at the end of the twentieth century. The development of vaccines involved trial and error, disappointments and sometimes accidents, but the number of diseases avoided in this way continued to increase.

Vaccines provide the body with active immunity, as they stimulate it to produce its own antibodies against the foreign antigens. Serums only provide passive immunity, the method consisting of introducing the serum of an animal which has previously contracted the disease into the human body. This procedure is not without disadvantages because proteins from another species have to be injected

The treatment of tuberculosis, shown left, by the satirical revue L'assiette au beurre *(1907) in the form of a prematurely aged woman, received a real boost in the 1920s, thanks to the vaccine developed by Calmette and Guérin, the BCG.*

into man. Here again materials have been gradually purified, and serums are now available against bubonic plague, diphtheria, tetanus, and other diseases. These serums can even be used once the disease has got a hold. Serum therapy achieved enormous successes against, for example, diphtheria, and the greatly feared diphtherial laryngitis (croup) before vaccination became widespread. Then it was rapidly realized that the danger from micro-organisms lay not so much in the micro-organisms themselves, but rather in the toxins which they manufacture, with the human body producing antitoxins against these and thus providing *humoral immunity*. In relation to this, Hippocrates' ancient doctrine of the

A vaccination scene in Paris, in the 1890s, probably against smallpox, to judge by the presence of the calf on the left.

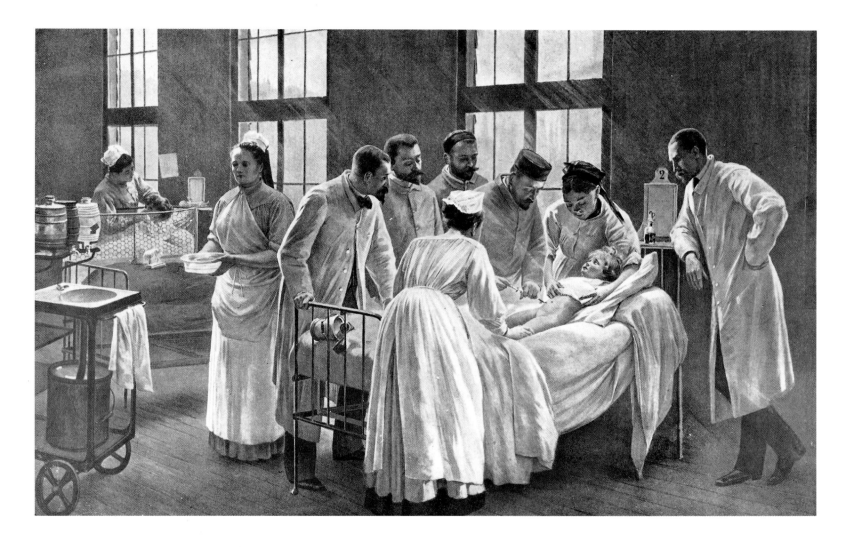

"humours", which attributed an essential role to the fluids circulating through the body, received a new lease of life when one of Pasteur's students, Elie Metchnikoff (1845–1916) succeeded in demonstrating the phenomenon of phagocytosis.

Mobile white cells, or phagocytes, which seem to specialize in this particular function, are attracted to micro-organisms or foreign bodies, absorb them and destroy them. These polynuclear cells move, throw out tentacles towards the "enemy" cells, and vanquish them. These cell immunity mechanisms, reflected in warlike metaphors, are another example of the exten-

Pierre-André Brouillet (1857–1914), Vaccination against croup at the Trousseau Hospital, *1895.*

sive competition which is a feature of life on earth, among both animals and cells.

When a foreign micro-organism penetrates the human body and causes other bodies to be produced, these persist there for a long time – sometimes for a whole lifetime, even when the original micro-organism has disappeared. If it returns to attack the body, it is again destroyed or "lysed". The phenomenon of clumping, described by Fernand Widal (1862–1929), can be used to establish the level of immunization to other micro-organisms in a patient. From this developed the search for so-called "cross"

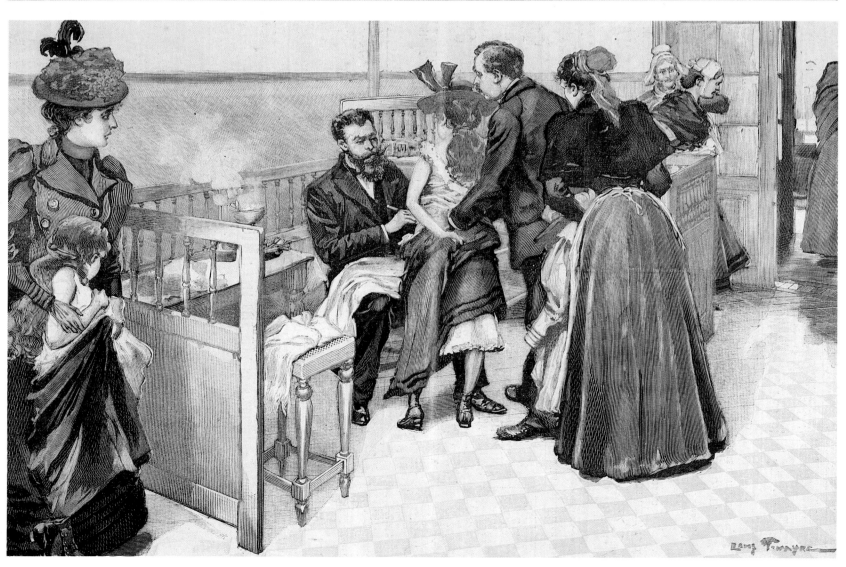

immunization as a means of diagnosing suspected infections. In this way it became possible to identify the serum antibodies of agglutinins which coagulate foreign proteins against different families of streptococci. In the course of the century this method became one of the main ways of diagnosing infectious diseases, such as typhoid fever, which affected or had affected a human body. The procedure became pre-eminent as soon as it was possible to determine these agglutinins. Nowadays serum diagnosis provides most laboratory diagnostic data.

Once again it was clumping observed in the laboratory which clarified observations made in the nineteenth century concerning the transfusion of blood. There were still too many accidents when sheep's blood was injected into women who suffered severe haemorrhage during childbirth, and when human blood was given to surgical patients who had lost a lot of blood. In fact the serum from the one agglutinated the corpuscles of the other. Karl Landsteiner (1868–1943) was the first person to distinguish four major blood groups (for red corpuscles), labelled A, B, AB and O, according to their compatibilities, in man. Some individuals can only receive blood from their own group, others can accept any blood without adverse result. With the proviso that each individual's specific situation must be taken into account, transfusion has become a common practice for correcting excessive blood loss arising through accident, surgery or childbirth.

Certain subgroups have been found within the four major blood groups, in proportions which vary between the different peoples of the world. Some in particular carry a factor which is called the "Rhesus" factor because it was discovered in rhesus monkeys. It is the presence of the Rhesus factor in both the mother and her newborn baby that gives rise to

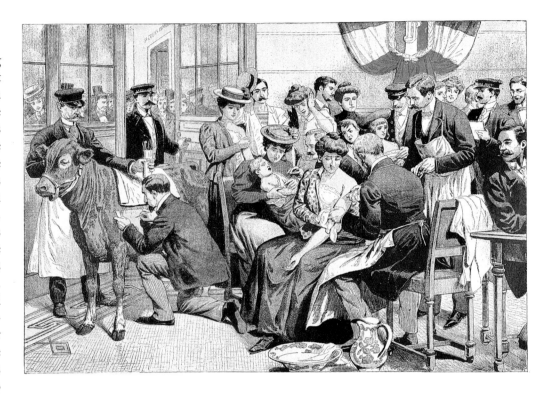

The benefits of "serotherapy". From allegorical painting: grateful mothers with their children surround Dr Roux, by Charles Maurin (top left), to educational features: vaccination against rabies as published in the Illustré national *in 1895 (bottom left), and against smallpox, as published in* Le petit journal *in 1905 (above).*

JULES BORDET AND IMMUNOLOGY IN BELGIUM

Jules Bordet (1870–1961) is undoubtedly one of the most famous research workers and doctors in the kingdom of Belgium. After working in the Pasteur Institute in Paris between 1894 and 1901, he founded and directed the Pasteur Institute of Brabant in Brussels (from 1901 to 1940). He was one of those who contributed to the great advances in serology in the 1900s by discovering the so-called "complement fixation" reaction with Octave Gengou in 1901, which was subsequently used to detect many pathogenic micro-organisms such as those causing typhoid fever, tuberculosis and syphilis, and also to diagnose infectious diseases.
In 1906, again with Gengou, he isolated the bacillus causing whooping cough which had first been described in 1578 by Guillaume Baillou, more than three hundred years before. He received the Nobel prize for medicine in 1919 for his research work in immunology.

haemolytic disease in the baby. This may merely take the form of benign jaundice, or the baby may die because its red cells are destroyed. It was discovered that this foetal-maternal immunization could be corrected by giving the newly born baby a complete blood transfusion to replace all the blood which it received from its mother. The blood which it receives in place of this matches the blood which its bone marrow will produce for the rest of its life.

Early in the twentieth century research workers discovered another humoral compatibility phenomenon. Charles Richet (1850–1935) discovered that dogs which had already suffered the toxic effects of contact with a sea anemone, effects similar to those observed in connection with jellyfish, suffered very much more serious and sometimes fatal symptoms when they came into contact with the toxin for a second time. The first contact between the dog's body and the foreign substance "sensitized" it. Richet gave this phenomenon the name "anaphylaxis", and this was gradually replaced by the name "allergy", particularly when Clemens von Pirquet (1874–1929) identified the mechanisms involved.

It was then established that a number of diseases can be explained by this type of sensitization. In the Middle Ages, a Persian physician had already described the type of head cold suffered by some people when the roses flowered in Isfahan. Rather more prosaically, we call it "hay fever", and we now know that allergies may be due to various causes (cat and dog hairs, certain types of house dust, and so on), and are manifested by different symptoms, some of them respiratory (asthma is the commonest), some digestive, some affecting the skin, and there are others.

Not all human beings therefore behave in an identical way biologically when their

Advertising campaigns, both straightforward and whimsical, serious and humorous, increased in number towards the end of the nineteenth century...

Si vous toussez
PRENEZ
SUPRÊMES PILULES
du DOCTEUR TRABANT
TOUTES PHARMACIES

bodies are attacked by a foreign substance of plant, animal or mineral origin. In his own lifetime Hippocrates had been able to distinguish different "temperaments", but he could attach no scientific significance to them and he had limited them to four. The nineteenth century invented the concept of "breeding ground" for disease, but this did not have a precise basis either, even though some still resorted to it a hundred years later. It is now known that every individual has his own immunological and allergological profile

... for both commercial and non-commercial purposes, from the fight against syphilis to Dr Trabant's miracle pills! Poster depicting Queen Victoria

which is partly of genetic origin and partly acquired.

Micro-organisms have ceased to be the determining factor in the phenomena which we call diseases, and are now regarded as merely the initiators. A "disease" is the reflection of an individual body's reaction to an intruder.

Bacteriology can establish specific causative factors in the investigation and classification of diseases as a whole, each micro-organism being responsible for certain symptoms which are peculiar to it,

NOUS
AVONS
QUAND
MÊME
UN BEAU
BÉBÉ parce que
NOUS NOUS
SOMMES
SOIGNÉS
A TEMPS!
POUR PROTÉGER
BÉBÉ ET VOUS-MÊME
CONTRE LES MALADIES HÉRÉDITAIRES
DÈS QUE VOUS VOUS SAVEZ ENCEINTE
CONSULTEZ LE MÉDECIN; DEMANDEZ-LUI
UNE ANALYSE DU SANG
UN TRAITEMENT APPROPRIÉ GUÉRIT LA SYPHILIS!

LE THERMOGÈNE
ENGENDRE
LA CHALEUR
ET
COMBAT:
TOUX, RHUMATISMES, POINTS DE CÔTÉ, etc.

HERMITINE
ANTISEPTIQUE   DÉSODORISANT   DÉSINFECTANT

LA GRIPPE

LE DOCTEUR. — « De même que nous avions la marmite norvégienne, vous avez attrapé la grippe suédoise et rien de plus!

Le microbe habitant le cuir chevelu, ça vous chatouille et vous éternuez,... voilà le secret !!!

Mais la science a tout prévu! Elle prend le parasite dans son propre repaire...

... pour le transporter dans un des doigts de la main, et...

... buvez trois gouttes de mon Élixir, vous allez comprendre!

Je traite les maladies par les pôles contraires! D'un imbécile, j'en fais un génie, et d'un génie, un imbécile à ne pas reconnaître sa chemise! C'est merveilleux!

Donc, si vous souffrez du mollet gauche, je vous pique l'oreille droite...

(Dessins de Marcel Capy)

Medical and pharmaceutical advertising became widespread in the years before the Great War. Medicine could sometimes have the answer to everything and let everyone know it, but this did not prevent the humorists from making fun of it, as shown, below, *in this cartoon from* La baïonnette *in 1919. This is not far from Jules Romains' Dr Knock!*

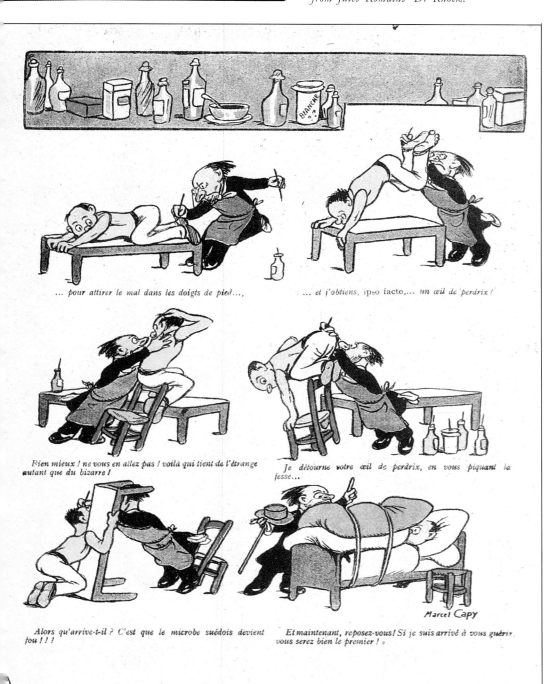

... pour attirer le mal dans les doigts de pied...,

... et j'obtiens, ipso facto,... un œil de perdrix !

Bien mieux ! ne vous en allez pas ! voilà qui tient de l'étrange autant que du bizarre !

Je détourne votre œil de perdrix, en vous piquant la fesse...

Alors qu'arrive-t-il ? C'est que le microbe suédois devient fou !!!

Et maintenant, reposez-vous ! Si je suis arrivé à vous guérir, vous serez bien le premier ! »

Marcel Capy

but every human body remains unique in the extent of its reactions.

A living body can also become sensitized against its own products, and can react in a way which sometimes has serious consequences. Through these diseases, called "auto-immune" diseases, the body destroys itself. As demonstrated by Paul Ehrlich (1854–1915), some forms of rheumatic polyarthritis enter into this category, and the list is getting longer and longer.

Claude Bernard was responsible for the doctrine of self-regulation in humoral phenomena. This states that the human body has many mechanisms for maintaining its "internal environment". It does not attack itself; disease and its disorders are the result of external aggression.

Claude Bernard was right as far as many chemical substances are concerned. For example, in most human beings the level of sugar in the blood is maintained at an almost constant level despite the irregularities of their eating and their physical activity.

By contrast, the discovery of auto-immune diseases, in which the body acts against its own self-preservation, would seem to undermine Bernard's principle. This is often the way things are in science. Theories rarely contradict each other, but they do not provide for all special cases. The universal law of gravitation laid down by Newton has never yet been shown to be wrong, but Einstein has shown that under certain circumstances Newton's principle does not apply.

Early in the twentieth century, Arsène d'Arsonval (1851–1940), Claude Bernard's tutor, extended the latter's work. Because he was interested in the physiological effects of electrical currents of all kinds on neuromotor activity, muscular contraction, heating effects, and so on, his studies included diathermy, faradization and short waves. As a result of his work, equipment was developed for the rehabilitation of muscles following injury, as was the diathermic electrical scalpel for sectioning tissue and coagulating vessels.

In the same field, Willem Einthoven's electrocardiography, the diagnostic interpretation of records of the electrical activity of heart muscle, was improved over several decades. A century on, arterial pressure is still measured by using

*B*iochemistry *transforms physiology*

III.

Pierre Potain's apparatus. The electricity produced by the activity of the brain is recorded by electroencephalographs. The changes in this activity during waking and sleeping have been investigated and as a result it has become possible to diagnose and monitor epileptic conditions. It was thanks to electroencephalography that epilepsy, which had been identified but not understood for a long time, was subjected to analysis which was important for prognosis.

Despite this progress based on conventional physics, it has been the improvements in biochemistry, rather than those in physics, which have brought about the main advances in the twentieth century.

Chemistry can be used to analyse the various components of urine; to identify the nature of the various juices in the digestive tract sampled at different points in the stomach or intestines, using a probe introduced via the mouth; to determine the composition of cerebrospinal fluid obtained by lumbar puncture; and to identify the many chemical materials contained in blood: urea, sugar, bile pigments, proteins and lipids, red corpuscle haemoglobin, and so on. Stools have also been analysed as these are the result of fermentation which takes place in the intestines, and reflects their functioning. The functions of the water, urea, electrolyte, lipid, sugar and protein cycles within the body, and their relation to food input, have been progressively discovered.

In its turn respiration was subjected to physical examination, with measurement of the volumes of gas breathed in and out when resting or after activity, and with chemical investigation of the concentrations of oxygen, carbon dioxide and rare gases which cannot be absorbed by the lungs. In this way it became possible to evaluate the absorption capacity of the pulmonary epithelium in each of the two lungs and in certain parts of the bronchi.

NINETEENTH-CENTURY NORTH AMERICAN AND BRITISH MEDICINE

Henry Acland (1815–1900)
British Physician
Thomas Addison (1793–1860)
British Physician
Elizabeth Garrett Anderson (1836–1917)
British Physician
Elizabeth Blackwell (1821–1910)
British Physician
Richard Bright (1789–1858)
British Physician
Thomas Hodgkin (1798–1866)
British Physician
Oliver Wendell Holmes (1809–1894)
American Physician
William Leishman (1865–1926)
British Army Physician
Patrick Manson (1844–1922)
British Physician
William Osler (1849–1919)
Canadian Surgeon
Ronald Ross (1857–1932)
British Physician
John Snow (1813–1858)
British Physician

Different viruses illustrated:
1–smallpox, 2–mumps,
3–the bacteriophage, 4–herpes,
5–influenza, 6–tobacco virus,
7–adenovirus,
8–palyoma, 9–poliomyelitis.

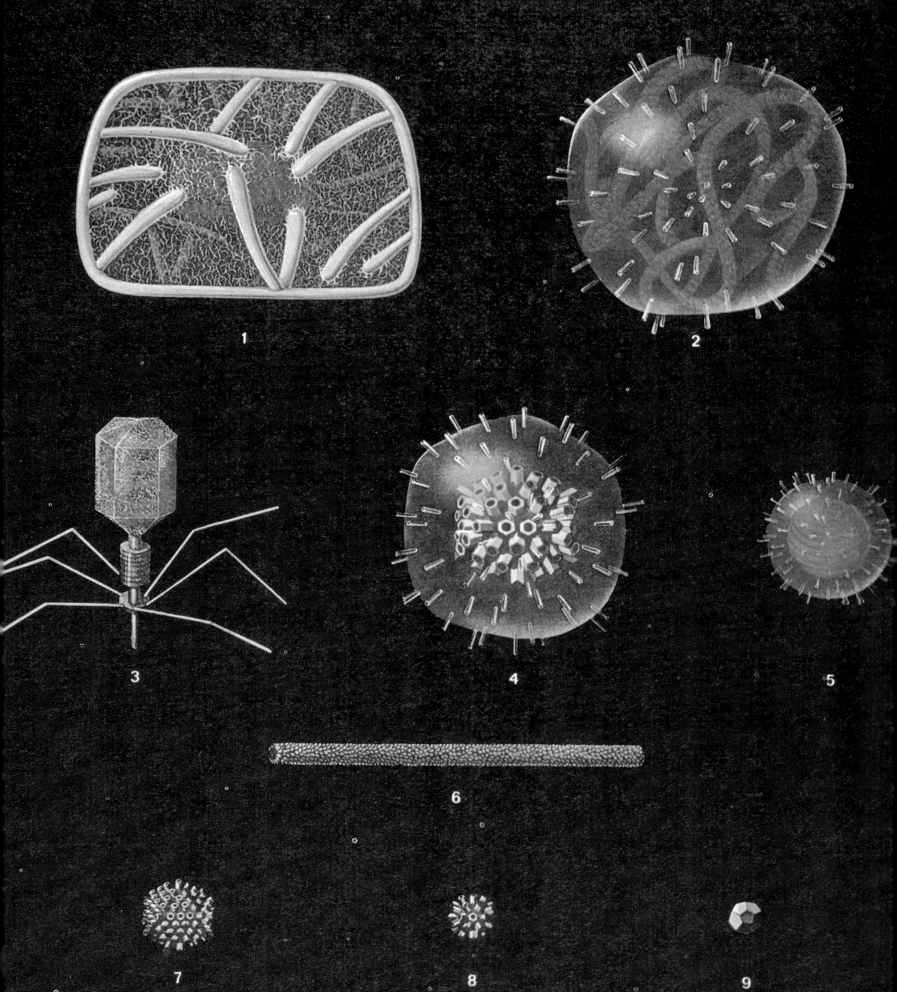

1/2 micron

A visit to hospital, as illustrated by Le petit
journal, *in 1903. Hospitals still had
communal wards, but many services were
provided and there was a strict hierarchy.*

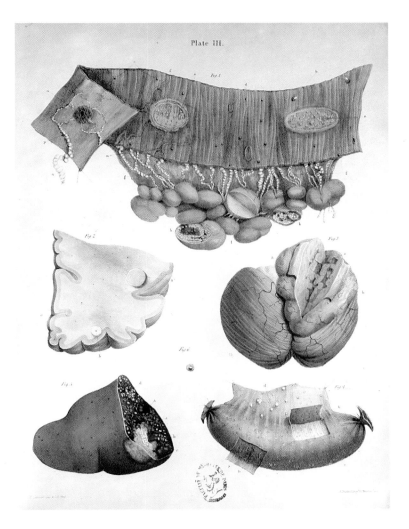
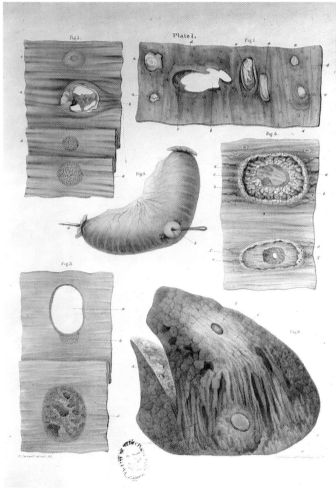

During the first decades of the twentieth century clinical medicine remained as it had been in the time of Laennec, Bretonneau and Charcot, and no further progress was recorded. Pathological anatomy, on both the macroscopic and microscopic scales, was content to describe lesions without explaining them. Chemistry alone contributed to improving diagnosis and prognosis by shedding light on physiology and disturbances of it. The proof of this is that all the clinicians of the period, that is those providing instruction at the patient's bedside, added

Two water-colour plates from the Medical *treatise by the Englishman R. Carswell, in 1838.* Left: *intestinal tuberculosis.* Right: *perforation of the intestine.*

a laboratory to their hospital services. Chemistry also presented new horizons for them. Through new techniques it became possible to identify disturbances in blood coagulation, and the reasons for the destruction of red cells (haemolysis); to measure blood hypercoagulability and hypocoagulability; to determine the fibrinogen and the fibrin which form blood clots; and to recognize certain infectious haemolytic diseases.

From then on doctors could either assist blood coagulation where this was inhibited by disease, or prevent it when it happened too readily and obstructed vessels, giving rise to thrombosis and embolism. Finally the discovery of heparin, a substance secreted by the liver, gave rise to many medical applications.

The interests of research workers also turned towards enzymes. Pasteur had been the first to demonstrate the role of these substances, which are essential for the chemical conversion known as "fermentation". Without them the reaction does not take place, yet they are found to be virtually unchanged when the process is complete.

It was soon realized that these catalysts, which were first called diastases and are now called enzymes, occur in the body in very large numbers. All major functions, such as respiration and digestion, only take place because of the existence of enzymes. Each portion of the digestive tract in fact specializes in the production of a juice which is associated with a particular category of food.

Chemistry also attempted to probe the mysterious functioning of the liver, that large organ given such importance in mediaeval medicine. Claude Bernard had already demonstrated its function in the metabolism of sugars. It was soon also found to be involved in urea metabolism. As a result of different chemical tests its involvement in the production of hormones, and its mechanical function as a reservoir of water and blood in the circulation of all body fluids, became established. Any obstruction in the arterial, venous or bile vessels within the liver gives rise to hypertension in the portal vein, called portal hypertension, which can be fatal; and conversely, any disturbance in venous circulation, for example due to the heart, increases the size of the liver and impedes its ability to produce or filter out the substances necessary for life.

The contribution of chemistry to medicine has been considerable, as we have

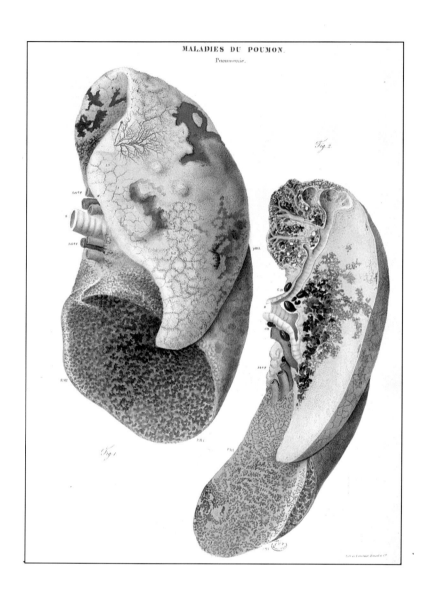

MALADIES DU POUMON.
Pneumonie.

Jean Cruveilhier, Anatomie pathologique du corps humain, *1828–1842. Description of pneumonia.*

seen, but there is no doubt that it is in the physiopathology of the kidneys that the clinical chemistry of the first half of the century made the greatest advances. Earlier work by Richard Bright (1789–1858) had already drawn the attention of specialists to the clinical features of kidney function and to the question of the single or multiple causes of inflammation of the kidneys, or nephritis. It gradually became possible to establish the link between arterial hypertension, disturbances in the

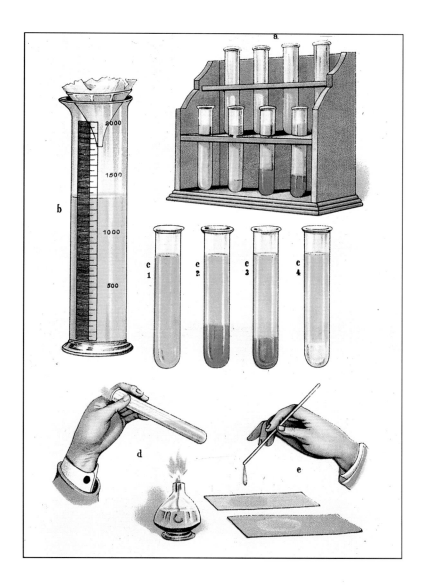

functioning of the left ventricle of the heart, and changes in the small arteries of the kidneys' parenchyma[*].

Widal, who has already been mentioned, played an important part in the field of kidney disease. Knowledge progressed rapidly. The excretion potential of the kidneys' glomeruli was investigated by observing the excretion of dyestuffs. The causal link between the general oedema shown by patients affected by kidney disease and the retention of water and

Plate on urine, *from a popular work dating from the late nineteenth century. This is far from the way the traditional doctor viewed urine!*

mineral salts was established. This led to the rule of the salt-free diet, which has been imposed, sometimes to excess, on patients suffering from kidney and heart problems.

In 1922 Donald Van Slyke established the concept of the kidney clearance coefficient. The existence of a "threshold" effect is well known in general physiology; that is, a chemical mechanism only comes into action when one of the constituents in the reaction reaches a certain concentration level. Studies of clearance showed the levels at which kidney cells came into action, and how vigorously they did so. The discovery of a concept which could be applied to other biochemical mechanisms marked a considerable step forward in the understanding of the physiopathology of the kidneys.

Thus, all the clinical and chemical analyses which we have mentioned have demonstrated the ability of the kidneys to adapt to and resist various challenges, as well as their vulnerability. The parenchyma can be affected rapidly or in the long term by streptococcal infections such as scarlatina, by poisoning – particularly mercury poisoning – or even by auto-immune diseases. The consequences can be fatal.

In parallel with this a distinction came to be made between the excretory and secretory functions of the kidneys, and conventional nephritis came to be divided into several distinct diseases depending on the histological portion of the organ which they affected.

Little by little clinical science, biochemistry and pathological anatomy became necessary to explain a disease, its initiation, its resulting signs and its deterministic features. But diagnosis accompanied by learned commentary is not enough for the well-being of patients, and treatment did not always benefit greatly from advances in knowledge.

After enzymes: vitamins and hormones

IV.

It was mainly American research workers, who were no doubt less preoccupied with bacteriology than their European colleagues, who discovered the existence of those chemical substances called "vitamins", which are essential to man. Like enzymes, these produce an effect in very small quantities, but their absence gives rise to a variety of disturbances called "deficiency diseases", the list of which rapidly became longer over a few decades.

Research workers already knew that mice raised solely on synthetic foods showed abnormal growth, which meant that natural foodstuffs must contain certain essential substances which were still unknown. Thus, in the previous century, Bretonneau had established that raw liver extract would correct rickets, and following this cod liver oil became the compulsory family remedy for sickly children.

In the twentieth century however, the majority of vitamins were discovered in the pulp or skin of certain fruits. For example Christiaan Eijkman (1858–1930) was intrigued by the paralysis affecting both pigeons and some patients in Java, because he noted that both ate polished rice; and he logically deduced that the "vital" material was to be found in the husk of the grain. This proved to be vitamin B.

Apart from this, the British navy had been avoiding scurvy on long sea voyages

Medicine and politics. If we are to believe this Soviet poster from 1925, rickets undoubtedly came from England.

by taking fresh fruit on board since the eighteenth century. And in fact it was in lemon juice that the antiscorbutic vitamin C was isolated in 1930. In the same way maize can be responsible for pellagra, due to a lack of vitamin PP, which can also give rise to haemorrhagic spots on the skin. The list could be illustrated by many anecdotes.

Over the years, vitamins whose existence was suspected from clinical experience and experiment came to be identified, their chemical structure came to be proved, and a distinction was established between those which are soluble in water and those which are soluble in fats. A large number were synthesized, and thus became industrial products.

It is now known that the diet of developed countries is sufficiently diversified to contain all the vitamins necessary for man. Dosing with vitamins, by which so much store is set in certain quarters, is a pointless fad in situations where true deficiency is not present.

Rickets, which was so common a century ago, has disappeared from the West. Developing countries on the other hand still suffer from many vitamin deficiency diseases. Hot countries have many cases of rickets, although there is no shortage of the ultraviolet rays which are needed to form vitamin D.

Like vitamins, hormones are essential substances for human life, and they act in very small quantities. But unlike the former they are produced by the body according to its needs. In his work on the pancreas Claude Bernard had already established the concept of internal secretion. The pancreas releases into the circulation a material which contributes to the control of the blood sugar level.

The pancreas is therefore partly an endocrine gland, like the hypophysis, the thyroid and the parathyroids, the sex

Two examples of postcards from a campaign for vitamins in the 1940s. From now on illustrations of drugs give way to symbolic representation. Right: fruit for vitamin C.

glands and the adrenals. Their secretions were named "hormones" in 1905. The first hormone to be isolated, and later synthesized, was insulin, so named because it originated in the "islets of Langerhans" in the pancreas. Frederick Banting (1891–1841) and Charles Best carried out the experimental work in 1921.

Work on the functioning and co-ordination of endocrine glands continued and disturbances resulting from insufficiencies or excesses were identified – goitre and cretinism, associated with the thyroid, contrast with the exophthalmia and heart problems due to its hyper-

THE MAIN VITAMINS

	Name	Deficiency disorders
A	retinol	growth disorders visual disorders
B1	thiamine	beriberi cardiac disorders – paralysis
B2	riboflavin	skin and eye disorders
B3	nicotinamide	pellagra – nervous disorders
B9	folic acid	anaemia
B12	cyanocobalamin	anaemia – disorders of the mucous membranes
C	ascorbic acid	scurvy
D	calciferol	rickets
E	tocopherol	muscular and nervous disorders
K	naphthoquinone	blood coagulation disorders
P	rutin	circulatory disorders
PP	nicotinic acid	pellagra – diarrhoea – mental confusion

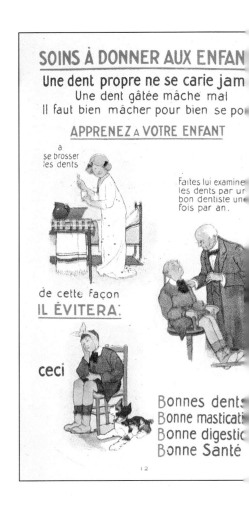

activity; the pituitary gland is responsible for dwarfism and giantism, and so on.

Some hormones were isolated and their chemical composition was determined, and some were found to be capable of synthesis, so that they could be manufactured and provided for those patients suffering from insufficient secretion from their own glands. Hormones act in combination with each other, and the pituitary gland seems to act as the "team leader".

Within half a century endocrinology became one of the main branches of clinical medicine. The list of diseases associated with endocrine glands has con-

Preventive medicine increased between the wars. Centre: principles of hygiene from a leaflet published by the Rockefeller Foundation. Below: two scenes from bathing cures in Germany from the mid nineteenth century.

tinued to grow, as each gland secretes several hormones which have gradually been identified. In addition, the internal organs were found to have hormonal action; the kidney, for example, has an endocrine function in the control of arterial pressure. Other organs, such as the pineal gland located at the base of the brain, and above all the thymus in the middle of the chest, behind the sternum, certainly have a major role, which it is still difficult to identify. This means that hor-monology, which developed in a spectacularly explosive way in the first half of the century, has yet to reach its limits.

An "elegant" experimental cure against tuberculosis published in Le petit journal, *in 1901.*

Although by the eve of the First World War the vaccines produced on the basis of Pasteur's work protected those vaccinated from many epidemic diseases, the number of such diseases was still limited, and vaccination was not an everyday practice. In France soldiers were protected against typhoid, but the civilian population was not, and neither were the troops from Central Africa. Treatment with serum was only effective for a few diseases.

The measures taken brought about some decrease in mortality, particularly in epidemics, but they did not prevent frequent suppuration of wounds due to widespread micro-organisms such as streptococci, staphylococci, coliform bacilli and the micro-organisms which produce gangrenous infections. These infections were always likely to complicate any operation, and the possibilities of surgery were as limited as they had been a century earlier. Then, during the Great War, Alexis Carrel (1873–1944) – who had become famous in the United States through his laboratory tissue cultures and the prolonged survival of a chicken heart perfused with the necessary chemical substances – won renown in his ambulance in the Compiègne forest through his technique of the prolonged drainage of suppurating wounds. However, he was still using hypochlorite irrigations, in accordance with an antiseptic practice which was already fifty years old.

Surgery was to remain subject to the rigorous rules of asepsis and antisepsis until the late 1930s.

Of the so-called medical afflictions, tuberculosis was still the most widespread. Despite its decline (in statistical terms) in most European countries since the beginning of the century, it was still a major scourge. The BCG made attacks less serious, but did not prevent them completely, and no specific product was effective against Koch's bacillus. Vigorous health education campaigns were organized throughout the West. People learnt not to spit on the ground, to avoid contagion; and early diagnosis was encouraged by medical consultation at the first sign of blood in the sputum. Nevertheless this advice seemed to have no effect on reducing mortality, and, being only directed towards attack on the lungs, did not prevent the occurrence of tuberculosis in ganglions (cervical adenitis) or in osteo-articular forms such as Pott's disease (lesions of the vertical column) or coxalgia (involvement of the hip). As far as antituberculosis clinics and systematic chest X-rays were concerned, the services they provided were always too limited.

Around 1890 Carlo Forlanini (1847–1918) in Pavia and John Murphy (1850–1916) in Chicago almost simultaneously came up with the same idea of "resting" the affected lung by compressing it with

Time *magazine for June 1938 commemorates two famous heroes in the United States: Lindbergh and Alexis Carrel (right), who was especially well known for his tissue and organ grafts.*

air introduced into the pleural cavity, where a negative pressure normally obtains. This pneumothoracic technique, together with a rest cure in places which were thought to have a healthy climate – like medium altitude mountains, pine forests or the seaside – resulted in the establishment of sanatoria devoted to the treatment of all forms of tuberculosis in many countries. When injection of air into the pleura was impossible because of tissue lesions, the surgeons then created an extra-pleural space by excision. They also collapsed a diseased lung by removing part of the thoracic skeleton. These thoracoplasties cured a considerable number of patients, at the price of mutilation which was sometimes significant.

However, these forms of treatment against frequently fatal infections of the internal organs only acted indirectly, and did not attack the micro-organisms responsible for disease. In addition to this, as data on infectious diseases built up, their determinism came to be more complex. There was no doubt that the discovery of a micro-organism in a patient explained his problems, but the same micro-organisms were sometimes identified in people who showed no complications. Thus healthy carriers, who should have fallen prey to cholera, amoebiasis, typhoid fever, diphtheria and other equally serious diseases, were recognized. Although the latter did not need any treatment, they could nevertheless contribute to the spread of the disease.

At the same time an increasing number of insects which transmit bacterial or parasitic diseases from one person to another, or through the intermediary of objects or foodstuffs, came to be identified. Thus, the role of the flea as a vehicle for typhus came to be recognized (Charles Nicolle, 1866–1936), together with the role of various flies, ticks spreading haemorrhagic diseases, and freshwater

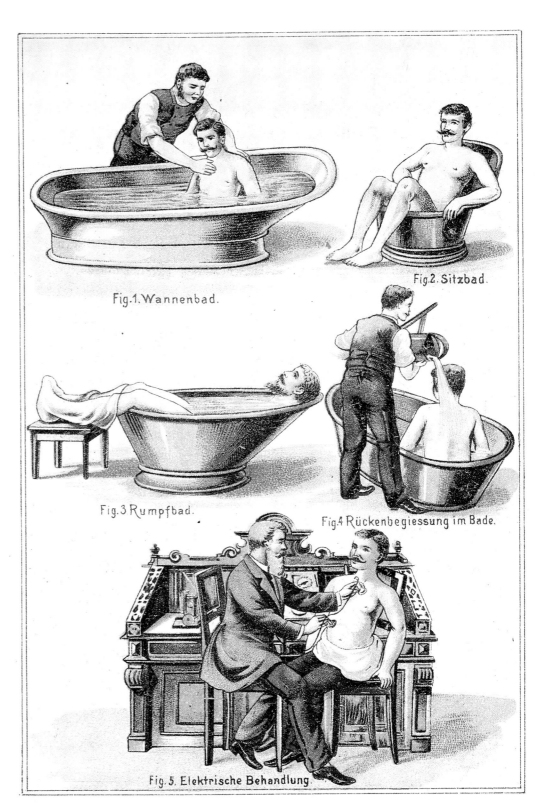

Fig.1. Wannenbad.

Fig.2. Sitzbad.

Fig.3 Rumpfbad.

Fig.4 Rückenbegiessung im Bade.

Fig. 5. Elektrische Behandlung.

Hygiene and different ways of taking a bath. Private bathrooms were still rare in the late nineteenth century. German lithographs, 1897.

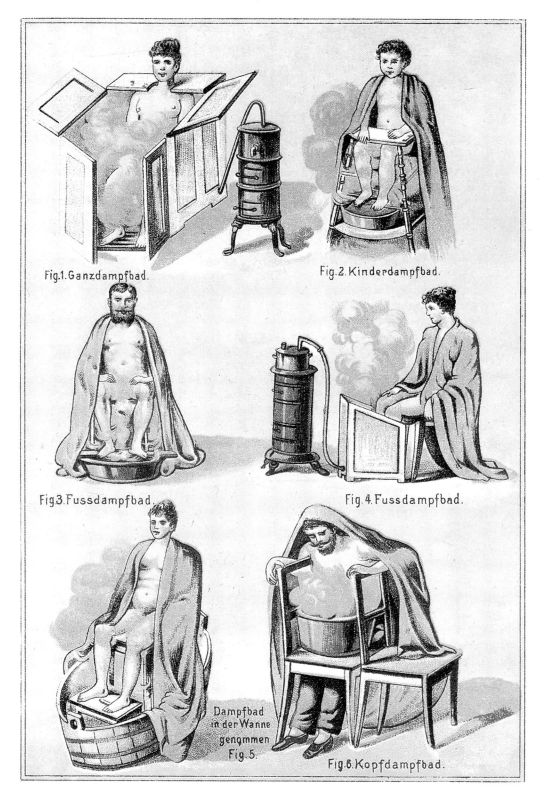

Fig.1. Ganzdampfbad.

Fig.2. Kinderdampfbad.

Fig.3. Fussdampfbad.

Fig.4. Fussdampfbad.

Dampfbad in der Wanne genommen Fig.5.

Fig.6. Kopfdampfbad.

molluscs spreading the micro-organisms responsible for urinary or digestive diseases, and so on, in man. It was Felix Dévé (1872–1951) who established the complete parasitological cycle of an invertebrate which, after an obligatory passage through dogs and sheep, gave rise to hydatic cysts in the liver or lungs of man, a condition which is still endemic on the southern shore of the Mediterranean. Alphonse Laveran (1845–1922), for his part, established the role of the female Anopheles mosquito in the transmission of malaria, demonstrating all stages in the development of plasmodium in both mosquitoes and human blood.

The whole world was dreaming of a drug which would act directly on micro-organisms in a diseased human body when sulphamides came on the scene. These first saw the light of day in Germany.

Ehrlich, who had ingeniously stained and then classified the various cells circulating in blood, established that substances which stained certain bacteria under the microscope must have chemical affinity with their membranes, an affinity which could be utilized. A few decades later Gerhard Domagk (1894–1964) developed several stains in the sulphamide family which killed certain bacteria, a particular material being effective against a particular micro-organism. The first micro-organisms to be dealt with in this way were the streptococci, the pneumococci responsible for lung diseases and the meningococci responsible for meningitis. These same sulphamides proved to be effective against gynaecological diseases following childbirth or abortion.

Members of the French Pasteur Institute, Jacques (1897–1977) and Thérèse Tréfouël (1892–1978), and Daniel Bovet (born in 1907), then established that the part of the material responsible for the

colour has no effect, while the substance which destroys the micro-organism or prevents it from reproducing (the bactericide or bacteriostat) has a relatively simple structure and can be synthesized industrially. From then on there has been no let up in the production of new sulphamides. Their toxicity, rules for their use, and the micro-organisms which they selectively affect, have been repeatedly refined over the last fifty years.

While sulphamides held the attention of French and German research workers, Alexander Fleming (1881–1955) in England noticed around 1928 that some micro-organism cultures died when they became contaminated with fungi. He managed to extract a "penicillin" from *Penicillium notatum*, which proved to have bactericidal powers both in the laboratory and in clinical practice.

When the industry began to manufacture this substance in 1942 English and American wounded benefited immedi-

Henri de Toulouse-Lautrec (1864–1901), Un examen à la faculté de médecine de Paris. *The scene is a solemn and serious one. In France, by tradition, the competitive examinations for hospitals always carried more prestige than university examinations.*

ately, but the French had to wait a little longer. For the first time it was possible for people to survive serious infections in hospitals. The bacteria responsible for pus in wounds seemed to be on the point of being vanquished. Thus, a new class of materials was born, called "antibiotics" because they are produced by the competition which takes place between different living organisms. The term has remained unchanged even though these materials can now be reproduced by synthesis, without the assistance of fungi or micro-organisms.

In 1945, when the whole world hoped to be at peace, medicine entertained extremely high hopes. The combination of sulphamides and penicillin would now make it possible to eliminate the great majority of common diseases, including syphilis, which was burdened with so many malpractices and fantasies. A final victory over infection seemed to be near.

LE MALADE VU PAR LE MÉDECIN

LE MÉDECIN VU PAR LE MALADE

Dessin de Toë.

Relationships between doctors and their patients changed appreciably during the twentieth century. To some extent these are now simpler and less formal. But this does not prevent ulterior motives, if we are to believe the periodical Le rire, *1929.*

VI.

Joint national and international responsibilities

During this time innovations in the art of healing had extensive repercussions on the work of doctors. They now had to acquire chemical knowledge in order to gain a better understanding of the new physiology and to achieve better prescribing, because for two decades antibiotics coexisted with the traditional pharmacopoeia based on simples and plant extracts. They also had to equip their surgeries with microscopes, chemical reagents and electrical equipment. They immediately considered reforming their training. The countries of northern Europe began to place great importance on the so-called fundamental sciences such as chemistry, physics, physiology and bacteriology, reducing the time spent on clinical experience. It was the reforms introduced by Simon Flexner (1863–1946) in the United States which had the greatest impact. His country certainly had need of it, with so many medical schools providing rudimentary education.

Flexner succeeded in introducing rigorous standards and teaching plans both in the universities and in the teaching hospitals. Through him American establishments acquired world-wide renown, examples being the Johns Hopkins University in Baltimore, Harvard and the Mayo Clinic in Minnesota. Unlike the English-speaking world, the Latin countries, and France in particular, remained obstinately faithful to the pre-eminence of clinical practice over the laboratory, in line with a century-old tradition. The hospitals' competitive examinations always had more prestige than the university ones, and clinical professors had a higher status than the holders of fundamental science chairs.

Increasingly doctors were to be found within associations in which new techniques were discussed, or where some measure of supervision was exercised over colleagues, and where relationships, particularly financial relationships, with government authorities were discussed. In fact most European governments continued to develop the public health policies of the previous century. They therefore had to call upon doctors as much for mass vaccination programmes as for the care which they provided to the poor. Gradually some idea of preventive medicine developed, and through force of circumstances it was government authorities who took responsibility for public measures to prevent disease, while the doctors confined themselves to their task of treating individual patients.

In 1902 and 1903 France set up a vast public health system in the country through a series of laws. Communal authorities found themselves responsible for highways, public drainage, the supervision of unhealthy and hazardous establishments, the setting up of hygiene departments, and so on. The professions of medicine and pharmacy were better regulated and,

A consultation at the hospital of the French Society for the Assistance of Wounded Soldiers.

LE DOCTEUR SANS PATIENCE.
— Voyons! qu'est-ce que vous voulez, vous? du repos, combien? un jour, deux jours?... — Mais je vous assure, docteur, que je suis malade. — Allons, huit jours? — Mais, docteur!... — Pas un mot de plus, ou je vous guéris tout de suite!

363 P. J.

TO WHOM SHOULD DISCOVERY BE ATTRIBUTED?

"In science, honour goes to the man who convinces the world, not to the first man who has the idea."

Erasmus Darwin (1731–1802).

Ibn-an-Nafiz and Michel Servet well understood that venous blood reaches the heart, from where it is distributed into the arteries, but it was Harvey who gained acceptance for the mechanism of circulation.

Leeuwenhoek had certainly seen bacteria, Davaine had certainly associated a bacterium with anthrax in sheep, but it was Pasteur who gained acceptance for bacteriology.

Pasteur and Duchesne definitely noticed the antagonism between bacteria and fungi, but it was Fleming who developed penicillin.

Social medicine developed, despite resistance by employers and some doctors themselves, as cartoonists like Grévin, from Le petit journal pour rire, *did not fail to point out.*

above all, the law compelled citizens to obtain vaccination against a list of diseases which grew until the 1980s. The law is not truly coercive, but it nevertheless provides an effective incentive, and has been copied by many European countries. Following the lead of Germany, and then France, the compulsory provision of medical monitoring for their employees by employers is becoming widespread. Occupational medicine for the prevention of accidents at work as well as of occupational diseases – that is, work-related accidents and illness for which compensation is payable – has developed despite resistance by the employers, and sometimes by the unions.

At the same time the social concerns of governments have become more specific. After having compelled large textile, mining and metalworking companies to protect workers against disease and meet the cost of their health care, and after having compelled them to ensure that their workers live decently after retirement, government authorities set up sickness insurance and then retirement pensions for employees.

After the Great War the extent of the material and human damage that had occurred led the French government to set up the Subsecretariat of Health in 1920, following the example set by Great Britain a year earlier. These developments were soon followed through most of Europe. France progressively extended social insurance to new categories of workers, in 1930, and then in 1936 and 1937. The finance for this insurance was covered by contributions from employers, by a levy on salaries, and by the state. On the eve of the Second World War France provided an appreciable number of its citizens with the best social security in Europe, if one ignores countries with dictatorial regimes at that time, such as Germany and Italy.

This solidarity between classes and professions within individual countries was also to be seen between nations. International congresses devoted to public health, which had met at irregular intervals during the nineteenth century, were already tending towards the formation of a permanent organization.

This was finally established in Paris in 1905: the International Office for Public Health (IOPH), which had an effective secretariat and the task of providing member states with information on current epidemics and endemics originating anywhere in the world. Many countries became members of the IOPH, together with most colonial territories.

In 1907 the Hague Convention adopted the terms of the Geneva Convention of 1864 on the protection of prisoners, the wounded, doctors and health personnel during conflict, and it made certain requirements. These measures were respected in many areas of operations, on land and at sea, during the First World War.

Then the League of Nations, which was set up following the Treaty of Versailles, considered co-operation between its members in the public health field by setting up a health bureau. At the same time the International Labour Office (ILO) was set up with responsibility for industrial health and collecting information, particularly on the new chemical industries.

Although the League of Nations was soon discredited, the IOPH remained the only world-wide organization. The latter even continued its documentation work during the Second World War, while the League of Nations disappeared in the turmoil.

The IOPH's monthly bulletin is therefore rich in epidemiological data on the first half of the twentieth century. In these

LES MÉTIERS QUI TUENT

By the end of the nineteenth century there was greater awareness of the importance of accidents at work. The dangers of white lead, used by painters on buildings, are here pointed out by Le charivari.

HOPITAL

BLANC
DE
CERUSE

245.
Ch. Vernier

455

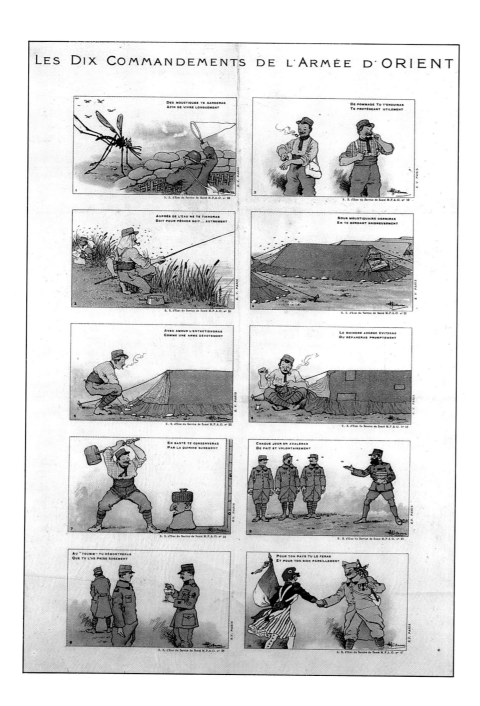

LES DIX COMMANDEMENTS DE L'ARMÉE D'ORIENT

The prevention of malaria became widespread, particularly in the army, from mosquito nets to quinine. This poster, which dates from the Dardanelles expedition of 1915–1916, is signed by Albert Guillaume.

it is possible to follow the epidemics of typhus and typhoid in Eastern Europe at the end of the First World War; the progress of the Spanish 'flu, which undoubtedly left some two million dead in Europe and North Africa in the years 1918–1920; and the bubonic plague pandemic which raged from Manchuria to the Middle East between 1894 and 1948, and even found a few victims in Paris.

The IOPH acted like an enormous world observatory, noting the flow of smallpox, cholera and yellow fever; maintaining permanent links with health stations and quarantine offices; and being particularly vigilant when large population movements took place in association with major pilgrimages like that to Mecca, and the flow of emigration to the United States.

This organization also monitored the progress of malaria both in tropical regions and in Europe, gave advice on the control of rats in ships and on ways of manufacturing and storing vaccines, and recorded progress in the struggle against the great micro-organism and parasite-induced endemics of Africa and the Far East. The IOPH disappeared in 1945 with the creation of the World Health Organization (WHO) by the United Nations Organization (UNO).

Thus, throughout the first half of the twentieth century medicine learnt to make use of and develop the new knowledge gained in previous decades. It made good use of innovations in associated disciplines, in particular chemistry, and developed the application of X-rays, which in themselves have nothing to do with medicine, for its own needs.

This period was therefore a particularly fruitful one for diagnosis, and ended with prospects which were at last encouraging in the field of treatment.

FROM X-RAYS TO PENICILLIN
1895 – 1945

POLITICS AND CULTURE	DATE	DATE	MEDICINE
Invention of cinematography by the Lumière brothers	1895	1895	Röntgen discovers X-rays
		1897	Eiskam: the first vitamin
Radioactivity	1900–1910	1900	Sigmund Freud: *The interpretation of dreams* Landsteiner identifies blood groups
The Russo-Japanese War	1901–1904	1901	Charles Richet: anaphylaxis
		1905	The establishment of the International Office for Public Health
Robert Peary reaches the North Pole	1909		
		1910	Alexis Carrel: tissue culture
Ernest Rutherford discovers the atomic nucleus	1911		
First World War	1914–1918		
The use of mustard gas	1915		
The October Revolution in Russia	1917		
		1918–1921	The "Spanish 'flu" epidemic
Treaty of Versailles League of Nations	1919		
		1921	BCG against tuberculosis Identification of insulin
Mussolini takes power in Italy	1922		
		1927	Egas Moniz: arteriography Cooley's work on thalassaemia
Stock market crash in New York: start of the Great Slump	1929	1929	Forsmann: catheterization of the heart Fleming: penicillin
		1931	The electron microscope
F.D. Roosevelt elected President of the United States	1932		
Adolf Hitler, Chancellor of Germany	1933		
		1935	The first sulphamides Discovery of the prostaglandins
Civil War in Spain	1936–1939	1936	Sorpes prepares heparin
German-Soviet pact	1939		
Second World War	1939–1945		
		1940	Hans Selye: adaptation syndrome, stress

chapter XIII

The explosion of knowledge and techniques

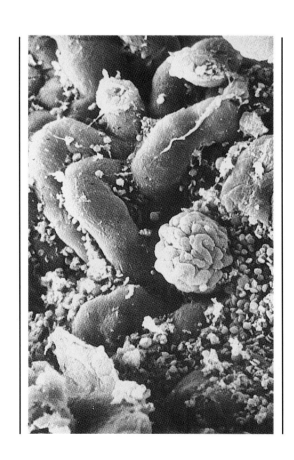

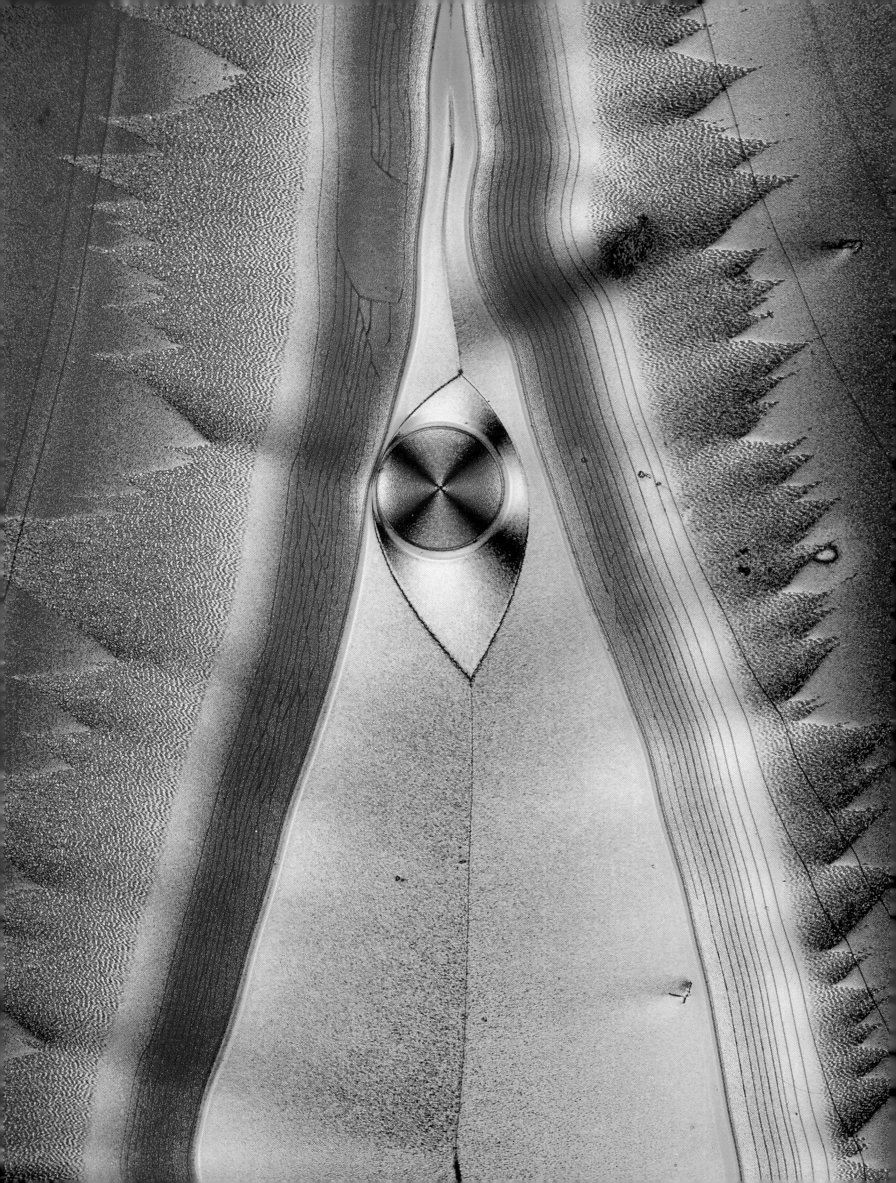

The understanding of the human body was achieved in several stages. The sixteenth century identified the principal structures that were visible to the naked eye, namely the viscera, the organs and some of their connections. More detailed knowledge was gained over the following centuries, and the microscope, though still awkward to use, began to excite people's curiosity.

The nineteenth century was able to look further: in France, François-Xavier Bichat discovered the types of tissue that make up the structure of the body; and in Germany, Rudolf Virchow discovered the cell, which he considered to be the basic element of all human physiology and pathology. The following generations progressed from histology (the study of tissues) to cytology (the study of cells). A number of constituents were discovered within the cell, such as the nucleus, the organelles and the corpuscles, each of which plays a specific role that is indispensable to the functioning of the others. Researchers thus found themselves looking at ever smaller bodies.

In the middle of the twentieth century, a breakthrough was made into the realm of the infinitesimal. It was now possible to conduct analyses (on the scale of a millionth of a millimetre) of the chemical composition and spatial structure of each substance that is created or destroyed in the body. Doctors could now keep a close watch on the chemical modification of polypeptide chains. Their interest turned to *molecular cell biology*, any disturbance of which can herald disease. But their curiosity did not end there. Nature kept confronting them with ever more precise problems, and they had no means of knowing if they would ever penetrate the mysteries of this life which they were finding so difficult to define.

This spectacular course of events was not confined to medicine, which was in

Crystal of vitamin C viewed under polarized light. Vitamins are essential to normal growth of humans and other animals. An adequate supply prevents the vitamin deficiency syndrome known as scurvy.

fact making use of all the other scientific disciplines and techniques. For example, electronics provided it with new means of exploration. The fluid mechanics that were used in the construction of pipelines could equally well be applied to the circulation of the blood. Astronomy and space exploration shed light on questions of physiology. Sound and light waves had their applications not only in military hardware, but also in surgical lasers. Data processing was equally useful in the management of bank accounts and patients' files, or for epidemiological work.

Man was progressing little by little towards that ideal which doctors had been pursuing for centuries: learning how to alleviate and prevent the suffering caused by disease.

From the early 1950s onwards, all the sciences underwent a revolution. The frontiers between chemistry and physics disappeared with the growing understanding of atomic structure. In medicine, scientists were pondering the transition of physiology to pathology, since the definition of a diseased state as opposed to a normal state was becoming increasingly imprecise. The very concept of disease appeared to be so uncertain that the classifications which had been in use thirty years before had all but lost their relevance. In medical practice, the logical separation between diagnosis and treatment was becoming blurred. This is why the history of these five decades of medicine is complex. That which was taken to be a discovery of genius would turn out to be a derisory attempt, or – who knows – an extraordinary intuition. During this period, all the branches of medicine were transformed; we will try to show how this came about.

A change had also occurred in research techniques. Researchers were no longer alone in their laboratories. They were members of teams, and several teams vast distances apart could work together on the same subject. Scientific complexity did not prevent rivalry. This was why, unlike in previous centuries, it was now rare that a discovery could be attributed to a single person.

Moreover, new discoveries no longer came suddenly to the attention of science. Preliminary notes were published first, to establish a date, and these would be followed by a series of more detailed, explanatory studies as the concept or the method was improved upon. It therefore became difficult to date a discovery precisely. Even the history of medicine changed in terms of how it reported the facts, and it no longer used methods that had been in use twenty years before.

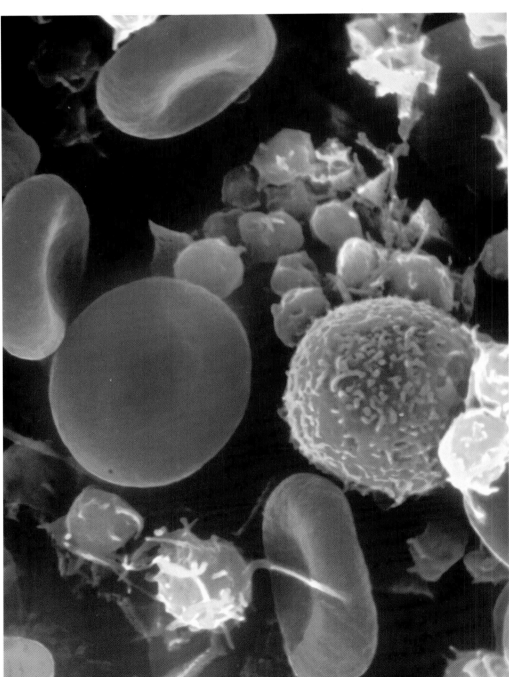

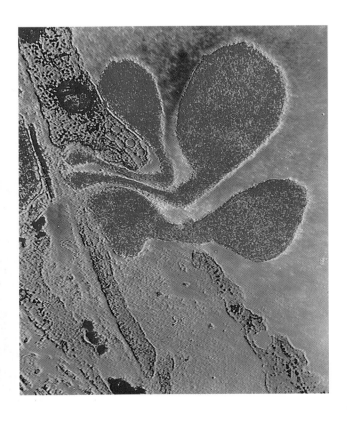

Left: *erythrocytes (red blood cells) cross the walls of a capillary (diapedesis).*
Above: *the formed elements of the blood, viewed with a scanning electron microscope, produce a kaleidoscope of colours: red erythrocytes, green lymphocytes and clusters of ochre platelets.*

The triumph of biochemistry

I.

Chemical analysis was no longer aimed merely at revealing the presence of a simple element within a complex body. It now attempted to identify the organic molecules in the midst of others.

Ultracentrifugation* and flame photometry* gave way to scientific techniques like column or paper chromatography, with analyses in the liquid or gas phase. It was found that when proteins are placed in an electric field they migrate according to their composition and molecular weight and can thus be identified. So, the process of "immunoelectrophoresis*" became an everyday procedure for studying biological fluids.

METICULOUS ANALYSES

The marking technique that involves the use of a radioactive isotope "marker" enabled substances to be followed as they migrated throughout the body and were transformed, just as we might watch the smoke of a ship at sea. Henceforth, such "probes" were indispensable for studying anabolic and catabolic chemical compounds and the functions of enzymes.

Medical diagnosis no longer rested solely on making an examination of the patient, listening to the chest and palpating the abdomen. The doctor required a growing quantity of biochemical data on the functioning of the kidney, the liver or the digestive tract, and this had to be supplied as quickly as possible. Electronics permitted the building of apparatus which, when primed with the necessary reagents, could make about twenty measurements in a few minutes on one sample of a patient's blood or urine.

In the space of a few years, these automatic analysis machines have now become essential in assessing the state of health of large population groups. They enable systematic health checks to be

This slide of frogs' eggs provides very convenient study material for experiments in the field of genetic engineering.

463

made on persons not otherwise being treated for a disease. They have also proved to be very useful in institutions where daily assessments have to be made of patients' laboratory data.

Simplification of analysis techniques brought biochemistry within the reach of everyone. Simple strips dipped in urine enabled diabetics to assess how well they were eliminating their excess sugar; in addition women were able to discover at a much earlier stage whether they were pregnant.

This type of test will no doubt become even more common in future for all kinds of purposes, for use both by the public in self-testing and by qualified medical staff. For the former it will represent a method of continuously monitoring phenomena such as the effect of diet on the body's metabolism, even though an optical instrument is required for the test; for the latter, it will be a quick and simple means of detecting disease.

Miniaturization, which came about via electronics, meant that only small quantities of liquid or cells were needed for biochemical analysis. For example, the study of sweat from an infant collected on a wad of cotton wool is sufficient to enable a diagnosis to be made of cystic fibrosis, a serious abnormality relating to secretion from the cutaneous, respiratory and digestive glands.

A small drop of blood taken from the pad of a finger shows the diabetic the status of his blood sugar level. When a foetus is only a few weeks old, the uterus of the pregnant woman can be punctured to remove a few cubic millimetres of amniotic fluid, a dozen cells resulting from the normal desquamation of the embryo, or even a few red blood cells if it is possible to puncture the umbilical cord.

Chemical and cytological* study of these samples can lead to the diagnosis of

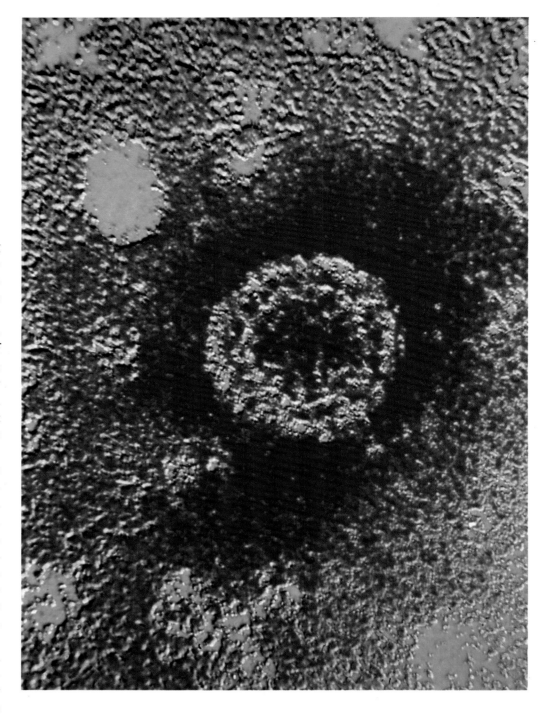

Particles of the hepatitis B virus which can cause fatal liver damage. Fortunately, a new vaccine has been developed against hepatitis B using genetic engineering methods.

foetal abnormalities, and this may be especially important if malformations have already occurred within the family.

If this antenatal diagnosis reveals serious abnormalities such as Down's syndrome, the parents can consider having the pregnancy terminated. These procedures contribute to limiting the number of children born with abnormalities, and are indicated especially in families in which hereditary diseases have been diagnosed, and in women who are more than thirty-five years old, since the risk of abnormality is higher for them than for younger mothers.

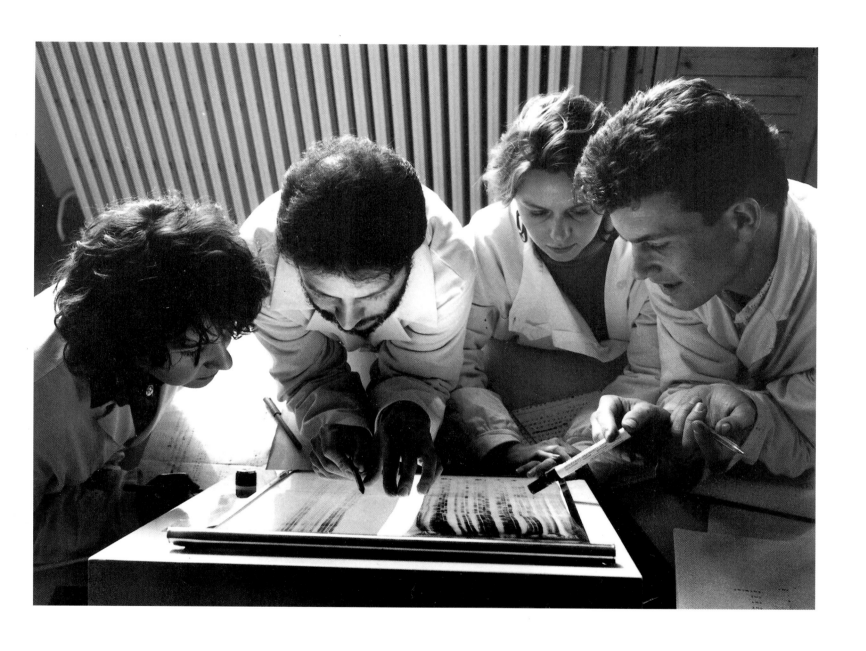

Students at the Pasteur Institute read an electrophoretogram of DNA. They remind the observer of Rembrandt's Anatomy lesson of four centuries earlier.

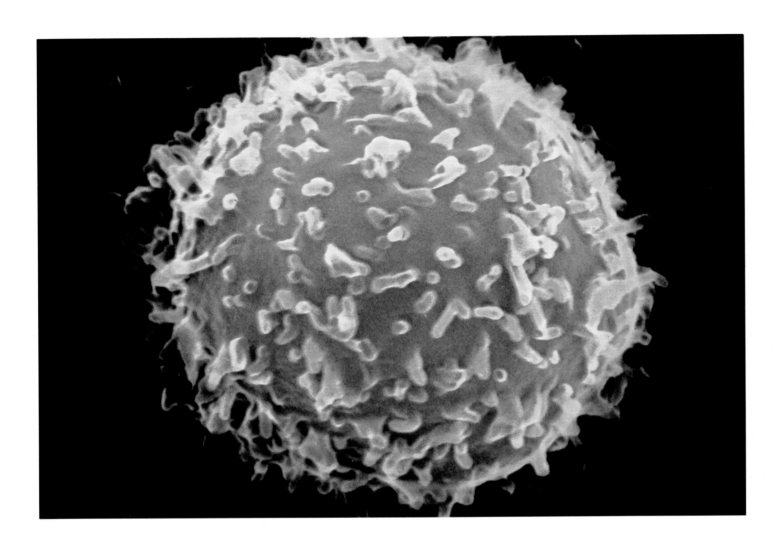

THE COMPLEXITY
OF BLOOD

These improvements in analytical techniques led to the gradual unravelling of the biochemistry of the blood, so that now we cannot deny the need for a "balance of the humours" such as Hippocrates wished for, nor refuse Claude Bernard a certain constancy of the "internal conditions". However, the number of substances whose concentration the organism has to control is considerable, and it would be too much to list them all here. We will therefore limit ourselves to a few examples.

Using artificial means, it is possible to isolate from blood the red cells that live and circulate in the plasma. These cells contain a pigment, haemoglobin, which

A T-lymphocyte magnified approximately 2500 times.

ensures the binding of oxygen in the pulmonary epithelium, from where it is transported throughout the body. Haemoglobin can be subject to various hereditary abnormalities that can be a severe handicap for the sufferer. The frequency of these haemoglobinopathies varies with the kind of population. For example, thalassaemia and sickle cell anaemia are particularly widespread in some African ethnic groups.

Thus "geographic haematology" came about, which enabled unexpected relationships to be established between populations, and patterns of very old human migrations to be reconstructed *a posteriori*.

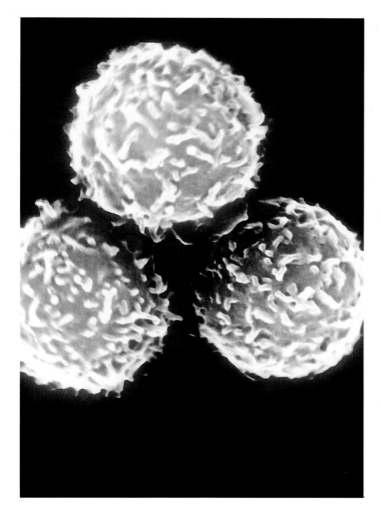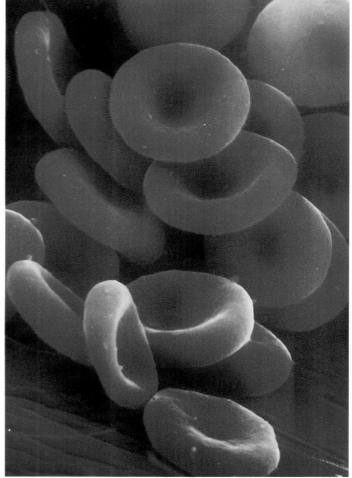

Over the last forty years, the white blood cells, or leucocytes, have perhaps sharpened the curiosity of the researchers even more than red blood cells, which used to be thought of as the more valuable. Since the start of the century, we have known about the phenomenon of phagocytosis, in which polynuclear leucocytes engulf micro-organisms in order to destroy them. Today, we understand better just how important leucocytes are in maintaining the integrity of the organism, reacting to foreign bodies and dangerous germs. Leucocytes – especially the T-lymphocytes which are made in the thymus, and the B-lymphocytes which are made in the bone marrow – are the agents

Above left: the T-lymphocyte is thymus-dependent and is responsible for the tolerance or rejection of transplants.
Above right: red blood cells (erythrocytes) have a characteristic shape. Under the microscope, they look like small cushions with a central depression.

of immunity. They secrete countless antibodies which, if they are well adapted to the invader, destroy it. The production of antibodies in response to infection by bacteria or viruses is such a vitally important phenomenon that it now forms the basis of immunology.

This new discipline is foremost in the struggle against infectious disease, whether of parasitic, bacterial or viral origin. The study of immunology revealed the existence of autoimmune diseases – which are more numerous than was orginally thought –such as some forms of arthritis. It underpins the hypothesis of the role of immunity in the predisposition to and course of some types of cancer.

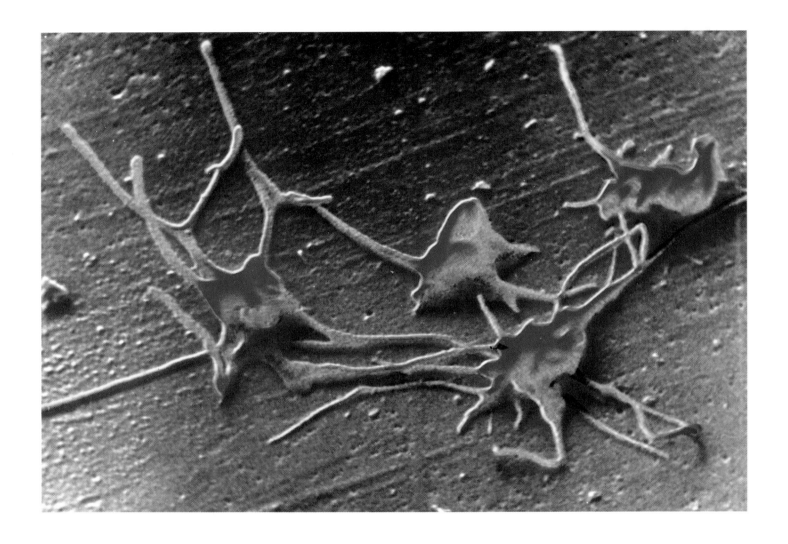

The platelets, the smallest components of the blood, play an essential part in coagulation.

Immunotherapy is currently one of the treatments for cancer. Also, when the body has proved to be too sensitive to certain forms of attack, such as in the case of asthma, it is possible to desensitize it.

An anarchic proliferation of white blood cells results in leukaemias, the prognosis for which used always to be death. New products now make it possible to combat malignant haemopathies, with the assistance of radiotherapy and surgery.

While leukaemias are due to an excess of white blood cells, some circumstances may reduce their production in favour of that of abnormal leucocytes. This is what happens in some congenital abnormalities, or in diseases caused by massive doses of ionizing radiation. The rise of the nuclear industry has led to accidents that

have threatened the lives of thousands of people. Treatment involves replacing the stem cells of the diseased leucocytes with other normal cells which then produce the required leucocytes. The applications for these bone marrow transplants have multiplied as their use in the treatment of various disorders has proved successful. The tissue types of the donor and recipient organisms must also be compatible if such a transplant is to succeed.

Since the turn of the century, we have known that the plasma of some donors does not match the red cells of some recipients. The Rhesus factor was then identified, together with the phenomenon of foeto-maternal immunization, and subsequently other blood groups were differentiated. The failures and successes of organ transplants between animals and humans (xenografts) as well as between humans of different genotypes (allografts) have led researchers to define more accurately the phenomena of intolerance. It was discovered that the phenomena of immunity which were associated with blood cells also occurred in response to foreign tissue, and this gave rise to the concept of histocompatibility. Blood groups were then joined by tissue groups, the most familiar system for which is the HLA system (drawn up by Jean Dausset in 1958) that includes several dozen subgroups. The ability to distinguish these ensures a greater success rate in transplantation and organ grafting, where the difficulties lie not so much in the operation as in the acceptance of the graft. Tissue rejection, which used to be so frequent, could now be suppressed.

This progress in our knowledge of immune mechanisms also led to the manufacture of new vaccines. In one decade alone, three types of vaccine against poliomyelitis were developed by Lépine in Paris (1954–1956) as well as by Salk and Levine in the United States (1953–1956). From the 1970s onwards, the dreaded hepatitis B, which is very contagious and is associated with possibly fatal liver damage, could be prevented by a vaccine.

The 1980s saw the development of combined inoculation against measles, mumps and rubella, which was especially valuable since the latter can lead to serious foetal abnormalities when it occurs in pregnant women. The 1990s will see the widespread use of a vaccine against hepatitis C. The day will doubtless come when AIDS can be prevented in the same manner.

The blood is responsible for a phenomenon which man has noted since his earliest beginnings. Most wounds lead to haemorrhage which stops spontaneously

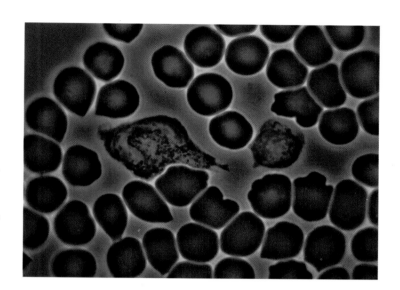

Red blood cells surround a granulocyte, a type of leucocyte, which they outnumber many times. Viewed with an optical microscope, magnified 1000 times.

THE NAZI DOCTORS

Under the Nazi regime in Germany (1933 to 1945), doctors were offered the opportunity to carry out experiments for the advancement of science on the internees of concentration camps. These practitioners, who usually had no training in physiology, carried out tests involving refrigeration, interruption of the circulatory flow, mutilation, pharmacological injections, interventions on the sexual organs and so forth, without definite experimental protocols, or any knowledge of toxicology or asepsis. Death was the most frequent outcome of these experiments, without any scientific benefit whatever being derived from them. Some of these doctors were condemned to death at the Nuremberg trials in 1946. The French government passed a law in 1988 regarding experimentation on healthy people which forbids the use of individuals who are in prison or who have been deprived of their freedom of consent.

Human blood is a powerful vehicle of life and the stuff of dreams, as in this painting by René Magritte (1898–1967), Le sang du monde, *whose degree of abstraction approaches that of objects viewed under a microscope.*

because blood coagulates. Physiologists and chemists had already studied the formation of the blood clot, but the twentieth century was to go even further in detailing substances such as fibrin, fibrinogen, thrombin and prothrombin which, under the influence of other proteins, are responsible for haemostasis* when blood vessels have been damaged. The role of the platelets, elements of the blood which were long neglected, has been shown to be vital in contributing to life-saving coagulation. Yet aggregates of platelets can also be dangerous when they obstruct vessels and hamper blood circulation.

The identification of each blood product has led to the definition of new diseases, since a product's absence can prevent coagulation and cause a wound to bleed indefinitely, as happens in haemophilia, or it may trigger spontaneous haemorrhages. Other anaemias result in the destruction of red blood cells or in abnormal haemoglobin.

New methods of treatment use many different kinds of procedures: dangerous blood may be replaced by different blood. For example, exsanginotransfusion in new-born babies replaces the dangerous blood they were born with by blood which is compatible with their immunological profile. It is also possible to inject bleeding patients with products that facilitate coagulation: the antihaemorrhagic agent vitamin K was discovered to be useful for this purpose.

These techniques have completely revolutionized the conditions for blood transfusion, which has progressed a long way since the first attempts in the seventeenth century when Denis replaced human blood with sheep's blood. In all the countries of the world, transfusion centres have been set up where blood is taken from donors, the group and subgroup are identified, and the non-infectivity of the

471

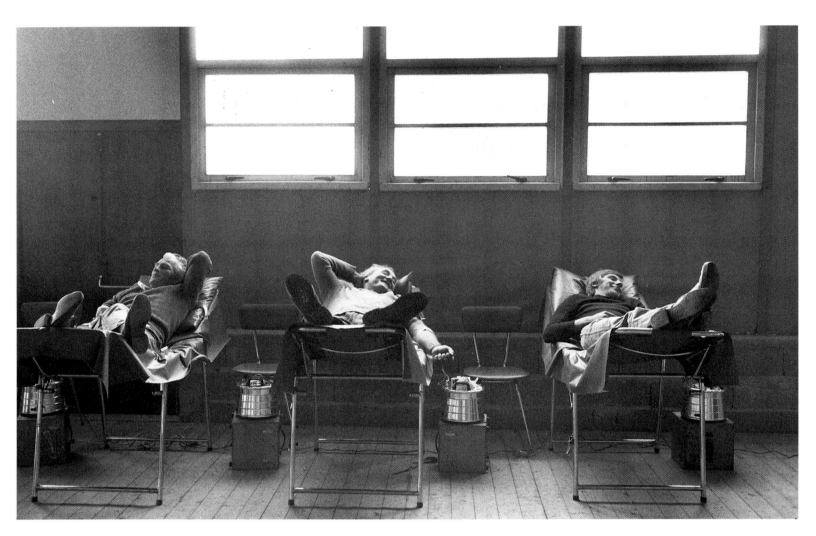

blood is checked before it is distributed to hospitals. We no longer talk about donors and recipients in general terms, since only transfusions between people of the same blood group are now legitimate.

In the 1960s and 1970s, generous transfusions were given for often modest requirements, but we have since become more economical with this precious fluid. We now extract the substances we require for each particular case: albumin, concentrates of blood cells, plasma fractions, and so on. Some of these may be kept for quite a long time under refrigeration, and can be transported easily to a battlefield or the scene of a disaster.

Sometimes doctors try to prevent coagulation, for example during prolonged surgical intervention, or in certain pathological conditions caused by thrombosis, in which the blood blocks either veins or arteries, often leading to embolism.

Here, too, there have been fruitful discoveries: an antivitamin K was isolated from certain plants and used in the manufacture of anticoagulants. Then in 1939 and 1940, two pioneers in this field, the Swede Johan Jorpes (1894–1973) and the Canadian Sir John Murray, isolated and used heparin, which is an anticoagulant substance secreted by the liver.

A young haemophiliac in a Paris hospital. Because of blood transfusions, he can lead a normal life.

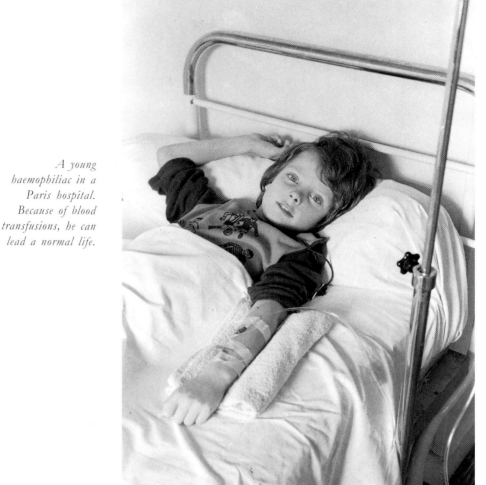

Top left: in the 1940s, the collection of blood donations was organized for the first time in France on a large scale, along American lines.
Bottom left: Paris, 1945.

THE FACTORS INVOLVED IN BLOOD COAGULATION

Factor
I   *fibrinogen*
II   *prothrombin*
V   *proaccelerin*
VII   *proconvertin*
VIII   *antihaemophilic factor A*
IX   *antihaemophilic factor B*
X   *Stuart factor*
XI   *plasma thromboplastin precursor*
XII   *Hageman factor*
XIII   *fibrin-stabilizing factor*
Each intermediate stage marks the combined action of a coagulation factor and a tissue factor.
Factors I, II, V, VII, IX and X are manufactured by the liver.
Factors II, VII, IX and X cannot be produced unless vitamin K is present.

(After C. Jacquillat et al. PUF, 1989.)

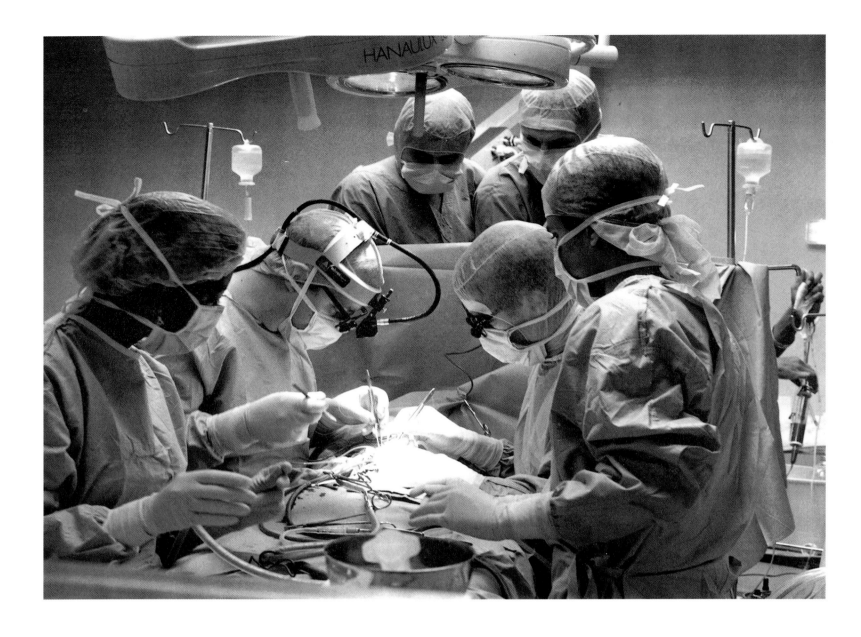

RESUSCITATION AND INTENSIVE CARE

Progress in biochemical analysis soon revealed that many known diseases led to hitherto unsuspected metabolic disorders. Fernand Widal's work, in which he based the prognosis of renal insufficiency purely on the level of urea in the blood, was no longer sufficient, and creatinine soon proved to be a much better indicator of the filtering ability of the kidney. New substances were discovered whose concentration in the blood was necessary to life, or conversely, whose presence was dangerous.

A completely unexpected discovery was made when certain concentrations of trace elements such as manganese and zinc in the blood proved to be vital, leading to deficiencies when present at lower levels, and disorders when present at higher levels.

Diseases, whose observable mechanical consequences were treated by surgeons using physical methods, were found to have chemical consequences that explained the damage they caused. When transit in the small intestine is blocked by a torsion or an adhesion in the peritoneal cavity, the surgeon can restore normal flow, but the retention of intestinal fluids upsets the balance of electrolytes in the blood. The levels of sodium, calcium chloride and potassium have to be determined and corrected before there is a return to normality. The disorder cannot be cured without the simultaneous application of mechanical and biochemical measures.

In the same way, pneumonia, pleural effusion (in which fluid compresses the lungs) and fractured ribs which hamper

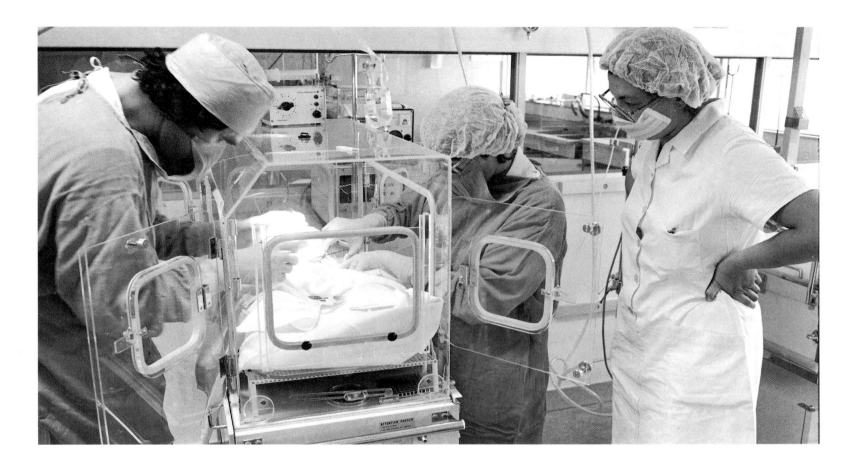

normal respiration, all have repercussions in the levels of oxygen and carbon dioxide in the blood. Many diseases involving diarrhoea can lead to death not so much as a result of the microbial infection that causes it but as a result of dehydration, which can easily be prevented or corrected.

These three examples show that all disorders which are apparently simple can have serious metabolic consequences. These require skilful correction by means of dosage, analysis of the blood gases and frequent determinations of electrolyte balance.

Different types of intensive treatment were therefore developed in the 1950s aimed at correcting disorders affecting proteins, electrolytes or general metabolism that were brought about by a wide

Opposite: the intensive care unit at the Laennec Hospital in France in 1988. Operating techniques have become increasingly complex. Here, surgeons need to wear special glasses when carrying out open-heart surgery on a new-born baby.
Above: neonatal intensive care enables increasingly fragile premature babies to survive.

range of diseases. According to studies by Selye in Canada and Laborit in France, it is possible to arrest certain nervous phenomena using so-called analeptic or ganglioplegic products. Good physiological conditions of respiration can be restored using a tube inserted into the trachea, and artificial respirators which insufflate the appropriate mixture of gases into the lungs. Drugs can be perfused into the veins and arteries, and nutritional products can be introduced directly into the intestine or even into the veins (parenteral alimentation).

These various intensive-care procedures do not merely apply to the acute imbalances. Chronic diseases have also benefited from them, and spectacular successes have been observed in the treatment of renal insufficiency. Death

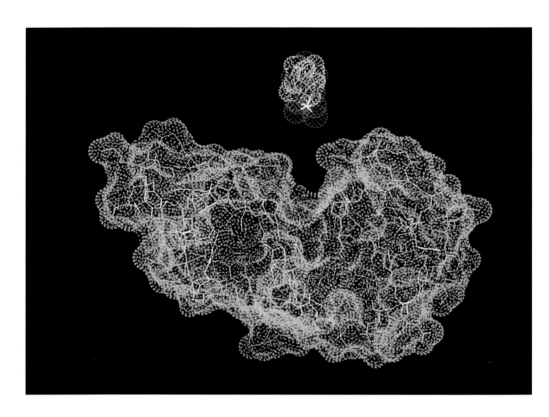

HOW SHOULD DEATH BE DEFINED?

Reconstruction of an enzyme, ribonuclease A, which is essential to cell metabolism.

Progress in long-term life-support techniques means that sick people and accident victims, who in former times would have died, can now be restored to life. Studies of the physiology of the brain and the heart have also made it more difficult to draw the line between life and death. At what point should the life-support machines be switched off because there is no more hope, and what will be shown on the death certificate as the time of death? New criteria have had to be established: "Brain death is a state of total unconsciousness characterized by:
– the absence of respiration which is not assisted by any apparatus;
– a total absence of reflexes, with hypotonia and unchanged dilatation of the pupils;
– a flat electroencephalogram trace;
– the recording of the above phenomena for a period of time that is judged to be sufficiently long for their reversal to be extremely unlikely, and in the absence of depressants;
– one of these four elements is not sufficient by itself to confirm brain death."

(French National Academy of Medicine, 1987.)

was once the only prognosis for such kidney patients, but they can now purify their blood by passing it through a semi-permeable membrane which filters out all the undesirable chemical elements not eliminated by the diseased kidney. This process of haemodialysis is done by filtering arterial blood through a machine and returning it into a vein. The process takes several hours, and can be carried out in a specialized centre or even in the patient's home.

The patient can then lead an almost normal social and professional life. Another less satisfactory method, peritoneal dialysis, consists in using the filtering ability of the serous membrane of the peritoneum in the abdominal cavity. These techniques prolong by several decades the lives of patients who were formerly doomed to die early.

The treatments mentioned are only some of the ways in which modern intensive care procedures can restore the body's equilibrium in a wide range of circumstances, from acute organ failure to chronic disorders. Intensive care units are now common in hospitals, but they can only function in continuous co-operation with clinical biochemistry laboratories. Even the first-aid services which go to the scene of accidents and disasters, in factories, on the roads or in patients' homes, are equipped so that they can restore changed vital functions in the shortest possible time.

Techniques of artificial respiration, circulation and alimentation mean that patients in a coma can be restored to an almost normal condition, whatever the cause of their unconsciousness – toxic, traumatic, infectious or other. The speed of intervention is of paramount importance, particularly in the case of collapse, as for example in cardiac arrest. Automatic instruments have been developed to assist in this. They measure blood

pressure and pulse, as well as record an electrocardiogram and an electro-encephalogram and sound an alarm at the least sign of failure.

However, the greatest difficulty in such therapeutic enterprises remains the prognosis, which varies with the depth of coma. Is it legitimate to subject patients to prolonged life-support when their recovery is fraught with problems? Such therapeutic persistence has already produced cures, or at least partial ones, after comas lasting several months. Nobody except the doctor can therefore decide to stop the machines, he alone can assess the

At the Pasteur Institute, identification of strains of bacteria which colonize the human intestine.

state of the patient, his or her biological data, cerebral activity, and so on. However, some people would like the doctor to switch off the machinery in cases where the patient is lucid and clearly suffering too much, or if a possible cure can only be brought about at the price of serious after-effects. This would then count as euthanasia.

At the end of the twentieth century, such questions give rise to serious technical uncertainties (for example, the biological and legal definition of death) and moral dilemmas, which cannot be easily resolved.

HORMONES AND ENZYMES

*B*y the middle of the century, we had arrived at what appeared to be a complete list of endocrine glands which secrete the hormones that are indispensable to life: the hypophysis, the thyroid gland, the parathyroids, the genital glands, the adrenal glands and the pancreas. However, the following decades saw additions being made to this list. In the 1960s, a substance was discovered which is produced by the prostate. Until then, only the external secretions produced by the prostate in the male were known. In fact, prostaglandins are observed in both sexes, and play a part in many functions. Then hormones produced by certain parts of the brain were identified: these neurohormones act in various places on cellular elements that may be quite some distance away, without even using the blood stream.

The classic distinction between internal and external secretions was thereby challenged. This chemical mechanism, which transmits impulses from one end to the other of the brain, the seat of thought and feeling, would appear to explain the processes of thought itself. A transfer of molecules ensures instant communication between the left hemisphere which governs speech and motor activity, and the right hemisphere which is responsible for perception, artistic expression and sensibility. Some scientists, echoing the materialist iatrochemists of the past, would go as far as to assert that man is nothing but chemistry. Roughly two centuries after his time, they have rediscovered Cabanis, for whom the brain secreted thought much as the stomach secreted gastric juices.

The existence of cerebral hormones has been verified, but we still do not understand the role of the epiphysis and the thymus which, even if it greatly diminishes in volume from birth to adult-

Sperm is stored in liquid nitrogen at a very low temperature (left) *and then introduced into the uterus* (right).

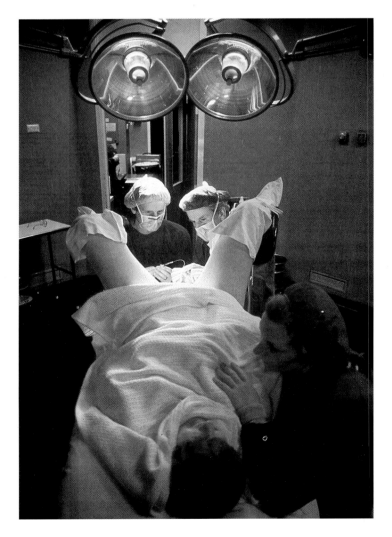

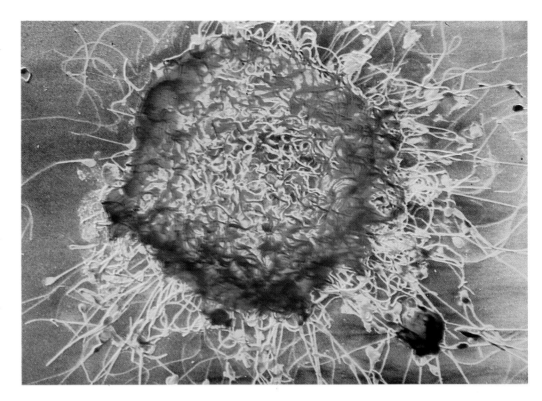

An oocyte surrounded by sperm. Only one will succeed in penetrating it to form a zygote.

hood, probably has an internal secretory role in addition to its function as a producer of the white blood cells that are so essential to the immune system. Far from the brain, other products made by the nerve cells exert control over the skeletal muscles and those of the viscera, and determine the production of various substances from the secretory glands. All the physiology of movement and digestion is therefore subordinate to such "neuromediators", the list of which is constantly growing.

It has also been possible to identify other modes of hormonal action which are triggered by very different mechanisms. Thus, when Hans Selye described his "general adaptation syndrome" in Montreal in 1946, he showed that the hypophysis and the adrenal glands can be initially responsible for a deep-seated autonomic imbalance manifested by agitation, muscular movements and disordered visceral secretions, as well as by psychological phenomena such as panic and depression. Then, when calm returns, the body adapts to the new external conditions.

These phenomena, which we erroneously call stress, can be observed after a physical attack, an accident, surgical intervention or the sight of a human drama, after an infectious or toxic illness, after an emotional event of a sad or a happy nature, and so on. These neurophysiological reactions can result in indisputable anatomical lesions such as stress ulcers of the stomach or intestine which in turn can lead to haemorrhages that are just as serious as those that arise from other forms of ulcers.

The sexual functions also obey hormones which are much more complex than was thought in 1940. Curiously, we still do not know the phenomena responsible for spermatogenesis, the formation of sperm. We know that some men produce more sperm than others, some may have sperm which are more mobile and long-lived than others, but less interest has been shown in this than in female sexuality.

Since 1950, we have known enough about the hormones responsible for the maturation of the ovum and the phenomena of menstruation to be able to prevent this maturation from taking place, and hence to prevent fertility. In the United States, Gregory Goodwin Pincus developed a method of contraception using drugs (1951) which hundreds of millions of women now use instead of the age-old methods, which were generally of a mechanical nature.

Doctors have also been trying for many years to solve the problem of infertility in some couples, which may be due to the man or the woman. By measuring the levels in the blood of the successive hormones which are responsible for the different stages of the menstrual cycle, and then by administering these hormones to provide stimulation at the relevant times, the fertility and maturation of the ovum can be increased. Then, at the right time, sperm previously obtained by masturbation, and kept at a very low temperature in sperm banks, can be injected into the uterus.

Sometimes sterility is due to an anatomical obstruction between the ovary and the uterus where the fertilized egg will

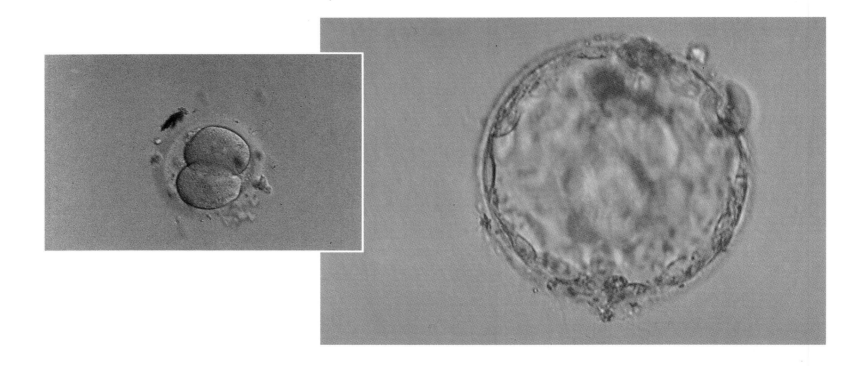

be implanted. In this case, fertilizable ova are removed from the woman during a small surgical intervention. They are then placed in contact with the husband's sperm or that of a donor if the husband's sperm is sterile. Once the embryo has started to form, it is implanted in the woman's uterus. These "*in vitro* fertilizations with embryo transfer" have already been successful in thousands of cases, but there have been many more failures, and there are risks associated with the technique such as a high rate of multiple pregnancies. The first such "test-tube baby" was born in 1978.

Efforts to resolve the problem of unwanted sterility have taken many forms, depending on the nature of the anatomical, hormonal or psychological obstacle which has to be overcome. Some answers to the problem, such as the gift of sperm or ova, or the loan of a uterus by surrogate mothers, create moral, social and legal problems which are a long way from being resolved. Over the last few years, the progress we have made in clinical endocrinology, in biological quantitative

The stages of fertilization.
Left: separation into two cells
of the fertilized ovum and,
right: the blastocyst stage
some hours later.

analysis and in the study and culture of cellular elements in the laboratory has revolutionized our knowledge in the field of procreation, or in other words, of reproduction in the human species.

Medically assisted procreation has still more to offer. We can anticipate that it will cause considerable upheavals in our ways of thinking, and even in the organization of families and societies. All over the world, ethical committees are trying to reconcile science and morality, and governments hesitate to pass laws concerning a field in which there is still so much uncertainty.

Generally speaking, the concept of the hormone has broadened considerably over the last few years. Hormonal mechanisms govern the communication between the organs and between areas of the same organ. Medicine is still a long way from obtaining a complete list, if such an inventory is even possible.

In parallel with our knowledge of hormones, our knowledge of enzymes has also made great strides. The list of "ferments", which were identified in the

last century and are now known as "enzymes", has steadily lengthened at the same time as biochemists have made detailed studies of biochemical pathways, as well as of the production and destruction of molecules.

Enzymes are complex proteins and the three-dimensional structure of some of them has been determined. The production of most biochemical substances involves multi-enzymatic systems. The progressive assembly of some enzymes has been precisely described. We know about pre-enzymes which are enzyme precursors, and about the differing activities of various forms of an enzyme, which are known as isoenzymes.

We can now identify hundreds of enzymes. According to the original theory, the ferment, of which only a very small quantity was required, intervened by necessity in the reaction between two substances without combining with them, and so could be found almost intact at the end of the reaction. The role of enzymes is now understood more fully. Their activity as well as the metabolites with

At twelve weeks the embryo already has all its organs.

which they are associated can be used as markers indicative of defective tissues and organs.

Information about enzymes therefore can contribute to the diagnosis of many disorders. The determination of lactase dehydrogenase or glutamic-pyruvic transaminase assists in the diagnosis and prognosis of myocardial infarction. Phosphatases play a part in the calcification of bone, and their concentration in the blood is a guide to the diagnosis of many skeletal disorders.

Gamma-glutamyl-transferase provides information about disorders of hepatic cells and can also indicate the condition of the liver when alcohol damage is suspected. Many more examples could be given. The mode of action of enzymes gradually came to be questioned: their role and chemical composition connect them with vitamins, while the distinction between hormone and enzyme tends to become blurred. We have much yet to learn about enzymology, which has become a highly specialized branch of biological science.

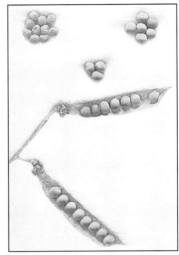

THE BIRTH OF GENETICS

As we have already seen in the preceding chapters, the reproduction of living species has always fascinated humanity. How was the first egg formed? Where did an organism come from? How did the embryo develop which would soon become an adult animal or human being? Aristotle was already pondering such questions.

Since prehistory, men have known that different varieties of wheat give different yields. Agriculture grew as a result of the selection and crossing of varieties. We have therefore tried to penetrate the secrets of heredity in all kinds of living species in an empirical manner.

Johann Gregor Mendel (1822–1884) was more methodical in his approach. He crossed varieties of peas in the Moravian monastery where he lived, and deduced various laws of heredity according to the appearance of the plant (which today we would call its phenotype). He observed that certain characteristics are transmitted to successive generations, and established differences between these characteristics. He called "dominant" those that occurred more frequently than others, and "recessive"

Brother Gregor Mendel (1822–1884). By crossing varieties of peas in his Moravian monastery, he was the first to establish the laws of heredity.

those that were transmitted with less frequency to descendants.

Mendel published these results in a Czech journal where they went unnoticed until they were rediscovered by Hugo De Vries (1848–1935) at the end of the last century. The new techniques for observing and colouring cells enabled Wilhelm von Waldeyer (1836–1921) to identify rod-like structures which could be stained in the nucleus of cells that were in the process of dividing. These structures were the chromosomes. It soon emerged that the male and female reproductive cells which are necessary for fertilization and procreation contain half the typical number of chromosomes for each species. The little rods were then discovered to carry chemical elements, which Johannsen called "genes", and these contained the characteristics that were transmitted according to Mendel's laws.

Several years later, after laborious studies on the drosophila fly, Thomas Hunt Morgan (1866–1945) managed to establish the chromosome theory of heredity. From then on, the study of chromosomes, and

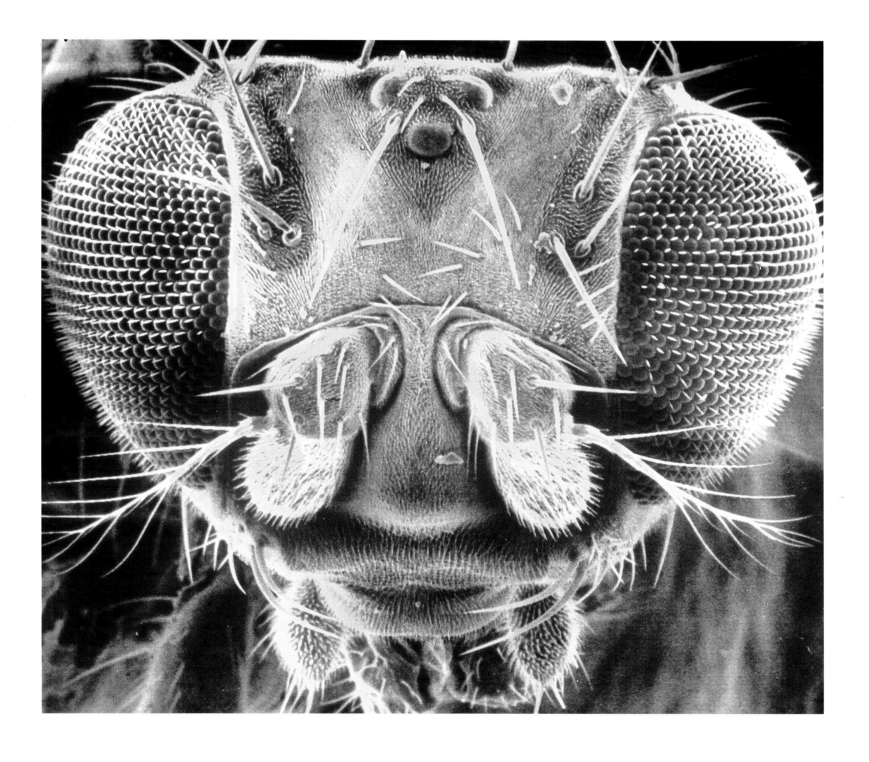

Thomas Hunt Morgan continued Mendel's work by studying successive generations of drosophila, a small and very prolific vinegar fly – seen here through a scanning electron microscope.

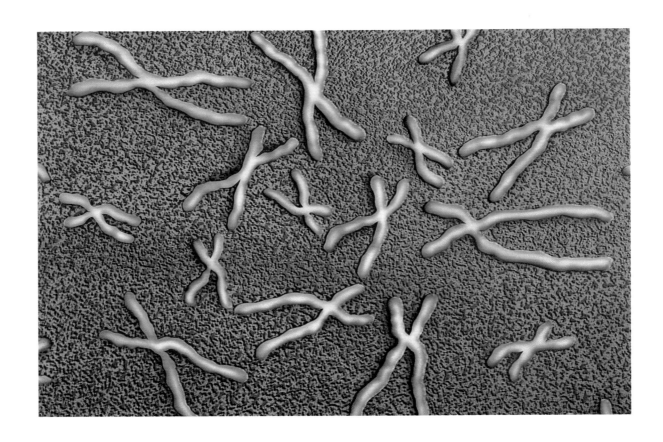

especially of the forty-six possessed by the human species, made steady progress. The electron microscope enabled scientists to observe the different stages through which ova and sperm pass in the course of fertilization, the stages during which the chromosomes from the man and the woman match up to form the pairs which will be present in all the cells in the embryo. Each of twenty-three pairs belonging to humans has been identified and given a number. Together these chromosomes comprise the "genome" and carry the genes, the complete set of hereditary factors which is transmitted from generation to generation. Each living species possesses a set of chromosomes which are characteristic in appearance, shape and number, and which constitute its specific "karyotype". When

In every species the chromosomes (above) carry the hereditary material, DNA. Opposite: two complementary DNA chains coiled into a double helix.

chromosomes fuse, they do not always line up side by side and join perfectly. Sometimes, abnormalities or accidents occur, such as inversion, deletion or duplication, with the chromosome arms becoming longer or shorter. In humans, the woman's karyotype is characterized by the presence of two X chromosomes, while that of the man is characterized by an XY pair. Like the other chromosomes, these may be malformed. Abnormalities of number are also encountered, with some chromosomes occurring on their own or in groups of three instead of two.

A serious error in the transmission of hereditary characteristics constitutes a mutation: some are incompatible with life and end in miscarriage, while others manifest themselves as malformations during the development of the foetus.

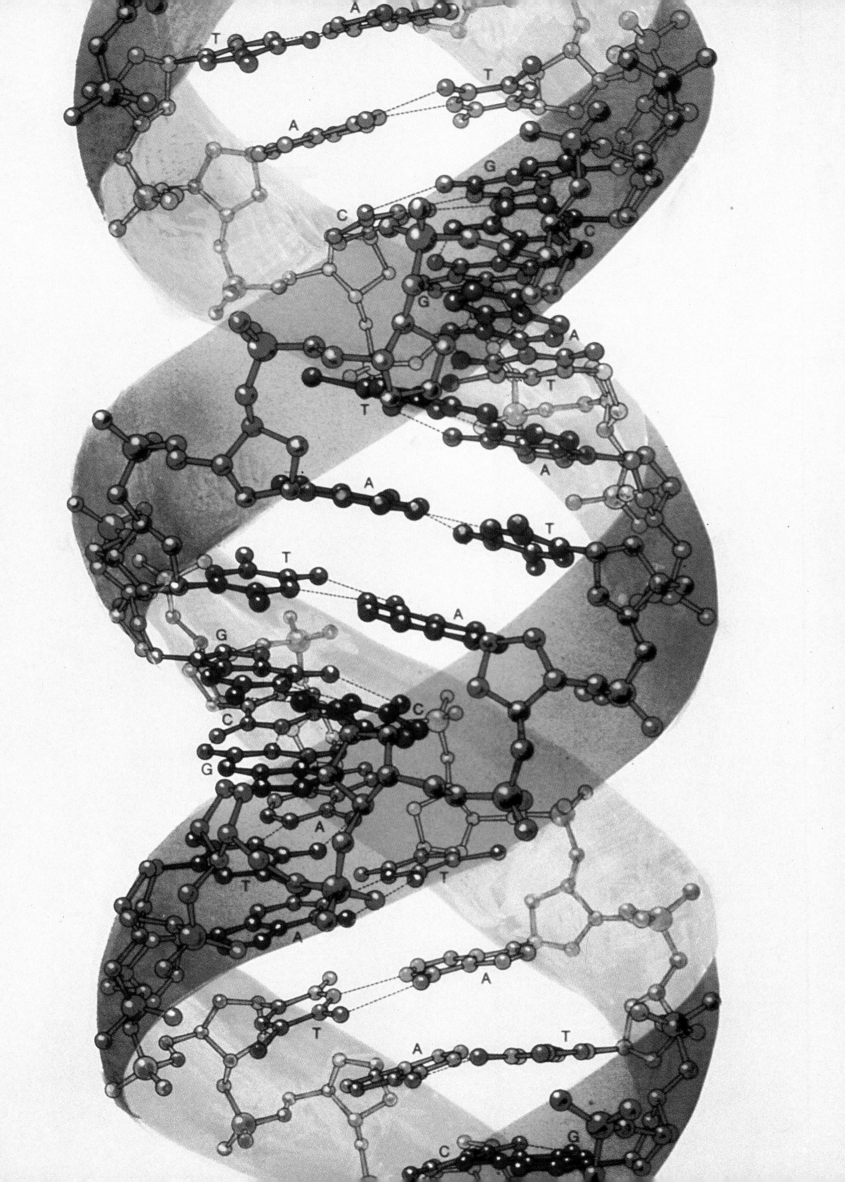

Over the last two centuries, very many disorders have been discovered in different generations of the same family. One of the most famous was the deformation of the jaw in the Hapsburgs which was passed down from Emperor Charles V. Another which was spread throughout the courts of Europe by the descendants of Queen Victoria was the haemorrhagic disease known as haemophilia, which is due to abnormal haemoglobin. Haemophilia is transmitted by women and only affects men, and is thus an example of a genetic disease that is linked to a sex chromosome.

In 1959, Raymond Turpin and Jérôme Lejeune linked Down's syndrome with a trebling of chromosome 21. Following this, other such trisomic conditions were identified. The study of several generations, especially in regions where marriages are made within small communities that do not have much contact with the outside world, has demonstrated the existence of more than three thousand hereditary diseases.

These are diseases which are carried in the genome and are therefore transmissible. They may be linked to one or more genes, and may or may not lead to disorders depending on whether or not the gene is "expressed". Generations may pass which are unaffected but which nonetheless carry the abnormality. The concept of "hereditary risk" was developed in the light of this knowledge, and this risk can sometimes be statistically calculated.

Chromosomal abnormalities do not only lead to manifest malformations which affect the skeleton, sexual glands, sensory and other organs: they may also affect the overall functioning of the organism. In the 1920s, Archibald Garrod (1857–1936) described "errors of metabolism". The ability to assimilate or destroy a substance is genetically determined. For example,

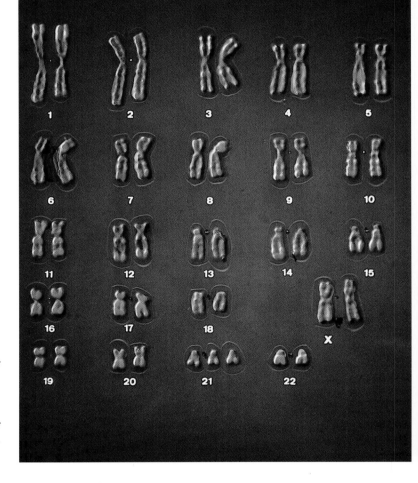

In a karyotype, the twenty-three pairs of human chromosomes are arranged according to a conventional order. Here, we can see the trebling of pair 21, which is characteristic of trisomy.

starting with James I, the descendants of the Stuart line were unable to break down phenylalanine, an abnormality which leads to neurological disorders. All enzyme synthesis and degradation is under genetic control. In cystic fibrosis, a hereditary disease, there is an abnormality of mucus secretions.

Inevitably, genetics progressed from the study of chromosomal morphology to a study of the detailed composition of the genome, to the extent that today this is an area of intense research in molecular biology. The big turning point came at the

end of the 1940s, and in 1953 when Averez, MacLeod and McCarty, then Jim Watson and Francis Crick succeeded in identifying the chemical structure of genes. The essential part of the genetic molecule consists of deoxyribonucleic acid (DNA), the carrier of hereditary information. The DNA molecule is composed of two parallel chains which are interconnected like the rungs of a ladder and arranged in a double helix. Ribonucleic acid (RNA) is formed using DNA as a template, and proteins, some of which form enzymes are specified by the RNA. The production

Deoxyribonucleic acid (DNA). Its transformation into ribonucleic acid (RNA) permits the synthesis of all the proteins which are necessary for life (right).

of an enzyme indicates that the gene controlling it is active (that is to say, that the gene is being "expressed"). A metabolic phenomenon can therefore be linked with a part of the genome, and insofar as it can be attributed to a chromosome or a part of a chromosome, it is also possible to locate it on the chromosome.

Molecular genetics is still in its infancy, but nevertheless the genes are gradually being charted. The phenomena of cellular and tissue incompatibility and immunity are being explained, as are hereditary disorders which affect the metabolism of proteins, carbohydrates and lipids, and abnormalities of haemoglobin and of all kinds of secretions. Molecular genetics also shows the extent to which the human species is a species, for cross-breeding between Eskimos and Pygmies produces fertile offspring. It also highlights the immense variety of these chemical constituents within a certain uniformity. This "genetic polymorphism" represents the wealth of the human species, since it enables man to adapt to the innumerable circumstances encountered during life on earth. For example, certain hereditary haemoglobinopathies are dangerous to life if they are too marked, but at the same time they have enabled some populations in the tropics to be more resistant to malaria.

We have already mentioned antenatal diagnosis which studies the product of conception from the first weeks of pregnancy. If there is a serious abnormality, an abortion can be considered.

This raises the question of eugenics, that is the selection of more capable individuals, which has been the subject of debate since time immemorial and which takes on new aspects as morals, religions and knowledge evolve.

With each advance that we make in the study of heredity, an area which was a mystery for so long, we come across unexpected questions concerning the boundaries between that which is inherited from our parents and that which is acquired through education as reflected in the discussions on Nature versus Nurture. The smallest details of everyday behaviour, the tastes for and dislikes of certain foods or activities, the choice of activities and partners in social life; all these can be attributed to innate factors. But we are nowhere near drawing a precise demarcation line.

SOME HEREDITARY DISEASES OF MAN

Four thousand hereditary diseases have been identified in the human species. One thousand of these affect vision.

1	2	3	4	5
Abnormality of colour vision and optic atrophy	–	–	–	–
Hypercholesterolaemia	*metabolism* *blood vessels*	20	+	+
Down's syndrome	*nervous system*	15	+	
Polycystic disease	*kidneys*	8	+	
Cystic fibrosis	*mucus secretion*	5	+	+
Haemophilia (S)	*blood*	1	+	+
Hypothyroidism	*thyroid gland*	3		+
Duchenne's disease (S)	*muscles*	2	+	
Fragile X chromosome (S)	*mental retardation*	5	+	
Phenylketonuria	*metabolism*	1	+	+
Sphaerocytosis	*red blood cells*	2	+	+
Sickle cell anaemia	*red blood cells*	1.5	+	+

Key – column 1: disease
        S: disease whose transmission is linked to sex
    column 2: function or organ affected
    column 3: frequency in 10 000 births
    column 4: antenatal diagnosis possible
    column 5: treatment possible from birth

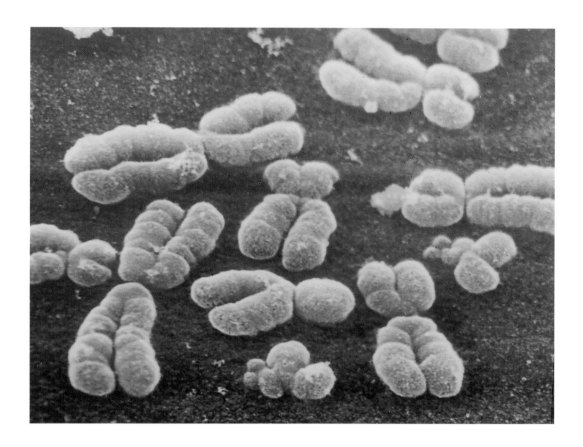

Researchers are clever enough to apply the knowledge recently acquired in molecular genetics to the plant and animal species which feed and serve the human race. Environment, diet, as well as the world economy have been changed according to whether we consume a particular variety of rice, or a particular kind of meat which comes from one part of the world, rather than another.

Each time we think up new techniques and unexpectedly come closer to nature, such new discoveries inevitably give rise to anxieties. Our knowledge of genes now enables us to modify them; we have succeeded in making micro-organisms manufacture useful substances, such as insulin.

In addition to this, we create chimeras by combining the genomes from different species. Almost certainly, genetic engineering, which some regard with disdain as well as a touch of dread, will eventually be applied to the genome of a human being.

Human chromosomes viewed with a scanning electron microscope, showing the structure of the two chromatids linked by a centromere.

We may be anxious about this, but we are not there yet. The transformations we have achieved to date have been on unicellular creatures which only have one chromosome, about which much is already known.

Possible modifications therefore appear to be limited. The forty-six human chromosomes have different structures and, judging by our current level of knowledge, they will escape our attempts at transformation for a long time to come. In any case, genetics, which at this level draws increasingly on genealogy, sees its field of action expanding considerably and, with good reason, we now ask ourselves with growing frequency about the hereditary determinism of all diseases, at least as far as the risk of disease is concerned. This risk is assessed in relation to life in societies as well as in relation to individual behaviours. From now on, genetics forces us to take a new view of health and disease.

Medical physics

Between the two World Wars, the faculties of medicine in Europe were endowed with chairs of "medical physics". This appellation has no meaning today, since all the medical disciplines make use of physics, and a separate identity is thus no longer justified. All the different kinds of waves, pulses and radiations have been harnessed to assist in medical care, both in doctors' surgeries and in the best equipped hospitals, to the extent that an attempt to classify and enumerate them would not serve any real purpose.

The discovery of electricity in the nineteenth century led to the production of artificial light. This enabled the first surgeons who were familiar with asepsis and anaesthesia to have shadowless lamps made which enabled them to operate at any time of the day or night throughout the year. However, it was not until the 1960s that some of them, for example those who operated on new-born infants, started to wear magnifying spectacles. Some years later, surgeons who operated on blood vessels started to operate under the microscope. Using these aids, they were able to extirpate or suture delicate

II.

SOUND AND LIGHT IN THE HUMAN BODY

The progress of the image: from Marey's rapid sequence photography in the 1880s to today's electron microscope.

tissue with a degree of precision undreamt of by their predecessors. Laryngologists were justly proud of their head mirrors, and otologists used operating microscopes when treating deafness by replacing the small bones of the middle ear. The instruments had also been improved: the ultramicroscope of the 1930s had given way to the scanning electron microscope and the phase-contrast microscope. The viruses which Pasteur guessed at and the most minute cellular structures which were only identifiable using special

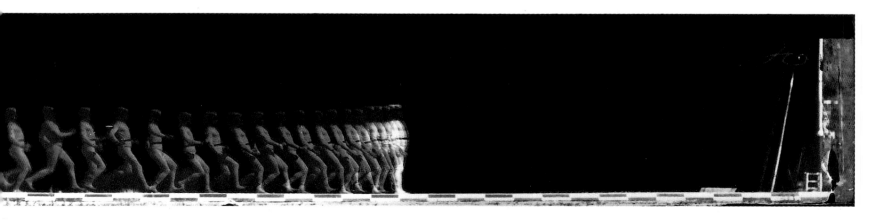

staining techniques were now being directly observed, photographed and filmed.

The period between the wars saw the manufacture of rigid tubes which had a light bulb on the end and were designed to be inserted into the bronchi, the oesophagus or the trachea. Their size was gradually reduced until they could be used for exploring the pleural cavity and for cutting adhesions in cases of pneumothorax, a treatment which is carried out in cases of pulmonary tuberculosis. A reduction of the order of a few tenths of a millimetre then enabled the interior of the abdomen to be observed, and this technique, known as coelioscopy, made it possible to diagnose and even to treat disorders of the Fallopian tubes and ovaries. Joints such as the knee were also inspected and arthroscopy was used to treat lesions of the menisci.

After reducing the calibre of the tubes, electric wires and bulbs, and after improving the magnifying lenses and making them thinner, it was discovered that light could be transmitted along glass fibres, which are much more supple. From then on, light in the service of doctors no longer travelled in straight lines. The clinician was able to look at the tiny bronchial ramifications or all of the large intestine, despite its bends. Fibrescopes even enabled intestinal polyps to be ablated or samples of cells to be removed to test for cancer in its very early stages. The same technique has also made possible the removal of small biliary calculi which have become trapped at the junction of the choledochous duct and the duodenum.

As for lasers, they emit very high energy light radiation and produce thermal, electrical and mechanical effects. Depending on the type of radiation and the wavelength, lasers have many applications, and these are bound to multiply. Using lasers, dermatologists destroy

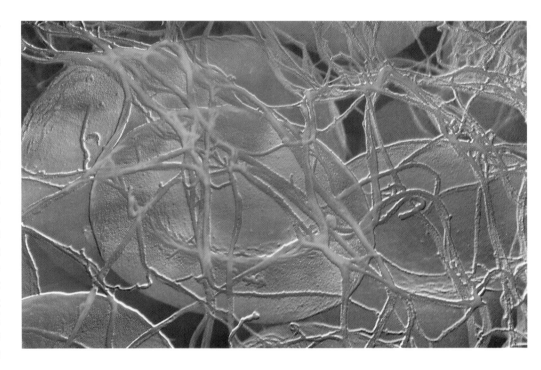

Using new techniques and new methods of staining, it is now possible to study the structure of a blood clot (above) or the cerebellar cortex (right).

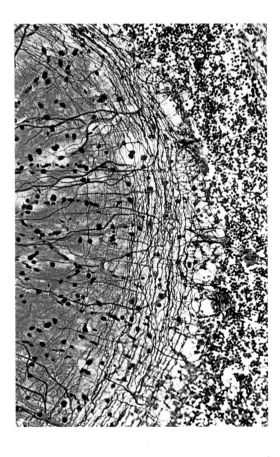

491

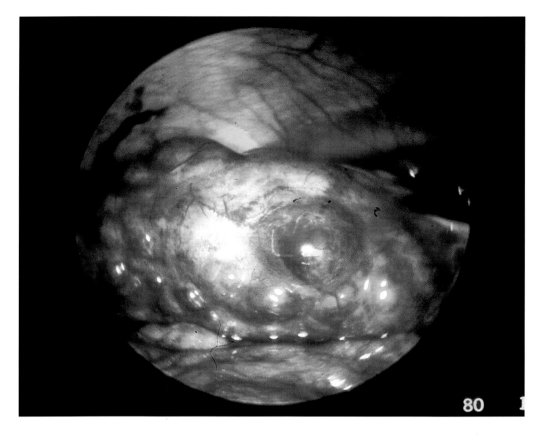

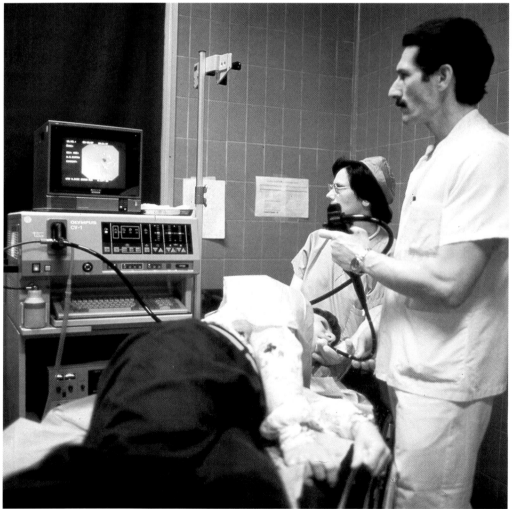

The fibre-optics of the endoscope enable an image of the abdominal viscera to be projected onto a screen.

abnormal pigmentations of the skin and limited tumours, ophthalmologists treat glaucoma and detached retinas, and cardiologists remove obstructions from the arteries of the heart.

All bodies emit heat which can be objectified and photographed using infrared radiation. Great hopes had been set on the thermographic exploration of various organs, as it was thought that this could assist in the early diagnosis of malignant tumours, whose anarchic development is accompanied by a greater calorific output. However, as yet these results have mostly been disappointing.

Since the days of Auenbrügger and Laennec, the sense of hearing has played an essential part in diagnosis by percussion and auscultation. For this reason, clinical examination or the study of signs of disease used to be restricted in this area to perceived sounds. However, the last few decades have seen the addition of ultrasound which, though inaudible to the human ear, can be recorded by machinery. It has been shown that all circulating fluid emits ultrasounds and that the Doppler effect is a common phenomenon in nature. When it is recorded in humans, ultrasound can reveal the slightest abnormalities in the blood vessels — for example, a narrowing due to arteriosclerosis, a tiny aneurysmal dilatation or an obstruction. A complete exploration of the arterial system of an elderly patient now includes an ultrasound analysis.

Ultrasound waves can also assist in the study of solid or hollow viscera, and the echo sent back by the opposite wall provides much useful information. Echography, in which echoes are recorded, is based on this simple principle. Graphs obtained by this technique provide information on the differences in density of the tissues in a cavity. The most spectacular use of echography is in the

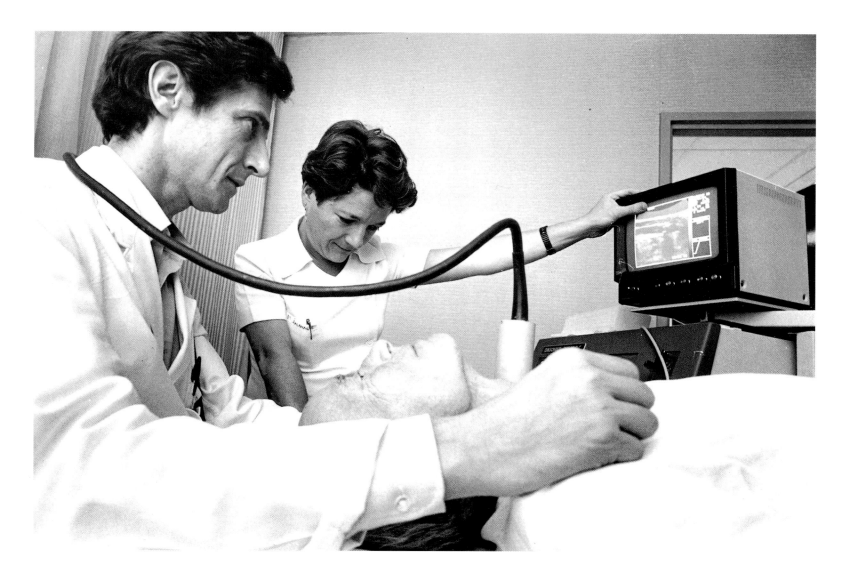

study of the pregnant uterus. As pregnancy progresses, a series of ultrasound examinations provides the gynaecologist with information on the growth of the foetus, its position, anatomical structure and in some cases even its sex. It is also possible to discover whether there is more than one foetus present. Today, it is impossible to imagine that medical checks carried out during pregnancy would not include regular ultrasound examinations, especially if there are risks associated with the pregnancy and labour.

In this ultrasound scan, the doctor is checking on a screen the ultrasound echoes produced by the circulation of the blood in the large vessels of the neck.

THE NEW ELECTRO-PHYSIOLOGY

It is a long time since our knowledge of electrophysiology was confined to the stimulation of nerves in frogs' legs. We now have a whole range of amperages, voltages and frequencies at our disposal. Electricity occurs everywhere in the body and enables us to explore all of the vital functions.

During the widespread poliomyelitis epidemic that struck Europe and the United States in the early 1950s, doctors built on Dubois-Reymond's work in electrophysiology by testing affected nerves and their muscles for their residual responsiveness, with the aim of treating them with stimulation.

An extreme fashion then developed, in which short waves, vibromassage, and various types of radiation were used for

Using an electroencephalogram, it is possible to record the electrical impulses produced by the activity of the brain cells.

purposes which were more magic than scientific.

The functioning of the various viscera and sphincters was examined to clarify peristalsis, the progression of muscular contractions, and any insufficiencies and paralyses of, for example, the bladder or the rectum. These explorations were aimed as much at diagnosis as at treatment. Methods of recording graphs showing the electrical activity of the brain were also developed. Electroencephalography detects the nature and disorders of sleep during its different phases in the course of a night. It also enables doctors to anticipate the triggering of epileptic fits.

However, the most spectacularly successful of these techniques was surely electrocardiography. Since the first recordings made

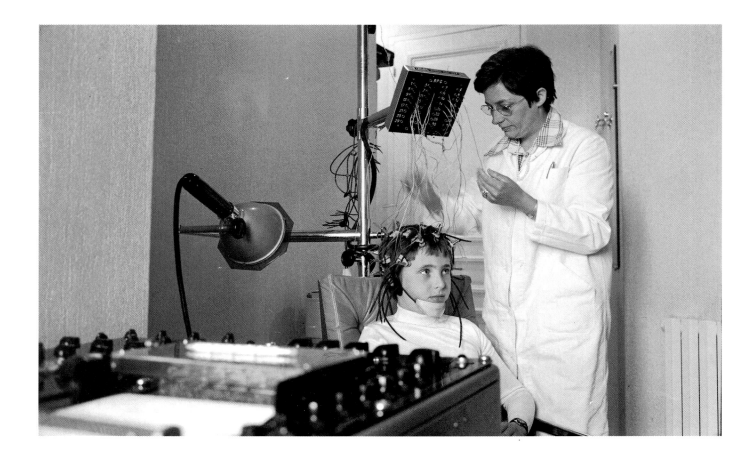

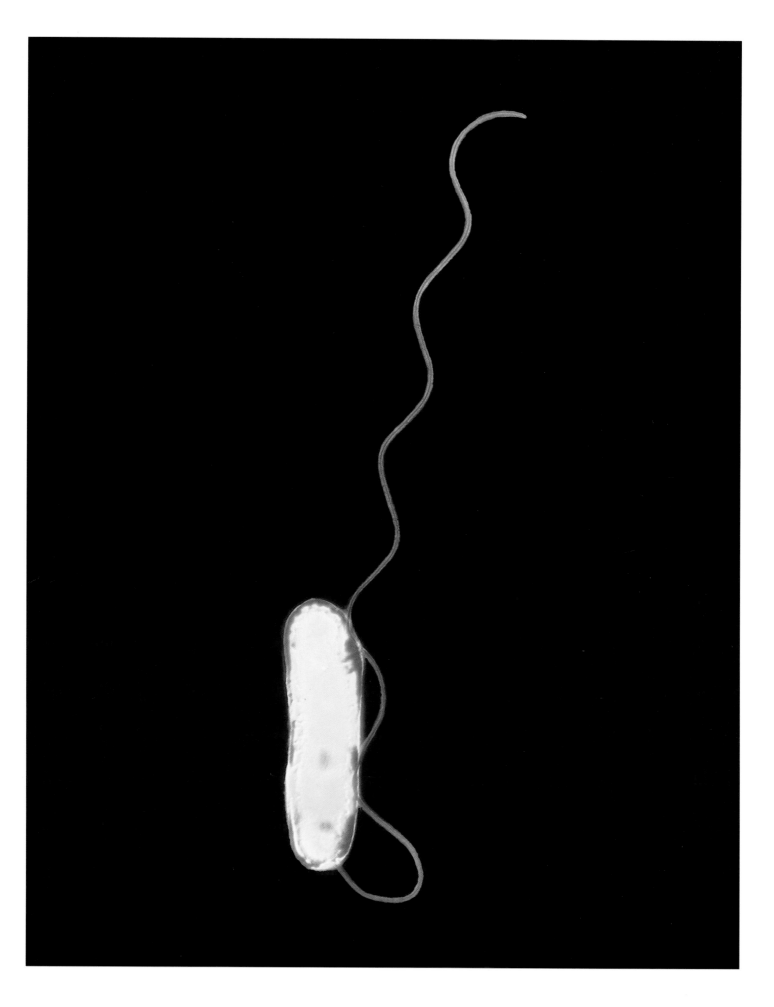

A bacterium of the genus Legionella,
responsible for serious pulmonary infections
which can be epidemic.

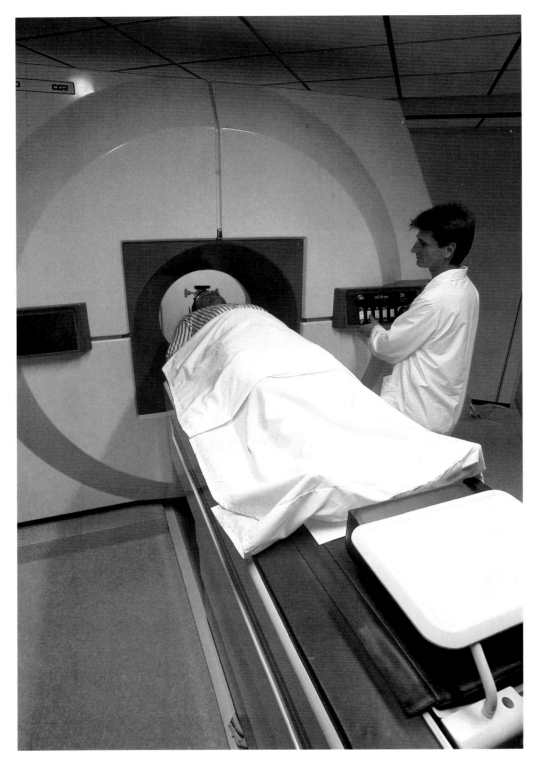

A CT scanner session. The use of X-rays enables the relative density of different tissues to be studied, such as those of the brain and cerebellum, as shown on the opposite page.

by Einthoven, the study of the heart's electrical activity has come a long way. Slight variations in the electrocardiogram reveal the most minute abnormalities in the autonomic nerve fascicles of the heart, and in the vascularization of the muscle caused by obstruction of the coronary vessels. They can also indicate, among other things, the effect on the contraction of the myocardium of defects in the valves. An electrocardiogram alone can thus afford a very precise anatomical and clinical diagnosis. Continuous recording of the activity of the heart in seriously ill patients in intensive care units can reveal all kinds of cardiac abnormalities, and the staff in charge can be alerted to the slightest incident. Such monitoring means that there is a high degree of safety associated with the care of these patients, who are often unconscious.

Therapeutic action has now been added to this passive surveillance. For the last two centuries it has been known that an electric shock can restart a stopped heart, thus reviving an apparently dead person. This technique is also used by surgeons who can stop and start a patient's heart at will. Since the 1960s, this form of stimulation has been in everyday use: suitable subjects who lead a normal life but who suffer from disorders of cardiac rhythm have a stimulator permanently fitted. This little battery-powered box, called a pacemaker, can at any given moment correct a potentially fatal variation in rhythm by means of pulses which regulate the cardiac contraction. Gradually, this technique of electrical monitoring and stimulation came to be applied to the nervous system, for example in the case of a failing bladder or of motor disorders caused by lesions of the spinal cord.

Since the 1930s, violent electrical shocks have been used to treat certain psychotic states. Related techniques have been used since 1982 to destroy kidney stones. Until

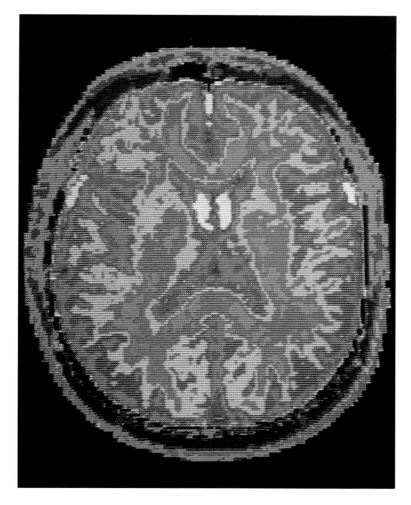

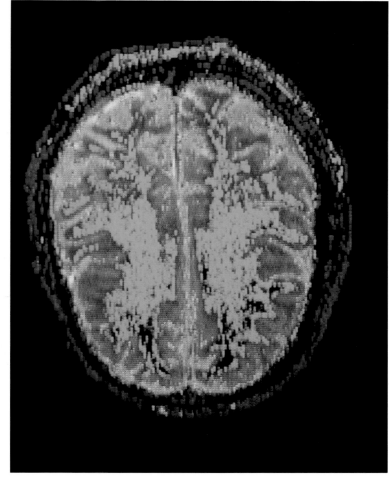

then, a probe had to be introduced into the ureter, whereupon one waited for the spontaneous expulsion of stone debris by natural means. Now it was possible to dispense with the probe altogether. Instead, a violent electrical discharge administered under general anaesthesia was used to pulverize calculi of a certain chemical composition. This form of lithotripsy was also applied to biliary calculi lodged in the gall-bladder. All these are non-invasive techniques that take the place of sometimes painful surgical intervention.

Magnetism, which was so dear to Mesmer and Marat, has been put to good use in the modern medical technique of nuclear magnetic resonance. The body is

Nuclear magnetic resonance (NMR) produces very detailed images of sections of the brain. Above left: it is possible to see the grey matter (the bodies of the nerve cells) around the outside in reddish-brown, and the white matter (nerve fibres) on the inside in blues and greens. Above right: the two hemispheres are clearly distinguishable.

placed in a large magnet and subjected to a powerful magnetic field. The natural movement of the atomic nuclei is thereby stimulated and, when they return to their original alignment, their protons emit a signal which can be recorded and transformed into an image. This technique was first developed in 1971 by Lauterbur and Damadian, and provides information on the skeleton as well as all the viscera of the body. It is the most innocuous instrument for exploring the human body, since it does not use any dangerous radiation and does not necessitate the introduction of any instruments or products into the organism. Today it is the most precise instrument for detecting the slightest abnormalities.

IONIZING RADIATION

Although new investigatory procedures continue to be developed, applications are still being found for the ionizing radiation discovered by Röntgen. Despite the anxieties which arose after the devastating explosions of Hiroshima and Nagasaki in 1945, it was found that this nuclear energy, which can be so dangerous, can also be of great assistance in medicine. Radiotherapy and curietherapy, which were developed between the two World Wars, have progressed little during the last few decades, despite the improvements made to equipment. However, progress has been made in diagnosis. With pulmonary tuberculosis receding, repeated X-ray examinations are made less and less frequently. The practice of direct radioscopy, the dangers of which are well known, is therefore also in decline. The traditional image on a fluorescent screen, exposing the practitioner to radiation, has been replaced by a

A thermographic study of a sleeping man. Different stages of sleep produce different degrees of warmth (in red), which also vary according to the part of the body.

harmless image intensifier that is placed at a distance. Now, manoeuvres which are followed directly by the operator can last several hours. Looking through the viewfinder, surgeons fit metal prostheses for the fixation of fractures and after ablating calculi they check on the patency of the bile ducts or the ureter.

Since radiocinematography proved to be too complex, machines have been developed which take several exposures in the space of a minute. This enables the progress of an opaque liquid in the blood stream to be followed. Angiopneumography and angiocardiography reveal abnormalities in the pulmonary circulation and in the configuration of the heart. Using the image intensifier, the operator can follow the progress of a probe which has been introduced into a vein or artery. Once the tip has reached the desired location, he injects a product which is opaque to X-rays and then watches its

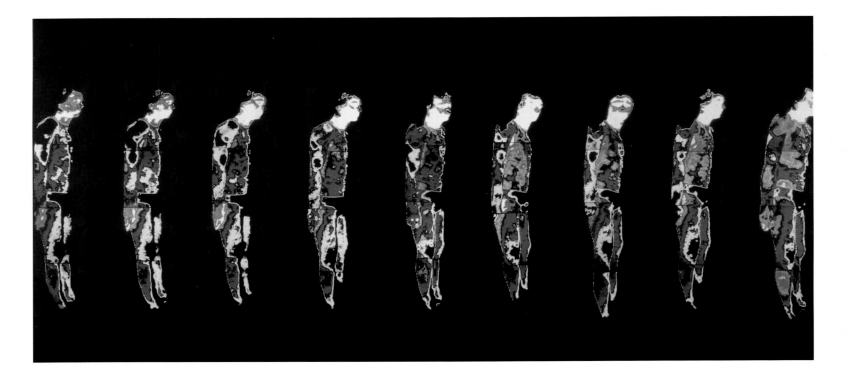

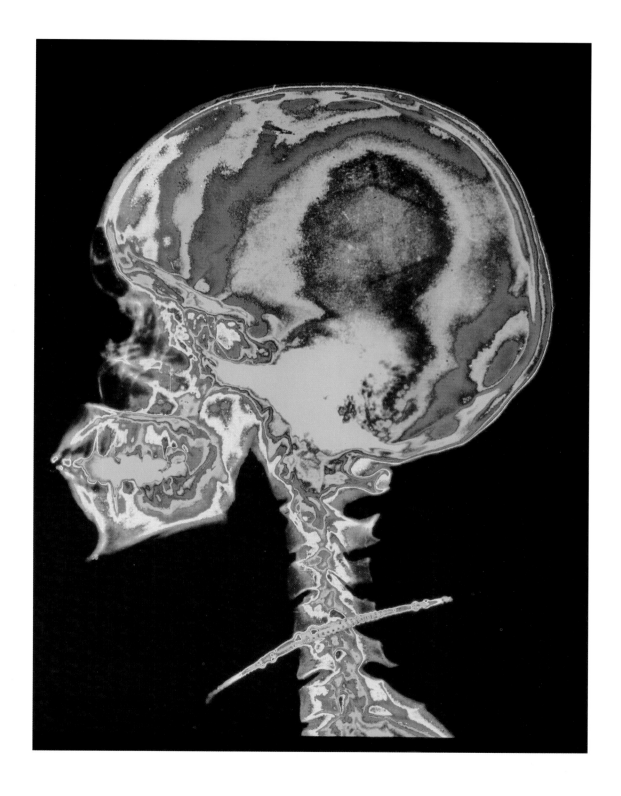

Simple radiograph of the head,
subsequently coloured using
computer enhancement techniques.

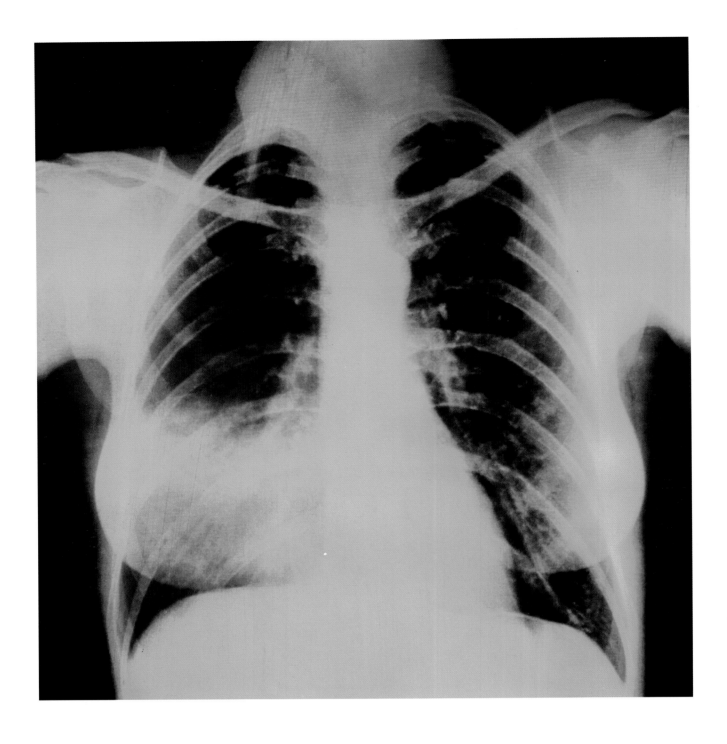

progress as it reveals obstacles or narrowings. He then takes a sample of blood and studies its chemical composition to assess the abnormal short-circuits between the cavities of the heart. Thus angiography has become an everyday technique for exploring the arterial, veinous and lymphatic systems, but the number of therapeutic procedures which are carried out with the aid of a screen is increasing rapidly. Intervention radiology is here to stay. Amongst other things, it can dilate the arteries of the heart, break up a calculus situated high up in the kidney, block an abnormal communication between an artery and a vein, and arrest the vascularization of a tumour. The potential uses of these new techniques are still

Simple radiograph showing pneumonia of the lower right pulmonary lobe in a woman.

being developed, and are far from being exhausted. Though themselves not without risk, they avoid the necessity for more complex surgical interventions.

In 1971, Godfrey Hounsfield, an English engineer, who had been a dispatch rider during the Second World War and was working for a company which made electric guitars, invented CT scanning, a wonderful extension of the tomography of the 1930s. With this system, the area under X-ray examination is approached from different angles. After passing through the body's tissues, the radiation emerges changed in quality depending on the tissues' density, and the considerable amount of information which can be obtained from these changes is then processed on a computer. The computer converts these physical data into pictures, either using colour or different shades of grey. Injection of a contrast medium can further enhance the results thus obtained. Observers then have at their disposal high-precision pictures which reveal abnormalities in the composition of the organs and tumours of less than a centimetre in diameter. The entire body may be studied in this manner. Even though the irradiation of the patient is not insignificant with CT scanning, it nonetheless represents an important revolution in diagnosis in the latter half of the twentieth century. It is also too early to be able to compare the relative advantages and disadvantages of scanography and nuclear magnetic resonance.

In other respects, medicine has not failed to profit from advances made by physicists in the manufacture and handling of isotopic substances. By marking a product, a cell or a category of cells with an isotope and introducing it into the body, the marked element can be tracked using the beta or gamma radiation it emits. This technique led to the development of the scintiscan and gammagram, which require the use of special cameras. Radioactive cobalt (already employed in the radiotherapy of cancers), iodine, phosphorus, gallium, gold and chromium are all tracers which electively fix onto certain organs, tissues or corpuscles and provide information about their capacity for fixation, elimination and secretion, on the length of their life or their abnormal location, and so on.

Thus nuclear medicine came about, bringing with it the delicate and expensive products which require careful handling and to which biology is gradually becoming accustomed. These techniques are now indispensable for studying the most intimate secrets of normal or pathological molecular biology.

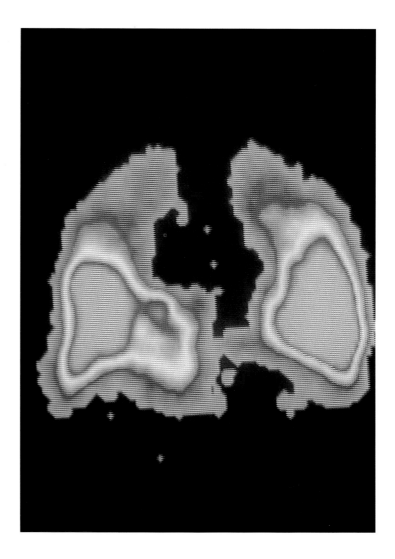

Representation of the lungs obtained by tomodensitometry using a radioactive isotope.

MEDICAL IMAGING BECOMES AN INDUSTRY

*I*n a short space of time, medical staff have had to become accustomed to many instruments totally unknown to them before 1940. They now follow on oscilloscopes the contractions of the heart of an accident victim in a coma, and check, using a commercial video recorder, the recordings from a gammagraphic camera. Such digital images can be read by the naked eye, printed on paper, or stored on magnetic tapes or discs.

Computers and the harnessed atom have brought with them new procedures for analysing the human body. They do a better job than the human eye when reconstructing images in three dimensions: for example, stereotaxis enables tiny lesions of the brain to be located. Doctors have had to learn how to interpret the latest methods, since the flat photographs of Röntgen no longer provided sufficient detail. An ultrasound picture of the pregnant uterus is not at all clear to the layman, while the experienced reader can discover from it a cardiac malformation of the foetus.

It was not surprising, then, that a doctor's training has become increasingly technical and that medicine diversified into specialties which demanded knowledge of an ever more precise nature which was far removed from the actual patient. Though we may be delighted at the enormous progress that has been achieved in diagnostics and therapeutics, some of us regret that medicine has become too much of a spectacle. Nevertheless, iconographic documents are kept although, as a result, medical records become unwieldy. They can, however, be very useful for following (in an objective manner) the course of diseases throughout the long years of an average person's life, now that life expectancy is so much greater.

Doctors examining a series of sections of the head obtained by nuclear magnetic resonance, which is able to detect the most minute cerebral abnormalities.

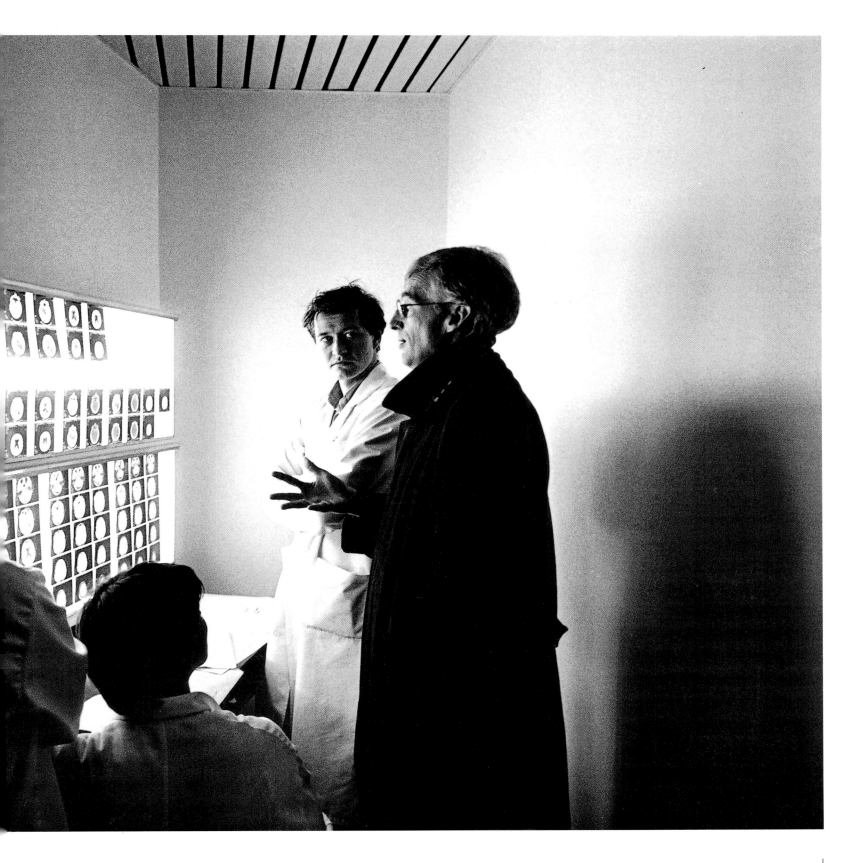

Effective treatments at last

III.

In 1945, any European doctor would write out his prescription at the end of a consultation and recommend a way of life and a diet to follow. He invented his own patent potion, or mixed chemical products with various extracts from plants, synthesized substances, and ingredients which gave the mixture stability, a pleasant taste and an agreeable smell. These were the principles which guided his "nostrum". If he had any doubts concerning the coherence of the whole, he used a treatise on therapy and manuals on posology to assist him. In 1990, the complicated problems of compatibility, efficacy and patient compliance have been resolved, since the doctor has at his disposal prescription medicines which come ready prepared. The formulary which he consults includes more than four thousand such preparations, and reminds him of the correct dosage for each, as well as the indications and contra-indications, and the side-effects which each may induce.

Our means of storing and retrieving knowledge are evolving. From the library at the Pasteur Institute (left) to the handling of an image analyser that allows images to be enlarged and contrast to be adjusted at will (right).

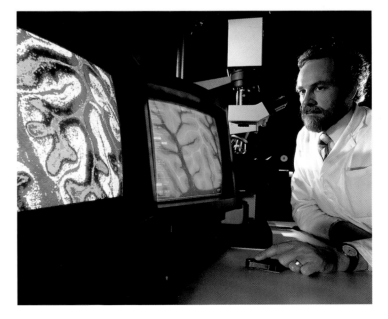

Animal experiments are essential when developing drugs that, for example, if proved not to be "mutanagenic", can be used in man.
Right: a modern "alchemist" examines a solution of DNA.

A TRANSFORMED PHARMACOPOEIA

*P*harmaceutical dispensaries no longer have any mortars, powder folders, pill machines or pill boxes. These have been replaced by display shelves on which prescription medicines are arranged in alphabetical order according to their commercial name, rather than their chemical composition or active constituent. Gone are the unique medicines which bore the doctor's or pharmacist's name, and which were produced in small batches in the room at the back of a pharmacy or a family shop, for distribution to the immediate surrounding area. Medicines now come from industrial laboratories which often belong to large multinational pharmaceutical groups. These are sometimes rivals, and sometimes collaborators.

In the research centre of the Garches hospital, France, various physiological data are recorded simultaneously during physical exertion.

The decision to manufacture a drug is taken by different scientific and financial bodies. One can exploit a product derived from traditional medicinal herbs, profit by a physiological experiment, reason by analogy and, basing one's assumptions on an existing substance, infer the properties of a related substance. A molecule's efficacy in treating a disease may also be discovered by chance. When a company has decided that an idea is worth pursuing, it has to develop the simplest method of manufacturing the product, and satisfy itself concerning the product's pharmacokinetics, that is, its behaviour in the living organism, including absorption, transformations, transport, degradation and excretion. It is also necessary to check

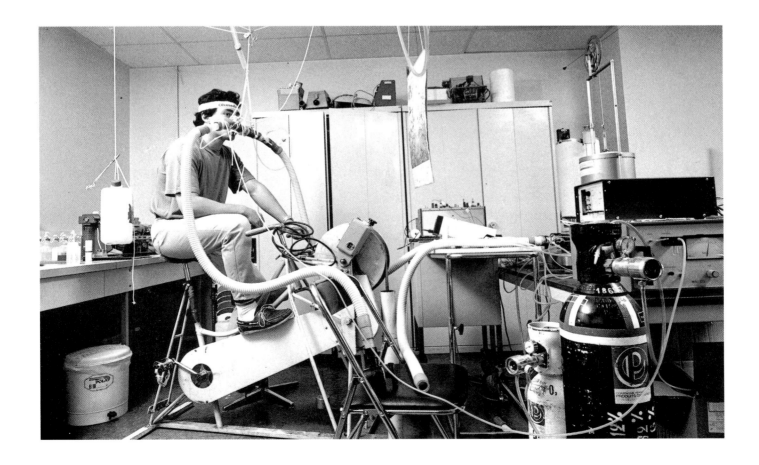

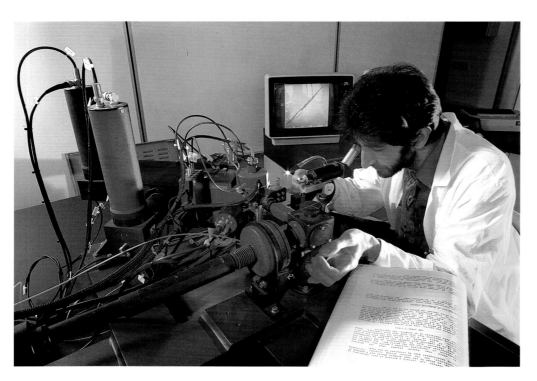

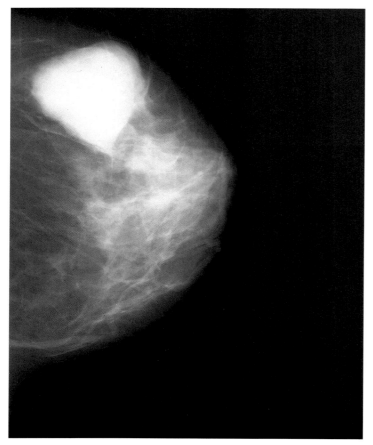

From the cell to cancer.
Above: *an ATC 3000 cell analyser and separator.*
Left: *radiograph showing cancer of the breast.*

the physiological effects on a number of animal species before testing the product on human beings, some of whom will be suffering from the disease at which the drug is aimed and others of whom will be healthy subjects.

A chemical substance which is introduced into the body can have many different effects, some beneficial, others harmful. Such side-effects can sometimes be very serious. A chemical with a harmful side-effect might, for example, cause abnormalities of the foetus in pregnant women (a teratogenic effect) or after prolonged use, tumours (a carcinogenic effect), to the extent that experiments and trials in human subjects have to be carefully monitored.

Only at the end of the tests, if the product has proved to be both effective and safe, is it allowed onto the pharmaceutical market of a country by the government authorities. In France it receives an *autorisation de mise sur le marché* (AMM) marketing authorization.

In Britain it has to be approved by the Medicine Control Agency. In the United States, the Food and Drug Administration (FDA) has the same function, and claims to exercise an authoritative power over the Western world which its decisions do not always justify. Within the European Community, the common acceptance of pharmaceutical products by all the member states will soon be a requirement.

Once the drug has been placed at the disposal of the doctors who will prescribe it, general practitioners monitor its effects. Most of the countries of Europe have developed systems which enable doctors to report on positive results, failures, advisable changes in the dosage, and above all on any unanticipated harmful effects. All drugs have to be regarded as causing an attack on the human body – they may correct a pathological

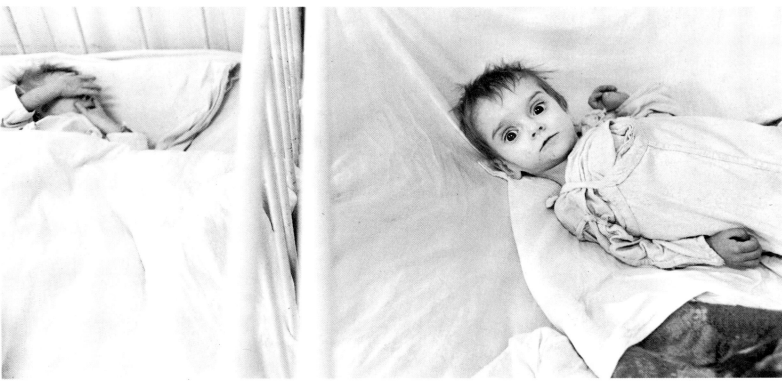

From the parasite of river blindness in Guinea (top) to the AIDS virus (below) – seen here in Romanian children, such "modern" epidemics take many forms for which medicine has not yet managed to find a cure.

condition, but this does not prevent them from being toxic. Needless to say, the harmful effects of drugs should be avoided whenever possible. The iatrogenic consequences of the new range of drugs, that is to say, those that result from medical intervention, are now a major concern.

The pharmaceutical industry contributes to the progress of medicine, but it takes increasingly longer to develop innovations – ten years on average – and ever larger investments are required for which there is no guaranteed return. This is why the industry is more interested in the diseases of rich countries, which are good customers, than in the parasitic ailments of poor countries which do not pay their debts.

The industry is also reluctant to market products which are aimed at rare diseases since the number of customers would be too small and would not offset the production and marketing costs. This leads to the phenomenon of "orphan drugs". The considerable progress made in drug research constantly comes up against the difficulty of reconciling financial interests with the health interests of the community.

Once a product has been launched on the market, there are still surprises. Despite the guarantees of efficacy and harmlessness provided by experimentation and sanctioned by governments, a drug may prove to be useless or doctors may reject it. Fashions change and the drug may be forgotten despite the initial excitement it generated.

In the 1950s, the fashion for gold salts in the treatment of tuberculosis barely lasted for a couple of years. Thalidomide, which was prescribed for minor disorders of pregnancy, subsequently proved to be responsible for serious malformations of the limbs in the new-born. Opprobrium was heaped upon it and it was withdrawn from the market in some countries, though

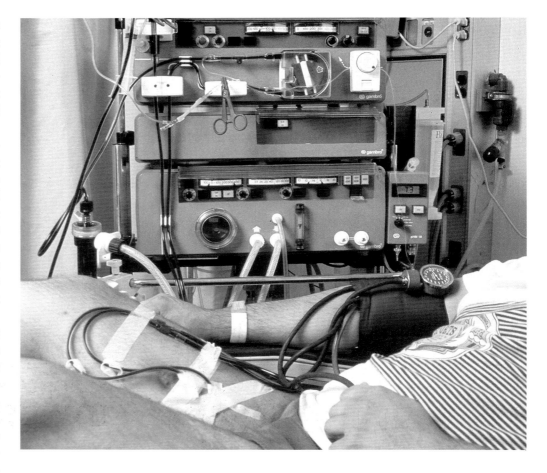

Patient undergoing a procedure for purifying the blood.

it is still rightly prescribed in others, since it helps to combat certain forms of leprosy. These hazards show that the revolutionary progress of the pharmaceutical industry over the last few decades has not been free from trouble, uncertainty and anxiety. All this would suggest that pharmaceutical innovation will slow down in the years to come, because of the ever-increasing worries about patient safety, the legal consequences which result from the side-effects of some substances, the increased cost of manufacturing drugs and the heavy expenditure which has to be borne by social welfare organizations.

Methods of administering drugs have

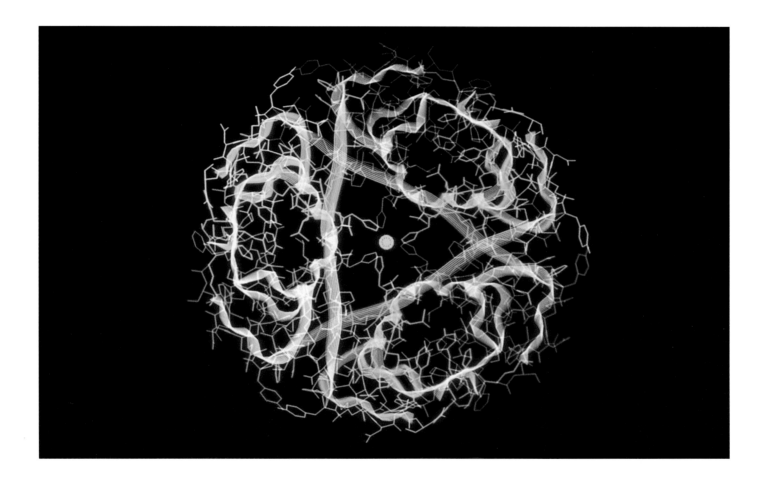

also evolved. Ingestion is the easiest and most widespread method. Suppositories for rectal absorption are little used outside France. Subcutaneous and intramuscular injections, which were only carried out by doctors and nurses between the First and Second World Wars, can now be administered by the patients themselves. As injections are still not the most pleasant way of taking drugs, laboratories have been trying to reduce the frequency with which they have be to carried out by evaluating products whose action lasts for several days. This is indeed the case with insulin and penicillin, for which a decrease in the frequency of injections has now been achieved.

Insulin molecule. This hormone regulates the metabolism of glucose in the body.

It is often necessary to introduce a drug intravenously, and this is almost always done by medical staff.

Some substances have to be introduced into the body under particular conditions of biochemical requirement and in a precise dose. In such cases, automatic pumps controlled by a miniature computer have been developed which, when placed outside or even inside the body, inject the necessary dose at the exact moment it is required. Insulin pumps can be of great help to diabetics, and the same method can be used to treat other diseases. Biochemistry, pharmacy and electronics thus come together in the service of the patient.

511

In Paris *(left), and in* Edinburgh *(below),* where he had just been appointed Vice-Chancellor of the University, Fleming, the father of penicillin, was received with just cause as a benefactor of humanity.

NEW MEDICINES

The range of medicines available to doctors, which had remained almost unchanged for a thousand years, was expanded by thousands of drugs in the space of half a century. These were distinguished by their natural or synthetic origins, their chemical nature, their mode of action and administration, their durability and the diseases which they combated.

The work of Fleming in the late 1930s culminated in widespread success when Sir Howard Florey, Ernest Chain and N. Heatley achieved the production of penicillin on an industrial scale. Continental Europe only benefited from this advance in 1945, after the war had ended. Soon its mechanism of action on bacteria was clarified and its chemical structure identified. Several kinds of penicillin with different compositions were developed and these were effective against a number of different bacteria.

In 1944, Selman Waksman discovered streptomycin which is derived from another mould and is effective against Koch's bacillus. When combined with other products, streptomycin proved to be an excellent treatment for all forms of tuberculosis. Tubercular meningitis, which was almost always a fatal disease, was cured for the first time in 1946.

At the end of the 1950s, treatment of pulmonary tuberculosis by intra- or extra-pleural pneumothorax, or by thoracoplasty which involved ablating part of the rib

*Penicillin is obtained from the cell of a mould (*Penicillium notatum*) which is capable of killing bacteria.*

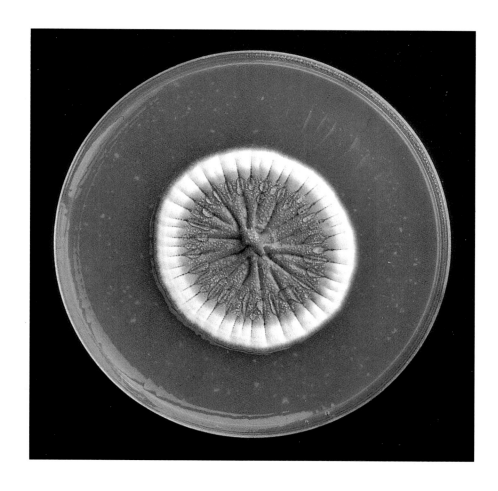

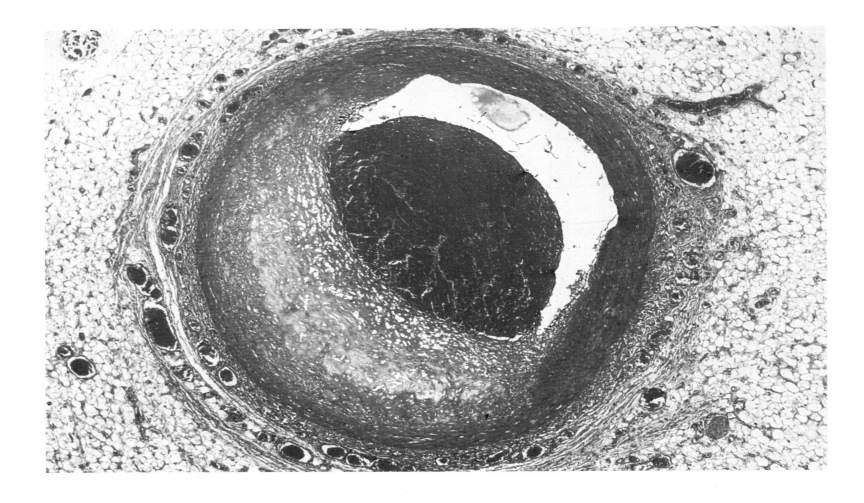

cage, was gradually abandoned. Drug treatment could be administered during a short hospital stay or in the patient's home, so the sanatoria which had been built for tuberculosis patients were closed or converted for other uses. Today, tuberculosis, which caused so much havoc in Western countries during the nineteenth century, is no longer a serious problem for them.

The chemical family of the sulphonamides, which were isolated in the 1930s, is also still very much in use. New varieties have been discovered which are effective against leprosy and tuberculosis. Researchers were even surprised to discover that these drugs had an effect on the sugar level in blood. The anti-diabetic sulphonylureas are currently used when strict diet alone is not enough, and they enable millions of diabetics, whose blood sugar levels can be controlled in this way, to avoid having to resort to insulin therapy.

Drugs which lower blood pressure by augmenting the secretion of urine have been developed to treat hypertension. In the 1960s, beta-blockers were isolated which inhibit adrenaline, a factor in hypertension. Products are also used which inhibit the transformation of the angiotensin secreted by the kidney into a hypertensive substance. All these substances contribute to stabilizing hypertension, but they have to be used with caution.

Moreover, hypertension itself may be due to various causes and may take various forms. It responds to many regulating factors, and therefore cannot be considered as a simple aberration of the numerical data. Even though they are effective for treating many patients, antihypertensive drugs have not resolved all the problems associated with this particular condition.

Similar observations can be made concerning the products which treat arteriosclerosis – a condition in which the

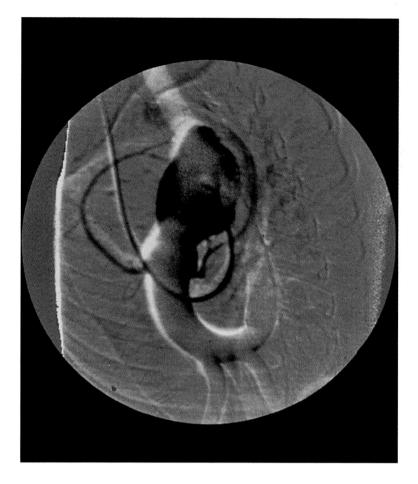 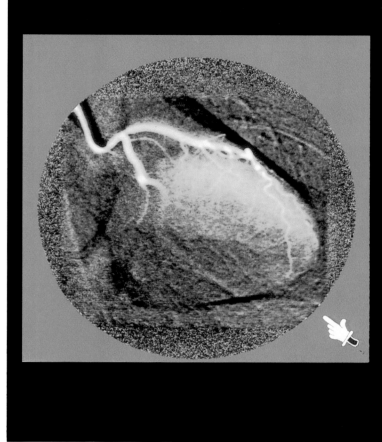

Left: *the aorta and cardiac artery of a two-year-old.*
Right: *digitalized vascularization of the heart of an adult.*

arteries of the lower limbs, heart and brain become obstructed. To this list we can also add the drugs that combat certain forms of arthritis and gout, that treat acute and chronic pain, cure insomnia, and prevent or treat eye conditions such as glaucoma. No group of diseases has remained unaffected by the improvements in drug treatment that have been made in recent years.

We will conclude by mentioning the drugs that are used to combat cancer, the most feared disease at the close of the twentieth century. In 1940, Higgins discovered that cancer of the prostate can be influenced by a female hormone.

This important product has saved thousands of men from painful surgical intervention. It was discovered by chance that a chemical product related to mustard gas, which was used as a weapon during the First World War, destroyed white blood cells. When doctors started to prescribe this product, it proved to be so effective in combating some kinds of leukaemia, which can be thought of as cancers of the blood, that some forms of the disease, which unfortunately in the past were inevitably fatal, can now be cured. Today, there are forty or so such "anti-mitotic" drugs used for combating cancer.

None of them, however, is free from drawbacks: they may destroy white blood cells, cause hair loss or lead to obesity. They have to be chosen and combined with great care, and their dose has to be precisely adjusted.

These drugs can be used in conjunction with surgery or radiotherapy. Nevertheless they have enabled considerable progress to be made in the treatment of malignant lesions: because of them many cancer patients can now hope for a permanent cure. Unfortunately, their rapid increase in number has meant that none of them has had the benefit of prolonged trials.

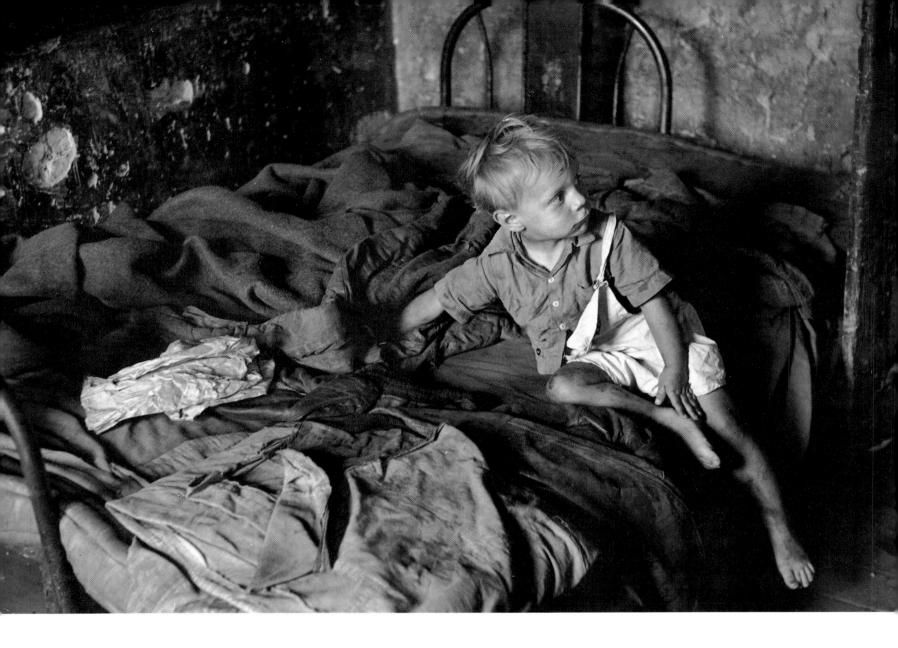

DISEASES ARE CHANGING

Doctors are proud of their recent successes in therapy and attribute to these humanity's good state of health. An assessment of humanity's health should, however, take into account the different situations that exist in the various parts of the world.

In industrialized countries, life expectancy has lengthened considerably. With people living longer, men and women in their seventies and eighties are much more numerous than they used to be. Infant mortality has been greatly reduced, as has the number of women who die in childbirth.

These spectacular results are attributable to a combination of several factors. Cities are properly supplied with drinking water, thus preventing epidemics of cholera, typhoid fever and diarrhoea. This abundance of water has led to an improvement in bodily hygiene, so people

Poverty, as in the home of this child of a Pennsylvanian miner in the 1950s, has always generated conditions in which diseases spread, one such being poliomyelitis.
Opposite: one of the first vaccinations against polio in Texas. Such vaccination programmes reduced the numbers of people who were paralysed and confined to wheelchairs for life.

are no longer affected by the parasites which used to transmit typhus, and were responsible for cutaneous infections such as abscesses, boils or anthrax. Similarly, visceral abscesses, cellulitis and osteomyelitis are rarely encountered.

Improvements in living conditions mean that people are no longer exposed to the inclemencies of the weather, household pests have been eliminated, and overcrowding, which contributed to the spread of tuberculosis, is no longer a problem. Food is varied and abundant and, since the development of refrigerators, meat can be kept fresh. Economic prosperity and the spread of education have contributed more to improving health than the medical profession itself. However, doctors have made strenuous efforts, especially in the domain of infectious diseases.

Immediately after the Second World

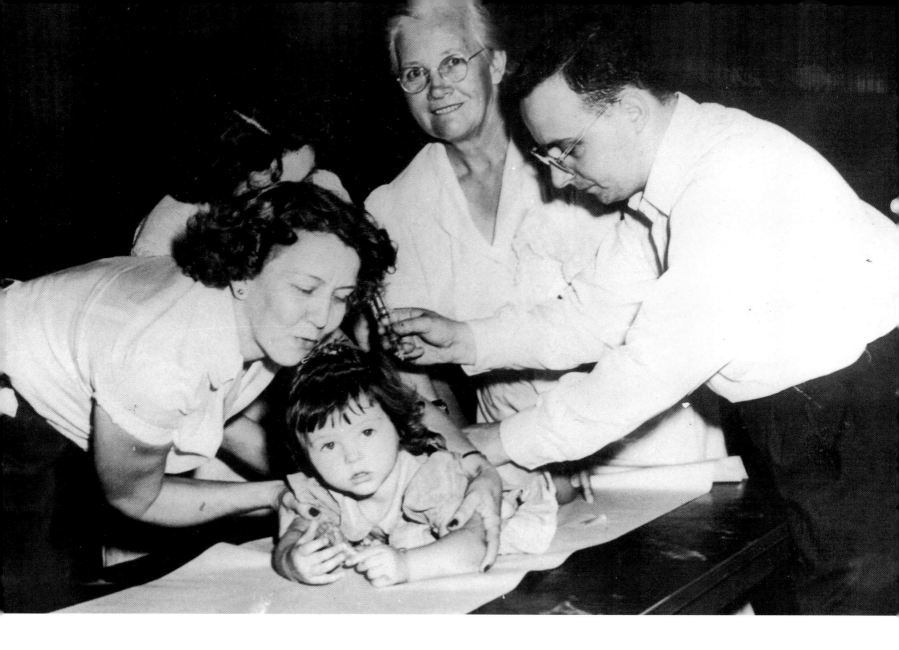

War, Europe and the United States were struck by an epidemic of poliomyelitis. The treatment of the victims who suffered from neuromuscular disorders was improved by the newly developed technique of motor rehabilitation. Today, many accident victims and patients suffering from certain diseases benefit from such rehabilitation.

It is to this epidemic that we also owe the combination of massage and kinesitherapy which still forms an important treatment today. The "iron lung" saved the lives of paralysed polio victims by restoring their respiratory function and, although it is no longer used today it has made a large contribution to the development of techniques of pulmonary resuscitation and assisted ventilation which are now employed in completely different circumstances. Almost at the same time, vaccines were developed using different

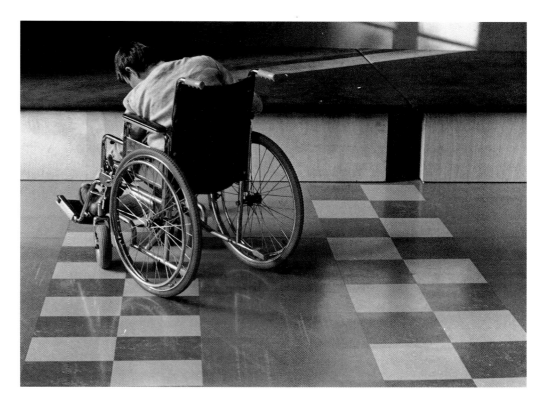

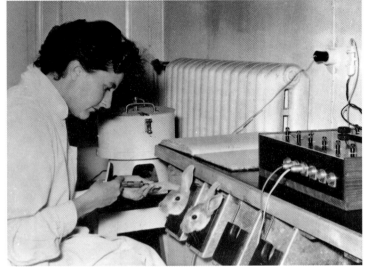

Using rabbits (above), researchers seek a vaccine against polio, an epidemic of which caused considerable damage in the 1950s (left). Today, polio is still rife in the Third World, as in India (right).

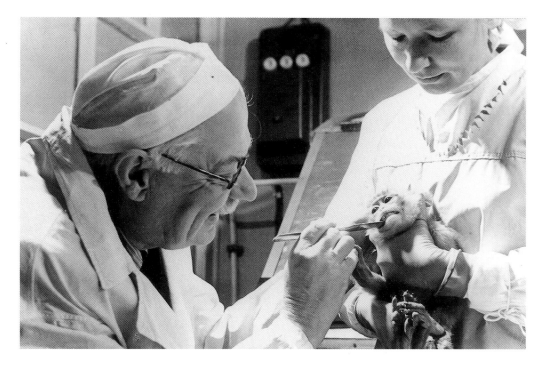

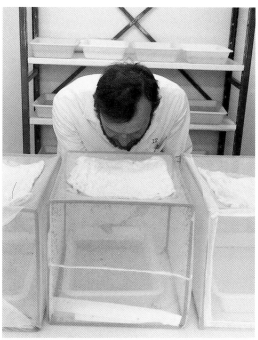

THE END OF SMALLPOX

For thousands of years, smallpox epidemics killed people in their millions: the last confirmed case was reported in Somalia in 1977. Since then, the World Health Organization has offered a prize of several thousand US dollars to anyone reporting an authentic case of the disease. As yet, no one has claimed it.

Many Western countries continue to cultivate the vaccine virus and keep several million doses of the vaccine in case smallpox reappears. It is also likely that some nations cultivate the smallpox virus in their laboratories in order to carry out scientific studies. A military use for the virus cannot be ruled out since bacteriological and chemical weapons are now held by many countries (for example, anthrax bacilli, and incapacitating or lethal gases).

Research has always used animals, from monkeys to mosquitoes, in its work on vaccines for man.

procedures, one in France by Lépine (1954–1956), and the other in the United States by Sabin (1957). Today, systematic vaccination has meant that poliomyelitis has practically disappeared in Western countries.

Penicillin has reduced the frequency of gonococcal infections and syphilis. These two venereal diseases have now been superseded by others such as chlamydial infections, genital herpes, and so on. Vaccination against smallpox has now become so widespread in many countries that this disease, of which the virus lives only in man, has disappeared off the face of the earth after having devastated peoples for thousands of years. The last known case was recorded in 1977, and it is the only infection which mankind has succeeded in eliminating from the face of the earth.

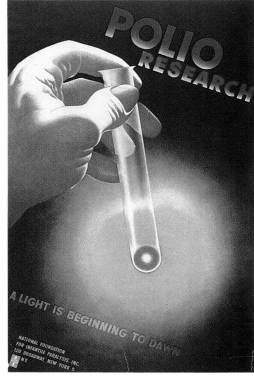

Successes have been less spectacular in other areas, even if we have managed to prolong life and to be more effective at relieving pain; as, for example, in the various forms of arthritis (especially rheumatoid arthritis) or the diseases of the nervous system, whose causes remain mysterious (such as multiple sclerosis). Even in the case of cancers, despite the complex combinations of surgery, radiotherapy and chemotherapy, and despite early diagnoses being made with the aid of cervical smears and George Papanicolaou's stain test (1933) in the case of cancer of the neck of the uterus, or mammography in the case of breast cancer, successes remain marginal. However, more than half the localized cancers can now be diagnosed and treated so successfully that a complete cure is achieved.

The most highly developed medicine

From the immediate post-war period to the present day, disease prevention has been evolving, as demonstrated by these campaign posters against tuberculosis, poliomyelitis and, more recently, AIDS. The slogans vary with the times.

cannot do anything for diseases whose cause is unknown, nor for disorders which are due to the behaviour or habits of the population which it treats. This is the case with alcoholism, that is, the consequences of excessive consumption of alcoholic drink. Whatever measures governments may take to limit the production of beer, wine and spirits, to reduce the number of outlets where they can be purchased and to increase prices, the scourge remains.

Despite cries of alarm from doctors who publicize the hepatic, nervous and pancreatic disorders which can result, not to mention the social tragedy which alcohol can cause, the pathological consequences of alcoholism are becoming increasingly common all over the world. Nevertheless, progress in biochemical investigation and metabolic rebalancing

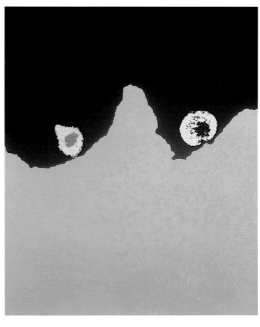

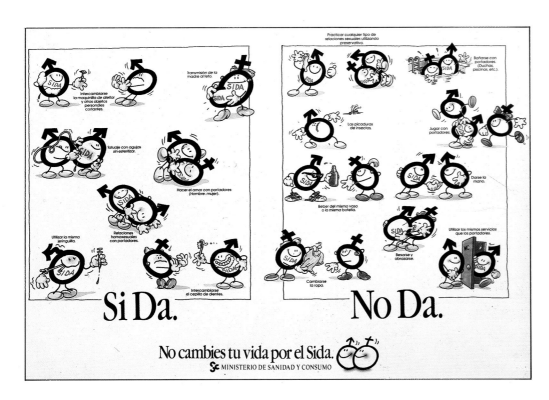

have also contributed to the treatment of alcohol-induced disorders. Cirrhosis of the liver (nine out of ten cases of which are related to alcohol) is no longer a fatal condition.

In the same way, smoking is also a disease of society. Everyone knows that smoking is responsible for chronic bronchitis with respiratory insufficiency and cancers of the lung and bladder. The combination of smoking and alcoholism leads to cancer of the upper respiratory and digestive tract (from the tongue and pharynx to the oesophagus).

If cigarettes were abolished and alcohol consumption reduced, a third of cancers would be avoided. While in some countries the consumption of cigarettes has decreased, the number of smokers has increased, particularly among women. Western societies behave as if they accept

AIDS, the new fear at the end of the twentieth century, as seen with the electron microscope (right), and in advertising material which borders on black humour in its interpretation (left).

THE NEW FEAR OF AIDS

The appearance of AIDS in the last few years has reawakened moral and social attitudes which have been observed in man since Antiquity: xenophobia and racism exhibited themselves in response to the belief that AIDS originated in Africa. AIDS appeared to be a just divine punishment for unnatural habits (homosexuality) and illegal practices (addiction to injected drugs).

In Sweden, it was proposed that all HIV-positive people and AIDS victims should be isolated on an island in the Stockholm archipelago, just as in mediaeval times plague victims were kept on San Lazzaro in the Venice lagoon.

In New York, a priest refused to marry an AIDS victim, and people want to test the blood of new tenants or employees to discover if they are HIV positive. Attitudes towards AIDS victims begin to resemble those towards lepers, who in the past were excluded from religion and society. Even though we know how AIDS is transmitted, this does not prevent incidents such as sufferers being chased out of their houses by crowds in Warsaw, because of the fear that they would contaminate the district.

Unknown and inexplicable dangers always arouse the same feelings of panic: man's atavistic reactions have not evolved.

the future risk of serious diseases for the sake of immediate pleasure.

Many diseases of the heart and blood vessels are probably diet linked, notably cerebral embolism, arterial hypertension and obstruction of the vessels in the limbs or the heart. However, biologists are still debating the pathogenic role of cholesterol and fats of various compositions, to the extent that they are unable to draw up dietary models which would have a prophylactic effect. Perhaps hereditary factors would explain individual predisposition. In any case, many drugs enable blood pressure to be stabilized, soothe or suppress angina and improve the patient's quality of life.

At both ends of life, demographic characteristics and the quality of life of populations have changed enormously in the last fifty years. Infant mortality rates have been greatly reduced by a healthy diet which has put an end to rickets, and by vaccination which has suppressed epidemic diseases such as measles, rubella, scarlet fever and diphtheria.

Old people also remain active for much longer. With the statistical growth of this group in the West, some diseases have been on the increase: Alzheimer's disease, which is caused by changes in the cerebral blood vessels, senile dementia, Parkinson's disease, some degenerative forms of arthritis, various cancers, and so on.

After this long list of disorders which medicine has conquered, or at least attenuated, we must not forget the ones which it has been unable to treat, for example the viral diseases. Antibiotics are ineffective against viruses, because they are so elusive – their make-up is so variable that they can adapt to products which are used to combat them. Vaccines against influenza are never completely armed against the virus of a particular year, since it is already different from that of the previous year.

A vaccination campaign in the United States in the 1950s. The doctor's task involves both prevention and education.

The doctor's role is also a social one, particularly in France, where home visits are quite common.

The AIDS virus, HIV, appeared suddenly in 1982. It has since spread throughout the world and will continue to prove fatal in almost all cases unless a vaccine is developed, or unless it disappears like the "Spanish 'flu" virus of 1918–1920, which was never identified and has never reappeared since.

Thus, our existence always appears to be dependent on these unforeseeable manifestations of the biological universe that surrounds us.

In the last fifty years, diseases have changed in the West, as evidenced by the population that is cared for in hospitals. Paediatric wards have become too large,

since only congenital diseases and growth disorders are now treated there. In contrast, owing to the ageing population, most countries lack sufficient provision for their old people. The way in which nursing establishments are utilised has also changed —an increasing number of sick people are cared for at home, and hospital stays tend to be shorter.

We must not be deluded by this victorious account of the struggle against disease in the last fifty years, for it unfortunately applies to barely a third of humanity. Many Third-World countries still experience the suffering which the developed countries once knew.

THE LAST OF "THE LUNATICS"

After discovering the concept of hysteria in Jean Martin Charcot's department and the efficacy of hypnosis with Pierre Janet (1859–1947), and after attending the schools of Hippolyte Bernheim (1840–1919) and Ambroise Liébeault (1823–1904), Sigmund Freud (1856–1939) returned to Vienna and having distanced himself from all these teachings, developed a system for exploring the subconscious which was soon to be known as psychoanalysis. His disciples, Alfred Adler (1870–1937) and Carl Gustav Jung (1875–1961), were eventually to part from him, but without acrimony. With the rise of Nazism, Freud left Vienna and sought refuge in London in 1938, where he died a year later.

Freud asked his mentally ill patients to search their memories for events during their childhood and adolescence which left a mark on them in spite of themselves. He considered these phenomena from the past, which were supposedly forgotten, to be responsible for their neuroses and psychoses. Freud linked these events to sexual experiences which his patients had lived through or repressed. He did not claim to treat his patients, but he encouraged them to come to terms with their subconscious, formed in earlier years, and to link it with their present neurosis, thereby liberating themselves.

In the 1950s, psychoanalysis won a considerable following in the United States.

Group therapy: patients learn to control their movements and their bodies in time to music.

The least fear or the slightest behavioural disorder resulted in a consultation with a psychoanalyst who, by interrogating the patient as the latter reclined by tradition on a couch (a piece of furniture which became symbolic of psychoanalysis), gradually set himself up as the uncontested guide to the patient's mental, social and sexual behaviour. These sessions, which could be repeated over a period of years, were a valuable source of income for the psychoanalyst, whether or not he was a doctor as well.

In Europe, the fashion was more restrained. Freud's followers split up into different schools which became the subject of fierce controversy. Many women played an important role in psychoanalysis: notably, Anna Freud (1895–1982), Marie Bonaparte (1882–1962) and Melanie Klein (1882–1960). At the end of the twentieth century, the work of Freud appears to be an interesting psychological hypothesis, sometimes successful because it assists patients in freeing themselves from their fantasies. It has proved to be fruitful in demonstrating the role of the subconscious and the omnipresence of sexuality in human relationships.

As a direct descendant of psychoanalysis, there developed in the 1950s a view of medicine which treated some disorders as psychosomatic – having a connection with or being caused by psychological stress. It was shown that purely mental disorders could lead to lesions of the organs such as ulcers and could perhaps even play a part in the origins of cancers. Many so-called "functional" symptoms such as palpitations, migraines and constipation, in relation to which scientific investigations have not revealed any abnormalities, are of mental origin. Conversely, no obvious anatomical lesion is exempt from mental repercussions. Today, psychosomatic medicine is not a discipline in itself. It reminds the doctor that the distinction between the body and the mind is artificial, and that the human individual is made up of both. Therefore, all diseases have to be treated by addressing the person as a whole. This piece of

Hypnosis also has a part to play in current methods for treating mental illness.

ELECTRIC SHOCK TREATMENT AND LOBOTOMY

The history of medicine is a graveyard of interesting ideas that have been abandoned because of their dangers and their failures. A violent electric shock leads to temporary coma from which the subject emerges with new ways of thinking. Thus, electric shocks were frequently used in the 1940s and 1950s for the treatment of certain mental disorders. The cruelty and the risks of the method (even when practised under general anaesthesia), and its failures in the medium term mean that convulsive shock therapy is nowadays reserved for very precise indications, when drug treatment has failed. Psychosurgery was used in the 1950s to treat schizophrenia and cases of severe depression. Nerves were sectioned in the frontal lobe to transform agitated or dangerous patients into passive sheep. The changes in personality were so serious and so risky that these unpredictable lobotomies were abandoned.

wisdom was already being spread about by the ancient Greek authors.

In the relationship between the doctor and the patient who is suffering from organic and mental disorders, Michael Balint (1896–1970) emphasized the therapeutic effect which the practitioner exerts despite himself, by the very fact of his presence: "the doctor is a drug". The respective personalities of doctor and patient play an essential role. Similar phenomena, which are as yet little understood, also explain the *placebo* effect of chemical products which have no real pharmaceutical action. The patient is convinced that the inert substance is making him feel better or, conversely, feel worse. In pharmaceutical trials in which the effects of a substance, which it is hoped will be useful, are compared with those of a placebo, these uncertainties have to be taken into account.

In order to increase the efficacy of practitioners, Balint suggested that his colleagues should ask themselves about their own behaviour when confronted with a particular case: in these "Balint groups", one practitioner tells other doctors about a typical conversation that he may have with a patient. He analyses himself in front of his peers, who in turn criticize him and and consider how they would have reacted in his place. These sessions are aimed at improving the therapeutic effect of the doctor-patient relationship.

Still under the influence of psychoanalysis, techniques of behavioural therapy or group therapy have become widespread, in which several patients recount their mental ordeals under the guidance of a leader in order to be more objective about them, and perhaps gain mastery over them.

These meetings, which have become popular mainly in English-speaking countries, have similarities with the public

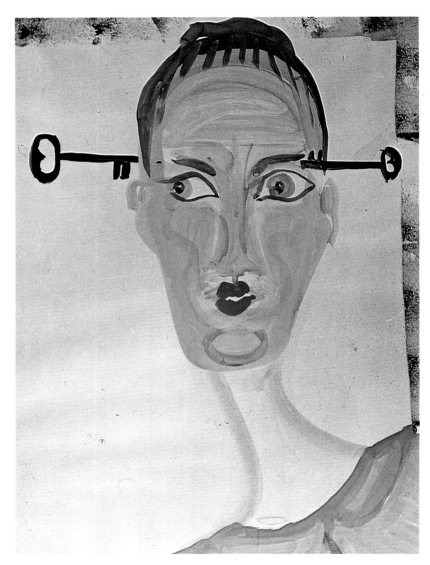

confessions which are acceptable among certain Protestant sects. They often prove to be useful – for example, meetings with other former alcoholics have been of great service in helping those with a drink problem to continue abstaining from alcohol.

The chemical treatment of mental disease began in 1952, when Jean Delay and Pierre Deniker in Paris noticed the psychotropic effects of chlorpromazine, which was being tested by Henri Laborit as a pre-anaesthetic and as a means of inducing unconsciousness in the operating theatre. This marked the start of psychopharmacology with its vast therapeutic potential and consequences for the study of cerebral functions which are far from being exhausted since, in the space of thirty years, many hundreds of pharmaceutical substances have appeared which act on various mental states.

Tranquillizers are represented by the large family of benzodiazepines. Some are mood elevators while others are hypnotics. Their long-term use may lead to tolerance and dependence which produce a formidable degree of addiction. Anti-depressants were being developed in 1957 during the study of anti-histamine derivatives. These substances correct depressive states, often benign and commonplace minor obsessions or phobias which are not in themselves dangerous but which can contribute to suicide.

Lithium salts were introduced onto the market in 1969. They are regarded as "mood" drugs, and are of great help in manic-depressive states in which sufferers alternate between extremes of excitement and apathy. Since 1963, major neuroleptics have been used which are chemically related to dopamine and are suitable for treating serious psychoses. There were soon a large number of such drugs available. Sometimes their use can extend over many years under medical supervi-

Painting has often mirrored various mental disorders. It is now used in psychopathology for diagnosing some mental diseases. Here, paintings by schizophrenics.

sion, and they have a beneficial effect on all kinds of mental disorder. They cure transient depressive episodes and enable schizophrenics and their families to lead virtually normal lives. They have transformed mental disease as suffered by patients and experienced by society. The age-old concept of the incurable lunatic has changed, since the mentally ill are now acceptable in society, and since they are affected by a disease which is just as temporary and curable as physical diseases can be.

Patients no longer have to be hospitalized for life. Certainly, hypocrisy does live on, since the mental asylums which have become psychiatric hospitals are now known in France as "special hospitals" to conceal their true identity. They have also been made "humane". Strait-jackets have disappeared and specially trained psychiatric nurses have replaced the sometimes aggressive supervisors of former times. Patients stay in such hospitals for shorter periods of time, and the hundreds of beds which were needed in the asylums have been taken away, as was the case with the sanatoria twenty years before. By taking a few tablets a day and occasionally seeing their doctor, many previous mental patients now lead quite normal lives, as the tuberculosis patients were eventually able to do.

This medical and pharmaceutical experience of the action of chemistry on mental mechanisms proves, at the cerebral level, the action of chemical mediators which was known about in the peripheral nervous system. The isolation of cerebral hormones also contributed to the birth and development of the neurosciences, and to a *chemical materialism*. In this context all decisions were therefore under the command of molecules; nothing separated the human mind from the animal except proteins; nothing differentiated our soul from our viscera.

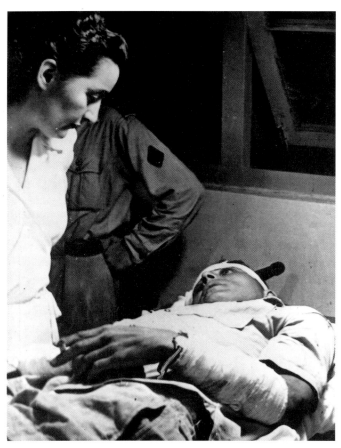

Wartime medicine, in Normandy in June 1944; and shortly after the retreat of Dien Bien Phu in May 1954 (below).

THE SUCCESSES
AND FAILURES
OF SURGERY

Surgeons, anxious about the future and astonished at the progress which medicine was making, finally believed that they could no longer play a useful role. Admittedly, they did not drain bone infections, or peritoneal, pleural or articular serous membranes, as they had done before, nor did they remove as many stomachs because of ulcers, or uteri because of fibroma. They no longer adjusted the position of kidneys, stomach or retroverted uteri. On the other hand, biologists, pharmacists and doctors themselves had placed at their disposal many chemical substances which enabled them to carry out procedures which would have been unimaginable a few decades earlier. Paradoxically, wars proved to be of use to surgery, in that they provided opportunities for new and important experiments. The Second World War encouraged the

Final preparations for a heart operation in a hospital in Düsseldorf, Germany.

development of contacts between European and American surgeons. Similarly, the Korean War and the two wars in Indo-China, involving the French and the Americans, indirectly benefited civilians in the industrialized countries during peace-time.

The first advances came with anaesthetics which, from 1945 onwards, proved to be more reliable and longer lasting. Using curare and various gases, it was possible to anaesthetize patients, rendering them unconscious and paralysed for almost ten hours, with their breathing being maintained by a ventilator. The heart could be stopped or stimulated as required, and blood losses were replaced by transfusions which were biologically more precise as to blood and tissue group, and which involved the use of better adapted blood products. Specialized centres

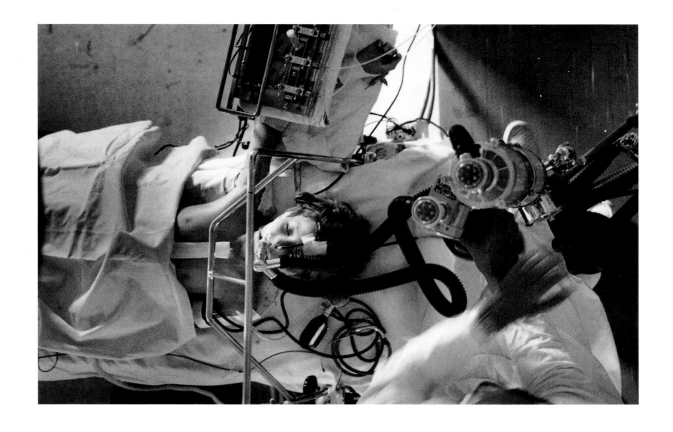

now took blood from carefully chosen donors, placing at the disposal of surgeons fluids and cells which were adapted to their requirements: whole blood, plasma, erythrocytes or platelets, concentrates of corpuscles, globulins, various coagulation factors, and so forth.

The many innovations in biochemistry also became indispensable to the surgeon. Before the start of an operation, the biological assessment of the patient's condition enabled increasingly frail subjects to undergo surgery safely. New-born babies were able to benefit from correction of oesophageal or cardiac malformations, and surgeons even

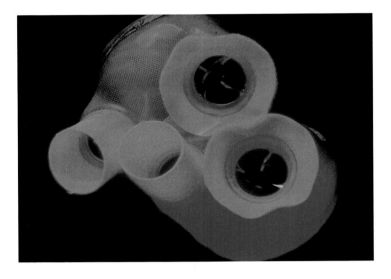

Below: *compression chambers for treating disorders of the circulation.*

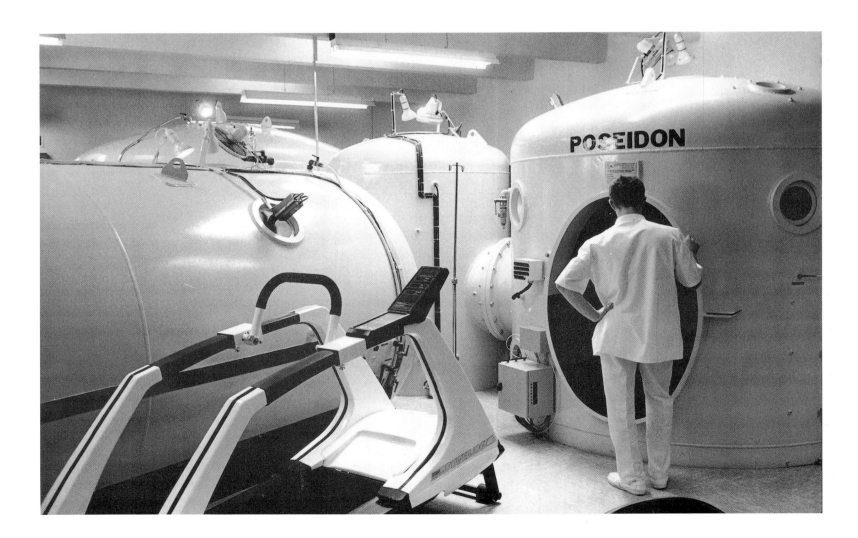

Progress in cardiac surgery.
Opposite, top: *an artificial*
heart; above: *replacement of a*
heart valve by an artificial valve.
Right: *a surgical laser.*

started to operate on babies while they were still in the womb. Similarly, there was no upper age limit, and octogenarians or nonagenarians could undergo surgery.

During surgical intervention, life-support techniques ensured that the balance of electrolytes was maintained as well as the appropriate haemodynamic and biochemical values.

Anticoagulants, heparin and the anti-vitamin K became indispensable in operations on the heart and blood vessels, including plastic surgery on the vessels which supply the brain or the heart, the replacement of heart valves or the un-blocking of a large vessel in embolism or atherosclerosis.

The diversity of drugs which combat infection also enabled surgeons to intervene in bacterial foci and to practise visceral ablations in septic areas, such as resection of large portions of the intestine in the case of cancer or of diffuse bacterial attacks on the digestive tract, or even excochleation of the small pelvis with ablation of the uterus, rectum and bladder in the case of cancers which have spread or become infected.

531

Improvements to surgical instruments enabled sutures to be carried out on smaller and smaller organs using needles and types of thread which could, if required, be assimilable by the organism. Arteries were removed and resewn, and so were small-calibre veins and nerves. In the 1940s and 1950s, Clarence Crafoord in Sweden, and Robert Gross and Alfred Blalock in the United States undertook the first corrections of malformations of the heart and large blood vessels of the thorax, some of which condemned "blue babies" to an early death. With the lungs and heart immobilized, external pumps ensured that the brain was perfused with oxygenated blood that had been rendered incoagulable. The majority of vessel repairs – for example, the reimplantation of parts of limbs which had been accidentally amputated – were done under the microscope. Kidneys were temporarily removed, remodelled on a table, and then they were put back.

The first kidney transplants were carried out in the 1950s.
Right: a kidney taken from a cadaver arrives in the operating theatre before being grafted to replace a diseased kidney.

ORGAN TRANSPLANTS

The chronology of "allografts", that is, grafts which involve transplanting organs or tissues from one person to another:
1948: corneal grafts are regulated in France
1959: first kidney transplant
1963: liver transplant attempted
1967: heart transplant
After years of trial and error in relation to technique and the indications for grafting, transplants are now well regulated, particularly in the choice of graft and in the treatment that avoids rejection by the recipient. Trials are continuing for the transplantation of the pancreas, lungs, small intestine and other organs.

Synthetic materials, such as plastics and industrial fabrics, and various metals were employed. Surgeons increasingly replaced segments of bone or artery, cardiac valves or complete joints such as the hip with prostheses made of nylon, Terylene and indestructible metal alloys which were well tolerated by the organism. If necessary, these prostheses were fixed in place with cements which had been carefully researched.

Surgeons also benefited from the progress made by all the medical and biological disciplines, especially immunology

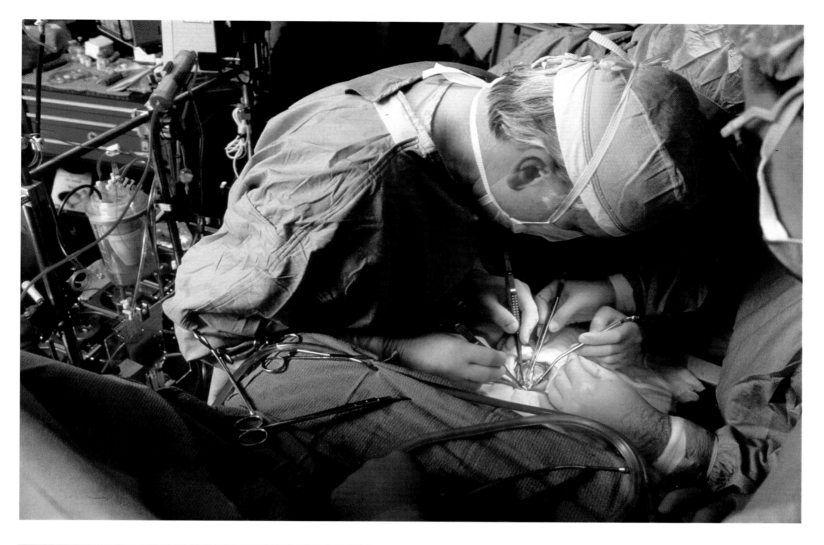

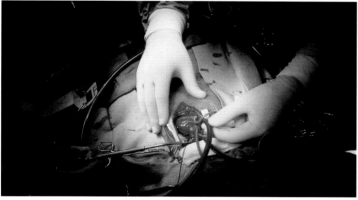

in the context of organ grafting. The first kidney transplants were carried out in the 1950s in the United States at the instigation of John Murray, and in France by Jean Hamburger. These were followed by heart transplants in the 1970s by the American Norman Shumway, then by transplants of the liver, pancreas, lungs and intestine. Shumway achieved a successful heart transplant at Stanford University, California, one month after Christiaan Barnard's first-ever heart transplant in South Africa, in December 1967. Such grafts would not have been possible

The surgeon inserts the new kidney in the abdominal cavity.
Below: *the perfusion of the new organ once it is in place has to be re-established with precision.*

if, in the intervening twenty years, our knowledge of genetics and molecular biology had not made considerable progress. Not only did the study of tissue compatibility increase the recipient's tolerance of the graft, but certain products such as cyclosporin A toned down the phenomena of rejection and the reactions of the graft itself.

This rapid overview of what the biological disciplines had to offer surgery, with its technical and professional limits that were becoming increasingly hard to define, would be incomplete without mentioning one or two successes in some specialties. Laryngology, above all in the fight against cancer, is becoming increasingly sparing in its ablations, while the prostheses used in tracheotomy have been improving and speech therapists are now able to do much to restore the voice. Progress in maxillofacial surgery also covers functional aspects such as swallowing and mastication as well as the psychological aspects.

In a related anatomical area, the art of dentistry has come a long way since the

The transplantation of bone marrow:
the diseased corpuscles are replaced by
healthy corpuscles from a donor.

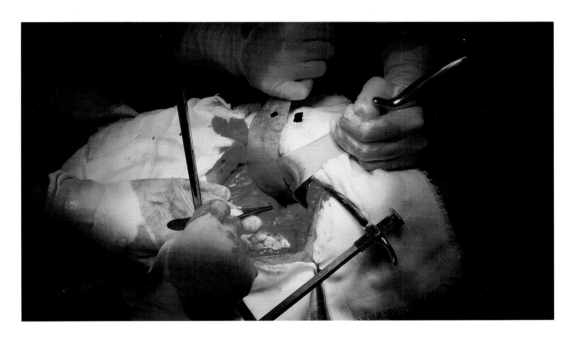

days of tooth-drawers at fairgrounds. Odontology and stomatology treat the teeth, jaws and mouth.

In a short space of time, instruments and techniques have been perfected which make the treatment of teeth painless. Teeth can now be partially or completely replaced using new materials, and fixed and removable prostheses have been much improved. Orthodontics corrects growth disorders of the upper and lower jaws and of teeth in children and adolescents.

Brain surgery is no longer limited to the draining of abscesses or of blood which has collected as a result of injury. Cerebral haemorrhages due to hypertension, atherosclerosis or ruptured aneurysms can now be treated. Brain surgery also aims to treat functional disorders such as those brought about by Parkinson's disease. All these interventions, which are carried out at precise, circumscribed points at the base of the brain, are assisted by radiological stereotaxis which can pinpoint the operation site.

Finally, gynaecology and obstetrics, which form an integral part of modern surgery, also evolved rapidly. In pregnancy, clinical and ultrasound examinations and interventions at the neck of the womb prevent premature delivery. Forceps may be used or a Caesarean section performed if the foetus is showing signs of distress or is in a bad position, or if there is a danger of the uterus rupturing. Most importantly, the work of special care baby units means that normal life without disorders resulting from brain damage can be offered to premature babies who are unable to breathe unassisted or control their body temperature. Twenty years ago, such children, if they survived, formed the majority of the severely mentally and physically handicapped who remain a burden on society. Thus, in surgery, as in all the branches of medicine, procedures can now be performed which would have been impossible fifty years ago. Science, technology and medicine are all the results of human ingenuity and are now being harnessed to help humanity.

Worldhealth

IV.

HEALTH SYSTEMS

An image of interdependence between the generations that has remained traditional in Mali. The large number of blind people – twenty million in Black Africa – mostly suffering from river blindness which is transmitted by a fly, renders such interdependence a necessity.

The technical development of medicine has been so rapid that poor health has ceased to seem inevitable for people in industrialized countries. Science has provided ways of treating and preventing disease, and people have a right to benefit from this. For their part, many governments have finally accepted the idea, which first arose during the Age of Enlightenment, that health is a social asset and that governments are under an obligation to preserve it. The National Health Service was founded in Britain in 1948. In France in 1953, it was a sign of the times that all matters relating to the general protection of public health, the health of families and children, and the ills of society were gathered together for the first time in a *Code de la santé publique.*

It was thus that health care became a collective concern. Medical assistance was no longer a simple agreement between patient and knowledgeable carer, it was a national enterprise which public administration had to take in hand. This trend began to be put into practice in a generalized way after the Second World War. Health administrations were set up, hierarchies were established, and officials were charged with ensuring that the food for sale was of good quality, that hygiene standards were adhered to by meat producers and abattoirs, and that clean drinking water was distributed to the entire population.

With the same aim in mind, the health professions have been the subject throughout the world of precise and compelling legislation. They have increased in number and have diversified, from doctors who qualify after years of study at university to medical assistants in hospitals and laboratory technicians. Physiotherapists and

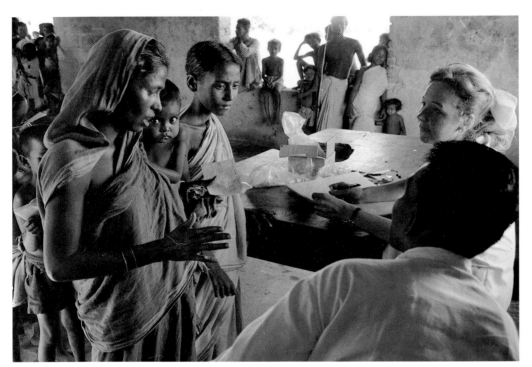

The Red Cross operates throughout the world: in India, the Caribbean and, right, in northeastern Brazil, a region that is regularly the victim of famine.

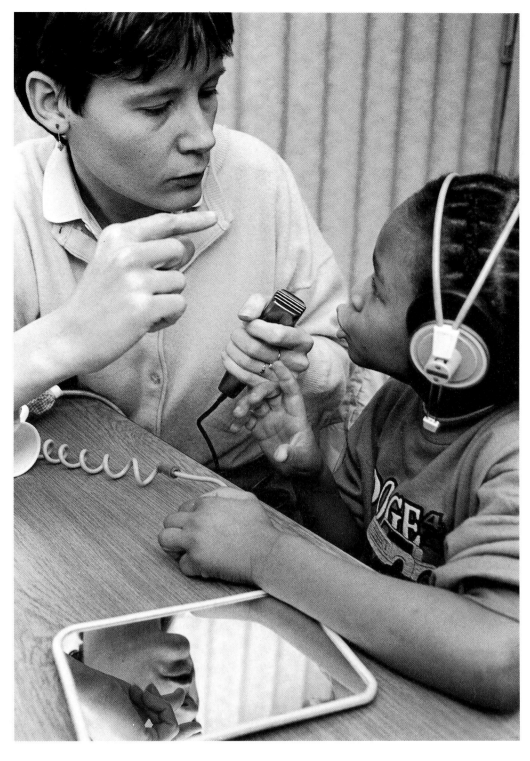

Scenes of the special education given to deaf children. Modern electronic techniques and traditional methods, from the mirror to the picture-book, coexist.

speech therapists cover many areas of specialization, and engineers are attached to hospitals and departments of public hygiene.

The great importance which is now attached to equipment has given rise to a biochemical industry which draws on electronics and manufactures biomaterials of remarkable composition. Doubtless because of the large variety of products and because of the industry's recent development, biomedical engineers do not yet represent a coherent economic force, unlike the pharmaceutical industry which is closely connected to the chemicals industry and is made up of large international groups that wield political power.

The majority of countries have given doctors the exclusive right to provide medical care. However, in all countries of the world, even the most industrialized and well educated, illegal professionals still attract clients and the most eccentric therapists have their followers.

Governments have tried to ensure an exact distribution of doctors' surgeries, hospitals and community clinics within their territories in a laudable attempt to establish the equal rights of citizens to health care, an ideal which will never be achieved because of people's different ways of life and because of each person's biological individuality. In France, the suburbs of Montpellier are better served than the Ardennes region, and in Africa, the bush and the savanna both lack the resources to provide health care. Accessibility of care is one of the main criteria required of a health system, and no country can claim that they have the perfect solution, for both social and financial reasons.

Furthermore, only the European Community has succeeded in bringing the health professions into line. Doctors, nurses and midwives who have been

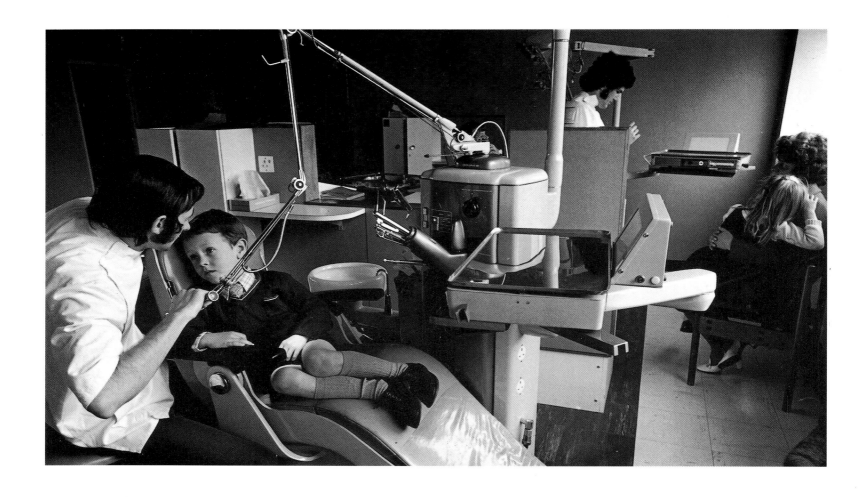

Dental care in England in the 1970s. Thanks to local anaesthesia, the treatment of caries no longer seems to frighten children.

trained at any of the institutions in the Community can live and work in any other member state. For example, they can emigrate from Copenhagen to Palermo, or from Athens to Dublin. Neither the Swiss Confederation nor the United States of America has arrived at this free movement of medical personnel.

In reality, when the system was established about ten years ago, expatriations were rare, since the caring profession is so closely linked to the culture, way of life, language and even the religion of a given country. Once again it has been demonstrated that medicine is neither a universal science nor a collection of techniques which can be applied anywhere.

However, the European Community has not managed to bring into line the regulations concerning the total number of doctors and other health professionals. Some member states, such as Britain and France, fix at a certain level the number of students admitted each year to college; others, such as Belgium and Italy, have manifestly too many doctors at their disposal who, although qualified, are unable to find work. However, Belgian and Italian doctors have thus far not sought to practise elsewhere.

France is the only country to have laid down by law the responsibilities of some of its doctors: those who are admitted to posts in regional and university teaching hospitals, that is in the highest level of public hospitals which in themselves form a hierarchy, have to carry out three types of duties: medical care, teaching and research. This arrangement is as a result of a law passed in 1958, at the instigation of the paediatrician Robert Debré (1882–1978). It marks a complete transformation of the jobs of hospital doctor and faculty professor, by forcing them to spend all their working hours in one place, and it has led to the construction of university and hospital premises in the same vicinity. This law has also transformed the large regional hospitals, the manner in which medicine is practised by the elite of the profession and the way in which it is taught.

Unfortunately, the associations cannot prevent ruptures and divergences of opinion and mentality which aggravate differences in practice. Those treating patients are gradually distancing themselves from those who work in laboratories. General practitioners, who work closely with families, often have less prestige than specialists working on one particular disease. We cannot tell how this situation will develop in the future, but it can only be detrimental to the uniqueness of the art of caring for patients and to the quality of care these patients receive.

ALEXIS CARREL: CHANGING MORALS

Alexis Carrel was born in 1873 near Lyons, France, and began his studies in medicine there. Doubtless frustrated by his initial failure to pass the hospital examinations, he left for Canada and the United States. He worked at the Rockefeller Foundation, became famous for his work on organ transplantation, the artificial culture of cells, and techniques for carrying out delicate sutures on blood vessels, and received the Nobel prize for medicine in 1912. During the First World War, he drove an ambulance for the French army and improved the treatment of infected wounds. He subsequently published several works in which he explained the inequality of the races, deplored the decline of morals, and recommended the execution of criminals, the severely mentally retarded and dangerous mental patients by the use of suitable gases. His book L'homme cet inconnu *was enormously successful in France between the two World Wars.*
He died in France in 1944 after being recalled by Marshal Pétain.

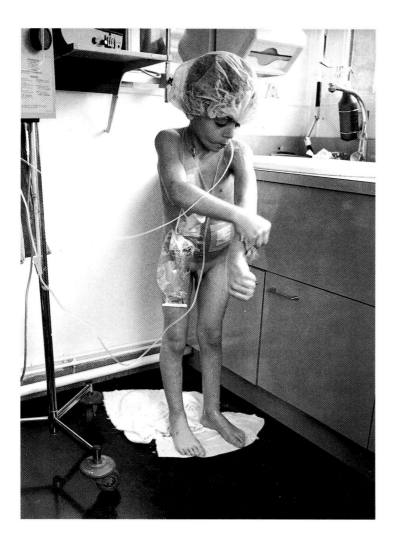

A boy suffering from cystic fibrosis, and receiving nourishment by transfusion, takes a shower.

All over the world, health professionals feel the need to join forces, meet and listen to one another. There are thousands of bodies, associations, learned societies and regional and international groups which hold periodic conferences attracting hundreds or thousands of delegates with particular professional qualifications or areas of specialization, who may be interested in a particular organ or a specific disease. This practice demonstrates the desire among doctors firstly to maintain a minimum code of ethics and secondly to ensure a degree of professional solidarity.

SOCIAL WELFARE

The egalitarian social ideal of 1945, and the period of prosperity in the 1950s, sanctioned the development in industrialized countries of systems of social welfare which enabled all citizens to receive medical care. In Britain, the National Health Service covers the entire population and was generous in its provisions, taking charge of all health supplies. But even in the richest European countries, the generalization of health services sometimes took several years. In France, it took more than twenty years to achieve. In the United States there is still no national health system, and national resources are currently reserved for the poorest families and the elderly.

Irrespective of how these national health services are financed, the sums at their disposal ensure the development of preventive and social medicine, the modernization and construction of public and private hospitals, and if necessary the freedom of movement of the health professionals whose number is increasing.

Non-industrialized countries have been unable to equip themselves with such protection plans because they lack the necessary resources. In the course of decolonization, the states that have gained

Brooklyn, night scene. Violence and drugs engender fear, isolation and apathy.

their independence adopt systems which have developed according to a general plan. First, foreign companies are "invited" to insure their staff against illness, industrial accidents and work-related diseases. Next, the public authorities provide medical care for the army and the police, and then the legal and teaching professions. Apart from having access to free community clinics, the agricultural population, which is in the majority in these third-world countries, usually has no access to medical care.

The considerable sums of money devoted to medical care by the rich countries weigh heavily on their national economy. During the 1980s, the levels of benefits generally dropped, and the freedom to manage and to equip hospitals declined, although in 1991, all these restrictions still did not pose any threat to the general level of health of the population.

These financial preoccupations of social security systems have given rise to a new discipline, "health economics", which studies the large items of expenditure, the system of benefits, the internal management of hospitals and the cost of some diseases.

Everywhere systems of evaluation have been set up at great expense. These are simple programmes of accounting control and not studies of the relationship between the clinical efficacy of techniques and their cost. Apart from mortality records, causes of death and admissions to public hospitals, none of the countries of the industrialized world possesses data of this nature. The science of health statistics is still in its infancy.

This explains the appropriation by management organizations of the caring professions; in all countries, the administration of public health is subordinate to finance administration. Money takes precedence over health.

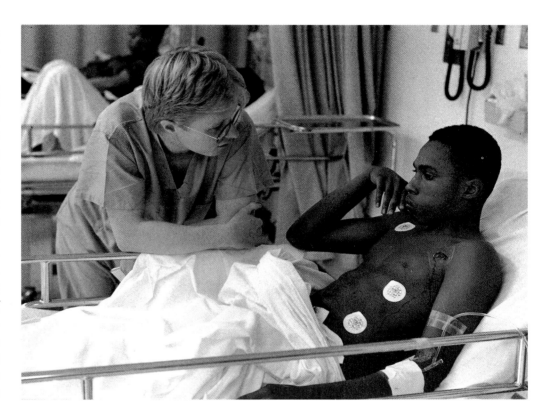

A hospital ward in Detroit: a young black victim of the "gang wars".

MEDICAL CONFIDENTIALITY AND COMPUTERS

Since the time of Hippocrates, it has been the duty of doctors to keep secret the information about patients' private lives which they gain during the exercise of their profession. Medical confidentiality has therefore been instituted in the interest of patients. It is absolute in France, but is respected variously in other Western countries. Public health statistics now require that medical records be entered into data bases (for example, "registers" of certain cancers); in France, their management is subject to the authorization and vigilance of the Commission nationale de l'informatique et des libertés (CNIL) (National Committee for Data Processing and Civil Liberties), to ensure that the confidentiality of data is respected.

THE DISEASES OF THE POOR

The description given of the successive advances in the struggle against disease should not lead to any misconceptions about the benefit that has been derived from them. The discoveries made by Western countries in the last two centuries have primarily been used by them. Prosperity and ingenuity went hand in hand and remained localized.

The deadly epidemic diseases which affected children in particular, and from which Europe has freed itself, are still rife in the developing countries: measles which can lead to bronchopneumonia; rubella; scarlet fever with its renal sequelae; acute arthritis which leads to cardiac disorders; diphtheria and the formidable laryngitis associated with it; whooping cough and its uncontrollable bronchial lesions; poliomyelitis which leaves very many people disabled; and so on. Systematic vaccination campaigns are not feasible in such countries, due to a lack of resources and to the people's general ignorance and prejudice.

The widespread use of the BCG vaccination (Koch's bacillus attenuated by Calmette and Guérin) during the first half of the twentieth century contributed to the reduction of endemic tuberculosis. However, in countries such as India, the immunological state of the population is different, and the vaccine less effective. In tropical Africa, the many carriers of the human immunodeficiency virus (HIV, the causative agent of AIDS) cannot be vaccinated against tuberculosis for fear of contracting a rapidly evolving form of the disease. The climatic and geographic conditions do not allow the populations access to sufficient quantities of water for proper food preparation and personal hygiene; as a result cholera, typhus, typhoid fever, dysentery, plague, and cutaneous and intestinal parasites cannot be avoided. Also, death in childbirth is common among women because of infection and other complications, and infant mortality is high.

In tropical zones, the climatic and natural conditions encourage a large quantity of insects that are themselves vectors of pathogenic micro-organisms which they transmit to humans. Mosquitoes harbour malaria, the most widespread disease on earth; the tsetse fly transmits sleeping sickness; small molluscs carry bilharzia; ticks pass on haemorrhagic diseases, and so on.

Transport facilities and the development of tourism enable micro-organisms to go round the world in a few hours. European airport staff who have never left their own countries may die from malaria brought in by an Indonesian mosquito. Each year in the United States, the deaths are mourned of victims of the plague which is transmitted by fleas from small rodents living in the Arizona desert. We have spoken of how germs can cross frontiers, but the limits are defined; unless they undergo a character change, the insect vectors of the tropics cannot live in temperate zones. This means that the poorest countries will continue to bear the brunt of poverty and disease for a long time to come.

In addition, people in the Third World

A leper weaver in India. The entire village is allocated to lepers.

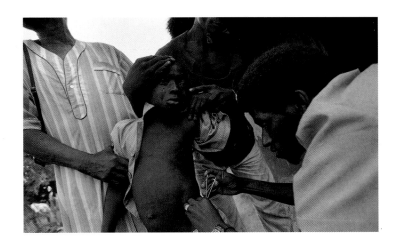

do not escape the metabolic diseases which many think are peculiar to the developed countries. For example, we often attribute disorders such as gout, high blood pressure and obstruction of the blood vessels by atheroma to too rich a diet. However, such disorders are also found among people who suffer from serious nutritional deficiencies. This shows how ignorant we are in matters of diet and heredity, since hereditary factors are doubtless also responsible.

Cancers and viral diseases are rife throughout the world, as the African AIDS epidemic proves. Like the men and women of high society, the poor make use of local toxic substances and, although their poverty at present prevents them from indulging in expensive narcotics, they like to imitate rich foreigners by smoking tobacco and drinking alcohol, the consumption of which increases annually.

These unfortunates will soon be adding the diseases of the northern hemisphere to their own burden of suffering.

Inequality of health provision is difficult to abolish in industrialized countries, and it is also true of countries with different levels of economic development. It is a vicious circle: poverty hinders the provision of medical services, and disease, which hinders productivity, becomes all the more formidable. The need for health care becomes enormous, even to the extent that nobody dares to quantify it.

Immediately after the Second World War, international organizations were founded such as the Food and Agriculture Organization (FAO) of the United Nations, the United Nations International Children's Emergency Fund (UNICEF) and the World Health Organization (WHO). Great hopes were pinned on these.

The WHO, with a membership today of over 160 nations, has followed on from the Office of International Public Hygiene and the Board of Hygiene of the League of Nations before the Second World War, and has carried out countless missions. From information gathered from all over the world, it draws up epidemiological and statistical data. It makes recommendations on hygiene and health care, assists impoverished countries with their programmes of aid for mothers and children, contributes to the training of

SOME PARASITOSES OF THE THIRD WORLD

Disease	Vector	Number of cases (millions)	Annual deaths (in thousands)
Malaria	mosquito	800	1 500
Trichuriasis (intestinal worms)	water	500	
Amoebiasis	water	480	75
Bilharzia (intestines, urinary tract)	water	200	750
Sleeping sickness	fly (glossina)	25	65
Kala-azar	fly	1.2	1
River blindness	fly (buffalo gnat)		
Trachoma	fly		

(Data from the WHO)

545

medical staff, implements projects for combating epidemics, and everywhere maintains teams of field-workers and educators including all kinds of medical personnel.

The WHO had hoped to wipe malaria from the face of the earth with a series of large-scale operations. However, these ended in failure. The plasmodium has a complex cycle of development; countries affected by malaria were incapable of persevering in the fight against the disease by supplying the required numbers of personnel, buying and distributing the DDT which was to kill the mosquitoes, and doing away with stagnant water where the larvae develop. Then the insect vectors themselves became resistant to the insecticides in use. By contrast, thanks

One of the Red Cross orphanages in India, where powdered milk is put to good use.

to the WHO's insistence on smallpox vaccinations, this disease no longer exists on earth. This victory is due to the WHO, without which it would never have been possible.

In Alma-Ata, Kazakhstan, in 1978, plans were laid for "health for all in the year 2000" at one of the periodic meetings of the World Assembly of the WHO. This project was deliberately utopian. Can we guarantee "health care for all in the year 2000"? It would indeed be a wonderful achievement and would not be without problems, since economic development, political stability and the development of the health services are inextricably linked.

The situation of the poorest peoples is further aggravated by their fertility rates. Moreover, their infant mortality rates have started to decrease, and their life expectancy is growing. The highest birth rates are always to be found in the countries where agriculture is least productive. The slightest increase in revenue obtained by modest economic progress is spent in advance when there are extra mouths to feed.

The imbalance between the rich, healthy North and the poor South, where as much as seventy-five percent of humanity lives, plagued by disease and parasites, is likely to last for a long time yet.

THE ALMA-ATA DECLARATION 1978

The assembly of the World Health Organization issued a proclamation aimed at the development of "primary health care", in particular in underprivileged countries:
1 *Health education.*
2 *Promotion of good standards of food and nutrition.*
3 *Provision of clean water.*
4 *Care for mothers and infants, family planning.*
5 *Vaccination against the major infectious diseases.*
6 *Prevention of local endemics.*
7 *Treatment of common diseases and lesions.*
8 *Supply of essential medicines.*

Fourteen years later, the realization of this programme of "health for all by the year 2000" has not made much progress, mainly for economic reasons.

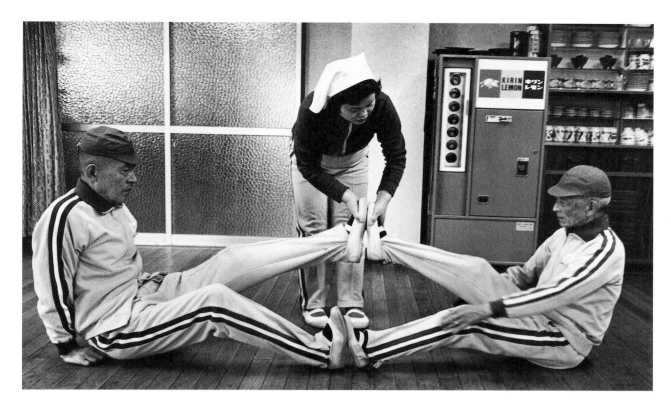

In Japan, the care given to the elderly forms part of the traditional culture of a strongly integrated society.
Left: *a scene in a Tokyo old people's home.*

THE MEDICINE OF TOMORROW?

The last half century in the history of medicine has seen major advances in all branches of the subject. However, there is nothing to boast about. The thousands of individuals, some famous, some not, who have contributed to medical progress, have only participated in that thirst for knowledge which is an irrational and irresistible voraciousness peculiar to man. In any case, doctors are not the only people who have contributed their skills to this progress. Other men and women have also played an important part in it, in areas that have nothing to do with medicine.

In the end, we have to become accustomed to the idea that we will never be able to know or do everything. Each new discovery, whether it concerns the biology of the smallest molecules or the transmission of hereditary characteristics from one generation to the next, leads to new questions.

We always want to go one step further: what is the reason for the shape of a certain nucleic acid, or how does a specific enzyme work? Just as astronomers expand the space they know by a few millions of kilometres each year without ever being able to fix a limit to the universe, in the same way the point at which we would be able say "that is when life commences" recedes further from

our grasp. Our accumulation of knowledge has led to notable successes in the fight against disease and pain; however, there are many reasons why we cannot be complacent.

Our successes are precarious. The satisfactory state of health of our society is based on evolving hygiene practices and administrative systems. If vaccinations are neglected and laws less well observed, we will see some of the former epidemics reappear. This can be seen when wars disrupt the organization of societies and states. The end of the Second World War was marked by typhus in Europe, and tribal warfare has encouraged the plague in central Africa.

Moreover, the continuous progress made in medicine is threatened by that in other technical fields. To escape the heat, we invented air conditioning, and this led to the development of fatal epidemics due to the previously unknown *Legionnella bacterium*. To assist the work of housewives, blocks of flats were equipped with rubbish chutes which transmitted germs from floor to floor and home to home.

In hospitals which admit patients suffering from increasingly complex symptoms, hospital epidemics can develop which are reminiscent of those of past centuries. There are many examples of this kind, and they prove that our techni-

547

cal innovations bring with them unsuspected risks.

Man becomes passionately interested in things without realizing their implications. He knows how to free himself from a number of cancers, but consumption of alcohol and tobacco is on the increase throughout the world. He becomes addicted to increasingly dangerous drugs and the list of addictive substances which lead to dependence, ruined lives and death is constantly growing.

When science tackles areas such as procreation, which hitherto it has not been able to address, the structure of society threatens to fall apart. Marriage, the couple and the family unit are structures upon which the survival of groups and states depend, and these are being undermined. Everywhere, people talk about morality, set up ethical committees and draw up laws which are designed to consolidate, to reassure, and to maintain scientific progress within the limits of what is reasonable.

Our scientific certainties sometimes cause us to forget that we are in the midst of a living universe which is characterized by widespread parasitism, since each species lives at the expense of others. The functioning of our intestines requires bacteria to ensure that chemical changes occur which our bodies cannot bring about by themselves, but viruses and bacteria live off us. A DNA helix changes, and thus a new biological arrangement comes into being for which we are not prepared and which causes terrible human suffering.

The diseases which have disappeared for ever, and those which suddenly arise like AIDS, whose future no one can predict, are evidence of the frailty of our species, even though it has succeeded in adapting itself to so many new situations in the last million years. If the fly which transmits river blindness along the length of the Niger, together with the nematode worm which it also carries, were ever to become adapted to temperate zones, the northern hemisphere would be populated by blind people.

No spectacular discoveries can prevent our anguish. We try to reassure ourselves by taking regular exercise and making regular checks on the level of cholesterol in our blood, or by taking tranquillizers or stimulants. As we free ourselves from tradition, and from the servitude and dangers imposed upon us by nature, our anxiety grows along with our impression of freedom.

We are not very different from our ancestors. Medicine still has a very long way to go in helping us live: its history is far from over.

A medical strike in Paris. The development of social security and state control often causes tension among the health professions.

THE EXPLOSION OF KNOWLEDGE AND TECHNIQUES
1940 – 1990

POLITICS AND CULTURE	DATE	DATE	MEDICINE
		1940	Identification of the Rhesus factor
		1942	Sulphonylureas against diabetes Industrial manufacture of penicillin
		1944	Kolff: artificial kidney Waksman: streptomycin
Atomic bombs on Hiroshima and Nagasaki Germany and Japan capitulate	1945		
Founding of the United Nations	1946		
India gains its independence	1947		
Birth of the State of Israel	1948	1948	World Health Organization
		1949	Cortisone used in arthritis
End of the colonial empires	1950–1960		
		1951	Pincus: the contraceptive pill
		1952	Tranquillizers in psychiatry
Death of Stalin	1953	1953	Cardiac pacemakers Salk: vaccine against poliomyelitis
Afro-Asian conference at Bandung	1955	1955	Start of open-heart surgery Worldwide campaign against malaria
Nationalization of the Suez Canal	1956		
		1958	J. Dausset: HLA tissue group
Independence of Algeria	1962	1962	Watson, Crick and Wilkins win Nobel prize for the structure of DNA
Assassination of US President John Kennedy	1963		
Six-Day War: Israel occupies the West Bank and Sinai	1967	1967	Christiaan Barnard and Norman Shumway: first heart transplants in man
First men on the moon	1969		
		1971	CT scanning, nuclear magnetic resonance
Capture of Saigon by North Vietnamese troops	1975		
		1977	Disappearance of smallpox
		1980	Development of ultrasound
		1982	AIDS Non-invasive lithotripsy
The Berlin Wall comes down	1989		

Appendices

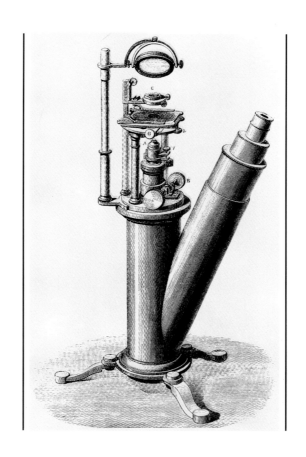

GLOSSARY

———◆———

Abortion: premature expulsion from the uterus of the products of conception.

Aetiology: study of the causes of disease.

Amoebiasis: a parasitic infection which can affect various organs, especially the intestine (dysentery), liver, lungs, etc.

Anaesthesia: loss of sensation or feeling.

Analgesia: reduction of pain.

Anastomosis: establishment of a connection between two hollow organs or two vessels.

Aneurysm: a kind of sac formed from the wall of a blood vessel.

Ankylostomiasis: parasitic disease caused by a small worm and affecting the skin, digestive tract and blood.

Antisepsis: the methods used to get rid of pre-existing germs by killing them.

Aphasia: total or partial loss of speech.

Asepsis: the methods used to prevent contamination by germs which cause infection.

Aseptic: free from germs. See *septic*.

Bilharzia: parasitic disease which affects the urinary organs or the digestive tract; it is caused by a kind of worm which uses a fresh-water mollusc as intermediary host.

Blepharitis: inflammation of an eyelid.

Blood group: a group of individuals having in common a blood-group antigen (a protein against which an antibody is formed), which may or may not be compatible with the antibodies from other types of blood not possessing this antigen.

Cataract: opacity of the crystalline lens in the anterior chamber of the eye.

Chronobiology: study of the biological phenomena which occur in an organism over time: in the course of a day, a year or a life.

Clinical practice: 1. observation of the patient as opposed to the carrying out of laboratory tests.
2. treatment of patients.

Congenital: observed at birth. See *hereditary*.

Contagion: transmission of an infectious disease from one person to another.

Copropharmaceutics: the use of excrement in medicine. Synonym: stercopharmaceutics.

Creatinine: a blood protein. The measurement of its concentration in urine provides an indication of the filtering ability of the kidneys.

Cytology: the study of cells.

Doppler effect: the modification noticed by a moving observer in the frequency of a vibration from a fixed source. The study of this effect is used in the diagnosis of abnormalities of the blood vessels.

Down's syndrome: human hereditary disease due to trisomy of chromosome 21, characterized by a flat face, mental retardation and often visceral abnormalities. Also called mongolism.

Dropsy: outdated term for a condition in which there is generalized swelling of the body due to the retention of fluid.

Dystocia: abnormal labour or childbirth.

Embolism: migration into the blood stream of a foreign body or blood clot which may obstruct a blood vessel.

Endemic: continuous presence of an infectious disease within a localized area or group. See *epidemic*.

Endorphins: neuropeptides found in the brain which bind to opioid receptors.

Epidemic: sudden, rapid spread of an infectious disease within an area or group, affecting many people in a short space of time. See *endemic*.

Epidemiology: study of the frequency and distribution of diseases of whatever cause.

Epigenesis: The theory that organ systems develop anew in the embryo, and are not preformed as such.

Fibrin: protein necessary for the coagulation of the blood.

Flame photometry: technique for studying the chemical composition of a biological fluid: the light spectrum of the chemical elements being investigated is observed by vaporizing the liquid in a flame at a high temperature.

Galenical: denoting remedies made from plants and not from synthetic substances.

Haemopathy: disease of the blood.

Haemostasis: the phenomena which contribute to coagulation of the blood or to arresting a haemorrhage.

Hepatoscopy: technique of divination involving examination of the liver of an animal: its weight, colour, anatomical structure, etc.

Hereditary: relating to factors that can be transmitted from parents to children. See *congenital*.

Hereditary disease: disease which runs in families and is transmitted genetically.

Histology: the study of the minute structure, composition and function of the tissues.

Hydrocele: a collection of fluid around the testicles.

Iatrochemistry: medical school of the seventeenth century which reduced all phenomena of life to simple chemical processes such as distillation and fermentation.

Iatrophysics: medical school of the seventeenth century which interpreted all phenomena of life as resulting from physics: mechanics, combustion, etc.

Immunoelectrophoresis: method for analysing biological fluids by placing them in an electrical field and mixing with serums. This enables a person's immunity in relation to foreign substances to be assessed.

Impetigo: microbial disease of the skin which is most commonly seen in children.

Incubation: 1. Ancient practice whereby sick persons were made to sleep in a temple at night in the hope that they would have a vision or dream, the meaning of which could be interpreted.

2. Period between the penetration of a germ into an organism and the appearance of the first symptoms of the disease.

Induration: transformation of tissue which becomes harder than normal.

Infarct: lesion of organ tissue due to the obstruction of one or more blood vessels.

Intumescence: the visible, progressive swelling of an area.

Laser: (acronym from Light Amplification by Stimulated Emission of Radiation): phased light source composed of beams of the same wavelength which is capable of transmitting high energy over a distance in a very narrow beam. It has numerous medical applications, particularly in surgery.

Leishmaniasis: parasitic disease caused by a flagellate and transmitted by insects. Various areas of cellular tissue may be affected: the skin, internal organs such as the spleen, etc.

Lithiasis: formation of calculi (stones) in the bile duct or urinary tract.

Luxation: dislocation of the bones in a joint.

Mantic: the art or science of divination.

Materia medica: branch of medical study which deals with drugs: their sources, preparation, composition and effects.

Mesotherapy: method which consists of injecting an anaesthetic into a cu-

taneous area supposed to correspond to the lesion of an internal organ.

Metritis: inflammation of the uterus.

Myocardium: muscular tissue of the heart.

Natural history of a disease: evolution of a disease from its appearance to its end, including the duration of each of its phases and any complications.

Necropsy: synonym: autopsy.

Nosology: the study, definition, description and classification of diseases.

Oedema: swelling of tissue, an organ or an anatomical region due to the accumulation of fluid.

Ontogeny: the development of an individual living organism.

Osteomyelitis: infectious disease of bone, usually due to a staphylococcus.

Panacea: medicine able to cure all diseases (the expression "panacea for all ills" is therefore tautological).

Parenchyma: those tissues which make up a large part of an organ and contribute to its functioning.

Pathology, external or internal: ancient tradition used to distinguish between external, visible diseases (deformities, tumours, wounds, traumatic lesions) and internal diseases without visible signs, which affected the internal organs. External pathology was the province of the surgeon, internal pathology that of the doctor. This is why the distinction between these two domains varies with the course of the disease, the scope for treatment, fashion, etc.

Pessary: originally this term merely referred to medicaments inserted into the vagina; today it also means a device worn internally to keep the uterus in position.

Pott's curvature: abnormal curvature of the spine due to osteoarticular tuberculosis of the vertebrae, or Pott's disease.

Prolapse: general term used to designate the abnormal descent of an organ; usually applied to the uterus and to the bladder in women.

Psychosomatics: study of the relationship between the mind and the body.

Radiotherapy: treatment which uses the X-rays discovered by Röntgen. Synonym: röntgenotherapy.

Rickettsiosis: infectious disease (transmitted by insects) characterized by periodic sudden rises in temperature.

Septic: harbouring or enclosing germs capable of causing disease. See *aseptic*.

Simples: plants having medicinal properties.

Specificity: a disease is specific in that it has a cause and apparently unconnected symptoms which have a single prognosis.

Stercopharmaceutics: the use of excrement in medicine. Also known as copropharmaceutics.

Stroke: sudden attack on cerebral activity, of vascular origin, most frequently due to obstruction of an artery.

Symptomatology: the study of the symptoms of disease.

Taxonomy: study of the scientific classification of organisms.

Thalassaemia: human hereditary disease characterized by an abnormality of the haemoglobin. It leads to increased destruction of red blood cells and may sooner or later be life-threatening.

Theriaca: mixture used until the nineteenth century which was made up of several dozen substances chosen by the practitioner, and which was thought to be effective against various poisons and diseases.

Thrombosis: intravascular coagulation of blood.

Tissue type: group of individuals having in common an antigen system in their white corpuscles.

Trichiasis: condition caused by ingrowing hairs, especially eyelashes.

Ultracentrifugation: study of a biological fluid by submitting it to very high rotational speeds in a centrifuge; the cells contained in the fluid separate into individual layers.

Uroscopy: diagnostic technique involving examination of the urine.

Vulvitis: inflammation of the vulva.

INDEX

◆

Abelard, Peter 145
Abulcasis 134, 166, 167, 238, 240
Achenwall, Gottfried 318
Actuarius, John 108
Adler, Alfred 524
Aetius of Amida 101
Albertini 273
Al-Biruni 133
Alcmaeon 66
Alcuin 139
Alexander of Aphrodisias 100
Alexander of Tralles 101, 102, 125, 126
Al-Fargani 133
Alhazen 133
Alibert, Jean-Louis 410
Al-Khwarizmi 133
Al-Wateb el Kurtubi 134
Anaximander of Miletus 66
Antyllus 100
Archagathos 85
Archigenes of Apamea 88
Archimedes 100, 125
Artaeus of Cappadocia 88
Aristotle 81, 82, 100, 125, 145, 148, 270, 482
Arnold of Villanueva 161, 163
Arsonval, Arsène d' 436
Asclepiades 85
Asclepius 63, 64, 71, 73, 78
Aselli, Gasparo 269
Assaph of Tiberias 115, 116, 117, 120
Asteur 375
Astruc, Jean 301, 303
Auenbrügger, Leopold 313, 339, 492
Avenzoar 135
Averez 486
Averroes 135, 136, 148
Avicenna 128, 130, 135, 136, 148, 161, 285

Babinski, Joseph 403
Bacon, Francis 263
Bacon, Roger 148
Baglivi 273, 281
Baillarger, Jules 409
Balint, Michael 525
Banting, Frederick 444
Barthez, Paul-Joseph 295, 314
Barnard, Christiaan 533
Baudelocque, Jean-Louis 333
Bauhin, Johannes 231
Bayen, Pierre 301
Bayle, Gaspard 339, 340, 354
Beauperthuy, Louis 377
Béclère, Henri 421
Becquerel, Antoine 425
Bede, the Venerable 138, 139
Bell, Charles 349
Benacosa, Jacob 120
Berengario da Carpi, Jacopo 230
Bernard, Claude 342, 350, 351, 352, 353, 381, 388, 390, 391, 435, 436, 440, 443, 466
Bernheim, Hippolyte 408, 524
Bernoulli, Henri 311
Besnier, Ernest 385
Bessarion, Jean 108
Best, Charles 444
Bichat, François-Xavier 338, 344, 348, 352, 354, 380, 461
Billard, Michel 409
Billroth, Theodor 399
Binet, Alfred 409
Blalock, Alfred 532
Boece 138
Boerhaave, Hermann 274, 275, 285, 291, 311, 313, 314, 333
Boissier de Sauvages 297, 315
Bollstaedt, Albert von 148
Bonaparte, Marie 524
Bordeu, Théophile de 295
Borelli, Giovanni 272
Botallo, Léonardo 231

Bouillaud, Jean-Baptiste 340, 405
Bourgeois, Louise 273
Bovet, Daniel 450
Bretonneau, Pierre 258, 357, 439, 442
Bright, Richard 388, 440
Brissot 244
Broca, Paul 405
Brouardel, Paul 410
Broussais, François 340
Brown, John 292
Brown-Séquard, Charles 390
Bruce, Sir David 377
Brunschwig, Hieronymus 240
Buffon, Georges Louis Leclerc, Comte de 296

Cabanis, Pierre-Jean 332, 362, 478
Caius, John 256
Calmette, Albert 426, 544
Cardano, Girolamo 275
Carrel, Alexis 447
Casserio, Giulio 231
Cassiodore 138
Caventou, Joseph 348, 386
Celsus 87
Cesalpino, Andrea 251
Chain, Ernest Boris 513
Chamberland, Charles Édouard 373
Chamberlen, Peter 273
Chaptal, Jean 332
Charaka 193
Charcot, Jean-Martin 403, 408, 421, 439, 524
Chauffard, Anatole 409
Chauliac, Guy de 135, 167, 168, 240
Chauveau, Auguste 391
Chrysoloras, Manuel 108
Clowes, William 242
Cohnheim, Julius 385
Colombo, P. 233, 237, 251

Colombo, Realdo 233, 251, 265
Conring, Hermann 266
Constantine the African 137, 141
Cooper, Astley 347
Corvisart, Jean Nicolas 313, 339, 340
Crafoord, Clarence 532
Crick, Francis 486
Cruveilhier, Jean 380
Cullen, William 296, 313
Curie, Marie 425
Curie, Pierre 425
Cuvier, Georges 372

D amadian 497
Darier, Jean 409
Darwin, Charles 373
Darwin, Erasmus 453
Dausset, Jean 469
Davaine, Casimir Joseph 370, 453
Daviel, Jacques 314
Debré, Robert 540
De Graaf, Reinier 271
Déjerine, Jules 403
De la Boë, Franciscus (Sylvius) 266, 275
Delay, Jean 527
Democritus 66, 70
Deniker, Pierre 527
Denis, J.B. 272, 473
Desault, Pierre-Joseph 314, 333, 344, 345
Descartes, René 263, 266, 271, 283
Dévé, Félix 449
De Vries, Hugo 482
Dieulafoy, Georges 401, 402
Diocles of Carystus 80
Diogenes of Apollonia 66
Dionis, Pierre 266
Dioscorides 88, 100, 102, 108, 117, 120, 134, 162, 185
Divaka 196
Domagk, Gerhard 449
Donnolo, Shabataï 120
Doyen, Eugène 409
Dubois, Jacques (Sylvius) 230, 233, 234, 236
Dubois-Reymond, Emil 391, 494
Duchenne de Boulogne, Guillaume 403
Duchesne, Ernest 453
Ducrey, Augusto 411
Dumas, Jean-Baptiste 369

Dunant, Henri 415
Dupuytren, Guillaume 345, 348

E berth, Karl Joseph 377
Edison, Thomas 390
Ehrlich, Paul 385, 435, 449
Eijkman, Christiaan 442
Einthoven, Willem 391, 436, 494
Empedocles of Agrigento 66, 126
Erasistratus 82, 83
Erb, Wilhelm Heinrich 411
Esquirol, Jean 405
Estienne, Charles 232, 233, 236
Eustachio, Bartolommeo 269

F abricius ab Aquapendente 265
Fabricius Hildanus 242, 256
Fahrenheit, Daniel 291
Fallopio, Gabriello 234
Farabeuf, Hubert 409
Fauchard, Pierre 314
Fernel, Jean 233, 244, 246, 248
Ficino, Marsilio 225
Finlay, Carlos Juan 377
Fleming, Alexander 450, 453, 513
Flexner, Simon 452
Florey, Sir Howard 513
Flourens, Pierre 349
Floyer, Sir John 301
Fodéré, François-Emmanuel 316, 324, 361
Forlanini, Carlo 447
Fothergill, John 313
Fourcroy, Antoine de 332, 344
Fournier, Jean-Alfred 411
Fracastoro, Girolamo 244, 246, 248, 375
Franck, Johann Peter 324
Franco, Pierre 242
Freud, Anna 524
Freud, Sigmund 408, 524
Fulbert de Chartres 139

G alen 90, 91, 92, 100, 102, 118, 126, 135, 137, 148, 161, 229, 230, 234, 244, 248, 251, 258, 285
Gall, Franz Josef 403
Galvani, Luigi 303, 343
Gariopontus, Warbod 142
Garrod, Archibald 486
Geoffroy Saint-Hilaire, Étienne 372

Gerard de Cremona 137
Gersdorff, H. von 240
Gershon ben Juda 120
Gershon ben Shlomo 120
Gessner, Conrad 242
Gontier d'Andernach 233
Grancher, Joseph 409
Gross, Robert 532
Guérin, Camille 426, 544
Guidi, Guido 242
Guillotin, Joseph-Ignace 354, 361
Guyon, Félix 409

H ai-Thuong Lan-Ong 220
Hales, Stephen 301
Haller, Albrecht von 303, 311, 349
Halsted, William 399, 400
Hamburger, Jean 533
Hanot, Victor 409
Harvey, William 91, 104, 130, 265, 266, 270, 272, 370, 380, 453
Heatley, N. 513
Hecquet, Philippe 301
Helmholtz, Hermann 391
Heracleides 83
Heraclitus of Ephesus 66
Hermonynus of Sparta 108
Herophilus 82, 83
Higgins 515
Hippocrates 66, 68, 69, 70, 71, 72, 73, 75, 76, 77, 78, 79, 80, 83, 86, 87, 88, 90, 102, 108, 118, 126, 137, 142, 148, 161, 189, 190, 197, 211, 244, 269, 274, 276, 285, 309, 352, 369, 375, 427, 433, 466
Hoffmann, Friedrich 305
Hofmann, August Wilhelm von 266
Homolle 386
Hooke, Robert 270
Horsley, Victor 399
Houang Fou Mi 215
Hounsfield, Godfrey 500
Hunaïn ibn Ishaq 126
Hunter, John 313
Huss, Magnus 407
Hutchinson, Sir Jonathan 411
Hygeia 63, 73

I bn al-Baïtar 130
Ibn al-Khatib 136

Ibn-an-Nafiz 453
Ibn Butlan 130
Ibn Juljul 134
Ibn Khaldun 136
Ibn Nafiz 130, 251, 265
Ibn Shaprut, Hasdaï 117
Ibn Sulaiman al-Israeli, Ishaq 115, 117
Ibn Rabban at-Tabari, Ali 117, 126
Imbert, Armand 421
Imhotep 46, 78, 185
Ingrassia, Giovanni F. 231
Isidore of Seville 138

Jackson, Charles 393
Jackson, John 403
Janet, Pierre 524
Jean de Vigo 241
Jenner, Edward 316, 354, 371
Johannsen, Wilhelm Ludwig 482
John the Psychrist 101, 450
Jorpes, Johan 473
Joubert, Laurent 233, 256
Jung, Carl Gustav 524
Jussieu, Antoine Laurent 296

Klein, Melanie 524
Koch, Robert 376, 426
Kocher, Theodor 399
Koeberlé, Eugène 399
Kölliker, Rudolf von 379
Korsakov, Serge 407
Kraepelin, Emil 407

Laborit, Henri 475, 527
Laennec, Théophile-René 339, 340,
    354, 439, 492
Lamarck, Chevalier de 370, 372
Lancereaux, Étienne 409
Lancisi, Giovanni 273, 276
Landsteiner, Karl 431
Lanfranchi, Guido 164
Langenbeck, Bernhard von 347
La Rivière 236
Larrey, Dominique 345
Las Casas, Bartolomé de 174
Lasègue, Charles 409
Lauterbur 497
Laveran, Alphonse 377, 449
Lavoisier, Antoine-Laurent de 301,
    386, 390, 394
Le Boursier du Coudray, A. 323

Leeuwenhoek, Antonie van 270,
    271, 369, 370, 453
Legrain, Marcel 407
Leibniz, Gottfried 263
Lejeune, Jérôme 486
Lemaire, Jules 396, 397
Leoniceno, Nicolo 244, 246, 248
Lépine, Raphaël 469, 517
Leriche, René 393
Levine 469
Liébeault, Ambroise 524
Liebig, Justus von 387, 388, 410
Linacre, Thomas 244
Lind, James 316
Linnaeus, Carl 296, 297, 313
Lisfranc, Jacques 345
Lister, Joseph 397, 399
Littré, Émile 292, 380
Locke, John 263
Löffler, Friedrich 376
Lombroso, Cesare 407
Louis, Pierre-Charles 258, 340,
    342, 381
Lowe, Peter 242
Lower, Richard 266, 272, 273, 301
Lucas-Championnière, Just 397
Ludwig, Carl 391
Lull, Raymond 161

Machaon 64, 69
McCarty 486
MacLeod, W.H. 486
Magendie, François 348, 349, 350
Magnan, Valentin 407
Maimonides 118, 136
Malgaigne, Joseph 345
Malpighi, Marcello 270, 273
Manson, Sir Patrick 377
Marat, Jean-Paul 305
Marbod of Rennes 162
Marey, Jules 391
Marie, Pierre 403
Marjolin, Jean 347
Mauriceau, François 273
Mendel, Johann Gregor 482
Mesmer, Franz Anton 305
Mésué, Jean 121,126
Metchnikoff, Elie 429
Mondeville, Henri de 167, 168, 240
Mondino di Luzzi 229
Monro, Alexander 313
Moreau de Tours, Jacques 407
Morel, Augustin 405

Morgagni, Giovanni Battista 298,
    306, 379
Morgan, Thomas Hunt 482
Morton, William 393
Müller, Johannes 379
Murphy, John 447
Murray, Sir John 473, 533

Nativelle, Claude 386
Neisser, Albert 411
Nélaton, Auguste 345
Newton, Isaac 263
Nicholas of Alexandria 108
Nicolle, Charles 449
Nightingale, Florence 412, 415

Odon de Meung 139
Ombredanne, Louis 396
Orfila, Matteo 408, 410
Oribasius 100, 101, 108, 126
Osler, William 400

Panacea 64, 73
Papanicolaou, G.N. 520
Paracelsus 246, 248, 250, 256, 258,
    282, 285, 314
Paré, Ambroise 135, 240, 241, 242
Parent-Duchatelet, Armand 361
Parrot, Jules 409
Pasteur, Louis 113, 369, 370, 371,
    372, 373, 375, 376, 378, 381,
    397, 399, 426, 429, 440, 447,
    453, 490
Patin, Guy 266
Paul of Aegina 102, 108, 126, 135, 166
Pavlov, Ivan 391, 393
Péan, Jules 399
Pecquet, Jean 269
Pelletier, Pierre Joseph 348, 386
Philinos of Cos 83
Pico della Mirandola 244
Pien Ts'io 215
Pincus, Goodwin Gregory 479
Pinel, Philippe 258, 297, 337, 338,
    340, 354, 405
Pirogoff, Nicolai 399
Pirquet, Clemens von 432
Platearius, Jean 142, 162
Plato 80, 145
Platter, Felix 253, 258
Pliny the Elder 102

Podalire 64, 69
Poirier, Paul 409
Poiseuille, Jean-Louis 391
Portal, Antoine 364
Potain, Pierre 391, 436
Pott, Percivall 313
Pouchet, Félix-Archimède 370
Power, Henry 267
Pravaz, Charles 387
Praxagoras of Cos 80
Priestley, Joseph 301, 386, 394
Primerose, Jacques 266
Psellus, Michael 102
Pythagoras 66, 125

Quesnay, François 323
Quételet, Adolphe 361

Raban Maur 139
Rabelais, François 253
Ramazzini, Bernardino 313
Ranke, Karl 423
Rayer, Pierre 375
Réaumur, René de 301
Récamier, Joseph 345
Recklinghausen, Friedrich von 385
Renaudot, Théophraste 285
Reverdin, Jacques 399
Rhazes 126, 130, 148, 192, 234
Richet, Charles 432
Ricord, Philippe 411
Riolan, Jean 266
Robin, Charles 380
Roger of Parma 142
Rokitansky, Karl 343
Röntgen, Wilhelm 421, 425, 498, 502
Ross 377
Rosso 236
Rostan, Louis Léon 125
Roux, Émile 372, 378
Rouyer 370
Rufus of Ephesus 88, 126
Rush, Benjamin 405

Sabin, Albert 517
Sabouraud, Raymond 410
Sahagun, Bernardino de 174

Salk, Jonas Edward 469
Santorio Santorio 251, 272
Schaudinn, Fritz 411
Schlegel, Paul 266
Schoenlein, Lucas 343
Selye, Hans 475, 479
Sénac, Jean-Baptiste 314
Séphradi 120
Serapion of Alexandria 83
Servetus, Michael 130, 233, 251, 265, 453
Seth, Simeon 102
Shumway, Norman Edward 533
Simpson, James 396
Sims, Jack Marion 347, 399
Skoda, Josef 343
Socrates 190
Sommelweis, Ignaz 397
Soranus of Ephesus 86, 87, 270
Soulié de Morant 212
Spallanzani, Lazzaro 298, 301, 303, 349, 379, 391
Spieghel, Adriaan van den 231
Stahl, Georg 292, 313
Sténon, Nicolas (Niels Steensen) 266, 271, 286
Stoll 343
Susruta 125,193
Sydenham, Thomas 274, 275, 285, 313
Sylvius (Franciscus de la Boë) 266, 275
Sylvius (Jacques Dubois) 230, 233, 234, 236
Syme, James 347

Tagliacozzi, Gaspare 242
Talbor, Robert 276
Tardieu, Ambroise 410
Tarnier, Stéphane 409
Tchang Tchong King 215
Tenon, Jacques 322, 331
Terrier, Felix 399
Terrillon, Octave 399
Thales of Miletus 66
Themison of Laodicea 86
Thessalus of Ephesus 85
Thomas Aquinas 148
Tissot, André 324
Tréfouël, Thérèse and Jacques 449, 450
Treviranus 370

Troisier, Charles 409
Tronchin, Théodore 313, 315
Trotter, Thomas 405
Trotula 142
Trousseau, Armand 258, 403
Tuê-Trinh 220
Tudela, Benjamin of 117
Tuffier, Théodore 409
Turpin, Raymond 486

Unna, Paul 410

Valsalva, Antonio 306
Van Helmont, Jean-Baptista 285
Van Slyke, Donald 441
Van Swieten, Gerhardt 313, 343
Varolio, Constanzo 231
Velpeau, Alfred 393
Vesalius, Andreas 230, 232, 234, 235, 237, 251, 258
Vicq d'Azyr, Félix 323
Vieussens, Raymond 266, 273
Villemin, Jean Antoine 375, 376
Villermé, Louis-René 361
Virchow, Rudolf 379, 380, 381, 382, 385, 461
Volhard, Franz 388
Volta, Alessandro 303, 343

Waksman, Selman 513
Waldeyer, Wilhelm von 482
Wale, Jan de 266
Wang Ts'ing Sen 216
Watson, Jim 486
Weber, Eduard-Friedrich 351
Wells, Horace 394
Wepfer 273
Widal, Fernand 388, 429, 441, 474
Willis, Thomas 276
Winslow, Jacques Bénigne 305, 310, 311
Withering, William 313, 386
Wöhler, Friedrich 387
Wolff, Caspar Friedrich 303
Würtz, Felix 242

Zeno of Elea 66

BIBLIOGRAPHY

◆

◆ Annales de Bretagne et des pays de l'Ouest, *La médicalisation en France du XVIIIe au début du XXe siècle*, Vol. 86, No. 3, France 1979.

◆ *Annales E.S.C.*, "Médecins, médecine et société", France, 1977.

◆ M. Bariety, Ch. Coury, *Histoire de la médecine*, Fayard, Paris, 1963.

◆ G. Baujouan, *Médecine humaine et vétérinaire à la fin du Moyen Age*, Droz, Geneva, 1966.

◆ Y. M. Bercé, *Le chaudron et la lancette. Croyance populaire et médecine préventive*, Presses de la Renaissance, Paris, 1984.

◆ J. N. Biraben, *Histoire de la peste*, 2 volumes, Mouton, France, 1976.

◆ A. Castigliani, *History of Medicine* (translated by E. B. Krumbhaar), 2nd edn, A. A. Knopf, New York, 1947.

◆ A. Corbin, *Le miasme et la jonquille: l'odorat et l'imaginaire social aux XVIIIe et XIXe siècles*, Aubier-Montaigne, Paris, 1986.

◆ Ch. Daremberg, *Histoire des sciences médicales*, Ballècre & fils, France, 1870.

◆ J. P. Desaive, J. P. Goubert, E. le Roy Ladurie, etc., *Médecins, climat et épidémies à la fin du XVIIIe siècle*, Mouton, France, 1972 (in the archives of the Royal Society of Medicine, eighteenth century).

◆ J. Dufy, *Epidemics in colonial America*, Louisiana State University Press, Baton Rouge, 1959.

◆ J. Dufy, *The healers. The rise of the medical establishment.* McGraw Hill, New York, 1976.

◆ F. Fay-Sallois, *Les nourrices à Paris au XIXe siècle*, Payot, Paris, 1980.

◆ M. Foucault, *The birth of the clinic* (translated from French by A. M. Sheridan Smith), Tavistock, London, 1963.

◆ R. French & A. Wear (eds), *British medicine in an age of reform*, Routledge, London, 1991.

◆ F. H. Garrison, *An introduction to the history of medicine, with medical chronology, suggestions for study and bibliographical data.* Saunders, Philadelphia, 1913. Reprinted 1960.

◆ J. P. Goubert, *Malades et médecins en Bretagne 1770-1790*, Klincksieck, 1974; *La conquête de l'eau*, Paris, 1986.

◆ D. Guthrie, *A history of medicine*, Thomas Nelson & Sons, London, 1958.

◆ B. Inglis, *A history of medicine*, Weidenfeld & Nicolson, London, 1965.

◆ J. Jelis, *L'arbre et le fruit: la naissance dans l'Occident moderne*, Fayard, 1984. *La sage-femme et le médecin. Une nouvelle conception de la vie.* Fayard, Paris, 1988.

◆ J. Jelis, M. Laget, M. P. Morel, *Entrer dans la vie*, Gallimard, Archives, Paris, 1978.

◆ L. S. King, *A history of medicine: selected readings.* Penguin, Harmondsworth, 1971.

◆ R, Klibansky, E. Panofsky, F. Saxl, *Saturne et la mélancolie*, Gallimard, Paris, 1989.

◆ Y. Knibiehler, C. Fouquet, *Histoire des mères, du Moyen Age à nos jours*, Montalban, France, 1980.

◆ M. Laget, *Naissances. L'accouchement avant l'âge de la clinique*, Seuil, Paris, 1982.

◆ F. Lebrun, *Se soigner autrefois: médecins, saints et sorciers aux XVIIe et XVIIIe siècles*, Temps Actuel, France, 1983.

◆ J. Léonard, *Les officiers de santé de la Marine française de 1814 à 1835*, Klincksieck, 1973; *Les médecins de l'Ouest au XIXe siècle*, H. Champion, 1976; *La vie quotidienne des médecins de province au XIXe siècle*, Hachette, 1977; *La France médicale au XIXe siècle*, Gallimard, Archives, 1978; *La médecine entre les pouvoirs et les savoirs*, Aubier-Montaigne, 1982; *Archives du corps, La santé au XIXe siècle*, Ouest-France, Rennes, 1986.

♦ F. Loux, *Le jeune enfant et son corps dans la médecine traditionnelle*, Flammarion, Paris, 1978; *Tradition et soins d'aujourd'hui*, Daler-Éditions, France, 1983.

♦ L. Loux, Ph. Richard, *Sagesse du corps. La santé et la maladie dans les proverbes français.* Paris, 1978.

♦ L. Loux, *Pratiques et savoirs populaires. Le corps dans la société traditionnelle,* Berger-Levrault, France, 1979.

♦ R. H. Major, *A history of medicine*, 2 volumes, Blackwell, Oxford, 1954.

♦ R. E. & M. P. McGraw, *Encyclopedia of medical history*, Macmillan, London, 1985.

♦ J. P. Peter, *Les mots et les choses de la maladie*, Revue historique, July 1971; *Le corps du délit*, Nouvelle Revue de Psychologie, No. 3, 1971; *Le grand rêve de l'ordre médical en 1770*, Autrement, 1976, No. 4; *Entre femmes et médecins*, Ethnologie française, 1976, Vol. 6, 3/4; *Quiconque n'est pas docteur n'est-il qu'un charlatan?*, Autrement, 1978; *Le désordre contenu: attitudes face à l'épidémie au siècle des lumières (Poitou 1784–1785)*, Ethnologie française, Oct/Dec. 1987, Vol. 17, No. 4; *Silence et cris. La médecine devant la douleur*, Le Genre Humain, No. 18, 1982; *Linges de souffrances, texture de chair. Problèmes et stratégies du pansement*, Ethnologie française, 1989, No. 1.

♦ M. C. Pouchelle, *Corps et chirurgie à l'apogée du Moyen Age*, Flammarion, Paris, 1983.

♦ M. Ramsey, *Professional and popular medicine in France (1770-1830), The social world of medical practice*, Cambridge, 1988.

♦ P. Rhodes, *An outline history of medicine*, Butterworth, London, 1985.

♦ C. Rosenberg, *Healing and history. Essays for George Rosen.* Science History Publications, New York, 1979.

♦ Cl. Salomon-Bayet, *L'institution de la science et l'expérience du vivant. Méthode et expérience à l'académie royale des sciences, 1666–1793*, Flammarion, Paris, 1970.

♦ R. Shryock, *Medicine in America. Historical essays.* Johns Hopkins University Press, Baltimore, 1966.

♦ H. E. Sigerist, *A history of medicine*, 2 volumes. Oxford University Press, New York, 1987. Reprint of 1951 edition.

♦ C. Singer & E. A. Underwood, *A short history of medicine*, 2nd edn, Oxford University Press, 1962.

♦ J. C. Sournia, J. Poulet, A. Martiny, *Histoire générale de la médecine, de la pharmacie, de l'art dentaire et de l'art vétérinaire*, 8 volumes, ESPF, France, 1976.

♦ G. Thuillier, *Pour une histoire du quotidien en Nivernais au XIXe siècle,* Paris, 1977.

♦ G. Vigarello, *Le propre et le sale, l'hygiène du corps depuis le Moyen Age*, Seuil, Paris, 1985.

♦ A. Wear, R. K. French & I. M. Louie (eds), *The medical renaissance of the sixteenth century*, Cambridge University Press, Cambridge, 1985.

LIST OF ILLUSTRATIONS

◆

The line vignettes on pages 15, 23, 61, 97, 173, 225, 263, 291, 311, 369, 421 and 461 are ornamental capitals taken from *Der Artzneispiegel* by Dryander. Photo © Library of the Old Faculty of Medicine, Paris.

p. 6: Georges Chicotot. *Le tubage*. Oil on canvas. Public Works Museum, Paris, France. Photo © J.L. Charmet.

Chapter I

p. 13: Detail of person. Cave painting from Séfar's shelter (Tassili-n-Ajer, Algeria). Neolithic period (6000–5000 BC) Photo © F. de Kéroualin. DR.

p. 14: Isidor Engel. Burial site at Hallstatt. Water-colour, 1878. Photo © Erich Lessing – Magnum.

p. 16: Vertebra and flint arrowhead. End of Neolithic period. Museum of National Antiquities. St Germain en Laye, France. Photo © J.M. Labat.

p. 16: Pollen from a type of lavender. Neolithic period. Prehistory Laboratory of the Museum of Mankind coll., Paris, France. Photo © Henry de Lumley.

p. 17: Mutilated hand print. Gargas cave, Pyrenees. Palaeolithic period. Cave art. Photo © Jean Vertut.

p. 17: Child's femur and humerus. Excavation by C. Masset at La Chaussée-Tirancourt, Somme, France. Photo © J.M. Labat.

p. 18: Trepanned skull. Neolithic period. Burial cave in the Petit-Morin valley, Seine et Marne. Museum of National Antiquities, St Germain en Laye, France. Photo © J.M. Labat.

p. 18: Section of left humerus. Neolithic communal grave. Excavation by C. Masset at La Chaussée-Tirancourt, Somme, France. Photo © Enlargement by F. Guillon.

p. 19: Paul Jamin. *The flight from the mammoth*. Decorative panel. Museum of National Antiquities, St Germain en Laye, France. Photo © RMN, Paris.

p. 19: Neolithic statuette. Anatolia. 6000 BC. Baked clay. Photo © Werner Forman Archive.

Chapter II

p. 21: Indian healer. Yellowstone river area. Engraving taken from *North-American Indians*, G. Catlin, 1851. Photo © J.L. Charmet.

p. 22: Statuette with magic uses originating from the Congo.

Sculpture in wood and mixed techniques. Private coll., Paris, France. Photo © J.M. Labat.

p. 24: Eskimo shaman. Alaska. Sculpture in wood. Danish National Museum, Copenhagen, Denmark. Photo © Werner Forman Archive.

p. 25: Traditional Ethiopian "Nakaté" cure. Museum of Mankind coll., Paris, France. Photo © Serge Tornay.

p. 25: Kamtchatkan shaman. Eastern Siberia. Engraving with water-colour, late eighteenth century. Decorative Arts Library, Paris, France. Photo © J.L. Charmet.

p. 25: "Doctor-cum-barber" shop. Photo © Charles Lénars.

p. 26: Fertility goddess and Ashanti doll. Ivory Coast. Photo © Hoa Qui.

p. 26: Gaston Vuillier. Cripples at the Saint-Éloi spring. Drawing from *Le culte des fontaines en Limousin*, in *Journal des Voyages 1901*. Photo © LL. de Selva – Tapabor.

p. 27: African shaman's drum. Photo © Museum of Mankind coll., Paris, France.

p. 27: Phytotherapy. Plants are changed into pharmaceutical products. Gelcom factory. Photo © A. Brucelle – Sygma.

p. 27: Fetishist grigris. Bobo Dioulasso market. Photo © Charles Lénars.

p. 28: David Ryckaert III, *The witch doctor*, 1638. Oil on wood. Fine Arts Museum, Valenciennes, France. Photo © Erich Lessing – Magnum.

p. 29: Bezoar on a gold tripod, encrusted with emeralds. Spanish artefact from the sixteenth century. History of Art Museum, Vienna, Austria. Photo © Erich Lessing – Magnum.

p. 29: "Anatomical plate" representing the lungs. Sculpture in wood from the source of the Seine. Gallo-Roman art. Photo © Archaeological Museum, Dijon, France.

p. 29: Silver plaque in relief, representing the lungs, nineteenth-century votive offering. Private coll., Paris, France. Photo © J.L. Charmet.

Chapter III

p. 31: Circumcision scene. Bas-relief from the mastaba of Ankhmahor at Saqqarah. Egypt, 6th dynasty. Photo © G. Dagli Orti.

p. 32: Babylonian bas-relief, 1200 BC. Detail from a stela in black stone found at Susa. Louvre Museum, Paris, France. Photo © Erich Lessing – Magnum.

p. 33: Statuette representing the demon Pazuzu. Bronze and copper. Assyrian art: *c.* 1500 BC. Louvre Museum, Paris, France. Photo © RMN, Paris.

p. 34: Seals with phallic subjects. Mesopotamia. 3500 BC. Photo © Werner Forman Archive.

p. 35: Clay tablet, taken from Book I of an Assyrian medical treatise. Neo-Assyrian period, *c.* 900 BC. Louvre Museum, Paris, France.

p. 36: Representation of a liver in clay. 1900 BC. Found at Hazor. Idam coll. on view in Jerusalem, Israel. Photo © Erich Lessing – Magnum.

p. 37: Models of animal livers in clay, found at Mari. Neo-Sumerian period about 1900 BC. Louvre Museum, Paris, France. Photo © RMN, Paris.

p. 38: Stela of Hammurabi. Babylonian art, *c.* 1750 BC. Louvre Museum, Paris, France. Photo © Charles Lénars.

p. 39: Cast in clay of the cylinder seal of doctor Makkur-Marduk. The original is in lapis lazuli. Mesopotamia. Neo-Babylonian period. Sixth century BC. Louvre Museum, Paris, France. Photo © G. Dagli Orti.

p. 40: Parents feeding children. Bas-relief from the Palace of Assurbanipal. Nineveh, seventh century BC. Louvre Museum, Paris, France. Photo © Erich Lessing – Magnum.

p. 41: Libation beaker belonging to Gudea, showing the symbol which became the caduceus of the medical profession. Steatite. Sumerian art. Tello, *c.* twenty-second century BC. Louvre Museum, Paris, France. Photo © RMN, Paris.

p. 41: Bronze exorcism plaque. Assyria, about 750 BC. Louvre Museum, Paris, France. Photo © RMN, Paris.

p. 42: Fragment of the "Edwin Smith" surgical papyrus. Egypt, 1500 BC. British Museum, London, England. Photo © J.L. Charmet.

p. 43: David Roberts (1796-1864), *Main entrance of the temple at Luxor*. Water-colour. Photo © Edimédia.

p. 44: Horus. Bronze statue. Egyptian art about 800 BC. Louvre Museum, Paris, France. Photo © RMN, Paris.

p. 45: Hesyre. "Chief dentist", "head of the king's scribes, Great One of the ten of Upper Egypt". Sculpted wood. Saqqarah. Old Kingdom, 3rd dynasty, about 2700 BC. Egyptian Museum, Cairo, Egypt. Photo © Jürgen Liepe.

p. 45: Canopic jars of Anpuhotep. Limestone and painted wood. Saqqarah. Middle Kingdom, 12th dynasty, about 1900 BC. Egyptian Museum, Cairo, Egypt. Photo © Jürgen Liepe.

p. 46: Imhotep. Bronze statue. Egyptian art. 2600 BC. Louvre Museum, Paris, France. Photo © H. Josse.

p. 47: The king of Punt and his wife Ati. Detail from a group in painted and sculpted limestone in the temple of Hatshepsut at Deir el-Bahari. Egyptian Museum, Cairo, Egypt. Photo © Jürgen Liepe.

p. 48: Mummy of Ramses II. 19th dynasty, about 1250 BC. Egyptian Museum, Cairo, Egypt. Photo © Roger Viollet.

p. 48: Mummy of Sennedjem prepared by Anubis. Painting in the tomb of Sennedjem, 19th dynasty. Deir el-Medina, Thebes, Egypt. Photo © Suzanne Held.

p. 49: Guardians of the gardens of Amon. Painting in the tomb of Sennefer, 19th dynasty, *c.* 1250 BC. Deir el-Medina, Thebes, Egypt. Photo © Suzanne Held.

p. 49: Circumcision. Detail from a relief at Saqqarah, Egypt. 6th dynasty. Photo © G. Dagli Orti.

p. 50: Blind harpist. Detail from a banquet scene, tomb of Nakt, Thebes, Egypt. 18th dynasty. Photo © Werner Forman Archive.

p. 50: Treating a workman with an injured eye. Drawing from a painting in the tomb of Nakt. Thebes, Egypt. 18th dynasty, *c.* 1420 BC. Photo © DR.

p. 51: Sick man. Bronze sculpture. Egyptian art. New Kingdom. Louvre Museum, Paris, France. Photo © Erich Lessing – Magnum.

p. 52: The goddess Isis. Bronze sculpture. Egyptian art, late period. Vivenel Museum, Compiègne, France. Larousse coll.

p. 52: Magic amulet. Egyptian artefact, *c.* 400 BC. Photo © Werner Forman Archive.

p. 53: Pendant which used to contain an oracular decree. Jewel set in gold. Tenth century BC. Louvre Museum, Paris, France. Photo © RMN, Paris.

p. 54: Young man with an atrophied leg. Carved and painted stela. Egyptian art, 18th dynasty. 1580–1330 BC. Carlsberg coll., Museum of Sculpture, Copenhagen, Denmark. Photo © the Museum.

p. 55: Stela of Horus on the crocodiles. Small stela in diorite. Sixth to fourth century BC. Egyptian art, Louvre Museum, Paris, France. Photo © RMN, Paris.

p. 56: Goddess of fertility. The book of the dead of Userhetmos. Painting on papyrus. Ancient Egypt, 19th dynasty, *c.* 1320–1200 BC. Egyptian Museum, Cairo, Egypt. Photo © Werner Forman Archive.

Chapter IV

p. 59: Skeleton with pitchers. Mosaic at Pompeii, first century BC. National Museum, Naples, Italy. Photo © Artephot – Nimatallah.

p. 60: The wounded Aeneas. Fresco from Pompeii, Italy. Photo © G. Dagli Orti.

p. 61: Telephus being treated by Achilles. Detail from a bas-relief from Herculanum. National Museum, Naples, Italy. Photo © G. Dagli Orti.

p. 62: Albert Tournaire, *Projet de restauration du sanctuaire d'Apollon à Delphes*. 1894. Graphite and water-colour. National College of Fine Arts, Paris, France. Photo © National College of Fine Arts, Paris.

p. 63: Apollo, the lizard slayer. Sculpture by Praxiteles. Greek art, fifth century. Vatican Museum, Rome, Italy. Larousse coll.

p. 64: Asclepius treats Temison. Engraving taken from *Spiegel der Arzt (sic)*, 1532. Library of the Old Faculty of Medicine, Paris, France. Photo © Lib. OFMP.

p. 64: Machaon and Podalirius. Engraving taken from *Spiegel der Arzt (sic)*, 1532. Library of the Old Faculty of Medicine, Paris, France. Photo © Lib. OFMP.

p. 65: Asclepius and Hygeia. Intaglio. National Library, Paris, France. Photo © National Library, Paris.

p. 65: Asclepius treating a young patient. Bas-relief, classical period. Museum of Piraeus, Athens, Greece. Photo © Artephot – Nimatallah.

p. 66: Pythagoras discovers the consonances of the octave. Engraving taken from *Theorica musica*, 1480. Decorative Arts Library, Paris, France. Photo © J.L. Charmet.

p. 67: Asclepius and Hygeia feeding a serpent. Funerary bas-relief from Pergamum. National Museum of Archaeology, Istanbul, Turkey.

p. 68: Crater portraying the Niobids. Greek art. Louvre Museum, Paris, France. Photo © RMN, Paris.

p. 69: Hippocrates. Fourteenth-century miniature. National Library, Paris, France. Larousse coll.

p. 70: Paul of Aegina. Detail from the frontispiece of the works of Galen. 1530 engraving. Library of the Old Faculty of Medicine, Paris, France. Photo © J.L. Charmet.

p. 71: The plane tree at Cos. Eighteenth-century engraving. Library of the Old Faculty of Medicine, Paris, France. Photo © J.L. Charmet.

p. 72: Scene depicting the teaching of medicine. Fifteenth-century manuscript. Library of the Old Faculty of Medicine, Paris, France. Photo © J.L. Charmet.

p. 73: The Hippocratic oath. From a fifteenth-century Greek manuscript. National Library, Paris, France. Photo © J.L. Charmet.

p. 74: Hygeia tending cripples. Nineteenth-century engraving from a vase, fifth century BC. Decorative Arts Library, Paris, France. Photo © J.L. Charmet.

p. 75: Drunken old man. Greek painting. Attic bowl, fifth century BC. National Museum, Copenhagen, Denmark. Photo © A. Held – Artephot.

p. 76: Coins from Cyrene depicting silphium. Tetradrachm, late third century BC. Berlin, Germany. Photo © Hirmer Photographic Archive.

p. 77: Embarkation of silphium. Cyrenian bowl, mid-fifth century BC. Medals Room, National Library, Paris, France. Photo © J.L. Charmet.

p. 78: Temple at Epidaurus. Detail from the left side. Pencil and water-colour by Defrasse, 1891–1893. Higher National College of Fine Arts, Paris, France.

p. 79: Theatre of the asclepion, Pergamum, Turkey. Photo © Suzanne Held.

p. 79: Asclepion, bath of the fourth terrace, Cos, Greece. Photo © G. Dagli Orti.

p. 79: Acroter of the propylaeum of the asclepion at Pergamum, representing a statue of Victory. Turkey. Photo © Suzanne Held.

p. 80: Asclepius, a peasant and a philosopher. Mosaic, third century BC. Cos, Greece. Photo © G. Dagli Orti.

p. 81: Votive stela dedicated to Amphiaraus. Fourth century BC. Museum of Archaeology, Athens, Greece. Photo © Erich Lessing - Magnum.

p. 82: Reconstruction of the library at Alexandria. Engraving, 1880. Decorative Arts Library, Paris, France. Photo © J.L. Charmet.

p. 83: Erasistratus. Engraving taken from *Spiegel der Arzt (sic)*, 1532. Library of the Old Faculty of Medicine, Paris, France. Photo © Lib. OFMP.

p. 83: Scene of magic. Roman mosaic, third century BC. National Museum, Naples, Italy. Photo © Artephot – Nimatallah.

p. 84: Asclepius arriving in Rome in the guise of a serpent. Eighteenth-century engraving. National Library, Paris, France. Photo © J.L. Charmet.

p. 84: A visit to the doctor. Roman bas-relief, first century BC. Museum of Roman Civilization, Rome, Italy. Photo © G. Dagli Orti.

p. 85: Roman haruspex. Engraving by Grasset de Saint Sauveur, eighteenth century. National Library, Paris, France. Photo © J.L. Charmet.

p. 86: Medical box: Asclepius and Hygeia. Carved ivory. National Museum, Sion, Switzerland. Photo © A. Held – Artephot.

p. 87: The preparation of medicine. Sixteenth-century manuscript of *Natural history* by Pliny the Elder. Marciana Library, Venice, Italy. Photo © G. Dagli Orti.

p. 87: Care given to a wounded man. Sixteenth-century manuscript of *Natural history* by Pliny the Elder. Marciana Library, Venice, Italy. Photo © G. Dagli Orti.

p. 89: Plato teaching geometry to his disciples. Mosaic from Pompeii, Athens school. National Museum of Archaeology, Naples, Italy. Photo © Artephot – Nimatallah.

p. 90: Portrait of Galen. Detail from the frontispiece of *Spiegel der Arzt (sic)*, 1532. National Library, Paris, France. Photo © J.L. Charmet.

p. 91: Hippocrates and Galen. Sixteenth-century miniature. National Library, Paris, France. Photo © Larousse archives.

p. 92: Antique painting, found in the baths of Titus. Nineteenth-century engraving. National Library, Paris, France. Photo © National Library, Paris.

p. 92: *The thermae of Diocletian*. Oil on canvas by Giovanni P. Panini. Corsini Palace, Rome, Italy. Photo © Anderson – Giraudon.

Chapter V

p. 95: A sick person is given an infusion. Thirteenth-century illustration in *Tractatus de pestilentia,* Abenzohar. University Library, Prague, Czech Republic. Photo © G. Dagli Orti.

p. 96: Collecting acorns. Fifteenth-century Italian pharmacopoeia. Royal Library, Turin, Italy. Larousse coll.

p. 97: Alexander of Tralles. *Practicia*. Central Italy, mid twelfth century. National Library, Paris, France. Photo © National Library, Paris.

p. 98: Emperor Justinian I. Byzantine mosaic. Church of San Vitale, Ravenna, Italy. Photo © Artephot – Nimatallah.

p. 99: Siege of Constantinople, 1453. Mid fifteenth-century miniature. National Library, Paris, France. Photo © ERL – Sipa.

p. 100: Pheasant's eye, medicinal plant. Sixth-century Greek manuscript *De materia medica*, Dioscorides. National Library, Paris, France. Larousse coll.

p. 101: Medicinal plants. Eleventh-century Greek manuscript. National Library, Paris, France. Larousse coll.

p. 102: Alexander of Tralles with his book on the art of medicine. Latin manuscript from the Carolingian period. France, early ninth century. National Library, Paris, France. Photo © National Library, Paris.

p. 103: Jesus raising a dying man. Byzantine mosaic, fourteenth century. Monastery of Christ-in-Chora, Istanbul, Turkey. Photo © Erich Lessing – Magnum.

p. 104: Healing the blind. Twelfth-century Greek manuscript. National Library, Athens, Greece. Photo © Artephot – A. Held.

p. 104: Resurrection of Lazarus. Twelfth-century gospel. Earl of Leicester, Holkham Hall, England. Photo © Artephot – A. Held.

p. 105: Fernando del Rincon. Saint Cosmas and Saint Damian, replacing a gangrenous leg. Oil on wood. Prado Museum, Madrid, Spain. Photo © Artephot – Oronoz.

p. 106: A doctor and a pharmacist in Athens. Greek manuscript *De Compositione medicamentorum*, Nicolas Myrepsus, 1339. National Library, Paris, France. Photo © National Library, Paris.

p. 107: The frontispiece of *Book on the composition of plants and fruits*, Giohanne Cademosto. Fourteenth-century manuscript. National Library, Paris, France. Photo © National Library, Paris.

p. 108: Christ and the paralytic. Ivory pyx lid. Seventh-century Byzantine art. Cluny Museum, Paris, France. Photo © Erich Lessing – Magnum.

p. 109: Basil. Illustration from the *Pseudo apuleius*. National Library, Vienna, Austria. Larousse coll.

p. 109: Plants from Asia Minor and their medicinal properties. Illustration from Dioscorides' *De materia medica*. Seljuk manuscript, 1228. Topkapi Museum, Istanbul, Turkey. Photo © G. Dagli Orti.

p. 110: Tintoretto. *Suzannah bathing*. Oil on canvas, 1560. Art History Museum, Vienna, Austria. Photo © Erich Lessing – Magnum.

p. 111: Michael Pacher (1435-1498) *The circumcision of Christ*.

Oil painting. 1481. Panel of retable, church of Saint Wolfgang, Austria. Photo © Erich Lessing – Magnum.

p. 112: Treatise on optics and ophthalmology. Hebrew manuscript, 1181. National Library, Paris, France. Photo © National Library, Paris.

p. 113: Treatise on summary of the Talmud. Fifteenth-century Hebrew manuscript. National Library, Paris, France. Photo © J.L. Charmet.

p. 114: Sexual taboos in the Talmud. Woodcut from the Passover Haggadah. Published in Venice, 1609. Reproduced in a Haggadah printed in 1864, in the Judaeo-Arabic dialect of Tunis. Alliance Israelite Universelle, Paris, France. Photo © J.L. Charmet.

p. 115: Nicolay. The Jewish doctor. Drawing, 1568. History Department of the Navy, Vincennes, France. Photo © G. Dagli Orti.

p. 116: Two Jewish doctors from Constantinople examine urine. Water-colour, late sixteenth century. Private coll. Photo © J.L. Charmet.

p. 117: Maimonides, 1135-1204. Eighteenth-century print. National Library, Paris, France. Photo © J.L. Charmet.

p. 118: The three masters of Jewish medicine: Isaac, Constantine and Halvabbas. Print published in Lyons, 1515. Library of the Old Faculty of Medicine, Paris, France. Photo © J.L. Charmet.

p. 119: The body of a circumcized man, showing the arteries and veins as well the signs of the zodiac. Compilation of medical texts. National Library, Paris, France. Photo © National Library, Paris.

p. 120: Gold amulet. Seventeenth-century Jewish jewellery. Max Berger, Judaïca coll., Vienna, Austria. Photo © Erich Lessing – Magnum.

p. 121: Aphorisms by Maimonides. Fifteenth-century Hebrew manuscript. National Library, Paris, France. Photo © Artephot – ADPC.

p. 122: Arab pharmacy. From Dioscorides' *De materia medica*. Miniature. Topkapi Museum, Istanbul, Turkey. Photo © R. and S. Michaud – Rapho.

p. 123: Arab pharmacy. Thirteenth-century miniature, Baghdad. Metropolitan Museum, New York, USA. Photo © Werner Forman Archive.

p. 124: Explanation of the properties of plants. Seljuk manuscript. Topkapi Museum, Istanbul, Turkey. Photo © G. Dagli Orti.

p. 124: Two students present their thesis. Seljuk manuscript. Topkapi Museum, Istanbul, Turkey. Photo © G. Dagli Orti.

p. 125: Development of the foetus. Fourteenth-century Latin manuscript, *Tractabus de medica*, Adbubetri Rhazes. Marciana Library, Venice, Italy. Photo © G. Dagli Orti.

p. 126: Arab doctors. Thirteenth-century Arabic manuscript. National Library, Paris, France. Photo © J.L. Charmet.

p. 127: Drawing illustrating the translation of a fifteenth-century manuscript, *De peste,* Rhazes. National Library, Paris, France. Photo © National Library, Paris.

p. 129: Diseases of the eye. Thirteenth-century Arabic manuscript, treatise by Al-Mutadibih. National Library, Cairo, Egypt. Photo © G. Dagli Orti.

p. 129: Avicenna (990-1037). *Canon.* National Museum, Damascus, Syria. Photo © G. Dagli Orti.

p. 129: A teacher and his pupils. Seventeenth-century Persian manuscript. Museum of Islam, Cairo, Egypt. Photo © R. and S. Michaud – Rapho.

p. 129: Man in the cosmos. Sixteenth-century Turkish manuscript. Museum of Turkish and Islamic Arts, Istanbul, Turkey. Photo © R. and S. Michaud – Rapho.

p. 130: An animal sacrifice. Fifteenth-century Persian miniature. Topkapi Museum, Istanbul, Turkey. Photo © R. and S. Michaud – Rapho.

p. 131: Turkish pharmacopoeia, fourteenth century. Malek Library, Teheran, Iran. Photo © R. and S. Michaud – Rapho.

p. 131: Doctor taking the pulse of a young girl. National Library, Cairo, Egypt. Photo © R. and S. Michaud – Rapho.

p. 132: Consultation. *The book of Calila el Dimna,* Bidpaï, fourteenth century. National Library, Cairo, Egypt. Photo © G. Dagli Orti.

p. 133: Abulcasis' surgery. Instruments. Fourteenth-century manuscript. Atger Museum, Montpellier, France. Photo © G. Dagli Orti.

p. 134: Abulcasis' surgery. Fourteenth-century manuscript. Atger Museum, Montpellier, France. Photo © G. Dagli Orti.

p. 135: Abulcasis' surgical instruments. Fourteenth-century manuscript. Atger Museum, Montpellier, France. Photo © G. Dagli Orti.

p. 136: Manipulation of a patient by a surgeon. Turkish manuscript, 1465. Fatih Museum, Istanbul, Turkey. Photo © G. Dagli Orti.

p. 137: Treatment of genital problems. Manuscript by Sharaf-ed-Din. National Library, Paris, France. Photo © R. and S. Michaud – Rapho.

p. 139: Isidore of Seville. Ninth-century manuscript. Chapter Library, Vercelli, Italy. Photo © G. Dagli Orti.

p. 140: View of Salerno, famous for its medical school. Illustration from Avicenna's work: *Canon,* fourteenth to fifteenth century. Municipal Library, Bologna, Italy. Photo © J.L. Charmet.

pp. 141-142: *Regimen sanitatis, c.* 1350. National Library, Naples, Italy. Photo © J.L. Charmet.

p. 142: Trotula or Trocta, from *Regulae Medicinales,* fourteenth century. Laurenziana Library, Florence, Italy. Photo © J.L. Charmet.

p. 143: Doctor giving remedies. French version of a Salernian treatise, thirteenth century. British Museum, London, England. Photo © Edimédia.

p. 145: Blood-letting. *Tractarus de pestilentia,* fifteenth century. University Library, Prague, Czech Republic. Photo © G. Dagli Orti.

p. 146: Harvesting of medicinal plants. Translation by Gerard of Cremona of the treatise by Galen. Italy, late thirteenth century. Municipal Library, Laon, France. Photo © G. Dagli Orti.

p. 147: Anatomical plate from *De arte phisicali et de chirurgia,* John Ardane of Newark. Royal Library, Stockholm, Sweden. Photo © G. Dagli Orti.

p. 148: A lesson at the University. *Novela super texto,* Jean André. Municipal Library, Cambrai, France. Larousse coll.

p. 149: Scene of hospital life c. 1400. Santa Maria della Scala Hospital. Pinacoteca, Siena, Italy. Photo © G. Dagli Orti.

p. 150: Albert the Great. Print. National Library, Paris, France. Photo © National Library, Paris.

p. 151: A crippled beggar. Woodcarving from a pew in the church of Saint Lucien in Beauvais, 1490. Cluny Museum, Paris, France. Photo © Roger Viollet.

p. 152: Franciscan monks caring for lepers. Sixteenth-century illuminated manuscript. Augustea Library, Perugia, Italy. Photo © G. Dagli Orti.

p. 153: Pilgrims. Capital above an arch in the cloisters of Tudela, Spain. Photo © Zodiaque.

p. 153: *Pilgrims in a sanctuary.* Master of Saint Sebastian. Barberini Palace, Rome, Italy. Photo © Artephot – Nimatallah.

p. 154: Hospital ward. 1490. Photo © ADPC – Artephot.

p. 155: The plagues descend on the town. *Le miroir historial,* Vincent de Beauvais. Condé Museum, Chantilly, France. Larousse coll.

p. 156: Lepers in *Des propriétés des choses*, Barthelemy the Englishman. National Library, Paris, France. Photo © National Library, Paris.

p. 157: "Saint Anthony's fire". Fifteenth-century woodcut. National Library, Paris, France. Photo © National Library, Paris.

p. 158: Page of a herbal from Plaetarius' *Circa instans*. Northern Italy, fifteenth century. National Library, Paris, France. Photo © National Library, Paris.

p. 158: Baths for the sick in *Des propriétés des choses*, Bathelemy the Englishman. National Library, Paris, France. Photo © National Library, Paris.

p. 159: Mediaeval therapy. In *Tractatus de pestilentia,* Abenzohar, thirteenth century. University Library, Prague, Czech Republic. Photo © G. Dagli Orti.

p. 160: *De balneis duteolaneis*. Illustration of the poem by Peter of Eboli. Italy. Fourteenth century. National Library, Paris, France. Photo © National Library, Paris.

p. 161: Consultation and discussion with a patient. Miniature illustrating Galen's work, fourteenth century. Municipal Library, Rheims, France. Photo © G. Dagli Orti.

p. 162: Illustration of mandrake. *De medicaminbus herbarum liber*. National Library, Paris, France. Photo © National Library, Paris.

p. 162: Medicinal plant: wild lettuce. Thirteenth-century Latin manuscript. National Library, Vienna, Austria. Larousse coll.

p. 163: Vision of Saint Hildegarde. Man subject to universal forces. Latin codex. State Library, Lucca, Italy. Larousse coll.

p. 164: Public dissection, Montpellier. *Chirurgia*, Guy de Chauliac, 1363. Atger Museum, Montpellier, France. Photo © G. Dagli Orti

p. 165: Surgical operations. Six fourteenth-century miniatures, in *Thiringia magistri rogerii*. Atger Museum, Montpellier, France. Photo © G. Dagli Orti.

p. 166: Manuscript by Guy de Pavie. Condé Museum, Chantilly, France. Photo © G. Dagli Orti.

p. 167: Operation on the skull. Illustrations taken from a French manuscript. British Library, London, England. Photo © R. and S. Michaud.

p. 167: Operation on the head by Saint Luke, the patron saint of doctors. Photo © Giraudon.

p. 168: Hieronymus Bosch, *Excision of the stone of madness*. Prado Museum, Madrid, Spain. Photo © G. Dagli Orti.

Chapter VI

p. 171: Drawing taken from a Chinese medical manuscript. Description of a meridian. National Library, Paris, France. Photo © National Library, Paris.

p. 172: The various sakras of the human body. Indian painting. Rajasthan, nineteenth century. Private coll., Paris, France. Photo © J.M. Labat.

p. 173: Statue made of volcanic rock. Person with his hair cut to resemble an hallucinogenic mushroom. Photographic library of the Museum of Mankind, Paris, France. Photo © Museum of Mankind, Paris, France.

p. 174: Scene of traditional treatment. Illustrated Peruvian codex, fine sixteenth-century drawing. *Nueva Cronica y buen gobierno*, Felipe Guaman Poma de Ayala. Private coll., Paris, France. Photo © J.L. Charmet.

p. 175: Ritual self-sacrifice. Sculpted stone, Huastec art. National Anthropological Museum, Mexico. Photo © C. Lenars.

p. 176: Ritual piercing of the nose. Aztec art. *Codex Nuttall*. Facsimile edition. National Library, Paris, France. Photo © National Library, Paris.

p. 177: Human sacrifices of the Aztecs. *Codex Tudela*, 1553. Facsimile edition. Museum of America, Madrid, Spain. Photo © G. Dagli Orti.

p. 178: Aztec calendar, Sun stone. Stone bas-relief. National Anthropological Museum, Mexico. Photo © C. Lenars.

p. 179: Handle of Tumi sacrificial knife. Private coll., Paris, France. Photo © J.L. Charmet.

p. 179: Scene of childbirth. *Codex Borbonicus*, early sixteenth century. Bourbon Palace Library, Paris, France. Photo © C. Lenars.

p. 179: Tlaloc, god of rain and fertility. *Codex Borbonicus*. Bourbon Palace Library, Paris, France. Photo © C. Lenars.

p. 180: Fumigation. *Indorum floridam*, Théodore de Bry, Frankfurt, 1591. Private coll. Photo © J.L. Charmet.

p. 180: Fumigation among the North-American Indians. Print, Catlin, nineteenth century. Private coll., Paris, France. Photo © J.L. Charmet.

p. 181: Ectromelia, corneal leucoma and mutilation of the skull. D. Rivera coll., Mexico. Photo © Museum of Mankind, Paris, France.

p. 181: Young man with tattoos, filed teeth, earlobes stretched. Huastec art. Photo © C. Lenars.

p. 181: Aztec human sacrifice as depicted by Diego Duran. *Historia de las Indias*. Manuscript, 1579. National Library, Madrid, Spain. Photo © G. Dagli Orti.

p. 182: Doctor priest in California. Print by Labrousse, in *L'encyclopédie des voyages*, J. Grasset de Saint Sauveur. Eighteenth century. Photo © LL. de Selva – Tapabor.

p. 183: Preparation and use of gayac. Sixteenth-century print. Bouvet coll., National Order of Pharmacists, Paris, France. Photo © J.L. Charmet.

p. 184: Diego Rivera (1886–1957). Scenes of dental care and tattooed woman among the Aztecs. Decoration in the Document Room of the National Agricultural School of Chapingo (1926–1927). Mexico. Photo © C. Lenars.

p. 185: Mummified Inca child. Ethnographic Museum, Santiago, Chile. Photo © C. Lenars.

p. 185: Statuette of an Aztec high priest clothed in the skin of a prisoner. Ethnographic Museum, Basle, Switzerland. Photo © C. Lenars.

p. 185: Gayac. Print in the *Blackwell Herbarium*. Nuremberg, 1757. Decorative Arts Library, Paris, France. Photo © J.L. Charmet.

p. 186: Inca priest treating a sick person. Peruvian terracotta. State Museum, Berlin-Dahlem, Germany. Photo © Werner Forman Archive.

p. 187: Funeral mask of Inca origin. Gold and copper. Fine Arts Museum, Dallas, USA. Photo © Werner Forman Archive.

p. 187: Aztec goddess of fertility. British Museum, London, England. Photo © Werner Forman Archive.

p. 188: The god Hanuman in Tantric form. Eighteenth century. Slim Gallery coll., Nepal. Photo © J.L. Charmet.

p. 189: Consultation and preparation of drugs in a courtyard following the precepts of Ayurvedic medicine, Udaipur, India. Eighteenth century. Udaipur Museum. Photo © J.L. Nou.

p. 189: Drug preparation in Rajasthan, India. Udaipur Museum, India. Photo © R. and S. Michaud.

p. 190: Vendor of remedies against scorpion stings. Indian manuscript, India, 1831. National Library, Paris, France. Photo © J.L. Charmet.

p. 191: Detail from medical scroll used for teaching purposes. Reproduction and birth. Tibetan miniature.

Philip Goldman coll., London, England. Photo © Werner Forman Archive.

p. 191: Feminine hygiene in India in the Mogul period. Nineteenth-century painting. Private coll. Photo © J.L. Charmet.

p. 191: Women bathing. Kangra, eighteenth century. National Museum, New Delhi, India. Photo © J.L. Nou

p. 192: A Brahman, also a doctor, places Tilak's mark on the brow of his patient. Pahari School, late eighteenth century. Shandrigarh Museum, India. Photo © J.L. Nou

p. 193: Vishnu as a surgeon. India, eighteenth-century illuminated text. National Library, Paris, France. Photo © J.L. Charmet.

p. 193: A painting of the yogi "model man" from the manuscript of Hatha-Yoga, eighteenth century. British Library, London, England. Photo © R. and S. Michaud.

p. 194: Medicine and rites according to the *Kama Sutra*. Jaipur, India. Kumar Sangram Singh coll. Photo © R. and S. Michaud.

p. 195: The goddess Mariadale invoked against smallpox. Eighteenth-century miniature. Private coll., Paris, France. Photo © J.L. Charmet.

p. 196: Opium smokers. Eighteenth-century Indian miniature. Udaipur Museum, India. Photo © J.L. Nou.

p. 196: Ayurvedic medicine, India. Preparation of drugs. Photo © R. and S. Michaud.

p. 197: Yogi. Eighteenth-century Indian painting. School of Mewar. Private coll., Udaipur, India. Photo © R. and S. Michaud.

p. 197: Tantric yogi today. Photo © R. and S. Michaud.

p. 198: Preparation of ambrosia. Pahari School, early nineteenth century. Bharat Kala Bhavan Museum, Benares, India. Photo © J.L. Nou.

p. 199: Healing divinity in Benares. Eighteenth-century miniature. National Library, Paris, France. Photo © J.L. Charmet.

p. 200: Hua T'o treats the wound of the hero Kuan Kung, Japanese print. Wellcome Institute, London, England. Photo © Wellcome Institute, London.

p. 201: Chinese medical manuscript. National Library, Paris, France. Photo © National Library, Paris.

p. 201: *Ibid.*

p. 202: Consultation of a mandarin doctor. Water-colour on rice paper. China, nineteenth century. Wellcome Institute, London, England. Photo © Wellcome Institute, London.

p. 203: Cosmological representation of the material world, Yin and Yang. Wellcome Institute, London, England. Photo © Wellcome Institute, London.

p. 204: Chinese medical manuscript, eighteenth century. National Library, Paris, France. Photo © National Library, Paris.

p. 205: An acupuncture meridian. Chinese medical manuscript, eighteenth century. National Library, Paris, France. Photo © National Library, Paris.

p. 206: A crippled Chinese man. Wash. Wellcome Institute, London, England. Photo © Wellcome Institute, London.

p. 207: Ivory medical statuettes. Private coll., Paris, France. Photo © G. Dagli Orti.

p. 208: A Chinese doctor prepares a death certificate. Wellcome Institute, London, England. Photo © Wellcome Institute, London.

p. 209: Emperor Taitsong, studying a book on medicine, tells the torturer how to spare certain organs. Water-colour, eighteenth century. Taken from the *Book of emperors*. National Library, Paris, France. Photo © J.L. Charmet.

p. 210: Smallpox rash. Nineteenth-century Chinese water-colour. National Library, Paris, France. Photo © J.L. Charmet.

p. 211: Chinese medicinal plants. National Library, Paris, France. Photo © National Library, Paris.

p. 211: Ginseng. Photo © R. and S. Michaud – Rapho.

p. 211: Buffalo horns. Photo © R. and S. Michaud – Rapho.

p. 213: Scene of acupuncture against dropsy. Water-colour, *c.* 1785. National Library, Paris, France. Photo © J.L. Charmet.

p. 214: Acupuncture. Statue used for teaching purposes. Photo © C. Lenars.

p. 214: Anatomical plate. Korean manual. British Library, London, England. Photo © R. and S. Michaud – Rapho.

p. 215: Child's hat which protects against evil spirits. Museum of Mankind coll., Paris, France. Photo © Museum of Mankind, Paris.

p. 216: Ma-Ku returning from gathering medicinal plants. Traditional image, nineteenth century. National Library, Paris, France. Photo © J.L. Charmet.

p. 217: A doctor treats a sore on the arm caused by an arrow wound. Print by Kunioshi. University of California, Los Angeles, USA. Photo © R. and S. Michaud – Rapho.

p. 218: *Gentiana algida*. Plate from a Japanese pharmacopoeia treatise. Water-colour, 1830. Private coll., Seoul, Korea. Photo © R. and S. Michaud – Rapho.

p. 218: *Salvia nipponica*. Plate from a Japanese pharmacopoeia treatise. Water-colour, 1830. Private coll., Seoul, Korea. Photo © R. and S. Michaud – Rapho.

p. 219: Utagawa Kunisada (1786-1864). Physiology of the digestion. Print. Bio Medical Library, University of California, Los Angeles, USA. Photo © R. and S. Michaud – Rapho.

p. 220: Huang Tui and Shen Nung. Ivory. Wellcome Institute, London, England. Photo © R. and S. Michaud – Rapho.

Chapter VII

p. 223: Anatomy of the human body, 1560. Library of the Old Faculty of Medicine, Paris, France. Photo © Kharbine – Tapabor.

p. 224: *Sabina Poppaea*. Oil on canvas, Fontainebleau school. Museum of Art and History, Geneva, Switzerland. Photo © Yves Siza – Museum of Art and History, Geneva.

p. 226: A. Dürer (1471–1528). Two didactic diagrams. School of Fine Arts, Paris, France. Photo © Bulloz.

p. 227: Fabricius ab Aquapendente. *Anatomy*. Painting. Marciana Library, Venice, Italy. Photo © G. Dagli Orti.

p. 227: L. Cranach (1472–1553). *Venus*. Painting on wood. Private coll., France. Photo © Artephot – Brumaire.

p. 228: Arnauld de Villenueva. *Trésor des pauvres*. Lyons, 1527. Decorative Arts Library, Paris, France. Photo © J.L. Charmet.

p. 229: Statutes of the Faculty of Medicine, 1672. Medical History Museum, Paris, France. Photo © J.L. Charmet.

p. 229: Giovanni and Gregorio de Gregori. Doctor in his study. Woodcut in *Fasciculo di medicina*, Verona, 1494. Library of the Faculty of Medicine, Padua, Italy. Photo © J.L. Charmet.

p. 229: Giovanni and Gregorio de Gregori. The doctor on his rostrum. Woodcut in *Fasciculo di medicina*, Verona, 1494. Library of the Faculty of Medicine, Padua, Italy. Photo © J.L. Charmet.

p. 230: Cranial muscles in *Illustrated anatomy of the human body*, Fabricius ab Aquapendente (1553–1619). Marciana Library, Venice, Italy. Photo © G. Dagli Orti.

p. 231: Michelangelo Buonarroti (1475–1564). Study of a man. Drawing. Louvre Museum, Paris, France. Photo © Bulloz.

p. 231: Giulio Casserio. *Tabulae anatomicae*. Frankfurt, Germany, 1632. Photo © LL. de Selva – Tapabor.

p. 232: Charles Estienne. *De dissectione partium corporis humani,* Paris, 1545. Library of the Faculty of Medicine, Paris, France. Photo © Lib. OFMP.

p. 232: Leonardo da Vinci (1452–1519). Anatomical figure. British Royal collection, Windsor, England. Photo © Edimédia.

p. 233: E. Hamman (1819–1888). Portrait of Andreas Vesalius in Padua. Fine Arts Museum, Marseilles, France. Photo © Giraudon.

p. 234: Pierre Pons (1574–1640). Portrait of Andreas Vesalius. Seventeenth century. Fine Arts Museum, Orleans, France. Photo © J.L. Charmet.

p. 235: Andreas Vesalius (1514–1564). *De humani corporis fabrica*. Engraving. Basle, 1543. Library of the Faculty of Medicine, Paris, France. Photo © J.L. Charmet.

p. 236: Andreas Vesalius (1514–1564). *Idem*, frontispiece. Library of the Faculty of Medicine, Paris, France. Larousse coll.

p. 237: *The works of mercy*. Sixteenth-century painting, Flemish school. Master of the Prodigal Son. Museum of Valenciennes, France. Photo © Giraudon.

p. 237: Figurine (*putti*) from the work of Vesalius. Engraving. Library of the Faculty of Medicine, Paris, France. Photo © Lib. OFMP.

p. 238: Portrait of Ambroise Paré (1509–1590). Engraving. Photo © LL. de Selva – Tapabor.

p. 239: Ambroise Paré. Designs for artificial legs. Coloured engraving. Wellcome Institute, London, England. Photo © Edimédia.

p. 240: Ambroise Paré. Drawing of foetus. Library of the Faculty of Medicine, Paris, France. Larousse coll.

p. 240: After Ambroise Paré. Two folding surgical knives, with a mermaid carved on the handle. Library of the Faculty of Medicine, Paris, France. Photo © Bulloz.

p. 241: Wash drawings attributed to Francesco Rossi, illustrating a Latin translation of Hippocrates by Guido Guidi. National Library, Paris, France. Photo © National Library, Paris.

p. 241: Monsters. Engraving. Library of the Faculty of Medicine, Paris, France. Larousse coll.

p. 242: Drawing of bandages, attributed to Primaticcio (1504–1570), illustrating *Chirurgia* by Guido Guidi, Rome, *c.* 1540. National Library, Paris, France. Photo © Edimédia.

p. 243: Illustration from *Chirurgia* by Guido Guidi. National Library, Paris, France. Photo © National Library, Paris.

p. 244: Treatment of a patient. Fifteenth-century ceramic. Uffizi Gallery, Florence, Italy. Photo © Erich Lessing – Magnum.

p. 245: Giovanni della Robia. Enamelled terracotta decorating the hospital at Pistoia, Italy. Photo © Artephot – Nimatallah.

p. 245: Detail from the enamelled terracotta. Welcome of the pilgrims. Photo © Artephot - Nimatallah.

p. 246: Giovanni da Cavino. Portrait of Girolamo Fracastoro on a medallion. Bottacin Museum, Padua, Italy. Photo © J.L. Charmet.

p. 246: R. Reisch. *Margarita philosophica*. Engraving. Library of the Faculty of Medicine, Paris, France. Photo © Tapabor.

p. 247: Lucas de Leyden. *The poor surgeon*. Petit Palais Museum, Paris, France. Photo © Bulloz.

p. 248: Portrait of Paracelsus. Oil painting. Louvre Museum, Paris, France. Photo © Lauros – Giraudon.

p. 249: Apothecary's shop. Sixteenth-century woodcut. Library of the Faculty of Medicine, Paris, France. Photo © Roger Viollet.

p. 250: Athanasi Kizcheri. Representation of zodiac man. Illustration from about 1600. National Library, Paris, France. Photo © Tapabor.

p. 251: Santorio (1561–1636). *De statica medicina*, 1612. Library of the National Natural History Museum, Paris, France. Photo © LL. de Selva – Tapabor.

p. 252: Rudolf II taking a cure. Oil on wood, sixteenth century. Art History Museum, Bern, Switzerland. Photo © Erich Lessing – Magnum.

p. 253: Jacomo Pontormo (1494–1556). Hospital scene, sixteenth century. Academy Museum, Florence, Italy. Photo © Artephot – Nimatallah.

p. 254: A. Dürer. *Melancolia*. Engraving, 1514. Petit Palais Museum, Paris, France. Photo © Bulloz.

p. 255: Rembrandt. *Dr Tulp's anatomy lesson*. Painting, 1632. Mauritshuis, The Hague, The Netherlands. Photo © Erich Lessing – Magnum.

p. 256: Bartisch von Königsbrück. Ophthamological treatise, 1568. Coloured engraving. Dresden, Germany. Library of the Faculty of Medicine, Paris, France. Photo © Viollet coll.

p. 257: Hans von Gersdorff. Extraction of arrows. Engraving, 1540. Strasbourg, France. Photo © Larousse coll.

p. 257: Mondino di Luzzi. *Anatomy*, 1532. Library of the Faculty of Medicine, Paris, France. Photo © Lib. OFMP.

p. 258: A. Salamanca. *Anatomia del corpo humano*. Two anatomical plates. Library of the Faculty of Medicine, Paris, France. Photo © Kharbine – Tapabor.

Chapter VIII

p. 261: First representation of an intravenous injection in man. *Clysmatica nova*, J.S. Elsholtz, Berlin, 1667. Library of the Old Faculty of Medicine, Paris, France. Photo © Lib. OFMP.

p. 262: Gérard Dou (1613–1675). *Le docteur*. Louvre Museum, Paris, France. Photo © Erich Lessing – Magnum.

p. 263: G. Abraham Mercklinus. *Blood transfusion*. Detail from the frontispiece of *De ortu et occasu transfusionis sanguinis*. Engraving, 1679. Library of the Old Faculty of Medicine, Paris, France. Photo © J.L Charmet.

p. 264: William Harvey (1578–1657). *Exercitatio anatomica de motu cordis et sanguinis circulatione,* 1648. National Library, Paris, France. Larousse coll.

p. 264: William Harvey, from the portrait by Rolls Park, 1627. The National Portrait Gallery, London, England. Photo © The National Portrait Gallery, London.

p. 265: Robert Hannah (1812–1909). William Harvey explains his theory of the circulation of the blood to King Charles I of England. Royal College of Physicians, London, England. Photo © Royal College of Physicians, London.

p. 266: Illustration of the heart. *De homine figuris*, René Descartes, Leyden, 1662. Library of the Old Faculty of Medicine, Paris, France. Photo © Lib. OFMP.

p. 267: Same engraving as the preceding one. The raised flaps enable the ventricles to be seen.

p. 267: Gaspare Aselli. *De Lactibus sine lacteis venis*. Coloured woodcut, Milan 1627. University Library, Padua, Italy. Photo © J.L. Charmet.

p. 268: Blood transfusion from a dog to a man. Engraving, Amsterdam, 1672. Photo © J.L. Charmet.

p. 269: Transfusion of blood from a lamb to a man. Engraving, Leipzig, 1692. Library of the Old Faculty of Medicine, Paris, France. Photo © J.L. Charmet.

p. 269: R. Odios. *De arte medica*. Ulm, 1642. *Tree of veins*. Library of the Old Faculty of Medicine, Paris, France. Photo © J.L. Charmet.

p. 270: Portrait of A. van Leeuwenhoek (1623–1723), the inventor of the microscope. Engraving, 1722. Library of the National Veterinary School of Maisons-Alfort, France. Photo © J.L. Charmet.

p. 271: Microscope. Nineteenth-century engraving. Photo © J.L. Charmet.

p. 271: M. Malpighi. *Discours anatomique de la structure des viscères*, Paris, 1683. Library of the Old Faculty of Medicine, Paris, France. Photo © J.L. Charmet.

p. 271: A. Leeuwenhoek. Drawing of sperm, 1678. Photo © J.L. Charmet.

p. 271: Ludovic Bonaciolus. *De conformatione foetus*. Engraving, Leyden, 1641. Library of the Old Faculty of Medicine, Paris, France. Photo © Lib. OFMP.

p. 272: Wolfgang Heimbach (seventeenth century). *The patient*. Oil painting. Art Gallery, Hamburg, Germany. Photo © Gallery.

p. 273: William Cowper (1666–1709). The arterial system. Engraving. National Library, Paris, France. Larousse coll.

p. 274: Abraham Bosse (1602–1676). Delivery scene. National Library, Paris, France. Larousse coll.

p. 275: Gabriel Metsu (1629–1667). *Doctor visiting a patient*. The Hermitage, St Petersburg, Russia. Photo © Edimédia.

p. 276: Cinchona. Engraving by Lemery, seventeenth century. Decorative Arts Library, Paris, France. Photo © J.L. Charmet.

p. 277: Pharmacy in Frankfurt-am-Main. German engraving from the late seventeenth century, Museum of Munich, Germany. Photo © Roger Viollet coll.

pp. 278–279: David Ryckaert III (1612–1661). Detail from *The alchemist*, 1634. History of Art Museum, Vienna, Austria. Photo © Erich Lessing – Magnum.

p. 280: Botanical garden. Coloured engraving. Library of the Arsenal and Carnavalet Museum, Paris, France. Photo © J.L. Charmet.

p. 280: The Hôtel-Dieu. A bird's eye view. Engraving. Carnavalet Museum, Paris, France. Photo © J.L. Charmet.

p. 281: Jacques Lagniet (1620–1672). *Recueil des plus illustres proverbes*. Seventeenth-century engraving. National Library, Paris, France. Photo © Viollet coll.

p. 281: Madeleine de Boulogne (1648–1710). Scene at the Abbey of Port-Royal-des-Champs: *Religieux soignant les malades*. Château de Versailles, France. Photo © G. Dagli Orti.

p. 282: Arnoult. *La belle saignée, c.* 1700. Coloured engraving. Decorative Arts Library, Paris, France. Photo © J.L. Charmet.

p. 283: Abraham Bosse. *Le clystère*. Seventeenth-century engraving. National Library, Paris, France. Photo © Roger Viollet.

p. 284: Larmessin. Four engravings: doctor – apothecary – surgeon – doctor. National Library, Paris, France. Photo © Harlingue – Viollet.

p. 285: Robert Fludd. Title page of *Anatomiae amphitheatrum*. Frankfurt, 1623. National Library, Paris, France. Photo © J.L. Charmet.

p. 286: Théophraste Renaudot. Engraved portrait, 1644. National Library, Paris, France. Photo © J.L. Charmet.

p. 289: *Écorché*. Print from *Tabulae anatomicae,* Berretini de Cortone. Library of the Old Faculty of Medicine, Paris, France. Photo © Library of the Old Faculty of Medicine, Paris.

p. 290: Wright of Derby. *The air pump experiment on a bird*. Detail. Oil on canvas, 1768. National Gallery, London, England. Photo © National Gallery, London.

p. 292: Two plates from Diderot's *Encyclopédie*: instruments, trepanning operation. National Library, Paris, France. Photo © R. Viollet coll.

p. 293: Frontispiece to a series of surgical plates in Diderot's *Encyclopédie*. Decorative Arts Library, Paris, France. Photo © J.L. Charmet.

p. 294: Anatomical plate from the *Encyclopédie*. Decorative Arts Library, Paris, France. Photo © J.L. Charmet.

p. 295: Neurological plate from the *Encyclopédie*, after Vieussens. Decorative Arts Library, Paris, France. Photo © J.L. Charmet.

p. 296: Henri Fragonard. Anatomical model of horse and rider. Coll. of the Museum of the Veterinary School of Maisons-Alfort, France. Photo © Gilles Capée.

p. 297: Sympathetic nerves. Water-coloured print. Medical Surgical Academy, Vienna, Austria. Photo © Erich Lessing – Magnum.

p. 297: J. Ladmiral. Arteries of the lower surface of the brain. Coloured print. Library of the Old Faculty of Medicine, Paris, France. Photo © J.L. Charmet.

p. 298: Lazzaro Spallanzani. Lithograph. Decorative Arts Library, Paris, France. Photo © J.L. Charmet.

p. 299: J.L. David (1748–1825), *Portrait of A.L. Lavoisier and his wife*. Oil painting. Metropolitan Museum, New York, USA. Photo © Erich Lessing – Magnum.

p. 300: Paolo Mascagni and Felice Fontana. Anatomical wax model, detail: the solar plexus. Florence, 1785. Medical Surgical Academy, Vienna, Austria. Photo © Erich Lessing – Magnum.

p. 301: Julien Offray de La Mettrie (1709–1751). Print. Carnavalet Museum, Paris, France. Photo © J.L. Charmet.

p. 302: G.B. Sandri. Terracotta model to teach obstetricians. Obstetrics Museum G.A. Galli, Bologna, Italy. Photo © Erich Lessing – Magnum.

p. 303: Instruments used to treat certain vaginal problems or malformations. University of Bologna, Italy. Photo © Erich Lessing – Magnum.

p. 304: *Magnetism*. Print, *c.* 1785. National Library, Paris, France. Photo © J.L. Charmet.

p. 305: Portrait of J.B. Winslow (1669–1750). Bouvet coll., National Order of Pharmacists, Paris, France. Photo © J.L. Charmet.

p. 306: Anatomical plate by Gautier d'Agoty. Library of the Old Faculty of Medicine, Paris, France. Photo © J.L. Charmet.

p. 307: Portrait of Giovanni Battista Morgagni (1682–1771). Palazzo del Bo, Padua, Italy. Photo © J.L. Charmet.

p. 307: Gautier d'Agoty. *L'ange anatomique*. Library of the Old Faculty of Medicine, Paris, France. Photo © J.L. Charmet.

p. 308: The famous German doctor Sansanietto examining a patient's urine. Print by Springer, eighteenth century. Museum of Medical Art, Rome, Italy. Photo © G. Dagli Orti.

p. 309: The doctor's visit. Eighteenth-century painting. Museum of Medical Art, Rome, Italy. Photo © G. Dagli Orti.

p. 310: Trying the corset. Print, after Leclerc, 1778. Photo © J.L. Charmet.

p. 311: Apothecary and physic garden. Beaune Hospice, France. Photo © J.L. Charmet.

p. 312: C.J. Desbordes. *Vaccine at the château of Liancourt*. Painting. Public Works Museum, Paris, France. Photo © Centre de l'image AP – HP.

p. 312: *Visite de Madame Necker à l'hospice de la Charité*. Painting, French school. Public Works Museum, Paris, France. Photo © Centre de l'image. AP – HP.

p. 313: The foxglove. Print after Jean Robin's *Le Jardin du Roi*, 1608. National Library, Paris, France. Photo © J.L. Charmet.

p. 314: Portrait of the French surgeon Desault (1738–1795). Print after Kimly, early nineteenth century. Library of the Old Faculty of Medicine, Paris, France. Photo © J.L. Charmet.

p. 315: Michel Serre (1650–1733). *La peste de Marseille en 1721*. Oil painting. Atger Museum, Montpellier, France. Photo © G. Dagli Orti.

p. 316: The origin of the vaccine. Ceramic plate. Institute of Vaccine, Paris, France. Photo © J.L. Charmet.

p. 317: Cretinism in the Valais. Print by Tresco in *Physiologie des passions*, J.-L. Alibert. Museum of the History of Medicine, Paris, France. Photo © J.L. Charmet.

p. 318: Procession with a doctor and an apothecary. Gouache by Senemone, eighteenth century. Private coll., Paris, France. Photo © G. Dagli Orti.

p. 319: Francisco de Goya. *The doctor as an ass*. Plate from "Freaks". National Library, Paris, France. Photo © J.L. Charmet.

p. 319: Rowlandson, *The hallucinations of the hypochondriac*. Eighteenth-century print. National Library, Paris, France. Photo © LL. de Selva – Tapabor.

p. 319: Rowlandson, *Suffering and fever*. Eighteenth-century print. Museum of Arts, Philadelphia, USA. Photo © J.L. Charmet.

p. 319: G.M. Woodward, *The funeral mute and death*. Print by Cruikshank. Museum of Arts, Philadelphia, USA. Photo © J.L. Charmet.

p. 320: Demachy. *La construction de l'Académie Royale de Chirurgie*. Gouache between 1780 and 1789. Private coll., Paris, France. Photo © J.L. Charmet.

p. 321: Interior of a pharmacy. Eighteenth-century painting. Museum of Medical Art, Rome, Italy. Photo © G. Dagli Orti.

p. 321: Theriaca, 1751. Coll. of the Faculty of Pharmacy, Paris, France. Photo © J.L. Charmet.

p. 321: Collection of pharmaceutical recipes. Saint-Roch Museum, Issoudun, France. Photo © Gauthier.

pp. 322–323: A.-M. Boursier du Coudray. *Traité des accouchements*, 1759. Library of the Old Faculty of Medicine, Paris, France. Photo © J.L. Charmet.

p. 324: J. Gautier d'Agoty. Anatomical plate: child's head, *c.* 1746. Museum of the History of Medicine, Lyons, France. Photo © J.L. Charmet.

p. 325: After Hogarth, 1694-1764. *The four stages of cruelty*. Water-colour print. Museum of the History of Medicine, Paris, France. Photo © J.L. Charmet.

p. 326: G. Regnault. *Les écarts de la nature*. Print, 1775. National Library, Paris, France. Photo © J.L. Charmet.

Chapter X

p. 329: Orthopaedic treatment. *Traitement orthopédique*, P. N. Gerby. Paris, 1826. Museum of the History of Medicine, Paris, France. Photo © J.L. Charmet.

p. 330 and 331: Véron-Bellecourt. *Napoléon visite l'infirmerie des Invalides le 2 février 1808*. Oil on canvas. Museum of the Palace of Versailles, France. Photo © G. Dagli Orti.

p. 332: *Leçon d'anatomie en 1826*. Nineteenth-century print. Carnavalet Museum, Paris, France. Photo © G. Dagli Orti.

p. 333: Portrait of Georges Cabanis (1757–1808). Print. Photo © J.L. Charmet.

p. 333: Portrait of Jean-Louis Baudelocque (1746–1810), doctor from the French Revolutionary age. Oil on canvas, eighteenth century, anonymous. Library of the National Academy of Medicine. Photo © J.L. Charmet.

p. 334: Charles Müller. *Philippe Pinel faisant enlever leurs chaînes aux fous de Bicêtre*. Oil on canvas, *c.* 1840–1850. National Academy of Medicine, Paris, France. Photo © J.L. Charmet.

p. 335: Courtyard of the hospital of La charité. Print by Janinet after Durand. Library of the National Academy of Medicine, Paris, France. Photo © Centre de l'image AP – HP

p. 335: Entrance of the School of Clinical Medicine in Paris. Print by N. Ransonnette in *Mémoire sur les hôpitaux civils de Paris*, Nicolas Clavareau. Library of the National Academy of Medicine, Paris, France. Photo © Centre de l'image AP – HP

p. 336: Honoré Daumier. *Les médecins homéopathes*. Drawing, 1837. Bouvet coll., National Order of Pharmacists, Paris, France. Photo © J.L. Charmet.

p. 337: Daniel Vierge. *La salle des folles à la Salpêtrière*. Gouache. Public Works Museum, Paris, France. Photo © Centre de l'image AP – HP

p. 338: Portraits of Pierre Descault and of François-Xavier Bichat. Painting and print. Library of the National Academy of Medicine, Paris, France. Photo © Centre de l'image AP – HP

p. 339: *Auscultation par Laennec*. From a painting by Robert Thom, 1954. Photo © Tapabor.

p. 340: Laennec. Self-portrait with stethoscope. Drawing, 1824. Library of the National Academy of Medicine, Paris, France. Photo © J.L. Charmet.

p. 341: Bleeding of the jugular and cephalic veins. Lithograph by H.N. Jacob and Jean Bourgery in *Traité complet de l'anatomie de l'homme*, 1831–1854. Library of the National Academy of Medicine, Paris, France. Photo © J.L. Charmet.

p. 342: Diseases of the heart, spontaneous perforation and pericarditis in a six-day-old infant. Plate by Jean Cruveilhier in *Anatomie pathologique du corps humain*, Vol. II. Part two. Library of the Old Faculty of Medicine, Paris, France. Photo © J.L. Charmet.

p. 342: Diseases of the liver and spleen. Plates by Jean Cruveilhier in *Anatomie pathologique du corps humain*. Library of the Old Faculty of Medicine, Paris, France. Photo © J.L. Charmet.

p. 343: Diseases of the arteries. Plate by Jean Cruveilhier in *Anatomie pathologique du corps humain*, Vol. II. Part two. Library of the Old Faculty of Medicine, Paris, France. Photo © J.L. Charmet.

p. 344: Henri Gervex. *Avant l'opération*. Oil on canvas, salon of 1887. Public Works Museum, Paris, France. Photo © J.L. Charmet.

p. 345: Portrait of Jean-Nicolas Corvisart des Marets, Napoleon's chief doctor. Painting on porcelain, anonymous. Library of the National Academy of Medicine, Paris, France. Photo © J.L. Charmet.

p. 345: The column to the glory of Napoleon. Detail from a print by Pellerin at Epinal. INRP. Historical coll. Photo © J.L. Charmet.

p. 346: *Le chirurgien Dominique Larrey opérant pendant la bataille de Hanau.* Oil on canvas, anonymous, early nineteenth century. Val-de-Grâce Museum, Paris, France. Photo © J.L. Charmet.

p. 346: Camels used as ambulances during the Egyptian campaign. Drawing by Dominique Larrey in *Mémoires de chirurgie militaire et campagnes,* 1812. Library of the Old Faculty of Medicine, Paris, France. Photo © J.L. Charmet.

p. 347: Dr Nélaton operating on Garibaldi, 1870. Photo © Sirot – Angel coll.

p. 348: *Portrait de François Magendie.* Oil on canvas, anonymous, first half of the nineteenth century. College of France, Paris, France. Photo © J.L. Charmet.

p. 349: Nasal operation, with section of face. Lithograph by H.N. Jacob from Jean Bourgery, *Traité complet de l'anatomie de l'homme,* 1831–1854. Library of the Old Faculty of Medicine, Paris, France. Photo © J.L. Charmet.

p. 350: Auguste Mengin. *Portrait de Claude Bernard.* Oil on canvas. College of France, Paris, France. Photo © J.L. Charmet.

p. 351: Sub-maxillary ganglion in a calf. Water-coloured sketch, Claude Bernard, in one of his experiment logs, 1840–1843. Archives of the College of France, Paris, France. Photo © J.L. Charmet.

p. 352: Stomach. Drawing by Jean Bourgery in Claude Bernard's *Traité complet de l'anatomie de l'homme* (1831–1854). Library of the Old Faculty of Medicine, Paris, France. Photo © J.L. Charmet.

p. 353: Nerves in a cat's head. Water-coloured sketch by Claude Bernard in one of his experiment logs, May 1842. Archives of the College of France, Paris, France. Photo © J.L. Charmet.

p. 355: Gaston Melingue. *Une des premières vaccinations d'Edward Jenner.* Oil on canvas. Library of the National Academy of Medicine, Paris, France. Photo © J.L. Charmet.

p. 356: Ernest-Antoine-Auguste Hébert. *La malaria.* Oil on canvas, Musée d'Orsay, Paris, France. Photo © Association of National Museums, Paris.

p. 358: Cartoon about cholera. Coloured print, *c.* 1830. Arts Library of the Prussian Cultural Heritage, Berlin, Germany. Photo © Picture Archive of the Prussian Cultural Heritage, Berlin.

p. 358: Label from "liqueur against cholera", *c.* 1832. National Library, Paris, France. Photo © J.L. Charmet.

p. 359: A doctor presents allied soldiers with medicine against syphilis, developed after visits to the Palais Royal during the occupation of Paris, 1815–1816. Coloured print, *c.* 1815. Museum of the History of Medicine, Paris, France. Photo © J.L. Charmet.

p. 360: Florence Nightingale (1820–1910) at work in the Crimea. Photo © Mary Evans Picture Library.

p. 361: W. Simpson. Florence Nightingale improves the army's medical services, 1854–1855. Photo © Mary Evans Picture Library.

p. 362: Edward Ritter. *Le musicien malade, c.* 1847. Oil on canvas. Austrian Gallery, Vienna, Austria. Ph © Meyer – Picture Archive of the Prussian Cultural Heritage, Berlin, Germany.

p. 363: J. Léonard. *Le médecin des pauvres.* Oil on canvas. Fine Arts Museum, Valenciennes, France. Photo © Lauros Giraudon.

p. 363: Albert Anker. *Le charlatan.* 1879. Oil on canvas. Public Art coll., Basle, Switzerland. Photo © Picture Archive of the Prussian Cultural Heritage, Berlin, Germany.

p. 364: Cartoon of a dissection "Voulez-vous déjeuner avec nous la mère Pilon?". Gérard Grandville in *Métamorphoses du jour,* 1829. Photo © J.L. Charmet.

Chapter XI

p. 367: Honoré Daumier. *Medical consultation.* Lithograph. National Library, Paris, France. Photo © L. de Selva – Edimédia.

p. 368: Pasteur's laboratory, rue du docteur Roux, Paris. Pasteur Institute, France. Photo © Erich Lessing – Magnum.

p. 369: *Pasteur discovers the law of ferments.* Card published by the chocolate manufacturer Aynebelle. Nineteenth-century lithograph. Photo © Kharbine – Tapabor.

p. 370: Albert Edelfelt (1894–1905). *Portrait of Louis Pasteur.* Oil on canvas. Pasteur Institute Museum, Paris, France. Photo © Erich Lessing – Magnum.

p. 371: Alphonse Mucha. Pasteur taking a sample of saliva from a rabid dog. Pastel and crayon. Pasteur Institute Museum, Paris, France. Photo © J.L. Charmet.

p. 371: Vaccinating a sheep against anthrax. Pasteur Institute, Paris, France. Photo © Sirot – Angel.

p. 372: Different types of microscope. England, nineteenth century. Arthur Frank coll. Photo © Roger Guillemot – Knowledge of the Arts/Edimédia.

p. 373: The tubercle bacillus. Drawing by I. Strauss in *Tuberculosis and its bacillus,* 1895. Library of the Old Faculty of Medicine, Paris, France. Photo © J.L. Charmet.

p. 373: Representation of tuberculosis lesions. Illustration in *La médecine illustrée.* Library of the Old Faculty of Medicine, Paris, France. Photo © Kharbine – Tapabor.

p. 374: Honoré Daumier. *L'eau du puits de Grenelle.* Lithograph, nineteenth century. National Library, Paris, France. Photo © Kharbine – Tapabor.

p. 375: Honoré Daumier. *Un omnibus en temps de grippe.* Lithograph, nineteenth century. National Library, Paris, France. Photo © National Library, Paris.

p. 376: Hedwig Koch. *Portrait of Robert Koch.* Oil on canvas, 1936. Berlin, Germany. Photo © Photographic Archive of Prussian Culture, Berlin.

p. 377: Robert Koch during a voyage to East Africa in 1906. Photo © Photographic Archive of Prussian Culture, Berlin, Germany.

p. 377: *Koch's bacillus.* Illustration by I. Strauss in *Tuberculosis and its bacillus,* 1895. Library of the Old Faculty of Medicine, Paris, France. Photo © J.L. Charmet.

p. 378: Portrait of Émile Roux. Photo © Henri Manuel –Sirot – Angel.

p. 378: Photograph of Russians from Smolensk, who were treated against rabies in Paris. Pasteur Institute Museum, Paris, France. Photo © L. de Selva – Tapabor.

p. 378: Protection against mosquitoes in colonial countries. Caricature by Does in *Le rire,* 31 August 1901. Decorative Arts Library, Paris, France. Photo © J.L. Charmet.

p. 379: Hugo Vogel. *Portrait of Rudolf Virchow.* Oil on canvas. Rudolf Virchow Hospital, Berlin, Germany. Photo © Photographic Archive of Prussian Culture, Berlin.

p. 380: Tissue section. Plate made by Georg Klemperer, 1889. Berlin, Germany. Photo © Photographic Archive of Prussian Culture, Berlin.

p. 381: Léon Lhermitte. *Une leçon de Claude Bernard.* Oil on canvas, 1889. National Academy of Medicine, Paris, France. Photo © J.L. Charmet.

p. 382: Rudolf Virchow in his institute of pathology, *c.* 1900. Charité Hospital, Berlin, Germany. Photo © Photographic Archive of Prussian Culture, Berlin.

p. 383: Rudolf Virchow and Lewis Wilkens, 1901. Charité Hospital, Berlin, Germany. Photo © Photographic Archive of Prussian Culture, Berlin.

p. 384: Rudolf Virchow is present at an operation on the skull in Paris, 2 August 1900. Photo © Photographic Archive of Prussian Culture, Berlin, Germany.

p. 384: Paul Ehrlich in his study in 1910. Photo © Photographic Archive of Prussian Culture, Berlin, Germany.

p. 385: Liver cells. Diagrams from Virchow's lecture on the foundations of cellular pathology, 1858. Photo © Photographic Archive of Prussian Culture, Berlin, Germany.

p. 386: Christian Rosenberg. *Pharmacy laboratory in Copenhagen.* Engraving, 1863. Museum of Medical History, Copenhagen, Denmark. Photo © J.L. Charmet.

p. 387: Wilhelm Trautschold. *Justus von Liebig in his laboratory at the Institute at Giessen, Hesse.* Woodcut from a drawing, *c.* 1840. Photo © Photographic Archive of Prussian Culture, Berlin, Germany.

p. 388: Wilhelm Trautschold. *Portrait of Justus von Liebig.* Oil on canvas. E. Merck AG coll., Darmstadt. Photo © Photographic Archive of Prussian Culture, Berlin, Germany.

p. 389: Direct auscultation. Catalan Medical History Museum, Barcelona, Spain. Photo © J.L. Charmet.

p. 390: Instruments for measuring blood pressure in man. Experiments by Étienne-Jules Marey. Nineteenth-century engraving. Museum of Medical History, Paris, France. Photo © J.L. Charmet.

p. 391: Ludwig Knaus. Portrait of *Hermann Helmholtz.* Oil on canvas, 1881. National Gallery, Berlin, Germany. Photo © Photographic Archive of Prussian Culture, Berlin.

pp. 392–393: François Feden-Perrin. *La leçon du professeur Alfred Velpeau.* Oil on canvas. Fine Arts Museum, Tours, France. Photo © Bulloz.

p. 394: R. Dubois. *Pumps with cog-wheels for anaesthesia.* Engraving, 1894. National Academy of Medicine, Paris, France. Photo © J.L. Charmet.

p. 394: K. Bryn Thomas. *Portable anaesthesia apparatus.* Engraving, 1893. Photo © Kharbine – Tapabor.

p. 395: Operating theatre, 1890. Photo © Photographic Archive of Prussian Culture, Berlin, Germany.

p. 396: Georges Marcel Burgun. The dentist T.G. Morton carries out an operation without pain. Engraving. Photo © DR.

p. 397: Doctor Dupuytren's surgical instrument case. Public Works Museum, Paris, France. Photo © J.L. Charmet.

p. 398: Adalbert Seligmann. *Operation on the stomach by Dr Theodor Billroth.* Oil on canvas. Photo © Erich Lessing – Magnum.

p. 399: Apparatus for recording the pressure of a liquid propelled along a tube. Experiment by Jules Marey. Medical History Museum, Paris, France. Photo © J.L. Charmet.

p. 400: Marguerite Delorme (daughter of subject). *Le professeur Delorme décrivant la décortication pulmonaire aux médecins stagiaires du Val-de-Grâce.* Oil on canvas, 1897. Val-de-Grâce Museum, Paris, France. Photo © J.L. Charmet.

p. 401: Cataract operation, incision of the cornea. Nineteenth-century engraving. Photo © Kharbine – Tapabor.

p. 402: Félix Vallotton. *La malade.* Oil on canvas, 1892. Private collection, Switzerland. Photo © Dupuis, Lausanne.

p. 403: Professor Charcot. Caricature by Luque published in *Les hommes d'aujourd'hui,* late nineteenth century. Photo © Kharbine – Tapabor.

p. 404: André Broussais. *Une leçon du docteur Charcot à La Salpêtrière.* Oil on canvas, nineteenth century. Neurological Hospital, Lyons, France. Photo © Erich Lessing – Magnum.

p. 404: G. Moreau de Tours. *Hypnosis session, Saint-Louis Hall, Paris, in 1891.* Engraving. Carnavalet Museum, Paris, France. Photo © G. Dagli Orti.

p. 405: Ambroise Tardieu. *A maniac during an attack.* Engraving in Esquirol's book *Des maladies mentales considérées sous les rapports médical, hygiénique et médico-légal,* 1838. Library of the Faculty of Medicine, Paris, France. Photo © Kharbine – Tapabor.

p. 406: Telemaco Signorini. *The San Bonifacio Asylum in Florence,* 1865. Oil on canvas, late nineteenth century. International Gallery of Modern Art, Venice, Italy. Photo © Erich Lessing – Magnum.

p. 407: Hemiplegic epileptic. Photograph by Bowneville and Regnard, Paris, 1878. La Salpêtrière photographic coll., Paris, France. Photo © L. de Selva – Tapabor.

p. 408: The shock treatment room at La Salpêtrière Hospital. Nineteenth-century engraving. Photo © Kharbine – Tapabor.

p. 409: Sigmund Freud and his daughter Anna in the Dolomites in 1913. Photograph by Max Halberstadt. Photo © Mary Evans Picture Library/Sigmund Freud Copyrights.

pp. 410–411: *The life of a handsome young man in Paris.* Engraving from the first half of the nineteenth century. Carnavalet Museum, Paris, France. Photo © J.L. Charmet.

p. 412: A. Plonchon. Smallpox vaccination session at the Val-de-Grâce Hospital in about 1900. Oil on canvas. Val-de-Grâce Museum, Paris, France. Photo © Erc – Sipa.

p. 413: Maximilien Luce. *La forge.* Oil on canvas. Petit Palais, Geneva, Switzerland. Photo © Edimédia.

p. 414: Bonhommé. *Usines du Creusot.* Water-colour, 1866. Private coll. Photo © J.L. Charmet.

p. 415: Arnold Böcklin. *Allegory of the plague.* Oil on canvas, 1898. Museum of Art, Basle, Switzerland. Photo © Photographic Archive of Prussian Culture, Berlin, Germany.

p. 416: Distribution of boiled water at Hamburg, Germany, 1892. Photo © Photographic Archive of Prussian Culture, Berlin, Germany.

Chapter XII

p. 419: Charles Richet. *Le lapin et le savant.* A philosophical fable, illustrated by H. Allouard, Paris, 1983. Private coll., Paris, France. Photo © J.L. Charmet.

p. 420 *Le cardiologue H. Vaquez avec son assistant,* Édouard Vuillard, Paris, France. Painting, *c.* 1917. Public Works Museum, Paris, France. Photo © J.L. Charmet.

p. 422: M.G. Séguy's radiographic and fluoroscopic operating table, from *Rayons cathodiques et rayons X,* J.L. Breton. Paris, 1897. CNAM Library, Paris, France. Photo © J.L. Charmet.

p. 422: Radiograph of the hand of Röntgen's wife. DR.

p. 422: Röntgen rays or X-rays. Photo © Kharbine – Tapabor.

p. 423: The cover of a radiological atlas published in Dresden by Dr Hübler, early twentieth century. Library of the Old Faculty of Medicine, Paris, France. Photo © J.L. Charmet.

p. 423: Fargeot. *Radioscopy.* Water-colour. Val-de-Grâce Museum, Paris, France. Photo © J.L. Charmet.

p. 424: G. Chicotot. *First attempts at the treatment of cancer by X-rays,* 1907. Public Works Museum, Paris, France. Photo © Centre de l'image AP – HP.

p. 425: Ducretet and Lejeune's apparatus for the therapeutic action of X-rays. From *Rayons cathodiques et rayons X,* J.L. Breton, 1897. CNAM Library, Paris, France. Photo © J.L. Charmet.

p. 425: Marie Curie. Sirot – Angel photo coll.

p. 426: A sanatorium *c.* 1900. Sirot – Angel photo coll.

p. 427: Florane. The treatment of tuberculosis. Drawing, 1907. Decorative Arts Library, Paris, France. Photo © J.L. Charmet.

p. 427: The fight against tuberculosis. Calmette. Stamp, 1934. Private coll. Photo © J.L. Charmet.

p. 428: Vaccination in Paris. Water-colour, late nineteenth century. Vaccination Institute, Paris, France. Photo © J.L. Charmet.

p. 429: Pierre-André Brouillet. *Vaccination against croup at the Trousseau Hospital.* Late nineteenth century. Photo © L. de Selva – Tapabor.

p. 430: Charles Maurin (1856–1914). State Hospices Museum, Lyons, France. Photo © J.L. Charmet.

p. 430: Anti-rabies vaccination at the Pasteur Institute. Coloured etching in the *Illustré national,* 1895. Photo © Kharbine – Tapabor.

p. 431: Vaccination against smallpox. Etching in *Le petit journal,* 1905. Photo © L. de Selva – Tapabor.

p. 432: "Watch out for syphilis". Poster by the French Society for Hygienic and Moral Prophylaxy. Private coll. Photo © Kharbine – Tapabor.

p. 433: Ogé. "If you cough…" Poster. Private coll. Photo © Kharbine – Tapabor.

p. 434: "Hermitine". Poster. Private coll. Photo © Kharbine – Tapabor.

p. 434: The prevention of hereditary diseases. Poster. Private coll. Photo © Kharbine – Tapabor.

p. 434: Marcel Capy. Cartoon on the Spanish 'flu epidemic, *La baïonnette,* 6 November 1919. National Order of Pharmacists, Paris, France. Bonnet coll. Photo © J.L. Charmet.

p. 434: Cappiello "Le thermogène". Poster, 1926. Decorative Arts Library, Paris, France. Photo © L. de Selva – Tapabor © by Spadem 91.

p. 435: "Poral fortifies the lungs". Late nineteenth-century advertising. Photo © L. de Selva – Tapabor.

p. 437: Models of various viruses. Photo © Magnum.

p. 438: *The hospital visit.* Engraving in *Le petit journal,* 1903. Photo © L. de Selva – Tapabor.

p. 439: Intestinal tuberculosis. Illustration from the *Medical treatise* by R.Carswell. England, 1838. Library of the Old Faculty of Medicine, Paris, France. Photo © J.L. Charmet.

p. 439: Perforation of the intestine and the pleura. *Idem.*

p. 440: J. Cruveilhier. Lung disease. Library of the Old Faculty of Medicine, Paris, France. Photo © J.L. Charmet.

p. 441: "Mon docteur". *Traité de médecine et d'hygiène,* Dr Menier. Paris, late nineteenth century. National Order of Pharmacists, Paris, France. Bonnet coll. Photo © J.L. Charmet.

p. 442: "What is rickets?" Soviet poster, *c.* 1925. Photo © J.L. Charmet.

p. 443: "Ultravitamin 4". Pharmaceutical advertising, 1947. Decorative Arts Library, Paris, France. Photo © J.L. Charmet.

p. 443: "Fruit instead of medicine". Hungarian poster, *c.* 1930–1940. Photo © J.C. Charmet.

p. 444: Hot spring cures. Lithograph, 1897. Photo © Picture Archive of the Prussian Cultural Heritage, Berlin, Germany.

p. 444: The care to be given to children. Lithograph after Sandmann, 1840. Photo © Picture Archive of the Prussian Cultural Heritage, Berlin, Germany.

p. 445: Principles of hygiene, between the two wars. Lithograph. INRP, Paris, France. Photo © J.L. Charmet.

p. 446: A cure for tuberculosis. Lithograph in *Le petit journal,* 1901. Photo © Tapabor.

p. 447: Alexis Carrel in the USA. Cover from *Time,* June 1938. Photo © J.L. Charmet.

p. 448: Natural care of the body, *c.* 1900. Lithograph, 1897. Photo © Picture Archive of the Prussian Cultural Heritage, Berlin, Germany.

p. 449: Steam baths. Lithograph, 1897. Photo © Picture Archive of the Prussian Cultural Heritage, Berlin, Germany.

p. 450: Henri de Toulouse-Lautrec (1864–1901). *Un examen à la faculté de médecine de Paris.* Oil on board. Toulouse-Lautrec Museum, Albi, France. Photo © Erich Lessing – Magnum.

p. 451: Cartoon in *Le rire.* "Le malade vu par le médecin, le médecin vu par le malade". Photo © Kharbine – Tapabor.

p. 452: The hospital of the French Society for the Assistance of Wounded Soldiers, 1909. Sirot – Angel photograph coll.

p. 453: Grévin. Social medicine *c.* 1865. Drawing in *Le petit journal pour rire.* Decorative Arts Library, Paris, France. Photo © L. de Selva – Tapabor.

p. 454: C. Vernier. Cartoon on painters' colic, *c.* 1860. National Order of Pharmacists, Paris, France. Bonnet coll. Photo © J.L. Charmet.

p. 455: Naudin. Occupations that kill. Cartoon in *L'assiette au beurre,* 1907. National Library, Paris, France. Photo © Charmet © by Spadem 91.

p. 456: Albert Guillaume. The ten commandments for the army of the West, 1915–1916. Poster. Val-de-Grâce Museum, Paris, France. Photo © J.L. Charmet © Spadem 91.

Chapter XIII

p. 459: Blood cells. Photo © Explorer – Biophoto Associates.

p. 460: Crystal of vitamin C viewed under polarized light. Photo © Cosmos – David Parker/Science Photo Library.

p. 462: Erythrocytes crossing the walls of a capillary. Photo © CNRI.

p. 462: Elements of the blood viewed under an electron microscope. Photo © Phototake – CNRI.

p. 463: Slide of frogs' eggs for genetic engineering studies, University of California, San Francisco, USA. Photo © Erich Hartmann – Magnum.

p. 464: Particles of the hepatitis B virus. Photo © Cosmos – Science Photo Library.

p. 465: Students at the Pasteur Institute, Paris, France. Photo © Martine Franck – Magnum.

p. 466: T-lymphocyte. Photo © Phototake – CNRI.

p. 467: Thymus-dependent T-lymphocyte. Photo © Phototake – CNRI.

p. 467: Red blood cells viewed with the electron microscope. Photo © Phototake – CNRI.

p. 468: Human blood platelets. Photo © Phototake – CNRI.

p. 469: Plasma: red blood cells surround a leucocyte. Photo © Cosmos – John Walsh/Science Photo Library.

pp. 470–471: René Magritte. *Le sang du monde.* Oil on canvas. Private coll., Brussels, Belgium. Photo © Giraudon ADAGP 1991.

p. 472: Blood donors in the Haute Savoie. Photo © Salgado JR – Magnum.

p. 472: Blood donation centre. Paris, France, 1945. Photo © Lapi – Viollet.

p. 473: Young haemophiliac in a Paris hospital. Photo © Pierre Michaud.

p. 474: Prof. Neveux's intensive care department at the Laennec Hospital in Paris, France, October 1988. Photo © Abbas – Magnum.

p. 475: Neonatal intensive care, boulevard Brune, Paris,

France. Photo © Pierre Michaud.

p. 476: Reconstruction of an enzyme, ribonuclease A. Photo © J.C. Révy – CNRI.

p. 477: Identification of bacterial strains at the Pasteur Institute in 1987. Photo © Abbas – Magnum.

p. 478: Sperm bank. Storage tubes in a vat of liquid nitrogen. Necker Hospital. Photo © Gilles Perret – Explorer.

p. 478: Artificial insemination. Photo © Alexander Tsiara/ Science Source – Explorer.

p. 479: Oocyte surrounded by sperm. Photo © Dr Sundström – CNRI.

p. 480: First division of the egg. Photo © Dr Boyer – CNRI.

p. 481: Embryo at twelve weeks. Photo © Dopamine – CNRI.

p. 482: Gregor Johann Mendel. Photo © Mary Evans Picture Library.

p. 482: Crossing of peas by Mendel. Breeding and the mendelian discovery. Photo © Mary Evans Picture Library.

p. 483: Drosophila. Photo © Phototake – CNRI.

p. 484: Human chromosomes. Photo © Omikron/Science Source – Explorer.

p. 485: The DNA double helix. Photo © Irving Geis/Science Source.

p. 486: Chromosomes of trisomy 21. Photo © CNRI.

p. 487: Deoxyribonucleic acid (DNA). Photo © Erich Hartmann – Magnum.

p. 487: Ribonucleic acid (RNA). Photo © Cosmos – Prof. Oscar L. Miller/Science Photo Library.

p. 489: Human chromosomes viewed under the electron microscope. Photo © Cosmos – Biophoto Associates/ Science Photo Library.

p. 490: Electron microscope. Photo © Publiphoto – CNRI.

p. 490: Race with sudden stop. Experiment by Marey. Photo © French Film Library.

p. 491: Blood clot viewed with the electron microscope. Photo © Cosmos – Nibsc/Science Photo Library.

p. 491: The cerebellar cortex. Photo © Biophoto Associates/ Science Photo Library.

p. 492: Endoscopic view of the interior of the human body. Photo © C. Lightdale MD.

p. 492: Endoscope. Photo © V. Gremet – CNRI.

p. 493: Ultrasound scan of a blood vessel of the neck. Photo © Pierre Michaud.

p. 494: Electroencephalogram. Photo © Pierre Michaud.

p. 495: Bacterium of the genus *Legionella*. Photo © Cosmos – Barry Dowsett/Science Photo Library.

p. 496: CT scan of the cranium. Photo © Thierry Borderon – Explorer.

p. 497: Image of the human brain produced by nuclear magnetic resonance (NMR). Photo © Cosmos – Science Photo Library.

p. 497: NMR image of the human brain. Photo © CNRI.

p. 498: Thermographic study of a sleeping man. Photo © Cosmos – Dr Ray Clark and Mervin Goff/Science Photo Library.

p. 499: Simple radiograph of the head. Photo © Cosmos – Agfa/Science Photo Library.

p. 500: Radiograph of a woman suffering from pneumonia. Photo © Cosmos – Science Photo Library.

p. 501: Representation of the lungs obtained by tomodensitometry. Photo © P. Bories – CNRI.

pp. 502–503: Sections of the head obtained by NMR. Photo © Pierre Michaud.

p. 504: Pasteur Institute Library. Photo © Abbas – Magnum.

p. 505: Scientist working an image analyser. Photo © Cosmos – Geoff Tompkinson/Aspect Picture Library.

p. 506: Maurice Hofning, departmental head of the molecular programme at the Pasteur Institute. Photo © Martine Franck – Magnum.

p. 506: Research using rabbits at the Pasteur Institute. Photo © Martine Franck – Magnum.

p. 506: Scientist examining a solution of DNA. Photo © Erich Hartmann – Magnum.

p. 507: Research centre at the Garches hospital, France. Photo © Pierre Michaud.

p. 508: ATC 3000 cell analyser and separator. Montpellier, France, March 1991. Photo © Thierry Borderon – Explorer.

p. 508: Radiograph of breast cancer. Photo © Cosmos – Breast Screening Unit, King's College Hospital, London/ Science Photo Library.

p. 509: River blindness in Guinea in 1988. Photo © Eugène Richards – Magnum.

p. 509: Children suffering from AIDS at Constanza, Romania, 1990. Photo © James Nachtwey – Magnum.

p. 510: Purification of the blood. Photo © Publiphoto – CNRI.

p. 511: Molecule of insulin. Photo © Phototake – CNRI.

p. 512: The arrival in Paris of Alexander Fleming. Photo © Keystone.

p. 512: Alexander Fleming being carried in triumph to Edinburgh University. Photo © Keystone.

p. 513: Culture of penicillin, obtained from *Penicillium notatum*. Photo © Cosmos – A. McClenaghan/Science Photo Library.

p. 514: Coagulation of blood in an artery. Photo © Cosmos – Biophoto Associates/Science Photo Library.

p. 515: Aorta and cardiac artery of a two-year-old. Photo © Explorer.

p. 515: Digitalized angiography of the heart. Lapeyronie Hospital, Montpellier, France, March 1991. Photo © Thierry Borderon – Explorer.

p. 516: Miner's family in Pennsylvania. Photo © H. Cartier-Bresson – Magnum.

p. 517: Dr Charles Swartz injects anti-polio serum into Debra Coaks. Houston, Texas, USA. Photo © Keystone.

p. 517: Kinesitherapy room, Saint Jean Centre, Paris, France. Photo © Pierre Michaud.

p. 518: Polio victim. Saint Jean Centre, Paris. Photo © Pierre Michaud.

p. 518: Polio research using rabbits. Photo © Keystone.

p. 518: Rehabilitating a child suffering from polio. Ahmedabad Red Cross Clinic, India. Photo © Martine Franck – Magnum.

p. 519: Test on a monkey infected with a virus. Laboratories of the Institute of Virology, Moscow, Russia, 1959. Photo © Keystone.

p. 519: Research on mosquitoes. Photo © Martine Franck – Magnum.

p. 520: Stamps worth twenty-five centimes marking the campaign against tuberculosis in 1965–1966. Photo © Keystone.

p. 520: Polio research. Lithograph, Herbert Bayer, 1949. library of Congress, Washington, DC, USA. Photo © Edimédia.

p. 520: AIDS campaign poster. French Committee for Health Education. Photo © Seigneury Conseil.

p. 521: Spanish AIDS campaign poster, 1985–1987. Photo © J.L. Charmet.

p. 521: AIDS virus viewed under the electron microscope. Photo © Cosmos – London School of Hygiene & Tropical Medicine/Science Photo Library.

p. 522: Country doctor in the United States. Photo ©

Eugene Smith – Magnum.

p. 523: General practitioner with a patient in Grenoble, France. Photo © Pierre Michaud.

p. 524: Group therapy. Photo © Rapho.

p. 525: Hypnosis. Photo © Krassovsky – BSIP.

p. 526: Paintings by schizophrenics. Photo © CNRI.

p. 526: Painting by Aloïse, a schizophrenic. Photo © CNAC/G. Pompidou.

p. 528: Nurse tending a wounded soldier in 1944. Photo © Keystone.

p. 528: The pre-fabricated bridge at Arromanches, France, 6 June 1944. Photo © Keystone.

p. 528: Two soldiers of the medical corps tending a wounded American, May 1954. Photo © Keystone.

p. 529: Preparations before a heart operation in Düsseldorf, Germany. Photo © Leonard Freed – Magnum.

p. 529: Artificial heart. Photo © Explorer – NIM/Science Source.

p. 530: Compression chambers. Photo © Pierre Michaud.

p. 531: Insertion of a mitral valve at Clermont Ferrand, France. Photo © P. Delarbre – Explorer.

p. 531: Surgical laser. Photo © Explorer – Charlotte Raymond/Science Source.

p. 532: Kidney before transplantation. Photo © Explorer – Will/Deni McIntyre.

p. 533: Kidney graft. Photo © Alexander Tsiaras – Cosmos.

p. 533: Re-establishing the irrigation of the kidney. Photo © Alexander Tsiaras – Cosmos.

p. 534: Transplantation of bone marrow. Saint-Louis hospital, Paris, France. Photo © C. Vioujard – Gamma.

p. 535: Kidney transplant. Photo © Kharbine – Tapabor.

pp. 536–537: River blindness in Mali, 1988. Photo © Eugene Richards – Magnum.

p. 538: Doctors in India. Photo © C. Steele/Perkins – Magnum.

p. 538: The Red Cross in the Caribbean. Photo © Martine Franck – Magnum.

p. 538: Famine in northeastern Brazil, 1984. Photo © Sebastiao Salgado – Magnum.

p. 539: Speech therapy for deaf children at the Gosselin Centre in France. Photo © Pierre Michaud.

p. 540: At the dentist in England. Photo © David Hurn – Magnum.

p. 541: Boy suffering from cystic fibrosis in the Paris Children's hospital, France. Photo © Pierre Michaud.

p. 542: Brooklyn, New York, USA. Photo © Eugene Richards – Magnum.

p. 543: Accident and emergency ward at Detroit Hospital, Michigan, USA. 14 November 1989. Photo © Leonard Freed – Magnum.

p. 544: Leper village in India. Photo © Martine Franck – Magnum.

p. 545: Examining a child, to check on the degree of parasitic infection, Guinea, 1988. Photo © Eugene Richards – Magnum.

p. 546: Red Cross orphanage in India. Photo © Martine Franck – Magnum.

p. 547: Old people's home in Tokyo, Japan. Photo © Martine Franck – Magnum.

p. 547: Woman from a Hakka village, 1980. Photo © Martine Franck – Magnum.

p. 548: March by doctors in Paris, France, 16 April 1987. Photo © C. Vioujard – Gamma.

p. 551: Nachet's new large microscope. Engraving, C. Robin in *Traité du microscope*. Paris, France, 1871. Photo © J.L. Charmet.

TABLE OF CONTENTS

◆

CHAPTER I   *The diseases of Prehistory* 13

    I. From palaeontology to palaeopathology   15
       "Homo sapiens": a portrait   16
    II. In search of palaeomedicine   18

CHAPTER II   *The continued existence of ethnomedicine* 21

    I. The modern Western world and ethnomedicine   23
       A medicine of "intermediaries"   24
       Revival of the tradition of "natural medicine"   28

CHAPTER III   *The archaeology of medicine* 31

    I. The medicine of the Fertile Crescent   33
       A hierarchical society   34
       Behind the disease: the transgression   34
       Diagnosis and religion   36
       Treating the disorder and placating the evil spirit   38
       Who are the "doctors"?   39
       There is still much that we do not know   40
       The influence of Mesopotamian medicine   41
    II. Egyptian medicine: early medicine   42
       How medicine was organized   44
       Pathology and therapy   48
       Logic and surgery   53
       Treatment of alopecia   53
       A patient's complaint   54
       What heritage?   56
    Chronological table   57

CHAPTER IV   *The Greeks establish our system of medicine* 59

    I. Medicine: between myth and philosophy   61
       Asclepius: a healing hero   63

Naturalist philosophers 66
Before Hippocrates 68

II. Hippocratic medicine 70
   A legendary life 71
   The Hippocratic Corpus 72
   Some Hippocratic aphorisms 72
   A famous oath 73
   A diagnosis of love 75
   The Hippocratic method 76
   A mumps epidemic on the island of Thasos 76
   Medical care in Greece 78

III. The doctrines of Alexandria 80
   Aristotle: the successor to Hippocrates? 81
   Medicine in Alexandria 82

IV. The Greeks in Rome 84
   Asclepiades – a fashionable name 85
   Celsus' "De arte medica" 87
   The Pneumatists and eclectics 88
   "Galen was wrong!" 90

Chronological table 93

CHAPTER V   *The Middle Ages in Mediterranean countries* 95

I. The Byzantines, heirs of Hippocrates 97
   The riches and weaknesses of the Eastern "Romans" 98
   Some brilliant successors 100
   From valetudinaria to hospitals 103
   The Latin races and Turks against the Byzantine culture 106

II. The Jewish faith and prophylactic measures 110
   Hygiene in the Talmud 110
   Deontological counsel of Jewish doctors 115
   Jewish doctors in Islamic countries 116
   The good doctor as seen by Ali ibn Rabban at Tabari 117
   Jewish doctors in Christian countries 120
   Medical axioms of Jean Mésué 121

III. The Muslim digression 122
   Hygiene in the Quran 123
   Respect for Greek books 124
   Clinical practice and philosophy 126
   Diagram taken from Avicenna's Canon 128
   Teaching hospitals 131
   Arab doctors in Spain 134

IV. Universities and medicine in the West 138
   The religious as guardians of knowledge 138
   The crossroads of Salerno 141
   Salernian health regime 145
   The birth of the thirteenth century 146
   Foundation of universities 147
   Between faith and reason 148
   The church and the hospital 152

The misfortune of the times   155
Ineffectual medicines   161
Skilful surgeons   164
Chronological table   169

CHAPTER VI   *Different types of medicine*   171

    I. The riches and contrasts of the Americas   173
Discovery and destruction   174
Customs and health   176
Sucking of wounds, infusions and steam baths   178
Exchanges of diseases and remedies   183
From the Eskimos to the Fuegians   186

    II. The traditions of India live on   189
Veda and Ayurveda   189
Charaka and Susruta   193
Ancient forms of medicine in modern India   197

    III. The wonders of Imperial China   201
The universe of numbers   201
A physiology without anatomy   204
Yin and Yang   204
Observation of the patient   206
The rank and functions of the organs   208
Code of good health   209
A "sensory" pharmacopoeia   211
From acupuncture to mesotherapy   212
"Standing on its own two feet"   215
China in the Far East   219
Chronological table   221

CHAPTER VII   *Anatomy in the Renaissance*   223

    I. *The discovery of the human body*   226
Dissection is regularized 228
Illustrated books   230
Renaissance anatomists   231
Vesalius (1514–1564)   233
Anatomy after Vesalius   235
The surgeon Ambroise Paré   238
A famous aphorism   241

    II. A Renaissance in all but medicine   244
Jean Fernel (1497–1558)   244
The doctor is expected to know everything   245
Fracastorius (1483-1553)   246
Paracelsus (1493–1541)   248
The "breath of life" theory is challenged   251
Those who administered to the sick   252
Vernacular languages and erudite medicine   256

Some "common fallacies" according to Joubert   257
The decline of Italian authority   258
Chronological table   259

CHAPTER VIII   *The seventeenth century and the Age of Reason*   261

   I. The fundamental principles of modern medicine   263
      Aristotle's principles as reformulated by Harvey   264
      Harvey and the dispute on the circulation   265
      Circulation, the steps to its discovery   267
      From the microscope to the mysteries of generation   270
      Towards the study of lesions   272
      What did the Paris doctors read?   275
      Cinchona in the treatment of fever   276

  II. A medicine still lacking in power   278
      The continuance of plagues   278
      Rudimentary therapeutics   282
      The illusions of iatrophysics and iatrochemistry   283
      Bossuet the iatromechanic   285
Chronological table   287

CHAPTER IX   *Medicine in the Age of Enlightenment*   289

   I. The fashion for "systems"   291
      Mechanists and vitalists   292
      Classification and world order   296
      Diseases are of the same order as nature   297

  II. Erudite and fashionable experimentation   298
      Physiology, the fruit of experimentation   298
      The man machine of La Mettrie   300
      Experimentation in the eighteenth century   303
      Clinical practice and fame   309
      The hygiene of clothing   310
      Medicine, numbers and hygiene   315
      Poor health in the countryside   318
      The authorities, epidemics and epizootics   322
      The authorities and food hygiene   324
Chronological table   327

CHAPTER X   *Conversion to clinical medicine*   329

   I. The French Revolution and medicine in Europe   331
      Essential reforms   332
      Homoeopathy   335
      A new vision of disease   337

Surgery – still a hasty affair 344
The concern for progress does not prevent scepticism 347

II. The experimental revolution: from Magendie to Claude Bernard 348
Magendie and his pathological philosophy 348
Claude Bernard (1813–1878) 350
The German school of physiology 351

III. From prevention to public health 354
The crusade against smallpox 354
Specificity according to Bretonneau 357
The emergence of public health 361

Chronological table 365

CHAPTER XI

Laboratory medicine 367

I. Bacteriology: Pasteur extends our knowledge of "nature" 369
Cholera and rabies 370
Knowing how to interpret chance 372
All the microbes in the world 375
The suffering of others 375

II. Towards microscopic pathological anatomy 379
Virchow and cellular theory 380
Some of the pathogens identified over thirty years 380
Scientific medicine according to Virchow 382
Medicine and politics according to Virchow 385

III. New progress: from analytical chemistry to physics 386
Analytical and synthetic chemistry 386
Medical physics and physiology 388
The eternal sceptics 393

IV. Anaesthesia and asepsis lead to a revival of surgery 394
William Morton and the birth of anaesthesia 395
Anaesthesia "fit for a queen" 396
Lister and Sommelweis: antisepsis and asepsis 397

V. The new specialists 400
Precise instructions are given concerning diet 402
Some famous French doctors: 1840–1900 409

VI. Preventive medicine becomes well organized 412

Chronological table 417

CHAPTER XII

From X–rays to penicillin 419

I. The radiology revolution 421

II. Serums and vaccines after Pasteur and Koch 426
Jules Bordet and immunology in Belgium 431

III. Biochemistry transforms physiology 436
Nineteenth-century North American and British medicine 436

IV. After enzymes: vitamins and hormones 442

The main vitamins   444

V. The fight against infections continues   447

VI. Joint national and international responsibilities   452
  To whom should discovery be attributed?   453

Chronological table   457

CHAPTER XIII   *The explosion of knowledge and techniques*   459

  I. The triumph of biochemistry   463
  Meticulous analyses   463
  The complexity of the blood   466
  The Nazi doctors   469
  The factors involved in blood coagulation   473
  Resuscitation and intensive care   474
  How should death be defined?   476
  Hormones and enzymes   478
  The birth of genetics   482
  Some hereditary diseases of man   488

  II. Medical physics   490
  Sound and light in the human body   490
  The new electrophysiology   494
  Ionizing radiation   498
  Medical imaging becomes an industry   502

  III. Effective treatments at last   505
  A transformed pharmacopoeia   507
  New medicines   513
  Diseases are changing   516
  The end of smallpox   519
  The new fear of AIDS   521
  The last of the "lunatics"   524
  Electric shock treatment and lobotomy   525
  The successes and failures of surgery   529
  Organ transplants   532

  IV. World health   537
  Health systems   537
  Alexis Carrel: changing morals   541
  Social welfare   542
  Medical confidentiality and computers   543
  The diseases of the poor   544
  Some parasitoses of the Third World   545
  The Alma-Ata declaration 1978   546
  The medicine of tomorrow?   547

Chronological table   549

APPENDICES   Glossary   553
  Index   557
  Bibliography   562
  List of illustrations   565

Editorial Director: Emmanuel de Waresquiel

———————◆———————

Design

Project Manager: Isabelle Martin
Editorial Assistant: Marine Le Guen
Designers: Stéphane Danilowiez and Georges Geoffroy
Editors: Olivier Benoist and Françoise Botkine
Production Co-ordinator: Lydie Conti

———————◆———————

Picture Researcher: Nicole Bonnetain
Production Manager: Marlène Delbeken

Jacket Designer: Gérard Fritsch